How To Know

THE NON-GILLED FLESHY FUNGI

Helen V. Smith
Alexander H. Smith

University of Michigan

WM. C. BROWN COMPANY PUBLISHERS
Dubuque, Iowa

Copyright 1973 by
Wm. C. Brown Company Publishers

ISBN 0–697–04866–7 (Paper)
ISBN 0–697–04867–5 (Cloth)

Library of Congress Catalog Card Number 73-86734

THE PICTURED-KEY NATURE SERIES

How To Know The—

AQUATIC PLANTS, Prescott, 1969
BEETLES, Jaques, 1951
BUTTERFLIES, Ehrlich, 1961
CACTI, Dawson, 1963
EASTERN LAND SNAILS, Burch, 1962
ECONOMIC PLANTS, Jaques, 1948, 1958
FALL FLOWERS, Cuthbert, 1948
FRESHWATER ALGAE, Prescott, 1954, 1970
FRESHWATER FISHES, Eddy, 1957, 1969
GRASSES, Pohl, 1953, 1968
GRASSHOPPERS, Helfer, 1963, 1972
IMMATURE INSECTS, Chu, 1949
INSECTS, Jaques, 1947
LAND BIRDS, Jaques, 1947
LICHENS, Hale, 1969
LIVING THINGS, Jaques, 1946
MAMMALS, Booth, 1949, 1970
MARINE ISOPOD CRUSTACEANS, Schultz, 1969
MOSSES AND LIVERWORTS, Conard, 1944, 1956
NON-GILLED FLESHY FUNGI, Smith-Smith, 1973
PLANT FAMILIES, Jaques, 1948
POLLEN AND SPORES, Kapp, 1969
PROTOZOA, Jahn, 1949
ROCKS AND MINERALS, Helfer, 1970
SEAWEEDS, Dawson, 1956
SPIDERS, Kaston, 1953, 1972
SPRING FLOWERS, Cuthbert, 1943, 1949
TAPEWORMS, Schmidt, 1970
TREMATODES, Schell, 1970
TREES, Miller-Jaques, 1946, 1972
WATER BIRDS, Jaques-Ollivier, 1960
WEEDS, Wilkinson-Jaques, 1959, 1972
WESTERN, TREES, Baerg, 1955, 1973

Printed in United States of America

CONTENTS

Introduction	1
The Fruit Body	1
Collecting and Handling Specimens	4
How to Study the Fungus Fruit Bodies	6
The Preparation of Specimens for the Herbarium	12
Formulae and Procedures	14
Calibrating Your Microscope	16
General Considerations	18
Key to Fleshy and Near-Fleshy Higher Fungi	19
The Ascomycetes	20
Pezizales	22
Hypocreales	60
The Basidiomycetes	66
Tremellales	67
Cantharellales	70
Aphyllophorales	101
Agaricales (Boletaceae)	146
Lycoperdales	255
Sclerodermatales	287
Podaxales	295
Nidulariales	296
Phallales	298
Hymenogastrales	302
Asterosporales	361
Glossary	382
Index	391

INTRODUCTION

The fleshy fungi are those which produce a fruit body (sporocarp) which is rather soft and soon decays. Some species in both the Ascomycetes and the Basidiomycetes come under this heading and are included here. The term mushroom, as generally applied, refers to the gilled fungi. There are so many of the latter that they will be treated in a second work similar to this one. There are many fungi which produce fruit bodies typically woody or tough in consistency and technically these are not within the scope of the present project, but they will be collected by every collector using this work. Consequently, enough of these are included here to give the user some idea of their diversity, and how, in more recent treatments of the group, they are classified into genera.

For the purposes of this work, the problem is to find specimens, and then learn how to study them. Fleshy and "almost fleshy" fungous fruit bodies are found in many habitats: on soil, in meadows, pastures, old fields, woods, dense forests of all types, dung heaps, on wood of living or dead trees of all species, as leaf parasites, parasites of other fungi—in short on almost any substrate that will furnish nutriment for a fungous plant. It goes without saying that they occur the world over: in deserts, in aquatic habitats, above timberline in the mountains, etc. There are some species fruiting most anytime of the year from early spring to winter if moisture is available, so go out and look and see what you can find. Do not neglect your own yard.

THE FRUIT BODY

The fruit body is a simple to complex device to produce and disperse spores. The spores serve to reproduce the fungous plant and to disperse the species over such areas of the earth as are suitable for its growth. Since the fruit body has no way of directing spores to favorable localities, it seems that the opposite approach has developed, namely that of blanketing large areas with spores (termed the *spore rain*), with only those falling in a favorable location actually performing their destiny by reproducing fungous plants. Waste of course is the rule, since relatively few spores are actually successful. Because the fungous plant is a mass of threads all produced by branching from an original thread which grew out of the germinating spore, few differences between species are evident in the vegetative phase of the plants. This phase is termed the *mycelium*, pl. *mycelia*.

In fact, the latter are usually buried in the material from which they derive nutriment and one seldom sees them, or at best sees only a slight moldy growth. The kinds of fungi are classified on the features of the spores and of the fruit bodies which produce them. Thus, regardless of one's purpose in studying fungi, the logical place to begin is by studying the fruit body.

To do this let us familiarize ourselves with its parts and their functions, for the two should always be considered together if one is to understand the changes in structure which have occurred in the evolution of the diverse types encountered among the fungi.

Since most people are familiar with the commercial mushroom let us consider a fruit body (a bolete in this case) which rather closely resembles it, yet falls within the scope of this volume—namely *Suillus luteus* the Slippery Jack (Fig. 1a). It consists of a broad cap (pileus) at the top of a stalk (stipe). In place of the radiating thin gills which are on the underside of the cap of the commercial mushroom, this bolete has a rather spongy mass of tissue composed of numerous tubes with the tube mouths or pores, on the lower surface. The surfaces of the mushroom's gills and the inside of the bolete tubes are covered with the spore-producing layer or hymenium. The tissue which produces the spores is called the hymenophore, and takes different forms in different kinds of fungi, in the mushroom it is in the form of gills, in coral fungi it covers the surfaces of the branches, in the hedgehog fungi it forms spines, in cup fungi it lines the inside of the cuplike fruiting body, in puffballs it occupies the interior of the fruit body and is called the gleba. The hymenophore in a mushroom or bolete consists of a palisade-like layer of hyphal end-cells (hymenium), and the spores are produced on special cells called basidia (sing. basidium), Fig. 2c, or in asci Fig. 2b, if the specimen is a cup-fungus. Other non-spore producing cells are also present in the hymenium. The spores are discharged from the basidia or asci and either fall free of the hymenophore as in most Basidiomycetes, or are discharged into the air currents as in many of the larger cup-fungi. This means that at the time of spore discharge the hymenophore as a unit or its individual parts, is so oriented that it is in a position to allow the spore-producing cells to carry out this function. In other words in *Boletus*, for instance, that the long axis of the tube is vertically arranged, thus the basidia are in a horizontal position. The stipe will bend as it elongates to accomplish this placement of the hymenophore, especially if some obstruction is encountered by the developing fruit body. The spores are discharged from the basidia with enough force so that most of them fall free of any obstructions.

The stalk (*stipe*) (fig. 1) is a simple device for elevating the hymenophore high enough so that air currents can carry away the

NON-GILLED FLESHY FUNGI

spores as they fall free of the hymenophore. The stipe, of course, must not only support the hymenophore mechanically, but it is also the structure through which the food materials must pass which are used in the production of spores. In some species there is a cup (*volva*)

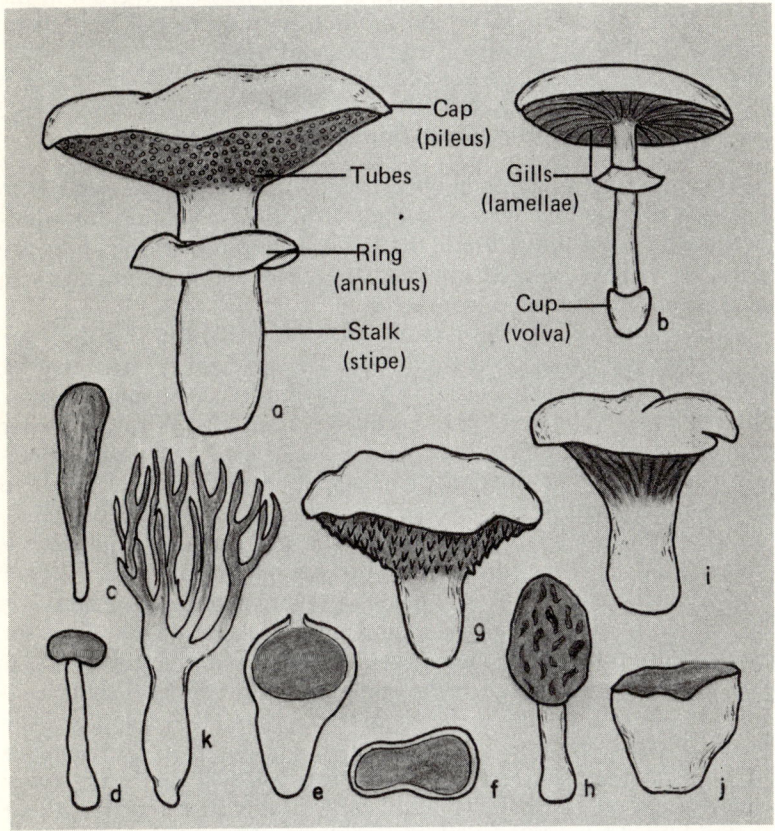

Fig. 1. (a) a bolete; (b) a gilled mushroom; (c) an unbranched coral fungus; (d) a member of the Geoglossaceae (*Cudonia*); (e) a puffball of the genus Lycoperdon; (f) a *Rhizopogon* (Hymenogastrales); (g) a *Hydnum* (hedgehog fungus); (h) a morel; (i) a chanterelle; (j) a cup-fungus; (k) a branched coral fungus. Note: the shaded portions are the hymenophore (where the spores are produced).

at the base of the stipe and/or a ring of tissue (the *annulus*) farther up—often near the apex. These tissues are the remains of veils or coverings which in the first case protect the entire fruit body in its early stages of development, and in the second, the layer protects the hymenophore from drying out rapidly before the spores are mature.

The cap is to be regarded as an expansion of the stipe, in a sense, and it acts principally as a support for the developing hymenophore, but also offers protection for it. It is also the distributing agent for the food stuffs being delivered to the developing basidia and finally the spores. The microscopic details of the fruit body are given in the section on how to study it, and are not essential to this first stage, namely finding the specimen and transporting it.

Collecting and Handling Specimens

The guiding principle in collecting and handling specimens is to follow a routine that will keep them in perfect condition for whatever purpose you desire to use them. The methods described here are the ones we have worked out over the years and recommend them at least until better ones can be found.

The importance of the type of container in which to place your collections cannot be overemphasized. We have always used market baskets of about a half bushel capacity. The basket should be fairly shallow as one should not pile up collections unduly. With the proper type of basket, a hunting knife with a thick blade (for prying specimens from wood or digging them out of the ground), a magnetic compass for locating your directions when it is time to go home, waxed paper for wrapping specimens, a pad of note paper and a pencil,—and clothing suitable for the season, region, and the fact that you will collect in brushy places—you are ready for the hunt.

At one season or another almost any area one might select for hunting—from the neighbor's or your own yard to a virgin forest (if you can find one), a golf course or a barren sandy field—will have some fungi fruiting on it if the weather has been at all favorable. We have collected specimens in Death Valley, California. So the place to go is your decision, but do not assume you will find fungi every time you go out. Perhaps you will try a woods first and it is about the middle of September and you are in northern Michigan. As you enter the woods, under a border of birches you see several large fruit bodies with orange caps. They are scattered (not growing close together). With your knife dig each one out and examine the base for remains of a volva and for a possible long rootlike projection. In the species at hand you will find neither. After cleaning away the dirt carefully, and making at least a mental note that there is nothing distinctive about the base, compare all the fruit bodies to see if they are similar in appearance. They will, in this case, doubtless have a layer of tubes (not gills) on the underside of the cap, and the stipe will be scabrous from blackish points and squamules. Cut one fruit body in half lengthwise and observe any color changes over a 5 minute

NON-GILLED FLESHY FUNGI

period. Let us say a change occurs, first to reddish and then gray and finally black. Include this data on a piece of note paper to be wrapped up with the specimens. If the specimens are large it is better to wrap each separately, and then in some manner wrap the whole group together as a unit to indicate they all came from the same place. Be sure to collect young as well as mature fruit bodies. Waxed paper of the type available in any supermarket is good for wrapping. Lay the specimen on a sheet of paper of such size that it will accommodate the specimen, and twist the paper tight at both ends after rolling the specimen up in it. This makes a reasonably tight package. If possible, stand the packages upright in the basket. You may have to brace them in some manner until you have enough so that they brace each other; and never pile heavy specimens on top of delicate soft ones. Always keep in mind that the main purpose is to get the specimens home undamaged. You will not collect them in the proper sequence to fit into your basket perfectly, so do not hesitate making rearrangements when necessary. The temptation, and in a good season it is difficult to resist it, is to collect more specimens than one will have time to study. When the basket is full, or it is time to go home, check your directions with your compass to avoid wasting time walking in the wrong direction.

Now for some DON'TS: Never use plastic bags for anything but woody specimens. Never pile up the specimens if it can possibly be avoided. Never use a basket with a cover, the latter is a hindrance rather than a help. Never leave specimens in a closed car on a hot day while hunting for more, getting lunch, or for any other reason. Under the above condition they overheat rapidly and then will not shed spores. Also, yeast and bacteria will multiply rapidly under such conditions rendering the specimens not fit to be eaten. When transporting specimens never have them packed tightly in a container even if the car is air-conditioned. We have seen beautiful collections ruined in a 200 mile drive. For those collecting for the table, plastic bags, in hot weather, are the worst container one can use. Paper bags allow the specimens to "breathe" and do not allow the sun's rays to directly affect the specimens. If you are collecting for the table, you have, presumably, already identified the species one or more times. When collecting for the table cut away parts that are very dirty or for some reason appear abnormal (such as having soft watery spots). But always check the identity of each fruit body you collect with the features learned for that species. Upon arriving home or at the laboratory, unload the basket and spread out the packages in some cool place. Select the specimens for study according to your preference, but it is best to study the delicate species first since they lose their characters faster than the others.

How to Study Fungus Fruit Bodies

In the preliminary study, the simple method of proceeding from obviously different kinds to those that show a goodly number of similarities, is best. For instance, first sort out into one group all the tough to woody specimens with pores on the underside of the cap. These can be studied last since there is no problem as to their losing characters. If you have any fleshy types with spines on the underside, place them in a second group. Fleshy to fragile upright types either simple or branched and with a smooth to wrinkled surface would go in a third group. These would be mostly coral fungi and related kinds. Fleshy specimens with gills on the underside of the cap would be true mushrooms—and are not treated in the following key. Finally, there will be a residual group, perhaps, which will be harder to place. Many of these may turn out to be puffballs—with the spore mass borne inside the fruit body or on a specialized part of it as a slimy mass. However, some of the possible remainder may be saucer-shaped to cup-shaped, and, as one opens the package to look at them, they may puff a cloud of spores at you (as a white mist). These are Ascomycetes. Obviously, from the key, the cup-shaped specimens are in the Pezizales. But how are you going to be sure? At this point it is necessary to use a microscope. It must be determined whether an ascus (fig. 2b) is present. In order to demonstrate the presence of the ascus cut a thin rectangle of tissue about 1-2 mm wide (very small) from the surface of the upper side of the cup and place it on a microscope slide in a drop of water. Crush the tissue with a scalpel to spread it out, place a cover slip over

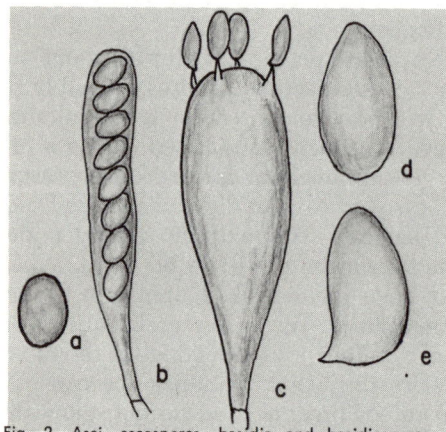

Fig. 2. Asci, ascospores, basidia and basidiospores. (a) an ascospore; (b) an ascus; (c) a basidium; (d) face view of a basidiospore; (e) profile view of basidiospore.

it, and observe under the microscope. In the less dense areas one will find some groups of cells as shown (fig. 3-e, f). These are: (1) the asci, and are the spore-bearing cells, the most important element of the hymenium. (2) The slender filaments beside the asci are paraphyses. Eight spores in an ascus is typical for the Ascomycetes, but 4 or 2 are found in some species, and very high numbers occur in others. From this same mount one can determine the size of the ascus, its shape, as well as the size and shape of the spores and whether they are smooth or roughened. The type of microscopic mount described above is termed a "crush mount" or "smash mount" (for obvious reasons), and is very useful for quickly checking on which major group of fungi one has in hand, as well as in making preliminary studies of spore size, shape, and type of ornamentation for either Ascomycetes or Basidiomycetes.

If one wishes, it is good practice to cut thin sections through the entire wall of the cup to show the relationships of the various layers of tissue to each other. The thicker the wall of the cup, the more difficult it is to get complete sections. To cut sections use a sharp razor or razor blade. Hold the tissue between the thumb and forefinger in such a way that when you cut across the tissue you are getting a section parallel to the long axis of the hymenial cells.

In crush mounts of Basidiomycetes most of the spores will be broken from their attachment, so it is best to go to sections immediately. Woody species, naturally, do not crush well. However, sectioning them is not too difficult. Cut out a piece of the hymenophore, moisten it with ethanol or a detergent to drive out the air, hold the tissue between the thumb and forefinger of your left hand in such a position that when you slice across it with the razor the desired sections are obtained (cross sections or longitudinal ones). If one is afraid of cutting his thumb, put a band-aid over it before doing the cutting. Mount the results of your slicing in a large drop of water or KOH (or better, some in a drop of each) on a microscope slide, and with a dissecting needle tease out the sections that appear too thick, cover the remainder with a cover slip and observe under the microscope. There will be many bad sections in the mount, so concentrate on finding some that show the detail you wish to study. Fig. 3-b illustrates the results one desires to obtain in making longitudinal sections of the hymenophore of a bolete. Cross sections (fig. 3-c) of the latter, and sections from a coral fungus (fig. 3-d) cut across a branch are shown.

It is very difficult to section the teeth of hydnaceous fungi. The best technique for microscopic study of this group is to place a spine on a slide in a drop of mounting fluid and crush it to such an extent that the details of the tramal hyphae and the hymenium can be seen. In crush mounts the spores become scattered all through the mount and may be advantageously studied where they are found adhering to bits of fungous tissue.

In sectioning, the important point to remember in using the razor or razor blade is to slice the material, do not just push the razor through it. Remember, also, that the sections too thick for study as sections can easily be pushed to one side, covered with a second cover slip, and crushed out thus giving one two different types of mount on one slide. If one uses his thumb to exert pressure on the

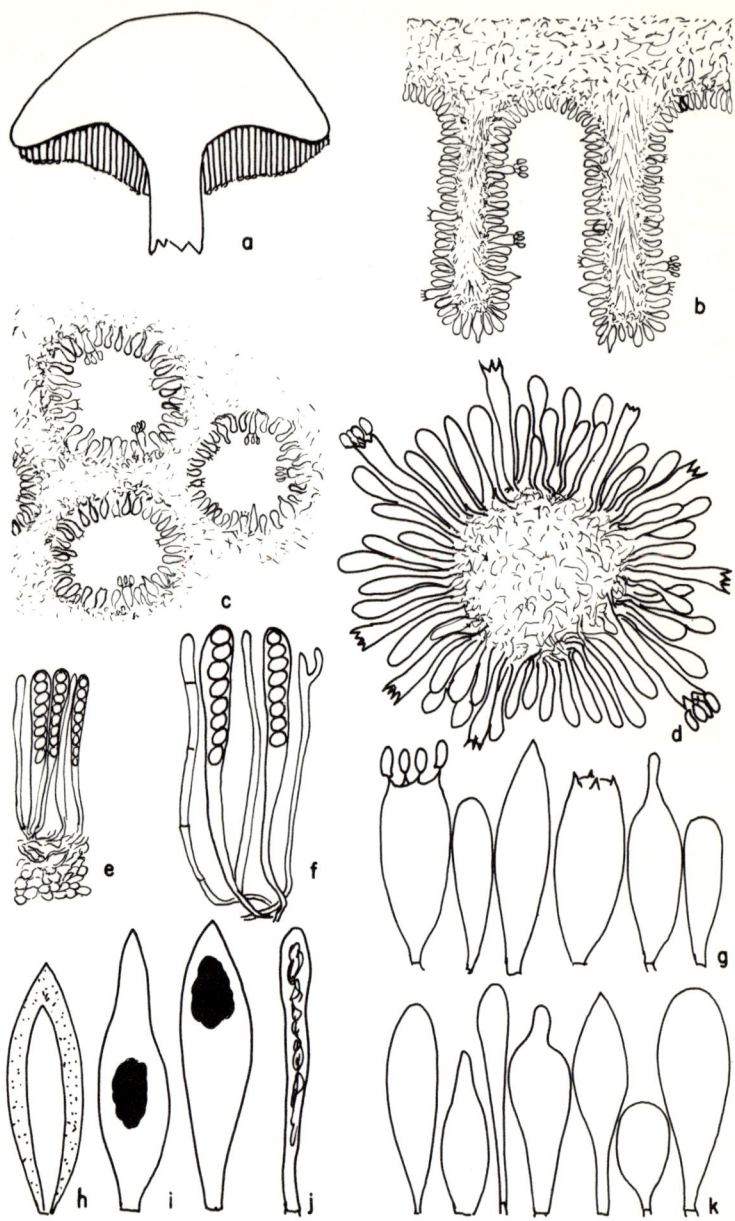

Fig. 3. (a) a longitudinal section through the cap of a bolete; (b) longitudinal sections of tubes of a bolete; (c) cross sections of tubes of a bolete; (d) cross section of a branch of a coral fungus; (e) asci paraphyses in a cup-fungus; (f) same as for e but the basal tissue (hypothecium) not shown; (g) from left to right in order named—basidium, basidiole, pleurocystidium, basidium, pleurocystidium and basidiole; (h) a lamprocystidium; (i) two chrysocystidia; (j) a pseudocystidium; (k) various shapes of leptocystidia.

cover slip in the process of crushing, be sure to have a cloth or piece of paper between your thumb and the glass to avoid leaving a thumbprint on the glass.

Spores from spore prints can be studied by scraping some spores from the print with a scalpel and transferring them to a very small droplet of mounting fluid on a slide, cover with a cover slip, and view under the microscope. The spores will move around a great deal if you have too much fluid in the mount, or if you have your microscope tilted. A spore print (fig. 4-b) may be obtained by cutting the stipe from the fruit body and placing the cap on white paper with the hymenophore oriented downward (its natural position). Cover this setup with a bowl or cup to shut off air currents (fig. 4-a). The spores will collect on the paper. Use white paper in order to be able to exactly determine the color of the deposit later. Do not shellac the deposit to the paper because this will interfere with removal of the spores for microscopic study. For a coral fungus, simply lay the fruit body on its side, place a sheet of white paper under it, and wrap in waxed paper. Spore prints of Ascomycetes are not ordinarily essential for general identification work.

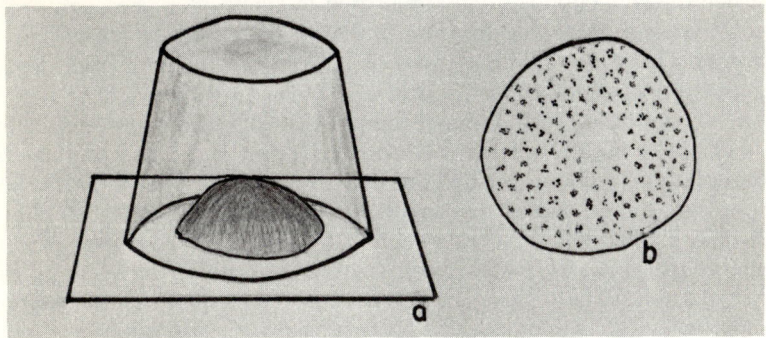

Fig. 4. (a) set-up for a spore print; (b) spore print from a bolete.

Sections made from fresh material may be studied under an oil-immersion lens. For this purpose an objective with a numerical aperature (NA) of about 0.95 or 1 is recommended. This gives you the maximum resolving power (the ability to distinguish between two points of light very close together) that can be obtained with your objective. It also gives you enough working distance (the distance between the objective and the cover slip) so that if the mount is reasonably thin the objective will not touch the cover slip when the material to be studied is in focus. If you are using a lens with a NA of 1.25-1.3 or 1.4, in order to get the full resolving power you must immerse the condenser lens as well as the objective. To do this place a drop of oil on the surface of the condenser lens and then raise the condenser bringing the oil drop in contact with the bottom of the microscope slide. This gives one an optical system with no air layers in it. When using an oil-immersion lens, use a #1 or #1.5 cover slip; the number is a gauge of thickness, the thicker the glass the higher the number. For general work I prefer an eyepiece for the microscope of 10 × or 12.5 × magnification in conjunction with a low power oil-immersion lens of 54 × magnification and an NA of 0.95.

At first one will spend most of his time demonstrating the characters as they are encountered in the key. Consequently, one can set up a system to follow in making a microscopic study of a specimen: (1) Study the spores first. Measure length and width of at least 10 spores from a deposit and record the measurements (see p. 17). Make a sketch of a spore in face view (fig 2-d) and one in profile view (fig. 2-e). Show the detail of the apex and/or any markings on the spore surface. Also measure the thickness of the wall, and record this if it is over 0.5 μ. Walls thinner than this are described simply as thin-walled. Now mount spores from the same deposit in Melzer's reagent and compare the color with those in the first mount which may be in water or KOH. After you have completed your study of the spores of a given collection, write out a description of them. When the collection is finally identified to genus or species, compare your description of the spores with that of the author of the description you have used. This will be of help in the future as one deals with the spores of various groups.

It is important to determine the presence of various types of cells in the hymenium, and for this, sections (thin ones) are preferred, though thick sections crushed out can also be used. First identify the spore producing cells in the layer. Are they asci or basidia? If they are basidia many will have 4 needle-like projections from the surface at the apex (fig. 2-c) and if one searches carefully, some examples will be found showing spores in various stages of development on these spicules. These cells are the *basidia* (sing. *basidium*), and the spicules are termed *sterigmata*. In the same mount will be many cells like the basidia (fig. 3-g: 2, 6) but not showing any sterigmata. These are *basidioles* (immature basidia, presumably). These two elements, basidia and basidioles, make up the entire hymenium of some species, but in others, scattered cells of a different shape and size are to be noted. These are termed cystidia (fig. 3-g: h-j and k). Their size, shape, thickness of wall, the presence of crystals at the apex, and nature of the content in water and KOH and in Melzer's should also be noted. There are many types of cystidia, and they are classified by two different systems: One by their location and secondly by their features. In the first system, those found on the faces of the hymenophore are termed *pleurocystidia,* those on the edges (such as tube mouths) are termed *cheilocystidia,* and cystidia on the stipe are termed *caulocystidia,* if any are found on the pileus they are *pileocystidia*. In the coral fungi, of course, there are no cheilocystidia. The term hymenial cystidia is also frequently used as a contrast to dermatocystidia which term refers to those of both the pileus and stipe. In the second classification, the most commonly encountered type is termed a leptocystidium (fig. 3-g: 3 & 5; k). It is thin-walled. *Lamprocystidia* have thick walls (fig. 3-h). *Chrysocystidia* have a peculiar content (fig. 3-i) when revived in KOH. *Pseudocystidia* have an oily (globular) content (fig. 3-j). These types may be found in various positions, but are usually in the hymenium.

The hyphae in the area between two hymenial layers are termed tramal hyphae and the tissue they form the *trama*. The location of pigment, if such is present, is important; is it dissolved in the cell sap or is it deposited irregularly or regularly on the wall as patches or spirals, or is it in the wall itself? For differentiating types of hyphae on the basis of their content, several mounting media should be used. Some hyphae may have an oily-globular content, some a homogeneous opaque content, and in Melzer's some may have blue to violet granules. Most hyphae, however, will appear to be empty when revived.

The goal in studying collections of fleshy fungi is to record the data on each worthwhile collection so that in the process of identifying the collection, as one uses books by various authors, one can compare his data with that of whatever author's work he happens to have in hand. Furthermore, the recording of data, as already stated, is a simple and effective device to accomplish two purposes: To get the collector to scrutinize his collections closely, and secondly, to enable him to compare his description with that of the author of the book he is using. At first one will be disappointed with his own descriptions as well as with those of the author whose work he is using for it is not an easy task to write a description of a mushroom that can be clearly interpreted by one who has not seen the actual specimens. But the system we are proposing is the shortest route to the accurate identification of fleshy fungi.

Never write out a "check sheet" on which are listed the characters you think you should observe so that you can simply check their presence later with a specimen at hand. This dulls one's powers of observation, and tends to encourage one to hurry through the collections without getting a good mental image of each. Also, if you use a check sheet, you will never learn to write a good description, and this in turn will prevent you from getting all the information you should from the technical descriptions of others. The dried specimen is an important part of the body of information you collect on each species.

For recording the data we use 4×6 inch cards cut from 2-ply bristol board, the material illustrators use for making pen and ink drawings. On one side of the card write the description of the macroscopic (gross) features that can be studied with the naked eye or a handlens. Describe the pileus, hymenophore and stipe in that order, each in a separate paragraph. On the other side of the card, in the upper left hand corner, write the name of the group: Order, family, or genus and species if the identification has proceeded that far. In the upper right hand corner write the name of the locality where the fungus was found; the date it was found, on what (or under the kind of tree) it was found, who collected it, and then your own collection number. If you photographed the collection make a notation to that effect. If you have a spore print staple it to the card after folding it with the spores to the inside of the fold. As you study the spores, hymenial features, and details of the dermal layers of pileus and stipe, record the data in paragraphs in the order just listed. Use a second card if there is no more room on the first, and staple it to the first one. Always treat the various parts of the fruit body in the same order to facilitate quick reference later when you are comparing many collections made over a period of years. The finished card (cards) may be filed either by collection number, family or genus. The next step is the preservation of the specimens.

The Preparation of Specimens for the Herbarium

It is important to think about keeping reference specimens just for your own use—to refresh your memory, possibly the next collecting season, when problems with closely related species arise. As one works with fresh material one is soon able to identify families or orders at sight, and very soon many of the larger common genera, but one will also find that there are many groups even yet in which mycologists (as specialists are called) have not made a sufficient study to enable the species to be clearly presented to beginners (or even to other specialists). In the large corals (Ramaria) for instance, the treatment given here is very incomplete since the diversity in this genus for North America has never been adequtaely documented from a scientific standpoint. In *Rhizopogon*, the most complete key yet published is presented here for the first time in order to show how complicated some of the larger genera are, and as an aid to those with a desire to hunt for the fungi most difficult to find: those producing fruit bodies under ground or barely breaking through.

In a few seasons, however, one will build up enough experience to enable him to select groups of particular interest—and at this time it is very desirable to think of preserving material for critical study, possibly to send to a specialist later. It is at this point that your study cards become of greatest importance.

NON-GILLED FLESHY FUNGI

An herbarium is nothing more than a collection of properly classified and labeled plants. The manner in which the plants are preserved is determined by the kind of plant to be preserved and how one desires to study it later. Our immediate concern is with the fruit bodies of fleshy fungi. There is only one way to preserve fleshy fungi that is worth discussion, namely by drying. After a collection has been studied and possibly photographed, one is ready to consider preserving it.

The best way of preserving fleshy fungi for future study is by drying. For small fruit bodies activated silica gel is recommended as a drying agent. We use "Tell-Tale," mesh size 6-16, made by Davison Chemical, Baltimore 3, Maryland. It is blue but turns white as it takes up moisture. The form of silica gel sold by florists and nursery supply houses under the name. Flower Dri can also be used. This is a fine white granular material with some larger blue crystals which are blue when the material is dry and fade to pink or white when it has absorbed moisture. Plastic freezer dishes of various sizes and with tightly fitting covers are needed. Fill these half full of dry silica gel, replace the cover tightly and stand the dish at the back of your work table or some other convenient place. When you have a specimen ready to dry, take a dish of appropriate size, scatter the specimens on *top* of the gel. Do not cover them with Flower Dri in particular as the small granules will adhere too persistently. If some do adhere, brush them off after the specimen has dried. The field label should be placed in the dish with the specimen. Replace the cover and allow to stand for 24 hours. The field label is a slip of paper giving the name of the fungus (as close as you can), where it was collected, what it was on (wood, soil, ashes, under pine, etc.), the name of the collector and the person who identified it, a note stating whether it was photographed or a card description was written, and the collection number. For the collection number keep a collecting diary in a notebook and in it number your collections consecutively, but have them grouped by month and day. If the specimens are not brittle in 24 hours, and the gel has turned from blue to white, transfer the specimen and the label to another dish to finish drying. Always keep the label with the specimen. The silica gel can be reactivated by spreading it out in a large baking pan and heating it in an oven to not over 250 degrees F. When the gel or the large crystals in Flower Dri turn blue, the material is ready for re-use.

Place the dried specimen in a cardboard box of suitable size, include the label, and on the cover paste a duplicate label. Add some crystals of paradichlorbenzene to fumigate the specimens and store in an airtight container so that the odor of the fumigant does not spread all over the house. Paradichlorbenzene is sold for killing clothes moths, but is also effective for other insects. After about two weeks remove all that is left of the fumigant and add some naphthalene flakes. These act as an insect repellent (naphthalene is the active ingredient in "moth balls"). *Never* mix paradichlorbenzene and naphthalene. Insects, especially small weevils *love* dried fungi and will ruin your collection if it is not protected against them. Keep your herbarium somewhere where it is dry and the odor of the insect repellant will not dusturb the household.

If the specimens are large, cut them in half lengthwise and place them on a drier (fig. 5). Our driers are made to accommodate two hot plates of one burner each or a 2-burner stove, and are operated on low heat. Never put so much on the drier that the air cannot properly circulate among the specimens, and never place paper under the specimen when you place the latter on the drier. Fold the label and place beside the specimen to the right or left, but always on the same side for all collections. If a large drier with several shelves is used, one should have a canvas treated to be flame proof to wrap around the drier to force the warm air up around the specimens. Our large drier is made of aluminum and built so that the shelves are removable for easy loading and unloading. When the specimens are dry (brittle) put them in boxes and fumigate as already directed. One can often get boxes of assorted sizes by arranging for them with a local druggist. Paper packets are used by some people, but they do not offer adequate protection to the specimens.

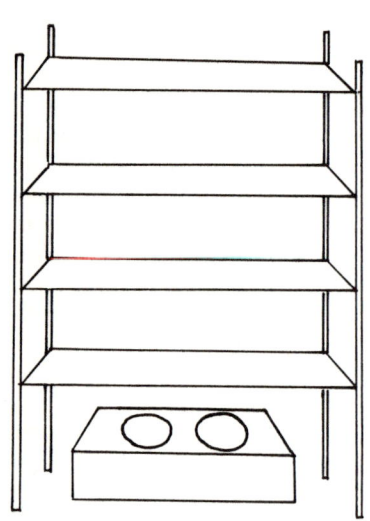

Fig. 5. A drier for fleshy fungi shown without the canvas to wrap around it to force the heat upward.

Formulae and Procedures

It is out of keeping here to try and list all the solutions that have been or are being tested in the study of the fleshy fungi. They are legion. Rather, it suits the purpose of this work better to give only those that are regarded as practical, and which can be obtained by most people. Naturally, some of the chemicals are dangerous to have where children can get at them. Keep your solutions out of reach of children at all times.

1. Water: As a mounting medium it ranks first. Tap or distilled water can be used. Always use it for the study of fresh specimens

since the appearance of the microscopic structures in this medium furnishes the standard for judging the effects of other media on these characters.

2. KOH: Potassium hydroxide is a strong base. Use a 2.5% aqueous solution. Use it both as a mounting medium for microscopic features, and for testing color reactions of the parts of the fresh fruit body. It is also the mounting medium to use routinely in reviving sections made from dried fruit bodies. It is a good idea to have two dropper bottles of this solution, one perfectly clear and one with a pinch of basic phloxine (a dye) added. The latter will help make more visible hyaline structures such as some spore and cell walls.

3. Ammonia: Commercial grade or concentrated will do. Use for testing color reactions, particularly on caps of boletes where one may get a flash of metallic green or blue, then a change to reddish brown on some species. Diluted to about 10 per cent it is also used as a mounting medium since it gives a clearer picture of some structures than does KOH.

4. Iron salts ("$FeSO_4$" is used as a symbol, but Fe_2Cl_2 may be used also): A solution of about 10 percent in water is used to test for certain color reactions. Various parts of the fruit body should be tested: Context, base of stipe, apex of stipe, hymenophore, etc. Expected reactions are: (a) No change. (b) A change to olive, grayish olive, green or blackish green. The change may develop slowly or rapidly and in some is enhanced by adding ethanol (70 to 95%) to the same spot. (c) A change to pink, salmon color, or grayish red. The reaction on dried material may not be as pronounced as on fresh.

5. Cotton blue (Poirrier's blue) in 85% lactic acid: Used for microscopic studies of spore ornamentation especially in Discomycetes. Heat the slide slightly after making the mount. Some structures show a strong affinity for the stain and are said to be cyanophillic. If a slide is too dark, wash it out with clear 85% lactic acid. Do this by absorbing the mounting fluid at one side of the mount with absorbent material while adding clear lactic acid at the other side.

6. Melzer's reagent: This solution is a "must" for the study of higher fungi. It gives distinctive color reactions, clears the material, and brings out fine detail remarkably well.

The Formula:
Water .... 22 gms.
chloral hydrate .... 20 gms.
Iodine .... .0.5 gms. (crystals)
Potassium iodide (KI) .1.5 gms.

Make up the formula in quadruple proportions, it keeps well.

For those without ready access to chemicals, it may be necessary to get a prescription for the chloral hydrate. "Melzer's" as it is termed in the key, can be used for reviving dried material. In fact it is excellent for this purpose, though it takes a short time for the cells to regain their normal shape and turgor. If used on fresh material, let the mount stand for about 5 minutes or more before viewing.

Reactions: *Amyloid.* A blue gray, blue, violet or violet black coloration usually on hyphal or spore walls. Spores of *Russula and Lactarius* have amyloid ornamentation.

Dextrinoid. A reddish brown, vinaceous red or dark red color, usually in hyphal walls or in the content of the cell, is covered by this term.

Inamyloid. No change or merely a change to yellowish (often merely the color of the mounting medium), or a change to pale brownish or orange.

Caution: Never mix KOH and Melzer's in the same mount since this ruins the reaction. The iodine is the active ingredient of the medium, though chloral hydrate has been found to produce some color reactions independent of the iodine.

When testing a chemical for a color change on fresh material, simply apply a drop to the surface you wish to test. Melzer's is used mainly as a mounting medium.

Sulfobenzaldehyde: Sulfobenzaldehyde 40% sol. in water ...... 6 cc
Distilled water .... 3 cc
Sulphuric acid (CP) ....10 cc

Calibrating Your Microscope

The problem of measuring spores and other objects under the compound microscope involves using a scale either placed in the eyepiece or having an eyepiece with a built-in scale, both are available but a removable glass disc with a scale engraved on it is the least expensive and is perfectly satisfactory. To place the glass disc in the eye piece, unscrew the top lens and lower the disc into the tube. Be sure that the disc is the correct diameter for your eye piece before you buy it. The disc will rest on a shelf in the tube, and it may be necessary to adjust the shelf upward or downward slightly to bring the scale into sharp focus. If the lines of the scale are blurred, unscrew the upper lens of the eyepiece, remove the disc and raise the shelf or lower it slightly, replace the disc and try again to see if the lines are clearer or more blurred. If the lines are more blurred, obviously the level of the scale was changed in the wrong direction.

NON-GILLED FLESHY FUNGI 17

Once the scale is in focus, the next item needed is a stage micrometer, which is nothing more than a glass slide with a scale of known values marked on it and covered with a cover glass. You need the stage micrometer only once, so borrow one from some source if possible. The scale will probably have 2 sets of lines: one set with lines 0.01 mm apart and the other set of lines 0.1 mm apart. In other words you know the values for the distance between lines for each scale on the stage micrometer but you will use only the set with the lines 0.01 mm apart.

Most of your measurements will be made in microns, and a micron (μ) is 0.001 mm. Each unit on your fine stage scale is thus 10 μ (or, in the fine set the lines are 10 μ apart). Your unknown value is the distance apart in μ of the lines of the scale on the eyepiece. Your problem is, therefore, rather simple: In order to establish the value in μ for the distance between two lines on the eyepiece scale, you compare this with the distance between two lines on the fine scale of the stage micrometer. Have the stage scale in the center of your microscopic field and match the two scales or parts of them. Do this by manipulating the eyepiece scale so that one line on it is superimposed exactly on a line of the stage, and note carefully how many spaces on the eyepiece scale it takes to cover exactly a space on the stage scale. This set of values will be different for each set of lenses on your microscope, but let us assume here you are using a low-power oil immersion objective of 54 $\times$ magnification and a 10 $\times$ eyepiece. Let us assume that with this system you have matched the two scales and that it takes 4 spaces of the eyepiece scale to cover one space on the stage scale. In other words 4 eyepiece spaces are equal to 10 μ. How much does 1 eyepiece unit (space) equal? Divide 10 μ by 4 and 2.5 μ is your answer. If the tube of your microscope is movable, be sure that you note the position it is in when you make your calibration, and always reset it in this position before you make measurements.

Make a chart for the value in μ of the eyepiece scale units for each set of lenses you intend to use for measuring covering from 1 to 25 spaces. This chart will save you a lot of time when you are working with specimens.

GENERAL CONSIDERATIONS

How to use the Key: A key is a device to enable one to find the name of an unknown object by making a series of choices between paired descriptive statements. In this key one always selects the best of a pair of like-numbered choices, two in the present key. These are termed a couplet. When one has decided which of the two statements in a couplet best describe the fungus he has in hand, look to the right side of that line to see if the name is given or if another couplet is indicated by a number. If a number, turn to it and repeat the process of selection. Do this until you come to a name or you come to the end of the key. If the latter, it should indicate that the fungus you have is not treated in this work. If your specimen does not seem to fit the description of the species you come to in the key, or you have exhausted the number of choices in the key, try going through the key again, and be sure of each choice. In some large groups, such as *Ramaria*, only a few representative species are included.

In using the key, you will find that in many instances the first member of a couplet may mention two or more features such as: "spore deposit yellow, hymenophore of tubes, and flesh staining blue when injured." The second choice may simply read "Not as above." This means that if at least one of the features mentioned in the first couplet is not present in the fungus in hand, choose the second member of the couplet.

Responsibility for Identifications: Neither the authors nor the publisher accept responsibility for any identifications users of this work may make or the results of these identifications especially in relation to edible and poisonous fungi. Great care in the study of fungi is necessary, and the responsibility for arriving at the correct species is entirely that of the user. We have tried to help the user all we can, but there is no book written on North American fungi which contains all the species.

Distribution: Since the distribution of fungi in North America is so poorly known, we have given it only in general terms and have placed more emphasis on habitat.

Illustrations: In the drawings, the distance between the lines on the scale indicates 1 centimeter (or 10 mm.). In a work of this kind it is impossible to illustrate all the basidiocarps and ascocarps life-size.

KEY TO THE FLESHY AND NEAR-FLESHY HIGHER FUNGI

1a. Spores borne in asci (fig. 8), the fruit bodies cup-shaped, saddle-shaped, pileate with the upper part pitted, somewhat fingerlike or forming a thin covering over the gill area of a true mushroom, etc. ....Fig. 6. ASCOMYCETES p. 20

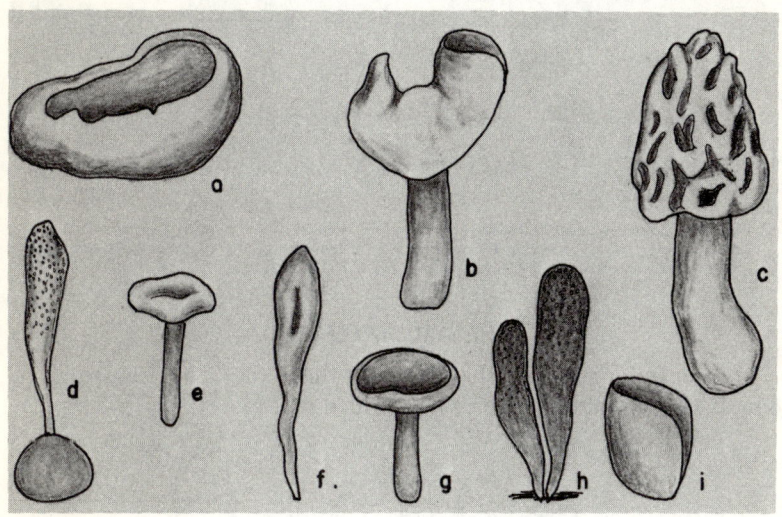

Fig. 6. Ascomycete fruit bodies. (a) a cup-fungus (Discomycete); (b) a *Helvella*; (c) a morel; (d) a *Cordyceps*; (e) a *Cudonia*; (f) a *Geoglossum*; (g) a stalked cup-fungus; (h) *Xylaria*; (i) *Otidea*

1b. Spores borne on basidia (fig. 2, c), the fruit bodies gelatinous, cartilaginous, fleshy or woody, varying in shape: club-shaped, vase-shaped, much-branched, or pileate with a cap and stalk, or the hymenophore borne inside a ball shaped fruiting body or the latter stipitate or opening like a star, or fruiting body variously shaped but bearing a slimy foul-smelling mass of spores on its exterior when expanded ....
..................................Fig. 7. *BASIDIOMYCETES* p. 66

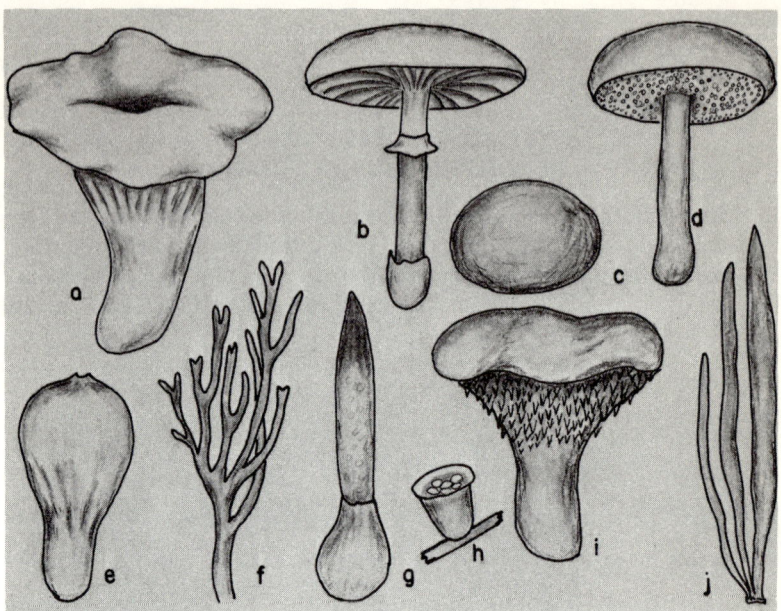

Fig. 7. Basidiomycete fruit bodies (a) chantrele; (b) a gilled fungus; (c) a puff-ball; (d) a bolete; (e) *Lycoperdon* (a puff-ball); (f) *Ramaria*; (g) a stink horn (*Mutinus*); (h) a "bird's nest fungus" (Nidulariales); (i) a *Hydnum*; (j) a *Clavaria*.

THE ASCOMYCETES

These fungi produce the spores of the sexual stage in asci (fig. 8; a, b, c, d, f) and the spores are termed ascospores (fig. 8; e, g, h).

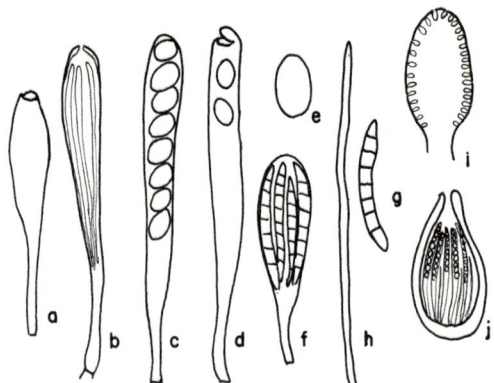

Fig. 8. (a) an ascus which has dicharged its spores; (b) an ascus with filamentous ascospores; (c) an ascus with ellipsoid ascospores; (d) an ascus showing the lid (operculum) at apex and most of the spores discharged; (e) an ellipsoid ascospore; (f) an ascus with septate ascospores; (h) a filamentous ascospore greatly enlarged; (g) a septate ascospore enlarged; (i) perithecia in the head of a *cordyceps*; (j) a single perithecium showing asci and ascospores.

NON-GILLED FLESHY FUNGI 21

The ascospores can be almost any shape, depending on the species and can be hyaline or colored violet, brown, black, etc., as viewed under the microscope. The features of the spores are among the most important for the identification of the various species. The asci (singular *ascus*) may be borne in a hymenium or in small flask-shaped bodies termed perithecia (fig. 8, i, j). The perithecia give a somewhat pimply appearance to the surface on which they are borne (fig. 9).

Ascomycetes grow on any substance that furnishes basic nutriments such as carbon and nitrogen, but the ones we are interested in here, those with fleshy (soft) fruit bodies, live on humus, old wood, dead insects (*Cordyceps*) or on other fungi. They are found at various times of the year, but many—and those of greatest interest to most naturalists—fruit in the spring.

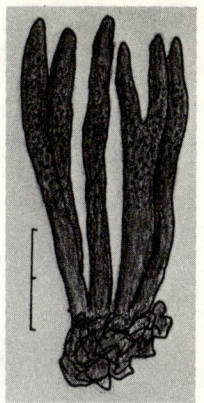

Fig. 9. *Xylaria polymorpha*.

Key to the Major Divisions Included Here

1a. Fruit body cup-shaped, saddle-shaped, pileate or with a pitted upper portion; hymenium covering most of the exposed surfaces of these structures ....Fig. 6; a, b, c, i *Pezizales*

1b. Fruit body not as above; the asci produced in perithecia (fig. 8; i, j) 2

2a. Fruit body arising from a dead insect or from a second fungus which the first one is parasitizing .....Fig. 6; d *Cordyceps* p. 60

2b. Not as above 3

3a. Perithecia borne on a clavate to subcylindric or pointed black carbonaceous to woody fruit body; growing on rotting wood Fig. 9 ....*Xylaria polymorpha* (Pers.) Grev.

The species of this genus have black fruit bodies 2-8 cm high and 0.5-2 cm broad or larger. They are exceptionally abundant on slash 5-10 years after an area has been logged. They persist all year so one is likely to find them without spores. The clubs develop during the late spring and summer and at that time are often found coated with non-sexually produced spores. We know of no use for the fruit bodies.

3b. Perithecia borne in a felty layer (subiculum) almost or completely obliterating the hymenophore of the host fungus ....*Hypomyces lactifluorum* (Schw.) Tulasne

Fruit body shaped like a gilled mushroom but in place of gills on the under side of the cap there occurs a bright orange-red layer marked by dots which are the openings of the perithecia of the parasite. The mycelium of the parasite apparently lives on the mycelium of the host mushroom and develops its fruiting state at the same time the host tries to fruit. The species included here occurs in large quantity in the late summer in eastern North America since that is the time the host(s) is (are) also fruiting. These parasitized fruit bodies are eaten by many mushroom hunters, but we have never encouraged this—what if the host happened to be a poisonous species?

Pezizales

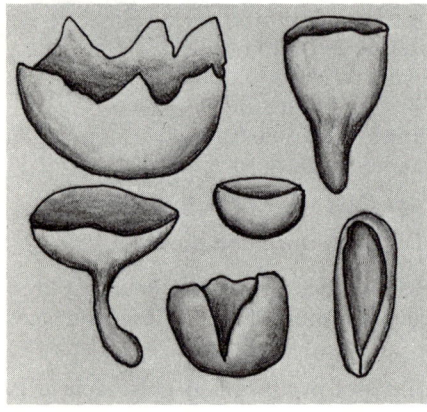

Fig. 10. Fruiting bodies of *Discomycetes* disc-like, cup-shaped or ear-shaped.

The fleshy Ascomycetes, as they are often called, have soft to submembraneous, gelatinous or tough fruit bodies of various shapes: saucer-shaped, cup-shaped, urn-shaped, clavate, capitate-stipitate, or pileate.

1a. Fruit body discoid to urn-shaped; ascus usually opening by a lid. Fig. 10 and Fig. 8d ....*Pezizaceae*

1b. Not as above 2

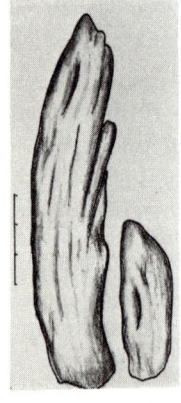

Fig. 11. *Underwoodia columnaris*.

2a. Fruit body 1-3 cm thick, clavate, surface smooth or nearly so; interior chambered with large compartments. Fig. 11 ....*Underwoodia columnaris* Pk.

Fruit body up to 10 cm long, fleshy, columnar, clavate, or slightly tapering above, the hymenium covering the entire outer surface, dingy cream-color or pale tan at first, becoming brownish, the surface more or less fluted, interior chambered; spores 25-27 × 12-14 μ, smooth at first, finally with warts; paraphyses thicker above than at base, brownish.

On soil among leaves, known from New York, Michigan, Kansas and in Canada in Manitoba, early summer, rare but very distinctive.

2b. Not with all of the features in 2a 3

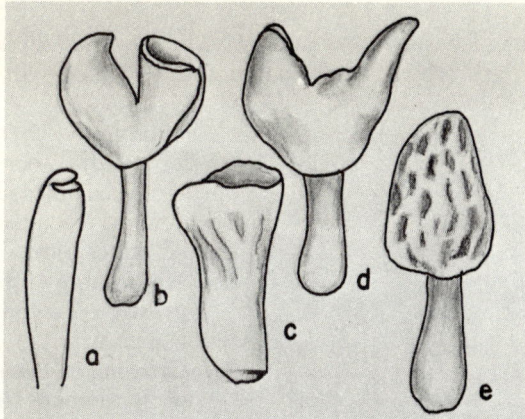

Fig. 12. Fruit bodies of the Helvellaceae, and (a) an operculate ascus.

3a. Fruit body soon becoming saddle-shaped to capitate-plicate or clavate and pitted; asci with a lid (visible after spore discharge); stipe mostly 1 cm or more thick. Fig. 12 ......*Helvellaceae* **p. 37**
3b. Fruit body capitate, pileate, clavate or cylindrical; stipe mostly less than 6 mm thick; asci with an apical pore through which the spores escape. Fig. 13 ....
..................*Geoglossaceae* **p. 50**

Pezizaceae

1a. Fruit body gelatinous to cartilaginous in consistency. Fig. 14 ....
......................*The Gelatinous Series*
1b. Fruit body fleshy to tough but not gelatinous or cartilaginous 2
2a. Fruit body sessile or nearly so ......
...*The Non-gelatinous Series* **p. 25**
2b. Fruit body distinctly stalked but often fluted, ribbed or cacunose, or terete in cross section ....
............Group 1 of the *Helvellaceae* **p. 38**

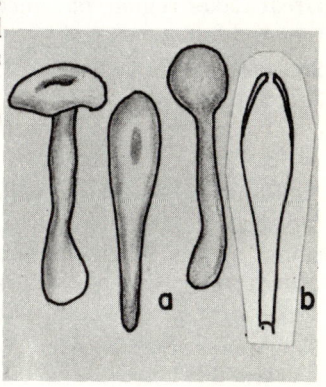

Fig. 13. Fruit bodies of the Geoglossaceae, and (b) an *inoperculate* ascus.

The Gelatinous Series

Some gelatinous species with inoperculate asci are included here.
1a. Fruit body with a thick, watery-gelatinous base ....
....Fig. 14. *Sarcosoma globosa* **Casp.**

Fruit body 4-10 cm broad at maturity, blackish, nearly globose when young, with hymenium as a flattened to depressed area at apex, interior of base watery and grayish; spores 23-26 × 10-12 μ; paraphyses dark brown, agglutinated and separated with some difficulty.

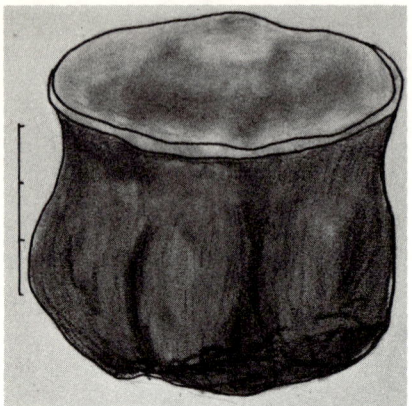

Fig. 14. *Sarcosoma globosa*

Solitary to gregarious on conifer duff, early spring northern: Canada south to New York and Michigan in the United States, rare.

1b. Not as above (the base not greatly enlarged at first).... 2
2a. Growing on decaying wood of hardwoods in clusters; hymenium dull lilaceous.... ....*Ascotremella fagineae* (Pk.) Seaver

Fruit bodies 1-4 cm, wide sessile to short-stipitate, in clusters 3-7 (10) cm wide, exterior of cups shining and pallid brownish; spores hyaline, 7 × 4-5 μ.

On wood of hardwood trees, eastern North America west to the Great Lakes region, not uncommon during wet weather in late summer and fall.

2b. Not as above 3
3a. Spores brown, 12-14 × 6-7 μ; growing on bark of dead hardwood trees (oak especially) ....*Phaeobulgaria inquinans* (Pers.) Nannflt.

Fruit bodies 1-4 cm wide, rounded to short cylindric becoming top-shaped, exterior rough and dull brown; hymenium blackish and shing; spores ellipsoid; paraphyses filamentous, yellow or violet-brown as revived, asci not operculate.

Solitary to clustered, widely distributed in North America.

3b. Spores hyaline, over 20 μ long; growing on the ground or on wood ....*Bulgaria*

Bulgaria

Fruit bodies sessile to short-stipitate, externally pubescent to roughened and blackish; hymenium paler; spores ellipsoid or nearly so.

1a. Hymenium black or brownish at first; apothecium not appressed against the woody substrate ....*Bulgaria melastoma* (Fr.) Seaver

Fruit body 1-2 cm wide, subglobose at first, opening by a circular aperature, the margin incurved, exterior tough, interior gelatinous;

hymenium concave, smooth, shining; stipe (if present) attached by a dense black mycelium; spores $20\text{-}25 \times 9\text{-}10\ \mu$.

Gregarious to clustered on sticks on the ground, on hardwood, widely distributed in North America.

1b. Hymenium dull brown or with a reddish tone 2
2a. On wood of conifers; spores $34\text{-}52 \times 8\text{-}10\ \mu$, slightly sausage-shaped in profile .... *Bulgaria mexicana* **Ellis & Holloway**

Fruit bodies obconic, urn-shaped at maturity, 2.5-7 cm wide, margin involute, hymenium cracking and whitish in the cracks; stipe short, thick, wrinkled; gelatinous in the interior.

Solitary to gregarious, western United States, especially along the Pacific Coast, rare, fall and early winter.

2b. On buried sticks of hardwoods; spores $20 \times 10\ \mu$ (approximately) .... *Bulgaria rufa* **Schw.**

Fruit bodies 2-3 cm, closed at first, opening and becoming shallowly cup-shaped, outer surface with clusters of hairs; consistency rubbery; stipe up to 1 cm long and 4-5 mm thick.

Eastern United States and Canada, early summer, often common.

Pezizaceae
The Non-Gelatinous Series

1a. Fruit body urn-shaped, large (6-10 cm high), blackish at maturity or in age (see figs. 23, 24) .... *Urnula* **p. 29**
1b. Not as above 2
2a. Fruit body attached to substrate (burned ground) by numerous rhizoids, shape discoid to crustlike (growth indeterminate) ....
.... *Rhizina inflata* **(Schaeff) Karsten**

Fruit body 2-6 or more cm broad, pale to dark date brown, paler on the margin; spores $35\text{-}43 \times 10\ \mu$, fusiform and with an apiculus $3\text{-}4\ \mu$ long at each end; paraphyses brown and intermixed with brown thick-walled non-septate hairlike structures.

On burned ground within a season or so following the fire, northern United States and Canada, common in its habitat.

2b. Not as above 3
3a. Fruit body black or blackish ....
.... *Pseudoplectania* and *Plectania* (see **p. 30**)
3b. Fruit body differently colored 4
4a. Fruit body disc-shaped to cup-like 7
4b. Fruit body typically lopsided, ear-shaped, half-cup-shaped or spoon-shaped (see *Peziza proteana* **p. 35** and *Otidea* also) (figs. 30-33) 5
5a. Fruit body with yellow to orange hymenium and the exterior blue to greenish at least near the margin. Fig. 15 ....
.... *Caloscypha fulgens* **(Fr.) Boudier**

Fig. 15. *Caloscypha fulgens.*

Fruit bodies lopsided to irregular or split on one side, up to 5 cm wide, substipitate, attached by coarse mycelium; spores 6-8 μ wide, globose; paraphyses filled with orange granules (in water mounts).

Solitary to clustered in cold wet springy places in early spring, common during wet seasons in northern U S. and Canada.

5b. Not as above 6
6a. Fruit bodies compound and shaped somewhat like a pair of moose antlers; arising from a large underground sclerotium ....
....Fig. 16. *Wynnea americana* Thaxter

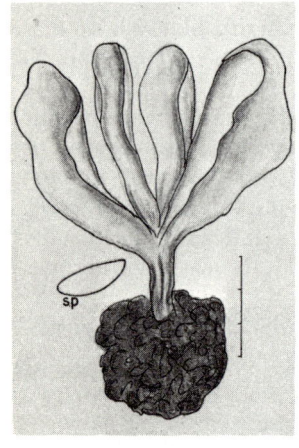

Fig. 16. *Wynnea americana.*

Divisions of the fruit body up to 25 in number, erect, elongate-ear-shaped, 6-13 cm long, blackish brown, the hymenium dark purplish red or brown; sclerotium 4-5 cm thick, brown, tough; spores 32-40 × 15 × 16 μ.

On the ground in woods, eastern North America, rare.

6b. Not as above (sometimes clustered but lacking a sclerotium) ....
.... *Otidea* p. 33
7a. Fruit body typically with a stipe (often quite short) 8
7b. Fruit body typically sessile 10
8a. Hymenium bright red to orange-red .... *Sarcoscypha* .... (p. 31) and related genera
8b. Hymenium some other color when young 9
9a. Fruit body goblet-shaped; hymenium dingy pale tan. Fig. 17
......................................*Geopyxis cupularis* (Fr.) Saccardo

Fruit body 3-15 mm wide, exterior slightly darker than hymenium; stipe 2-4 mm long, 1 mm thick; spores about 17-19 × 9-10 μ; paraphyses enlarged to apex and up to 7 μ wide near apex.

On burned areas, common and widely distributed; summer and fall.

9b. Not as above ....(see *Discina* (p. 28) and *Sarcosphaeria* also)

10a. Fruit body at first sunken in the soil 11

10b. Fruit body superficial from the first 12

11a. Fruit body 3-10 cm wide; hymenium grayish lilac to pallid lilaceous near maturity. Fig. 18 ......*Sarcosphaeria crassa* (**Santi ex Steudl.**) ....**Pouzar**

Fig. 17. Geopyxis cupularis.

Fruit body subglobose, splitting open into 7-10 rays, the wall quite thick and fleshy; exterior pallid, usually fairly clean of debris; stipe when present short and thick; spores 15-18 $\times$ 8-9 μ; paraphyses branched and enlarged above, when fresh with a bluish pigment in the interior.

Solitary to clustered under either conifer or deciduous trees, widely distributed, common in some areas such as the northern Rocky Mountains in the U. S during early summer.

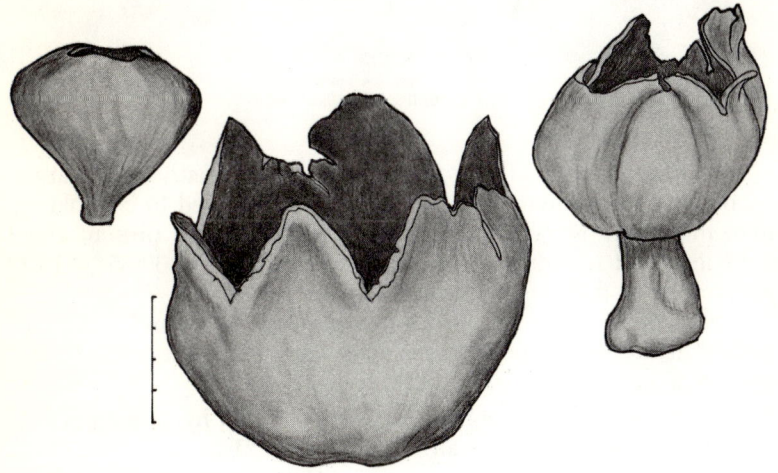

Fig. 18. Sarcosphaeria crassa.

11b. Fruit body under 4 cm wide; hymenium pallid at first (never lilaceous). Fig. 19 ....*Sepultaria arenicola* (**Lev.**) **Massee**

Fig. 19. *Sepultaria arenicola*.

Fruit bodies closed at first, and then visible as a hole in the ground; margin incurved, entire or splitting; exterior densely brown-hairy; spores 25-30 × 12-17 µ; paraphyses slender.

Gregarious in sandy soil, summer, widely distributed.

12a. Spores fusoid and with a short extension at each end. Fig. 20 ....
............*Discina perlata* **Fries**

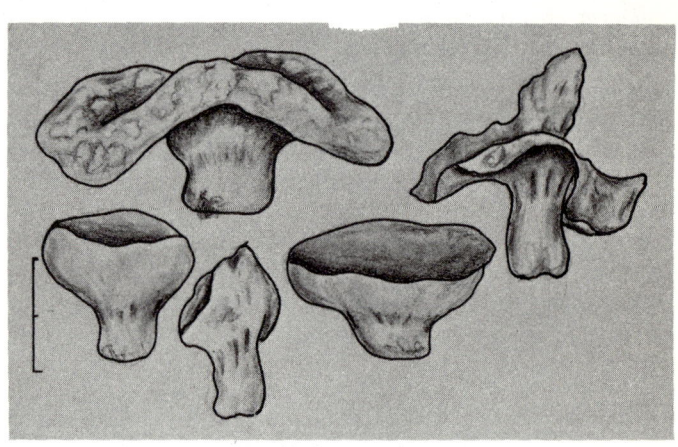

Fig. 20. *Discina perlata*.

Fruit body 4-10 (25) cm wide, discoid with a curved in margin, becoming repand, hymenial area becoming wrinkled to convoluted; hymenium dark brown to tan, exterior pallid; stipe if present about 1 cm long and 1-2 cm thick, lacunose in some; spores 30-35 × 12-14 µ; paraphyses dark yellowish brown.

Scattered or gregarious on humus or rotten wood under conifers, widely distributed in northern regions, early spring.

12b. Not as above 13
13a. Exterior of fruit body lacking distinct hairs; hymenium orange to scarlet, fading to orange-yellow. Fig. 21 ....
....*Aleuria aurantia* (Fr.) **Fuckel**

Fruit body soon saucer-shaped or shallowly cup-shaped; 2-10 cm wide; exterior whitish and pruinose; spores 18-22 × 9-10 µ, reticulate; paraphyses strongly enlarged at apex and filled with orange globules.

NON-GILLED FLESHY FUNGI

Fig. 21. Aleuria aurantia.

Gregarious to clustered on newly exposed soil such as along roads, skid-ways, etc., widely distributed and common, summer and fall. It is one of our most common, large, highly colored Cup-Fungi.

13b. Not as above 14
14a. Fruit body gray to yellowish gray over exterior; hymenium buff-colored when fresh; ascospores of 2 sizes in one apothecium (20-24 × 12-14 μ and 12-14 × 8-10 μ. Fig. 22 ......
....*Pustularia bronca* (Pk.) Kanouse

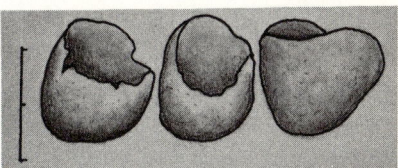

Fig. 22. Pustularia bronca.

Fruit body deeply cup-shaped, 1-3 cm wide and 1.5 cm deep; exterior roughened to somewhat verrucose; paraphyses of two types: one forked once below the middle, the other with various thickenings and irregular branching.

Solitary or in small groups, on humus in the woods, mossy banks, etc., summer, widespread in eastern North America.

14b. Not as above 15
15a. Exterior of fruit body (or its margin) with stiff dark brown hairs ....*Scutellinia* p. 32
15b. Not as in either of above choices............................*Peziza* p. 35

Urnula

1a. Fruit bodies at maturity splitting into segments and resembling earth stars somewhat; spores 50-70 × 12-16 μ. Fig. 23 ....
....*Urnula geaster* Peck

Fruit bodies at first elongate and closed or nearly so, splitting lengthwise into 3-6 rays, when expanded 10-12 cm wide; exterior covered by brownish hairs; hymenium pallid becoming yellowish; spores fusoid.

Attached to sticks on the ground. Texas.

1b. Fruit body not splitting deeply but crenate on margin; spores 28-35 × 12-14 μ. Fig. 24 ....*Urnula craterium* (Schw.) Pk.

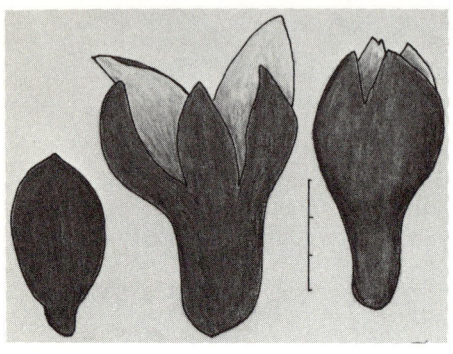

Fig. 23. *Urnula geaster*.   Fig. 24. *Urnula craterium*.

Fruit body 10-12 cm long, 3-8 cm wide, at first the exterior dark brown and scurfy but becoming black; substipitate to stipitate; hymenium dark brown to black; spores narrowly ellipsoid; paraphyses filiform, pale brown.

Attached to wood on the ground, early spring, widely distributed, common east of the Great Plains.

Pseudoplectania and Plectania

1a. Fruit body sessile or nearly so. Fig. 25 ....
....*Pseudoplectania nigrella* (Fr.) **Fuckel**

Fruit body 0.5-2 cm wide, sessile, exterior clothed with fine black hairs, black or nearly so, margin incurved at first but often wavy in age; hymenium dull brown to blackish; spores globose, 12-14 μ; hairs of exterior of cup usually coiled or twisted, pale brown, septate, 4-6 μ wide.

Scattered or gregarious on decaying moss-covered conifer sticks and logs, early summer, common in northern regions.

Fig. 25. *Pseudoplectania nigrella*.

NON-GILLED FLESHY FUNGI   31

1b. Fruit body distinctly stipitate 2
2a. Spores globose, 16-18 μ wide. Fig. 26 ....
................................Pseudoplectania melaena (Fr.) Saccardo

Fruit body cup-shaped becoming expanded, margin often wavy, 2-3 cm, black or blackish; hymenium olivaceous-brown; stipe up to 2-3 cm long, 3 mm thick, attached at base by a dense mass of coarse brown hairs.

Scattered or gregarious on decaying wood in conifer forests, northern regions, not common.

2b. Spores ellipsoid, 30-35 × 15 μ. ....
........................Plectania nannfeldtii Korf

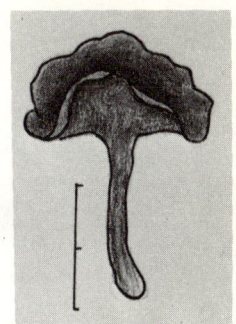

Fig. 26. Pseudoplectania melaena.

Fruit body shallow-cup-shaped, 2-3 cm wide; exterior hairy and brownish black; stipe up to 4 cm long and 2-3 mm thick, covered brown hairs, attached by a dense mass of coarse black mycelium.

Scattered on rotten wood in conifer forests.

Sarcoscypha and Related Genera

1a. Fruit body 1-4 cm wide, exterior whitish. Fig. 27 ....
....Sarcoscypha coccinea Saccardo

Fruit body cup-shaped, the margin incurved, exterior floccose and dry; stipe 2-3 cm long, at times very short; spores 26-40 × 10-12 μ; paraphyses containing numerous red granules.

On buried or partly buried hardwood sticks (fallen branches, etc.) in wet places, early spring, common and widely distributed in North America.

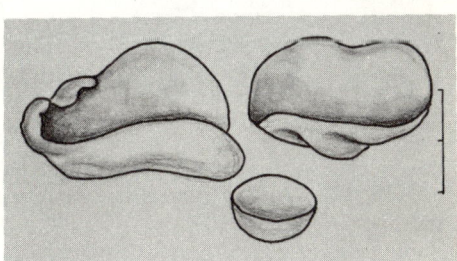

Fig. 27. Sarcoscypha coccinea.

1b. Fruit body smaller 2
2a. Exterior of fruit body conspicuously white-hairy. Fig. 28 ....
....Anthopeziza floccosa (Schw.) Kanouse

Cups 0.5-0.75 cm wide and up to 1.25 cm deep; hymenium scarlet, exterior hairs long and distinct; stipe slender (up to 5 cm long), hairy; spores 20-35 × 14-16 μ; paraphyses branched and forming a reticulum around the asci, having frequently small knoblike branches.

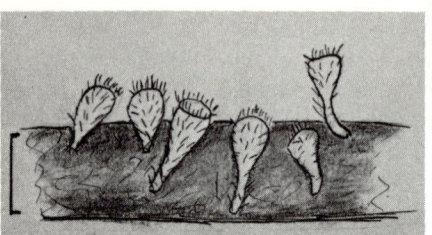

Fig. 28. Anthopeziza floccosa.

Usually clustered in groups of 3-6 from buried sticks of hardwoods; late spring, common and widely distributed.

2b. Not as above 3

3a. Fruit bodies with a long hard black pseudorhiza (rootlike process); stipe portion 2-6 cm long above it; spores 24-25 × 10-14 μ ....*Microstoma protracta* (Fr.) Kanouse

Stipes branched several times giving rise to up to 11 cups, upper portion light colored, covered with hyaline hairs; cups 1-2 cm wide typically deeply vase-shaped, often with a flat collar; hymenium rose red, exterior of cup orange-red; a layer of gelatinous hyphae present in the context; spores 24-45 × 10-14 μ; paraphyses branched, with a red content.

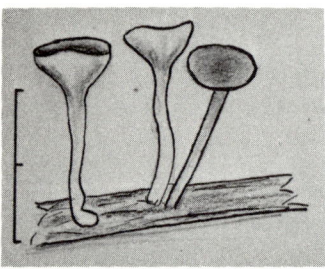

Fig. 29. Sarcoscypha occidentalis.

On buried wood, often of cottonwood, early spring, northern, rare.

3b. Lacking a pseudorhiza; stipe 1-3 cm long; spores 18-20 × 10-12 μ. Fig. 29 ......*Sarcoscypha occidentalis* (Schw.) Saccardo

Cup up to 1 cm wide; hymenium scarlet; exterior pallid and smooth or nearly so, color of hymenium may show through the wall; paraphyses branched, forked near the base.

On sticks in wet places in hardwood forest, early summer, common.

Scutellinia

1a. Hymenium orange to red ....*Scutellinia scutellata* (Fr.) Lambotte

Fruit bodies globose, opening to expose the bright red hymenium, (0.5) 1-2 cm broad; margin conspicuously fringed with hairs brown in color, hairs swollen above the base and tapered to a point; spores 20-24 × 12-15 μ, minutely warty.

Usually densely gregarious on rotten wood and adjacent soil, very common and widely distributed in North America.

1b. Hymenium pallid to grapish ....
..................................*Scutellinia hemisphaerica* (Fr.) Kuntze

Cups 1-3 cm wide, about half as deep, margin wavy or regular, fringed with brown hairs; spores $25\text{-}27 \times 12\text{-}15\ \mu$, becoming sculptured.

Gregarious or scattered on rich humus and near or on rotten wood; summer, common, widely distributed.

Otidea

In addition to the key characters, the spores are usually smooth and the paraphyses filiform and frequently branched, the tips may be straight, bent, or hooked.

1a. Fruit bodies elongate-ear-shaped. Fig. 30 ....
....2

1b. Fruit bodies truncate at the apex. Fig. 31
....4

2a. Exterior of fruit body ochraceous-orange to orange-buff; hymenium having a pinkish tint
................................*O. onotica* (Fr.) Fuckel

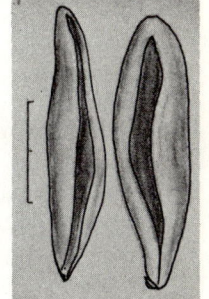

Fig. 30. Elongate-ear-shaped apothecia of *Otidea*.

Fruit bodies arising from a mass of debris held together by mycelium, 6-10 cm high, 5-6 cm wide (wider if expanded); hymenium with ground color pinkish cinnamon to ochraceous-buff; spores $12\text{-}14 \times 6\text{-}7\ (8)\ \mu$; paraphyses usually strongly hooked.

Gregarious to cespitose on the ground in conifer forests, New England and the Pacific Northwest.

2b. Exterior of fruit body light brown; hymenium lacking pinkish tints 3

3a. Paraphyses hooked at their apex ....
................................*O. leporina* (Fr.) Fuckel

Fruit bodies 1-4 cm high, 1-3 cm wide, the stipe up to 6 mm long; hymenium wood brown to avellaneous; spores $12\text{-}14 \times 6\text{-}8\ \mu$ ($8\text{-}11 \times 5\text{-}6\ \mu$ in var. *minor*).

Gregarious or cespitose on the ground in woods, Maryland and the Pacific Northwest.

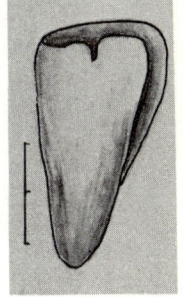

Fig. 31. *Otidea* fruit body truncate at apex.

3b. Paraphyses not hooked at the apex. Fig. 32 ....
....O. auricula (Cke.) Massee

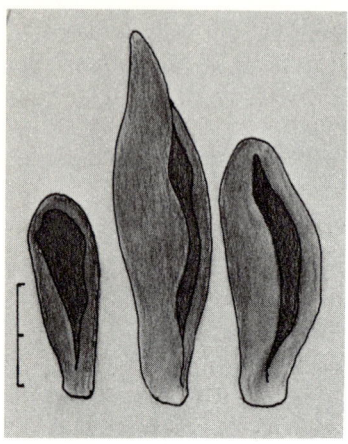

Fig. 32. Otidea auricula.

Fruit bodies 3-7 cm high, 1-2 cm wide (3-4 cm if flattened out), the edges inrolled, bay to chestnut-brown, lighter at the short stipelike base; spores $22\text{-}25 \times 12\text{-}16 \mu$.

On the ground, northern U. S. and in Canada.

4a. Fruit body with exterior and hymenium the same shade of dark brown; paraphyses having short lateral branches near the apex.
................O. abietina (Fr.) Fuckel

Fruit bodies 2-3 cm high, 2-4 cm broad; stipe short, whitish tomentose at base; spores $18\text{-}20\ (22) \times 10\text{-}12 \mu$.

Solitary or gregarious on the ground, northern U. S.

4b. Not as above 5
5a. Fruit bodies 1-2 cm high, 1-4 cm broad; exterior brown, the hymenium paler and frequently with areas of orange-red; paraphyses strongly hooked at the apex ....O. grandis (Pers.) Rehm

Stipe thick, up to 1 cm long, yellowish; spores $14\text{-}17 \times 6\text{-}7 \mu$, elongate-ellipsoid to subfusoid.

Solitary to clustered on the ground, eastern North America west to Michigan, rare.

5b. Not as above 6

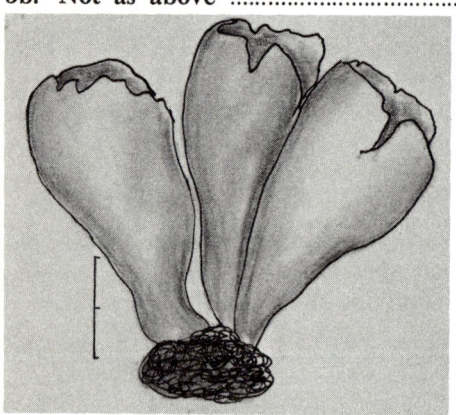

Fig. 33. Otidea alutacea.

6a. Fruit body pale clear yellow when fresh, 1-1.5 cm high, 1-2.5 cm broad ....O. cantharella ....(Fr.) Saccardo

Spores $10\text{-}11\ (12) \times 6\text{-}7 \mu$; paraphyses merely bent at the apex.

Solitary to gregarious on the ground, western United States.

6b. Fruit body darker in color and larger 7

7a. Fruit body densely clustered, frequently irregularly contorted. Fig. 33 ....O. alutacea (Fr.) Massee

NON-GILLED FLESHY FUNGI

Fruit body 2-6 cm high, 2-4 cm wide, exterior dull brown (yellow in var. *microspora*); hymenium gray-brown; spores 14-16 × 7-9 μ (or 9-10 × 5.5-6.5 μ in var. *microspora*).

7b. Fruit body solitary to gregarious 8
8a. Fruit body 3-7 cm high, 3-5 cm wide, exterior wood brown, hymenium drab ....*O. rainierensis* Kanouse

Fruit body creamy white toward the base, stipe up to 1 cm high, usually hollow; spores 10-12 × 6-7 (8) μ; paraphyses abruptly enlarged at apex.

On humus in woods, Pacific Northwest.

8b. Fruit bodies 2-3 cm high, 2-4 cm wide, yellowish tan to yellowish buff over both hymenium and exterior ....
....*O. kauffmanii* Kanouse

Stipe up to 1 cm high, 3-5 cm thick; spores 8-10 (12) × 5-6 (7) μ; paraphyses abruptly enlarged at apex, frequently bent but not hooked.

On the ground, Michigan.

Peziza

Peziza was the original genus for most of the cup-fungi, and it is from it that most of the genera treated so far were segregated. Hence the name in the older literature is used in varying concepts depending on the author. In the following treatment *Peziza clypeata* is placed by some in *Pachyella*. See Group I of *Helvella* also. Fruit bodies usually cup-shaped, sometimes discoid or repand.

1a. Fruit bodies variable in shape from shallowly cuplike to lopsided or spoon-shaped, often in compact masses, lilac tints present in fresh unweathered material ....
....*Peziza proteana* (Boud.) Seaver

Cups up to 9 cm wide and 5 cm deep, hymenium often wrinkled, pallid to light brown, often lilac tinted, exterior concolorous or slightly darker than hymenium except at the paler base; spores 10-12 × 4.5-6 μ, oblong, often with truncate projection.

F. *sparassoides* (Boud.) Korf grows in clumps up to 20 cm wide in which the apothecia are often spoon-shaped and fused at or near the bases.

On humus rich in lignin, in either conifer or hardwood forests, rare. f. *sparassoides* is rated as a good edible fungus.

1b. Not as above 2
2a. Hymenium blackish and shining when mature; fruit body disclike, 1-2.5 cm wide, on wet wood (submerged at times) ....
....*Peziza clypeata* Schw.

Fruit body closely attached to the substrate except for the free often slightly turned up margin, 1-4 cm broad; spores 25-27 × 12-14 μ (rarely up to 30-35 μ long); paraphyses septate, sticking together in revived material.

On decayed very wet wood of deciduous trees, eastern North America, fairly common, late summer and fall.

2b. Not as above 3
3a. Fruit body 1-4 cm wide, hymenium violaceous becoming deep violet and finally almost black; on burnt ground ....
....*P. violacea* Fries

Sessile or substipitate when young, at first closed and subglobose, becoming discoid or occasionally repand, often becoming irregular; spores 12-13 × 8 μ.

Gregarious on burnt ground and on charcoal, widely distributed in North America and common in its habitat, throughout the season.

3b. Not as above 4
4a. Hymenium becoming venose to conspicuously reticulate; spores 22-30 × 12-17 μ, brownish in mass ....*P. venosa* Fries

Fruit bodies substipitate, soon depressed and resting on the substrate except for the extreme margin, often irregularly splitting at maturity, up to 20 cm wide, exterior whitish or dingy, hymenium reddish brown; paraphyses adhering in groups when revived.

Solitary or gregarious on the ground in woods, eastern North America.

4b. Not as above 5
5a. Fruit body pallid, shallow-cup-shaped to saucer-like; spores smooth; growing on fallen tree trunks of hardwoods. Fig. 34 ....
....*P. repanda* Fries

Fruit body becoming repand, the margin entire or splitting, hymenium pallid to buffy tan; spores 14-16 × 9-10 μ.

On rotten logs or on soil or piles of chips, eastern North America, common, late spring. It is one of the very common species.

5b. Fruit body dingy yellow-brown over exterior but lilaceous to lilac-brown at the base; spores warty; growing on humus ....
....*Peziza badioconfusa* Korf

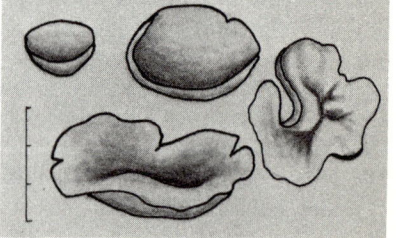

Fig. 34. *Peziza repanda.*

NON-GILLED FLESHY FUNGI

Fruit bodies cuplike, 3-10 cm wide, rarely *Otidea*-like, exterior roughened to unpolished; hymenium dull cinnamon-brown to date-brown; spores 17-23 × 8-11 μ.

Solitary to gregarious on humus rich in lignin or beside old logs or stumps, late spring, common in eastern North America.

The Helvellaceae

1a. Stipe 1-5 cm thick, often with interior folds; pileus or head ochraceous to reddish brown or bay red, wrinkled, brain-like, or if saddle-shaped the stipe not white and often internally folded. Fig. 35 .... *Gyromitra* p. 43
1b. Not as above 2
2a. Fruit body pileate or semipileate (the attachment at the apex of the stipe and sides hanging down like a skirt) or the hymenium borne on a pitted surface continuous with stipe, stipe usually terete near the apex. Fig. 36 .... *Verpa* and *Morchella* p. 46
2b. Fruit body not pitted, mostly saddle-shaped or mitrate; stipe often fluted to ribbed or also lacunose or in one group terete and 3-10 mm thick. Figs. 37, 38 ...*Helvella* p. 38

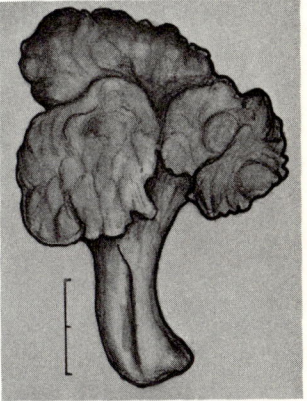

Fig. 35. *Gyromitra esculenta*.

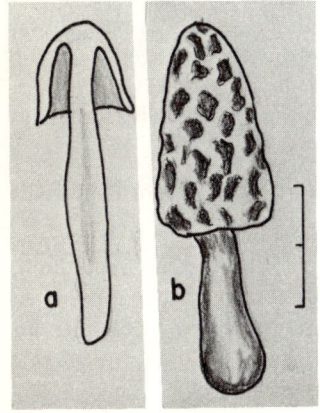

Fig. 36. (a) *verpa*; (b) *Morchella*.

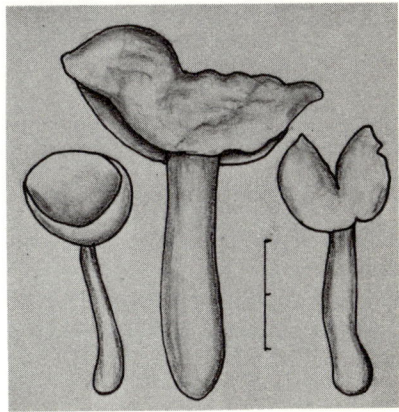

Fig. 37. species of *Helvella*.

Helvella (The False Morels)

1a. Stipe poorly formed to almost lacking .... *Helvella* (Group 1)
1b. Stipe clearly evident 2
2a. Stipe fluted to ribbed and often lacunose ....
....*Helvella* (Group 2) p. 40
2a. Stipe terete in cross section, 3-10 mm thick, rarely somewhat lacunose near base ....*Helvella* (Group 3) p. 42

Helvella (The False Morels)
Group 1 (Or the Cup-Like Helvellas)

1a. Subsessile, stipe short and obviously ridged, the ribs widening onto the outside of the cup. Fig. 38 2

1b. Stipe distinct, if ridged the ridges not extending onto the outside of the cup. Fig. 39 3

2a. Ribs angular and with sharp edges. Fig. 38 ....
.................................*Helvella acetabulum* (St. Amans) Quélet

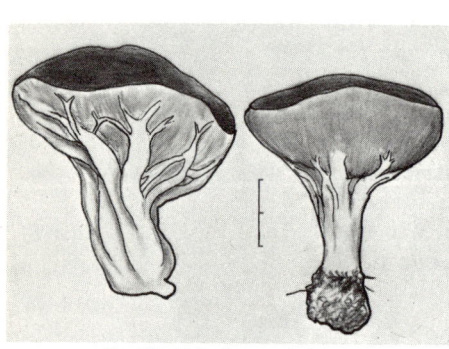

Fig. 38. *Helvella acetabulum*.

Cup 1.5-5 cm broad, hymenium gray-brown to dark brown, sometimes with a violet tint, darker than the outside of the cup; ribs prominent, whitish to cream color, extending nearly to the margin of the cup; stipe usually well developed, the interior chambered, 2-6 cm long; spores 18-22×12-$4\ \mu$; paraphyses straight, enlarged and 5-6 μ near apex.

On the ground in woods and open places, widely distributed in eastern North America, spring, uncommon.

2b. Ribs with blunt edges ....*Helvella costifera* Nannfeldt

Cup 1.5-7 cm wide, hymenium pale grayish to grayish brown; upper part of exterior of cup pubescent, colored like the hymenium, the ribs and lower part pallid to cream color, the ribs conspicuous, branching; spores 15-19×10-$13\ \mu$; paraphyses 3-4 μ thick and enlarged above.

On rich soil, eastern U. S., summer not common.

3a. Stipe merely ridged. Fig. 39 ....*Helvella queletii* Bresadola

Cup 2-8 cm broad, saucer-shaped, in age sometimes recurved, irregular, the margin split at times, hymenium pale irregular, the margin split at times, hymenium pale brownish to dark grayish brown, with or without a violet tinge, exterior of cup even, yellowish gray to avellaneous, pubescent; stipe 2-6 cm long, 8-10 mm thick, ribbed with 4-7 regular blunt ribs, pale grayish tan to nearly white, pubescent; spores 17-21 × 11-13.5 μ.

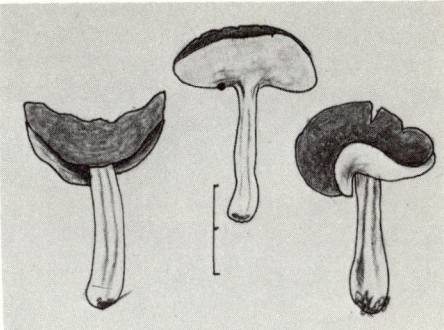

Fig. 39. *Helvella queletii.*

Northern U.S., on sticks and debris in wet places, summer, rare. The hymenium, exterior of the cup, and the stipe are typically each a slightly different shade of color.

3b. Stipe even, round in cross section or with a few indistinct basal grooves 4
4a. **Hymenium black, exterior of cup dark brown to black, margin often with whitish tufts or warts. Fig. 40** ....
....*Helvella corium* **(Weberb.) Massee**

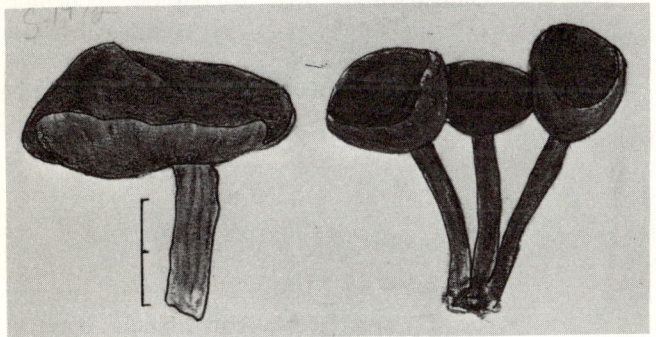

Fig. 40. *Helvella corium.*

Cup 1-6 cm wide, the margin somewhat wavy, exterior villose; stipe up to 3 cm long, 2-5 mm thick, concolorous with exterior above, pale at base, pubescent to villose; spores 18-22 × 10-13 μ; paraphyses septate much enlarged and brownish above.

Solitary or in small clusters on the ground, central to western U. S., fairly rare.

4b. Not as above 5

5a. Hymenium yellowish brown to pale grayish brown; spores subfusoid, 18-24 × 10-14 μ paraphyses septate, much enlarged and brownish above. Fig. 41 .... *Helvella macropus* (Fr.) Karsten

Fig. 41. *Helvella macropus*.

Cup 2-3 cm broad, exterior colored like the hymenium or gray; stipe 2.5-4 cm long, 3-5 mm thick, often thickened near the base, upper part colored like the cup, whitish below; spores typically finely verrucose.

On rich soil or on decaying wood, often along roads in eastern North America, summer, common.

5b. Hymenium gray, grayish brown to steel gray, exterior of cup grayish to dark brown; spores ovoid, up to 21 μ long, smooth; paraphyses clavate, hyaline to pale tan ....
........*Helvella villosa* (Hedw. ex O. Kuntze) Dissing & Nannfeldt

Cup 1-2.5 cm wide, compressed when young, becoming saucer-shaped to discoid at maturity splitting into several irregular lobes, exterior gray to dark brown or steel gray, pubescent to villose; stipe 1-3 cm long, concolor with exterior above, yellowish pallid at base; spores 17-21 × 9-12.5 μ.

On rich humus, summer, eastern and central U.S.

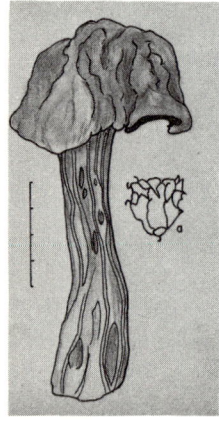

Fig. 42. *Helvella lacunosa*.

Group 2

1a. Spores 10-14 μ wide 2
1b. Spores 7-9 (10) μ wide 4
2a. Hymenium blackish to pale gray; under-surface of pileus glabrous. Fig. 42 ....
...................................*Helvella lacunosa* Fries

Pileus 1.5-5 cm broad, saddle-shaped with 2-3 lobes, margin attached to stipe in places, surface even or wrinkled toward the center, under-surface pale gray, grayish brown or nearly black, sometimes pale at the base; stipe deeply furrowed, the ribs sharp, sometimes doubled-edged, anastomosing, interior of stipe having longitudinal chambers; spores 15-19 × 9-12 μ.

NON-GILLED FLESHY FUNGI

On the ground or less often on decaying wood in both conifer and deciduous forests, widely distributed and quite common, especially in California and the Pacific Northwest.

2b. Hymenium white pallid or buff 3
3a. Under-surface of pileus pubescent Fig. 43 ....*Helvella crispa* Fr.

Pileus 1.5-6 cm broad, saddle-shaped or irregular with 2-3 lobes, margin inrolled then expanded, adnate, hymenium whitish to light buff, wrinkled and often irregular; stipe 3-8 cm long, 5-25 mm thick, tapering toward the pileus, pubescent, having strong anastomosing ribs and longitudinal furrows, interior chambered; spores 18-21 × 12.5 μ.

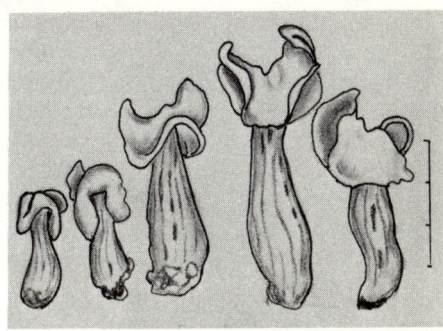

Fig. 43. *Helvella crispa*.

In deciduous forests, fall, widely distributed in North America.

3b. Under-surface of pileus glabrous ....*Helvella lactea* Boudier

Pileus 1.5-3 cm broad, margin connivent, saddle-shaped, often irregularly lobed and covering more than half of the stipe; stipe 2-3 cm long, 8-12 mm thick, whitish, drying bright yellowish, deeply furrowed, the ribs sharp-edged, anastomosing; spores 15-18 ×10-12 μ.

On the ground in thin woods, Great Lakes region.

4a. Spores globose, up to 10 μ in diam.; eastern North America. Fig. 44 ....*Helvella sphaerospora* Peck*

Pileus 6-8 (12) cm broad, widely spreading, margin evenly reflexed, usually free from stipe, hymenium brown to blackish brown, undersurface pallid and slightly tomentose; stipe 4-10 cm long, 2-4 cm thick, fluted, lacunose.

On rotting hardwood logs and debris, common at times in the Great Lakes region during late spring when there is heavy rainfall.

4b. Spores ellipsoid 14-17 × 8-9 μ; western North America. Fig. 45 ....*Helvella californica* Phillips

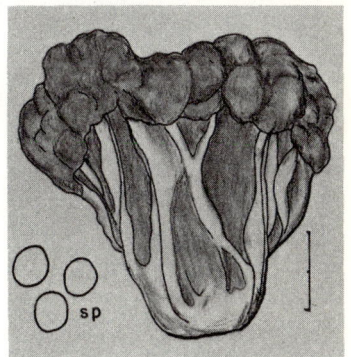

Fig. 44. *Helvella sphaerospora*.

* In a paper just received Harmaja has shown that this and the following species differ from *Helvella*. He gives their names as *Pseudorhizina sphaerospora* (Pk) Pouzer, and *P. californica* (Phill.) Harmaja.

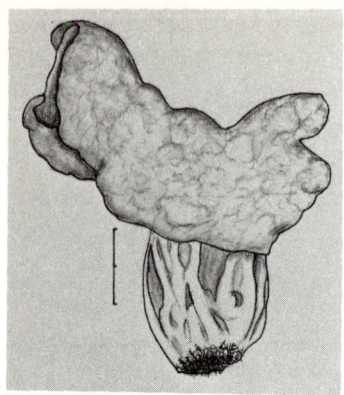

Fig. 45. Helvella californica.

Pileus up to 10 (20) cm or more broad, strongly spreading and inflated, hymenium uneven to convoluted, light to dark grayish brown to medium date brown; stipe up to 10 cm long and 6 cm thick, deeply and irregularly fluted, ribs white to pallid or near base dingy vinaceous yellowish in age.

Solitary to scattered on soil along streams, skid-ways through the woods, and recently disturbed soil generally, common in the spring and early summer in the Pacific Northwest south into California.

Group 3

1a. Fruit body black to dark gray 2
1b. Fruit body paler than the above, tan to yellowish to whitish 3
2a. Under surface of pileus glabrous ....*Helvella atra* Fr.

Pileus 1-2 cm broad, usually saddle-shaped or irregularly lobed, hymenium black, under-surface smoky brown at first; stipe 4-5 cm long, 2-3 mm thick, smoky black except at the base which is paler and slightly enlarged, tomentose; spores 17-19 $\times$ 9-11 μ, ellipsoid; paraphyses strongly enlarged and 8-10 μ in diam. at apex, smoky brown.

In rich soil in deciduous woods, eastern North America, summer and fall.

2b. Under-surface of pileus villose. Fig. 46 ....
Helvella pezizoides Fr.

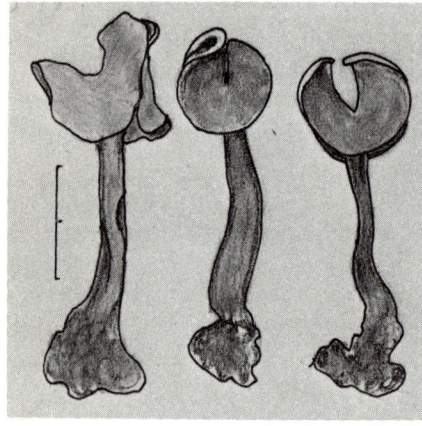

Fig. 46. Helvella pezizoides

Pileus up to 2.5 cm broad, involute to saddle-shaped, margin usually free, hymenium dark brownish to black, under-surface grayish brown to dark brownish; stipe 1.5-6 cm long, 3-5 mm thick, concolorous with under-surface of cap except for the whitish to yellowish base; base sometimes with 1-2 indistinct grooves, spores 17-20 $\times$ 9-12 μ paraphyses 4-6 μ broad, apex enlarged, walls brownish.

NON-GILLED FLESHY FUNGI

On humus in woods, South Carolina and Minnesota, apparently widely distributed.

3a. Margin of pileus remaining inrolled over the hymenium for some time; exterior pubescent. Fig. 47 ....*Helvella stevensii* **Peck**

Pileus up to 2 cm broad, hymenium whitish to cinnamon-brown when fresh, under-surface whitish, delicately pubescent; stipe 1.5-3 (5) cm long, 2-4 mm thick, concolorous with under-surface, pubescent; spores 18-19.5 × 11.5-13 μ; paraphyses slightly enlarged above to 5-7 μ wide.

Scattered to gregarious on humus in mixed conifer and hardwoods or in hardwood forests, along woods roads and edges of clearings, early summer, abundant at times in western Great Lakes Area.

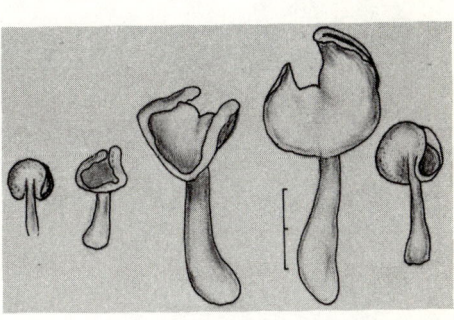

Fig. 47. *Helvella stevensii.*

3b. Margin of pileus straight or somewhat incurved (toward the stipe); under-surface glabrous. Fig. 48 ....*Helvella elastica* **Fries**

Pileus 1-3.5 cm broad, saddle-shaped to campanulate with adnate lobes, hymenium pale brown to buff, at times with a violet tinge; under-surface whitish to cream-buff, glabrous; stipe 1.5-10 cm long, 3-10 mm thick, concolorous with outside of pileus or paler, glabrous or pubescent, indistinctly grooved at base; spores 18-21 × 11-13.5 μ; paraphyses slightly enlarged above to 6-8 μ in diam.

On the ground in deciduous and coniferous woods, widely distributed in North America.

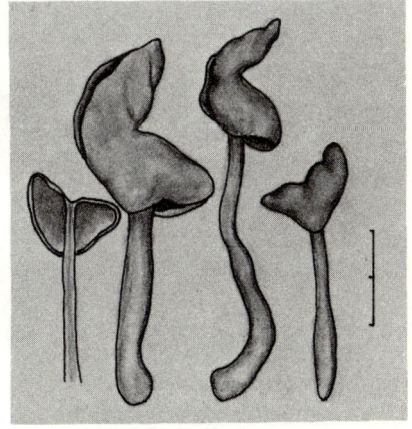

Fig. 48. *Helvella elastica.*

Gyromitra (The brain-fungi)

1a. Pileus typically saddle-shaped (a single saddle or several compounded) 2
1b. Pileus cerebriform to convoluted variously 3

2a. Pileus compound-saddle shaped; spores ornamented; on humus in late spring. Fig 49 .... *Gyromitra underwoodii* Seaver

Pileus up to 12 cm broad, irregularly lobed and folded; hymenium bay to chocolate-brown, undersurface pallid; stipe up to 13 cm long and 2-5 cm thick, white, hollow or loosely stuffed; spores 28-30 × 14 μ, becoming finely warted to reticulate.

On rich humus in low woods, eastern North America. *Poisonous*.

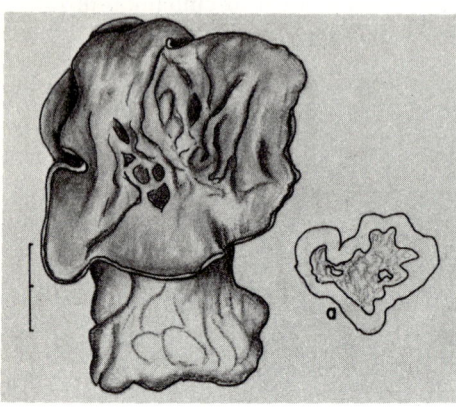

Fig. 49. *Gyromitra underwoodii*.

2b. Pileus in the form of a single saddle; spores smooth; growing mostly on rotting wood. Fig. 50 .... *Gyromitra infula* Fries

Pileus typicaly 3-10 cm broad, margin usually incurved, quite even to somewhat wrinkled or convoluted, reddish brown to dark brown; stipe 1-6 cm long, up to 2 cm thick, surface even to quite irregular, concolorous with or paler than the hymenium; spores 15-18 × 6-7.5 μ, containing 2 large oil drops (in water mounts).

Solitary to scattered, on rotting wood, or humus rich in lignin, summer and fall, common and widely distributed in North America. *Not recommended* as an esculent.

Fig. 50. *Gyromitra infula*.

3a. Stipe with a single hollow or somewhat compressed and with 1-2 narrow hollows; growing under conifers in the early spring. Beefsteak Morel. Fig. 51................... *Gyromitra esculenta* **Fries**

Pileus 3-10 cm broad, subglobose but irregular in outline, very wrinkled to folded over all but not pitted, yellowish, yellowish brown to bay-brown or darker; stipe rather short, 2-5 cm long, 1-2.5 cm thick, pallid furfuraceous to nearly glabrous, even to somewhat wrinkled; spores 17-22 × 7-9 µ, smooth.

Scattered or gregarious under aspen and pine, widely distributed in North America but more common northward and in the mountains, early spring to (in the mountains) early summer. This species is a dangerous one to eat as many people have been made ill by it. In spite of this it is a popular edible species in most areas where it is abundant. Parboil it in salt water before trying it if you feel you must experiment with it. The poison is volatile.

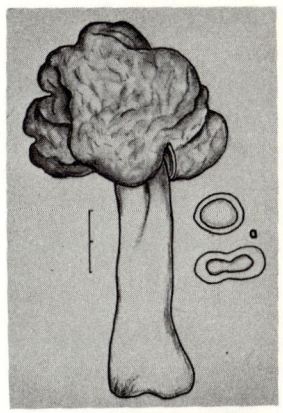

Fig. 51. *Gyromitra esculenta*.

3b. Stipe with several interior folds especially near the base. Fig. 52 4

4a. **Pileus soon deeply convoluted to irregularly pitted; spores ornamented, but not apiculate** ....
......*Gyromitra caroliniana* (Bosc) Nees

Pileus 5-25 cm broad, ridges often anastomosing and giving a reticulate appearance, brown to brownish black, underside pallid; stipe 8-10 cm long, 2-5 cm thick near apex usually somewhat enlarged at the base (up to 9 cm thick), deeply furrowed at times, pallid; spores 25-30 × 12-14 µ, faintly sculptured to finely warted in age; paraphyses much-branched.

On rich humus, eastern North America but most common in the middle to southern United States. Edible (at least for many people), but easily confused wtih *G. underwoodii*.

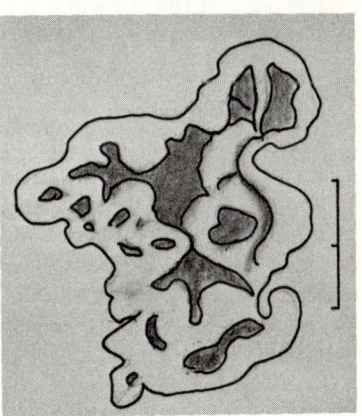

Fig. 52. Folded interior of stipe of *Gyromitra caroliniana*.

4b. **Pileus folded to cerebriform-wrinkled; spores smooth but many with a projection at each end. Fig. 53** ....
......*Gyromitra gigas* Krombholz

Pileus 4-10 cm wide, 4-6 cm high, subglobose, attached to the stipe in various places, ochraceous to smoky brownish or dingy bay, frequently cracked and white in the cracks; stipe short, 5 cm or more thick, hollow, whitish, somewhat enlarged at the base; spores 26-36 × 14-16 μ, paraphyses branched, septate, stout.

On humus under or near conifers; spring in the midwest, spring and early summer in the Rocky Mountains—often near melting snow banks. Edible and choice. It is known as the Snow Mushroom in the Rockies.

Harmaja has given the name *G. montana* to the American *G. gigas*.

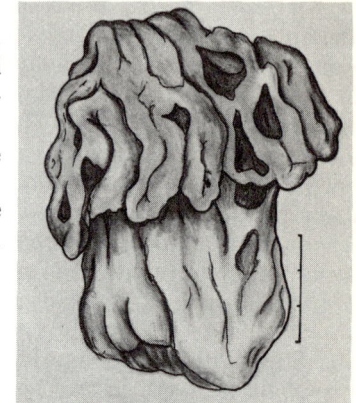

Fig. 53. *Gyromitra gigas*.

Morchella and Verpa (The Morels)

These two genera are so frequently confused by the public that they are treated together here. Some investigators recognize 3 genera in this group. Distinctions are made on whether the pileus is attached to the apex of the stipe (*Verpa*); attached down the upper half of its radius (*Mitrophora*); or whether the stipe and cap are completely fused (*Morchella*).

1a. Pileus or head attached at or near the apex of the stipe and the sides hanging down like a skirt 2

1b. Pileus or head not having a free-hanging margin 4

2a. Pileus surface usually rather deeply wrinkled or pitted; asci 2-spored. Early Morel. Fig. 54 ......
................*Verpa bohemica* (Krombh.) Schroter

Pileus 1-2 cm wide at base, obtusely conic, surface with longitudinal freely anastomosing ribs or folds, pale to dark yellow-brown; stipe 6-8 cm long, hollow or loosely stuffed, whitish to cream color, finally pale tan; spores 60-80 × 15-18 μ.

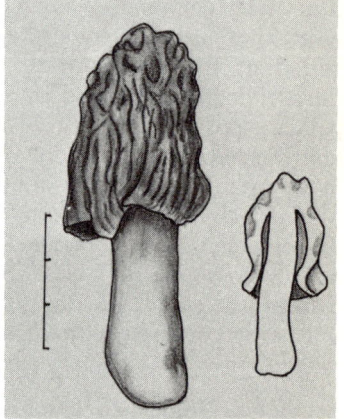

Fig. 54. *Verpa bohemica*.

In rich low woods, early spring before the trees have leafed out. Widely distributed throughout North America. Early Morel. Edible; but some are made sick from it.

2b. Pileus surface smooth to wrinkled, asci 8-spored 3

NON-GILLED FLESHY FUNGI

3a. Pileus with conspicuous ridges and some cross veining to form pits. Fig. 55 .... *Morchella semilibera* **Fries**

Pileus with conspicuous ridges and in age obtusely conic with a flaring margin, pits elongated, dull yellowish brown, the ribs of the pits discoloring darker than the depressions; stipe 8-10 cm long, 1-2 cm thick at apex, in age clavate and up to 4 cm thick at base, pallid to yellowish, at times with pinkish discoloration in age, ribbed near the apex, granular furfuraceous; spores 24-27 (30) $\times$ 12-15 μ.

On the ground in oak or beech woods, widely distributed and usually fruiting about a week before the larger morels appear. Edible.

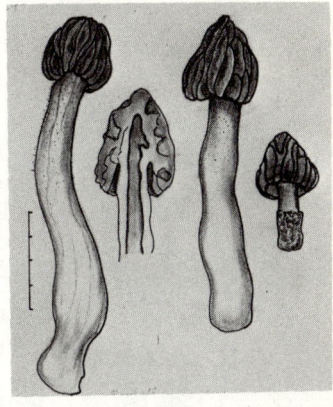

Fig. 55. *Morchella semilibra.*

3b. Pileus smooth or nearly so, the margin rarely ingrown with the stipe in places. Fig. 56 .... *Verpa conica* **Fries**

Pileus 5-25 mm wide at base, margin often slightly reflexed exposing the pallid under-side, entirely free from the stipe except at the apex, dark brown over hymenial area, even or slightly wrinkled; stipe 5-6 cm long, slightly narrowed above; spores 22-26 $\times$ 12-16 μ.

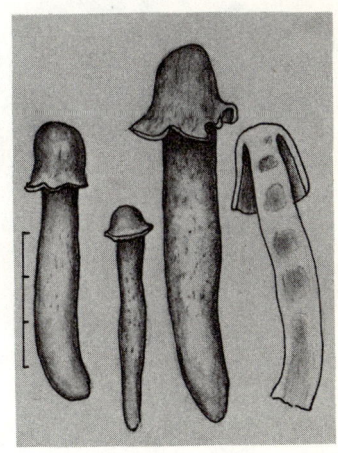

Fig. 56. *Verpa conica.*

On the ground in deciduous woods in the spring, frequent but not usually found in quantity, widely distributed. The best fruitings we have seen were under old apple trees where fruit had been rotting for years.

4a. Pileus 1-5 cm high, narrowly conic, pallid to grayish young but the borders of the pits darkening finally to black. Fig. 57 .... **Black Morel** ....*Morchella angusticeps* **Peck**

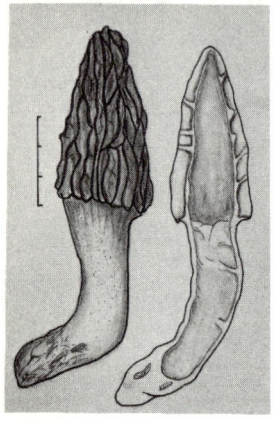

Fig. 57. *Morchella angusticeps.*

Heads with greatly elongated pits; stipe equal, nearly as thick as the head, pallid to buff, in a large form the pits blackish like the ribs by maturity; spores $24\text{-}28 \times 12\text{-}14\mu$.

On sandy soil in woods. Widely distributed, often associated with aspen (*Populus*) in the Great Lakes Region. Edible and choice. It is often frozen or dried for winter use.

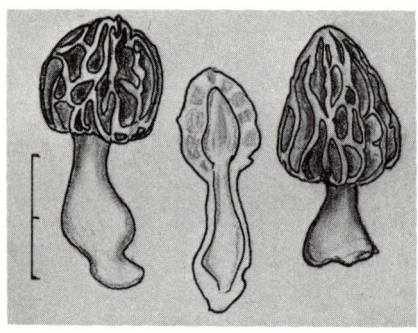

Fig. 58. *Morchella deliciosa.*

4b. Pileus not blackening as above 5

5a. Pits or depression of the pileus gray to fuscous, ridges pallid; fruit bodies typically small. Delicious Morel. Fig. 58 .... *Morchella deliciosa* **Fries**

Pileus 2-3 cm long, pits elongated, ridges much lighter than the pits, irregularly anastomosing; stipe up to 2/3 as thick as the pileus, often enlarged at the base and somewhat lacunose, whitish or yellowish; spores $20 \times 10\ \mu$ approximately.

On the ground in grassy places, usually at the edge of woods, widely distributed but not common.

5b. Not as above 6

NON-GILLED FLESHY FUNGI

6a. Pits large and shallow, ridges thin; stipe enlarged and at times lacunose at the base. Fig. 59 ....*Morchella crassipes* **Fries**

Pileus subconic, usually elongated and 6-12 cm long and 5-6 cm broad or at times larger, pits roundish or irregularly elongated, up to 1 cm wide; yellowish in the valleys; ribs irregularly anastomosing, edges sharp; stipe stout, up to 10-11 cm long, 4 cm at apex and 5-7 cm at base, yellowish or whitish; spores 20-22 × 12-14 μ, smooth.

On the ground in open places, at the edge of woods, in low elm swamps and near where elms have been cut. It is widely distributed and is without question the best of the morels for the table.

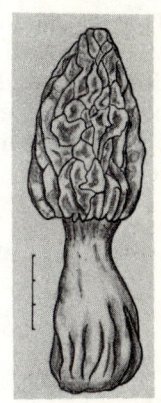

Fig. 59. *Morchella crassipes.*

6b. Pits shorter and deeper; pileus not distinctly longitudinally ridged; stipe not especially enlarged at the base. Common Morel Fig. 60 .... *Morchella esculenta* **Fr.**

Pileus subglobose ovoid or elongated, if narrowed upward the apex obtuse, up to 7-9 cm long and 4-5 cm wide, pits rounded, irregular or at times longitudinally elongated, yellowish, becoming light brownish when dry, ridges irregularly anastomosing, edges rounded, lighter than the pits; stipe only slightly enlarged at the base; spores 20-25 × 12-14 μ.

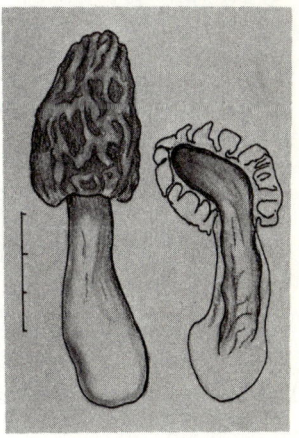

Fig. 60. *Morchella esculenta.*

In old orchards, forests, lightly burned grassy areas and swampy ground, early spring, widely distributed in North America. *It is one of the most popular mushrooms for the table.* Edible.

The GEOGLOSSACEAE (Earth Tongues)

Fruit bodies composed essentially of a stalk and a fertile portion, the latter being in the form of an abrupt or gradual enlargement. The hymenium usually distinct from the stalk by being smoother and of a slightly different color or texture. The basic difference between this family and the other Pezizales is that the spores pass through a pore in the apex of the ascus in being discharged instead of the ascus opening by a lid. See fig. 13. For illustrations of microscopic features see fig. 61.

Key to Genera

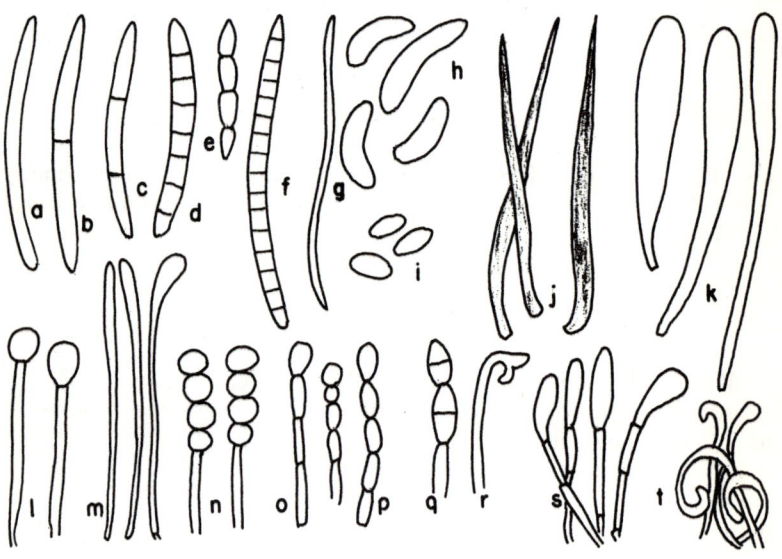

Fig. 61. Microscopic characters of the Geoglossaceae. (a-i) ascospores; (j) setae of *Trichoglossum*; (k) outline of asci; (l-t) paraphyses.

1a. Spores (at least some of them) brown 2

1b. Spores in an ascus all hyaline 3

2a. Hymenium with brown setae among the asci Fig. 61-j ....
....*Trichoglossum* p. 53

2b. Hymenium lacking setae ....*Geoglossum* p. 54

NON-GILLED FLESHY FUNGI

3a. Hymenium extending down on opposite sides of the flattened fruit body, the upper portion being fan-shaped. Fig. 62 ....*Spathularia* p. 56

3b. Not as above 4

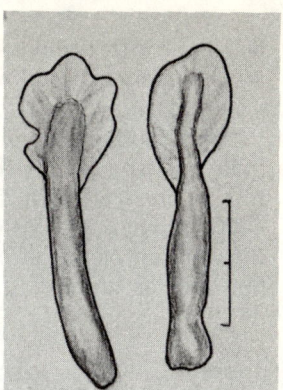

Fig. 62. *Spathularia*.

4a. Fruit body capitate or pileate. Fig. 63, a, b 5

4b. Fruit body typically clavate, or quite irregular. Fig. 63, c, d 8

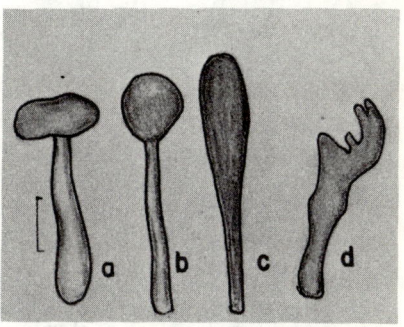

Fig. 63. (a-b) fruit body capitate; (c-d) fruit body clavate to irregular.

5a. Fruti body gelatinous. Fig. 64 ....*Leotia* p. 57

5b. Fruit body fleshy to leathery or pliant 6

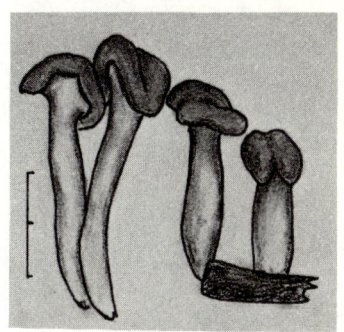

Fig. 64. *Leotia*.

6a. Spores threadlike; growing in cold water, in wet places or on submerged wood often in several feet of water ....
....*Vibrissia truncorum* **Fr.**

Fruit bodies 3-20 mm high, the cap 2-5 mm wide, flesh-colored, (pale pinkish tan to buff); stipe 1-2 mm thick, white, minutely tomentose; spores (80) 125-250 (274) $\times$ 1 μ, multiseptate.

Gregarious to clustered on wet wood, leaves, etc., northern in distribution or in the high mountains, spring and summer.

6b. Not as above 7

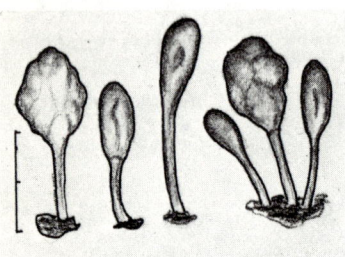

7a. Head covered completely by hymenium, capitate to clavate. Fig. 65 ....*Mitrula* **p. 58**

Fig. 65. Mitrula.

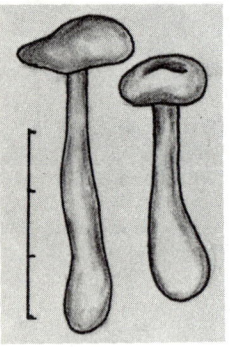

7b. Pileate (the fertile upper surface and a sterile under surface with somewhat different appearance (texture) See *Leotia atrovirens* p. 57 also Fig. 66 ....
....*Cudonia* **p. 58**

Fig. 66. Cudonia.

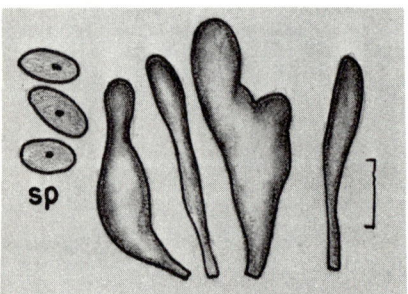

8a. Paraphyses lacking; fruit body variable in shape in a single collection, pale to bright yellow. Fig. 67 ....
........*Spragueola irregularis* (Peck) Nannfeldt

Fig. 67. Spragueola irregularis.

Fruit body 1-7 cm long, very variable in shape (clavate, twisted, lobed or branched, often compressed), usually with a stipe up to 15 mm wide, some shade of yellow (usually bright); stipe 2-8 mm thick, white; spores (4) 6-8 (10) × 3-4 µ, 1 celled.

Scattered to gregarious rarely clustered, on the ground, on mosses or on the needle carpet, widely distributed in conifer areas of North America.

8b. Paraphyses present; fruit body clavate to subcapitate. Fig. 68 ..9
9a. Fruit body blackish to blackish brown .....see *Geoglossum* p. 54
9b. Fruit body orange to yellow, dingy olivaceous or brownish ....
....*Microglossum* p. 59

Trichoglossum

The determination of species is based entirely on microscopic characters in this genus. Fruiting bodies clavate. See Fig. 68.

1a. Spores 0-5 septate, rarely more, most commonly 3-septate, (45) 57-75 (90) × 6-7 µ ....*Trichoglossum farlowii* (Cke.) Durand

Fruit body 3-8 cm long, blackish; paraphyses cylindric and enlarged at apex, curved above.

On moist or wet soil, at times in moss or on rotten logs in eastern North America, summer and fall.

1b. Spores mostly more than 5-septate 2
2a. Spores 7-septate, rarely more 3
2b. Spores more than 7-septate or if varible in septation many with more than 7 septa 5
3a. Spores fusoid or subfusoid, (80) 100-120 (150) × 4-5.5 µ; paraphyses cylindric to the enlarged apical cell; fruit body 1.5-4 cm long ....*Trichoglossum octopartitum* Mains

On soil, Ohio, Tenn., W. Va., summer, not common.

3b. Spores subcylindric or clavate-cylindric, mostly less than 100 µ long 4
4a. Spores (60) 72-100 (125) × 5-6 µ; fruit body 3-10 cm long, on soil ....*Trichoglossum walteri* (Berk.) Durand
4b. Spores (45) 55-65 (75) × 5-6 µ; paraphyses cylindric; fruit body 1.5-2.5 cm long ....*Trichoglossum confusum* Durand

On soil, in North Carolina, rare.

5a. Spores 15-septate or if varible then many 15-septate 6
5b. Spores very variable in septation but few or none 15-septate 7
6a. Asci 8-spored; spores 80-170 (210) × 5-7 µ; paraphyses cylindric and somewhat enlarged above ....
....*Trichoglossum hirsutum* (Fr.) Boudier

Fruit body 1-8 cm long, clavate or at times capitate to subcapitate.

On rotting wood or soil, or on sphagnum, widely distributed in North America and usually the first one in the genus to be collected by one beginning the study of fungi. Several variants are known.

6b. Asci 4-spored or occasionally with fewer spores; spores (110) 125-145 × 6-7 μ, 0-17 septate but mostly 15-septate ....
.........................*Trichoglossum tetrasporum* **Sinden & Fitzpatrick**
Fruit body 2-8 cm long.
On moist earth, New York.

7a. Asci 4-spored; spores (90) 110-145 (160) × 6-7 μ, mostly 7-11 septate ....*Trichoglossum velutipes* **(Pk.) Durand**
Fruit body 2-5 cm long; paraphyses cylindric, septate.
On soil or rotting wood, eastern North America south to Tennessee.

7b. Asci 8-spored; spores (80) 110-130 (150) × 4.5-6 μ, 4-16 septate, mostly 10-13 septate ....
................................*Trichoglossum variabile* **(Durand) Nannfeldt**
Fruit body 2-4 cm tall.
On soil or ocasionally in sphagnum, eastern North America, summer, rare.

Geoglossum (The Earth-Tongues)

As for *Trichoglossum,* species are distinguished on microscopic features. Both brown and hyaline spores occur in some species of *Geoglossum.* Fruit bodies clavate, generally similar in form to those of *Trichoglossum.* Fig. 68.

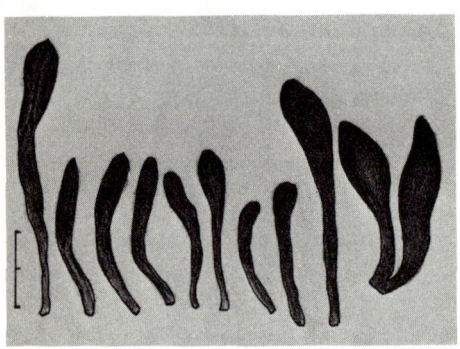

Fig. 68. *Geoglossum* (fruit body clavate to subcapitate).

1a. Spores all brown 2
1b. Spores both hyaline and brown on a single fruit body and in some the hyaline spores predominate 10
2a. Spores 7-septate or if variable with rarely more than 7................3
2b. Spores with many more septa than 7, usually with 15 8
3a. Paraphyses continuing down the stipe and forming a gelatinous layer 4
3b. Paraphyses not forming a continuous gelatinous layer on the stipe 5
4a. Spores (55) 60-90 (100) μ long, often with 3 septa, narrowly cylindric with pyriform end cells....*Geoglossum glutinosum* **Fries**
Fruit body 1.5-5.5 cm long.

Growing on soil under hardwoods and/or conifers, eastern North America, summer, rather frequent during some seasons.

4b. Spores mostly less than 60 μ long; paraphyses with end cells globoid, the others cylindric ..*Geoglossum affine* (Durand) Lloyd

Fruit body 1.5-2.5 cm long, viscid to very gelatinous when wet. Growing on soil in wet areas, New York, August, rare.

5a. Paraphyses usually strongly curved above, moderately or sparsely septate, not constricted at the septa, the end cell enlarged only moderately or not at all 6

5b. Paraphyses straight or somewhat curved above, closely septate in upper portions, somewhat constricted at septa, the end cells enlarged 7

6a. Paraphyses agglutinated by dark amorphous matter, clavate to pyriform or contorted at the apex ....
....*Geoglossum cohaerens* Durand

Spores subfusoid or subcylindric, mostly 3-4 septate; fruit body 2-4.5 cm long; spores (30) 38-40 (55) × 5-6 μ.

Eastern United States, rare.

6b. Paraphyses not agglutinated ....
....*Geoglossum nigritum* (Fr.) Cooke

Spores clavate, many or most 7-septate, 30-90 × 4.5-6.5 μ; paraphyses cylindric or at the apex slightly enlarged.

Scattered to gregarious on wet soil and among mosses (on rotten conifer logs in var. *heterosporum*) summer and fall, widely distributed.

7a. Paraphyses having upper cells variously enlarged, (globoid, ellipsoid or obovoid); spores (45) 55-78 (90) μ long ....
....*Geoglossum glabrum* Fries

Fruit body 1.5-10 cm long, stipe smooth.

Scattered to crowded on soil throughout the continent, summer and fall. Several varieties are known.

7b. Paraphyses having many 2-celled oblong or barrel-shaped segments; spores (6) 75-90 (105) × 6-9 μ; fruit body 2-7 cm long, stipe usually squamulose ....*Geoglossum simile* Peck

Scattered to clustered in swamps, bogs and on well-drained soils, humus, rotten wood or mossy areas, eastern North America, summer.

8a. Paraphyses forming a gelatinous layer down the stipe, those above much twisted and coiled ....*Geoglossum difforme* Fries

Spores (70) 92-115 (135) × 6-7 μ, 15-septate or with fewer septa; fruit bodies 3-12 cm long, scattered to crowded on wet or dry soil or on rotting logs of hardwoods, eastern North America, late summer.

8b. Paraphyses not forming a continuous gelatinous layer on the stipe, the stipe pubescent to squamulose 9

9a. Spores (85) 90-130 (145) × 5-6 μ, mostly 15-septate ....
.... *Geoglossum pumilum* Winter

Paraphyses cylindric below, clavate to ellipsoid above; fruit body 5-20 mm long.

On soil, Virginia, rare.

9b. Spores (120) 125-160 (180) × 6-7 μ, mostly 15-septate ....
............................*Geoglossum pygmaeum* Gerard & Durand

Paraphyses closely septate, lower cells cylindric, upper pyriform; fruit bodies 15-20 mm long.

On soil, eastern United States, rare.

10a. Hyaline spores non-septate, spores (45) 66-90 (110) × 5-6 μ, variable from hyaline to light brown to dark brown and 0-13-septate ....*Geoglossum fallax* Durand

Paraphyses not agglutinated, cylindric below, end cell clavate; fruit body 1-7 cm long, scattered to crowded on humus and rotting logs in the northern United States and Canada, summer.

10b. Hyaline spores frequently septate; paraphyses agglutinated by amorphous matter; stipe with tufted setose hairs 11

11a. Spores (50) 65-85 (95) × 4-5 μ, hyaline spores 0-15-septate ......
......................................*Geoglossum alveolatum* (Rehm) Durand

Paraphyses cylindric below, the end cells clavate to pyriform; fruit body 15-50 mm long, frequently with white pubescence.

Solitary to a few gregarious on rotting wood or on soil, to be expected in eastern North America in southern Canada and the Great Lakes region, summer and fall.

11b. Spores (40) 50-65 (75) × 6 μ, the hyaline spores 0-7 septate ....
....*Geoglossum intermedium* Durand

Paraphyses cylindric with pyriform end cells; fruit body 20-45 mm long. On moist soil in eastern North America.

Sphathularia

Fruit bodies fleshy or fleshy-leathery, the upper part flattened, spathulate or compressed-capitate; fertile part fan-shaped, decurrent on opposite sides of the stipe (fig. 69); asci clavate; spores needle-shaped, 1-celled or at times with several septa; paraphyses thread-like.

1a. Spores mostly more than 30 μ long 2

1b. Spores 18-26 μ long ....*Spathularia spathulata* (Imai) Mains

Fruit body up to 3 cm long, spathulate to flattened-capitate, 5-12 mm wide, yellow-brown to reddish brown; stipe brownish yellow to reddish brown.

Known only from California.

NON-GILLED FLESHY FUNGI

2a. Stipe whitish, yellowish or brownish; smooth or with fluffy mycelium at base, mycelium white to yellowish ....
....*Spathularia flavida* **Fries**

Fruit body 1-8 cm long, the fertile portion up to 3 cm wide, light yellow to pale buff; spores $30\text{-}95 \times 1.5\text{-}2\text{-}5\ \mu$, 0-several-septate, the wall with a gelatinous layer.

Gregarious to clustered or in rings on conifer needles, summer and fall, northern U. S. and eastern Canada but not uncommon in northern Idaho. Several varieties are known.

2b. Stipe dark brown, taste farinaceous; mycelium orange. Fig. 69
...................................*Spathularia velutipes* **Cooke & Farlow**

Fruit body up to 6 cm long, much compressed above and up to 3 cm wide, whitish, cream or light brownish yellow, often with patches of the veil; spores $(26)\ 30\text{-}40\ (46) \times 1.5\text{-}2\ \mu$, 0-several-septate, the wall with a gelatinous layer.

Gregarious, cespitose or scattered on rotting hardwood stumps and logs or on humus rich in lignin, eastern North America, common.

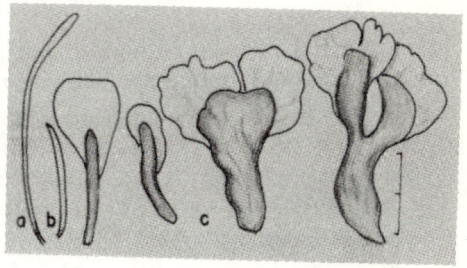

Fig. 69. *Spathularia velutipes.*

Leotia

1a. Fruit body buff, ochraceous or cinnamon, at times olivaceous. Fig. 64 ....*Leotia lubrica* **Fries**

Fruit body 2-7 cm long, pileus smooth or somewhat furrowed above, 8-40 mm broad; stipe 5-10 mm thick, minutely squamulose or furfuraceous; spores $16\text{-}23 \times 4\text{-}6\ \mu$.

Scattered, gregarious or in large clusters, often on barren soil under scrub oak, but likely to be found in hardwood forests generally. Large clusters have been found fruiting hypogeously buried in 2 inches of sand (Hoseney, 1969). This is the most abundant species of *Leotia* in North America.

1b. Not as above 2

2a. Stipe green like the head or lighter ....
....*Leotia atrovirens* **Fries**

Fruit body up to 4 cm long, head 3-10 mm wide; stipe 2-4 mm thick, usually squamulose; spores 16-22 × 4-5 μ.

Scattered or cespitose on soil, eastern North America including the Great Lakes region, rare, summer and early fall.

**2b. Stipe and lower surface of pileus white, yellow or orange ....
....Leotia viscosa Fries**

Fruit body 3-9 cm long; head 2-3 cm wide, 5-10 mm thick, olive-green to dark green; stipe 5-10 mm thick, green puncate or furfuraceous, spores 17-26 × 4-6 μ.

Clustered to scattered on soil or rotten wood, eastern North America to Michigan and also along the Pacific Coast, summer and fall.

Mitrula

1a. Head light brown to pinkish buff; stipe light to dark brown; growing on decaying needles of conifers ....Mitrula abietis Fries

Fruit body 3-20 mm long, head 1-7 × 0.5-2 mm; stipe 0.3-0.7 mm thick; spores 10-14 × 2-2.5 μ; one-celled.

Scattered to densely gregarious on carpets of fallen conifer needles, widely distributed in North America where conifers occur.

1b. Not as above 2

2a. Hymenial bearing portion clavate to capitate, light orange to yellow, smooth; stipe white; growing on decaying leaves in very wet soil or in water. See Fig. 65 ....Mitrula paludosa Fries

Fruit body 1-4 cm long or longer, hymenium bearing portion 5-15 mm long 3-10 mm wide; stipe 1-2 mm thick, somewhat viscid to slimy; spores 10-17 (20) × 2-3 μ, one-celled or rarely 1-septate.

Scattered to crowded, early spring, widespread in northern regions.

**2b. Head ochraceous to orange-buff, rugose or at times smooth; stipe lighter than the head; growing on mosses ....
....Mitrula gracilis Karsten**

Fruit body 1-3 cm long, heads 2-6 × 1.5-7 mm, variable in shape; stipe 1 mm thick; spores 9-12 (14) × 1.5-2 μ.

In arctic and alpine habitats throughout North America, summer, rare.

Cudonia

1a. Fruit body yellowish or ochraceous-buff; spores (40) 50-65 (70) μ long 2 μ wide ....Cudonia lutea (Peck) Saccardo

Fruit body 1-6 cm long, pileus up to 1.5 cm broad, upper surface smooth.

Gregarious or scattered on decaying leaves, usually of beech, eastern North America, not uncommon.

1b. Not colored as above; the spores smaller (up to 40 μ long) 2
2a. Spores (28) 32-40 (46) μ long; pileus cream to dark brown ....
....*Cudonia circinans* **Fries**

Fruit body 1.5-7 cm long, pileus up to 2 cm broad, thin; stipe 2-12 mm thick, drab to dark brown; spores 2 μ wide.

Gregarious or clustered on soil or humus and rotting wood, widely distributed in North America, our most common species, late summer and fall.

2b. Not as above 3
3a. **Pileus drab or dark gray; stipe fuscous** ......*Cudonia grisea* **Mains**

Fruit body 1.5-5 cm long; pileus up to 1.5 cm broad, smooth; stipe 3-8 mm thick below, narrowing upward; spores 18-22 (24) × 1.5-2 μ, usually 1-celled.

Gregarious on rotting coniferous wood, Pacific Northwest, spring, rare.

3b. **Pileus pinkish cinnamon or pinkish buff; stipe avellaneous to wood brown** ....*Cudonia monticola* **Mains**

Fruit body 1.5-10 cm long; pileus 1-3 cm broad, compressed, rugose; stipe 5-7 mm thick below, hollow in age; spores (15) 18-24 (28) × 2 μ.

Closely gregarious to cespitose on soil and rotten conifer wood, Pacific Northwest, usually found in large masses but generally rare.

Microglossum

1a. Fruit body green, yellow or orange 2
1b. Not as above 3
2a. **Fruit body yellow or orange. Fig. 70** ....*Microglossum rufum* **(Schw.) Underwood**

Fruit body 2-7 cm long, 4-12 mm wide; stipe 2-4 mm thick; spores (18) 20-36 (40) × 4-6 μ.

Scattered to clustered in Sphagnum, on humus and on rotten wet wood, widely distributed in North America, summer, common —our most common species.

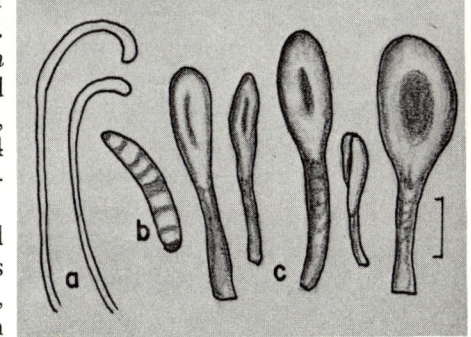

Fig. 70. *Microglossum rufum.*

2b. Fruit body pea green to dark green (but see *M. olivaceum also*)
....*Microglossum viride* **Fries**
Fruit body 1.5-5.5 cm long, 2-12 mm wide; stipe 2-5 mm thick, furfuraceous becoming glabrous; spores (12) 14-20 (22) $\times$ 4-5 μ, sausage shaped to subfusiform; paraphyses hyaline below, greenish above.

Scattered to clustered on soil, summer, eastern North America and California; August in the Great Lakes area.

3a. Spores less than 20 μ long ....*Microglossum olivaceum* **(Fr.) Gillet**
Fruit body 1-6 cm long, sometimes twisted and contorted; fertile part 3-10 mm wide, olivaceous to walnut-brown; stipe 1-4 mm thick; spores 10-18 (20) $\times$ 3.5-5 μ.

Scattered to clustered on soil, widespread in North America, summer and fall.

3b. Spores mostly more than 20 μ long 4
4a. Fruit body yellowish brown to date brown ....
....*Microglossum fumosum* **(Pk.) Durand**
Fruit body 2-8 cm long, fertile part 3-15 mm wide; stipe 2-5 mm thick, furfuraceous becoming smooth; spores (16) 20-40 (48) $\times$ 4-5 μ.

Scattered to clustered on soil and rotting wood, northern United States and Canada, summer.

4b. Not as above 5
5a. Paraphyses not or only slightly exceeding the asci, hyaline, slender, septa inconspicuous ....
....*Microglossum atropurpureum* **(Fr.) Karsten**
Fruit body 1-7 cm long, fertile part 2-15 mm wide, dark brown, purplish or black; stipe 2-8 mm thick, brownish black or black; spores (16) 20-44 (52) $\times$ 4-6 μ.

On soil, eastern North America and Washington, late summer and early fall.

5b. Paraphyses longer than the asci, brown, robust, septa conspicuous ....*Microglossum arenarium* **Rostrup**
Fruit body 1-5 cm long, brownish black to black, fertile portion 2-15 mm wide; stipe 1-3 mm thick; spores (25) 28-42 (45) $\times$ 4-6 μ.

Scattered to clustered on soil, eastern Canada and Michigan.

HYPOCREALES
Cordyceps

Fruit body arising from dead insects (larvae or adults), spiders, or from hypogeous Ascomycetes (*Elaphomyces*); perithecia with well developed walls; asci long and slender, cylindric, subfusoid, or narrowly clavate; spores threadlike or narrowly fusoid, hyaline, multiseptate and often breaking into segments when mature.

1a. Growing on hypogeous Ascomycetes (*Elaphomyces*), the perithecia embedded in the clavate to capitate fruit body ....Group I
1b. Growing on insects, the perithecia embedded to free ....
....Group II p. 62

Species Growing on Fungi—
Group 1

1a. Fruit body clavate, the fertile part only slightly distinct from the stipe. Fig. 71 ....*Cordyceps ophioglossoides* (Fr.) Link

Fruit body 2-8 cm long, 3-8 mm thick above, upper part reddish brown to olivaceous-brown; stipe 2-8 mm thick, olivaceous to dark brown; usually attached to the host by rhizomorphs; spores breaking into segments 2-4 (5) $\times$ 1.5-2 μ.

Throughout eastern North America, but rarely collected.

1b. Fruit body capitate, the fertile portion abruptly enlarged from the stipe 2
2a. Fruit body 2-11 cm long 3
2b. Fruit body 1.5-2.5 cm long, 2-5 mm thick
    ....*Cordyceps fracta* Mains

Heads purplish black; stipe up to 1 mm thick, yellowish green to olivaceous; spore segments 2-5 $\times$ 1.5-2.5 μ.

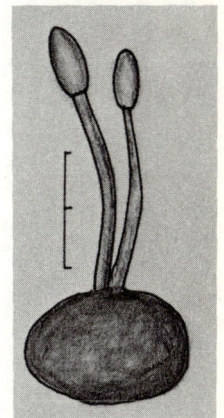

Fig. 71. *Cordyceps ophioglossoides*.

Known from Tennessee, rare.

3a. Surface cells of the head forming a palisade-like covering 4
3b. Surface cells of the head not as above. Fig. 72 ....
    ....*Cordyceps capitata* (Fr.) Link

Fruit body 2-11 cm long, head 5-20 mm wide, brown to olive-black; stipe 2-8 mm thick, ocher-yellow to olive-black; spore segments 8-25 (32) $\times$ 2.5-3 μ.

Throughout North America where *Elaphomyces* grows.

4a. Spore segments (18) 24-48 (54) $\times$ 4-5 μ ......
    ......*Cordyceps canadensis* Ellis & Everhart

Fruit body 5-8 cm long, head 6-17 mm wide, brown to olive-brown or black; stipe 3-8 mm thick, yellow, olive-brown or black.

Eastern North America.

4b. Spore segments 3-8 $\times$ 2 μ ....
    ....*Cordyceps valliformis* Mains

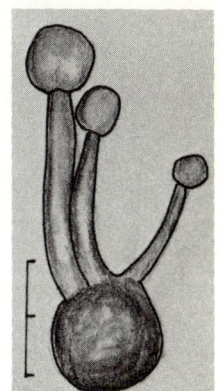

Fig. 72. *Cordyceps capitata*.

Fruit body 5-7 cm long, head 3-15 mm wide, dark brown; stipe 1.5 mm thick, dark brown.
Eastern North America.

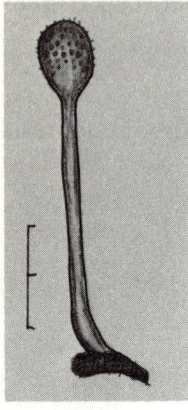

Fig. 73. Cordyceps gracilis.

Species Growing on Insects— Group 2

1a. Fruit body capitate. (See fig. 73) 2
1b. Fruit body not as above 5
2a. Head ochraceous to mahogany red, the stipe chrome yellow to straw yellow; growing on larvae of beetles, moths or butterflies. Fig. 73 ....*Cordyceps gracilis* **Durand & Montagne**
Fruit body 1.5-9 cm long, 2-5 mm wide; perithecia completely embedded at right angles to the surface; spore fragments 6-8 (12) × 1-1.5 μ; frequently having a dense growth of yellow mycelium around the host.
Eastern United States, early summer.

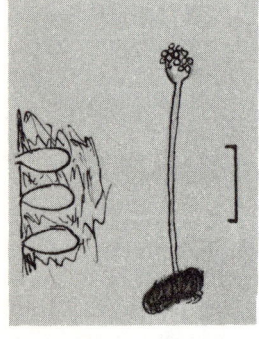

Fig. 74. Cordyceps entomorrhiza.

2b. Not as above 3
3a. Head light vinaceous-drab, stipe brownish; growing on beetle larvae; perithecia completely embedded at right angles to the surface. Fig. 74 ....
..........*Cordyceps entomorrhiza* **(Fr.) Link**
Fruit body 3.5-4 cm long, head 2-4 mm wide, very warty; stipe 0.8 mm thick; spore segments 6-10 × 1.5 μ.
Pacific Northwest, rare.
3b. Not colored as above; perithecia embedded obliquely to the surface (Fig. 75); growing on wasps or ants 4

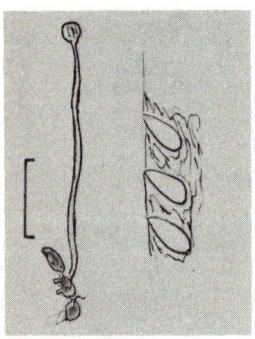

Fig. 75. Cordyceps myrmecophila.

4a. Head ochraceous; stipe light yellow; growing on ants. Fig. 75 ......
..............*Cordyceps myrmecophila* **Cesalpino**
Fruit body 2-10 cm long, head 2-8 mm thick, lacking a central core, the hyphae loosely interwoven; spore segments 8-10 × 1.5 μ.
Known from Tennessee, Michigan and the Pacific Northwest.

NON-GILLED FLESHY FUNGI

4b. Head and stipe cream color to brownish yellow; growing on wasps .... *Cordyceps sphecocephala* (Berkeley) Saccardo

Fruit body 2-10 cm long, head 2-8 × 1.5-3 mm, having a central core of parallel longitudinal hyphae; perithecia frequently with curved neck, completely embedded; spore segments 8-12 × 1.5-2 μ. Southeastern United States, rare.

5a. Fruit bodies commonly several to many from a carcass 6

5b. Fruit bodies single or only a few 8

6a. Fruit body 1.5-2.5 cm long; perithecia superficial and free from each other. Fig. 76 .... *Cordyceps michiganensis* Mains

Fruit body slender, 2-4 mm thick, pointed ochraceous to orange-yellow, asci cylindric, having a 3-4 μ thick cap; spores tardily breaking into segments 12-50 × 1-1.5 μ.

On beetle larvae in rotten logs; Great Lakes region and North Carolina.

6b. Fruit body up to 11 mm long; perithecia partly or completely embedded at right angles to the surface 7

Fig. 76. *Cordyceps michiganensis.*

7a. Growing on adult moths, the white mycelium covering the host and often attaching it to the substratum; spores breaking into segments 2-6 × 0.5-1 μ .... *Cordyceps tuberculata* (Lebert) Maire

Fruit body 2-11 mm long, up to 2 mm thick, yellowish white or gray above, stipe brown, up to 1 mm thick; perithecia partly embedded in a cottony layer; asci with a 4 μ thick cap; spores breaking into segments 2-6 × 0.5-1 μ.
Known only from North Carolina.

7b. Growing on scale insects; spores 42-80 × 2.5-3.5 μ, the cells 4-6.5 μ long but not breaking into segments ....
.... *Cordyceps clavulata* (Schw.)Ellis & Everhart

Fruit body 2-4 mm long; brownish black, the head warty, up to 1.5 mm.
Eastern North America to the Great Lakes region.

8a. Some shade of gray, brown, ochraceous-tawny or black 9
8b. Some shade of ochraceous, yellow, orange or vinaceous fawn 13

9a. Heads 3-5 mm thick; perithecia produced in a palisade-like layer. Fig. 77 ....*Cordyceps ravenelii* Berkeley & Curtis

Fruit body 4-10 cm long, clavate, upper portion dark purplish brown to chocolate brown or black; stipe up to 4 mm thick, brown; spores 132-252 × 2-2.5 μ, the cells 13-30 μ long, not or only irregularly breaking into segments.

On beetle larvae, eastern North America, rare.

9b. Head up to 2 mm thick; perithecia produced in a layer of interwoven hyphae 10

10a. Fruit body 3-30 mm long, 0.2-0.5 mm thick ....
....*Cordyceps unilateralis* (Tul.) Saccardo

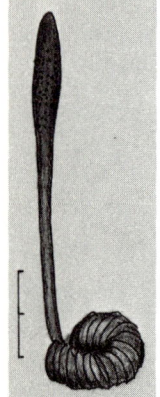

Fig. 77. *Cordyceps ravenelii*.

Growing on ants and often producing a brown mycelium which attaches them to the substrate; brown, perithecia embedded except at the apex; spores 100-162 × 2.5-3 μ, the cells 5-14 μ long, not breaking into segments.

On ants and Hymenoptera, from the Great Lakes region south to Honduras.

10b. Fruit body larger, 1.5-13 cm long; growing on larvae 11

11a. Fruit body ochraceous-tawny to dark cinnamon-brown; perithecia embedded at right angles to the surface ....
....*Cordyceps stylophora* Berkeley & Broome

Fruit body 1.5-4.5 cm long, up to 2 mm thick; spores 102-160 × 2-3 μ, the cells 12-20 μ long, not breaking into segments, maturing in the spring.

Eastern and Central United States, rare.

11b. Fruit body gray or brown at least when young; perithecia superficial and free 12

12a. Perithecia 800-855 × 375-410 μ; fruit body 5-13 cm long and 1 mm thick ....*Cordyceps paludosa* Mains

Spores nearly as long as the ascus, the cells 12-18 μ, not breaking into segments.

On larvae of moths and butterflies, Michigan.

12b. Perithecia 320-560 × 250-400 μ; fruit body 1-5 cm long and 0.3-2 mm thick ....*Cordyceps superficialis* (Pk.) Saccardo

Becoming grayish brown or black with age; spores breaking into segments 14-32 × 1.5-2 μ.

On beetle larvae, eastern North America.

13a. Fruit body 2 or more mm thick, yellow or orange; perithecia embedded in a cushion or in a continuous layer 15

13b. Fruit body less than 1 mm thick, ochraceous or vinaceous fawn; perithecia embedded in a cushion 14

14a. Fruit body 20-35 mm long; perithecia 290-325 × 190-225 μ .....
....Cordyceps macularis **Mains**

Fruit body light ochraceous, salmon or vinaceous fawn; spores 60-90 × 2-3 μ, the cells 6-14 μ long, not breaking into segments.

On beetle larvae, Michigan and New York.

14b. Fruit body 5-17 mm long; perithecia 330-600 × 230-400 μ ....
....Cordyceps variabilis **Petch**

Fruit body ochraceous to ochraceous-orange, furfuraceous; perithecia completely embedded at a right angle to the surface; spores breaking into segments 5-10 × 1.5-2 μ.

On beetle larvae in rotten wood, eastern North America.

15a. **Apex of fruit body sterile, perithecial layer in cushions or patches below the apex. Fig. 78** ....Cordyceps melolonthae **(Tul.) Saccardo**

Fruit body 3-13 mm thick, clavate, sulphur yellow to orange above; stipe light buff; perithecia embedded (except for the apex) at right angles to the surface; spores breaking into segments 4-8 × 1-1.5 μ.

On beetle larvae, eastern North America, June, sometimes on June Bug larvae in epidemic proportions.

Fig. 78. Cordyceps melolonthae.

15b. Not as above 16

16a. **Fruit body orange-buff to orange; spores breaking into small segments. Fig. 79** ....Cordyceps militaris **(Fr.) Link**

Fruit body clavate, often with a longitudinal furrow, up to 8 cm long, and 2-6 mm wide above; perithecia embedded at right angles to the surface except for their apex; spore segments 2-4.5 × 1-1.5 μ.

Usually on pupae but at times on larvae of moths and butterflies, eastern North America, one of our more common species.

16b. **Fruit body yellow; spores not breaking into segments**....Cordyceps washingtonensis *Mains*

Fruit body 15-30 mm long, 2-6 mm wide; stipe whitish, 2-4 mm thick; spores 80-110 × 1-1.5 μ.

On pupae and larvae of moths and butterflies, Washington.

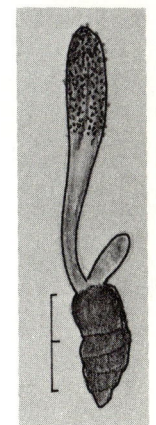

Fig. 79. Cordyceps militaris.

THE BASIDIOMYCETES

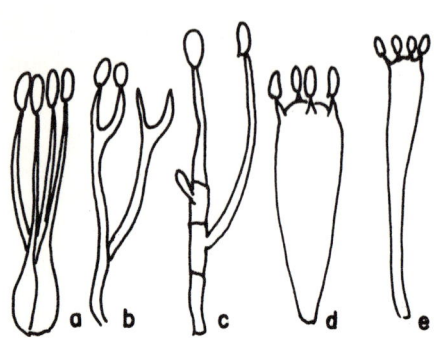

Fig. 80. Major types of basidia: (a) Tremellales; (b) Darcrymycetales; (c) Auriculariales; (d) Boletaceae; (e) Cantharellaceae.

In this large and diverse group of fungi the spores of the sexual stage are produced on basidia (fig. 80) and the basidia are produced on some part of, or in, a structure termed a fruit body (or basidiocarp, the comparable structure in an Ascomycete being an ascocarp, though both are termed fruit bodies). Basidia, however, have different shapes depending on the group, see fig. 80, a-e. Most of the species treated here, however, have the simple type shown in fig. 80, d-e.

Key to the Included Orders of Basidiomycetes

1a. Fruit body extremely gelatinous, slimy or cartilaginous; basidium at maturity divided into 4 cells by longintudinal septa (fig. 80 a) .... *Tremellales* and other Jelly Fungi p. 67

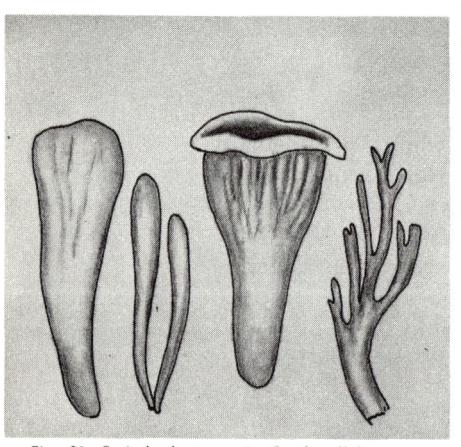

Fig. 81. Fruit body types in Cantharellales.

1b. Not as above 2

2a. Fruit body cartilaginous; on wood; basidia as in Fig. 80, c .... Auriculariales (see key to *Tremellales*)

2b. Fruit body mostly fleshy to woody but sometimes gelatinous or cartilaginous; basidia as in fig. 80, d-e (but in many of the gastromycetes basidia are not present in specimens mature enough to identify) 3

NON-GILLED FLESHY FUNGI

3a. Basidia borne on the smooth surface of the fruit body or on rudimentary gills or pores but the fruit body fleshy, club-shaped to vase-shaped or variously (often elaborately) branched. Fig. 81 ....*Cantharellales* p. 70

3b. Not as above 4

4a. Fruit body with hymenophore in the form of spines, tubes (poroid) or smooth, and texture of fruit body woody to tough or subfleshy to fleshy 5

4b. Fruit body with spore mass borne internally and with basidia mostly disintegrating before spores are mature; or spores discharged from basidia at maturity and borne on lamellae (gills) 7

5a. Fruit body woody, tough, subfleshy but if the latter it does not decay readily and the hymenophoral trama is interwoven to subparallel in hyphal arrangement ....*Aphyllophorales* p. 101

5b. Not as above 6

6a. Hymenophore in the form of spines or "teeth" (Fig. 1g) borne on the underside of a pileus or a framework of branches ....*Hydnaceae*

6b. Fruit body pileate, very fleshy and readily decaying, hymenophoral trama with hyphae at least slightly divergent; hymenophore present as a layer of shallow to deep tubes. Fig. 1a ....The *Boletaceae* of the Agaricales p. 125

7a. Hymenphore in the form of gills (lamellae) with relatively sharp edges; fruit body fleshy to touch. Fig. 1b ....The *Agaricales* (not treated here)

7b. Hymenophore (spore mass) typically borne within the fruit body and often the fruit body itself modified into special shapes or with special structures to aid in spore dissemination (the basidiospores are not forcibly discharged from the basidia as in the previous orders). Fig. 1, e-f ....The "Gasteromycetes" or "Stomach-Fungi"

THE TREMELLALES (The Jelly-Fungi)

The fruit bodies are mostly water and rather shapeless. They must be collected just after a rain as they dry out rapidly and then often appear only as a varnished spot on the substratum. Those in which a distinctive shape is constant are keyed out here, and one member of the order *Auriculariales* is included because it will be mistaken for either a gelatinous Discomycete or a Jelly-Fungus by most collectors.

NON-GILLED FLESHY FUNGI

1a. Fruit body whitish to watery gray, pileate and with short white teeth on the underside of the pileus. Fig. 82 ....
..............................*Pseudohydnum gelatinosum* (Fr.) Karsten

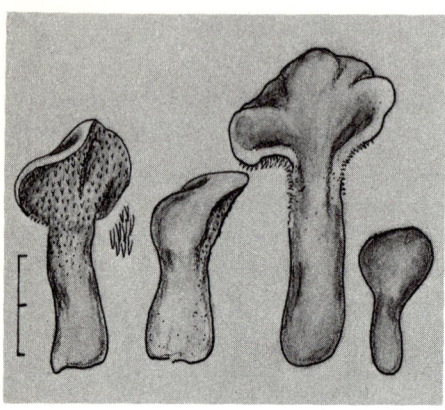

Fig. 82. *Pseudohydnum gelatinosum.*

Pileus lateral and spathlate to fan-shaped, translucent, 2-6 cm broad, finally dingy brownish, upper surface roughened; spines 2-5 mm long; spores subglobose, 5-7 μ, white in deposits.

This is one of the common and distinctive jelly-fungi of the conifer forests of North America, often abundant during cool wet seasons late in the fall.

1b. Not as above 2

2a. Fruit body pinkish to vinaceous or red, spathulate and upright, outer surface smooth. Fig. 83 ....
...............................*Phlogiotis helvelloides* (Fr.) Martin

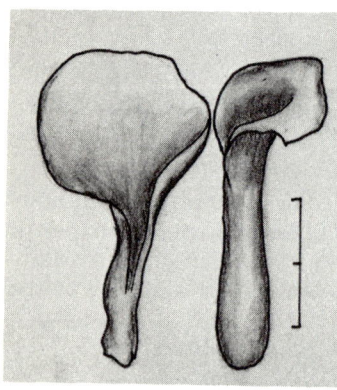

Fig. 83. *Phlogiotis helvelloides.*

Fruit body 3-8 (15) cm high and 3-7 (10) cm wide, spathulate or in age semivase-shaped (open down one side); hymenium smooth; stipe lateral and continuous with pileus, rubbery in consistency, pale red to deep rose color; spores white in a deposit, 9-12 (16) $\times$ 4-6.5 μ; secondary spores 6-7 $\times$ 3.5-4.5 μ.

Scattered to clustered on debris of conifers in calcareous areas across the continent, August to October or later. In some regions this is a highly prized esculent—but it is not suited for cooking; it is usually pickled or candied.

2b. Not as above 3

3a. Terrestrial or clinging to herbaceous plants but originating in the soil 4

3b. Clearly lignicolous 6

NON-GILLED FLESHY FUNGI

4a. Upright and branched (Clavaria-like) but consistency very cartilaginous. Fig. 84 ....
................................*Tremellodendron schweinitzii* (Pk.) Atkinson

Fruit body white to dingy pallid, branches often flattened, up to 12 cm high and 5-10 (15) cm wide, often arising from the base of last years fruit body, in age frequently green from algae living in the moist tissue; spores (7) 8-11 (12) × 4-6 μ, germinating by repetition.

On humus under hardwoods, not uncommon in the Great Lakes area and east of the Great Plains generally in deciduous forests, summer and fall, not edible.

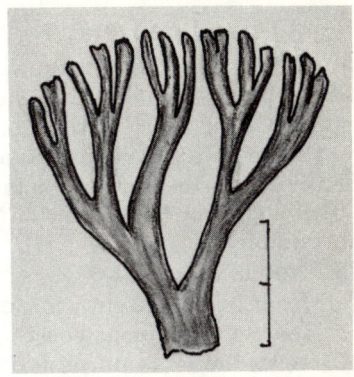

Fig. 84. *Tremellodendron schweinitzii*.

4b. Not as above (or fruit body as a rosette of broad flabby branches) 5
5b. Fruit body taking the shape of the object it clings to—surrounding herbaceous stems, coating surfaces of leaves, etc. ....
....*Tremella concrescens* (Fr.) Burt

Fruit body indefinite in shape and extent, white to pallid and finally dingy ochraceous in places, finally forming a translucent layer over the substrate or supporting object, margin often fimbriate; hyphae 2-3.5 μ wide, clampless; spores cylindric in face view, slightly curved in profile, 14 × 5 μ, through broadly ovate, 9-12 × 7-8 μ to globose, 9 μ.

Mostly east of the Mississippi River, late summer and fall after extended rainy periods.

5b. Fruit body a rosette of hollow thick obtuse branches gelatinous-cartilaginous in consistency; the whole 6-15 cm wide, white to pallid; spores 9-11 × 5-6 μ. Fig. 85 ....
......*Tremella reticulata* (Berk.) Farlow

On the ground, often around stumps in hardwood forests, summer and

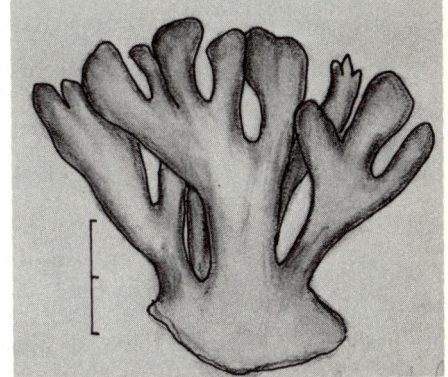

Fig. 85. *Tremella reticulata*.

fall after heavy rains, eastern North America west to the Great Plains, occasional.

6a. Fruit body shaped more or less like a cup-fungus, dark brown ....*Auricularia auricula* (Hook.) Underwood

Fruit body 2-10 (15) cm broad, tough-gelatinous centrally or laterally attached, yellow-brown to blackish brown (as it dries), upper surface (outer surface) sterile and covered with erect brown hairs; hymenial surface smooth; spores $12\text{-}14 \times 4\text{-}6\ \mu$.

Common in the mountains of our western states on wind-thrown fir trees with the bark still intact, late summer and fall, but widely distributed over the continent. Mostly on wood of hardwoods. Probably edible.

6b. Not as above 7

7a. Fruit body 3-12 cm wide, consisting of a mass of leaflike fertile folds of gelatinous consistency and reddish cinnamon to vinaceous brown or purplish tinted ....*Tremella foliacea* Fries

Spores 8-9 (13) $\times$ 7-9 μ (Martin), globose to ovate.

On dead wood, especially around stumps, widely distributed, generally not common in North America but at times numerous after prolonged rainy periods.

7b. Fruit body *Clavaria*-like, orange-yellow to golden yellow ....
....*Calocera viscosa* (Fr.) Fries

Fruit body 3-6 (10) cm tall; basidiospores deep ochraceous in deposit, 9-12 $\times$ 3.5-4.5 μ, becoming 1-septate.

On or beside wood of conifers, especially small sticks in the moss; not rare in the conifer forests of the west but never in large numbers, widely distributed, late fall after prolonged rains.

This genus belongs in the Dacrymycetales, an order also placed with the jelly-fungi in a broad sense.

CANTHARELLALES

The fruit body upright, simple to much-branched, club-shaped or semipileate to pileate; hymenium on the smooth to wrinkled (rarely) lamellae surface of the basidiocarp.

Key to Families

1a. Fruit body simple (but not pileate), forked, or variously branched and if the latter then often in compound clusters; the apices not distinctly enlarged ....*Clavariaceae* p. 71

1b. Fruit body typically flared to pileate at apex, margin ± lobed, hymenophore smooth, as shallow pores, or lamellate ....
....*Cantharellaceae* p. 92

NON-GILLED FLESHY FUNGI

CLAVARIACEAE
Key to Genera

1a. Fruit body arising fom a thick stalk, much-branched above, the branches decidedly flattened so that the whole resembles a bouquet of egg-noodles. Fig. 86 ....*Sparassis radicata* **Weir**

Near conifers in mountain forests of western North America, fall. Edible.

1b. Fruit bodies not flattened as in above 2

2a. Fruit body mostly simple and interior in apex soft and punky, fruit body 5 mm or more thick in widest part ....*Clavariadelphus* p. 89

2b. Not as above (if simple then not punky within and less than 6 mm thick) 3

3a. Lignicolous; spores amyloid (in species included); branching, the type of branching pyxidate to diviricate. Fig. 87 ....*Clavicorona* p. 88

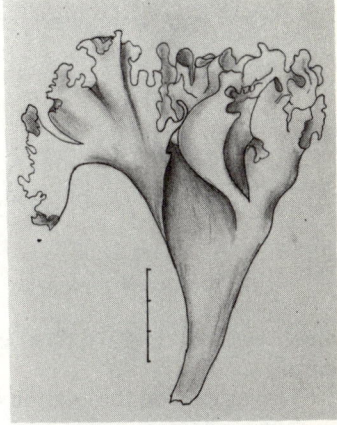

Fig. 86. Sparassis radicata.

3b. Not as above 4

4a. Fruit bodies profusely branched; FeSO$_4$ on fresh hymenium dull olive to blue or bright green; spore deposit cream color to yellow or yellow-brown, rarely white; spores not amyloid ....*Ramaria* p. 80

4b. Not as above 5

5a. Spore deposit white, spores subglobose to globose, minutely ornamented; fruit body sparsely to profusely branched ....*Ramariopsis* p. 79

5b. Not as above 6

6a. Terrestrial or if on wood then the wood covered with algae; simple to forked or sparingly to profusely branched, but if branching the spores white in deposit and not minutely verrucose (some may be angular to angular-tuberculate ....*Clavaria* p. 72

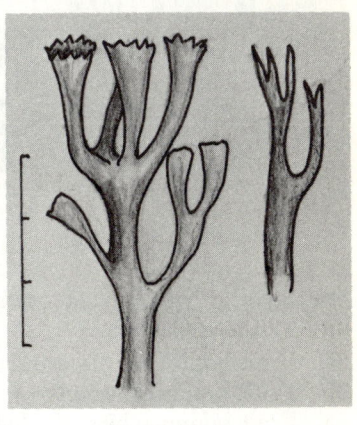

Fig. 87. Clavicorona.

6b. On wood, fruit bodies simple to forked, consistency distinctly gelatinous ....see the key ot the Jelly-Fungi

CLAVARIA

Key to Species

1a. Fruit body associated with algae on soil or wood (the genus *Multiclavula* Petersen) 2
1b. Fruit body not as above 3
2a. Cystidia present in the hymenium; growing on alga-covered soil. Fig. 8 ....*Clavaria phycophylla* Leathers

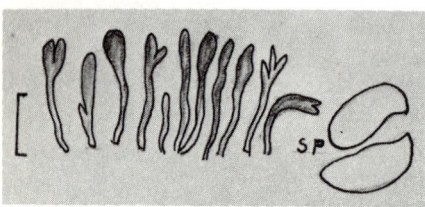

Fig. 88. *Clavaria phycophylla*.

Fruit body 8-12 mm tall, 1-2 mm thick, rarely bifurcate; stipe poorly defined as a whitish zone 2-3 mm long; hymenophore translucent, pale orange or paler; context somewhat gelatinous and pliant, odor and taste none; spores (6) 6.5-10 × 2-3.5 (4) μ, allantoid in profile view; cystidia 20-40 × 7 μ, embedded in hymenium, fusoid-ventricose.

Gregarious on the coating of algae one often finds over naked soil in moist places, summer and fall, Great Lakes Region.

2b. Cystidia absent; growing on algae covering wet wood. Fig. 89 ....*Clavaria mucida* Fries

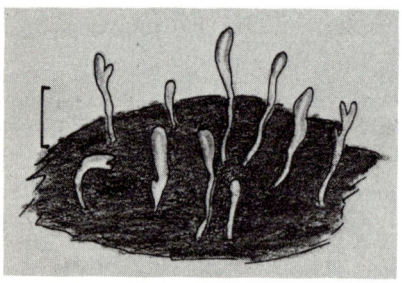

Fig. 89. *Clavaria mucida*.

Fruit body 5-15 mm tall, 1-1.5 mm thick, sometimes forked; stipe indistinct as the lower fourth of the fruit body, white to yellowish; hymenophore white to yellowish or buff or in age brick reddish; context waxy, tough and pliant; taste woody, odor none; spores 5.5-7.5 × 2-3 μ, white, narrowly elliptic to oblong.

Gregarious on decaying wet usually decorticated wood covered by a growth of algae, summer and fall, northern United States and southern Canada.

3a. Fruit bodies simple or rarely bifurcate, brittle 4
3b. Fruit bodies sparingly to much-branched 19
4a. Fruit bodies white, shaded smoky-color over a brighter ground color, dull yellow-brown, gray, pinkish gray, or fuscous to purplish 5
4b. Fruit bodies yellow, pink, orange or red (bright colored) 11

NON-GILLED FLESHY FUNGI

5a. Fruit bodies white to pallid 6

5b. Fruit bodies more deeply colored 8

6a. An appreciable number of fruit bodies in a large collection bifurcate to sparingly branched ....
Clavaria rugosa, C. subtilis, and C. rufipes which are not treated here.

6b. Fruit bodies rarely branched (but they may occur in large clusters) 7

7a. Spores 8.5-10 × 4-5.5 μ ....*Clavaria atkinsoniana* **Leathers**

Fruit body about 3 cm tall and 2 mm thick; stipe distinct as a watery-translucent whitish zone; hymenophore very translucent-whitish and shining; context white, very brittle.

Scattered on soil and humus, summer, central and southeastern United States, apparently rare.

7b. Spores 4.5-7 × 2.5-3.5 (4.5) μ. Fig. 90 ....
....*Clavaria vermicularis* **Fries**

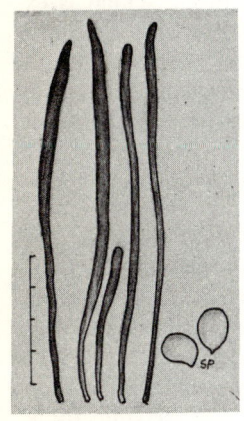

Fig. 90. *Clavaria vermicularis*.

Fruit bodies (1) 3-10 cm tall, 1-5 mm thick; stipe more or less distinct as a translucent portion; hymenophore white but unpolished, soon withering and brownish at apex; context exceedingly fragile, white, taste mild, odor suggestive of tincture of iodine.

Gregarious to clustered on moist soil, summer and fall, common in eastern and central United States but more widely distributed.

8a. Fruit body dark brown; odor and taste of unripe peanuts ....
................*Clavaria fuscoferruginea* **Leathers**

Fruit body 3-6 cm tall, 2-7 mm thick, cylindric to clavate; stipe poorly defined; hymenophore dull cinnamon-brown to a dingy paler yellow-brown (bister), smooth to longitudinally striate or grooved, usually curved or crooked (rarely upright); context pale brown or concolorous with surface; spores 5.5-7 (8) × 3-3.5 (4) μ, elliptic to slightly ovate.

Gregarious to cespitose on moist earth, summer, Great Lakes Region, rarely collected.

8b. Not as above 9

9a. Cystidia present in hymenium; fruit body dark violaceous purplish when young and moist. Fig. 91 ......*Clavaria purpurea* Fries

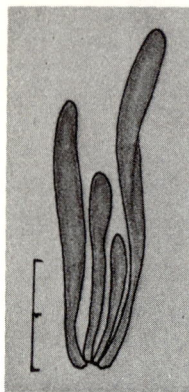

Fig. 91. *Clavaria purpurea.*

Fruit bodies (2) 4-11 cm tall, 2-6 mm thick, more or less cylindric; stipe pallid and appearing more moist than the hymenophore; hymenophore when moist bluish fuscous to purple or purple-drab, fading to vinaceous-buff, lavender-buff or smoky brownish; context brittle, odor and taste slight and hardly distinctive; spores 5.5-9 $\times$ 3-5 μ, more or less elliptic in face view; cystidia 45-130 $\times$ 5-10 μ, cylindric to narrowly clavate.

Gregarious to clustered (10-30 in a cluster at times), on wet soil usually near conifers, common in the northern Rocky Mountains of the United States but apparently rare elsewhere in southern Canada and the northern United States, summer and fall.

9b. Cystidia absent 10
10a. Hymenophore yellowish shaded gray (when fresh) ....
....*Clavaria fumosa* Fries

Fruit body 4-10 cm tall, 2-5 mm thick; stipe indistinct and whitish; hymenophore sometimes compressed and furrowed, ashy-buff (more gray than yellow, but of the type of coloration which is extremely variable depending on the proportions of pigments present); context whitish, in age sometimes collapsing and fruit body becoming flattened, brittle; spores 5-7 $\times$ 3-3.5 μ, in profile view the ventral line straight to slightly concave.

Densely cespitose on humus under hardwoods, July, Great Lakes Region, rare.

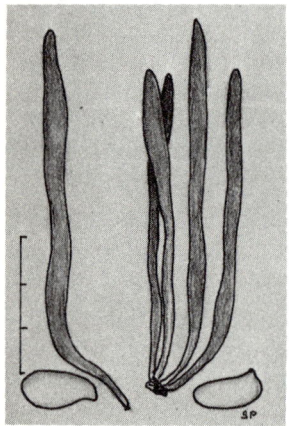

Fig. 92. *Clavaria rubicundula.*

10b. Hymenium vinaceous-buff or grayer with pink tints around basal portion, no yellow tones evident; exceedingly fragile. Fig. 92 ....
.... *Clavaria rubicundula* Leathers

Fruit body 4-15 cm tall, 2-7 mm thick, cylindric to narrowly clavate; stipe poorly defined as a pale pink to pinkish buff zone; hymenophore grayish pink to avellaneous (never purplish violet); context exceedingly fragile, taste mild, odor slight and of tincture of iodine; spores (5) 5.5-8.5 $\times$ 3-4 μ, elliptic.

Densely cespitose (often over a dozen fruit bodies in a cluster), summer and early fall, Great Lakes Region, common under second growth maple and beech on poor sandy soil.

NON-GILLED FLESHY FUNGI

11a. Fruit body with red color predominant when perfectly fresh 12
11b. Fruit body with yellow to orange dominant 13
12a. Spores oblong to ellipsoid ....*Clavaria rosea* Fries

Fruit bodies 1.5-6 cm tall, 1-5 mm thick, erect or decumbent; stipe fairly distinct as a translucent whitish zone at the base, or pale pink; hymenophore rich pink (very brilliant), terete or compressed; context concolorous with surface, very brittle, odor and taste not distinctive; spores $5.5\text{-}7 \times 2.5\text{-}3.5\ \mu$, subellipsoid.

Gregarious to clustered on moist earth in woods, summer and early fall, Great Lakes Region, not common.

12b. Spores subglobose (see *Clavaria applachiensis* also) ....
....*Clavaria miniata* (Berk.) Corner

Fruiting body 4-11 cm tall, 0.5-5 mm thick, terete, rarely bifurcate; stipe distinct as a gold colored zone 1.5-3 cm long; hymenophore pale pinkish orange to salmon color, often twisted; context paler than the surface, very brittle, odor and taste not distinctive; spores $5.5\text{-}8 \times 4\text{-}7\ \mu$, faintly apiculate.

Clustered in small groups on humus, summer and early fall, Great Lakes Region, not common.

13a. Taste farinaceous-disagreeable...see *Clavaria corniculata* p. 77
13b. Taste not as above 14
14a. Spores globose or nearly so 15
14b. Spores narrower in relation to their length 18
15a. Hymenial surface creamy yellow or tinged with vinaceous-buff to salmon ....*Clavaria appalachiensis* Coker

Fruit body 3-9 (12) cm tall, 1.5-5 mm thick, terete and often channeled, becoming flattened; context moderately pliant in the stipe, brittle in the hymenial portion, odor and taste mild; spores $5\text{-}6.5 \times 5.5\text{-}7\ \mu$, with a small apiculus.

Gregarious in cedar swamps, generally solitary to subcespitose on humus and very rotten wood, summer and early fall, widely distributed.

15b. Not as above 16
16a. Spores angular-tuberculate ....*Clavaria helvola* (Fr.) Corner

Fruit bodies 2-7 cm long, 1.5-4 mm thick; stipe distinguished from hymenophore by its shiny or silky texture; bright yellow to orange-yellow (cadmium yellow) over the hymenophore; context lacking a distinct odor or taste; spores $5.5\text{-}7.2 \times 4.5\text{-}5.7\ \mu$, with a prominent apiculus.

Scattered to gregarious on soil, often among grasses, widely distributed but not common in North America.

16b. Spores smooth but apiculate 17

17a. Fruit body 1.5-6.5 cm tall, 1-5 mm thick; stipe distinct as a bright yellow zone; hymenophore bright orange ....
....*Clavaria pulchra* **Peck**
Fruit body terete or flattened, sometimes slightly twisted; context pallid or pale yellow, rather pliant, taste and odor no distinctive; spores 5.5-7 (8.5) × 4-5.5 (6.5) µ, broadly ellipsoid to subglobose, apiculus 1.5-2 µ long.
Gregarious on humus in deciduous and mixed forests, summer and fall, common in Great Lakes Region but generally widely distributed.
17b. Fruit body 3-12 cm tall, 1-5 mm thick if terete, often flattened and wider, bright but pale yellow (lemon yellow). Fig. 93 ....
....*Clavaria fusiformis* **Fries**
Fruit body often narrowly fusiform (pointed at apex); stipe distinct only as a pale yellow zone 10-15 mm long; context pale yellow, moderately brittle, taste bitter, odor none; spores (5) 5.5-7 (8) × 4.5-5 (7) µ, apiculus 1-1.5 µ long, globose to subglobose.
Gregarious to clustered, summer and fall, common generally in northern United States and southern Canada but not limited to these areas.

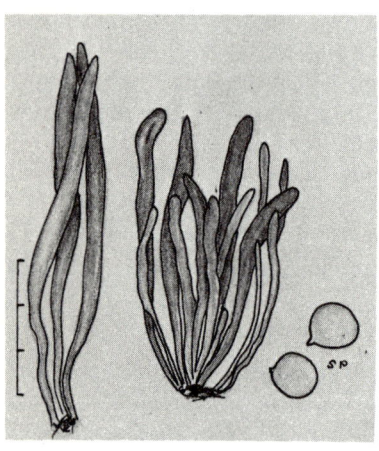

Fig. 93. *Clavaria fusiformis.*

18a. Stipe distinct, golden yellow
......*Clavaria gracillima* **Peck**
Fruit body 2.5-8 cm tall, 3-5 mm thick, terete or compressed; hymenophore pale yellow to buff-yellow (duller), apex acute to obtuse; context yellow, taste farinaceous to almost sharp, odor of tincture of iodine; spores 5.5-8.5 × (2.5) 3-4.5 µ, thin-walled.
Gregarious on humus in deciduous and mixed forests, Great Lakes Region, late summer, apparently rare.
18b. Stipe poorly defined as a pale yellow zone, base slightly bulbous ....*Clavaria luteotenerrima* var. *borealis* **Leathers**
Fruit body 2-5 cm tall, 1.5-6 mm wide, terete to compressed; hymenophore lemon yellow, apex obtuse to subacute; context brittle, taste none, odor sharp and reminding one of tincture of iodine; spores 6-9 × 3-4 µ, ellipsoid, apiculus 1-2 µ long.
Gregarious to subcespitose on sandy loam in deciduous forests, Great Lakes Region, late summer, not common.
19a. Color in violet to purple series 20
19b. Color various but not as above 21

NON-GILLED FLESHY FUNGI

20a. Spores 7-10 × 6-8 μ ....
................*Clavaria amethystina* var. *lilacina* **Quélet & Cooke**

Fruit body 2-6 cm tall, much-branched; stipe short and stout, pale violaceous to whitish; hymenophore lilac-purple, fading in aging, branches firm, often twisted, not cristate; context concolorous with the surface, moderately brittle, taste and odor not distinctive; spores 7-10 × 6-8 μ, white, smooth, subelliptic; basidia 2-spored.

Solitary on humus in deciduous or mixed forests, Great Lakes Region, rare.

20b. Spores 5-7 (7.5) × 3-4.5 μ ....*Clavaria zollingeri* **Léveillé**

Fruit body 3-8 cm high, 0.5-2 cm wide, sparingly branched in the upper third, uniformly violet, paler and duller faded; stipe indistinct, hymenophore with a short unbranched lower portion and branching above this to form smooth branches terete and somewhat divergent, ultimate branches 2-6 cm long and 1-3 mm thick, rounded to subacute at apex; taste somewhat radishlike, odor none.

Gregarious to subcespitose on mossy mounds in the forest, Great Lakes Region, summer and early fall, uncommon.

21a. Fruit body white, pallid, brown or cinereous **22**
21b. Fruit body yellow; taste farinaceous-disagreeable. Fig. 94 ......
....*Clavaria corniculata* **Fries**

Fruit body 3-5 cm tall, 2-2.5 cm wide, sparingly to much-branched and with or without a dendroid appearance; stipe dull lemon yellow above, whitish below, gradually enlarged upwards; hymenophore dull yellow to ochraceous, branches arising on the upper half to upper third of the fructification, $FeSO_4$ on hymenium olive-green; spores 5.5-7 (7.5) × 4-5.5 (7) μ, apiculus 0.5-1 μ long.

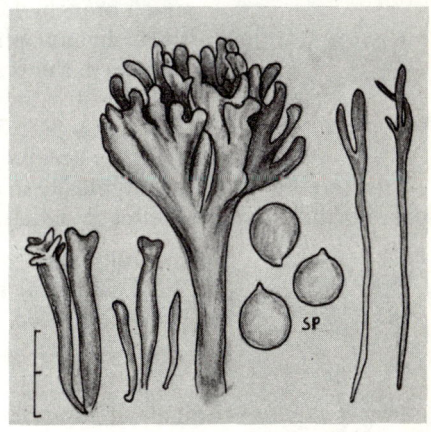

Fig. 94. *Clavaria corniculata.*

Solitary to scattered or gregarious on humus in the forest, eastern and northern United States and southern Canada, common, summer and fall.

22a. Stipe densely covered with brown hairs ....
....*Clavaria ornatipes* **Peck**

Fruit body 2.5-4 cm tall, 5-15 mm wide, sparingly branched; hymenophore pinkish gray or duller, branching dichotomous to polychotomous, divergent, usually flattened and evenly enlarged upward;

context dark brown, drying to yellowish, tough, reviving when moistened, odor and taste scarcely distinctive; spores 8.5-11 (12.5) × 6.5-8.5 μ.

Gregarious on humus across the northern United States and southern Canada, not uncommon.

22b. Not as above 23

23a. Taste penetratingly bitter; hymenium dark green in $FeSO_4$ .... *Clavaria umbrinella* (Sacc.) Corner

Fruit body up to 5 cm tall, 2-5 mm thick, in the stipe; hymenophore pallid to dull brown or drab; branching occurring about half way up; spores (5.2) 5.6-8 (10.5) × 5.6-7 (9) μ, globose, strongly apiculate.

Scattered to gregarious in mixed woods, eastern United States, summer, not common.

23b. Not as above 24
24a. Fruit body much-branched, white at first but ashy to dark gray by maturity. Fig. 95 .... *Clavaria cinerea* Fries

Fruit body 2-11 cm tall, 3-10 cm wide, much-branched; stipe 1-1.5 cm long, 5-6 mm thick; hymenophore densely polychotomously branched, the branch tips acute; context white, rather brittle, odor and taste none; spores (5.5) 7-10 (11) × 5.5-7.5 (10) μ, globose to subglobose; basidia 2-spored.

Fig. 95. *Clavaria cinerea*.

Scattered to gregarious typically in conifer forests during wet seasons, northern United States and Canada, common. Edible.

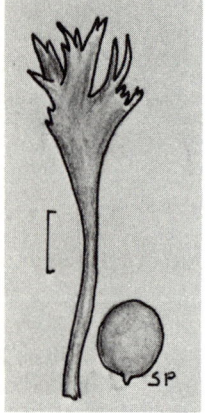

24b. Fruit body white and sparingly branched (if simple or nearly so the name *C. rugosa* is often used) Fig. 96 .... *Clavaria cristata* Fries

Fruit body 2-8 cm tall, 2-5 cm wide, sparingly branched; stipe distinct as a rule, 5-40 mm long, mostly flattened to irregular; hymenophore uniformly white when fresh or rarely with a suggestion of yellow, branching cristate; context white, solid, moderately brittle, odor and taste not distinctive; spores (5.5) 7-10 (11) × 5.5-7 (10) μ, basidia 2-spored.

Gregarious on humus summer and fall, widely distributed.

Fig. 96. *Clavaria cristata*.

RAMARIOPSIS

Key to Species

1a. Fruit body snow white at first but often tinged pinkish by maturity, exceedingly fragile. Fig. 97 ....
....*Ramariopsis kunzei* (Fries) Donk

Fruit body 4-7 cm tall, 3-6 cm wide, much-branched, compound; stipe, lacking or up to 1 cm long, surface scurfy; hymenophore not staining in $FeSO_4$, branching polychotomous at base, dichotomous above, surface of branches unpolished; context white solid, taste and odor not distinctive; spores 3-4 (5.5) × 2.5-4.5 μ, ornamented by minute spines.

Gregarious to clustered on humus in the woods, common in the Great Lakes Region but widely distributed in eastern and northern United States and southern Canada.

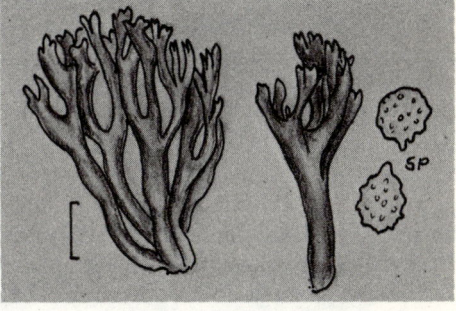

Fig. 97. *Ramariopsis kunzei.*

1b. Not as above 2
2a. Fruit bodies lavender, small (about 1.2 cm high) ....
....*Ramariopsis pulchella* (Boud.) Corner

Fruit bodies with stipe up to 5 mm long and 0.5 mm thick, very delicate, attached by a small mat of mycelium, branching open and dichotomous, branched 2-4 times, tips acute; context markedly pliant; spores 2-3 × 2.8-3.7 μ, very minutely echinulate.

Solitary to scattered, on soil in woods, under hemlock in Michigan, rare, widely distributed.

2b. **Fruit body brilliant orange or redder, fading to bright yellow**
....*Ramariopsis crocea* (Fr.) Corner

Fruit body 1.5-3 cm tall, 0.5-1 cm wide, sparingly branched to well-branched but delicate in appearance; stipe orange, 0.5 cm long, 1-1.5 mm thick; hymenophore branched dichotomously producing a dendroid effect, often lax in appearance but branches erect, surface lubricous; context orange, elastic, taste and odor none; spores 2-4 × 2.5-3 μ, asperulate.

Scattered to gregarious on humus in conifer and deciduous forests, northern and eastern United States and southern Canada, not common.

RAMARIA

Key to Species

1a. Lignicolous species, clearly growing on decaying wood (logs, stumps etc.); at least some contextual hyphae thick-walled 2
1b. Not as above, but may be on small sticks or rotten wood that has crumbled, or an occasional fruit body on woody material 4
2a. Taste sharply but often slowly acrid ....
....Ramaria acris (Peck) Corner

Fruit body 4-8 cm tall, 2-8 cm wide, solitary to cespitose; stipe short or absent, arising from a thick mat of cottony white mycelium and with rhizomorphs penetrating the substratum; hymenophore vinaceous-cinnamon to more vinaceous-brown (in age), staining darker vinaceous-brown where bruised, tips whitish if actively growing; branches usually somewhat flattened in cross-section, the angles between them rounded, surface smooth; context concolorous with surface, very tough, odor faintly fragrant; spores 5.5-8.5 $\times$ 3.4-4.5 μ, minutely ornamented, dingy yellow-tan in deposit; clamps present.

Solitary to gregarious on decaying conifer logs and stumps (rarely on hardwood), eastern and northern United States and very likely widespread in southern Canada, late summer and fall.

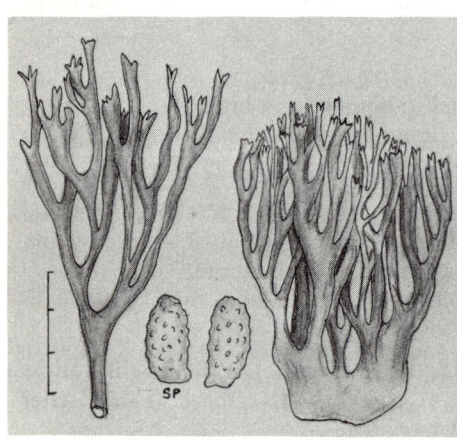

Fig. 98. Ramaria apiculata.

2b. Taste bitter or otherwise unpleasant but not acrid 3
3a. Tips whitish when growing but soon vinaceous-cinnamon like the branches; branching more or less open at maturity. Fig. 98 ....
........Ramaria apiculata (Fr.) Donk

Fruit body medium to large (6-10 cm tall, up to 6 cm wide); stipe fleshy tan to reddish brown, short or very short; hymenophore vinaceous-tawny, staining vinaceous-brown bruised; context tough, taste bitter, odor slightly fragrant; spores 8.5-10 $\times$ 3.5-4 μ, yellow (ochraceous) in deposit, minutely ornamented; some hyphae in fruit body thick-walled; clamp connections present.

Gregarious to cespitose on conifer wood and less frequently on hardwood, summer and fall, eastern and northern United States and southern Canada, not rare.

3b. **Tips of branches or ultimate branches soon yellow; branching typically compact. Fig. 99** ....*Ramaria stricta* (**Fr.**) **Quélet**

Fruit body 4-12 cm tall 4-8 (10) cm wide; stipe almost lacking; hymenophore buff-pink to pinkish tan except for yellow extremities; vinaceous-brown when bruised; context tough, taste metallic, odor slight; spores 7-10 × 3.5-4 μ, ellipsoid, minutely ornamented.

Scattered to gregarious on hardwood, more rarely on conifer wood, widely distributed but common in the Great Lakes Region, summer and fall.

4a. **Consistency tough; spore deposit white to pallid; some hyphae thick-walled** 5
4b. **Consistency pliant to fragile; spore deposit yellowish to pale tan; hyphae of the context thin-walled** 6
5a. **Spores 10-14 μ long, smooth; tips of branches pallid to pale pinkish tan but becoming flushed delicately pale pea green** ....
    ....*Ramaria byssiseda* (**Fr.**) **Quél.**

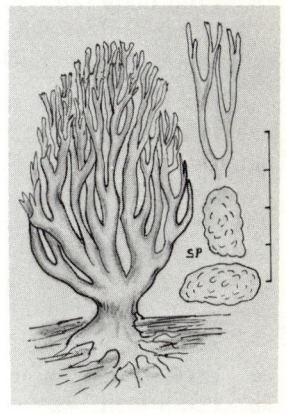

Fig. 99. *Ramaria stricta.*

Fruit body 1.5-5 cm high, 0.5-4.5 cm wide; stalk scurfy, nearly white; hymenophore pinkish buff or near it and at the tips whitish, darkening in age; context pliant, taste slightly metallic, odor not distinctive; spores (9) 10-14 (15) × 3-4 μ, sigmoid in profile view; clamps present.

Scattered to clustered on humus and debris in conifer and hardwood forests, August to November, common in the Great Lakes region but widely distributed.

5b. **Spores 7-10 × 2-3.5 μ; tips creamy white or with a tinge of grayish blue** ....*Lentaria patouillardii* (**Bres.**) **Corner**

Fruit body 3-6.5 cm tall, 2-4 cm wide, much-branched; stipe white to pale tan, 1-2 cm long, arising from a dense mat of mycelium, numerous rhizomorphs penetrating the substrate; hymenophore cream-buff to dingy cinnamon; context tough, pliant, taste bitter, odor fungoid to fragrant; spores smooth; clamps present.

Gregarious in mixed woods, summer and fall, widely distributed but not common. *Lentaria* is a satellite genus intergrading with *Ramaria*.

6a. **Fruit body gradually becoming olive or green or so stained in age or slowly staining green to olive when bruised; spores 5.5-7.5 μ long** ....*Ramaria ochraceo-virens* (**Jungh.**) **Donk**

Fruit body 4-10 cm tall, 2-8 cm wide, much-branched; stipe white to ochraceous, 1-2 cm long, 3-7 mm thick, numerous white rhizomorphs extend into the substratum; hymenophore ochraceous to light cinnamon or finally dingy brown especially over lower branches; context where injured slightly vinaceous, taste bitter, odor fungoid; spores 5.5-7.5 (10) × (2) 3-3.5 μ, finely echinulate.

Scattered to gregarious under conifers or hardwoods, common during the fall in the northern United States and very likely in southern Canada also.

6b. Not as above 7
7a. Fruit body tough to pliant; copious mycelium and rhizomorphs around the base and penetrating the substratum 8
7b. Fruit body fairly brittle to brittle, if pliant lacking copious mycelium and/or rhizomorphs at the base 12
8a. Spores 8-10 × 3.5-4 μ ....*Ramaria suecia* (Fr.) **Donk**

Fruit body 3-6 cm tall, 2-5 cm wide; stipe 1-3 cm long, pallid to pale dull pinkish, in age dingy cinnamon; hymenophore dingy pale pinkish tan becoming dingy cinnamon; tips acute, pallid at first, in age nearly concolorous with branches; context pith-like, distinctly bitter on dried specimens, odor not distinctive; spores ochraceous in mass, verrucose; clamps present.

Gregarious under pine late summer and fall, common during wet seasons in eastern and northern United States and southern Canada.

8b. Spores 5-8 μ long 9
9a. Fresh fruit body not staining where injured 10
9b. Fresh fruit body staining vinaceous to vinaceous-brown where injured 11
10a. Odor not distinctive; spores distinctly echinate ....
....*Ramaria abietina* **Quélet**

Fruit body 3-6 cm tall, 2-4 cm wide; stipe dingy tan or dingy pale cinnamon, 0.5-3 cm long 0.2-1 cm thick; hymenophore pale yellow to cinnamon-buff; branches mostly with acute tips; context white, spongy; taste bitter, odor slight; spores 5.5-6.5 (8.5) × 3-4 (5) μ, clamps present.

Gregarious to cespitose, rarely on beech stumps; usually on the needle carpet under conifers, widely distributed but common in the Great Lakes Region, June to September.

10b. Odor of licorice when fresh; spores minutely verrucose ....
....*Ramaria gracilis* (Fr.) **Quélet**

Fruit body 2.5-5 cm tall, 1.5-3.5 mm wide much-branched; stipe up to 2 cm long, 2-5 mm thick, whitish to pale tan, typically with a cottony felt of mycelium around the base; hymenophore whitish to pale buff or in age pinkish buff, tips pallid and acute; context solid, pith-like, taste musty-stale; spores (4.5) 5.5-7 (7.5) × (2.5) 3-3.5 μ; clamps present.

Gregarious to subcespitose on needles and debris under conifers June to October in Great Lakes Region, not uncommon.

11a. Basal branches and mycelium and lower branches at times vinaceous when bruised; hymenophore creamy yellowish to dingy yellow ....*Ramaria flaccida* (Fr.) **Ricken**

Fruit body 4-6 cm tall, 2-5.5 cm wide; stipe up to 2 cm tall, up to 5 mm wide, yellowish; hymenophore smooth; context white, flaccid, taste bitter, odor fragrant; spores ochraceous in mass; clamps present.

Gregarious on conifer needles in the fall, Great Lakes region and eastern North America.

11b. Fruit body staining vinaceous on tips and upper branches; hymenophore honey yellow to pale honey brown ....
....*Ramaria pusilla* (Pk.) **Corner**

Fruit body 2-9 cm tall, 4-10 cm wide, much-branched; stipe dingy yellowish to whitish, short; often grooved or channeled near the base; hymenophore with branches having acuminate tips; context white, becoming vinaceous on bruising, pith-like, taste slowly but distinctly bitter, odor somewhat fragrant but faint; spores $5.5\text{-}7 \times 2.8\text{-}3.5\ \mu$; clamps present.

Gregarious-cespitose under conifers and hardwoods, summer and fall, eastern North America and the Great Lakes region, not common.

12a. Context at maturity in the lower portions (stipe and primary branches) translucent and gelatinous when fresh; taste resembling that of tobacco ....*Ramaria gelatinosa* (Coker) **Corner**

Fruit body 7-12 cm tall, 5-14 cm wide; stipe not distinct; hymenophore creamy-white becoming pinkish to deep flesh-color; context elastic, taste acid then bitterish (and tobacco-like), odor tobacco-like on dried material; spores $7.5\text{-}9 \times 4.4\text{-}5\ \mu$, warty.

Under mixed conifers and hardwoods, summer, Southeastern. A Pacific Northwest species, as yet undescribed, has gelatinous flesh and formerly the name *Clavaria gelatinosa* has been applied to it erroneously.

12b. Context of fruit body not gelatinous 13
13a. Fruit body dull olive to violaceous in region of lower branches and stipe 14
13b. Fruit body differently colored 15
14a. Tips of branches olive-yellow to dingy buff ....
....*Ramaria fennica* (Karst.) **Ricken**

Fruit body 6-12 cm tall, 7-8 cm wide, massive; stipe violaceous near point of branching, base whitish; hymenophore olive-gray to smoky yellowish (in age) or finally dingy yellow-brown; context firm, taste bitterish, odor none; spores $8.5\text{-}12 \times 3.5\text{-}4.5\ \mu$, verrucose; clamps present.

Scattered under hardwoods, Great Lakes region, summer and fall, not uncommon during wet seasons.

14b. Tips of branches remaining violaceous a long time ....
....*Ramaria fumigata* (Pk.) **Corner**

Fruit body 5-12 cm tall, over 9 cm wide, massive; stipe 2.5-5 cm thick, distinct as a white area below the primary branches; hymenophore evenly lilac to violaceous, slowly becoming smoky-yellowish to dingy yellow-brown; context white, fairly tough, taste bitterish to slightly peppery; spores 8.5-11 × 3-4 μ; clamps present.

Scattered under hardwoods, summer, Great Lakes region, rare, and in eastern North America.

15a. Branches of fruit body elastic; branches lavender-pink upward, more dingy vinaceous below; odor of cocoa-butter; spores striate .... *Ramaria cacao* (Coker) Corner

Fruit body 7-8 cm tall, 5-6 cm wide; stipe whitish; deeply vinaceous when bruised in stipe and lower parts; stipe 1-2.5 cm thick; context white, firm, taste mild.

Solitary to gregarious under hardwoods, summer, southeastern but extending north to Michigan, rare.

15b. Not as above 16
16a. Spores with ornamentation in lines (spores striate); hymenophore pallid to yellowish but tips vinaceous. Fig. 100 ....
....*Ramaria botrytis* (Fr.) Ricken

Fruit body up to 15 cm tall and 12 cm wide; stipe up to 6 cm thick, white, solid and fleshy; context white, taste and odor pleasant; spores (11) 12-15 (16) × 3.5-5.5 μ; clamps present.

Scattered, gregarious or in arcs under conifers and in mixed forests, late summer and fall, widely distributed, not uncommon.

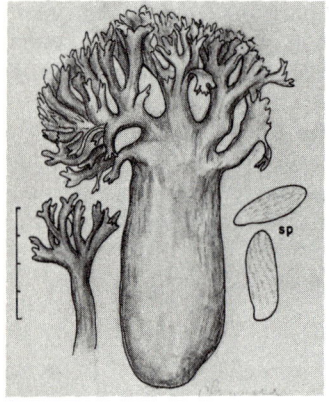

Fig. 100. *Ramaria botrytis*.

16b. Spores not striate 17
17a. Injured portion of hymenophore staining in a distinctive manner or stains showing on older specimens 18
17b. Fruit body not staining on injury or in aging 21

18a. Hymenophore lemon yellow, tips bright yellow, staining blood red to wine red on stipe and lower branches ....
....*Ramaria sanguinea* (Coker) Corner

Fruit body 6-14 cm tall, 4-17 cm wide; stipe 2-3 × 2-4 cm, often very short; context white to yellowish, brittle, taste and odor mild; spores 8.5-12 × 3.5-4 μ, verruculose.

Solitary to gregarious under hardwoods, southeastern states, eastern and central United States, summer and fall, not uncommon. *Hypomyces transformans* frequently parasitizes this species.

18b. Not as above 19

19a. Hymenophore pale dull yellow, tips obtuse and concolorous with branches, tips soon staining grayish vinaceous ....
....*Ramaria secunda* **(Berk.) Corner**

Fruit body up to 14 cm tall and 15 cm wide; stipe lacking or up to 1 cm long and 2.5 cm thick, yellow; context brittle, white, taste faintly acid becoming bitterish in old specimens, odor slight; spores 10-12.5 × 3.5-4 μ, verruculose; clamps present but rare.

Gregarious on sandy soil in pine-scrub oak association, late summer and fall, widely distributed but rare.

19b. Fruit body with brown to dark brown hymenophore 20

20a. Spore deposit ochraceous; tips at first yellowish; spores verrucose ....*Ramaria brunnea* **(Zeller) Corner**

Fruit body 11-12 cm tall, 7-10 cm wide, with a deeply rooted stipe; hymenophore vinaceous-brown, the tips finally concolorous; taste bitter; spores 9-12 × 4-5 μ.

Under conifers, Oregon, Washington and Idaho east to Michigan, late summer and fall, uncommon.

20b. Spores dark yellow brown in deposit, echinlate, spines to 1.5 μ high; tips of branches abruptly white ....
....*Ramaria grandis* **(Pk.) Corner**

Fruit body up to 18 cm high, to 12 cm broad, uniformly deep brick brown; stipe up to 6 × 2 cm, deeply rooted, quickly turning dull brownish lavender or purple if injured; context white quickly turning lavender if cut, taste bitterish then astringent; spores 11-13.5 × 6.3-7 μ.

On humus in frondose woods, southeastern states, rare.

21a. Fruit body pale orange to orange-buff, tips chrome yellow; clamps not present. Fig. 101 ....

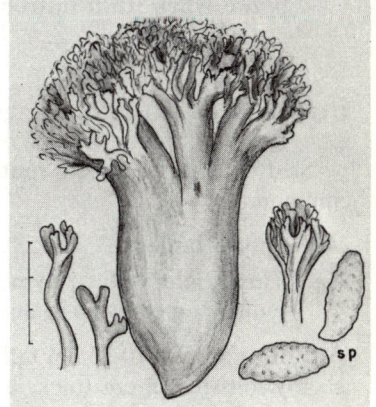

Fig. 101. *Ramaria aurea*.

Ramaria aurea **(Fr.) Quélet**
Fruit body 11-13 cm tall, 4-8 cm wide or more; stipe white, 3-5 cm long, up to 4 cm wide; hymenophore smooth; context white, brittle, taste and odor not distinctive; spores (8.5) 10-12 (14) × 3.5-5.5 μ, verruculose.

Gregarious on humus under hardwoods, common in the Great Lakes Region, late summer and fall.

21b. Not as above 22
22a. Fruit body brilliant coral pink over all at first; spores 8.5-10 × 3-4 μ ....*Ramaria subbotrytis* (Coker) Corner

Fruit body 7.5-10 cm high, 5-9 cm broad; context concolorous with the surface; odor and taste slightly krauty; spores verrucose; clamps absent.

Solitary to gregarious in deciduous woods, summer and early fall, Great Lakes Region and eastern North America.

22b. Not as above 23
23a. Fruit bodies with lavender-pink tips at first and remainder of hymenophore pinkish cinnamon to vinaceous-brown when mature; spores 9-10.5 × 4-5 μ ....
....*Ramaria subspinulosa* (Coker) Corner

Fruit bodies 6-10.5 cm tall, 3-8 cm wide; stipe usually roughly felted, stout, more or less grooved where extending to main branches, darkening to dull cinnamon; taste acid-bitterish; spores 9-10.5 × 4-5 μ.

Not rare in pine or mixed or deciduous woods in July and August (Coker). Southeastern United States.

23b. Not as above 24
24a. Spores 7.5-8.5 × 4-4.5 μ; branch tips lemon yellow, hymenophore when fresh saffron (yellowish-salmon) ....
....*Ramaria conjunctipes* (Coker) Corner

Fruit bodies up to 7 cm high, the bases slender and string-like, attached to rhizomorphs, in age becoming pale tan over all; context firm, flexible, taste and odor not distinctive.

Scattered to cespitose, southeastern United States, summer, uncommon.

24b. Spores larger 25
25a. Tips bright yellow, hymenophore pinkish to salmon-color but fading to yellowish in age ....*Ramaria formosa* (Fr.) Quélet

Fruiting body 10-15 cm tall, 2.5-15 cm wide, massive; stipe pinkish to whitish, 1-2 cm thick; hymenophore much-branched; context bitterish and often leaving an astringent feeling in the throat; spores (8.5) 9.5-12.5 (13.5) × 3.5-5 (5.5) μ, verruculose; clamps present.

Scattered to gregarious or in arcs, under hardwoods or conifer, northern and eastern United States and southern Canada, not uncommon. Not edible.

NON-GILLED FLESHY FUNGI

25b. Not with above colors 26

26a. Fruit body whitish to pale buff but the tips at first pale and vinaceous-lilac to lilac-gray. Fig. 102 ....
....*Ramaria botrytoides* (Pk.) **Corner**

Fruit body up to 14 cm high and wide, massive; stipe white to pallid, 2-4 cm thick, pointed below; context white, solid, spongy, rather brittle, taste slightly acid-bitterish, odor slight; spores 8.5-11 × 4-5.5 μ, spore deposit pale yellow; clamps absent.

Gregarious in mixed woods, summer and fall, not uncommon, Great Lakes Region and eastern North America.

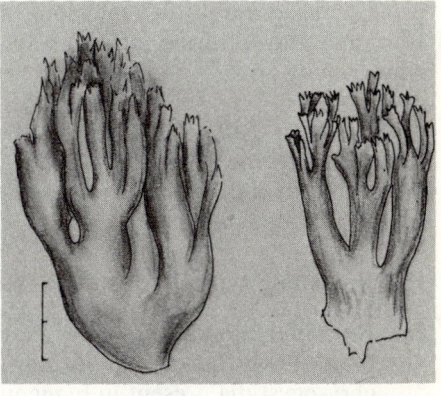

Fig. 102. *Ramaria botrytoides*.

26b. Hymenophore yellowish to brown 27

27a. Spores 8-10 × 4-5 μ; fruit body mostly in the form of compact head 5-15 cm wide ....
.....................................*Ramaria caulifloriformis* (Leathers) **Corner**

Fruit body with a stipe whitish to creamy brown, finally dark yellow-brown, 1-3 cm thick, pointed at the base; hymenophore creamy tan to slightly darker (cinnamon-buff) and finally dingy yellow-brown, tips finally becoming vinaceous-brown; context white at first, taste and odor not distinctive; spores verrucose; clamps numerous and distinct.

Gregarious under scrub oak and jack pine on sandy soil, late summer and fall, Michigan, fruiting during very wet seasons.

27b. Spores 9-12 (14) × 3-4.5 μ; fruit body with tips obtuse and pallid to yellowish ....*Ramaria obtusissima* (Pk.) **Corner**

Fruit body up to 15 cm tall, 6 cm or more wide, massive; stipe white below, creamy tan above, 1-2.5 cm thick; hymenophore creamy tan to tan, surface smooth to rugulose longitudinally; context white, solid, rather brittle, odor fragrant, taste faintly bitter; spores verruculose, ochraceous in deposit (duller than in 27a); clamps absent.

Clustered on humus under conifers, summer and fall, and also under hardwoods, not common, eastern United States and Great Lakes region.

CLAVICORONA

Key to Species

1a. Branching divaricate in normal specimens. (See Fig. 87-b) ....
................................*Clavicorona divaricata* Leathers & Smith

Fruit bodies 2-5 cm high, 1-4 cm wide, solitary to cespitose or 3-4 fused at base, rarely 6-7 mm long and 1-2 mm thick; secondaries 1.5-2 mm and ultimates often about 1 mm thick, color snow-white when young, finally pale vinaceous-fawn or if water-soaked lilac-gray; context very soft and delicate; odor fragrant; taste bitterish; spores 4.5-6.5 × 2.2-3.5 μ; leptocystidia 18-28 × 4.5-7 μ, chrysocystidia not present.

On rotten cottonwood logs, Pacific Northwest, during cool rainy weather in the fall, rare.

1b. Branching typically pyxidate (see fig. 87-a) 2

2a. Fruit body grayish brown when young except for the pallid tips; taste slowly becoming burning acrid; both leptocystidia and chrysocystidia present in hymenium; on conifer logs and stumps
................................*Clavicorona avellanea* Leathers & Smith

Fruit bodies 2-6 cm high and 1-4 cm broad or clusters larger, primary branches soon pubescent to strigose; context brittle; odor slightly pungent to disagreeable; unchanging when bruised; spores 3.5-5 × 3-4 μ, smooth to minutely roughened.

Scattered on conifer logs (often of *Thuja plicata*) in the Pacific Northwest, abundant during some seasons But generally rare. *C. piperata* (Kauffman) Smith & Leathers was described as having yellowish spores.

2b. Color pale yellow to pallid or white when young but often becoming wood brown to dark gray-brown over basal branches; taste peppery; on wood of hardwoods, especially aspen ....
................................*Clavicorona pyxidata* (Fr.) Doty

Fruit body 6-10 cm high, 2-6 (8) cm wide, branching pyxidate; taste slowly slightly to sharply peppery; odor slight, resembling freshly dug potatoes; spores 3.5-5 (5.5) × 2-3 μ, smooth; chrysocystidia 30-50 × 5-7 μ; clamps present.

Scattered to cespitose often in large masses on rotting logs in the spring or early summer, especially on aspen in late June and in July in the Great Lakes area, but widespread throughout North America north of Mexico, common. Edible.

NON-GILLED FLESHY FUNGI

CLAVARIADELPHUS

Key to Species

1a. Fruit body (when mature) mucronate at apex and apical area typically whitish. Fig. 103 ....
................................*Clavariadelphus mucronatus* Wells & Kempton

Fruit bodies 3-6 (8) cm tall, 10-15 (25) mm wide at apex, merely acute at apex at first but soon developing a small distinct central mucro; the sides tan to light brownish; spore deposit white; spores 11-15 × 3.5.7 μ.

1b. Fruit bodies not mucronate and apical area not white 2
2a. Fruit bodies truncate (flattened or shallowly depressed) at apex 3
2b. Fruit bodies obtuse to rounded or blunt-pointed at apex when mature 6

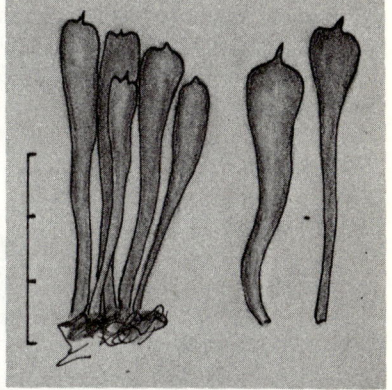

Fig. 103. *Clavariadelphus mucronatus.*

3a. Spore deposit pale ochraceous. Fig. 104 ....
....*Clavariadelphus truncatus* (Quél.) Donk

Fruit body 9-15 cm tall, 3-6 cm wide at apex, apex often slightly concave at maturity and the margin uplifted slightly, narrowing downward to a bulbous (1-2.5 cm) base; hymenial surface pinkish brown, apex bright to golden yellow when young; spores 9-11.5 × 6-7 μ; cystidia none; the flat part of the apex sterile.

Scattered to gregarious or subcespitose on duff under conifers, August to October, Great Lakes region.

3b. Spore deposit white 4
4a. Fruit body bright red at apex shading to reddish orange at the sides and dull flesh color at the base; growing under conifers in the Rocky Mountains ....
..........*Clavariadelphus lovejoyae* Wells & Kempton

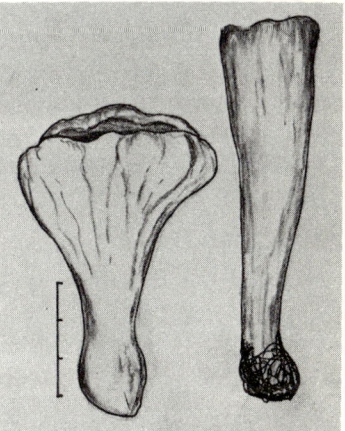

Fig. 104. *Clavariadelphus truncatus.*

Fruit body 0.5-3 cm broad at apex, at first covered to near the base of the stipe with a white bloom; spores of two types, mostly

10.7-13 × 5-6 μ, broadly ellipsoid, but some 15-17 × 6-7 μ and constricted near the midportion.

Gregarious to cespitose in groups of 4-6, on soil under balsam and spruce, August, Wyoming.

4b. Fruit body yellow to orange to pinkish at apex 5

5a. Apex of fruit body yellow to orange; growing under conifers from Alaska to Oregon, Idaho and Michigan. Fig. 105 ....
................................*Clavariadelphus borealis* **Wells & Kempton**

Fruit body 4.5-14 cm tall, 1.5-5 cm wide at apex, broadening in age to become turbinate and usually with a puckered ridge around the margin, the sides dark vinaceous-brown to alutaceous or flushed lilac; spores 9-11.3 × 4.7-6.6 μ.

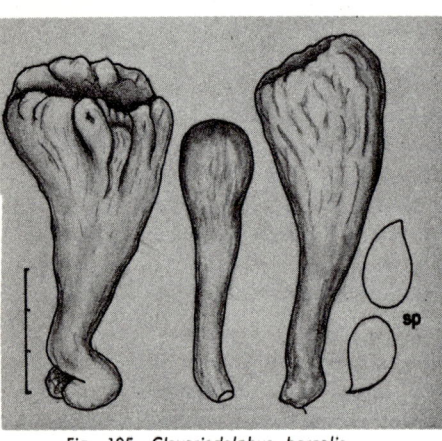

Fig. 105. *Clavariadelphus borealis.*

Scattered, gregarious, or rarely subcespitose under conifers; fall.

5b. Fruit bodies pink to lilac at first; growing in deciduous woods in the southeastern United States ....*Clavariadelphus unicolor* **(Rav. ex. Berk) Corner**

Fruit body 2.5-6 cm tall, 2-4 cm wide near apex, frequently becoming turbinate and with an elevated and furrowed marginal ridge, pale ochraceous with tints of flesh pink, violet or reddish brown, drying and becoming darker as well as redder; spores 9.4-11 × 4.5-5.5 μ..

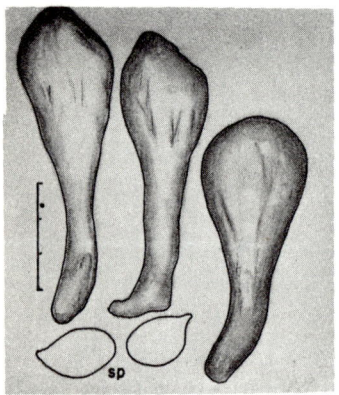

Fig. 106. *Clavariadelphus pistillaris.*

Gregarious under hardwoods or in mixed forests, southeastern United States, November and December.

6a. Fresh fruit body staining brown to vinaceous-brown when handled; typically under hardwoods. Fig. 106 ....
..........*Clavariadelphus pistillaris* **(Fr.) Donk**

Fruit bodies 8-30 (40) mm in diam. near the apex, the apex rounded, frequently inflated with age, pallid with a yellow apex at first, soon ochraceous to ochraceous-brown overall, 6-15 (20) cm tall; spore deposit white; spores 9-13.8 × 4.5-7.5 μ.

Gregarious to scattered in hardwoods or mixed woods, summer and fall to early winter, widely distributed.

6b. Fresh fruit body not staining when handled or (in *C. subfastigiatus*) staining slightly 7
7a. KOH on fresh hymenial surface staining it forest green (bright green); cut context staining slightly vinaceous ....
..........................*Clavariadelphus subfastigiatus* Wells & Kempton

Fruit body 4-9 cm tall, 5-25 mm wide at widest place, pallid at first but becoming brownish orange, apex obtuse; spores 8-10.5 × 6-6.5 μ.

In clusters or gregarious, rarely solitary, on humus under conifers, fall, Pacific Northwest and Alaska.

7b. KOH not staining hymenophore green; cut context unchanging 8
8a. Fruit bodies large (up to 20 cm tall), in clusters ....
....*Clavariadelphus cokeri* Wells & Kempton

Fruit bodies pink then alutaceous, the apex at first acute then obtuse or flattened or branched antler-like, bases deeply inserted in the humus; spores 9.4-11.3 × 4.7-5 μ.

Under hemlock, September, New England.

8b. Fruit bodies small and typically scattered to gregarious or in small clusters in addition 9
9a. Spore deposit pale yellowish; spores 12-15 × 3-4.5 μ ....
....*Clavariadelphus ligula* (Fr.) Donk

Fruit body 3-12 mm wide near apex, apex obtuse, terete to flattened or at times ligulate to spathulate, pale ochraceous buff to vinaceous-buff uniformly to the pallid pase, base strigose to tomentose and with abundant white mycelium.

Scattered to gregarious to gregarious-subcespitose on humus under conifers, July to November, widely distributed.

9b. Spore deposit buff to ochraceous; spores 16-24 × 4-6 μ. Fig. 107 ....
......*Clavariadelphus sachalinensis* (Imai) Corner

Fruit body 3-15 mm wide at apex, 5-10 cm tall, cylindric to clavate or subventricose to variously contorted, light yellow to buff or dull ochraceous, apex

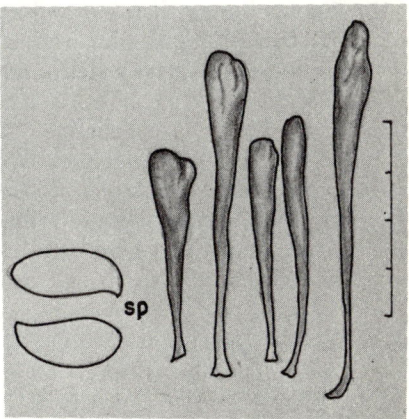

Fig. 107. *Clavariadelphus sachalinensis*.

conclorous or becoming pale olivaceous at times, base with abundant white mycelium in the surrounding duff.

Densely gregarious on conifer duff, summer and fall, widely distributed, common in Alaska and the Pacific Northwest to northern Idaho and Michigan.

The CANTHARELLACEAE

See Key (p. 70) for diagnostic characters.

Key to Genera

1a. Hymenophore veined and bluish fuscous; consistency fleshy; stipe solid; spores 4-5 μ diam. and angular-tuberculate. Fig. 108 ....*Polyozellus multiplex* (Underw.) Murrill

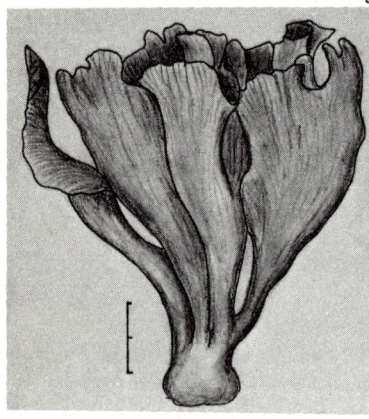

Fig. 108. *Polyozellus multiplex*.

Fruit body compound, 6-15 cm high and up to 1 m. in diam., pilei 2-5 cm wide and 3-10 cm high, vase-shaped or lopsided; stipes 3-5 cm long, 6-20 mm thick, compound, violaceous-fuscous; spore deposit white; basidia olivaceous in KOH; clamp connections present.

Growing in clusters; known across the continent in Canada and northern United States; late summer and fall; rather rare. The relationships of this species are with *Thelephora* not to the species of *Cantharellus*.

1b. Spores longer than 5 μ and not angular tuberculate 2
2a. Hymenophore of veins rather than lamellae and brownish violaceous; consistency fleshy and stipe solid ....*Gomphus*
2b. Not as above 3
3a. Fruit body funnel-shaped, hollow, thin, color blackish-brown to fuscous; clamp connections absent ....*Craterellus* p. 93
3b. Fruit body with strong ochraceous to reddish tones in pileus or stipe and hymenophore white to yellow or orange as well as being smooth to lamellate, clamps typically present. See *Clavariadelphus* also, p. 89 ....*Cantharellus* p. 95

GOMPHUS

Cap dull and unpolished, the margin often grown out on one side more than the other and variously lobed; color purplish to purplish brown fading to olivaceous-brown or paler; hymenophore not truly

gill-like; stipe often compound (with several pilei coming from a main stem).
1a. Spores smooth ....
.......................*Gomphus pseudoclavatus* (Smith & Morse) Corner

Cap 3-8 (19.) cm broad, margin often lobed, flesh white; odor none, taste mild; spore deposit pale buff; spores 9-12 × 5-6.5 μ; pleurocystidia and clamp connections absent.

Under hardwoods (oak-hickory), known from Michigan and California after heavy rains in the fall, rare.
1b. **Spores slightly rugose-wrinkled to obscurely warty. Fig. 109** .....
........................*Gomphus clavatus*
(Fr.) S. F. Gray

Cap (3) 5-10 (15) cm broad, fruit bodies merely truncate clubs when young, smooth or becoming slightly squamulose from breaking of the cuticle; flesh whitish to buff;

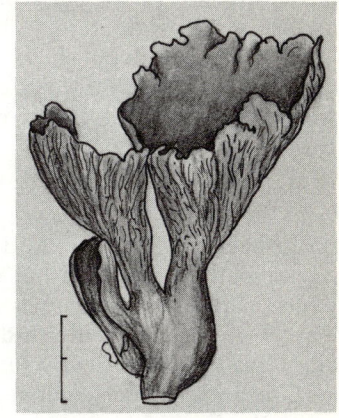

Fig. 109. *Gomphus clavatus*.

stipe 4-10 cm long, 0.8-3 cm thick; spores 10-13 × 5-6 μ, pale alutaceous in deposit; cystidia absent and clamp connections present.

Cespitose to gregarious under conifers in eastern, northern and western United States and southern Canada. Often frequent and abundant in late summer and fall.

CRATERELLUS

Fruit body more or less funnel-shaped, usually blackish brown, bluish black or grayish brown; hymenophore smooth, or veined or with low obtusely margined gills; clamp connections absent.

Key to Species

1a. Spore deposit colored 2
1b. Spore deposit white 3
2a. Spore deposit salmon-buff; spores 11-14 × 7-9 μ. Fig. 110 ....
................*Craterellus fallax*
A. H. Smith

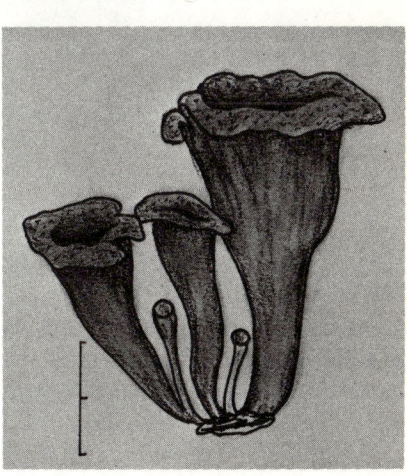

Fig. 110. *Craterellus fallax*.

Fruit body 2-6 (8) cm wide, 4-8 (10) cm high, surface rough to slightly squamulose, the flaring margin entire to wavy, lobed or frayed, often ragged in age, blackish fading to dingy grayish brown; hymenophore smooth (never with well developed veins near the pileus margin), dark cinereous with a salmon-buff tinge as spores mature; context very thin, brittle, odor and taste not distinctive; stipe indistinct, short, unpolished.

Scattered to gregarious or cespitose in deciduous and mixed woods in the Great Lakes region. Common in summer and fall. Edible.

2b. Spore deposit pale buff; spores 8-11 × 5-6 μ ....Craterellus cornucopioides **Pers.**

Fruit body 2-7 cm wide, 3-8 cm high, blackish to dark drab, surface smooth to wrinkled but unbroken, fading to cinereous, margin somewhat reddish brown when faded; hymenophore veined near the margin of the pileus, bluish drab, waxy in appearance; stipe 2-4 cm long, finally hollow nearly to the base.

Gregarious under conifers or hardwoods in eastern North America to the Great Lakes region, in summer and early fall, reported as common. Edible.

3a. Odor sickening sweetish; hymenophore with veins or vein-like gills. Fig. 111 ....Craterellus foetidus **A. H. Smith**

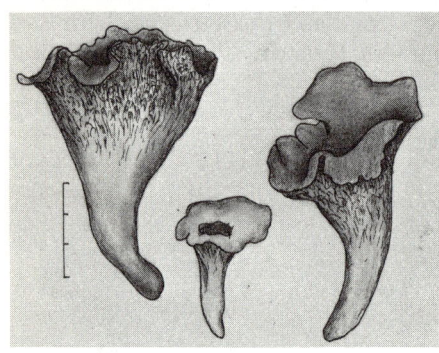

Fig. 111. Craterellus foetidus.

Fruit body 3-7 cm broad, funnel-shaped to very irregular, watery gray when moist, fading to ashy gray, uneven or squamulose to reticulate near the margin, the margin often quite wavy; hymenophore with veins or poorly formed gills which are narrow, much-branched, anastomosing and often nearly poroid, glaucous-cinereous to bluish gray; spores 8-10 × 5-6 μ.

Cespitose under hardwoods in the Great Lakes region in summer. Not common.

3b. Odor somewhat fragrant to lacking 4
4a. Hymenophore smooth or practically so; pileus watery brownish when fresh ....Craterellus calyculus (**Berk. & Curt**) **Burt.**

Fruit body up to 1 cm broad, margin wavy; hymenophore cream-buff; stipe up to 3 cm long, 4 mm thick, tapering to 2 mm at base, dingy brownish below, cream-buff above; spores 7-9 × 4.5-5 μ.

Solitary on the ground in damp shady woods in late summer and fall in eastern United States, rare.

4b. Hymenophore becoming wrinkled to veined; pileus blackish brown to bluish fuscous when fresh 5

5a. Fruit bodies in compound clusters 6-10 cm broad, 8-12 cm high; cuticular hyphae not readily disarticulating at the septa ....
..........................*Craterellus cinereus* var. *multiplex* A. H. Smith

Fruit bodies 1-4 cm broad with central or lateral stipes, somewhat funnel-shaped and becoming deeply perforated, blackish, glabrous or becoming squamulose, taste faintly disagreeable; hymenophore with folds at first, becoming more distinctly lamelliform in age; stipe compound, smooth, grayish; spores 8-11 $\times$ 5-6μ.

Cespitose on the ground in mixed pine and hardwoods in the Great Lakes region, late summer.

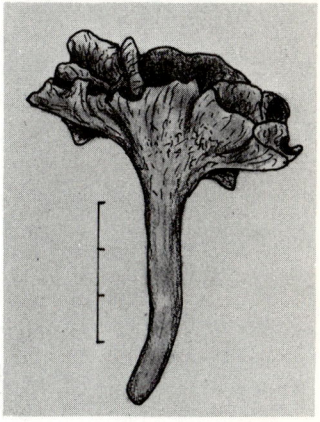

Fig. 112. *Craterellus caeruleofuscus*.

5b. Fruit bodies rarely compound; cuticular hyphae readily disarticulating at the septa into units of 2-3 cells. Fig. 112 ....
..........................*Craterellus caeruleofuscus* A. H. Smith

Fruit bodies 3-8 cm broad, funnel-shaped with the hollow extending well into the stipe, margin very irregular, at times fimbriate to toothed, bluish black when moist, fading to wood brown, smooth to wrinkled; hymenophore of radial veins frequently forked; stipe 5-8 cm long, 4-12 mm wide at apex; spores 7-9 $\times$ 5-6 μ.

Scattered to gregarious on sphagnum in bogs in the Great Lakes region in September.

CANTHARELLUS
(Chanterelle)

Fruit body typically some variation of trumpet-shaped; fleshy to moderately tough or in one group membranous; pileus merely the spreading margin of the apex of the stipe; gills or ridges extending from the cap margin to the stipe and down it or rarely the hymenopore smooth; Basidia typically much elongated and narrowly clavate (fig. 113), often bearing more than 4 sterigamata; spores non-amyloid, rough or smooth and white to buff or yellow in deposits depending on the species.

Fig. 113. Basidium in Cantharellus.

Key to Sections

1a. Pileus surface and context breaking up into coarse scales; stipe becoming hollowed by this process. Fig. 114 ....Sect. *Excavatus*

1b. Pileus not developing characteristic scales 2

2a. Stipe hollow or soon becoming so; cap often perforated in the disc; context membranous and pliant ....Sect. *Mesopus* p. 99

2b. Stipe solid; cap not perforated ....
....Sect. *Cantharellus* p. 97

Section **EXCAVATUS**

Key to Species

1a. Fruit bodies often cespitose or several arising from a common stipe, numerous small aborted fruit bodies often present. Fig. 114 ....*Cantharellus bonari* Morse

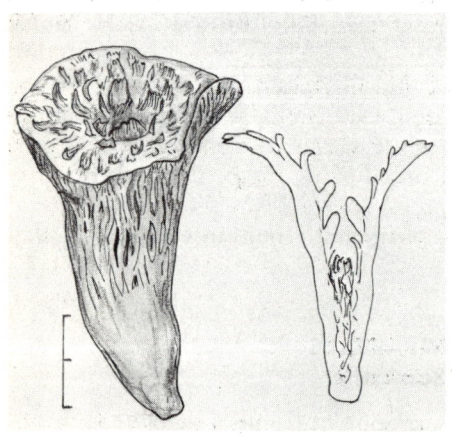

Fig. 114. *Cantharellus bonari*.

Fruit bodies 3-15 cm wide, lemon yellow at the base, scales orange to orange-buff; hymenophore milk white becoming dingy cream color; stipe white; spores 10-12 (14) $\times$ 5-6 μ.

Closely gregarious to cespitose under conifers, often partly hidden in deep humus; under conifers in the Rocky Mountains and Pacific Coast ranges, spring, summer and fall, often common; edible (for most people).

1b. Fruit bodies typically gregarious or scattered 2

**2a. Cap clay color to ochraceous-tawny when young, but very brittle, scales large and well-developed but very brittle. Fig. 115 ....
................................Cantharellus kauffmanii A. H. Smith**

Fruit body 10-35 cm broad, often lobed or splitting; context thin, odor sharp to lacking; hymenophore soon shallowly poroid, picric yellow when young, pallid to pinkish buff in age; stipe 8-15 cm long (rarely 40 cm), 2-5 cm thick, solid at first but soon hollowed; spores 12-15 × 5-7 μ, slightly ornamented, ochraceous in deposits.

Solitary to scattered to subcespitose on rich humus in conifer forests, especially with hemlock, Pacific Northwest, fall, uncommon. Not recommended.

**2b. Pileus reddish to orange or orange-yellow; scales relatively soft and poorly developed (by comparison with previous species) ....
....Cantharellus floccosus Schweinitz**

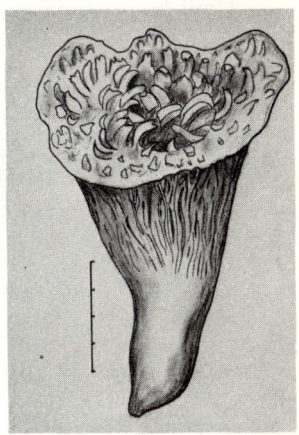
Fig. 115. *Cantharellus kauffmanii.*

Fruit body 5-15 cm broad, coarsely floccose-scaly to merely floccose; hymenophore cream color to darker, somewhat poroid; odor and taste mild; stipe 8-15 cm long, 1-3 cm thick (stipe not distinctly separated from the pileus); spores 12-15 × 6-7.5 μ, weakly ornamented, ochraceous in deposits.

Solitary to gregarious, rarely cespitose, in conifer forests (especially with hemlock, eastern North America, the Great Lakes region, and more rarely along the Pacific Coast, fruiting in the summer and fall. Edible for some people, not so for others.

Section CANTHARELLUS

**1a. Fruit body white, thick and stocky; gills white, staining yellow to orange where injured; spore deposit white. Fig. 116 ....
...............Cantharellus subalbidus Smith & Morse**

Pileus 5-10 (14) cm broad, flat to broadly depressed, glabrous or subsquamulose in age; gills close, often forked or anastomosing; stipe 2-6 cm long, 1-3 cm thick, soon brown from discolorations; spores 7-9 × 5-5.5 μ, smooth.

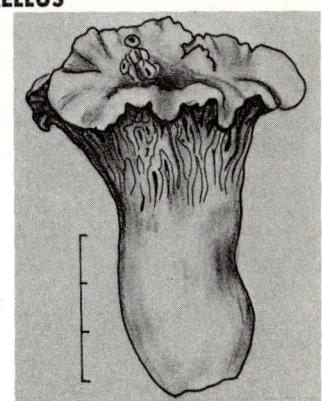
Fig. 116. *Cantharellus subalbidus.*

Gregarious, often in scrub pine stands or second growth of mixed conifers in late summer and fall in the Pacific Northwest, common. *One of the excellent edible fungi of the region.*
1b. Fruit body yellow to orange or cinnabar red 2
2a. Fruit body cinnabar red to pinkish orange when fresh. Fig. 117
....*Cantharellus cinnabarinus* **Schweinitz**

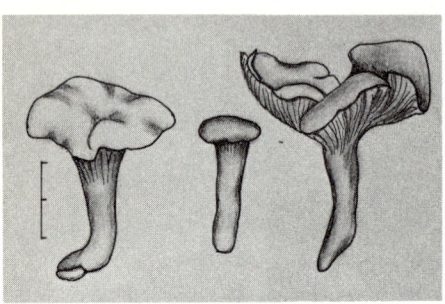

Fig. 117. *Cantharellus cinnabarinus.*

Fruit bodies 1-5 (7) cm broad, nearly plane becoming shallowly funnel-shaped, margin at first incurved, becoming lobed, crenate or scalloped, color fading rapidly in sunlight and finally near pallid; taste slowly burning acrid; gills close to distant, narow, conscpicuously intervenose, not staining when injured; stipe 2-6 cm long, 3-9 mm thick, not staining; spore deposit pinkish; spores $7-9 \times 4.5-5.5$ μ.

Scattered to gregarious on humus under hardwoods in the United States and southern Canada in summer and early fall. Not abundant but appearing nearly every season. Edible.
2b. Pileus yellow to yellow-orange or orange 3
3a. **Pileus and gills tinged purplish when cut or bruised; pleurocystidia present** ....*Cantharellus purpurascens* **Hesler**
Pileus 4-12 cm broad, plane or slightly depressed, appressed-fibrillose, margin even; context thick on disc, thin toward margin, white, staining purplish when cut; gills narrow, thin, close, dichotomously forked, white; stipe 4-10 cm long, 8-20 mm thick, tapering downward, colored like the pileus, becoming purplish; spores (8) 9-12 (15) $\times$ 3.5-4.5 μ, pleurocystidia, 40-100 $\times$ 7-10 μ, subfusiform.

Gregarious to scattered on soil in conifer and hardwood forests in August, southeastern United States, rare.
3b. Not staining purplish; pleurocystidia absent 4
4a. **Gills poorly formed; taste slightly bitter** ....
....*Cantharellus lateritius* **Berkeley**
Pileus 2.5-5.5 cm broad, plane, slightly depressed or funnel-shaped, margin typically undulating and arched, bright orange-yellow fading to pale buff; gills crowded, narrow, almost fold-like, forking, orange-yellow to pale ocher-yellow; stipe 1.7-4.5 cm long, 10-16 mm thick at apex, tapering to 5-8 mm at base; spore deposit pinkish ochraceous; spores $7-9 \times 4.5-5$ μ, smooth.

Gregarious on soil in deciduous woods, southern United States but extending as far north as Michigan, August, not common.

4b. Gills well-formed; taste slightly peppery. Fig. 118 ....
....*Cantharellus cibarius* **Fries**

Pileus (2) 3-8 (10) cm broad, broadly obtuse when young with an irregular incurved margin becoming wavy and scalloped in age, pale to rich egg yellow at maturity, becoming paler; gills narrow, egg yellow (whitish in on variety), slowly staining more ochraceous when bruised; stipe 3-8 cm long, 5-15 mm thick, colored like the pileus or paler; spore deposit ochraceous; spores 8-10 × 4.5-5.5 μ, smooth.

var. *pallidifolius* Smith has a pinkish spore deposit and whitish gills.

Scattered, gregarious to clustered on the ground in hardwood and conifer forests, widely distributed and variable. **One of our best edible fungi.**

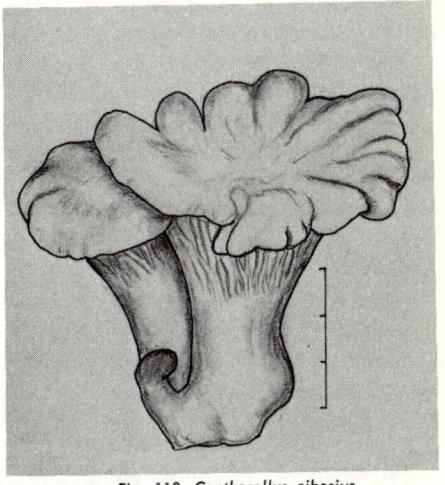

Fig. 118. *Cantharellus cibarius.*

Section MESOPUS

1a. Stipe with mustard yellow mycelium at the base ....
....*Cantharellus subperforatus* **Smith**

Pileus 2.5-6 cm broad, blackish brown becoming dingy yellowish brown; odor faintly fragrant, taste mild; gills bluish drab with an ochraceous flush; stipe 4-6 cm long, 4-8 (10) mm thick, dull ochraceous-orange; spores 8-11 × 7-9 μ.

Gregarious in cold conifer forests and bogs in the Great Lakes region in late summer and fall, rare.

1b. Basal mycelium if present pallid or white 2
2a. Hymenophore smooth or merely wrinkled 3
2b. Hymenophore of more distinct gills 4
3a. Spores 7-9 × 4-5 μ; growing in southern United States and Mexico ....*Cantharellus odoratus* **Schweinitz**

Fruit bodies simple or branched, 3-7 cm high, pilei 2-9 cm broad, egg yellow, the margin deflexed and often lobed or irregular; hymenophore ochraceous-orange or with a reddish tinge; stipe 2-4 cm long, 3-8 mm thick, concolorous with the pileus; odor like that of *C. cibarius.*

Gregarious or cespitose in moist places in the woods in summer and fall.

3b. Spores 9-13 × 6.5-8 μ; growing in northeastern U. S. and eastern Canada. Fig. 119 ....*Cantharellus lutescens* Fries

Pileus (1) 2-4 (8) cm broad, scurfy at first, dull orange to yellow when young, more alutaceous in age, thin, taste unpleasant, odor slight but fragrant; hymenophore yellowish orange or pale salmon; stipe 3-8 cm long, 4-10 mm thick at apex, 3-4 mm thick at base; spore deposit salmon tinged; spores 9-13 × 6.5-8 μ.

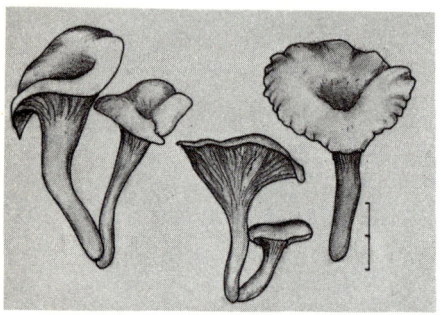

Fig. 119. *Cantharellus lutescens*.

Gregarious to scattered on wet moss in bogs or cold springy areas from Newfoundland to North Carolina and westward to Michigan, common in the late summer and fall.

4a. Spore deposit white 5
4b. Spore deposit yellow to yellowish 6
5a. Context very fragile; growing under hardwoods ...... *Cantharellus convolvulatus* Smith

Pileus 3-7 cm broad, very convoluted and irregular, dingy yellow-brown fading to dingy grayish ochraceous, margin lobed, wavy or crinkled, disc perforate in age; hymenophore very irregular in appearance, (smooth, fold-like, intervenose, or poroid, vinaceous-fawn to gray-brown); stipe 2-5 cm long, 6-12 mm thick, brittle, dull orange; spores 9-12 × 6.5-8.5 μ.

Gregarious to scattered under hardwoods in the Great Lakes region in the summer, rare.

5b. Context fairly pliant; growing in bogs and mossy cold conifer forests especially under larch ....
.................................*Cantharellus tubaeformis* sensu Smith

Pileus 1-3 (5) cm broad, convex to plane or broadly depressed with arched incurved margin when young, the margin finally spreading or uplifted and crenate or lobed, at times becoming funnel-shaped in age, disc not perforated at first but often becoming so, dark sordid yellowish brown; context thin and membranous, fragile; gills narrow, forked near the cap margin, yellowish gray becoming pale drab; stipe 3-6 cm long, 3-7 mm thick, dark to pale ochraceous above, whitish at the base; spores (8) 9-11 × 6-8 μ.

Gregarious to scattered on sphagnum in bogs or on other mosses in cold springy areas in eastern North America and Great Lakes region, late summer and fall.

6a. Spores 8-11 × 7-9 μ; pileus yellowish gray fading to grayish ....
....*Cantharellus sphaerosporus* Peck

NON-GILLED FLESHY FUNGI

Pileus 1.5-3 cm broad, plane to depressed, with an incurved margin, the margin becoming elevated and finally often funnel-shaped, the disc becoming perforated, yellowish gray fading to grayish or pale drab; gills narrow, close to distant, often forking near the margin, grayish ochraceous to avellaneous; stipe 3-6 cm long, 3-6 mm thick, equal or nearly so, dull to bright ochraceous-orange; spore deposit pale yellow.

Gregarious to scattered in cold bogs. Known from the Great Lakes region and Newfoundland, apparently rare.

6b. Spores 9-12 × 6.5-8 μ; pileus blackish brown to dingy yellowish brown but fading to ochraceous-gray. Fig. 120 ....*Cantharellus infundibuliformis* sensu Smith

Pileus 2-3.5 cm broad, convex, depressed or finally broadly funnel-shaped with an irregular wavy or sulcate margin; gills distant narrow, pale violaceous-brown and somewhat waxy in appearance; stipe 5-8 cm long, 4-9 mm thick, light orange-yellow at the base at times, paler and duller in age; spore deposit yellowish to ochraceous.

Fig. 120. *Cantharellus infundibuliformis.*

Solitary, gregarious or clustered in cold conifer woods and in bogs throughout the conifer regions of Northern United States and in Canada. Common and often abundant in the fall. Not edible.

APHYLLOPHORALES

Fruit body membranous, tough, or woody but fleshy in some, hymenium smooth, wrinkled, shallowly poroid, with deep narrow tubes, spines or poorly formed lamellae, one type often intergrading with another, trama of hymenophore parallel to interwoven; spore deposit variously colored; spores ornamented or smooth; many reduced types of fruit body occur in this order, a feature obviously associated with the habitat on wood for so many of the species.

Key to Families

1a. Hymenophore of tubes .... *Polyporaceae* p. 102
1b. Hymenophore of spines or "teeth" .... *Hydnaceae* p. 125

NON-GILLED FLESHY FUNGI

POLYPORACEAE

Fruit body stipitate to sessile; hymenophore composed of tubes; tube trama parallel to interwoven (but not divergent).

Polypores, as this group is called, cause heart rots in living trees as well as causing decay of dead wood, either the sap wood or the heart wood. Some grow on the ground in the manner of a bolete. Emphasis in this work is placed on the edible semifleshy species, and the more common ones having woody fruit bodies.

Key to Selected Genera

1a. Fruit body shelving; pore layer sulphur yellow (white in one form); pileous surface yellow or when young and fresh reddish on the margin; fleshy when young; often growing in large masses. Sulphur-Shelf. Fig. 121 ....
....*Laetiporus sulphureus* (Fr.) Murrill

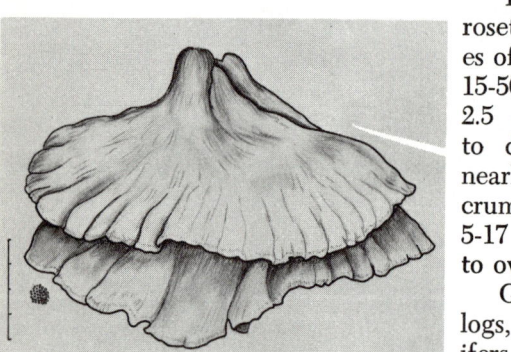

Fig. 121. *Laetiporus sulphureus*.

Typically forming large rosettes or imbricate masses of fruit bodies wtih pilei 15-50 cm broad and up to 2.5 cm thick, weathering to dingy buff or finally nearly white and then crumbly in texture; spores 5-17 $\times$ 3.5-4.5 μ, ellipsoid to ovoid, inamyloid.

Growing on stumps, logs, and dead trees of conifers and hardwoods alike. Widely distributed and common during the late summer and fall, but occasionally found as early as the middle of June. A form with a white hymenial surface is sometimes collected throughout the range of the species in North America. It is var. *semialbinus* Peck.

1b. Not as above 2

2a. Pore surface covered by a membranous layer of tissue which is sometimes perforated by one (rarely 2) worm holes ....
....*Cryptoporus volvatus* (Pk.) Hubbard

Fruit body globose or compressed-globose, 1.5-8.5 cm broad and long 1-3.5 cm thick, upper surface with a thin resinous crust, whitish or yellowish when fresh, drying to ochraceous or chestnut or tinged with red; margin thick and rounded, extending downward and back to form a veil-like covering over the pore surface; spores 8-12 $\times$ 3-5

NON-GILLED FLESHY FUNGI

μ, elongate-ellipsoid or short-cylindric; context colored in mass but hyaline under the microscope.

Sessile or attached by a point on dead standing or fallen conifers, at times on living trees; throughout the northern U. S. A. and in Canada, spring and early summer. The "worms" nearly always found in the interior can be used as fish bait.

2b. Not as above 3
3a. Interior of fruit body bright orange; hymenium borne on flattened teeth ....*Echinodontium tinctorum* **Ellis & Everhart**

Pileus hoof-shaped, 4-20 × 3-10 × 2-10 cm, surface often moss-covered, consistency woody, perennial, olivaceous-black, margin olive-brown, pubescent, undersurface pale olive-buff, the teeth up to 3 cm long, 1-3 mm wide; spore print white; spores 6-8 × 5-6 μ, ellipsoid, strongly amyloid.

On conifers, particularly fir and hemlock, causing a heart rot. Common in northern Idaho, but widely distributed in the conifer belt of western North America.

3b. Not as above 4
4a. Fruit body with a shiny and/or crust-like upper surface; spores truncate at the apex ....*Ganoderma* **p. 108**
4a. Not as above 5
5a. Fruit body a large compound structure typically with many pilei from a massive framework or point of origin 6
5b. Not a compound structure as in above choice but pilei may be shelving in large masses or (if stipitate) with 1-3 pilei 8
6a. Fruit body with many small (2-6 cm) pilei, these terminating the branches of the central fleshy structure or framework, the individual pilei varying in color from white to black ...*Polypilus* **p.110**
6b. Fruit body consisting of a few to many large pilei (2-35 cm); stipe a gnarled almost sclerotium-like structure 7
7a. Spores with amyloid ornamentation; context pallid to brownish ....*Bondarzewia* **p. 110**
7b. Spores smooth and non-amyloid; context dark brown. Fig. 122 *Phaeolus schweinitzii* (Fr.) Patouillard

Fruit body with pilei 5-25 × 0.5-4 cm thick,

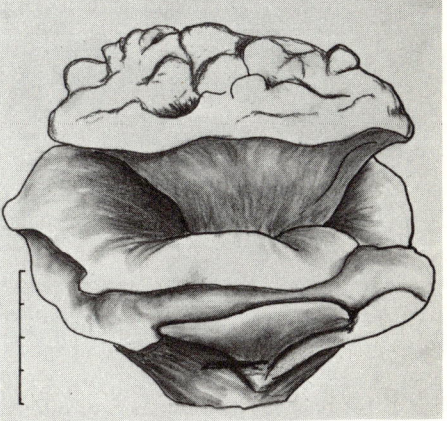

Fig. 122. *Phaeolus schweinitzii*.

ochraceous to orange when rapidly growing and dark rusty brown when mature or in age; surface strigose to tomentose (rough), weathering to nearly glabrous, when touched with KOH red turning to black; context yellowish becoming rusty brown in age, 0.2-3 cm thick; pore surface yellowish to greenish yellow, darker where bruised; pores 1-3 per mm; spores $5.5\text{-}8 \times 4\text{-}5\ \mu$, hyaline, ellipsoid, smooth; cystidia projecting 20-26 μ, brownish to near the hyaline apex; clamps present.

Typically at the base of conifers, living trees and stumps and (more rarely) on exposed wood above ground, rarely on wood of hardwoods, common where conifers grow in North America.

This fungus causes a serious carbonizing cubical decay known as red-brown butt rot or cubical butt rot. The rot may extend up into the trunk 10-15 ft. It causes heavy wind-throw in mature stands.

8a. Fruit body more or less stipitate 9
8b. Fruit body sessile or nearly so, often shelving 14
9a. Pileus fleshy and brittle 10
9b. Pileus coriaceous, pliant to almost woody 11
10a. Spores smooth (see Polyporus p. 113 also) .... *Albatrellus* p. 111
10b. Spores nodulose, pileus whitish young and (in one) nearly black in age ....*Boletopsis griseus* (Pk.) **Bondarzew & Singer**

Pileus 4-12 cm wide, circular to irregular, dingy white to pallid gray usually from the disc outward, sometimes virgate, glabrous or nearly so, dull and unpolished; context thick, white and fleshy; pore surface white to discolored, pores very small; stipe 4-8 cm long, 1-2.5 cm thick, central to excentric, solid, concolorous with pileus or remaining paler; spores 5-6.5 μ, angular-tuberculate.

On the ground in conifer and hardwood forests, not uncommon in the Pacific Northwest during wet seasons, but widely distributed in conifer areas of North America, fall. A second species, *Boletopsis leucomelas* (Fr.) Bondarzew & Singer has a bluish black pileus.

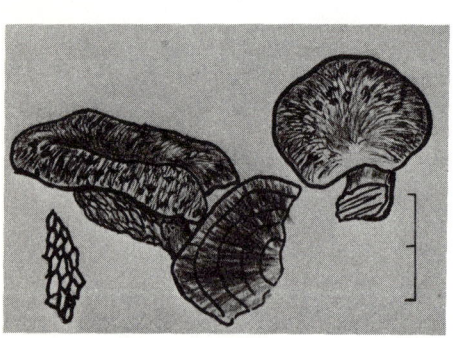

Fig. 123. *Favolus alveolaris.*

11a. Pores large, radially elongate and arranged in radial rows (see *Polyporus squamosus* p. 114 also). Fig. 123 ......*Favolus alveolaris* (Fr.) Quélet

Fruit body brittle when dry; pileus $1\text{-}8 \times 1\text{-}10 \times 0.7$ cm, usually reniform to fan-shaped, reddish yellow at first, becoming a brick red and fibrillose, weathering to cream color or white and either squamulose or glabrous; pore surface white drying yellowish; stipe rudimentary; spores 9-11 × 3-3.5 μ, cylindric.

On dead branches of deciduous trees such as beach, hickory, maple, etc., eastern North America, Great Lakes region and the Rocky Mountains, summer and fall, very common.

11b. Pores circular to angular, not arranged in rows 12

12a. Context dull brownish, pallid, or whitish .... *Polyporus* p. 113

12b. Context rusty brown to tawny 13

13a. Setae not present in the hymenium .... *Coltrichia* p. 116

13b. Setae present in the hymenium. Fig. 124 ....
.... *Polystictus tomentosus* (Fr.) Fries

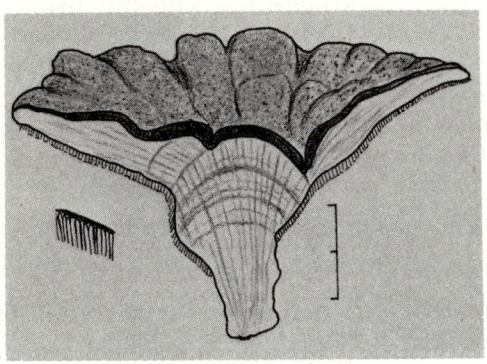

Fig. 124. *Polystictus tomentosus*.

Pileus 3-10 cm broad, up to 4 cm thick, circular to semi-circular, tomentose; pore surface hoary over a brown ground color, darker when bruised; stipe when present up to 5 cm long and 0.5-2 cm thick, lateral, excentric or central, ochraceous to dark rusty brown, tomentose or velvety; spores 4-6 × 3-5 μ, ellipsoid to oblong, smooth; stetae 35-65 × 10-16 μ, dark brown in KOH, pointed and straight.

Stipitate to substipitate when terrestrial or on buried wood, sessile when on stumps and trunks of living or dead conifers. It is widely distributed in the conifer areas of North America.

14a. Pileus white to whitish and somewhat rough to hairy-strigose
.... 15

14b. Not as above 16

15a. Fruit body perennial (2-many layers of pores) ....
.... *Oxyporus* p. 117

15b. Fruit body annual (a simple layer of pores). Fig. 125 ....
............................*Spongipellis unicolor* (Schw.) Murrill

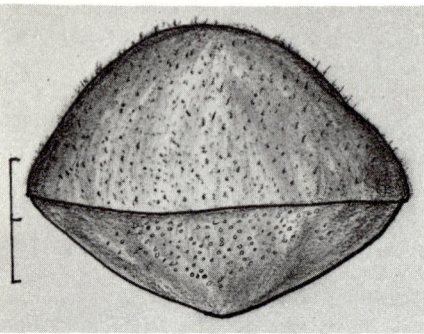

Fig. 125. Spongipellis unicolor.

Pileus 3-20 × 4-30 × 3-8 cm, convex to ungulate white becoming grayish to yellowish, hirsute to tomentose, tomentum becoming matted, margin thick and rounded; context white, spongy to soft-corky, strongly duplex (when dried); pores white, circular to angular or in age almost daedaloid; spores 5-7 × 4-5 μ; smooth, hyaline, broadly ellipsoid, hyphae of context thick-walled, clamps present.

On trunks and branches of living or dead hardwoods, especially oak, widely distributed.

16a. Fruit body when sectioned showing annual layers of tubes (indicating it is perennial, but see *Ganoderma* p. 108 also) .... *Fomes* p. 118

16b. Fruit bodies annual (but context may be zoned) 17

17a. Hymenophore gill-like or nearly so .... *Lenzites* p. 121

17b. Hymenophore clearly poroid or the pores radially elongate 18

18a. Under-surface of pileus with radially elongated sinuous pores or sublamellate (see *Favolus* p. 104 also). Fig. 126, 126 a .... *Daedalea* p. 122

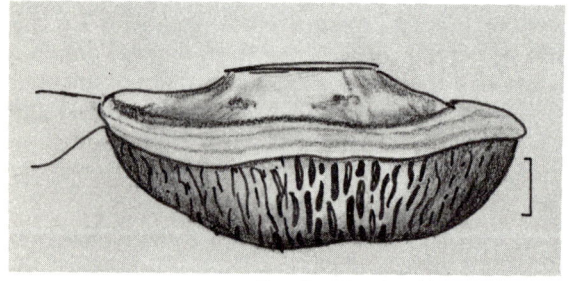

Fig. 126, 126a. Daedalea quercina.

18b. Under surface of pileus with essentially round to angular, usually minute pores 19

NON-GILLED FLESHY FUNGI

19a. Context pores and pileus surface orange reddish to cinnabar. Fig. 127 .... *Pycnoporus cinnabarinus* (Fr.) Karsten

Fruit body sessile, tough and leathery; pileus 2-7 × 2-12 × 0.5-2 cm, orange to cinnabar, fading, context red to yellowish red, 0.4-1.5 cm thick, black with KOH; tubes rarely in 2-3 layers; pores 2-4 per mm; spores 4.5-6 × 2-3 µ; hyphae of context thick-walled.

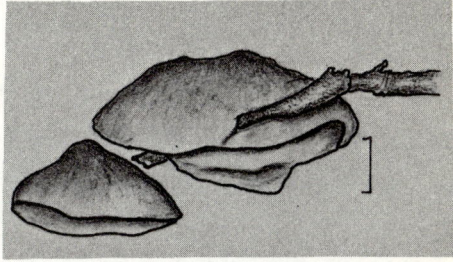

Fig. 127. *Pycnoporus cinnabarinus*.

Widely distributed in northern and central United States and in southern Canada. *P. sanguineus* is a more common species in the south. Its pileus is thinner and smoother than in *P. cinnabarinus*. The latter occurs frequently on cherry in the Great Lakes region.

19b. Not as above 20

20a. Pileus tan to brownish and instantly violet to purple when touched with KOH. Fig. 128 ....
.... *Hapalopilus nidulans* (Fr.) Karsten

Pileus sessile, 1.5-6 (8) × 2-8 × 0.5-4 cm, surface dull yellowish tan to dull cinnamon to tawny-brown, unpolished to finely pruinose, margin often reddish where bruised; context concolorous with pileus, soft when fresh, friable when dry, 2-30 mm thick; pores 2-4 per mm; spores 3-4 × 2-3 µ; cystidia none; context hyphae thick-walled, clamps present.

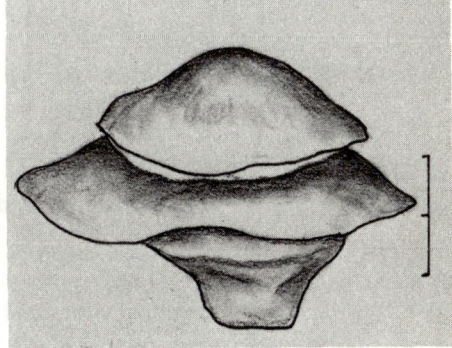

Fig. 128. *Hapalopilus nidulans*.

Usually on dead wood of hardwoods, but often only one fruit body at a time, rarely on conifer wood, widely distributed.

20b. Not as above 21

21a. Pileus rough-tomentose, dark brown to blackish; context not truly white. Fig. 129 ....*Ischnoderma resinosum* (Fr.) Karsten

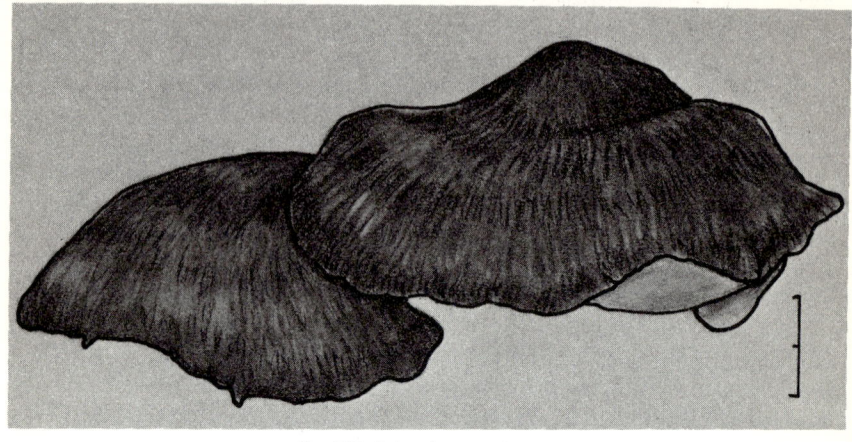

Fig. 129. *Ischnoderma resinosum.*

Fruit body consisting of pilei single or in shelving masses, pileus 7-25 × 0.8-4 cm, sometimes shallowly furrowed or with dark metallic zones, often radially rugose, the margin thick and often exuding drops of a liquid in humid weather; pore surface pallid, darker where bruised; spores 4-7 × 1.5-2 μ.

Common on fallen hardwood logs, especially elm, also on conifers, very widely distributed in late summer and fall.

21b. Pileus white to pallid or grayish; context not duplex, white when fresh (but see *Spongipellis* p. 106 also) ....
....*Tyromyces* p. 123

GANODERMA

Fruit bodies perennial, surface of pileus appearing varnished or composed of a crustlike layer; spores with a truncate (flattened) apex and the wall in our most common species ornamented.

Key to Species

1a. Upper surface of pileus pallid gray to gray-brown, dull in appearance, woody, perennial with a chocolate-brown layer of hyphae between annual layers of tubes. Artist's Fungus. Fig. 130 ....*Ganoderma applanatum* (Pers.) Patouillard

NON-GILLED FLESHY FUNGI

Fig. 130. Ganoderma applanatum.

Pileus sessile, broadly fan-shaped to semicircular in outline, hard and woody, up to 50 cm in width; pore surface white at first and quickly becoming brownish where injured, often yellowish or umber on dried specimens; spores 6-9 × 4.5-6 μ, ovoid, ornamentation present as projections extending through the thick inner wall.

Growing on old logs or stumps of deciduous trees, often from wounds of living trees; rarely on conifers. It is found throughout southern Canada and the United States, very common. Marks or pictures drawn upon the white pore surface will last for years.

1b. Pileus surface orange to red or nearly black, shining as if varnished, watery or soft-corky when fresh, rigid and corky when dry; annual 2
2a. Fruit body usually at least somewhat stipitate; context 0.5-3 cm thick; spores 9-11 × 6-8 μ. Fig. 131 ......
Ganoderma tsugae **Murrill**

Pileus 5-20 × 6-30 cm, reniform or fan-shaped, pallid to orange on the margin at times; pore surface white to brown, discoloring where handled.

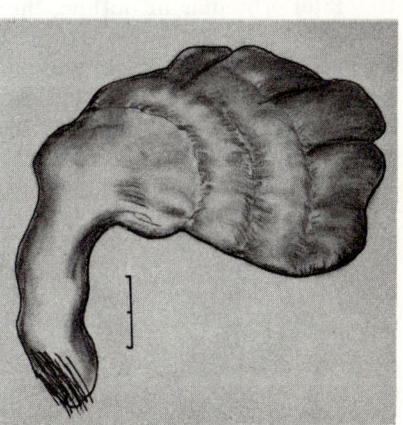

Fig. 131. Ganoderma tsugae.

On or about stumps and dead trunks of conifers, hemlock in particular, throughout the range of that genus in North America.

2b. Fruit body more frequently sessile; context 1.5-10 cm thick; spores 10-16 × 7.5-9 μ; on conifers in the Pacific Northwest
.... *Ganoderma oregonense* **Murrill**

It differs from the preceding in the larger spores and much thicker context, also the pilei measure 5-80 × 5-100 cm.

Not uncommon in the range given above.

A third species *G. lucidum* is more frequent on hardwood substrata and is not as shiny as either of the two above species.

POLYPILUS

Fruit body fleshy to subfleshy, stipitate or in rosettes, some repeatedly branched to form of complex framework, the tips of the branches giving rise to numerous small pilei.

Key to Species

1a. Pileoli flattened and one-sided, spathulate or fan-shaped, center part of fruit body a branched framework. Hen of the Woods
.... *Polypilus frondosus* (Fr.) **Karsten**

Fruit body often up to 60 cm wide, the pileoli 2-7 cm wide and 2-7 mm thick, pale to dark gray; pore surface white to yellowish; spores 5-7 × 3.5-5 μ, ovoid to ellipsoid, smooth.

Growing around stumps or trunks of deciduous trees, rarely around conifers. Found throughout the United States. Edible and popular but somewhat tough and usually requires long cooking.

1b. Pilei orbicular in outline, the stipe central ....
.... *Polypilus umbellatus* (Fr.) **Karsten**

Fruit body up to 36 cm wide, the pileoli 1-4 cm broad, less than 5 mm thick; often depressed at the center, whitish to smoky brown; pore surface white; stipe arising from an irregular compound underground tuber; spores; 7-9.5 × 3-4 μ, cylindric.

On the ground around stumps or old trees throughout northern United States and southern Canada, early summer. Beech is a common substrate. Edible when young and tender.

BONDARZEWIA

Fruit bodies tough at maturity, large and compound, tapering to a gnarled rooting base; ornamentation of the spores amyloid.

Key to Species

1a. Growing around dead oaks or oak stumps, at times with other hardwoods .... *Bondarzewia berkeleyi* (Fries) **Singer**

NON-GILLED FLESHY FUNGI

Fruit bodies 25-80 cm broad; pilei 6-25 cm wide, pale buff to grayish, unpolished to finely tomentose, weathering to glabrous, often radially rugose or pitted; spore surface whitish; stipe 4-10 cm long, 3-5 cm thick above the ground; spores 6-8 μ in diam., globose or nearly so.

Throughout the United States and southern Canada. It causes a serious butt-rot of living trees. The rot is sometimes called the "string and ray rot."

Another species, *Polyporus giganteus* has a similar stature but the spores are not amyloid and the pilear margin stains grayish if injured.

1b. Growing on or around conifer trees or stumps .... *Bondarzewia montanus* (**Quél.**) **Singer**

Fruit body stipitate to (rarely) sessile, irregular, 6-25 cm wide, dark tan to brown and covered with a plush-like pubescence; context white; pore surface whitish; stipe 6-12 $\times$ 2-4 cm, surface plush-like; spores 5-7 μ.

Found in British Columbia and our Pacific Northwest, generally rare but common in the Priest Lake district of Idaho.

ALBATRELLUS

Fruit bodies fleshy to subfleshy, brittle, context weakly colored yellowish to grayish or white, spores smooth, amyloid or not, stipe central to eccentric or lateral, terrestrial or appearing so.

Key to Species

1a. Pileus some shade of blue when young 2
1b. Pileus not blue when young 3
2a. Pore surface blue ...... *Albatrellus caeruleoporus* (**Peck**) **Pouzar**

Pileus 2-7 (15) $\times$ 0.3-2 cm, glabrous or subtomentose, margin lobed; stipe deep indigo blue when fresh; when dried and in the herbarium often red (from contact with naphthalene?); spores 4-6 $\times$ 3-5 μ, globose to subglobose.

Solitary to clustered on humus in damp woods, eastern North America and Great Lakes region, late summer and fall, rare.

2b. **Pore surface white at first becoming salmon in age** ....*Albatrellus flettii* (**Morse**) **Pouzar**

Pileus circular or irregular, 10-20 cm broad, convex then plane and finally depressed at the center, greenish blue to caeruleus, paler toward the margin and gradually becoming dingy ochraceous; stipe 6-14 cm long, 2-3.5 cm thick, white, drying dingy ochraceous or stained reddish; spores 3.5-4 $\times$ 2.5-3 μ.

Solitary to clustered, on humus under conifers in the Pacific Northwest, fall, common at times late in the summer after heavy rain.

3a. Typically under hardwoods; pileus yellow-brown to ochraceous and often greenish near margin; stipe gnarled and uneven but fragile especially if occurring in clusters; spores $5\text{-}6 \times 4.5\ \mu$. Fig. 132 .... *Albatrellus cristatus* (Fr.) Pouzar

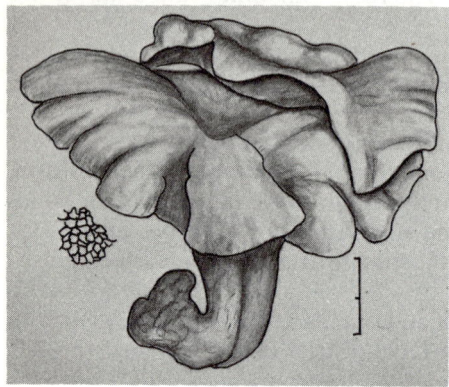

Fig. 132. *Albatrellus cristatus*.

Pileus 4-20 cm broad, circular or irregular, plane or convex, surface becoming cracked and areolate at times; pore surface white, later becoming yellowish to greenish yellow, often extending down the stipe.

Solitary to clustered on soil and humus, late summer and fall, rarely under conifers, eastern North America and the Great Lakes region, often common after heavy rains.

3b. Especially under conifers; pileus white to pale reddish tan or with yellow tones evident; spores $3\text{-}4.5 \times 2.5\text{-}3\ \mu$ 4
4a. Pileus white becoming buff to cream color or pale crust brown with an ochraceous undertone. Fig. 133 ....
.... *Albatrellus ovinus* (Fr.) Kotlaba & Pouzar

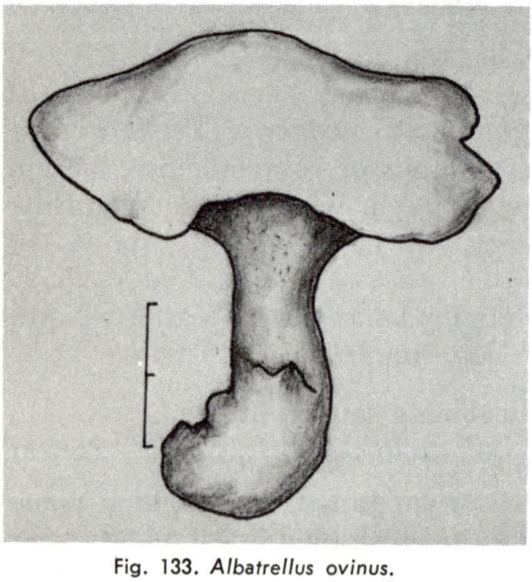

Pileus 4-12 (15) cm broad, usually circular and regular but often very irregular if occurring in large masses, surface unpolished, pore surface becoming yellow in age, stipe 3-8 cm long, 1-3 cm thick near base, often confluent below to form a cluster.

Solitary to confluent in masses, on humus in eastern North America, the Great Lakes region, and conifer belt in the western mountains, widely distributed in Canada.

Fig. 133. *Albatrellus ovinus*.

In the mountains of Idaho a form with violaceous-brown to brownish gray pileus often occurs with the typical form.

NON-GILLED FLESHY FUNGI

4b. Pileus whitish on margin and pale pinkish tan over disc, slowly becoming pinkish cinnamon over all. Fig. 134 ....
.... *Albatrellus confluens* (Fr.) Kotlaba & Pouzar

Pileus 4-12 (15) cm broad, variable in shape, glabrous, unpolished, becoming subsquamulose at times; pore surface white, in age often stained cinnamon; stipe typically eccentric to lateral, 3-6 cm long, 1-3 cm thick, white but in age stained tan; spores 4-5.5 × 3-4 µ, ellipsoid, amyloid.

Solitary or in clusters or confluent masses with bases fused, often under hemlock, northern United States and Canada. This species has been much confused in the literature, the common one in North America is *A. ovinus*.

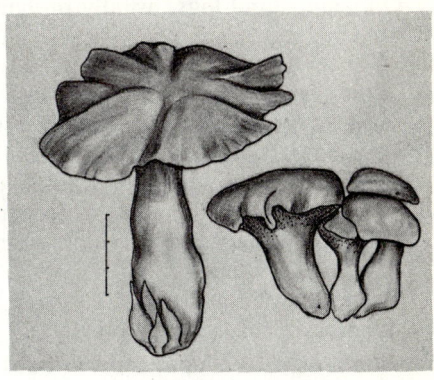

Fig. 134. *Albatrellus confluens*.

POLYPORUS

Fruit bodies stipitate, growing usually on wood or adjacent to it; consistency tough-fleshy to leathery, or thin and coriaceous; spore deposit white or weakly colored; spores smooth.

Key to Selected Species

1a. Context thin and pliant to membranous and tough 2
1b. Context 5-20 mm thick and subfleshy to tough 5
2a. Pileus tan to blackish brown with the margin paler; pores about 5-7 per mm; stipe 4-15 (20) mm thick, blackish below at maturity. Fig. 135 ....
.... *Polyporus picipes* Fries

Pileus circular to subcircular, convex becoming depressed at the disc and the margin wavy, 4-20 cm

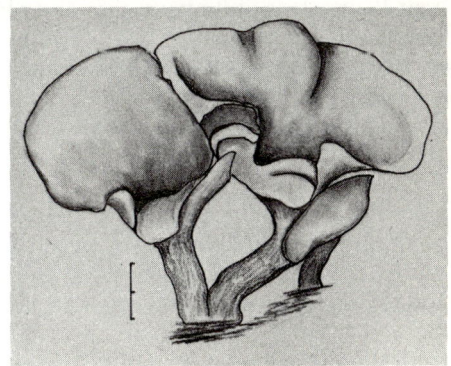

Fig. 135. *Polyporus picipes*.

broad, 1·8 mm thick; pore surface white to pale dingy brownish finally; stipe central to eccentric, 1-6 cm long, 0.4-1.5 cm thick; spores 6-8 × 3-4 µ, cylindric to ellipsoid.

On stumps and logs, usually on hardwood, widely distributed in North America.

2b. Not as above 3
3a. Pores large (0.5-1 mm wide) and angular; pileus dingy brown and margin ciliate when fresh, (see *Favolus* p. 104 also) ....
....*Polyporus arcularis* Fries

Pileus 1-8 cm broad, 1-4 mm thick, circular, convex to umbilicate, surface somewhat squamulose; pore surface white or off-color; stipe central, 2-6 cm long, 2-4 mm thick, yellowish brown to darker; spores 7-11 × 2-3 µ, cylindric.

On dead wood of hardwoods, widely distributed in North America, fruiting in the spring typically.

3b. Pores small (2-5 per mm); pileus margin seldom ciliate 4
4a. Pileus pale to dull tan and glabrous; stipe often excentric and in age black over lower portion ....*Polyporus elegans* Fries

Pileus circular to variable in outline, 1.5-7 cm broad, 2-10 mm thick, weathering to whitish at times, often radiate-striate; pore surface gray to light bay or (if perfectly fresh) pallid; spores 6-10 × 2.5-3.5 µ, cylindric.

On dead wood, usually on small branches of hardwood trees in old slashings, typically solitary; widely distributed in North America.

4b. Pileus blackish brown; stipe usually central ....
....*Polyporus brumalis* Fries

Pileus circular, 1.5-6 (10) cm broad, convex or depressed, 2-4 mm thick, when young hispid, finally nearly glabrous, margin involute when young or on drying; pore surface whitish; stipe 2-6 cm long, 2-6 mm thick, grayish or brownish; spores 5-7 × 1.5-2.5 µ, short-cylindric.

Common on wood of hardwoods, summer and fall, east of the Great Plains. It is quite persistent and old fruit bodies may be found throughout the year.

5a. Growing on wood which is above ground 6
5b. Appearing terrestrial 7
6a. Pileus distinctly squamulose with blackish to dark brown scales
....*Polyporus squamosus* Fries

Pileus 6-30 cm broad, 0.5-4 cm thick, more or less funnel-shaped to fan-shaped, pallid except for the scales or in age ground color brownish; pore surface white or buff; stipe lateral to eccentric, often rudimentary, 1-4 cm thick, black at the base; spores 10-15 × 4-6 µ; hyphae having a central enlarged section with very thick walls.

Solitary to gregarious or in clusters from wounds on living trees or on fallen trees, elm in particular, eastern North America to the

Rocky Mountains, spring and early summer. Not poisonous, but too tough to eat and also the flavor is poor.

6b. Pileus not conspicuously scaly and those scales present not darker than the ground color. Fig. 136 ....
.... *Polyporus fagicola* **Murrill**

Pileus 4-12 (20) cm broad, 2-5 cm thick, depressed in the center, fan-shaped to incompletely funnel-shaped, pale tan or ochraceous-buff, pore surface whitish then dingy yellowish in age; stipe central or excentric, 2-5 cm long, 4-10 mm thick, pallid, hispid becoming glabrous; spores 10-14 × 4-5.5 μ, oblong; hyphae thin-walled.

On old logs of hardwoods, especially beech, common in the spring in the Great Lakes region.

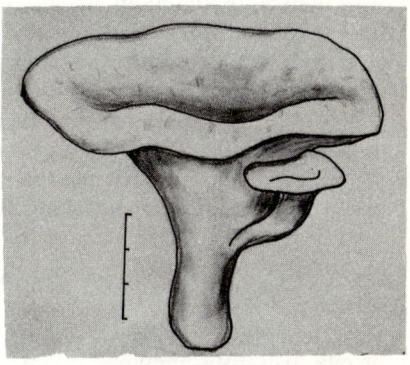

Fig. 136. *Polyporus fagicola*.

7a. Fruit body with a long narrow though (often) somewhat gnarled pseudorhiza; stipe mostly central; pileus velvety to unpolished. Fig. 137 .... *Polyporus radicatus* **Schweinitz**

Pileus 3.5-25 cm broad, circular, convex or depressed, fleshy-tough when fresh, yellowish brown to sooty brown, velvety to scurfy or more rarely somewhat scaly with the center glabrous; pore surface white or yellowish; stipe central, 6-13 cm long, 5-25 mm thick; spores 12-15 × 6-8 μ, ovoid to elliptic in face view, subfusoid in profile.

Usually solitary on the ground around stumps, attached to buried wood, eastern and central United States, not common.

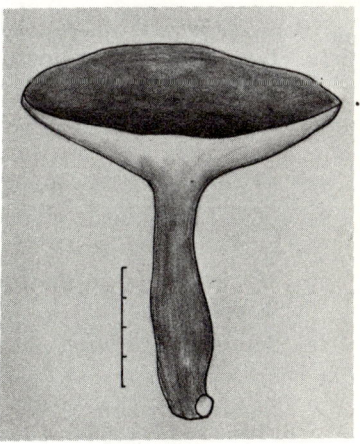

7b. Not as above 8

Fig. 137. *Polyporus radicatus*

8a. Pileus conspicuously scaly and sulphur yellow to yellow-brown and often with a greenish tinge .... *Polyporus ellisii* **Berkeley**
Pileus 1-5 cm broad, context white becoming yellowish green on exposure; pore surface white becoming yellowish or greenish in age

or on handling; stipe excentric, 7-8 cm long, 4-6 cm thick, yellow; spores 8-9 × 5-7 μ, ovoid and strongly apiculate.

On the ground under conifers, widely distributed but often abundant in northern Idaho, late summer and fall.

8b. Pileus subsquamulose, dingy brown to pinkish brown or finally brown .... *Polyporus pescaprae* Fries

Pileus subcircular or irregular, 3-10 (20) cm or more broad, at first with fine fibrils which may form definite scales or a plush-like covering; context white becoming pink on exposure; pore surface white, yellowish or pinkish, pores large, angular; stipe 3-8 cm long, 1-4 cm thick, lateral or excentric, pallid, darker or yellowish and enlarged below; spores 8-11 × 5-6 μ, ovoid, apiculate.

Solitary or somewhat confluent on the ground in woods, southeastern United States and along the Pacific Coast.

COLTRICHIA

Fruit bodies stipitate; pileus thin, coriaceous, tawny to rusty brown, usually somewhat zonate, context rusty brown, black where touched with KOH solution; hymenophore poroid or broken up into concentric plate-like structures around the stipe; spores smooth, oblong to ellipsoid, pale to moderately brown under the microscope; setae none.

Key to Species

1a. Pore surface breaking up to form concentric plates extending around the stipe as concentric gills ....
....*Coltrichia greenei* (Berk.) Imazeki

Pileus circular or irregular, 2.5-17 cm broad, up to 2 cm thick, velvety tomentose, becoming glabrous, pore surface brown; spores 9-15 × 5-7 μ, elongate-ellipsoid.

On the ground in woods in eastern United States, summer, rare.

1b. Hymenophore in the form of pores and not breaking up into lamellae 2

2a. Spores 8-12 μ long; pores 0.5-2 mm broad ....
....*Coltrichia montagnei* (Fr.) Murrill

Pileus 2-10 cm broad, 2-7 mm thick, yellowish cinnamon to bright rusty brown or darker, at first soft silky or fibrillose; spore surface white to alutaceous or umber; stipe 2-5 cm long, 0.3-1.5 or more thick; spores 8-12 × 4.5-6 μ, elongate-ellipsoid.

Growing on the ground, sometimes attached to buried wood of coniferous trees. Eastern United States and in Ontario, Canada.

2b. Spores 6-9 μ long; pores 2-4 per mm 3

NON-GILLED FLESHY FUNGI

3a. **Pileus rich cinnamon to darker, surface shining with silky striation** .... *Coltrichia cinnamomeus* (Fr.) Murrill

Pileus 1-5 cm broad, 1-3 mm thick, zones usually narrow and inconspicuous; pore surface yellow-brown to reddish brown or cinnamon; stipe reddish brown, velvety to villose, 1-4 cm long, 1-3 mm thick; spores 6-8 × 4.5-6 μ.

On clay banks or along packed paths in woods, rarely on very rotten wood; widely distributed in North America. Fruit bodies of this species dry nicely and can be used in making winter arrangements with remains of herbaceous plants.

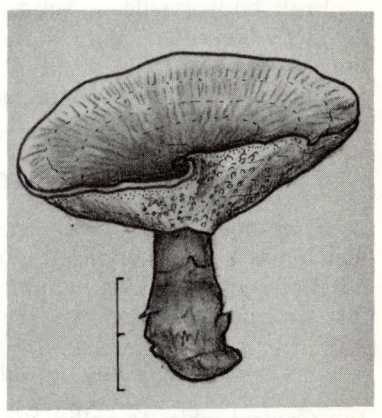

Fig. 138. *Coltrichia perennis*.

3b. **Pileus pale cinnamon, weathering to paler to grayish brown, not shiny, finely velvety tomentose when fresh. Fig. 138** *Coltrichia perennis* (Fr.) Murrill

Pileus 1.5-11 cm broad, 1-4 mm thick, usually zonate; spore surface yellow-brown to cinnamon or gray; stipe 1.5-7 cm long, 2-6 (10) mm thick, brown, velvety; spores 6-9 × 3-5 μ.

On the ground in woods, often where fires have been kindled, along beaten trails or on clay banks, rarely on rotten wood. Widely distributed in North America.

OXYPORUS

Fruit body shelving to resupinate, perennial, white, the surface uneven and hairy, or overgrown with moss obscuring the surface, white or pale leather color at first; cystidia with a crystalline cap at the apex; spores small, up to 7 × 4 μ.

O. nobilissimus is an example of a species of fungus which could easily be eliminated from our flora by the policy of cutting all "mature" trees. The damage it does, as a possible butt-rot of hemlock to our knowledge has not been assessed. The species is so rarely collected that we have little or no information on the chemical properties of the fruit bodies.

Key to Species

1a. **Growing on hardwoods, usually on maple; surface often moss covered, 6-15 cm broad** .... *Oxyporus populinus* (Fr.) Donk

Pilei usually somewhat imbricate, convex, 2-12 × 3-8 cm, 2.5-4 cm thick; pore surface white to cream or yellowish when fresh, tubes

2-5 mm long in each season's growth, the layers very distinct; spores 4.5-5 × 3-4 μ when ellipsoid, 3-5 μ when globose.

Usually near the ground on trunks of living maple.

Widely distributed in the United States and Canada east of the Rocky Mountains.

1b. Growing on old conifers, especially on hemlock; surface strigose, not moss covered; massive (30-140 cm broad and up to 100 cm deep) ....*Oxyporus nobilissimus* Wm. B. Cooke

Fruit body sessile or substipitate, ungulate, imbricate; context distinctly stratified; pore surface white; spores 6-7 × 3.5-4 μ, smooth; cystidia 15-23 × 3-6 μ, subfusoid, wall slightly thickened.

In the western hemlock region. Some fruit bodies found weighed up to 150 lbs and had 35 tube layers.

FOMES

Fruit body woody and perennial with yearly layers of tubes which may be distinct or not; pores typically minute (2-4 per mm); often at wound sites on living trees. A number of important timber rots are caused by members of this genus.

Key to Selected Species

1a. Context white to pallid, pinkish or orange 2
1b. Context dark yellow-brown to rusty brown, black where touched with KOH 6
2a. Fruit body ungulate, context chalky in dried specimens, the taste very bitter; growing on conifers. Felted Heart Rot ....
....*Fomes officinalis* (Fr.) Faull

Fruit body sessile, cheesy when fresh, at first convex and knoblike, 5-12 × 4-20 × 5-30 cm; white or yellowish; pore surface white or discolored on drying; spores 4-5 × 3-4 μ, ellipsoid to ovoid.

On trunks of living or dead conifers mostly in western North America. This usually produces a trunk rot and is one of the 3 most important sources of defect in standing coniferous timber. A single fruit body may be over 50 years old. The common name refers to the extensive mat of mycelium in the trunk, often several feet long. The fruit bodies, because of the bitter taste, were formerly used in making bitters.

2b. Not as above 3
3a. Context reddish orange or rusty orange; growing on live juniper only ......*Fomes juniperinus* (von Schrenk) Saccardo & Sydow

Fruit body sessile, more or less ungulate, 3-10 × 4-15 × 2-12 cm, corky to woody, yellowish orange and tomentose at first, becoming brownish orange to grayish black or black and glabrous, the margin remaining yellowish, rough to rimose in age; pore surface yellowish to brownish; spores 6-9 × 4.5-7 μ, ellipsoid to subglobose, truncate at one end or somewhat quadrangular.

Widely distributed throughout the range of *Juniperus*.

3b. Not as above 4
4a. Pores whitish to yellowish 5
4b. Pores rosy or vinaceous at first. Fig. 139 ....
....*Fomes roseus* (Fr.) Cooke

Fruit body sessile, convex to somewhat ungulate, 1-6 × 1.5-10 × 1-3 cm, brownish pink or pinkish red at first, becoming smoky brown then blackish except on the margin, tomentose becoming glabrous, furrowed or sulcate in old specimens; context silvery pinkish to pale rose; spores 5-7 × 2.5-3.5 μ, elongate-ellipsoid.

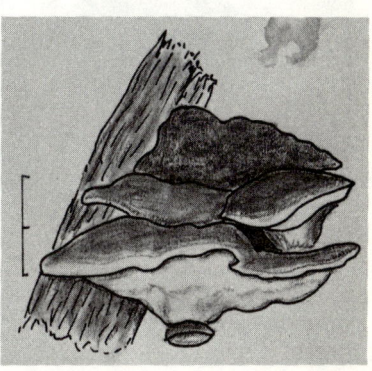

Fig. 139. *Fomes roseus*.

On dead wood, usually of conifers, in northern United States and southern Canada. *F. subroseus* (Weir) Overholts, is very similar but has spores 4-7 × 1.5-2 μ, cylindric and slightly curved. Also, the context is more deeply colored.

5a. Pileus with a resinous crust and often reddish in some part, margin often with a reddish to dull ochraceous tone; no distinct hyphal layer present between layers of tubes. Fig. 140 ....
....*Fomes pinicola* (Fr.) Cooke

Fruit body sessile or decurrent, applanate to ungulate, 4-30 × 6-40 × 2.5-22 cm, context turning pinkish where wounded when in actively growing state, dark cherry red changing to dark reddish brown when touched with KOH; pore surface white to umber or sometimes light yellow, yellow where bruised when fresh; spores 5-7 × 4-5 μ, ovoid to subglobose.

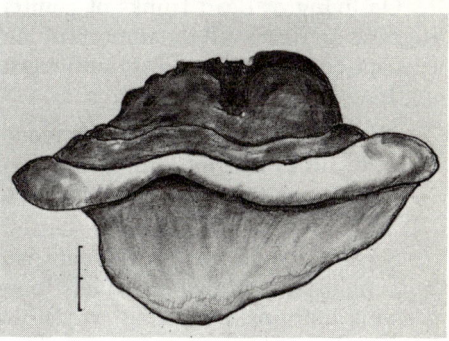

Fig. 140. *Fomes pinicola*.

Usually on dead trees or on stumps or logs of both hardwood and conifers throughout North America. Very common and causing large amounts of decay.

5b. With a thin layer of chocolate-brown hyphae present between tube layers .... see *Ganoderma applanatum* p. 108
6a. Pileus incrusted, ungulate, grayish brown; pore surface gray to grayish brown; very common on birch. Fig. 141 ....
.... *Fomes fomentarius* (Fr.) Kichx

Fig. 141. *Fomes fomentarius*.

Fruit body sessile, 3-15 × 6-20 × 2-15 cm, pale brown to grayish brown becoming gray or grayish black, velvety at first, becoming glabrous; context dark tan or brown, the tube layers not distinct; spores 12-18 × 4-5 μ, cylindric.

Mostly on trunks or logs of dead hardwoods, at times from wounds of living trees, common and widespread throughout Canada and the United States.

6b. Not as above 7
7a. Fruit body with a context less than 1 cm thick ....
....*Fomes pini* (Fr.) Karsten

Fruit body sessile or decurrent, ungulate or applanate, 6-15 × 4-25 × 1-15 cm, fulvous to tawny with an elevated zone or zones of appressed tomentum, becoming blackish and glabrous finally; pore surface ochraceous to rusty brown; spores 4-6 × 3.5-5 μ, globose or subglobose.

On living or dead trunks of conifers throughout North America. It grows on nearly all the important lumber trees in the conifer group (except cedars and cypress) and causes a greater timber loss in living trees than any other fungus.

7b. Fruit body with the context more than 1 cm thick 8
8a. Old tubes stuffed with white mycelium which shows as white streaks in the tube layers of sectioned pilei; spores hyaline in KOH .... *Fomes igniarius* (Fr.) Kichx

Sessile or somewhat decurrent, pale to ungulate, 3-15 × 5-20 × 2-12 cm, usually brown and finely tomentose when young and on the growing margins, becoming grayish or black and glabrous; context hard and woody, brown; pore surface gray-brown; spores 5-6.5 × 4-5 μ or 4.5-5 μ, subglobose or globose; setae in hymenium rare to abundant, 12-18 × 4-6 μ, walls brown.

On trunks of a wide variety of deciduous species over much of North America, quaking aspen is one of the most favored host species.

NON-GILLED FLESHY FUNGI

8b. Old tubes not stuffed as above; spores brown in KOH 9

9a. Usually growing on locust or other members of the legume family; setae lacking in the hymenium ....
....*Fomes rimosus* (Berk.) Cooke

Fruit body sessile, fan-shaped to ungulate, 3-20 × 5-30 × 1.5-15 cm, young specimens and the growing parts of old ones rich brown and compactly tomentose, becoming blackish and very rimose and often having concentric furrows; context yellowish brown; pore surface yellow-brown to deep brown; tube layers often not very distinct; spores 4-6 μ and globose or 4.5-6 × 3.5-5 μ and broadly ellipsoid.

On living or dead trees in eastern United States and in the southwest.

9b. Setae present in the hymenium; most often growing on oak ......
..........*Fomes everhartii* (Ell. & Gall.) von Schrenk & Spaulding

Sessile, convex or ungulate, 2-15 × 4-36 × 2-15 cm, at first uniformly brown, becoming gray or black except for the brown margin, sulcate, rough and rimose in age; context rusty brown; pore surface brown; spores 4-6 × 3.5-4.4 or 4-5 μ, subglobose to globose; setae 15-35 × 5-12 μ.

In eastern and central United States and in Ontario, Canada.

LENZITES

Fruit bodies annual or persisting several years (perennial), corky to leathery or coriaceous if thin, sessile, fan-shaped in large fruit bodies; hymenophore of thick radiating rigid plates or lamellae varying to subporoid; spores cylindric, smooth, hyaline under the microscope. *Daedalea* has a very similar hymenophore causing the two genera to be easily confused.

Key to Selected Species

1a. Context and gills pallid or light colored; gills white to whitish
....*Lenzites betulina* (Fr.) Fries

Pileus sessile or effused-reflexed, 2-8 × 2-12 × 0.3-1.5 cm, grayish to brownish, zonate, the zones narrow, multicolored; pore surface usually lamellate, the lamellae branched toward the margin of the cap and about 1 mm apart; spores 4-7 × 1.5-3 μ, short cylindric.

On dead wood, usually of hardwoods, very common and widely distributed in North America. It often has a growth of green algae over the surface of the pileus in age.

1b. Context dark umber to rusty brown; gills white to brownish or violaceous 2

2a. Entire fruit body rich rusty brown or darker; typically on wood of conifers. Fig. 142 ....*Lenzites saepiaria* (Fr.) Fries

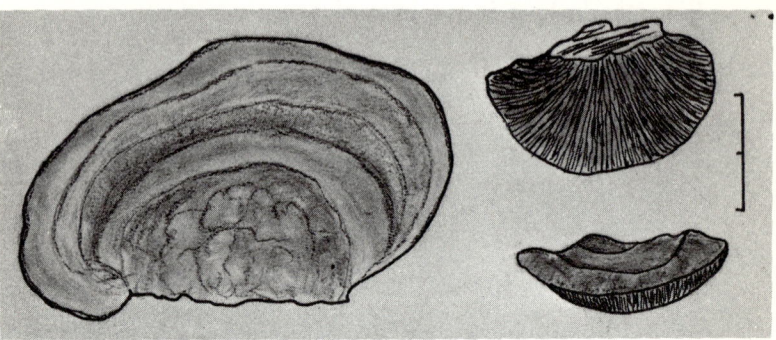

Fig. 142. *Lenzites saepiaria*.

Pileus 1-7 × 2-10 × 0.3-1 cm, the growing margin often white, yellow or orange; pore surface usually lamellate, but at times daedaloid, poroid or toothed.

Common throughout North America where conifers grow.

2b. Entire fruit body gray to pale dingy cinnamon; typically on wood of deciduous trees ....*Lenzites trabea* Fries

Pileus 1-5 × 2-8 × 0.2-0.8 cm, becoming blackish if persisting for more than 1 year, tomentose becoming glabrous, lower surface usually somewhat poroid, rarely lamellate; spores 7-10 × 2.5-5 μ, cylindric.

Widely distributed in North America.

DAEDALEA

Fruit bodies annual or in some species perennial but then the tubes not in layers; consistency tough-membranous to corky or woody; context pallid to brown; pores radially elongated so the pore surface appears sublamellate to lamellate or at times poroid with round pores but typically sinuous (daedaleoid); spores oblong, ellipsoid or cylindric (never globose); setae absent.

A number of species in other genera may have radially elongated pores especially near the point of attachment of the fruit body, particularly *Lenzites*.

Key to Selected Species

1a. Pileus less than 0.5 cm thick, surface villose to tomentose and often green from algae growing in the tomentose layer ....
....*Daedalea unicolor* Fries

NON-GILLED FLESHY FUNGI

Fruit body sessile or effused-reflexed, surface white to olivaceous, ochraceous or brownish, often covered with algae, black next to the substrate in age, 0.5-6 × 2-8 cm; pore surface white to cinereous or smoky, the mouths often breaking up into teeth; spores 4.5-5.5 × 2.5-3.5 μ.

Usually on dead wood of deciduous trees. Widely distributed in North America.

1b. Pileus at least 1 cm thick, usually thicker, the surface not villous or tomentose 2

2a. Space between the "gills" 1 mm or more wide; pileus 1-8 cm thick, up to 20 cm broad, perennial; surface whitish at first, darker in age, Fig. 126 ....*Daedalea quercina* Fries

Pileus sessile, corky, rimose in age, the margin often thick and obtuse; context pallid or light brown; pore surface whitish to umber, the pores with thick walls, usually daedaloid; spores 5-6 × 2-3 μ.

Usually on logs, stumps or trunks of hardwoods, mostly on oak and chestnut in eastern United States.

2b. Space between the "gills" less than 1 mm; pileus up to 2-3 cm thick, not perennial; surface not highly colored at first 3

3a. Pileus grayish or brownish, when fresh staining pinkish where the pore layer is injured .... *Daedalea confragosa* Fries

Pileus 2-10 × 3-15 × 0.2-2 cm, plane or slightly convex, often zonate at least near the margin; pore surface whitish to pale brown, poroid, daedaloid or lamellate, the mouths up to 1.5 mm wide; spores 7-9 × 2-2.5 μ.

Usually growing on dead hardwood, occasionally from wounds in living trees, rarely on conifer wood. Widely distributed.

3b. Pileus typically white to pallid; pore surface not staining pink where injured ....*Daedalea ambigua* Berkeley

Pileus sessile, 3-20 × 5-35 × 0.3-3 cm, often dark at the base; pores small, 2-3 per mm, their walls thick and entire; spores 5-7 × 1.5-2 μ.

On dead deciduous wood, southern in distribution.

TYROMYCES

Fruit body white to grayish but context whitish when fresh, sessile to substipitate, fan-shaped to subungulate; fleshy to subfleshy, surface glabrous to roughened; pores small and round or nearly so; spores hyaline under the microscope; when touched with KOH yellow or not reacting; solitary to shelving or clustered (if substipitate) mostly on wood of hardwoods.

Key to Species

1a. On conifer wood (especially hemlock); pileus marked with large (2-5mm) smooth spots especially near the margin; taste very bitter. Fig. 143 ....*Tyromyces guttulatus* (Pk.) Murrill

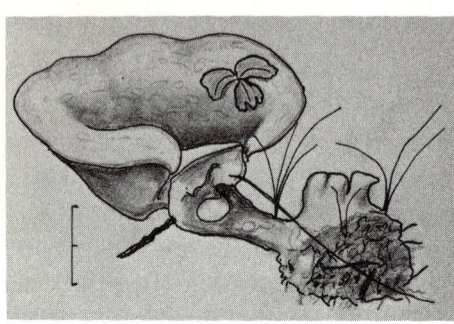

Fig. 143. *Tyromyces guttulatus*.

Fruit body 3-12 × 5-15 × 0.5-1.5 cm, sessile to substipitate, usually fan-shaped, white to yellowish or mottled these colors; pores 4-5 per mm, angular, pore surface white to buff; spores 3-4.5 × 2-2.5 μ; cystidia small, embedded in the hymenium, sub-fusoid.

Not uncommon in the Great Lakes region where hemlock grows, but widely distributed in the conifer areas of North America.

1b. Not as above 2

2a. Spores blue in a deposit (often lodged on pileus margin and imparting a blue tone to it) ....
..................................*Tyromyces caesius* (Schrad ex Fr.) Murrill

Fruit body sessile; pileus 1-5 × 1-4 (8) × 0.2-1 (2) cm, white or gray, uniformly villose pubescent; context white, 1-10 mm thick, taste mild; pores angular or sinuous, 2-4 per mm, pore surface white, grayish (or bluish from spores); spores 3-5 × 0.7-1.5 μ; cystidia none but hyphal pegs abundant.

On dead wood of both hardwoods and conifers, seldom found in quantity, but common and widespread in North America. A very similar species, *T. perdelicatus* Murrill, also has blue spores and is rather common in the Pacific Northwest. It is generally thinner and more effuse-reflexed.

2b. Spores not blue in deposit 3

3a. Margin of young pileus staining green when injured; spores 4.5-7 × 4-5 μ ....*Tyromyces spraguei* (B. & C.) Murrill

Pileus sessile, 4-12 × 4-15 × 0.6-3 cm, white to cinereous or darker often som:what reddish on the edge; context white, watery-tough, when fresh zonate, 0.3-2.5 cm thick, taste bitterish; tubes 0.2-1 cm long, pores 3-4.5 per mm; spores smooth; cystidia none.

On hardwoods, particularly oak, around stumps and dead trees or on logs, not uncommon in the Great Lakes region, but widely distributed.

NON-GILLED FLESHY FUNGI

3b. Pileus not staining when injured. Fig. 144 ....
........................*Tyromyces albellus* (Peck) **Bondarzew & Singer**

Pileus applanate or convex, 2-7 × 1-12 × 0.5-3 cm, white to watery white, slightly villose to nearly glabrous; context white, odor fragrant, 2-15 mm thick; pore surface white when fresh, 3-5 per mm; spores cylindric or allantoid, smooth, hyaline, 3.5-5 × 1-2 μ; cystidia none, hyphal pegs present; hyphae of context much-branched.

Fig. 144. *Tyromyces albellus*.

Usually on dead wood of deciduous trees, often on decaying branches particularly of birch in slashings, widely distributed in North America, but not found in quantity, solitary fruit bodies are common. A very closely related species, *T. tephroleucus*, has the context hyphae parallel and mostly unbranched. In the field they resemble each other quite closely.

The HYDNACEAE

Fruit body fleshy, leathery, or woody, with a central (rarely lateral) stipe, or sessile; the spore bearing surface covering spines or icicle-like downward oriented teeth attached to the underside of a pileus or hanging from a framework of branches or a fleshy mass of tissue (a tubercle). See *Echinodontium* also, p. 103.

Key to Genera

1a. Spines projecting down from a loose framework of branches or the fruit body a rather solid mass of tissue (a tubercle) with the spines attached over its surface; fleshy; spores amyloid ....
....*Hericium* **p. 126**

1b. Not as above (if spores amyloid then the fruit body stipitate)..2

2a. Fruit body sessile or formed by the curved outward margin of the fruit body extending away from the substrate to a greater or lesser degree, part of the hymenophore often resupinate on the substrate ....*Steccherinum* **p. 128**

2b. Fruit body more or less stipitate 3

3a. Growing on rotting pine cones; stipe slender, lateral (but may appear central), hairy and slender, dark brown; spores amyloid. Fig. 145 ....*Auriscalpium vulgare* S. F. Gray

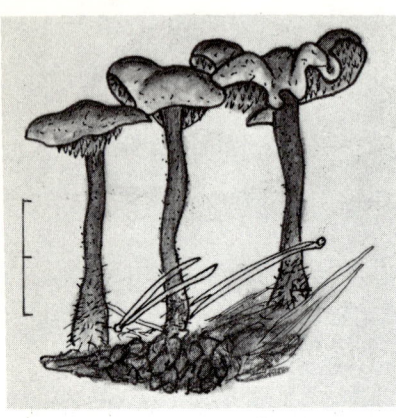

Fig. 145. *Auriscalpium vulgare*.

Pileus 1-4 cm broad, covered with dark brown fibrils, margin often fimbriate; context white, thin, pliant; spines when mature dark violaceous-brown to merely dull brown, 2-3 mm long; stipe 3-7 cm long, 1-3 mm thick; spores $4\text{-}5.2 \times 4.8\text{-}5.5$ μ, becoming minutely ornamented.

Widely distributed in the pine belt of Canada and the United States, typically on partly buried cones, or in thick mats of debris formed in part by decaying cones.

3b. Habitat and stipe not as above 4

4a. Spore deposit white 5

4b. Spore deposit brown 7

5a. Fruit body tough, fibrous and pileus thin in the area away from the stipe ....*Phellodon* p. 129

5b. Fruit body rather thick and fleshy 6

6a. Spores smooth ....*Dentinum* p. 131

6b. Spores minutely tuberculate ....*Bankera* p. 132

7a. Context soft and fleshy or brittle, soon decaying ... *Hydnum* p. 133

7b. Context tough, fibrous, often duplex (two layers each of a different texture), or in some species woody ... *Hydnellum* p. 138

HERICIUM

Fruit body in the form of a framework of branches with the spines of various sizes hanging down from them, the arrangement loose or compact; spore deposit white; the hyphae of the fruit body often amyloid at least in part. Growing on wood of both conifers and hardwoods. The known species are edible.

Key to Species

1a. Fruit body a rather solid mass of tissue with spines arising from it, the spines up to 6 cm long at times; typically growing on scars on living trees. Bear's Head. Fig. 145 ....
....*Hericium erinaceus* **Pers.**

Fruit body fleshy and tough, white when fresh, discoloring on aging to yellowish to tan and finally dingy brown at least over exterior; spores 4-5.5 × 5-6.5 μ, subglobose; hyphae of the context hyaline, thick-walled, up to 12-14 μ wide, septate, clamps occasional.

Widespread in eastern and central U. S. and the Pacific coast where oak is found, late summer and fall, or in Florida in the winter.

1b. Fruit body more or less openly branched at maturity 2

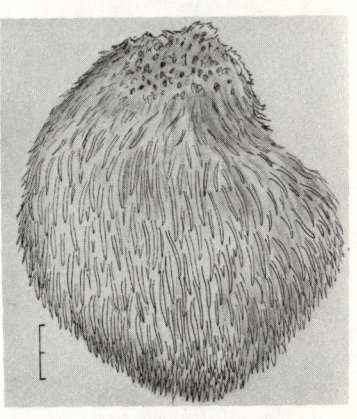

Fig. 146. *Hericium erinaceus.*

2a. Fruit body salmon buff when young, and becoming paler to finally whitish; characteristically on the wood of conifers in the Pacific Northwest ....
..............................*Hericium abietis* (Weir ex Hubert) **Harrison**

Fruit body up to 75 cm high and 40 cm wide arising from a solid tubercle at first but it develops into a branched framework; spines up to 1 cm long; spores 4.5-5.5 (6) × 4-4.5 (5) μ, subglobose, finely roughened to smooth, strongly amyloid.

Occurring in the fall and causing a typical white pocket-rot of conifers. Not common.

2b. Fruit body white to whitish when young 3

3a. Spines short (3-10 mm), branch system open and often delicate; spores 3.5-4 (4.5) × 4-5.5 μ ....
....*Hericium ramosum* (Merat) **Letellier**

Fruit body up to 30 cm or more wide, the fine end-branches very delicate attached to dead wood by a small tough repeatedly branched "root," when fresh pure glistening white, becoming buff to brownish in age.

Widely distributed but not common, late summer and fall. On hardwood.

3b. Spines 5-40 mm long; branch system more compact than in above and not delicate; spores 4.5-5.5 × 5.5-5.5 (6.5) μ. Fig. 147
....Hericium coralloides **Pers.**

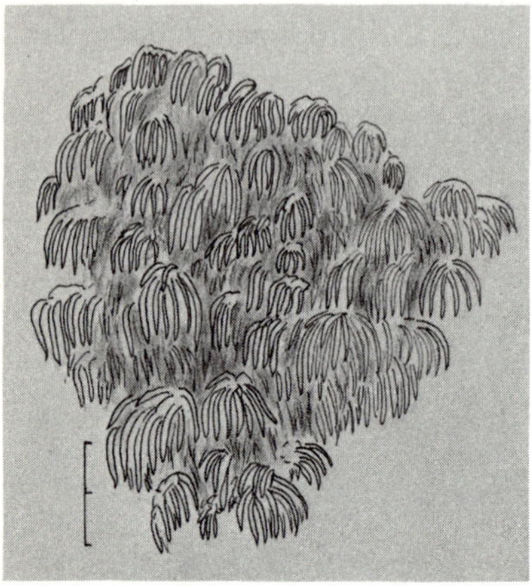

Fruit body often large and bulky, arising from a rooting base which branches above to produce the framework of the fruit body, branches densely covered with pendent clusters of stout sharp spines; pure white at first, becoming dingy yellowish to brownish.

Widely distributed on logs of hardwoods, questionably on conifer wood, late summer and fall. Edible.

Fig. 147. *Hericium coralloides.*

STECCHERINUM

Fruit body rather persistent, thick or thin, tough to leathery, sessile, stalked or at times at least in part resupinate; teeth usually somewhat flattened; spores inamyloid, smooth, white in deposit; cystidia often present in the hymenium.

Key to Species

1a. Fruit body massive, up to 28 cm broad, consisting of shelving pilei (in horizontal layers) all arising from a common solid base; spores 4.5-5.5 × 2.5 μ, ellipsoid; cystidia thick-walled, incrusted at tips, up to 18 μ wide and projecting somewhat beyond the basidia, numerous. Fig. 148 ....
..............................*Steccherinum septentrionale* (**Fr.**) **Banker**

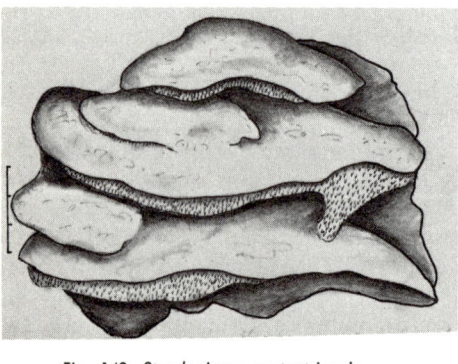

Fig. 148. *Steccherinum septentrionale.*

Fruit body with surface scabrous-roughened to tomentose; pileus up to 30 cm broad, the larger ones in the center and smaller ones to the side, thick and tough, whitish but soon dingy yellowish and discoloring further to brownish in age.

Widely distributed in northern United States and

NON-GILLED FLESHY FUNGI

southern Canada especially in the range of hard maple (*A. saccharum*), late summer and fall. Not edible.

1b. Not as above 2
2a. **Pileus dark gray over the center when dried; spores 6-7 (8) × 4.5-5.5 (6) μ; teeth up to 1 cm long (as dried); cystidia lacking** ....*Steccherinum crassiusculum* K. A. Harrison

Fruit body 10 × 5 × 7 cm, imbricate; stipe 4 × 3.5 cm, apparently tapering to point of attachment.

Solitary on fallen logs, Mexico, October, rare.

2b. **Spores 3-3.8 × 1-1.2 μ; tips of spines becoming smoky gray from injury of the microscopic white hairs (which blacken)** ....
..........................*Steccherinum adustum* (Schw.) Banker

Fruit body sessile or stalked, simple or several pilei arising from the same point or from the pileus surface of older pilei near their bases; pilei up to 8 cm wide, circular to fan-shaped, surface uneven, often ridged, white to light tan, often dark on the margin, smoky where rubbed; context pure white; odor and taste not distinctive; stipe when present up to 2-3 cm long, stout, white, velvety; spines 1.5-3.5 mm long, generally confluent in groups of 2-3 for most of their length, white, becoming rose color then purplish in age and when dried.

Common on logs and branches of hardwoods in eastern United States in the summer and early fall, less common in the Great Lakes region.

PHELLODON

Spore deposit white; spores echinulate, up to 5 μ in diameter; context usually in 2 layers; spines delicate, pale, becoming ashy or brownish gray; odor usually fragrant and pleasant; often with copious mycelium around the base of the stipe.

Key to Species

1a. **Pileus bluish black, somewhat zonate; context bluish black in KOH; odor when fresh not fragrant** ....
....*Phellodon atratus* K. Harrison

Pileus 1-5 cm broad, irregular, surface rough, subtomentose; odor and taste not distinctive; spines 1-2 mm long, decurrent; stipe 2-5 cm long, compound, irregular, frequently flattened, enlarged at ground level by a felty layer of mycelium; spores 4-5 μ in diam., globose, finely echinulate; hyphae containing dark granules; clamps absent.

Gregarious, compound and often concrescent under conifers in the Pacific Coast states and British Columbia in Canada.

1b. Not as above 2

2a. **Pileus margin white and having the consistency of soft felt; pileus finally zoned with dingy yellow-brown and dark cinnamon areas; odor fragrant.** Fig. 149 ....
....*Phellodon tomentosus* (**Fr.**) **Banker**

Pilei 1.5-3 (4.5) cm wide, sometimes fused together but stipe usually separate, the margin becoming brown when rubbed; flesh thin, taste faintly bitter; spines white at the tips, pale fawn in age, up to 2 mm long; stipe 1-5 cm long, 2-3 mm thick in midportion, enlarging into the pileus, tapering downward, arising from buried spongy light brown feltlike pads of mycelium; spores 3.5-4.5 μ globose, minutely echinulate.

Under conifers in eastern North America, also in the Pacific Northwest. Often common after heavy fall rains.

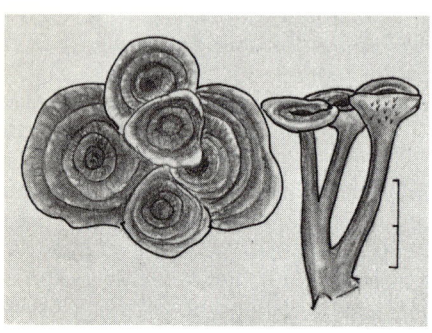

Fig. 149. *Phellodon tomentosus.*

2b. **Not as above** 3
3a. **Stipe thin, radicating, the root slender, fragile and readily breaking off if specimen not carefully collected, dark brown to black, lacking a mycelial or cottony outer layer** ....
....*Phellodon melaleucus* (**Fr.**) **Karsten**

Pileus 1-6 cm broad, each distinct or many fused together, white tomentose at first, becoming dark brown in the center and silky gray on the margin; context dark brown in the center and silky gray on the margin without a distinctive odor or taste; spines up to 1 mm, grayish; stipe up to 3.5 cm long and 3 mm thick, dark brown to black, often branched; spores 3-4.5 μ globose.

Growing in woods in eastern North America and the Pacific Northwest. Not uncommon after heavy fall rains.

3b. **Stipe thickened by a felty layer** 4
4a. **Inner layer of context not black; spines not over 2 mm long** ......
.... *Phellodon confluens* (**Pers.**) **Pouzar**

Pileus up to 6 cm broad, pilei often fused forming an irregular mass, surface tomentose, whitish becoming brownish toward the center as new growth collapses; spines whitish, then buff and finally gray-brown; stipe short; spores globose, echinulate, 3-4 μ.

Gregarious in deciduous or mixed woods, eastern North America and the Pacific Northwest, common during some seasons.

4b. **Inner layer of context black; spines up to 4 mm long** 5

NON-GILLED FLESHY FUNGI

5a. Surface of pileus typically floccose and depressed, gray ....
................................*Phellodon niger* (Fr.) Karst. var. *niger*

Pileus 5-7.5 cm, velvety to strigose, whitish gray to dark brownish gray at the center, margin light gray, upper layer of context dry and soft, colored like the surface; lower layer and in the stipe hard, black; spines light gray, darker when bruised, odor and taste mild.

Gregarious under red pine and spruce in Nova Scotia in Canada, and in the Great Lakes region (both U. S. and Canda).

5b. Surface of pileus typically convex, pallid to cinereous or brownish, more or less pubescent ....
Phellodon niger (Peck) Banker var. *alboniger* (Pk.) Harrison

Similar to the previous variety but the pilei are lighter in color when young and darker in age, also they tend to be larger and to grow in confluent masses.

Gregarious in coniferous woods, eastern North America and the Great Lakes region. Not common.

DENTINUM

Fruit body fleshy and brittle, stipitate with the stipe central, excentric, or lateral; spores smooth, nonamyloid, white in deposit.

Key to Species

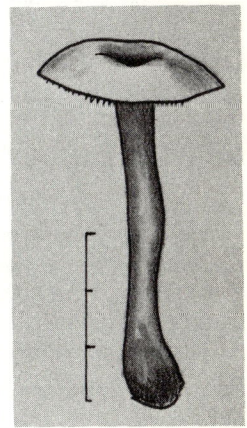

Fig. 150. *Dentinum umbilicatum.*

1a. Pileus umbilicate, deep reddish buff to pale orange-buff; stipe mostly under 1 cm thick; spores 7.5-9 $\times$ 6-7.5 μ; often growing in low boggy areas under cedar, balsam and spruce. Fig. 150 ....
......*Dentinum umbilicatum* (Pk.) Pouzar
Pileus 2.8-4.5 cm broad, somewhat irregular and wavy, slightly felted or unpolished; context 2-3.5 mm thick near the center; taste somewhat soapy, odor mild; spines up to 7 mm long, shorter ones intermingled, not decurrent on the stipe, creamy buff; stipe 2-5.5 cm long, 4.5-7 (19) mm thick near apex, paler than pileus, staining orange-buff or darker on bruising.

Gregarious and not uncommon in its favored habitat, eastern North America and the Great Lakes region; edible.

1b. Not as above 2

2a. **Pileus pallid to tan or rusty cinnamon; spores globose, 6.5-8.5 μ. Fig. 151** ....*Dentinum repandum* (Fr.) S. F. Gray

Pileus 1.5-15 cm broad, margin wavy and often indented nearly to the stipe; flesh thick, tender, brittle, white, typically ochraceous where bruised (progressing to orange-brown at times); spines 5-6 mm long, cream color or white, dark reddish brown when dried; stipe up to 7.5 cm long and 1-3.5 cm thick, colored like the pileus or paler; clamps present.

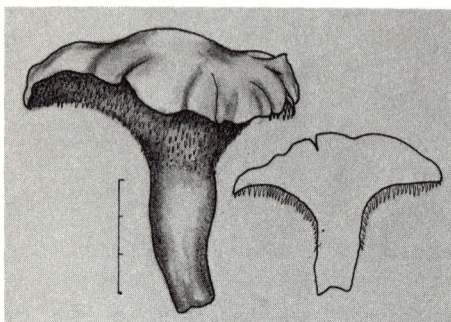

Fig. 151. *Dentinum repandum*.

Widely distributed throughout the United States and Canada, summer and fall, common. Edible and choice.

A nearly pure white form var. *album* (Quél.) Harrison, is often aboundant late in the season and is particularly good for the table.

2b. **Pileus white or pallid** 3
3a. **Context turning dull yellow to orange when cut or bruised** 4
3b. **Context unchanging when injured** ....
....*Dentinum albo-magnum* **Banker**

Pileus up to 11 cm broad, spines white, drying deep red-brown; spores 6-7.4 $\times$ 3.7-4.5 μ; taste mild.

Growing in pine and oak woods in southeastern United States in the fall, quite rare.

4a. **Taste peppery; spores 4-5.2 $\times$ 3.5-4 μ** ....
....*Dentinum albidum* (Pk.) **Snell**

Pileus 1-7 cm broad, often lobed, nearly chalk white at first, then creamy; teeth up to 6 mm long; pileus surface very smooth, like leather; stipe 2-5 cm long, 3-20 mm thick.

In deciduous and mixed woods, southeastern U. S. and the Great Lakes region, summer and early fall.

4b. **Taste mild or slowly bitterish; spores up to 6.5 μ diam** ....
............see *Dentinum repandum* var. *album* (Quél.) **Harrison**

BANKERA

Fruit body terrestrial, the pileus with a central stipe, somewhat fleshy and brittle, context not distinctly duplex or zonate; spore deposit white, the spores subglobose and minutely roughened.

NON-GILLED FLESHY FUNGI

Key to Species

1a. Pileus gray-brown, smooth but becoming scaly in age; context of stipe having a thin hard core. Fig. 152 ....
Bankera carnosa (Banker) Snell, Dick & Taussig

Pileus 3-10 cm broad, margin split and incurved, lacking spines at the edge on underside; context fleshy and fragile, brownish, odor fragrant; spines up to 4 mm long, pale gray.

Solitary, gregarious or cespitose and often irregular from crowding, in coniferous and mixed forests, eastern North America and the Great Lakes region, midsummer into the fall, uncommon.

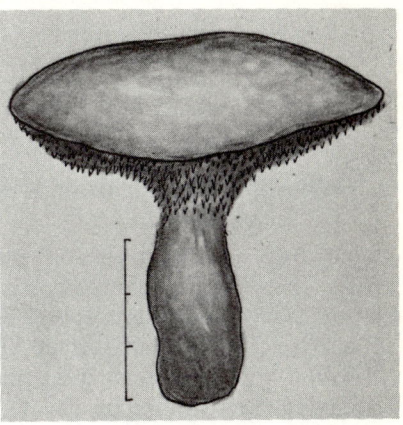

Fig. 152. *Bankera carnosa.*

1b. **Pileus with a white cottony margin and usually yellow-brown to dull cinnamon-brown in the center; stipe lacking a hard core. Fig. 153** ....*Bankera fuligineo-alba* (Schmidt ex Fr.) Pouzar

Pileus 8-15 cm, surface usually smooth, holding trash by means of densely matted fibers, surface layer easily becoming water-logged; spines extending to pileus margin in age; odor mildly foetid-aromatic; stipe short, 2-3 cm long, 1.3-2 thick.

Solitary to gregarious in conifer forests, usually pine in North America, late fall, rare, but, when it fruits, large numbers of fruit bodies are produced.

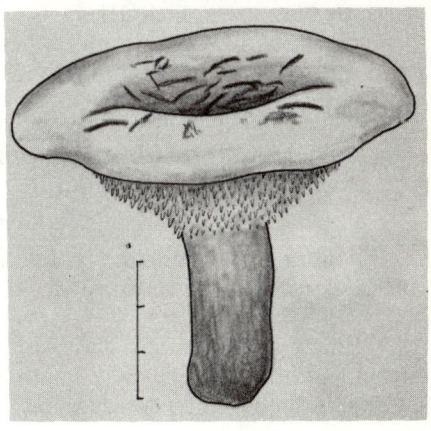

Fig. 153. *Bankera fuligineo-alba.*

HYDNUM

Pileus often large (10-30 cm), consistency fleshy and brittle; the stipe central or excentric to lateral; spores brown in deposit, angular-tuberulate; terrestrial. This genus is quite similar to *Den-*

tinum but the spores of the latter are white and smooth. Many species of *Hydnum* are acrid to bitter and hence not desirable for food. The edibility of many has not been tested.

Key to Species

1a. Context and/or pileus lilac to violet or distinctly vinaceous 2
1b. Context differently colored 5
2a. Pileus spines and stipe dark violet when young ....
.... *Hydnum fuscoindicum* **Harrison**

Pileus 3-13 cm broad, disc depressed, odor and taste mild; spines brittle, the tips pale lilac; stipe 2-5 (10) cm long, 1-3.5 cm thick, tapering to a narrow base; spores $5-6.5 \times 4.5-5$ μ, subglobose; clamp connections lacking; cut surface black when dried.

Solitary, gregarious to subcespitose under conifers in the Pacific Northwest, not uncommon in late summer and fall.

2b. Not as above 3
3a. Pileus surface soon conspicuously rimrose; context avellaneous to vinaceous buff ....*Hydnum rimosum* K. **Harrison**

Pileus 4-12 cm broad, vinaceous; odor and taste not distinctive; spines vinaceous buff; stipe 4-8 cm long, 1-4 cm thick, hoary, colored like the spines; spores $5-6.5 \times 4.5-5$ μ; clamp connections lacking, subcutis blue-green in KOH.

Gregarious under pine and other conifers in the Pacific Northwest during late summer and fall.

3b. Not as above 4
4a. KOH instantly dark green and finally black on the context when fresh; the context purple to vinaceous or lilac ....
........................*Hydnum fuligineo-violaceum* **Kalchb. in Fries**

Pileus 3-12 cm broad, matted fibrillose, later with small appressed scales, vinaceous-brown; spines very crowded; spores $5-6 (7) \times 4.5-5.5$ μ.

Solitary or gregarious under fir and spruce in the southeastern states but under hardwoods more frequently in the Great Lakes region, in the fall after heavy rains.

4b. KOH giving a green reaction on the pileal cutis but the context merely lilac-gray .... *Hydnum cyanellum* **Harrison**

Pileus up to 9 cm broad, vinaceous-violet to bluish black; context lilac gray, odor fragrant, taste disagreeable; spines cinnamon with whitish tips; spores $5-5.5 \times 4-5$ μ.

Solitary under Sitka spruce, Northern California.

5a. **Pileus conspicuously scaly when quite young; taste mild to only somewhat disagreeable. Fig. 154** ....*Hydnum imbricatum* **Fr.**

Pileus 6-20 cm broad, center depressed in age and usually perforate, connecting to the hollow of the stipe; light brown with darker brown scales, becoming dark brown over all; context thick, white to brownish, soft but fragile becoming somewhat pliant; spines pale brown becoming darker; stipe colored like the pileus, 4-9 cm long, 1.5-3 cm thick, enlarged downward, interior light brown; spores $5-7 \times 6-8$ μ, subglobose, clamps present.

In North America it fruits both in conifer and hardwood forests, and is rather common when the rainfall is heavy. Edible, but the flavor poor.

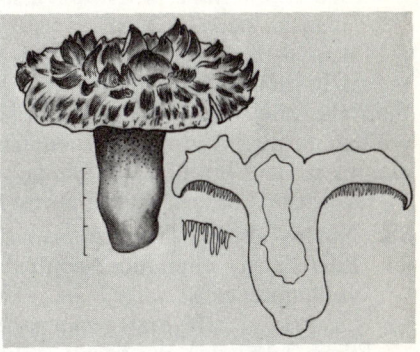

Fig. 154. *Hydnum imbricatum.*

5b. **Pileus usually smooth before maturity but if scaly then the taste of the raw context very bitter or acrid** 6
6a. **Stipe olive to black at base at maturity** 7
6b. **Not as above** 8
7a. **Surface blackening and the context becoming blue-green in KOH. Fig. 155** .... *Hydnum scabrosum* **Fr.**

Pileus up to 20 cm broad, isabelline becoming dark reddish brown to dark dull brown, the scales darker in age; spines concolorous with the pileus or nearly so; spores 5-6 μ.

Solitary to gregarious in conifer or mixed forests, eastern North America.

7b. **KOH not giving the above described reaction** ....
.... *Hydnum fennicum* (Karst.) Saccardo

Pileus smooth becoming more or less scaly, russet brown

Fig. 155. *Hydnum scabrosum.*

with darker scales, margin white and incurved in youth context pallid to light brown, darker on exposure; taste intensely bitter-farinaceous; spines 3-5 mm long pallid fawn becoming dark brown with paler tips; stipe rather long, tapering downward, concolorous with pileus except for the blackish olive to bluish green base.

Solitary to gregarious in deciduous or conifer forests, widely distributed and common after heavy rains in the late summer and fall.

8a. **Pileus sepia to bister; taste mild; cuticle olive-black in KOH (see *Hydnellum piperatum* also p. 144)**..
....*Hydnum ustale* K. Harrison

Pileus 6-15 cm broad, the disc with appressed squamules or irregularly rimose; taste mild; spines becoming wood brown but paler than the pileus surface; stipe 3-5 cm long, 1-15 cm thick, equal, whitish turning brownish when handled; spores 4.5-8×5.5-7μ; clamps present but not abundant.

Gregarious under pine in northern Michigan, late fall.

8b. **Not as above** 9
9a. **Pileus rusty cinnamon; context paler and with scattered large vesiculose cells** ....
..................................*Hydnum martioflavum* Snell, Harrison & Jackson

Pileus 4-15 (25) cm broad, subtomentose to matted tomentose, orange-buff to tawny or cinnamon, darker when old; odor farinaceous; spines bright orange-cinnamon becoming duller and darker in age; stipe 2.5-7 cm long, 0.7-3 cm thick, dull cinnamon, pointed and white mycelioid at base; spores 4-$5.5 \times 4.5 \mu$.

Under fir and spruce in eastern Canada and west to the Pacific Coast late summer and fall, not common.

9b. **Not as above** 10
10a. **Pileus distinctly fibrillose-strigose, matted fibrillose or woolly** 11
10b. **Pileus glabrous and dull or somewhat scaly** 13
11a. **Pileus dark brown and matted fibrillose when mature** ....
....see *Hydnellum mirabile* p. 144
11b. **Pileus creamy white, pallid or pinkish at first** 12
12a. **Pileus covered with creamy white plush when young; growing under hardwoods** ....*Hydnum cristatum* Bres. in Atk.

Pileus 3-10 (19) cm broad, usually depressed in the center, lobed and irregular, becoming strigose-hairy and yellowish to buffy brown; odor strongly farinaceous, taste farinaceous becoming peppery and astringent; spines dull straw color, becoming almost blackish with pale tips; stipe 2.5-6.5 cm long, 0.7-1.5 cm thick, surface unpolished; spores 3.8-4.2×4-5μ.

Solitary or in colonies, at times connate, in deciduous or mixed woods in eastern North America.

12b. **Pileus pinkish at first, soon grayish; becoming woolly and floccose-scaly** ....*Hydnum lanuginosum* K. Harrison

Pileus 3-15 cm broad, the scales darkening when dry; context brittle; stipe 3-6 cm long, 0.5-2.5 cm thick, glabrous; taste strongly farinaceous; spores 4.5-6×4.5-5μ.

Solitary to gregarious, often connate, under conifers in eastern Canada.

13a. Context quickly purple-drab if cut; pileus olive-tinted when dried .... *Hydnum fumosum* (Banker) Pouzar

Pileus 8.5-9.8 cm broad, softly felted-tomentose, grayish tan becoming drab with a purplish tint; odor pleasant, taste bitterish; spines pallid when young, staining blackish brown when bruised, the tips greenish on drying; stipe 3.5-6 cm long, 2-3 cm thick, enlarged at the base, grayish tan darkening to blackish brown when handled; spores 7.5-10.5 (11.5) $\times$ 6-8.5 (9) μ.

In mixed woods in North Carolina, summer.

13b. Not as above 14

14a. Context brownish white; taste slightly farinaceous; pileus light brown .... *Hydnum stereosarcinon* (Wehmeyer) Harrison

Pileus 2-14 (18) cm broad, very irregular, light brown darkening to dull brown, faintly zonate, in humid weather sometimes exuding a light yellow juice; spines up to 1 cm long; stipe 4-8 cm long, 1-2 cm thick, tapering to a point, base of young specimens at times with droplets of reddish brown juice; spores 4.5-5 $\times$ 3.5-4.5 μ.

Solitary, gregarious or fused, under conifers in eastern North America, common especially in Nova Scotia, Canada. It is a variable species.

14a. Not as above 15

15a. Pileus cuticle merely brownish in KOH ....
.... *Hydnum crassum* K. Harrison

Pileus 5-15 cm broad, yellowish becoming dull yellow-brown, slightly tomentose, finely or rarely coarsely cracked; odor mildly medicinal, taste mild or slightly acrid; stipe up to 3 cm thick, tapering downward to a white mycelioid base; spines up to 1.5 cm long, at times branched and with 2-4 tips; spores 3-5 $\times$ 2.5-4 μ.

Solitary, gregarious or clustered, under spruce or fir in Nova Scotia, Canada, rare but fruiting in quantity during some seasons.

15b. Pileus cuticle olive to black when touched with KOH 16

16a. Taste very bitter ....*Hydnum subincarnatum* K. Harrison

Pileus 4-14 cm broad, smooth at first, then cracking into scales, vinaceous-brown; context pallid with a tint of vinaceous; odor farinaceous and pungent; taste very bitter-farinaceous; spines up to 5-6 mm long, close, fine, whitish to pale vinaceous fawn; stipe 5-10 cm long, 1-5 cm thick, excentric or central, tapering downward; spores 5.5-6 $\times$ 4-5 μ.

Solitary, gregarious or cespitose under oak and pine in the Pacific Northwest.

16b. Taste mild at first, slowly slightly bitterish 17

17a. Context yellowish ....*Hydnum subfelleum* K. Harrison

Pileus 4-17 cm broad, brown with vinaceous tints when young, darkening to browner at maturity; spines light grayish brown, tips white darkening when bruised; stipe 1-9 cm long, 1-4 cm thick, with a white mycelioid base; spores $5\text{-}6 \times 4\text{-}5.3\ \mu$.

Gregarious or cespitose under conifers in Nova Scotia, Canada.

17b. Context grayish .... *Hydnum calvatum* K. Harrison

Pileus 15-28 cm broad, brown; odor not distinctive in the type variety but strong and fragrant in var. *odoratum* K. Harrison; spines brown with pale tips; stipe 2-4 cm long, 2-4 cm thick, base whitish; spores $4.5\text{-}5 \times 3.5\text{-}4\ \mu$.

Gregarious or clustered in conifer forests of the Pacific Northwest, summer and early fall.

HYDNELLUM

Context tough and fibrous when fresh, and almost woody as dried; spores brown in deposits, typically non-amyloid, tuberculate; stipe continuous with the pileus and the context often zoned. Growing on the ground in masses or individually in either conifer or hardwood forests in late summer and fall.

Key to Stirpes

1a. Blue to violaceous or fuscous violaceous color present on the context, pileus, spines or stipe when young (weak in *H. ferrugipes*) .... Stirps *Caeruleum*
1b. Lacking blue tints in the color pattern 2
2a. Pileus and tips of spines sulphur yellow when young ....
.... *H. geoginium* (Fr.) Banker

Caps up to 7 cm broad, growing in complicated masses up to 25 cm broad; becoming almost black but retaining greenish tones; spores $3\text{-}4.5 \times 3\ \mu$; mycelium sulphur yellow.

Under spruce and fir, Nova Scotia, Canada.

2b. Pileus and tips of spines not as above 3
3a. Fruit bodies rusty orange to rusty red or rusty ochraceous in some part (also see *H. ferrugipes* p. 140) ....
.... Stirps *Aurantiacum* p. 141
3b. Fruit bodies duller in color: cinnamon-brown to russet, but some showing bright red droplets when humidity is high, when actively growing the pileus surface may be white and unpolished .... Stirps *Spongiosipes* p. 142

STIRPS CAERULEUM

1a. Odor very distinctive, heavy but fragrant 2
1b. Odor not readily noticed 6
2a. Context of stipe dusky violaceous at apex, dingy cinnamon-tan at the base .... *Hydnellum regium* K. Harrison

Fruit body complex, the pilei 3-9 cm broad in rosettes up to 25 cm broad and 15 cm high from a complex central stipe, surface of pileus matted fibrillose, eroded, violaceous black, radially striate toward the margin, context firm, brittle, zonate; stipe compound, tapering downward to a point, pinkish cinnamon downward; spores 4.5-6 × 3.5-4.5 µ.

Solitary or gregarious under conifers in western United States.

2b. Not as above 3
3a. Pilei in large masses up to 25 cm broad, dingy vinaceous-brown; spines bright blue .... *Hydnellum scleropodium* K. Harrison

Margin of pileus dull pink becoming reddish when handled, at first spotted with red droplets; spines up to 11 mm long, some forked; stipe 3-9 cm long, 2-4 cm thick, narrowest at apex, rooting, hard and swollen like a sclerotium, white tinged with ferruginous, blackish when handled; spores 4-5 × 3.5-4.5 µ angular; context of stipe, pileus and spines green to blue-green in KOH; clamps present.

Solitary under oak or in mixed woods, eastern North America, rare.

3b. Not as above 4
4a. Context zoned bluish black ....
.... *Hydnellum cyanopodium* K. Harrison

Pileus 4-8 cm broad, irregular, lobed, dark bluish vinaceous changing to lavender and then whitish at the margin, beaded with red droplets; spines brownish; stipe 2-5 cm long, 1-2 cm thick, tapering downward, deep bluish black; spores 4-5 × 3.5-4.5 µ.

Solitary, gregarious or concrescent under spruce and pine in California.

4b. Context not as above, blue zones in stipe distinct 5
5a. Growing margin white and not beaded with droplets of red juice; odor heavy-aromatic ....
.... *Hydnellum suaveolens* (Fr.) Karst.

Pileus (3.5) 6-15 (30) cm broad, pure white over all at first and felted by a soft thin coating, becoming tan to brownish tinted with violet gray or olive, rather dingy in age; taste not distinctive; spines crowded, drab-brown with pale tips; stipe 1-2 cm or more long and up to 1.5 cm or more thick, indigo blue to blue-black, not white-felted; mycelium deep blue; spores 3-3.7 × 3.8-5 µ; clamps present.

Solitary or in colonies, at times confluent, under conifers late summer and fall, eastern North America and northern Rocky Mountains, often common.

5b. Odor of menthol; growing margin soft and beaded wtih red droplets .... *Hydnellum cruentum* K. Harrison

Pileus 3-10 cm broad, club-like to top-shaped, white to pale brown, becoming brown and staining darker on bruising, surface rough, radially ridged; spines lilac to dark blue, the tips finally brown-tinted; stipe up to 5 cm long and 1.5 cm thick, white shaded with blue; spores 4-4.5 × 3.5-4.5 µ, cross-shaped.

Solitary, gregarious or connate, under spruce, eastern Canada.

6a. **Context zoned blue to mauve with brown** ....
....*Hydnellum caeruleum* (Pers.) Karst.

Pileus 3-11 cm broad, mauve then whitish becoming light brown and finally dull dark brown at the center, margin white with a faint blue tint when fresh, soft-velvety becoming matted and pitted; spines whitish becoming dark brown with white tips; stipe 2-4 cm long, 1-2 cm thick, context reddish brick color; spores 4.5-6 $\times$ 4.5-5 μ, irregular.

Gregarious or fused, in conifer forests in eastern Canada, eastern United States, the Great Lakes region and the Pacific Northwest.

6b. **Context azonate or zoned with different colors** 7
7a. **Pileus slate gray to blackish; spines not violaceous at any time ....see specimens of** *Phellodon niger* **p. 131 which do not shed spores**
7b. **Not as above** 8
8a. **Context with slight slate violet tints in places** ....
....*Hydnellum ferrugipes* Coker

Pileus 4-7 cm broad, regular, felted-tomentose becoming glabrous, the growing parts becoming blackish when rubbed; context duplex, the upper layer corky in texture and buff colored, lower layer hard and dark brown, when dry with tints of slate blue; spines up to 4 mm long, tips pallid until age; stipe 2-4 cm long, 1-1.5 cm thick, rusty red; spores 4-5 $\times$ 5-6.5 μ.

In deciduous or mixed woods, summer and fall in eastern North America.

8b. **Not as above** 9
9a. **Taste farinaceous; pileus whitish but becoming light brown; spines grayish blue with lighter tips** ....
....*Hydnellum subzonatum* Harrison

Pileus 1.3-5 cm broad, radially ridged, margin white, elevated; context thin, pale brown; spines up to 3 mm, fine, forked; stipe 1-5 cm long, 1.5-3 cm thick, enlarged upward, having a light mycelium at the base; spores 3.6-4.5 $\times$ 3-4 μ, oblong to nearly square, with coarse blunt tubercles.

Gregarious or connate under spruce in eastern Canada.

9b. **Taste mild; pileus russet to brick red on the disc** ....
....*Hydnellum cyanodon* K. Harrison

Pileus 3-6 cm broad, top-shaped, fibrillose to matted to glabrous, becoming dark brown with a lighter margin; context dark brown with darker zones; spines up to 5 mm long, close, fused, indigo colored with lighter fringed tips; stipe 2.5-6 cm long, 1.1.5 cm thick, tapering downward to a pointed root, chestnut brown, the base rusty-indigo; spores 4-5 (5.5) $\times$ 3.5-4.5 μ, with 4-6 tubercles.

Solitary to gregarious in moss under spruce, eastern Canada.

NON-GILLED FLESHY FUNGI

STIRPS AURANTIACUM

1a. Pileus surface typically colliculose to rough when mature; spores 5.5-7.5 × 5-6 μ. Fig. 156 ....
....................................Hydnellum aurantiacum (Fr.) Karsten

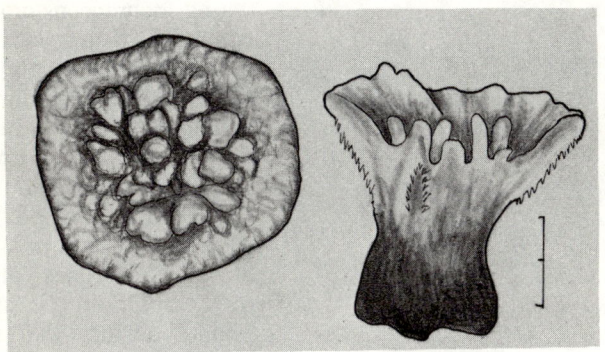

Fig. 156. *Hydnellum aurantiacum*.

Pileus 3-15 cm wide, finely tomentose to velvety, becoming matted down and roughened, color white in rapidly growing stage but soon orange to rusty cinnamon, darker in age; context duplex, orange to rusty cinnamon and remaining orange-toned when dried; spines whitish becoming brown, the tips often remaining whitish; stipe 3-6 cm long, 1-2 cm thick, very firm, orange, becoming bright rusty cinnamon and finally dark brown.

Gregarious to clustered or concrescent, under conifers throughout North America, summer and fall, common during warm wet seasons.

1b. Pileus surface and spore size not as above 2

2a. Pileus context thin and not duplex ....
....Hydnellum conigenum (Peck) Banker

Pileus 3-7 cm broad, depressed to deeply funnel-shaped varying to complicate or flabelliform, concrescent to rosettes up to 10 cm broad; surface irregular, radially ridged, fibrillose, becoming zonate, pinkish cinnamon, orange cinnamon to orange-red. Context with strongly farinaceous taste. Stipe 3-6 cm long, 5-20 mm thick, with a mass of felted tomentum at base. Spines to 3 mm long, decurrent, orange; spores 4-5.5 × 3.5-4.5 μ.

Gregarious to concrescent in coniferous forests. Common in the Pacific Northwest south to New Mexico, rare in Michigan.

2b. Pileus context duplex, thicker than in the above at first. Fig. 157 .... *Hydnellum earlianum* **Banker**

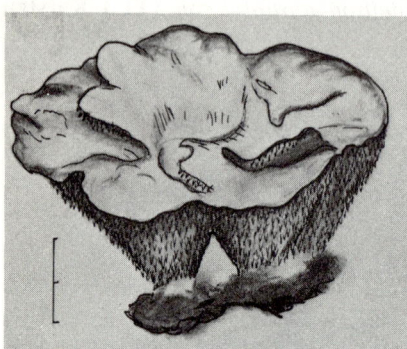

Fig. 157. *Hydnellum earlianum.*

Pilei numerous, attached to a branched or simple stipe, the entire mass up to 12 cm wide, dull and velvety when young, ochraceous-orange becoming brown or black when rubbed (when truly fresh); spines up to 3.5 mm long, ochraceous-tawny becoming dark brown; stipe up to 7.5 cm long, 2 cm thick.

Under hardwoods, southeastern and central United States, sometimes abundant in the soulthern Great Lakes region during wet summer weather.

STIRPS SPONGIOSIPES

1a. Spines up to 11 mm long; context of pileus and spines blue in KOH .... *Hydnellum longidentatum* **Coker**

Fig. 158. *Hydnellum spongiosipes.*

Pileus 6.5-7.5 cm wide, fan-shaped, pinkish white on margin when fresh, staining watery red when rubbed, then buffy pink and finally nearly black in age; taste slight, odor slightly fragrant; spines very close, blackish gray with a tint of purple at first, tips concolorous; spores $3.5\text{-}4 \times 4\text{-}4.8\ \mu$.

In a road on the ground, North Carolina, September.

1b. Not as above 2

2a. Typically under hardwoods; pileus covered by rusty brown velvet or tomentum; stipe near the base with a thick spongy layer concolorous with surface of the pileus. Fig. 158 ....
.... *Hydnellum spongiosipes* (**Pk.**) **Pouzar**

Pileus 2-10 cm broad, convex to nearly plane, rarely depressed, azonate, cinnamon-brown to darker vinaceous-brown; context du-

NON-GILLED FLESHY FUNGI

plex, upper layer thick and spongy, lower layer hard and thin; spines up to 6 mm long, decurrent, pale brown becoming dark brown, darkening when bruised; stipe 3-10 cm long, 5-20 mm thick above, 4-5 cm below, with a hard core in the interior; spores 5.5-7 × 5-6 μ, thick-walled.

Common under oak in the Great Lakes region in the summer and fall, also apparently throughout the eastern states where oak grows.

2b. Not as above 3
3a. Fresh actively growing pileus surface white and usually beaded with red droplets; old pilei dingy brown to dingy dark vinaceous-brown (see *H. scrobiculatum* p. 145 also) 4
3b. Not as above 6
4a. Odor when fresh sweetish pungent ....
....*Hydnellum diabolus* Banker

Pileus 3-11.5 cm broad, surface soft, white, becoming brown and finally black with some whitish or pale areas on the margin; context of pileus thick, soft, zoned vertically with dark and light brown layers when fresh; taste sharply acrid (even when dried); spines short, crowded, light fawn color with pale tips at first, becoming dark brown; stipe 2-4 cm long, 1-3 cm thick, mostly in the duff; spores 4.2-5 × 3.7-4.2 μ, light fawn color to vinaceous buff under the microscope.

In pine needles many of which are incorporated into the fruit body. Eastern North America, September to December.

4b. Not as above 5
5a. Context of pileus dark cinnamon ....
....*Hydnellum pineticola* K. Harrison

Pileus 3-14 cm broad, vinaceous-cinnamon to Mars brown (dark rusty), at times with pinkish droplets in humid weather, finally staining blackish brown after handling, instantly black in KOH; spines up to 9 μ long, tips pale; stipe 2-4 cm long, 1-2 cm thick, bulbous; surface felty from a layer of soft tissue; spores 4.5-6 × 4-5 μ.

Gregarious or concrescent under various pines on sandy plains, or at times in mixed conifers, eastern Canada and northern Michigan.

5b. Context of pileus dingy brown. Fig. 159 ....
Hydnellum peckii Banker
Pileus 2-15 cm broad, whitish pubescent when young, becoming glabrous and brownish gray; stipe 6-8 cm long,

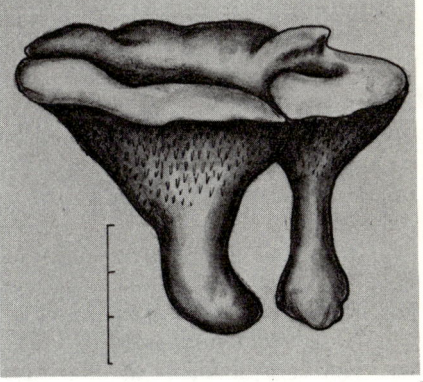

Fig. 159. *Hydnellum peckii*.

1.5-3 cm thick, felty tomentose, tapering to a hard white-mycelioid root; spines gray-brown at base, lighter at the tip, 2 to 3 mm long; spores 4.2-5.5 × 3.8-4.4 μ.

On the ground in woods in the fall, Nova Scotia in Canada, and New York in the United States.

6a. Pileus strigose matted or roughened; stipe exuding a watery yellowish juice when broken ....
....................................*Hydnellum mirabile* (Fr.) **Karsten**

Pileus 3-14 cm broad, brownish white becoming dark brown, margin isabella color (dingy yellowish), darkening where bruised and exuding a coffee-colored juice when young; context dull brown staining darker, enclosing quantities of twigs and debris, taste slightly acrid, odor faint; stipe 1-5 cm long, 1-2.5 cm thick, tapering downward, lighter than the pileus under the dark brown tomentum; spines up to 6 mm long, light brown becoming dark brown with light tips; spores 5-7 × 4.5-6 μ.

Solitary to gregarious in mixed conifers and hardwoods, eastern Canada, and the Pacific Northwest.

6b. Not as above 7
7a. Context when fresh soft as in *Hydnum* but becoming rather hard when dry ....*Hydnellum piperatum* **Coker**

Pileus up to 10 cm broad, irregular with radiating ridges and channels, light snuff brown with lighter zones toward the margin, in age blackish brown to black, margin whitish; context thin; spines crowded, 1.5-2 mm long, whitish at tips until maturity then brownish over all; stipe 3-4 cm long, 8-10 mm thick above, enlarged below; spores 4.2-5.5 (6) × 4.4-5 μ.

On the ground in hardwoods, eastern North America and Great Lakes region, after wet weather in late summer and fall. The name *H. humidum* has also been applied to this species.

7b. Not as above 8
8a. Consistency juicy when fresh, often staining the fingers as a result of handling the fruit bodies ....
....*Hydnellum subsuccosum* **K. Harrison**

Pileus 4-8 cm broad, surface very rough with radial ridges and tufts, margin ridged and irregular, walnut brown (vinaceous-brown); context thick; spines up to 3 mm long, fine, colored like the pileus or redder; stipe 2-3 cm long, 1-2 cm thick, hard, irregular, dark vinaceous-brown, base radicating and blackish at the tip; spores 4.5-5 × 3.5-4.5 μ.

Gregarious to confluent under conifers in the Pacific Northwest.

8b. Not as above 9
9a. Fruit body a shelving mass of pilei from a single stipe (see *H. scrobiculatum* also p. 145) 10
9b. Not conspicuously as above but small pileoli may develop on the main pileus to some extent 12

NON-GILLED FLESHY FUNGI

10a. Pilei gray to mouse brown ....
....*Hydnellum frondosum* K. Harrison

Individual pilei 1.8-4 cm broad, the mass up to 14 cm across, context colored as the surface of the pileus, darker brown in the stipe, spines up to 1 mm long, brownish white becoming deep brown with lighter tips; stipe up to 3.5 cm long, tapering below to a thick rooting base, dark brown and blackening in the soil; spores 3.5-4.5 × 3-4 μ.

Near pine and hemlock in mixed woods, Nova Scotia, Canada.

10b. Not as above 11

11a. Context hard, brick red to almost black ....
....*Hydnellum cumulatum* K. Harrison

Individual pilei up to 9 cm broad, avellaneous to burnt umber or almost black when wet; spines fine, short; stipe 2-4 cm long, up to 1 cm thick; spores 4-5.5 × 4-5 μ, subglobose.

Solitary to gregarious in masses under pine and hemlock in Nova Scotia, Canada. Often it remains partly hidden in the duff.

11b. Context soft and fibrous, pale brown ....
....*Hydnellum multiceps* K. Harrison

Masses of fused stipes and overlapping pilei up to 30 cm across and 8 cm high, single pilei up to 5 cm broad, rough, pale brown becoming dark brown, margin whitish; spines 2-5 mm long, isabelline becoming dark brown, tips whitish; stipe 2-3 cm long, 4-6 mm thick, wider upward, light brown; spores 3-4.5 × 3-4 μ.

In spruce woods in Nova Scotia, Canada.

12a. Surface irregular to roughened with projections, not conspicuously zonate; context duplex. Fig. 160 ....
....*Hydnellum scrobiculatum* (Fr.) Karst.

Pilei gregarious or confluent, 3-10 cm wide, sometimes with smaller pilei on top, pale salmon buff to dull cinnamon, darker in age and blackish red where rubbed; context zonate, spongy, soft and colored as the surface above, becoming deep reddish brown and harder below, thick in the center, with red juice which may form droplets on the surface; spines 1.5-3 mm long with slender shorter ones intermixed, some sometimes fused; stipe 1-3 cm long, the base tuberous and usually buried; spores 4.8-5.5 × 4-5 μ.

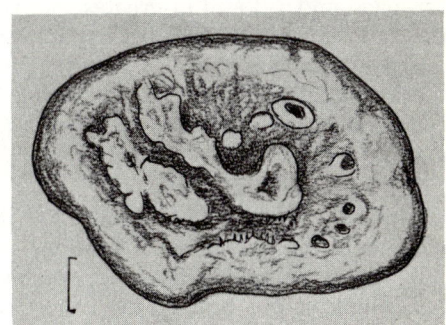

Fig. 160. *Hydnellum scrobiculatum*.

On the ground in damp coniferous or mixed woods, widely distributed in North America. Several varieties are known.

12b. Surface not bumpy or with projections but typically distinctly zonate, often with radiating ridges; context very thin and homogeneous except for a very thin felt layer when young. Fig. 161 ....*Hydnellum zonatum* (Fr.) Karsten

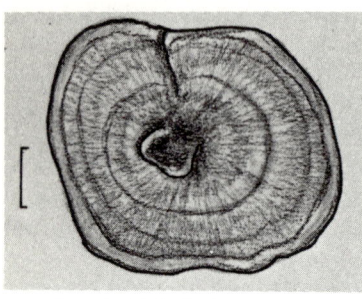

Fig. 161. *Hydnellum zonatum.*

Pilei single or confluent, up to 9.5 cm broad, surface at first dull and thinly felted, later glabrous and almost shiny, margin pale and with a pinkish tint, darkening by distinct zones to the dark vinaceous-brown center; spines 1-2 mm long, pinkish near the edge at first, finally all deeper brown than the pileus; stipe up to 4 cm long, 1.5-8 mm thick, dull, colored like the pileus; spores 4-5 × 3.7-4.2 μ.

Common under hardwoods in North America, summer and fall. Several varieties are known, and it appears to intergrade with *H. scrobiculatum.*

AGARICALES

Boletaceae

Fruit body fleshy and readily decaying; underside of pileus furnished with a layer of tubes with openings (pores, fig. 162, b, c) either small (1-3 per mm) or medium to large, often more or less radially arranged and 1-3 mm in greatest dimension, or larger if compound; the tube layer often readily separating from the cap tissue; stipe central (rarely excentric); spore deposit pale yellow to cinnamon to olive to olive-brown, dark yellow-brown, vinaceous-brown, vinaceous-red, umber, or fuscous; hyphae of the tube trama typically diverging slightly toward the hymenial layer from a thin central strand (fig. 162, f).

Mostly terrestrial fungi fruiting in hot showery weather in the summer or fall, but they can be collected from late spring until late fall. Species of *Suillus,* however, usually fruit during late summer or fall. Many of our best edible fungi are found in this family. One should avoid any with red pores as well as those in stirps *Fraternus* of *Boletus.* The latter have red caps and usually stain blue on the pore surface when bruised. A number of non-poisonous species are inedible because of a disagreeable or bitter taste. Some edible species turn black in cooking, but this in no way effects their edibility. In fact, the color change is in a sense a check on one's identification.

NON-GILLED FLESHY FUNGI

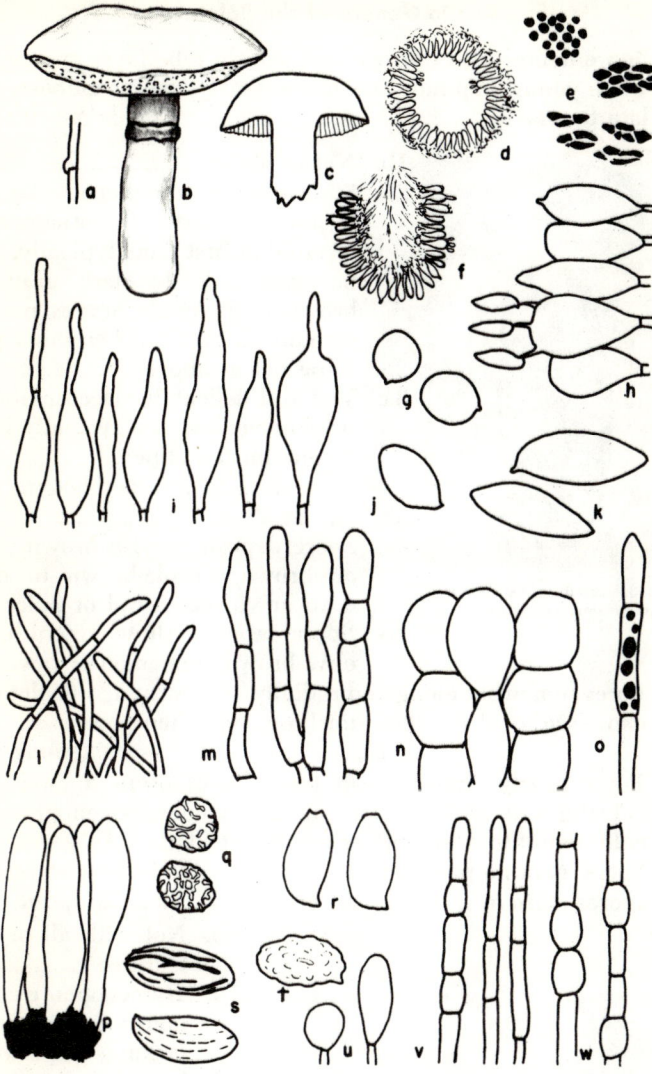

Fig. 162. Characters of Boletaceae: (a) hypha showing clamp connection; (b) fruit body of *Suillus luteus* showing annulus on the stalk; (c) longitudinal section through a fruit body; (d) cross section of a tube showing hymenium; (e) shape of pores (in black), the longest represent the state known as boletinoid; (f) longitudinal section through tube including the edge; (g) spores of *Gyroporus* (ellipsoid) and *Suillus sphaerosporus* (globose); (i) caulocystidia of *Leccinum*; (j and k) spores of *Boletus*; (l) a turf (one type of cuticle of the pileus in Suillus); (m) a true trichodermium (as in *Boletus*); (n) cellular cuticle as in *Leccinum* (some species, and in some *Boletus*); (o) a cuticular hypha from *Leccinum* showing globules (as revived in Melzer's); (p) a cluster of pleurocystidia in *Suillus* as revived in KOH; (q) spores of *Strobilomyces*; (r) spores with a truncate or notched apex (in *Boletus*); (s) spores of *Boletellus*; (t) spore of *Boletus betulae*; (u) inflated end-cells as found on some species of *Leccinum*; (v and w) cuticular hyphae of *Leccinum* showing short scarcely inflated cells, tubular cells, and truly inflated cells.

Key to Genera of the Boletaceae

1a. Spore deposit rusty brown to blackish; tube layer grayish white when young; cap hairy to floccose-scaly; spores globose, reticulate to warty .... *Strobilomyces* p. 254

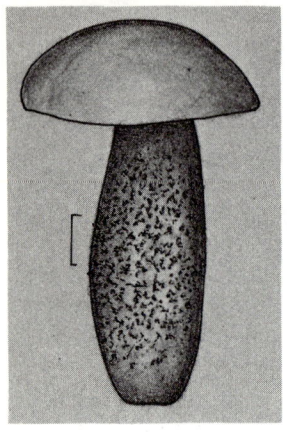

Fig. 163. *Leccinum*, showing punctate-ornamented stipe.

1b. Not as above 2
2a. Stipe scabrous-roughened (fig. 163), to punctate and if the ornamentation is pallid at first then, typically, it soon becomes pale to dark gray, dark brown or blackish; spores not ornamented .... *Leccinum* p. 187
2b. Stipe not as above 3
3a. Veil and delicately floccose-fibrillose, sulphur yellow, and typically leaving a zone on the stipe ....
.... *Pulveroboletus* p. 251
3b. Not as above 4
4a. Spore deposit grayish brown, vinaceous-brown, purple-brown to purple-drab or vinaceous-red or paler 5
4b. Spore deposit yellow, greenish, olive, olive-brown, cinnamon or tawny 6
5a. Pores somewhat elongated radially at least in age (boletinoid); cap viscid or if dry then fibrillose; veil often present ....
.... *Fuscoboletinus* p. 171
5b. Pores nearly circular; cap typically glabrous, unpolished or velvety; veil typically lacking and young hymenophore typically pallid to olive-buff or grayish at first ...... *Tylopilus* p. 177
6a. Spore deposit pale yellow; stipe usually hollow at maturity; spores more or less ellipsoid (fig. 162) .... *Gyroporus* p. 149

Fig. 164. *Boletinellus merulioides*.

6b. Not with all of above features 7
7a. Hymenophore conspicuously boletinoid; veil lacking; stipe usually lateral or excentric; spores broadly elliptic to subglobose. Fig. 164 .... *Boletinellus merulioides* (Schw.) Murrill

Cap 5-12 cm, plane to convex, margin incurved, in age margin spreading and center with a shallow depression, soft pruinose to finely tomentose, typically dry but tacky when wet, olivaceous to yellow-brown or dull brown, staining brown when injured. Context thin, pliant, pale olive-yellow, often bluish green where cut; tubes 3-5 mm deep, decurrent, yellowish to olivaceous; staining olive to reddish brown if injured. Stipe 2-4 cm long, 4-25 mm thick, expanded upward, yellowish above, base often blackish; spores 7-10 × 6-7.5 μ.

Gregarious to scattered under ash trees (*Fraxinus*), often common, eastern North America, summer and fall.

7b. Not as above 8
8a. With at least two of the following features: (1) hymenophore having boletinoid pores; (2) stipe glandular dotted; (3) veil leaving an annulus on the stipe (fig. 169); or adhering to margin; (4) cap viscid to slimy; (5) pleurocystidia in bundles (fig. 162) in part at least; (6) spore deposit pale dingy cinnamon to near clay-color to olive ....*Suillus* p. 151
8b. Not as above 9
9a. Spores with longitudinal wings or folds or striate (fig. 162); stipe lacerate-reticulose, squamulose, scabrous, pruinose, to glabrous ....*Boletellus* p. 252
9b. Spores not ornamented as in above choice (see *Gastroboletus* in the Hymenogastrales p. 304) ....*Boletus* p. 211

GYROPORUS

Spore deposit yellow, spores short ellipsoid, stipe hollow at maturity, and tubes pallid when young characterize the genus.

Key to Species

1a. Context of cap and stipe and the tubes instantly indigo blue when injured. Fig. 165 ......*Gyroporus cyanescens* (Fr.) Quélet

Fig. 165. *Gyroporus cyanescens*.

Cap 4-12 cm broad, convex, surface dry, uneven to pitted; rarely appressed fibrillose, dingy yellowish to cinnamon-buff (pale yellowish crust color); tubes white at first; stipe 4-10 cm long, 1-2.5 cm thick, often with an inconspicuous zone where cap margin made contact with it; spores 8-10 $\times$ 5-6 μ; cap cuticle a collapsing trichodermium, the elements with yellow content in KOH.

Solitary to cespitose, often abundant along sandy roadsides through mixed woods, not uncommon in the Lake States and eastern North America generally; late summer and fall. Edible.

1b. Not staining as in above choice 2
2a. Cap coarsely fibrous to squamulose; ground color dark yellow-brown .... *Gyroporus umbrinisquamosus* Murrill

Cap 5-8 cm broad; tubes white becoming yellowish; stipe concolorous with cap; spores 9.5-16 $\times$ 4.5-7.5 μ, ellipsoid to allantoid.

Known only from Florida, rare.

2b. Not as above 3
3a. Cap pallid to yellowish or pinkish, glabrous to slightly fribillose .... *Gyroporus subalbellus* Murrill

Cap 2.5-10 cm broad, convex; tubes white becoming mustard color; stipe pallid or flushed pink, sometimes spotted olive to umber near base; spores 7.5-13.5 $\times$ 4-5.5 (6) μ.

North Carolina to Florida west to Mississippi; common in some areas, May to October.

3b. Cap more highly or deeply colored 4
4a. Cap bright rich vinaceous-red ....
.... *Gyroporus purpurinus* (Snell) Singer

Cap 1-5 cm convex, dry, subtomentose, uneven; tubes white, slowly becoming yellow; stipe 3-6 cm long, 3-8 mm thick, often slightly browner than cap; spores 8-11 $\times$ 5-6.5 μ.

In open hardwood stands, Great Lakes region southward and eastward; rare; summer and fall.

4b. Cap yellowish-fulvus to tawny to ferruginous to chestnut-color. Fig. 166 ....
.... *Gyroporus castaneus* (Fr.) Quélet

Cap 3-10 cm broad, convex, margin often splitting, surface dry and unpolished; tubes white becoming yellow; stipe colored like cap, glabrous; spores 8-12.5 $\times$ 5-6 μ; clamps present but often rare.

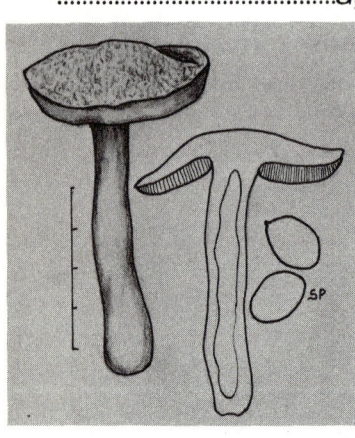

Fig. 166. *Gyroporus castaneus.*

Gregarious to scattered in hardwoods and mixed stands; Great Lakes area and eastward and south to the Gulf; not rare in the summer and fall.

SUILLUS

Key to Sections

1a. Fresh spore deposit an olive-mustard color; spores ± globose *Paraygyrodon*. One species known. Fig. 167 ....
.................................*Suillus sphaerosporus* (Pk.) Smith & Thiers

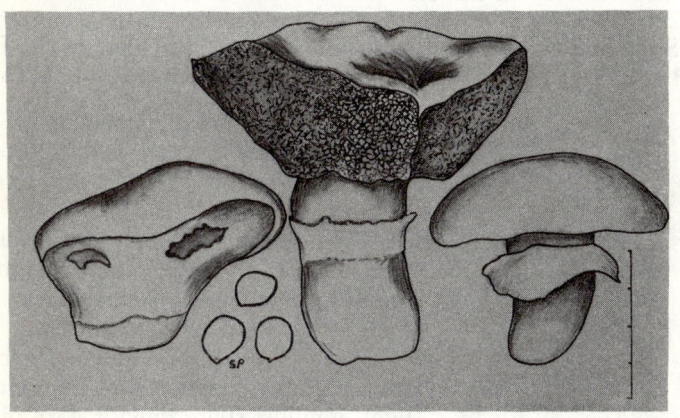

Fig. 167. *Suillus sphaerosporus*.

Cap (4) 8-20 cm, glabrous, slimy, ocher to golden yellow, slowly dull yellow brown to bister. Context up to 2 cm thick, whitish to yellowish but staining brown; tube layer 4-10 mm deep, yellow staining brown; stipe 4-10 cm long, 1-3 cm thick, yellow staining brown; veil a thick tough membrane, outer layer gelatinizing; spores 6-9 × 6-8 μ.

Solitary to gregarious under hardwood, especially oak in the western Great Lakes region, spring, summer and fall. Not recommended for the table.

1b. Spores and spore deposit not as above 2

2a. Annulus typically present; glandular dots lacking on stipe or present only in age and not conspicuous ....*Boletinus* p. 152

2b. Annulus present or lacking, but if present then glandular dots and smears are present on stipe .... *Suillus* p. 159

Section BOLETINUS

Cap typically dry and fibrillose, but all degrees of variation occur from this condition to a glabrous slimy cap; the veil either slimy or floccose but absent in *Suillus castanellus*; the stipe never glandular dotted.

Key to Species

1a. Cap surface dry to moist but not viscid, typically covered by fibrils or fibrillose squamules 2

1b. Cap surface glutinous to viscid, or at least with a layer of gelatinized tissue in the cuticle 9

2a. Stipe hollow in the base; clamps present in hyphae of the fruit body. Fig. 168 .... *Suillus cavipes* (Opat.) Smith & Thiers

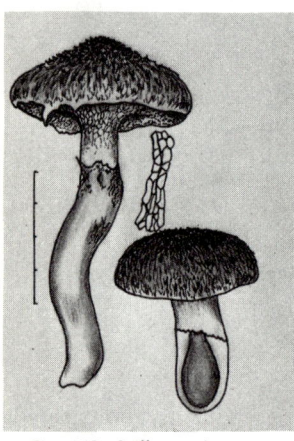

Fig. 168. *Suillus cavipes*.

Cap 3-10 cm broad, cinnamon-rufous, tawny, orange-cinnamon, or dark brown, rarely ocher-yellow or paler, the tips of the fibrils often pallid; context white to yellowish; tubes 3-5 mm deep, yellow, more olivaceous in age; pores angular, simple to compound, elongated radially at maturity; stipe (3) 4-9 cm long, (5) 8-15 (20) mm thick solid in apex, colored like the pileus or paler, typically with a slight annulus; spore deposit dark olive-brown; spores $7{-}10 \times 3.5{-}4\ \mu$; cuticle a turf of colored fibrils.

Scattered to clustered under larch, both eastern and western, common in the fall. Edible.

2b. Stipe typically solid or if hollowed in some specimens then clamp connections lacking or rare on hyphae of fruit body 3

3a. Cap covered with rose-red to brick red fibrils or squamules when young 4

3b. Cap glabrous or if fibrillose the fibrils not rose-red to brick red 6

4a. Stipe 3-5 mm thick; growing in cold northern bogs ....
.... see *Fuscoboletinus paluster* p. 173

4b. Stipe 8-20 mm or more thick 5

5a. Regularly associated with white pine; stipe with dull red fibrils forming a sheath or zones and these fading to gray in age. Fig. 169 .... *Suillus pictus* (Pk.) Smith & Thiers

Cap 3-12 cm broad, never truly viscid but sometimes tacky when wet, red becoming grayish to buff in age, the yellow flesh often showing through especially in age, tips of squamules at times finally gray; context up to 1.5 cm thick, yellow, changing to reddish if injured; tubes yellow, becoming dull ochraceous then brown, about 5 mm deep; pores large and angular, becoming radially extended, changing to reddish or brownish when injured; stipe 4-10 (12) cm long, 8-25 mm thick, with a whitish delicate somewhat fibrillose partial veil, the fibrils of the outer veil reddish; spores clay color in deposit, 8-11 × 3.5-5 μ; pileus cuticle a tangled turf with short cells at the ends of the hyphae.

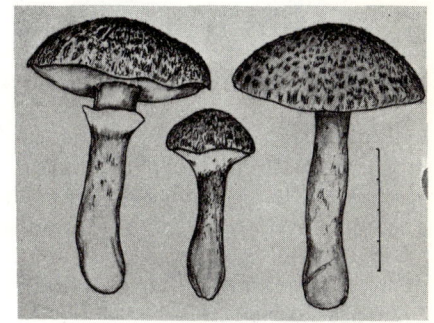

Fig. 169. *Suillus pictus*.

Scattered under eastern white pine, summer and fall. Edible.

5b. Regularly associated with Douglas fir; veil submembranous and pallid to brownish red ....
.... *Suillus lakei* var. *pseudopictus* Smith & Thiers

Cap 3-9 (10) cm broad, tomentose to fibrillose-squamulose, the fibrils brick red to reddish brown, becoming grayish to dingy yellow in age; context often showing between the squamules; tubes bright yellow, typically less than 1 cm deep; pores yellow, staining dingy pinkish brown or darker when bruised, angular, 1mm or more wide; stipe 2-6 (8) cm long, 10-15 (25) mm thick, yellow above the annulus, yellow with red streaks below, base staining greenish when injured, veil dry and thin, usually leaving a thin evanescent ring or the fragments decorating the cap margin; spore deposit olivaceous, drying to dingy cinnamon; spores 7-9 × 3.5-4 μ; cuticle of pileus of fibrils arranged in a turf; large dark laticifers present in the context of the cap.

Gregarious under Douglas fir and other conifers, Pacific Northwest, fall, often common early in the fall season. Edible.

6a. Tubes tawny to vinaceous-red, taste acrid; spores 11-13 × 5-6.5 μ .... see *Boletus piperatus* p. 214
6b. Not as above 7
7a. Cap dark vinaceous-brown; spores 8-11 × 4.5-5.5 μ ....
.... *Suillus castanellus* (Pk.) Smith & Thiers

Cap 3-7 cm broad, densely tomentose to velvety; context about 8 mm thick, white unchanging; tubes about 6 mm deep, pinkish, becoming ochraceous-tawny where bruised; stipe 2-4 cm long, 4-8 mm thick, colored like the pileus or paler, glabrous, or subtomentose at the base; spores $8\text{-}11 \times 4.5\text{-}5.5$ μ; pileus cuticle a tangled turf of thin-walled hyphae which collapse readily.

7b. Not as above 8

8a. Tubes grayish; cap with closely appressed brown to purplish fibrils ....*Suillus solidipes* (Pk.) Smith & Thiers

Cap 5-10 cm broad, squamose with radiately arranged closely appressed hairs, sometimes purplish brown or reddish brown in the center; stipe equal, slightly annulate, grayish above, often stained with darker spots; spore deposit ochraceous; spores 8-10 (12) $\times$ 3.3-4.5 μ; cuticle of cap of parallel appressed strands of pale ochraceous hyphae.

Maine, August, rare.

8b. Tubes greenish yellow; cap with pinkish cinnamon to pale tan fibrils ....*Suillus decipiens* (B. & C.) Kuntze

Cap 4-7 cm, appressed fibrillose; context light yellow, unchanging or becoming slightly testaceous; tubes yellow during all stages, not more than 5 mm long; pores irregular and compound; stipe 4-7 cm long, 0.7-1.5 cm thick, typically clavate and hooked at the base, surface cottony tomentose, yellow; veil peronate and forming a slight gray to whitish annulus; spores $9\text{-}12 \times 3.5\text{-}5$ μ; cystidia $43\text{-}72 \times 10\text{-}13$ μ; cuticle of cap of interwoven hyphae subgelatinous to gelatinous in KOH as revived.

Densely gregarious in humus under pines in mixed pine-oak forests, Gulf Coast region, summer.

A somewhat similar species, *Suillus floridanus*, has smaller spores ($8\text{-}10 \times 3\text{-}4$ μ), and smaller cystidia ($23\text{-}33 \times 7\text{-}10$ μ), as well as oleiferous hyphae in the trama. It is known from Florida.

9a. Pores at maturity typically 1 mm or more in widest diameter 10

9b. Pores typically under 1 mm in widest dimension 14

10a. Cap with agglutinate fibrils or fibrillose squamules 11

10b. Cap glabrous or nearly so, if fibrillose-streaked the fibrils occurring beneath the gluten 12

11a. Stipe staining blue in lower part when cut; cap nearly glabrous, viscid (see S. subvariegatus also p. 159). Fig. 170 ....
.... *Suillus caerulescens* **Smith & Thiers**

Cap 6-14 cm, dull vinaceous or dull yellow on the disc to brighter yellow toward the margin; context pale yellow, unchanging or becoming flushed with pinkish, taste and odor mild or slightly acidulous; tubes 6-10 mm deep, yellow at first, then slightly vinaceous-brown; pores yellow, irregularly angular, sometimes compound; stipe 2.5-8 cm long, 2-3 cm thick, flesh yellow, discoloring vinaceous-brown except at base, colored like the tubes above the annulus; annulus bandlike, fribillose to tomentose, pallid to white but soon discoloring like the cap; spore deposit dingy cinnamon; spores 8-11 × 3-5 µ.

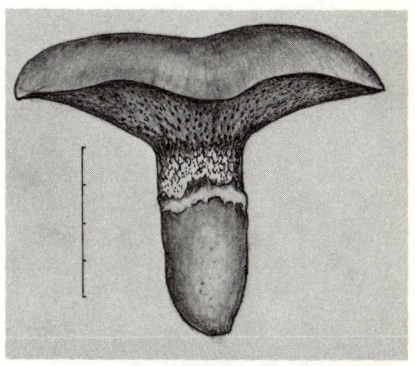

Fig. 170. *Suillus caerulescens*.

Gregarious in humus under mixed conifers but Douglas fir usually present, Pacific Northwest, late summer and fall. It is one of the common species of *Suillus* along the northern coast of California. Probably edible.

11b. Stipe staining merely slightly greenish at base when cut; cap distinctly fibrillose-squamulose with reddish to brown squamules, with a viscid layer beneath the squamules. Fig. 171 ......
.... *Suillus lakei* (Murrill) **Smith & Thiers**

Cap 6-15 (20) cm broad, at first covered with reddish to orange-buff or brownish squamules, becoming glabrous at times, ground color dingy yellowish; tubes 5-10 mm deep, dingy ochraceous young; pores staining brownish when bruised, 1-2.5 mm wide, angular; stipe 6-12 cm long, 1-4 cm thick, yellow above the veil, also yellow below but soon brown from handling; annulus thin, membranous; spore deposit dull cinnamon; spores 8-11 × 3-3.7 µ; cap cuticle a layer of gelatinous hyphae with an outer layer of smooth to in-

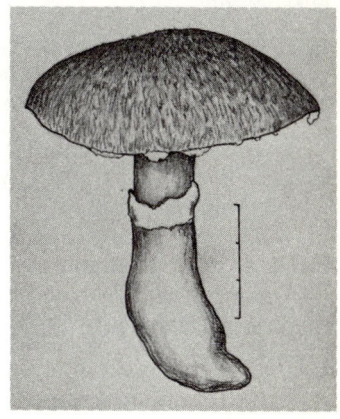

Fig. 171. *Suillus lakei*.

crusted hyphae which stain ochraceous in KOH, scales formed by clusters of semierect hyphal tips.

Scattered to gregarious, associated with Douglas fir, Pacific Northwest and the Rocky Mountains, late summer and fall, often common. Edible.

12a. Cap glabrous and viscid; stipe staining blue in lower half when cut; spores 7-9 × 4-4.5 µ (see S. *ponderosus* also). Fig. 172 ....*Suillus imitatus* Smith & Thiers

Cap 4-12 cm, broadly convex, slimy and glabrous, unicolorous, orange-cinnamon to cinnamon, becoming dingy; context pale yellow, slowly dingy where exposed, odor acidulous, taste mild; tubes 7-12 mm deep, yellowish, staining dull reddish brown on the angular or irregular pores; pores 2-3 × 1.5-2 mm; stipe 3.5-6 cm long, 1.5-2.4 cm thick, context rather bright yellow, becoming bright blue in basal part only, elsewhere discoloring like the context of the cap, somewhat fibrillose and ridged below the annulus, yellow above, pallid below, mottled and discoloring over all; annulus bandlike, well to weakly developed; pleuro- and cheilocystidia both present; cuticle of cap of repent gelatinous narrow hyphae.

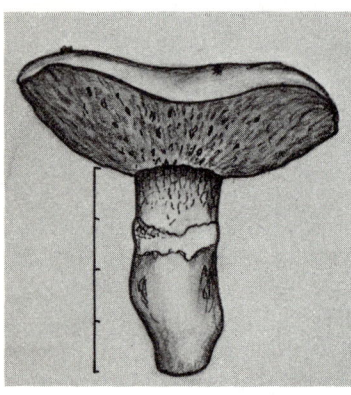

Fig. 172. *Suillus imitatus*.

Gregarious on humus and mosses under mixed conifers, Pacific Northwest, October, often under second growth Douglas fir. Probably edible.

12b. Not as above 13
13a. Cap 10-20 cm broad, ocher-yellow; annulus lacking ....
 ....*Suillus appendiculatus* (Pk.) Smith & Thiers

Cap margin incurved and appendiculate from remains of a membranous veil; tubes small, yellow; pores angular, staining brown where injured stipe 5-7.5 cm long, 0.8-1.5 cm thick, yellow; pleuro- and cheilocystidia present; pileus cuticle a thick layer of rather twisted gelatinous hyphae.

Under or near fir trees, Pacific Northwest, late fall into the winter; not well-known.

13b. Cap cinnamon or streaked yellow and cinnamon (color variable); annulus present and gelatinous. Fig. 173 ....
 ....*Suillus ponderosus* Smith & Thiers

Cap 9-29 cm, broadly convex, glabrous or with veil remnants near the margin only, viscid; context yellow, unchanging, odor sharply acidulous, taste mild; tubes up to 1.5 cm deep, dull yellow, yellow staining brownish on pores; stipe 9-14 cm long, 3-6 cm thick, pale yellow, spore deposit snuff brown; spores 8-10 (12) × 3.8-5 μ; pleuro- and cheilocystidia present.

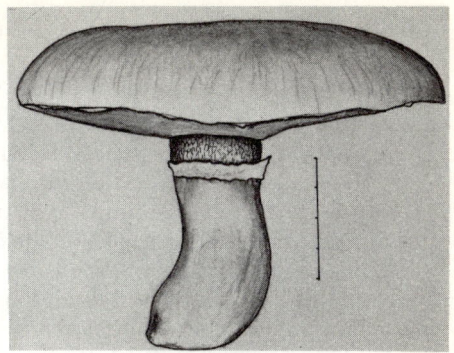

Fig. 173. *Suillus ponderosus*.

Scattered in forests of Douglas fir, hemlock and pine mixed, Pacific Northwest, fall, often abundant. Probably edible.

14a. **Context whitish to yellowish, staining first blue then fuscous, in age lemon yellow throughout, then not bluing readily** ....
....*Suillus lithocarpi-sequoiae* **Singer**

Cap 7-14 cm broad, slimy, soon dry, somewhat rugulose, variegated cinnamon and reddish brown; context soon soft, taste mild, odor agreeable, fruity; tubes yellow, becoming dingy olive-ocher to brown, up to 8 mm deep; stipe 8-11 cm long, 2.2-3.3 cm thick, pallid, yellowish or brownish; annulus becoming appressed to the stipe; spores 7.5-9.8 × 3.2-3.8 μ; pleuro- and cheilocystidia present; cap cuticle thick, slimy, of narrow hyphae.

On the ground in mixed woods of redwood and tan oak, California, winter, rare.

14b. **Not as above** 15
15a. **Cap and veil white, at times spotted with green or yellow-brown** ....*Suillus hololeucus* **Pantidou**

Cap 3-10 cm, very viscid; context white, unchanging; stipe 6-8 cm long, 2 cm thick, white, often spotted below the annulus; annulus flaring, persistent, viscid at the edge; spores (8) 9-10.5 (11) × 3.5-4.5 μ.

In mixed coniferous woods, New York, October, rare.

15b. **Not as above** 16
16a. **Veil grayish** 17
16b. **Veil yellow to yellowish** 18
17a. **Cap grayish, viscid (but not copiously slimy), Florida** ....
....................*Suillus pseudogranulatus* (Murr.) **Smith & Thiers**

Cap 6-11 cm broad, smooth, glabrous or with thin patches of gray veil along the margin; context white, yellowish near the tubes; tubes

4-6 mm deep, bright yellow; stipe 3-6 cm long, 2.5-4 cm thick, white becoming bright yellow, glabrous or with small blackish dots or sometimes reticulate; spores 7-9.5 (11) $\times$ 2.7-3.3 μ.

In hammocks near pine, Florida, October to April.

17b. **Cap clay color to yellow-brown, slimy when fresh, western U. S.** ....*Suillus pseudobrevipes* **Smith & Thiers**

Cap 6-11 (14) cm, glabrous or at times with patches of veil near the margin, fibrillose-streaked; context white or pale yellow; taste mild to acidulous, odor fungoid; tubes 6-10 mm deep, dingy yellow, becoming dull ocher; stipe 2-8 cm long, 1-3 cm thick, white becoming yellowish; annulus often merely a fribrillose zone; spore deposit pale brownish; spores 7-9 $\times$ 2.5-4 μ.

Gregarious to scattered under lodgepole pine, northern Rocky Mountains, summer. Probably edible.

18a. **Spore deposit chestnut brown moist; spores 4-4.5 μ wide. Fig. 174** .... *Suillus proximus* **Smith & Thiers**

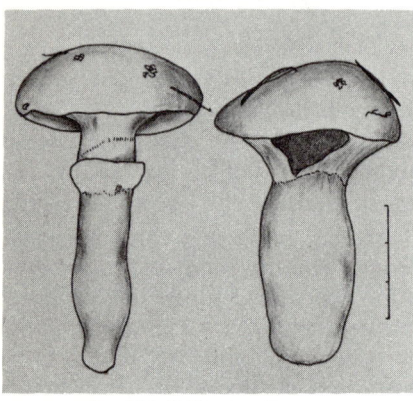

Fig. 174. *Suillus proximus.*

Cap 6-9 cm, slimy, glabrous, streaked with pinkish cinnamon over a yellow ground color, margin soon watery brownish where bruised; context yellowish, odor acid-metallic, taste mild; tubes 5-6 mm deep, dingy yellowish; pores staining pale cinnamon brownish where bruised; stipe 8-9 cm long, 1-1.5 cm thick, canary yellow above, staining green in lower part when cut, surface often vinaceous-cinnamon below; annulus with a gelatinous margin; spores 7-10 $\times$ 4-4.5 μ; cuticle of cap a thick layer of interwoven gelatinous hyphae.

Gregarious in swamps under cedar with larch in the vicinity, Great Lakes region, fall. Not recommended.

18b. **Spore deposit olive-brown when moist; spores 2.8-3.5 μ wide. Fig. 175** ....
..........*Suillus grevillei* **(Klotzsch) Singer**

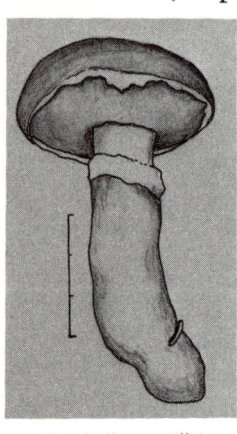

Fig. 175. *Suillus grevillei.*

Cap 5-15 cm, glabrous, slimy, bay-red to yellow-brown on the disc, yellow on margin or bright yellow overall; context yellow, soon becoming reddish, taste slightly bitterish, odor not distinctive; tubes 10-15 mm deep, yellow becoming olive-ocher; stipe 4-10 cm long, 1-3 cm thick, yellow at first, soon with chestnut variegations; annulus gelatinous on the outside, inner side floccose; spores 8-10 × 2.8-3.4 μ.

Cespitose to gregarious, often in arcs and always associated with larch, common in the fall where larch grows.

Section SUILLUS

Stipe glandular dotted or if not then no veil, is present; spore print usually dull cinnamon when air dried, in some olive to olive-brown moist; cuticle of cap gelatinous; clamps absent to rare; veil present or absent.

Key to Species

1a. Injured places on fruit body turning blue 2
1b. Not changing color as in above choice 4
2a. Spores 9-14 × 3.5-5 μ; stipe fibrillose to squamulose ....
................................*Suillus subvariegatus* Snell & Dick

Cap 5-12 cm, dry to subviscid, slimy in wet weather, covered with hairy squamules that may be evanescent, yellowish gray to pale orange becoming brownish or orange, at times tinged with olive, scales darker than ground color; context yellowish to pale orange, changing to blue when injured; tubes pale yellow or orange at times bluish when injured; pores angular; stipe pallid to pale or bright yellow, at times reddish.

Under white pine and oaks; Massachusetts, rare.

2b. Spores 7-10 μ long; stipe glandular dotted 3
3a. Cap yellow to orange-buff with patches of gray-brown to reddish tomentum or squamules over surface. Fig. 176 ....
........................*Suillus tomentosus* (Kauff.) Singer, Snell & Dick

Cap 5-15 cm, becoming glabrescent; context pallid to yellow, changing to blue when injured; tubes 1-2 cm deep, pale dingy yellow becoming olive-yellow; pores dingy brown, slowly yellow, about 2 per mm; stipe (3) 5-10 (15) cm long, 1-3 cm thick, concolor with cap or more orange; spores 7-10 (12) × 3-4 (5) μ.

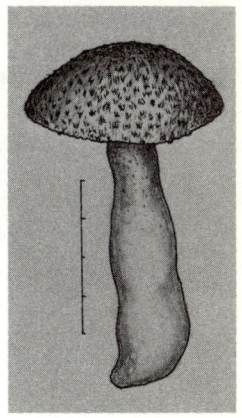

Fig. 176. *Suillus tomentosus*.

Scattered to gregarious under 2-needle pines along the Pacific Coast, in the Rocky Mountains in north central U. S. and southern Canada, common west of the Great Plains, summer and fall. Not recommended.

3b. Cap bright red sprinkled with darker spots ....*Suillus ruber* Singer & Sipe

Cap viscid, subfibrillose-warty when dry; context white becoming blue when injured;

tubes greenish yellow when mature, the pores narrow; spores 7.8-9.8 × 2-3.4 μ; stipe yellow, fleshy, context yellow becoming blue when injured.

Under conifers, Pacific Northwest; fall; rare.

4a. Veil or false veil well developed, in young fruit bodies leaving an annular zone or a true annulus on the stipe or the remains adhering to the cap margin as a soft cottony mass of material in the form of submembranous segments or a cottony roll, veil never becoming fused with the stipe tissue 5
4b. Veil absent or very rudimentary as found on immature fruit bodies, never leaving obvious remains 21
5a. Veil or false veil typically adhering to cap margin, rarely leaving any particles of veil tissue on the stipe ....:....6
5b. Typically with a distinct annulus on the stipe 13

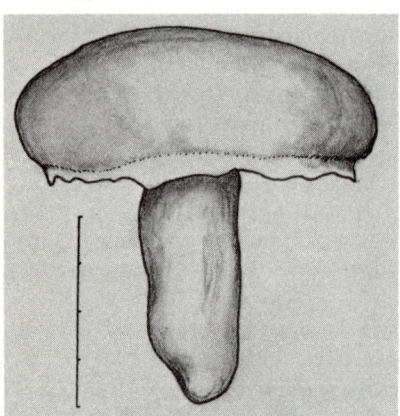

Fig. 177. *Suillus brunnescens*.

6a. Cap white at first but often streaked in age, the slime soon changing to chocolate-brown. Fig. 177 ....*Suillus brunnescens* Smith & Thiers

Cap 5-15 cm; context white when young, finally yellowish; tubes up to 15 mm deep but mostly 10 mm, pale ochraceous; pores 2 per mm; stipe 3-6 (8) cm long, 1-2.5 (3) cm thick, white, base straining vinaceous then brownish; veil thin, membranous, white; spores 6.6-8.8 × 2.3-3.2 μ.

Scattered under sugar pine, fall, southern Oregon.

6b. Not as above 7
7a. Outer layer of veil soon becoming lilac-brown; cap dark brown. Fig. 178 ....*Suillus borealis* Smith Thiers & Miller

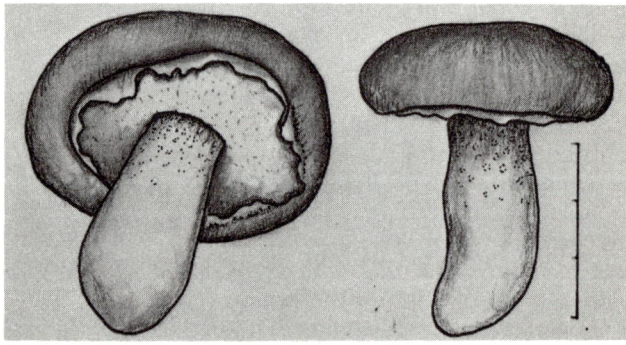

Fig. 178. *Suillus borealis*.

Cap 4-12 cm broad, whitish only before being exposed to light, dark vinaceous-brown to chocolate brown; tubes 4-7 mm deep; pores about 2 per mm, pale dull yellow; stipe 1-5 cm long, 1-3 cm thick, white becoming yellowish and glandular dotted, in age the dots pinkish brown; spores $7\text{-}8 \times 2.8\text{-}3\ \mu$.

Gregarious to subcespitose under western white pine in the northern Rocky Mountains, late fall, common. Edible and *choice*.

7b. Not as above 8
8a. Stipe 3-7 (9) mm thick; cap tubes and stipe ocher-yellow. Fig. 179 .... *Suillus americanus* (Pk.) Snell in Slipp & Snell

Cap 3-10 cm, bright yellow with buff to cinnamon patches of fibrils; context mustard yellow, staining vinaceous-brown when injured; tubes 4-6 mm deep, dull yellow and staining vinaceous-brown where injured; pores 1.5-2 mm wide when mature, drying dark yellow-brown; stipe 3-9 cm long, lemon yellow, glandular dots darkening in age or on handling and the surface vinaceous-brown where handled; spores 8-11 (12) $\times$ 3-4 μ.

Fig. 179. *Suillus americanus*.

Gregarious under eastern white pine (*P. strobus*) in northern and eastern U. S. and southern central and eastern Canada, late summer and early fall, very common. Not recommended.

8b. Not as above 9
9a. Cap spotted or streaked with fibrils when young; stipe often vinaceous in or at the base in age 10
9b. Cap typically glabrous or merely with a few veil remnants along the margin 11
10a. Pores less than 1 mm broad; stipe white at first; tubes unchanging when bruised .... *Suillus glandulosipes* Thiers & Smith

Cap 7-12 cm, pale ochraceous-buff to cinnamon, margin strongly inrolled with a conspicuous white cottony roll when young; context white becoming yellowish in age; tubes up to 1 cm deep, buff to yellowish; stipe 4-11 cm long, 1-2 cm thick, becoming yellowish, often staining dark brown where handled; spores 6-9 (12) $\times$ 3-4 μ.

Gregarious to cespitose in humus under lodgepole pine; California, fall and winter, not common.

10b. Pores 1-2 mm broad; stipe yellow when young; tubes staining vinaceous-cinnamon when bruised. Fig. 180 ....*Suillus sibiricus* (Singer) Singer

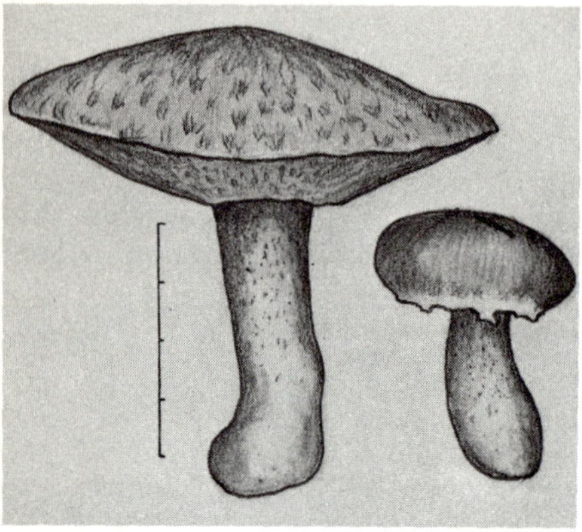

Cap 3-10 cm, ground color chamois to dingy olive-yellow, with brownish patches of veil tissue especially near the margin; context pale olive-yellow, slowly dull cinnamon when cut, taste acidulous; tubes 1-1.5 cm deep, dingy ochraceous; stipe 5-10 cm long, 7-15 mm thick, dingy ochraceous above, sometimes annulate; spores $8-11 \times 3.8-4.2\ \mu$.

Fig. 180. *Suillus sibiricus*.

Gregarious under white pine in the Pacific Northwest, fall, very common in northern Idaho, often mistaken for *S. americanus*. Not recommended.

11a. Cap glabrous at all times (or merely streaked with slime); white becoming olive; odor of fresh specimens pungent; taste subnauseous and weakly acid....*Suillus pungens* Thiers & Smith

Cap 4-14 cm, grayish olive to olive; context white becoming yellowish; tubes up to 1 cm deep, whitish becoming yellowish and having droplets of whitish latex which become ochraceous or brown when dried; stipe 3-7 cm long, 1-2 cm thick, whitish to yellowish like the tubes; spores $9.5-10 \times 2.8-3.5\ \mu$.

Solitary to gregarious in humus under Monterey pine; California, fall and winter. Not recommended.

11b. Cap at first with fibrillose or floccose scales or a cottony roll along the margin; odor and taste not distinctive 12

12a. Cap with a zone of soft cottony whitish to vinaceous-buff material along the margin, in age usually having pallid cottony patches along the margin; stipe white becoming yellowish above and reddish brown below. Fig. 181 ....
....................*Suillus albidipes* (Pk.) Singer

Fig. 181. *Suillus albidipes*.

NON-GILLED FLESHY FUNGI

Cap 4-10 cm broad, pallid, becoming pale ochraceous or vinaceous-cinnamon; context white, slowly becoming yellow; stipe 3-6 cm long, 10-15 mm thick, white, in age with dark dots in lower portion; spores $6.6\text{-}8.8 \times 2.5\text{-}3$ μ.

Scattered in 2- and 5-needle pine forests from New England to the Pacific Coast, often common in pine plantations in the Great Lakes region, late summer and fall. Edible.

12b. Cap at first covered with a white fibrillose veil which leaves squamules or floccose squamules on the cap especially near the margin. Fig. 182 ....
............................*Suillus albivelatus* Smith, Thiers & Miller

Cap 4-12 cm broad, at times with a portion of the margin intergrown with the stipe, pallid at first, becoming vinaceous-brown to dull yellow-brown; context white but soon lemon yellow, staining reddish around worm holes; stipe 1-4 cm long, 1.5-2.5 cm thick; spores $7\text{-}8.5 \times 2.8\text{-}3$ μ.

Gregarious to subcespitose in the white pine areas of the Pacific Northwest; summer and fall, most abouundant in northern Idaho. Edible.

Fig. 182. *Suillus albivelatus*.

13a. Pores more than 1 mm broad in mature fruit bodies 14

13b. Pores less than 1 mm broad in mature fruit bodies 15

14a. Cap olive-buff becoming avellaneous to dingy cinnamon; stipe staining pinkish cinnamon below from bruising ....
............................*Suillus megaporinus* Snell & Dick

Cap 2-7 cm, subviscid, at times with fibrillose scales, the fibrils reddish brown; context pale reddish tan; tubes compound, 1 mm or more, 7-10 mm, bright yellow, becoming rusty, at times nearly lamellate; stipe 8-20 cm long, about 10 mm thick, central or somewhat eccentric, tomentose to hispid, concolorous with cap, annulus flaring, membranous and at times evanescent; spores (5) $7\text{-}10 \times 3.3\text{-}3.8$ μ.

In grass or moss at edge of mountain meadows near lodgepole and fir in California, August and September.

14b. Cap olivaceous to grayish-olive or avellaneous to dingy cinnamon finally; stipe base with rusty orange tomentum at times. Fig. 183 .... *Suillus umbonatus* **Dick & Snell**

Cap 3-5 (9) cm often streaked; context pale yellow, soon dingy cinnamon when cut, odor not distinctive, taste slightly sour; tubes 3-4 mm deep, buff staining sordid pinkish cinnamon when bruised; stipe (2.5) 3-5 (9) cm long, 4-8 (12) mm thick, pallid or yellowish, base sometimes discoloring, gelatinous veil soon dingy cinnamon; spores 7-9 (10) $\times$ 4-4.5 μ.

Gregarious under lodgepole pine, Pacific Northwest and Rocky Mountains, late summer and fall, often common and usually found in large quantities when it fruits. Not recommended.

Fig. 183. *Suillus umbonatus*.

15a. Stipe base conspicuously staining yellow when injured ....
.... *Suillus lutescens* **Smith & Thiers**

Cap 3-6 cm, pale olivaceous to olive-brown, grayer in age; context pallid and slightly yellower when bruised, odor slightly fragrant, taste mild; tubes 5-7 mm deep, pale yellow; pores pale yellow, no color change when bruised; stipe 5-12 cm long, 10-15 mm thick, pallid; annulus thick, readily collapsing; spores 7-10 (11) $\times$ 3-4 μ.

Under conifers in bogs, Michigan, fall. Not recommended.

15b. Not staining as in the above choice 16

16a. Stipe 1-2.5 cm thick; annulus with a thin gelatinous purplish brown layer on the under side which gelatinizes in humid weather. Slippery Jack. Fig. 184 .... *Suillus luteus* (**Fr.**) **S. F. Gray**

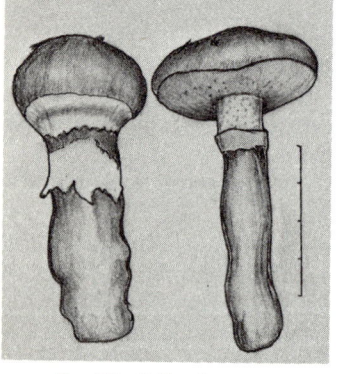

Fig. 184. *Suillus luteus*.

Cap 5-12 cm broad, color variable in the yellow-brown to red-brown series; context white, taste pleasant, odor not distinctive; tubes 3-7 mm deep, whitish to yellow, pores yellow becoming dark-dotted; stipe (3) 4-8 cm long, sheathed with a whitish veil up to the annulus, glandular dotted and pale yellow above the membranous persistent annulus; spores 7-9 $\times$ 2.5-3 μ.

NON-GILLED FLESHY FUNGI

Gregarious under conifers, common in conifer plantations and often associated with scotch pine, Canada and the United States. Edible and choice.

16b. Not as above 17

17a. Annulus in young specimens thick and baggy, flaring away from stipe at lower as well as upper margin before maturity ..18

17b. Annulus not as above or rarely slightly baggy 19

18a. Southern in distribution; stipe with ordinary *Suillus*-type dots and hyaline scales composed of inflated basidium-like bodies; Cap 1.6-4 cm .... *Suillus cothurnatus* **Singer**

Cap ochraceous on margin, pale ochraceous-tawny to clay color on disc, or mottled with these colors; context marbled with buff-colored areas, unchanging, soft and watery; tubes pale yellow; pores pale yellow to somewhat orange; stipe 2.3-4 cm long, 4-7 mm thick, pallid to brownish, becoming darker; veil whitish, becoming grayish, lower edge flaring more than the upper, about as high as broad; spores 7-9.8 × 2.7-3.2 μ.

On naked or mossy ground, mossy trunks, etc. in hammocks, rarely in flatwoods and scrub, near pine, Florida to North Carolina, summer, fall and early winter.

18b. Northern in distribution; stipe with only the ordinary *Suillus*-type dots; cap 3-8 cm. Fig. 185 (see *S. subolivaceus* also p. 166) .... *Suillus subluteus* (Pk.) **Snell in Slipp & Snell**

Cap 3-8 cm, Salmon-buff to pale buff becoming darker dingy yellow-brown context thick at first, pale ochraceous, darkening on standing, taste acid at first but soon fading, odor not distinctive; tubes 6-10 mm, pale olive yellowish young, becoming pale yellow; pores yellowish with brownish spots; stipe 4-7 cm long, 6-12 mm thick, pinkish ochraceous, the dots vinaceous and slowly blackening, annulus baggy and flared at both a lower and upper margin, collapsing in age; spores 7-10 (11) × 2.3-3.3 μ.

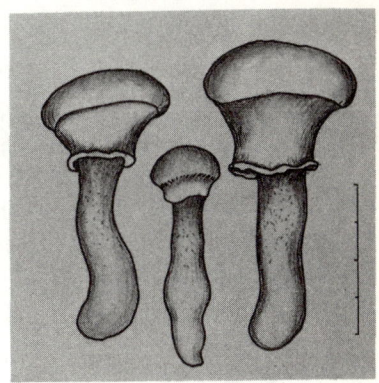

Fig. 185. *Suillus subluteus*.

Gregarious under jack pine, Michigan, New York and New England, late August and September. Not recommended.

19a. Cap bister to olive-brown or olive; tubes olive grayish to grayish buff over pores when young; western in distribution. Fig. 186 .... *Suillus subolivaceus* **Smith & Thiers**

Fig. 186. *Suillus subolivaceus*.

Cap 5-10 cm, streaked, color variable from dark dingy yellow-brown to olive-brown or dingy olive; context up to 1 cm thick, stipe 6-10 cm long, 8-14 mm thick, equal, yellowish above, pallid to brownish below, the pinkish brown dots soon blackening; spores (8) 9-11 × 3-4 μ.

Gregarious under mixed conifers including western white pine and western hemlock, Pacific Northwest, fall. Not recommended.

19b. Not as above 20

20a. Tubes and tube mouths orange-yellow; context of cap orange-buff .... *Suillus pinorigidus* **Snell & Dick**

Very similar to *S. subluteus* but drying blackish. Northeastern United States, fall.

20b. Not as above, the cap white and the taste of slime strongly acid. Fig. 187 .... *Suillus acidus* (**Pk.**) **Singer**

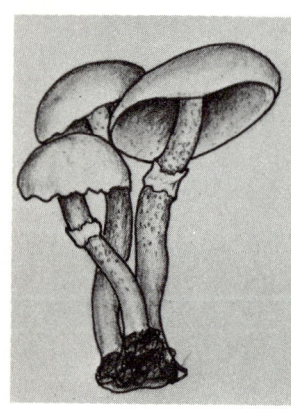

Fig. 187. *Suillus acidus*.

Cap 4-10 cm, yellowish in age; context white at first; tubes 4-6 mm deep in large caps, pallid at first, finally dull yellow; stipe 4-10 cm long, 5-10 mm thick, whitish at first; spores 7-9 × 2.8-3.3 μ.

Gregarious under mixed pines, in the northeastern states and westward to the Great Lakes. Not recommended.

21a. Cap white when young and only slowly becoming yellowish to cinnamon-buff 22

21b. Cap if whitish at first soon more highly colored after exposure to light 24

NON-GILLED FLESHY FUNGI

22a. Stipe surface pure white at first, lemon yellow at apex in age; not granular dotted; pores small (2-3 per mm). Fig. 188
............*Suillus pallidiceps* Smith & Thiers

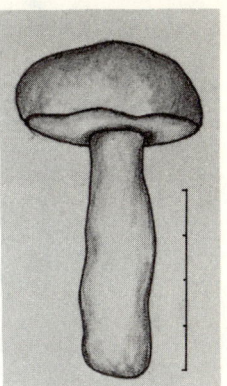

Fig. 188. *Suillus pallidiceps.*

Cap 3-8 cm, slowly becoming pale yellow and finally dull cinnamon-buff, not staining when handled but in contact with waxed paper becoming purplish umber; context white becoming yellow, unchanging when cut; stipe (1) 2-7 cm long, 12-16 mm thick, glabrous; veil absent; spores 8-11 $\times$ 3.5-4.2 μ.

Gregarious under lodgepole pine, northern Rocky Mountains, summer.

22b. Stipe surface distinctly glandular dotted or smeared; pores 1-2 (2.5) mm wide 23

23a. Stipe slender, 4-12 cm long, 5-12 mm thick, usually narrowed toward the base. Fig. 189 ....*Suillus placidus* (Bonorden) Singer

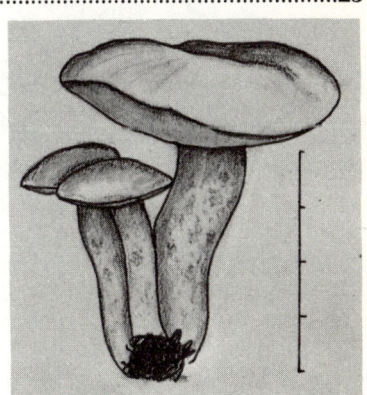

Fig. 189. *Suillus placidus.*

Cap 3-10 cm broad, glabrous and viscid to slimy, white to ivory white at first, becoming yellowish, slime often grayish to blackish in age; tubes pale yellow at maturity, often beaded with pinkish droplets; stipe white on surface, interior yellow; spores 7-9 $\times$ 2.5-3.2 μ.

Scattered to gregarious under eastern white pine from Maine to Tennessee, west to the Great Lakes region and in southern and eastern Canda where white pine grows. Not recommended.

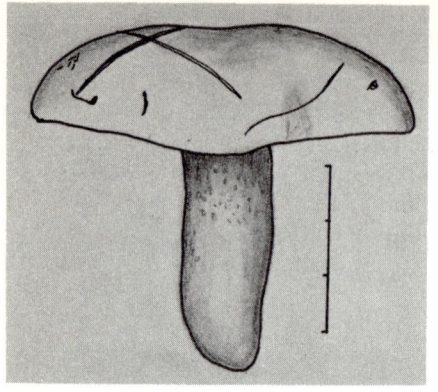

Fig. 190. *Suillus flavogranulatus*.

23b. Stipe stout, 3-5 cm long, 12-18 mm thick, equal or nearly so. Fig. 190 .... *Suillus flavogranulatus* Smith Thiers & Miller

Cap 6-9 cm, pallid beneath the slime, becoming pale yellow to dingy ochraceous; context white except at apex of stipe; stipe white on surface, sulphur yellow within, slowly pinkish brown when cut; spores $7.5\text{-}9 \times 3\text{-}3.2\ \mu$.

Scattered under lodgepole and white pine, northern Rocky Mountains, fall. Edible.

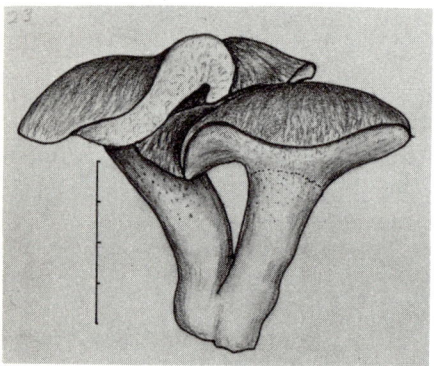

Fig. 191. *Suillus punctatipes*.

24a. Pores 1-3 (4) mm long radially; cap orange-brown or finally violaceous-brown. Fig. 191 .... *Suillus punctatipes* (Snell & Dick) Snell & Dick

Cap 8-20 cm broad, slimy, margin naked; context white at first; tubes up to 1 cm deep, yellow; pores yellow; stipe 6-10 cm long, 1-3 cm thick, white becoming yellow and with large glandular smears often 1 cm or more broad; spores $7.5\text{-}9 \times 3\text{-}3.2\ \mu$.

Common along woods roads through lodgepole and white pine in mixed stands, Pacific Northwest, late fall. Not recommended.

24b. Not as above 25
25a. Stipe not obviously glandular dotted 26
25b. Stipe typically rather obviously glandular dotted 27

26a. Cap having appressed tomentum often in only minute spots or patches and these at times red, the ground color bright yellow. Fig. 192 ......*Suillus subaureus* (Pk.) Snell in Slipp & Snell

Cap 3-12 (17) cm, flesh up to 3 cm thick, yellow when young, changing to tawny when exposed; tubes (3) 4-10 mm deep, ochraceous, unchanging when bruised; pores small but becoming radially elongated, dingy yellow; stipe 4-8 cm long, 1-2.5 cm thick, yellow, brownish where bruised; context yellowish, reddish where cut, white mycelioid at base; spores 7-10 × 2.7-3.5 μ.

Scattered to gregarious under aspen and scrub oak, New England to the Western Great Lakes, summer, common at times. Not recommended because of difficulty of identification.

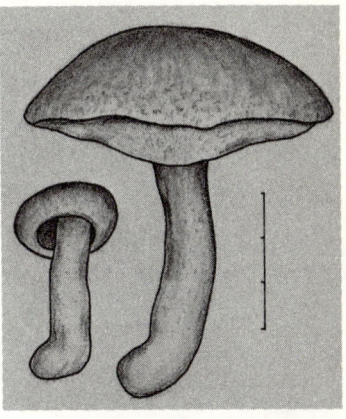

Fig. 192. *Suillus subaureus*.

26b. Cap naked and glutinous, dark vinaceous-brown, slowly becoming pale tan to ochraceous. Fig. 193 ....
......................................*Suillus brevipes* (Pk.) Kuntze

Cap 5-10 cm, margin in buttons faintly white-tomentose but veil lacking and no roll of cottony material present; context white, becoming yellow in age at least in apex of stipe; tubes 4-10 mm deep, dingy yellow becoming darker and more olivaceous; stipe 2-5 cm long, 1-3 cm thick, white becoming yellowish; spores 7-9 (10) × 2.8-3.3 μ.

Scattered to cespitose under 2- and 3-needle pines throughout the range of these species in North America, summer and fall, or even in winter during warm weather. Edible.

Fig. 193. *Suillus brevipes*.

27a. Taste unpleasant; stipe typically 2 mm thick..........................
......................................*Suillus acerbus* Thiers & Smith

Cap 8-13.6 cm, glabrous but often streaked with slime, tawny, hazel, or reddish cinnamon, occasionally grayish, often more yellow toward the margin; context 1.5-2.5 cm thick, staining yellow in irregular areas; tubes 5-10 mm long, white to buff, becoming yellow, unchanging when bruised; pores yellow; stipe 4-10 cm long, white to ivory, changing in age or when handled to pale yellow, the context white at first, glandular dots soon brown; spores $9.3\text{-}12 \times 3.3\text{-}4\ \mu$.

Scattered to cespitose in humus under pines, California.

27b. Taste pleasant; stipe 8-15 (20) mm thick 28

28a. Cap pallid at first, soon becoming vinaceous-cinnamon to dark orange-cinnamon, often obscurely mottled. Fig. 194 ....
.... *Suillus granulatus* (Fr.) Kuntze

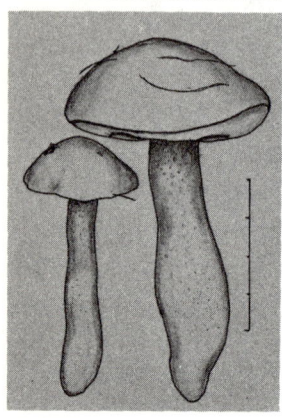

Fig. 194. *Suillus granulatus*.

Cap 5-15 cm broad, pale at first, cinnamon in age, often streaked or sometimes areolate; context whitish but soon pale yellow then dingy yellow; pores yellowish becoming brownish spotted, when very young often with droplets of a cloudy liquid on them; stipe 4-8 cm long, 1-2 (2.5) cm thick, whitish but soon bright yellow above, base becoming dingy cinnamon, glandular dots becoming pinkish tan to brown; spores 7-9 (10) $\times$ 2.5-3.5 μ.

Scattered to gregarious under pine, widespread throughout the United States and Canada during summer and fall but mostly in September. Edible.

28b. Not as above 29

29a. Cap very soon glabrous; stipe at first distinctly brown from numerous glandular dots and smears. Fig. 195 ....
.... *Suillus punctipes* (Pk.) Singer

Fig. 195. *Suillus punctipes*.

Cap 3-10 cm broad, with tufts of tomentum when very young, soon glabrous, dull ochraceous; context thick and soft, pallid yellow; tubes 4-6 mm deep, dull brownish becoming olivaceous to yellow, pores dark dingy brown becoming dingy yellow; stipe 4-9 cm long, 10-14 mm thick at apex, bright yellow ground color showing at maturity, when handled the fingers becoming stained sordid brown.

Scattered under spruce and balsam in bogs or low wet ground, New England to Michigan south to North Carolina, late summer and early fall.

29b. Not as above 30

30a. Cap surface long remaining spotted with appressed fibrillose squamules; glandular dots on stipe yellow at first. Fig. 196 ....
....*Suillus hirtellus* (Pk.) Kuntze

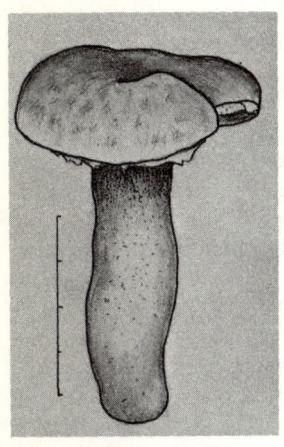

Fig. 196. *Suillus hirtellus*.

Cap 5-15 cm, squamules grayish or often reddish, ground color bright yellow tending to stain vinaceous-brown from handling, glabrous in age; context pale yellow, odor mild; tubes 3-8 mm deep, pale yellow to ochraceous; pores pale yellow when young, orange-buff when mature, staining slightly vinaceous-brown where bruised; stipe 3-8 cm long, 1-2 cm thick, pale yellow (even the dots yellow at first), the dots blackening in age, base tapered to a point; spores 7-9 $\times$ 3-3.5 μ.

Gregarious under pines and aspen, Great Lakes region, summer and fall. Not recommended.

Var. *thermophilus* (Singer) Smith & Thiers has red glandular dots when mature, and var. *cheimonophilus* (Singer) has spores 8-13.5 $\times$ 3-3.3 μ. These two are southern in distribution.

30b. As above but tubes only 2-3 mm deep; stipe purplish red at base ....*Suillus flavoluteus* (Snell in Snell & Dick) Snell & Dick

Pileus 5-7 cm, fibrillose-squamulose, dull yellow to golden, squamules brownish (a few reddish); context yellow, odor sweetish; pores $\pm$ large, boletinoid; stipe 4-5 cm long, 15-20 mm thick, golden yellow, touched with vermillion in places, purplish red at base, greenish at apex; spores 7-9 $\times$ 2.5-3 μ; pleurocystidia clustered.

Solitary under mixed hardwood and hemlock, New York.

FUSCOBOLETINUS

Cap viscid to slimy and glabrous to squamulose or dry and fibrillose to squamulose; tubes separable from the pileus when fresh; pores usually large, angular and radially elongated; stipe usually not glandular dotted, often annulate, viscid or dry; spore deposit purple, dark vinaceous-drab, vinaceous-brown, chocolate-color to chocolate-gray; spores often dextrinoid; pleurocystidia ususally in clusters and with brown incrusting material near the base as revived in KOH, content often vinaceous in KOH, on fresh material. Growing under conifers, especially larch in the fall.

Key to Sections

1a. Cap dry and fibrillose at maturity ....Sect. *Palustres* p. 172
1b. Cap viscid from a gelatinous cutis after veil remnants disappear 2
2a. Tubes yellow and stipe not glandular dotted ....Sect. *Fuscoboletinus* p. 173
2b. Tubes whitish to grayish, or finally yellowish if stipe is glandular dotted 3
3a. Tubes pallid to grayish or grayish olivaceous in age, stipe not noticeably glandular dotted ....Sect. *Grisellii* p. 175
3b. Tubes finally yellowish; stipe distinctly glandular dotted ....Sect. *Pseudosuillus* p. 176

Section PALUSTRES

Cap dry and fibrillose to squamulose; hymenophore yellow, boletinoid to sublamellate.

Key to Species

1a. Cap whitish from fibrils or squamules at first, slowly becoming bright rose red. Fig. 197 ....
......*Fuscoboletinus ochraceoroseus* (Snell) Pomerleau & Smith

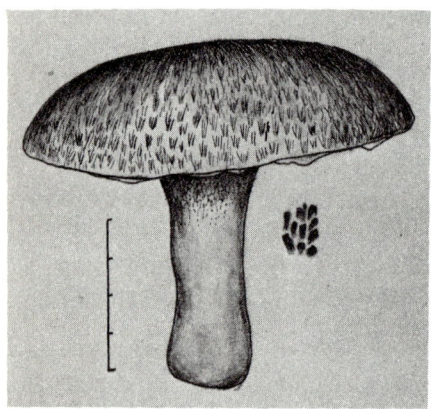

Fig. 197. *Fuscoboletinus ochraceoroseus.*

Cap 8-20 cm, convex to slightly umbonate; context thick, bright yellow with a pinkish zone near the cuticle, unchanging or becoming slightly greenish blue when injured, odor acidulous, taste slightly acrid (bitter when cooked); tube layer about 5 mm deep, straw yellow or brighter, finally brownish; stipe 3-10 cm long, 1-3 cm thick, typically slightly reticulate above, somewhat fibrillose below the annulus, yellow within; annulus whitish and evanescent; spores $7\text{-}9.5 \times 2.4\text{-}3.2 \mu$, subcylindric to somewhat ventricose; pileus cuticle of compactly interwoven hyphae with dissolved red pigment which breaks down readily in KOH.

Scattered to gregarious under larch in the Pacific Northwest, late spring to fall; common where western larch is present, especially along roadsides. Not recommended, it is bitter when cooked.

1b. Cap covered by deep red fibrils when young; stipe typically under 1 cm thick. Fig. 198 ....
....*Fuscoboletinus paluster* (Pk.) **Pomerleau**

Fig. 198. *Fuscoboletinus paluster*.

Cap 2-6 cm, typically expanded-umbonate; context yellowish to deep yellow, unchanging when injured; odor and taste typically farinaceous; tubes with large angular pores radially enlarged or hymenophore almost gill-like but with cross-veins, decurrent, yellow; stipe 3-6 cm long, 3-8 mm thick, apex typically reticulate, with a reddish veil-line and somewhat red-fibrillose below this, yellow within; spores pinkish brown in deposit, 7-9 × 3-3.5 μ; pleurocystidia 50-70 × 9-12 μ, not incrusted; clamp connections present.

Scattered to gregarious in cold northern bogs, cedar swamps, etc., often on very decayed conifer logs; northern Great Lakes area eastward to the Atlantic in Canada and the United States, generally rare.

Section FUSCOBOLETINUS
Key to Species

1a. Cap red to ferruginous or chestnut beneath the fibrils (if some are present); context yellow 2
1b. Cap gray to olivaceous-brown; context whitish, see old specimens of sect. ....*Grisellii*
2a. Cap at first coated with coarse floccose patches of grayish veil remnants, becoming red in age as the scales collapse. Fig. 199 ....*Fuscoboletinus spectabilis* (Pk.) **Pomerleau & Smith**

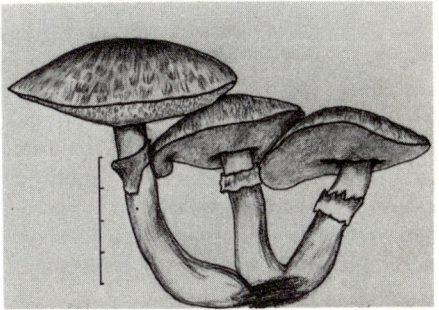

Fig. 199. *Fuscoboletinus spectabilis*.

Cap 4-10 cm, convex to plane; context slowly pinkish brown when exposed; odor slightly disagreeable or aromatic, taste astringent; tube layer 6-12 mm deep, pale yellow, typically changing to pink if injured and finally yellowish brown, tubes with pores radiating somewhat and often compound; stipe 4-10 cm long, 1-1.5 cm thick, yellow above the annulus, having red fibrils below; annulus with a gelatinous outer layer, becoming dark red upon collapsing on stipe; spores 9-13 (15) × 5-6 μ, dextrinoid; pleurocystidia 40-80 × 6-9 μ, nearly cylindric, reddish brown in Melzer's, KOH on flesh dark green.

Solitary to scattered under larch, northern and northeastern United States and in Canada, early fall, common some seasons. Edible.

2b. Cap lacking coarse scales (observe young specimens) 3

3a. Cap slimy, chestnut-brown; tubes pale bright yellow when young; annulus and stipe below it slimy. Fig. 200 ....
...............*Fuscoboletinus glandulosus* (Pk.) **Pomerleau & Smith**

Fig. 200. *Fuscoboletinus glandulosus*.

Cap 3-13 cm, typically covered by a thick slimy layer in wet weather, red when young, becoming chestnut brown or paler and brighter orange, or ochraceous ground color evident, blackish from drying gluten in age; context about 1 cm deep, reddish around the worm holes, taste mild, odor mild to slightly pungent; tubes brilliant yellow becoming olivaceous, pores yellow and angular, up to 2 mm in longest dimension; stipe 4-8 cm long, 8-15 mm thick, yellow above annulus, becoming various shades of red below, base yellow; annulus gelatinous, deep red becoming darker; spore deposit dull purple-drab (grayish lilac); spores 7.5-11.5 × 3.5-5 μ, yellowish in Melzer's; pleurocystidia 40-60 × 3-4 μ.

Gregarious under conifers, mostly firs and arbor vitae; northeastern North America to the western Great Lakes region; August and September, sometimes common in eastern Canada.

3b. Cap red to bay-brown, annulus and stipe dry, veil floccose ....
.....................*Fuscoboletinus sinuspaulianus* **Pomerleau & Smith**

Cap 3-13 cm, obviously innately fibrillose to glabrous; context soft, yellow to orange-buff, odor when crushed slightly farinaceous; tube layer about 1 cm deep, dull yellowish brown when young, pores angular, typically compound, at times with bay-red spots; stipe 4-14 cm long, 1-3 cm thick, dull yellowish brown above the annulus and grayish or reddish below; annulus dry and floccose, yellow within; spores chocolate brown in deposit, 8-10 (13) × 4-4.5 μ; pleurocystidia 40-60 × 4-6 μ, subcylindric to fusoid-ventricose; clamp connections none.

Solitary to gregarious under conifers (pine, fir, and spruce); so far known only from Canada, fruiting in late summer and fall.

Section GRISELLII

Hymenophore whitish to gray and not becoming truly yellow at any stage of development, usually grayish brown at maturity.

Key to Species

1a. Cap viscid to slimy-viscid; tubes white at first; pores small and round but finally elongating radially somewhat; context typically bluish green where bruised. Fig. 201 *Fuscoboletinus aeruginascens* (Sec.) Pomerleau & Smith

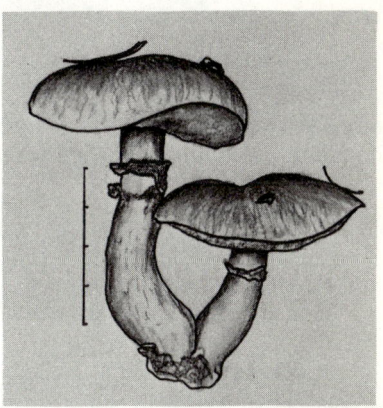

Fig. 201. *Fuscoboletinus aeruginascens*.

Cap 3-12 cm, broad, glabrous, smoky gray to olivaceous or olive brownish, finally with fuscous spots in age; context white to yellowish; taste and odor not distinctive; tube layer 6-9 mm, deep, pores 1-2 (3) mm wide; stipe 4-10 cm long, 8-12 mm thick, typically somewhat reticulate above, pallid, to pale olive above the annulus, somewhat viscid below, grayish to olive grayish below the annulus; spore deposit dingy vinaceous-brown; spores 8-12 (14) × 3.5-5 μ.

Scattered to gregarious under larch, northern United States and in Canada, late summer and fall, common. Edible. *F. serotinus* (Frost) Sm. & Thiers has a slimy-viscid chocolate brown cap and also grows under larch in eastern North America.

1b. Cap only slightly viscid; tubes or flesh very rarely changing to bluish if injured, pores greatly elongated radially near the stipe (almost lamellate); cap typically with a conic umbo. Fig. 202 .... *Fuscoboletinus grisellus* (Pk.) **Pomerleau & Smith**

Cap 3-8 cm, appressed fibrillose to subsquamulose, pale dull olive to grayish or tinted yellowish; context white to faintly olivaceous; tubes 3-6 mm deep; stipe 2-4 (6) cm long, 5-15 mm thick, whitish, veil submembranous, seldom leaving a distinct annulus; spore deposit wood-brown (chocolate-gray); spores 8-11.5 × 4.3-5 μ; pleurocystidia 40-60 × 5-7 μ, subcylindric.

Fig. 202. *Fuscoboletinus grisellus*.

Densely cespitose to gregarious near larch around hummocks (often on their sides), northeastern North America west to the Great Lakes wherever the eastern larch grows; usually fruiting during late summer and early fall, not common but abundant when found.

Section PSEUDOSUILLUS

Only a single species is known ....
..................................*Fuscoboletinus weaverae* **Smith & Shaffer**

Cap 3.5-7 cm, viscid, glabrous, grayish pink becoming pinkish cinnamon to vinaceous-brown; context about 1 cm thick, pallid but yellow around worm holes, unchanging, odor and taste mild; tubes white at first; pores angular but not radially elongated, yellowish young, unchanging when injured, developing vinaceous-brown glandular dots; stipe 4-10 cm long, 9-15 mm thick above, usually tapered downward, vinaceous-brown from a coating of glandular dots, at times staining yellow where bruised; veil fibrillose to cottony, white to yellow, sheathing lower part of the stipe, not leaving an annulus; spore deposit vinaceous-brown to purplish brown; spores 6.5-8 × 2.7-3.2 μ; pleurocystidia 20-60 × 3.3-9.6 μ; cap cuticle a thick gelatinous layer.

Scattered to cespitose in sandy soil of woods of oak, pine, aspen and birch mixed, Minnesota, fall, rare.

TYLOPILUS

Spore deposit vinaceous, vinaceous-brown, rusty ferruginous, or chocolate brown to purplish brown; veil absent in American species; tubes white to pallid and occasionally pale dingy yellow when young; content of pleurocystidia often strongly dextrinoid; clamps absent.

Key to Species

1a. Stipe scabrous with pinkish to pallid ornamentation, bright yellow inside and out at the base. Fig. 203 ....
..............................*Tylopilus chromapes* (Frost) Smith & Thiers
Cap (3) 5-11 (15) cm broad, dry, pink to old rose becoming pallid leather color; tubes white or pallid becoming yellowish and finally dull pinkish gray; pores 2-3 per mm; stipe 4-13 (17) cm long, 1-2.5 cm thick deep chrome yellow below, paler to pink above at first, ornamentation pinkish becoming pallid; spores 11-16.8 × 4-5.5 μ; cuticle of pileus a tangled turf of narrow (4-7 μ) hyphae yellow in KOH.

Fig. 203. *Tylopilus chromapes*.

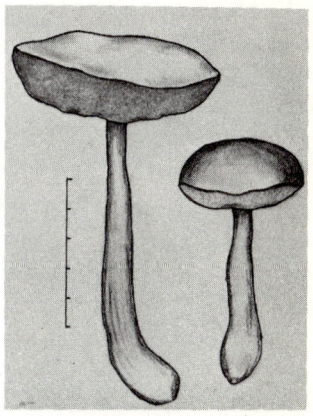

Fig. 204. *Tylopilus gracilis*.

Solitary to scattered in deciduous woods, mixed woods or conifer woods in eastern North America to the Great Lakes region, spring and summer, common at times.

1b. Not as above 2
2a. Stipe slender and pale tawny to cinnamon; many spores in a mount appearing punctate under an oil-immersion lens. Fig. 204 ....*Tylopilus gracilis* (Peck) Hennings
Cap (3) 4-8 (10) cm broad, becoming areolate, tawny-brown to cinnamon or dull yellow, usually evenly colored; context unchanging when cut; tubes longer than the context is deep, depressed around the stipe, white becoming flesh-colored; pores small, pallid

at first; stipe 6-15 cm long, 4-8 (10) mm thick near apex, often curved, base whitish, often longitudinally striate; spores 9-16 × 5-8 μ.

Typically under hemlock in the eastern states west to the Great Lakes and southward in the mountains, solitary to scattered, not common.

2b. Not as above 3

3a. Cap at first dark sooty, brown, drab, fuscous, dark coffee color to olive-brown; spores pale to dark chocolate-color in deposit 4

3b. Cap not colored as above or if so then the spore deposit pinkish to vinaceous 12

4a. Pores coffee brown on young fruit bodies 5

4b. Pores grayish to whitish when young 6

5a. Stipe pruinose but not reticulate. Fig. 205 ....
.... *Tylopilus pseudoscaber* (Secr.) Smith & Thiers

Fig. 205. *Tylopilus pseudoscaber*.

Cap 5.5-15 cm broad, subtomentose, finally unpolished, at times slightly areolate, olive-brown to dark earth brown; context white, turning bright blue then reddish brown and finally dull brown when cut, staining paper blue-green; odor pungent; taste mild; stipe 4-10 (12) cm long, 1-3 cm thick, equal to clavate, colored as the pileus; spores (12) 14-18 × 6-8 μ; pleurocystidia 50-70 × 10-16 μ, clavate-mucronate to fusoid-ventricose; cheilocystidia similar or broader; cuticle of pileus a trichodermium of hyphae 7-9 μ wide.

Scattered to gregarious along roads and in open woods of mixed conifers and hardwoods, most abundant in the Pacific Northwest in the fall but known from the western Great Lakes area and eastern North America also.

5b. Stipe reticulate at least over apical third ....
.... *Tylopilus olivaceobrunneus* (Zeller) Thiers

Cap 9-14 cm blackish brown to olive-brown, blackish where bruised, velvety; context pallid becoming drab on exposure, taste mild; tubes 1-1.5 cm deep; pores small, coffee-bean-brown when young; stipe 8-15 cm long, 2-3 cm thick above, pallid within staining brownish black where cut; surface often ribbed in addition to the reticulation, also pruinose; spores 13-16 × 5-6.5 μ, smooth; pileus trichodermium having the end cells of the elements cystidioid.

Solitary to scattered under Sitka spruce, Pacific Northwest.

6a. Spores truncate at apex (or notched) ....
.... *Tylopilus amylosporus* (Smith) Smith

Cap 4-12 cm broad, velvety, olive-fuscous, areolate in age; tubes dull to greenish yellow, their pores large and irregular at maturity, readily staining blue; stipe 4-9 cm long, 1-1.5 (2) cm thick, red within and at times reddish on the surface, but usually olive-gray; spores 12-17 × 4.5-6 μ.

Gregarious under red alder in the Northern Rocky Mountains in the fall.

6b. Spores not truncate or notched at apex 7

7a. Spores 13-16 (18) × 6-8 μ. Fig. 206 ....
.... *Tylopilus porphyrosporus* (Secr.) Smith & Thiers

Cap 5-12 cm broad, dark grayish brown to tobacco brown, velvety, subciscid when wet; context pallid, staining reddish when cut and also blue to greenish blue; tubes grayish pallid becoming dark dingy brown, 1-2 cm deep; pores pallid to grayish at first, bluish if bruised; stipe 4-12 cm long, 10-18 mm thick at apex, dark colored more or less like the pileus, pruinose-punctate, not reticulate (spores 15-19 × 6-7.5 μ Moser, 1967).

Solitary to scattered in moist places under conifers,

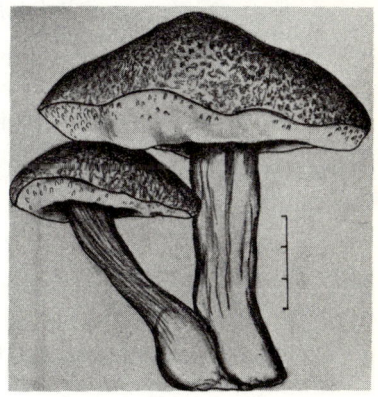

Fig. 206. *Tylopilus porphyrosporus.*

more abundant in the Pacific Northwest than elsewhere, but widely distributed.

7b. Spores 10-14 μ long OR 4-6 μ wide 8

8a. Stipe reticulate above; pores whitish ....
.... *Tylopilus atrofuscus* (Dick & Snell) Smith & Thiers

Cap to 8.5 cm velutinous, sooty black; context whitish, staining reddish to gray or blackish; tubes whites becoming honey yellow before maturing, about 15 mm deep; pores whitish at first; stipe up to 10 cm long, 2.5-3.5 cm thick, pruinose to furfuraceous as well as reticulate; whitish below, colored above like the pileus; spores 11-17 × 4.5-6 μ.

Under *Pinus muricata*, California.

8b. Stipe not reticulate but may be pruinose or glabrous 9

9a. Tubes with a yellowish tint prior to maturity ....
...................................*Tylopilus cyaneotinctus* Smith & Thiers

Cap 4.5-8.5 (13) cm broad, finely tomentose to at times areolate, light brownish drab becoming darker brown with a blue-green tint near margin pores dotted with dark smoky brown particles (heaps of spores?), when bruised deep blue-green and soon deep brownish red; stipe 4.5-6 cm long, 7-10 mm thick, the base pinched to a point, finely dotted upward to the striate apex; spores 10-13.5 × 3-5.5 μ; pleurocystidia with an elongated neck.

Solitary to scattered on poor sandy barren soil under oak in the Great Lakes region in late summer and fall.

9b. Tubes pallid to grayish prior to maturity 10

10a. Base of stipe extended into a rootlike projection ....
...................................*Tylopilus umbrosus* (Atk.) Smith & Thiers

Pileus 5-9 cm broad, subtomentose, becoming finely areolate, blackish brown to walnut brown; context whitish, slowly pinkish then brown where injured; stipe colored like the pileus, 8-10 cm long, 1.5-2 cm thick, somewhat longitudinally ridged, minutely furfuraceous; spores 11-14 × 4.5-5.5 μ; cuticular hyphae lacking incrustations as revived in KOH.

Apparently very rare, it is known only from New York state.

10b. Not as above 11

11a. Cheilocystidia clavate to vesiculose-pedicellate, (up to 15 μ broad; some spores (not the typical range) 7-11 μ wide and with walls 1-2 μ thick ....
...................................*Tylopilus sordidus* (Peck) Smith & Thiers

Cap 3-6 (12) cm broad, velvety, soon rimose-areolate, olive-brown to dingy yellow-brown or gray-brown; context yellowish white slowly staining pale bluish green then to vinaceous-gray; tubes 1-2 cm deep, grayish to olive-gray at first, chocolate color in age; pores 1-2 per mm, grayish to olive-gray at first, staining blue; stipe (2) 3-6 (15) long, 10-20 mm thick at apex, reddish when cut; surface faintly brownish pruinose, almost concolorous with cap, often with a weak bluish zone at apex; spores 11-15 × 5-6.5 μ (12-18 × 6-11 μ); some cuticular hyphae with incrusting pigment granules.

Solitary to scattered on sandy open soil in thin oak woods summer and early fall, eastern North America, uncommon, rare in the Northwest.

11b. Cheilocystidia as revived in KOH seen gelatinizing and wide thick-walled spores not present in mounts. Fig. 207 ....
.... *Tylopilus fumosipes* (Pk.) **Smith & Thiers**

Cap 2-5 cm broad, velvety to subtomentose, at times rivulose, dark olive-brown; context whitish; tubes at first nearly plane; pores whitish, becoming yellowish brown in places and then blackish; stipe 2-5 cm long, 6-8 mm thick, smoky brown, minutely scurfy; spores 12-14 (18) $\times$ 3-5 (6) μ.

Known from New York, apparently rare. It has been a much misunderstood bolete.

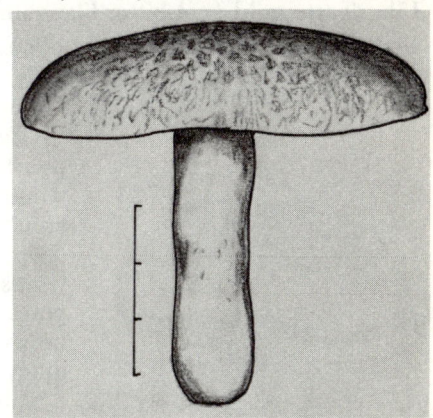

Fig. 207. *Tylopilus fumosipes*.

12a. Cap soon sooty brown, chocolate brown to blackish; tubes staining reddish or red and then blackish 13
12b. Cap dark vinaceous-brown, cinnamon, tan or buff to whitish 14
13a. Taste bitter or disagreeable; tubes fuscous-brown (sides and pores) .... *Tylopilus eximius* (Peck) **Singer**

Cap 5-12 cm broad, convex, unpolished to subtomentose, at times subviscid if wet, surface uneven to pitted, more or less chocolate brown, with a slight sterile margin; context thick, pallid to grayish; tubes 10-17 mm deep, depressed; pores about 3 per mm, stuffed when young; stipe 4.5-10 cm long, 1-3 cm thick, solid, furfuraceous-punctate; spores 11-17 $\times$ 3.5-5 μ.

Solitary to scattered, fairly common in eastern Canada and New England rare in the Great Lakes region and apparently so in the southeast.

13b. Not as above (tubes pallid at first) ....
.... *Tylopilus alboater* (Schw.) **Murrill**

Cap (3) 4-8 (15) cm broad, dry, with a hoary bloom at first, drab to nearly black; context pallid changing to vinaceous-gray to black when cut; tubes 5-8 (10) mm deep, pallid, soon flesh color; pores white becoming pale vinaceous, staining black when bruised; stipe 4-10 cm long, 2-4 cm thick, clavate becoming equal, solid, blackening when cut, surface gray to blackish, reticulate at apex or merely unpolished over all; spores 7-11 $\times$ 3.5-5 μ.

Not uncommon in the southeastern states and up the Atlantic Coast but less common inland, summer and early fall.

- 14a. Stipe not reticulate (apex may be slightly striate) 15
- 14b. Stipe reticulate at least at apex in most fruit bodies 20
- 15a. Taste bitter or disagreeable 16
- 15b. Taste mild (not bitter like quinine) 17
- 16a. Spores 10-14 × 3-4.5 µ; pileus dark vinaceous-brown slowly becoming dull cinnamon. Fig. 208 ....
  ....*Tylopilus rubrobrunneus* Smith & Thiers

Fig. 208. *Tylopilus rubrobrunneus*.

Cap 8-20 (30) cm broad, unpolished, finally areolate; context white, often stained olivaceous around worm holes; tubes 1-2 cm deep, adnate, avellaneous becoming whitish then pink to flesh-color; pores small (1-2 per mm), dingy brownish becoming pallid, staining dingy brown when bruised; stipe (6) 8-20 cm long, 1-5 cm thick at apex, up to 8 cm at base, surface pallid above, vinaceous-brown below, unpolished, often olivaceous in age near the ground-line.

Gregarious to cespitose on sandy soil under scrub oak, summer and fall, often abundant in the Great Lakes region.

- 16b. Spores 7-9.5 × 2.3-3.5 µ; pileus with strong yellow tints when mature ...... *Tylopilus peralbidus* (Snell & Beardslee) Murrill

Cap 4.5-13 cm broad, dry, subtomentose; context white at first, staining vinaceous when cut; tubes 6-10 mm long, pallid, slowly becoming flesh color to grayish vinaceous when cut; pores pallid at first, 1-2 per mm; stipe 4.5-11 cm long, 1.3-4 cm thick, white to concolorous with pileus, glabrous and smooth, furfuraceous with yellowish particles or points; spore deposit yellowish (this color needs to be verified from fresh specimens).

Usually associated with oak, in lawns, gardens or in woods, Florida.

- 17a. Pileus with strong yellow tones (but not red); spores 14-17.5 × 4-6 µ .... *Tylopilus conicus* (Rav. in B. & C.) Beardslee

Cap 2.5-9.5 cm broad, alveolate-reticulate, moist, bright yellow-brown to yellow; context white, odor pleasant (fruity); tubes about 10-15 mm deep, pale grayish vinaceous when young; pores about 2 per mm; stipe 4-7 cm long, 6-18 mm thick, pallid near apex and base, with intermediate area pale cinnamon to yellowish, smooth to slightly rugose, glabrous; spores 14-18 × 4-6 μ.

17b. Not as above 18
18a. Context of pileus ochraceous ....
....*Tylopilus subunicolor* **Dick & Snell**

Cap 5-6 cm glabrous, near ochraceous-tawny, becoming somewhat rimose; context unchanging, when remoistened with odor of celery; tubes 3-4 mm long, white when young, developing pinkish tints but finally light ochraceous-brown; pores pallid when young, 1 mm or less broad; stipe 2-5 cm long, 7-15 mm thick, minutely furfuraceous, concolorous with pileus; spores dull cinnamon in deposit, 8-10 × 3.5-4 μ; mycelium yellowish to ochraceous.

Under oak, Louisiana.

18b. Context of pileus white or finally brownish in places, or changing color when injured 19
19a. Pileus bright orange to orange tinged brown, becoming wood brown or dull cinnamon in age; context unchanging ....
....*Tylopilus ballouii* (**Pk.**) **Singer**

Cap 5-12 cm broad, convex to slightly depressed, often irregular, dry, unpolished or minutely tomentose, sometimes areolate-rimose; tubes at first whitish becoming smoky brown where cut or bruised; depressed around the stipe; stipe 2.5-12 cm long, 7-15 mm thick, surface merely scurfy, striate to subreticulate at apex; yellow to orange except at apex and base; spores 8-10 × 4-5 μ; mycelium white; spore deposit "pale yellow inclining to orange" (Peck). Note: I have not seen this species fresh, but doubt that it is a Tylopilus—A. H. S.

From New York southward, its range is not clearly established but it appears to be typically southern.

19b. Pileus dark bay-brown ....
....*Tylopilus badiceps* (**Pk.**) **Smith & Thiers**

Cap 4-8 cm broad, convex, dry, velvety; context white, unchanging or slowly brownish where bruised, odor suggestive of molasses; tubes adnate, white becoming dingy with age; pores minute; stipe 4-5 cm long, 1.5-3 cm thick, equal or ventricose, radicating, glabrous, solid, brownish; spores 8-10 × 3.5-4.5 μ, smooth, narrowly elliptic in face view; pileus cuticle a compact palisade of pileocystidia 30-40 × 7-10 μ, fusoid-ventricose varying to utriform.

Pennsylvania: Its area of distribution has not been established.

20a. Taste mild to slightly disagreeable 21
20b. Taste distinctly bitter 24
21a. Cut flesh of pileus soon slate-violet; odor of older specimens peculiar .... *Tylopilus tabacinus* (**Pk.**) **Singer**

Cap 4.5-17.5 cm broad, velvety, brown to dark brown; tubes whitish and developing brown stains or the pores brown from the first; stipe 4-16 cm long, 2.5-6 cm thick, nearly concolorous with the cap, smooth below, brown reticulate on a paler ground color above; context white becoming slate-violet when cut; spores (8.8) 11.8-14.5 (17) × 3.5-5 µ (Singer).

Under live oak and laurel-oak, frequently on high hammocks and shady lawns in the southeast in the summer.

21b. Cut flesh of cap unchanging or becoming pinkish to avellaneous or brownish; odor usually merely fungoid 22
22a. Cap surface with coarse shallow depression; cuticular hyphae when mounted in Melzer's usually having orange-brown pigment globules in them; stipe reticulate only at the apex and obscurely dotted below. Fig. 209 ....
.............................*Tylopilus subpunctipes* (Pk.) Smith & Thiers

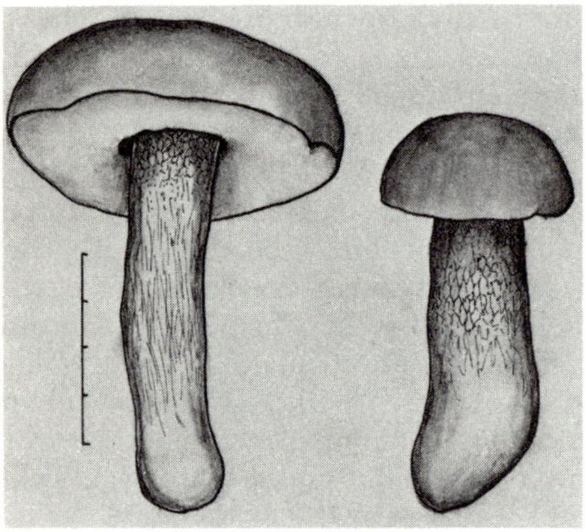

Cap 5-10 cm broad, convex, surface often uneven, resinous to touch but not viscid, rusty brown; context white slowly becoming dingy brown where cut or broken; taste mild; tubes nearly plane across pore surface, becoming slightly depressed at stipe; pores small, pallid staining reddish brown; stipe 2-7.5 cm long, 1-3 cm thick, pallid above brownish below or grayish brown almost overall, finely reticulate above; spores rusty brown or cinnamon (sub mic.), 8-12 × 3-4.5 µ. New York, August, not well known.

Fig. 209. *Tylopilus subpunctipes*.

22b. Not as above 23
23a. Context of cap or stipe sometimes staining blue when injured; stipe 2-5 cm long, up to 3.5 cm thick; under pine in California. Fig. 210 .... *Tylopilus humilis* Thiers

Cap 5-12 cm broad, margin often convoluted, dry, subviscid if wet, appearing matted-tomentose when mature, cinnamon-brown to darker yellow-brown; context white, staining avellaneous when cut, more rarely staining blue; tubes 5-10 mm deep, narrowly depressed at stipe,

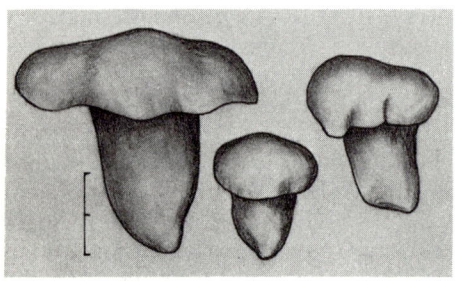

Fig. 210. *Tylopilus humilis*.

pallid at first, becoming dingy salmon color by maturity; pores 1-2 per mm, angular, when bruised staining cinnamon-brown; stipe often poorly developed, at times eccentric, dry, glabrous, smooth to the usually reticulate apex, pallid above, some shade of dull brown downward; spores 8-12 × 3-4 μ, obscurely inequilateral in profile view.

Under pine, California.

23b. **Never staining blue; stipe 4-12 cm long or more; growing under oak in central and eastern North America** .... *Tylopilus indecisus* (Pk.) **Murrill**

Cap 5-15 (25) cm broad, subviscid moist but soon dry and unpolished, pale dingy cinnamon to dark dull cinnamon; context pure white, staining slowly vinaceous-buff on injury; tubes 9-12 mm deep, becoming somewhat depressed, white but when mature vinaceous, staining brown where bruised; pores pallid, small, staining brown when injured; stipe 4-10 cm long, 1-2.5 (3.5) cm thick, clavate then equal, surface minutely furfuraceous, finely reticulate above in addition, pallid above soon brown below (especially after handling); spore deposit vinaceous-fawn; spores 10-13 × 3-4 μ.

New England to Michigan and southward in hardwood forests (mostly under oak in Michigan), summer and fall after heavy rains.

24a. **Stipe reticulate only at apex; context of cap white and unchanging; southern in distribution** ....*Tylopilus minor* **Singer**

Cap 3.5-5.5 cm broad, convex, dry, unpolished, dingy cinnamon to dingy cinnamon-brown; context white; tubes whitish becoming dingy flesh color, somewhat depressed around the stipe; pores pallid, small; stipe 5-6.8 cm long, 7-13 mm thick, white but slowly becoming dingy brown, apex typically with a wide-meshed reticulum; spores (8) 10-13 × 3.5-4 μ or 10.2-15 (16.3) × 4.5-5 μ.

Northern Florida, May to August, oak usually present in vicinity. Note: This species may be merely a variation of *T. felleus*).

24b. **Not as above** 25

25a. **Cap white or whitish** 26

25b. **Cap more distinctively colored** 27

26a. **Cap wrinkled and stipe only weakly reticulate at or near apex; northern in distribution** ..*Tylopilus intermedius* **Smith & Thiers**

Cap 6-12 (15) cm broad, broadly convex, dry, unpolished to pruinose, slowly staining pale tan where bruised; flesh white, brownish where bruised, $FeSO_4$, pinkish on young caps; tubes deeply depressed to free from stipe, white becoming vinaceous; pores white then pinkish vinaceous, 1-2 per mm; stipe 8-14 cm long, 1-4 cm thick, enlarged downward, surface white, staining yellow-brown where handled, apex usually faintly reticulate; spore deposit vinaceous; spores 10-15 × 4-4.4 (5) μ.

Gregarious under oak, Michigan, late summer and fall.

26b. Cap smooth and stipe coarsely reticulate ....
.... *Tylopilus rhoadsiae* (**Murrill**) **Murrill**

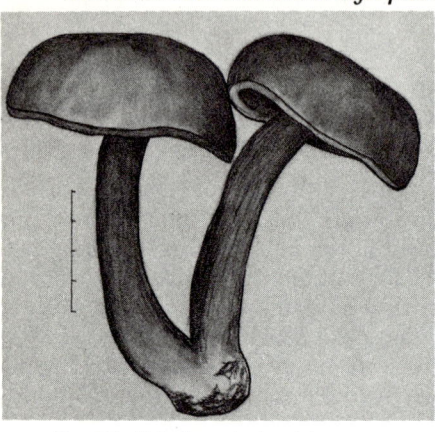

Cap 6-9 cm broad, broadly convex or flattened on disc, white when young, surface dry and unpolished or subviscid in wet weather, with a narrowly projecting sterile margin; tubes 9-16 mm deep, deeply depressed around the stipe, whitish becoming flesh-tinged; pores pallid, unchanging when injured; stipe 5.5-9.5 cm long, 16-27 mm thick, white, strongly reticulate over upper half at least; spores 11-13.7 × 3.7-4.5 μ.

Fig. 211. *Tylopilus plumbeoviolaceus*.

Southeastern in distribution, July to September in Florida.

27a. **Cap dull violet when young; stipe violet at first, slightly reticulate. Fig. 211** .... *Tylopilus plumbeoviolaceus* (**Snell**) **Snell**

Cap 4-15 cm broad, broadly convex, dry, unpolished, becoming dingy cinnamon finally; flesh white, typically unchanging or only slightly brownish where bruised; tubes 1-2 cm deep, cream color becoming dingy vinaceous; pores 1-2 per mm, pallid at first; stipe 8-12 cm long, 10-17 mm thick at apex, surface glabrous, dark violet like the cap when young, color gradually fading, developing olivaceous stains in or around the base; spores 10-13 × 3-4 μ.

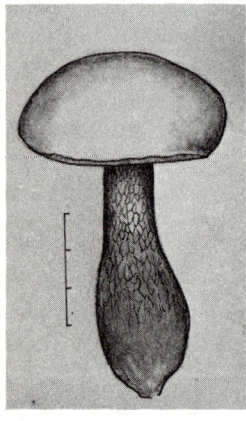

Scattered to cespitose on sandy soil in open aspen-hickory-oak woods, late summer and fall, from Michigan eastward and southward.

27b. **Pileus dingy dark to pale cinnamon when young and merely paler shades of the same color in age; stipe distinctly reticulate. Fig. 212** ....
.........*Tylopilus felleus* (**Fr.**) **Karsten**

Fig. 212. *Tylopilus felleus*.

Cap 5-15 (30) cm broad, broadly convex, dry, unpolished, when wet subviscid, sometimes areolate in dry weather; flesh white, stained brownish when injured; tubes 1-2 cm deep, whitish then vinaceous; pores whitish to grayish young, staining brownish bruised, at maturity about 1 per mm; stipe 4-10 (15) cm long, 1-3 cm thick, clavate, pallid above, brownish downward, in age often with olive stains; spores 11-15 (17) $\times$ 3-5 μ.

Common in summer in eastern and central North America, on humus or rotting conifer (hemlock) stumps and logs.

LECCINUM
Key to Sections

1a. Cap margin sterile for 2-6 mm in buttons and this membrane soon broken into segments as cap expands. Fig. 213 ....
....Sect. *Leccinum* p. 188
1b. Cap margin not as above or sterile for only a millimeter or less and not becoming crenate as cap expands. Fig. 214 2

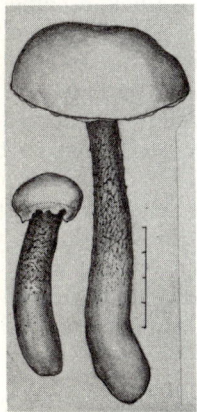

Fig. 213. *Leccinum* sect. *Leccinum* showing appendiculate cap margin.

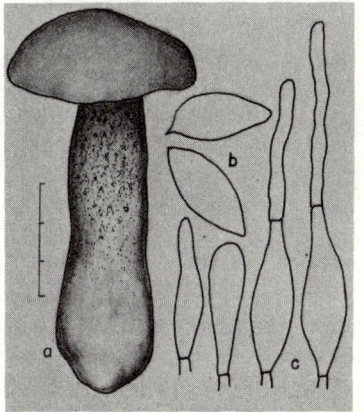

Fig. 214. *Leccinum* sections *Luteoscabra* and *Scabra;* (a) fruit body showing no sterile tissue on cap margin; (b) spore in profile and face view; (c) caulocystidia with secondary cross wall.

2a. Cuticle of cap a cellular layer (an epithelium) or of inflated cells so numerous as to give the impression of such a layer, or of filamentous hyphae with one to several cells in a hypha short and oval to subglobose; cap surface often smooth to reticulate
....Sect. *Luteoscabra* p. 208
2b. Cuticle of cap fibrillose, composed of tubular hyphae, but some of the cells may be short (less than 4 times as long as broad) but if so they are at most only slightly inflated ....
....Sect. *Scabra* p. 200

Section LECCINUM

Key to Subsections

1a. Young basidiocarps covered with a submembranous outer veil which breaks leaving patches on the cap, cap finally becoming glabrous .... *Velosi*
One species known. Fig. 215 ....
.... *Leccinum potteri* Smith, Thiers & Watling.

Cap 4-12 cm, convex, dry and matted-fibrillose beneath the veil or over all when veil has disappeared, dull brick orange to dingy orange-tawny; context pallid, when cut staining vinaceous then lavender and finally gray, with $FeSO_4$ bluish; tubes pallid, maturing to wood brown; pores pallid young, staining yellowish then brownish when lightly injured; stipe 5-10 cm long, 1-2.5 cm thick, ornamentation going from pallid to yellowish brown to blackish brown, when dried the basal portion lime green to sulphur yellow; spores 13-16 × 4-5 μ; caulocystidia clavate to balloon-shaped; hyphae of cap cuticle 7-12 μ wide, end-cells mostly clavate, content in KOH lemon yellow to ochraceous-brown, in Melzer's a few reddish globules form.

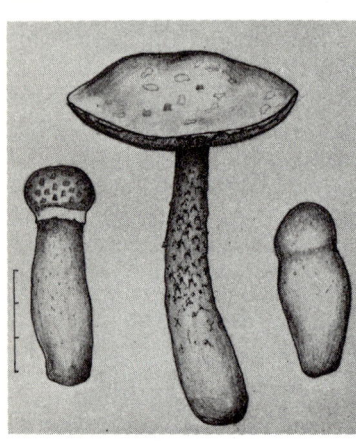

Fig. 215. *Leccinum potteri.*

Under large-toothed aspen, Michigan, late summer and fall, common at times.

1b. Cap at all times lacking remains of an outer veil 2
2a. Cap and stipe exuding a watery latex when cut; cap blackish where bruised .... *Lactiflua*
One species known ....
.... *Leccinum truebloodii* Smith, Thiers & Watling.

Cap 3-9 cm, convex, glabrous becoming areolate, dull tan to medium date-brown, blackish where bruised; context pale cream color, when cut pinkish before changing further; tubes pale yellow, blackish where bruised; stipe 6-8 cm long, 3-3.5 mm thick above, subventricose, surface with blackish fibrillose squamules; spores 14-18 × 5-7.5 μ; cuticular hyphae 8-17 μ wide, end-cells bullet-shaped to cystidioid, content of cells homogeneous in Melzer's.

Under aspen, Owyhee County, Idaho.

2b. Not exuding a latex when injured but cut context often staining one or more colors 3

3a. Cap gray to blackish or distinctly grayish brown when young ....Obscura p. 190
3b. Cap pallid to dingy tan to cinnamon, ferruginous, bay-red, orange, orange-red, rose-red, liver-color or darker vinaceous brown 4
4a. Cut surface of context in apex of stipe and adjacent pileus lacking a color change to gray, fuscous or blackish ...Vulpina p. 189
4b. Cut surface of context of cap or that of apex of stipe eventually changing to gray or fuscous 5
5a. Cut surface of the context in apex of stipe (and usually in cap) becoming lilac-gray, avellaneous or yellowish or bluish gray and then fuscous, without a distinct reddish preliminary stage ....Versicolores p. 197
5b. Cut surface developing reddish tints before becoming lilac-gray or fuscous ....Leccinum p. 192

Subsection VULPINA

Key

1a. Context of cap and/or stipe turning yellow when cut; the subiculum supporting the stipe ornamentation bright yellow in KOH ....Leccinum sublutescens Smith, Thiers & Watling

Cap about 7 cm, convex, dry, conspicuously areolate, orange-cinnamon; context whitish at first; tubes about 1 cm long, white at first; pores small, pallid, staining ochraceous then slowly going to olivaceous; stipe about 8 cm long, 1 cm thick, whitish beneath fine sparse blackish ornamentation; spores $12\text{-}15 \times 3\text{-}4.5$ μ; caulocystidia clavate to fusoid-ventricose; hyphae of cap-cuticle 5-12 μ wide, content rounding into globules in many of the cells when mounts are made in Melzer's.

Solitary in mixed woods, Emmet County, Michigan, October.

1b. Not as above 2
2a. Cap orange-tan to clay color; stipe ornamentation concolorous with the cap ......Leccinum subfulvum Smith, Thiers & Watling

Cap 6-12 cm, convex, dry, distinctly fibrillose, later squamulose, context white; tubes 1-2 cm long, dingy yellowish brown as dried; pores concolorous and not staining; stipe 5-10 cm long, 1-2 cm thick at apex, clavate but base pointed below; spores $13\text{-}17 \times 4.5\text{-}5.5$ μ; caulocystidia elliptic to fusoid-ventricose; hyphae of cap-cuticle 5-10 (12) μ wide, content homogeneous to granulose in Melzer's.

Gregarious under lodgepole pine, Washington, fall, rare.

2b. Not as above 3
3a. Cap surface granulose-roughened; spore deposit dingy cinnamon when air-dried ....
................Leccinum idahoensis Smith, Thiers & Watling

Cap 8-13 (20) cm, convex, viscid to the touch, dark liver brown; context pallid, faintly vinaceous-gray in about 15 minutes after being cut, with $FeSO_4$ slightly greenish; tubes about 2 cm deep, pallid young, when cut slowly staining faintly grayish; pores small and staining olive when lightly bruised, pale olive-buff when young; stipe 8-12 cm long, 2.5-3.5 cm thick, pinched off at base, ornamentation dingy cinnamon-buff but finally blackish over lower half; spores 13-16 (17) $\times$ 3.8-5.2 μ; caulocystidia mostly fusoid-ventricose; hyphae of cap cuticle 4-7 (10) μ wide, in mounts in Melzer's filled with orange-brown globules.

Under western cedar, hemlock, and western white pine mixed, scattered, September and October.

3b. Not as above 4
4a. Cap 7-10 cm, spores 3.5-4.5 μ wide ....
....*Leccinum vulpinum* **Watling**

Cap flattened in age, dry, brick red or paler; context pallid, when cut slowly slightly brownish, with $FeSO_4$ bluish olive; tubes pallid becoming wood brown; spores pallid young and staining yellow when lightly bruised; stipe 10-13 cm long, 1-1.5 cm thick at apex, nearly equal, ornamentation brown but drying blackish, surface over lower part flushed yellow to greenish as dried; spores 14-17 (19) $\times$ 3.5-4.5 μ; hyphae of cap-cuticle 5-8 (12) μ wide, content in Melzer's merely granular.

Scattered in mixed woods with pine, Michigan, fall, rare.

4b. Cap 10-30 cm, spores 4.5-6 μ wide ....
...........................*Leccinum ponderosum* **Smith, Thiers & Watling**

Cap soon viscid, ferruginous-red; context white, when cut not changing appreciably; tubes 1-2 cm deep, pallid young pores pallid to avellaneous, stained ochraceous where lightly bruised; spores 14-17 $\times$ 4.5-6 μ; caulocystidia mostly clavate; hyphae of cap cuticle 4-12 μ wide, in Melzer's the content rounding into distinct globules in some.

Scattered under ponderosa or lodgepole pine, Oregon, Washington and Idaho, fall, not common.

Subsection OBSCURA

Key to Species

1a. Cut context in apex of stipe staining pinkish but not darkening to gray or fuscous; spores 16-21 $\times$ 5-7 μ ....
.... *Leccinum subatratum* **Smith, Thiers & Watling**

Cap 7-9 cm, obtuse to broadly umbonate, viscid to the touch but often granulose in appearance, blackish to gray first, in age; context pallid, unchanging except near apex of stipe where it is pinkish; tubes pallid, depressed; pores minute, pallid, staining dingy ochraceous when bruised; stipe 8-11 cm long, 8-12 mm thick at apex, 2 cm thick at base, surface with coarse black ornamentation becoming finer near apex, pallid ground color showing slightly; caulocystidia clavate to fusoid-ventricose; cuticle of cap a turf of hyphae becoming appresed, 10-15 (30) µ wide, some cells short and inflated (to nearly globose), end cells bullet-shaped, as revived in Melzer's the cell content of some aggregating into globules.

Fruitng in wet areas under birch and aspen, Chippewa county, Michigan, apparently rare, September.

1b. Not as above 2
2a. **Cuticular hyphae of cap often with brownish bands of incrusting pigment** ....*Leccinum obscurum* **Smith, Thiers & Watling**

Cap about 7 cm, convex, glabrous, grayish fuscous; context pallid, staining vinaceous when cut but slowly going to fuscous; tubes white, pores pallid, staining vinaceous then fuscous if injured; stipe 14 cm long, 2.5 cm thick, ornamentation coarse and blackish; spores 12-16 (19) $\times$ 4.5-6 µ; caulocystidia clavate to fusoid-ventricose; hyphae of cap cuticle with some enlarged cells up to 20 µ broad, cell content lacking globules in mounts in Melzer's.

Solitary under aspen, southeastern Michigan, October, rare.

2b. **Cuticular hyphae not incrusted as in 2a above** 3
3a. **Cuticular hyphae showing pigment globules when mounted in Melzer's; cut surface of stipe apex staining pinkish then fuscous**
.... *Leccinum uliginosum* **Smith & Thiers**

Cap 5-15 cm, convex, dry, unpolished, fuscous to drab-gray; context white, slightly reddish when cut then changing to fuscous, with $FeSO_4$ olivaceous; tubes pallid becoming wood brown, pores pallid at first and staining yellowish when bruised; stipe 9-16 cm long, 1-2.5 cm thick, surface charcoal gray to black from ornamentation, ground color pallid but often obscured; spore deposit dark dingy cinamon-brown; spores 14-17 (18) $\times$ 3.5-5 µ; caulocystidia fuscoid-ventricose and often the neck proliferated; hyphae of cap cuticle 5-11 µ wide, mostly tubular, end cells often clavate and up to 15 µ wide or more.

Gregarious under aspen and willow, Emmet county, Michigan, August, apparently rare.

3b. **Cuticular hyphae lacking pigment globules as revived in Melzer's; the cut surface of the stipe apex staining fuscous directly (see** *L. ambigum* **also p. 192)** ....
........................*Leccinum subspadiceum* **Smith, Thiers & Watling**

Cap 8-15 cm, convex, dry, date brown or darker in age; context pallid, with $FeSO_4$ pale gray; tubes 1-2 cm deep, pores pale tan young, staining olive when lightly bruised; stipe 10-18 cm long, 1-2 cm thick, surface with dull yellow-brown ornamentation to near apex and this finally blackish in age; spores 14-16 $\times$ 4.5-6 µ; caulocystidia elongate-subfusiform to clavate; cap cuticle of hyphae 6-12 µ broad, content in Melzer's mostly granular, a few short inflated cells seen in some hyphae.

Gregarious in a mixed forest, central Michigan, June, rare.

Subsection LECCINUM

Key to Stirpes

1a. Cap gray to dark brownish gray or blackish (but see *L. ambiguum* also) .... see Subsection *Obscura* p. 190
1b. Cap some other color 2
2a. Stipe ornamentation black and conspicuous in button stages of the basidiocarp .... Stirps *Atrostipitatum* p. 192
2b. Stipe ornamentation pallid, grayish, or brownish at first but darkening later to dark brown or blackish 3
3a. Cuticular hyphae as mounted in Melzer's showing pigment globules 2 µ or more in diameter ..... Stirps *Aurantiacum* p. 193
3b. Cuticular hyphae in Melzer's lacking pigmented globules or only an occasional hypha showing weak globule formation .... Stirps *Rufescentoides* p. 195

STIRPS ATROSTIPITATUM

Key to Species

1a. Cap grayish brown to olive-buff ....
.... *Leccinum ambiguum* Smith, Thiers & Watling

Cap 6-15 cm, convex, dry and appressed-fibrillose, color olive-sepia (dark dull grayish brown), paler and near olive-buff in age; context white, in buttons staining dingy cinnamon and then lilac-fuscous when cut, in mature caps staining dingy lilac-fuscous directly when cut, with $FeSO_4$ readily staining grayish blue; tubes pallid then olive-buff; pores pallid at first, dull brown where injured; stipe 6-15 cm long, 1-2.5 cm thick, clavate when young, ornamentation coal-black on buttons, coarse; spores 14-17 × 4-5.5 µ; caulocystidia clavate, fusoid-ventricose and utriform all intermingled; cuticle of cap of hyphae 7-16 µ wide, cells more than 4 times longer than broad, content not forming globules in Melzer's.

Under birch, Chippewa County, Michigan, July.

1b. Cap some other color 2
2a. Cap orange-red when perfectly fresh ....
.... *Leccinum testaceoscabrum* (Secr.) Singer

Cap 4-10 cm, convex, dry and fibrillose but becoming glabrous and subviscid, fading to dull orange or orange-cinnamon; context white, when cut staining reddish and finally fuscous; pores olive-pallid young, staining olive when lightly bruised; stipe 5-10 cm long,

1-1.5 cm thick at apex, ornamentation blackish in buttons; spores (12) 13-16 (18) $\times$ 3.5-4.5 μ; caulocystidia clavate to mucronate and fuscoid-ventricose all intermingled; cuticle of cap of hyphae 6-15 (18) μ wide, cells mostly 4 times longer than broad but some oval short cells also present, end cells cystidioid to bullet-shaped, content in Melzer's slowly aggregating into globules 3-10 μ wide.

In mixed woods of aspen, birch and oak with conifers also present, August, Michigan.

2b. Cap not as brightly colored as in 2a 3
3a. **Cut context of cap bright green where touched with FeSO$_4$** ....
.....................*Leccinum pellstonianum* **Smith, Thiers & Watling**
Cap 4-9 cm, dry, matted-fibrillose, becoming rimulose, pale tan to subalutaceous; context when cut white, changing to reddish cinnamon and finally black, quickly spotting green with FeSO$_4$; pores white staining dingy yellow-brown when injured lightly; stipe 8-12 (16) cm long, 1-3 cm at apex, clavate, surface ornamented with coarse black fibrils often in zones giving a scaly rather than a punctate appearance; spores 12-15 $\times$ 3.5-4.5 μ; caulocystidia versiform, clavate, elliptic-pedicellate, mucronate and fusoid-ventricose; cuticle of cap of appressed hyphae 4-8 (10) μ wide, tubular or nearly so, end cells tubular to weakly cystidioid, content in Melzer's not forming pigment globules.

Gregarious under aspens, Pellston, Michigan, August.

3b. **Cut context of cap bluish gray directly when touched with FeSO$_4$** ....*Leccinum atrostipitatum* **Smith, Thiers & Watling**
Cap 6-18 (25) cm, convex, dry, appressed-fibrillose, patchy in appearance at maturity, pale dingy orange-buff to orange brownish or pinkish tan; cut context vinaceous-buff going to fuscous; pores pallid when young, staining olive if lightly bruised; stipe 8-15 cm long, 1-2.5 cm at apex, buttons with coarse black ornamentation to apex; spores 13-17 $\times$ 4-5 μ; caulocystidia clavate to fusoid-ventricose; cuticle of cap of hyphae 6-12 μ wide, end cells tubular to narrowly clavate, rarely short and somewhat inflated cells present but these not oval to subglobose, cell content not forming globules in Melzer's.

Under birch, not uncommon in western Great Lakes area during wet years.

STIRPS AURANTIACUM

Key to Species

1a. **Cap pallid with a faint tinge of pink** ....
................*Leccinum vinaceo-pallidum* **Smith, Thiers & Watling**
Cap 4-14 cm, glabrous to appressed-squamulose, dry becoming subviscid; context white, showing reddish lilac then fuscous when

cut, with $FeSO_4$ olive; pores pallid staining olive to olive-brown when lightly bruised; stipe 7-15 cm long, 1-2 cm thick, ornamentation pallid at first but becoming dull brown and finally dark brown; spores 13-16 $\times$ 4-5 μ; caulocystidia (30) 40-60 $\times$ 10-30 μ, clavate to saccate or a few fusoid-ventricose; cuticular hyphae 7-12 μ wide, end cells 10-15 μ wide, weakly cystidioid, no short cells observed, content in Melzer's aggregating into small beads about 2 μ diam. in fresh material, in dried material the content homogeneous to stringy.

Under aspen and birch, summer, Michigan.

1b. Cap more highly or deeply colored 2
2a. Cap dark red to ferruginous-red 3
2b. Cap paler, rusty orange, tan, yellow or paler 5
3a. Associated with bearberry (*Arctostaphylos*) ; spores 15-19 $\times$ 4.5-6 μ; stipe clavate ....
....*Leccinum arctostaphylos* **Wells & Kempton**

Cap 9-20 cm, subviscid, bright orange-red to brick red; context when touched with $FeSO_4$ pale blue; tubes whitish becoming ochraceous-brown; pores small, colored like the sides of the tubes, staining brownish when injured; stipe 7-10 cm long, 1.5-2.5 cm at apex, 3.5-5 cm at base, white at first, the tips of the ornamentation becoming light brownish orange over the lower half, darker as dried; cap cuticle of hyphae 3-11 μ wide, content in Melzer's aggregating into amber-orange globules.

Known from exposed areas in Alaska, summer.

3b. Not as above 4
4a. Stipe equal or narrowed rather near the apex. See fig. 213 ....
.... *Leccinum aurantiacum* (**St. Amans**) **Gray**

Cap 5-20 cm, dry and uneven becoming subviscid, bright to dull ferruginous-red; context when cut vinaceous before going to fuscous, with $FeSO_4$ bluish gray; pores pallid when young, staining olive when lightly bruised; stipe 10-16 cm long, 1-3 cm at apex, ornamentation pallid at first but soon brown and finally black (changes progressing from base upward); spores 13-16 (18) $\times$ 3.5-5 μ; caulocystidia mostly clavate; cuticle of cap of hyphae 5-15 μ wide, cells elongate, end cells clavate to tubular, cell content in Melzer's aggregating into large to small globules.

Under aspen or pine, common at times, summer and fall, throughout the northern United States and in adjacent Canada.

4b. Stipe short-clavate, the base up to 8 cm broad ....
....*Leccinum fallax* **Smith, Thiers & Watling**

Cap 6-20 cm, convex, dry, matted-fibrillose; context thick, white, slowly staining dingy vinaceous then gray when cut; pores pallid to grayish, when bruised slightly staining yellowish to green and then brownish; stipe 6-14 cm long, 1-4 cm near apex, surface white at first, ornamentation gradually becoming brownish to dark brown

NON-GILLED FLESHY FUNGI

finally but not black; spores 14-17 × 3.2-4.5 μ; caulocystidia mostly clavate, up to 20 μ broad, content hyaline to yellowish in KOH; cap cuticle of hyphae having content aggregating into globules when mounted in Melzer's, end cells subcylindric to narrowly clavate.

Under spruce, Rocky Mountains, August.

5a. **Cap rusty orange to reddish brown; stipe or ornamentation reddish at first** .... ***Leccinum subrobustum*** Smith, Thiers & Watling

Cap 6-12 cm, appressed fibrillose and dry, in age nearly glabrous and subviscid, at times distinctly squamulose, dark rusty orange, context when cut soon reddish cinnamon then going to fuscous, pores pallid at first, staining olive when lightly bruised; stipe 9-12 cm long, 1-3 cm thick, ornamentation finally blackish; spores 13-16 × 4-5 μ; caulocystidia elongate-subelliptic, clavate, or clavate and fusoid-ventricose intermingled; cuticle of cap of hyphae 7-15 μ wide, many short-ellipsoid cells present, end cells short and bullet-shaped, content in Melzer's forming beads and globules in a few hyphae.

Under aspen and birch, Michigan, July and August.

5b. **Not as in above choice** .... **Variants of *L. aurantiacum* not treated here.**

STIRPS RUFESCENTOIDES

Key to Species

1a. **End cells of cuticular hyphae of cap gigantic (13-35 μ in width); cuticular hyphae containing some short-inflated cells** ....
.... ***Leccinum rufescentoides*** Smith, Thiers & Watling

Cap 4-9 cm, dry, slightly fibrillose to glabrous, bright orange over all, context pallid, when cut quickly staining reddish then fuscous; stipe 8-11 cm long, 1-1.5 cm thick, ornamentation pallid becoming reddish and finally dark brown and as dried blackish; spores 11-13 × 4-5.5 μ; hyphae of cap cuticle with homogeneous content as revived in Melzer's.

Gregarious under mixed ash, birch, alder, aspen, balsam and spruce, Michigan, July.

1b. Not as above 2

2a. **Cap orange-brown when young; spores 4.5-6 (7) μ wide** ....
.... ***Leccinum discolor*** Smith, Thiers & Watling

Cap 8-12 cm, convex, glabrous, dull, finally faintly areolate-rimose, dull cinnamon at maturity; context white; pores grayish when young, stipe 7-9 cm long, 1-2 cm thick, surface whitish beneath blackish ornamentation; spores gray-brown in deposit; caulocystidia ventricose-mucronate to fusoid-ventricose; cap cuticle with hyphae having end cells cylindric to weakly cystidioid, content not rounding into globules in Melzer's.

Under aspen and conifers mixed, northern Idaho, September.

2b. **Not as above** 3

3a. **Cap pale pinkish cinnamon to vinaceous; stipe ornamentation vinaceous-buff and slowly becoming wood brown** ....
................................*Leccinum incarnatum* **Smith, Thiers & Watling**
Cap 5-15 cm, dry, matted-fibrillose, becoming areolate-rimose; context when cut vinaceous to vinaceous-gray, with $FeSO_4$ blue on white context; pores small, gray-brown at first, staining dingy yellow-brown where injured; stipe 4-8 (12) cm long, 2-2.5 cm thick, 4 cm near base, ornamentation white at first; spores 13-16 × 3-4.5 μ; hyphae of cap cuticle 6-11 μ wide, end cells clavate to narrowly fusoid, cell content nearly homogeneous as revived in Melzer's.

Under white-bark pine (*P. albicaulis*), Idaho, August.

3b. Not as above 4
4a. **Cap dark liver brown and conspicuously fibrillose at first** ....
................................*Leccinum fibrillosum* **Smith, Thiers & Watling**
Cap 8-25 cm, convex, dry and matted-fibrillose becoming squamulose, at times with an overtone of grayish fibrils; context staining vinaceous then purple-drab, with $FeSO_4$ greenish blue; pores dingy buff-color when young, staining yellow-brown where lightly injured; stipe 4-12 cm long, 2-5 cm thick, surface densely coated with woolly-scabrous material which forms squamules that blacken; spores 14-18 (20) × 3.8-5 μ; caulocystidia mostly ovate-pointed; cuticle of cap of tubular hyphae 6-12 μ wide, end cells tubular to weakly cystidioid, content of cells not forming globules in Melzer's, hyphal cells all 5 times or more longer than wide.

Gregarious under lodgepole pine, Idaho, late August.

4b. Not as above 5
5a. **Cap rufous (ferruginous) to orange-tan in age (see *L. subrobustum* also p. 195)** 6
5b. **Cap yellow to orange to cinnamon or tan** 7
6a. Spores 14-18 (20) × 4-5.5 (6) μ ....
................................*Leccinum boreale* var. *boreale* **Smith, Thiers & Watling**
Cap 4-10 cm, glabrous to unpolished, becoming subviscid; context white, when cut pinkish orange slowly going to fuscous, with $FeSO_4$ slate-blue; pores small, whitish at first; stipe 4-12 cm long, 10-15 mm at apex, 1-2 cm at base, surface white except for dark brown to blackish ornamentation; caulocystida saccate, elongate-clavate and fusoid-ventricose all intermingled, cuticle of cap of hyphae (3) 5-8 (12) μ wide, end cells tubular or nearly so, cell content lacking globules as revived in Melzer's.

Under cottonwood, Alaska, August.

6b. Spores 13-15 × 3.8-4.5 μ ....
...*Leccinum boreale* var. *microspora* **Smith, Thiers & Watling**
7a. **Stipe viscid at base; spore deposit olive when fresh** ....
................................*Leccinum laetum* **Smith, Thiers & Watling**
Cap 5-15 cm, dry, appressed-fibrillose to squamulose, glabrescent, orange when young, yellower to ochraceous in age and then

gray to fuscous, with FeSO₄ blue; pores pallid at first, staining olive when lightly bruised; stipe 8-16 cm long, 1-2.5 cm at apex, surface ornamentation fine and pallid but slowly brownish; spores 13-16 (17) × 4-5 μ; caulocystidia both clavate and fusoid-ventricose intermingled; cuticle of cap of hyphae 6-15 μ wide, end cells often bullet-shaped, cells 40-120 μ or longer and not appreciably inflated, cell content not forming globules in Melzer's.

Under willow and aspen, fall, Michigan.

7b. Not as above 8
8a. Cap pale tan to pale dingy tawny ....
.... *Leccinum cinnamomeum* Smith, Thiers & Watling

Cap 6-18 cm, dry and unpolished, appressed-fibrillose to squamulose, becoming subviscid and glabrous; context when cut quickly staining vinaceous then going to fuscous, with FeSO₄ bluish green; pores pallid, staining yellowish when lightly bruised; stipe 8-10 cm long, 2-2.5 cm thick, ornamentation soon becoming brown to fuscous; spores 12-15 × 4-5 μ; caulocystidia clavate and fusoid-ventricose intermingled; cuticle of cap of hyphae (5) 7-12 (22) μ wide, end cells often bullet-shaped, the broader hyphae often containing some short cells but these not appreciably inflated, content not forming globules when mounted in Melzer's.

Scattered under birch and aspen, Michigan, summer, found mostly during wet seasons.

8b. Cap yellow to orange to reddish orange 9
9a. Cap ocher-yellow with grayish overtone from a thin coating of epicuticular fibrils ....
.... *Leccinum ochraceum* Smith, Thiers & Watling

Cap 5-15 cm, dry, unpolished to fibrillose, finally with appressed patches of fibrils near margin; context when cut staining vinaceous then going to fuscous, with FeSO₄ bluish; pores pallid, when lightly injured staining olive-brown; stipe 10-15 cm long, 1.2-2.3 cm near apex, surface soon with blackish ornamentation of lines and points; spores 14-16 × 4.5-5.5 μ; bister to dark violaceous laticifers in the tube trama as seen in material revived in Melzer's; caulocystidia clavate to mucronate, rarely fusoid-ventricose, hyphae of cap cuticle 6-15 μ wide, end cells often bullet-shaped, short cells rare in the filaments and when present not greatly inflated, cell content not forming globules in Melzer's.

Scattered in aspen-birch woods, Michigan, summer.

9b. Cap orange to orange-brown ....see *L. insigne* p. 199

Subsection VERSICOLORES

Key to Species

1a. Stipe clavate (up to 7 cm thick near base); cap pallid becoming crust-brown; under spruce and fir ....
.... *Leccinum clavatum* Smith, Thiers & Watling

Cap 8-20 cm, dry, becoming subviscid, appressed fibrillose when young; context white, staining bluish gray directly in young specimens when cut; pores small (2 per mm), whitish at first, when bruised staining dingy yellowish then dingy brown; stipe 4-8 cm long, 1.5-3 cm at apex, surface white and scabrous, the ornamentation slowly becoming dull brown; spore deposit rusty brown; spores 14-18 (19) $\times$ 4-5 μ; caulocystidia clavate, mucronate or fusoid-ventricose all intermingled; cuticular hyphae 5-15 μ wide, end cells tubular to narrowly clavate, content of cells as revived in Melzer's yellowish and homogeneous.

Under spruce and fir, Idaho, August.

1b. Not as above 2
2a. Tubes pale yellow before maturing to wood brown; spores 5-7 μ wide ....*Leccinum imitatum* Smith, Thiers & Watling

Cap 6-10 cm, dry and matted fibrillose, dingy rufous, later dull cinnamon; context white, with $FeSO_4$ greenish; pores same color as the sides; stipe 6-12 cm long, 1-2 cm thick, surface whitish with blackish ornamentation when mature; spores 14-18 $\times$ 5-7 μ; caulocystidia mostly clavate, a few fusoid-ventricose; cap cuticle of hyphae 4-9 μ wide, end cells narrowed near apex or weakly cystidioid, cell content in Melzer's reddish, and homogeneous to granular.

Under aspen, Michigan, June.

2b. Not as above 3
3a. Pores cinnamon-brown at first; cap dark ferruginous-red ....
...................*Leccinum subtestaceum* Smith, Thiers & Watling
var. *subtestaceum*

Cap 4-12 cm, glabrous or nearly so, dry, finally liver color; context white, vinaceous-gray when cut, with $FeSO_4$ greenish blue; stipe 7-12 cm long, 2-3 cm thick at apex, ornamentation soon blackish, white ground color showing; spores 11-15 $\times$ 4-5 μ; caulocystidia mostly fusoid-ventricose, some clavate to mucronate; cuticle of cap of appressed hyphae 4-10 (12) μ wide, end cells mostly clavate to subcylindric and content of some of them in Melzer's rounding into beads and globules.

Under aspen, Michigan, September.

3b. Not as above 4
4a. Pores tan at first; cap pale to medium date brown ....
........see *Leccinum subspadiceum* Smith, Thiers & Watling p. 191
4b. Not as above 5
5a. Cap white to pallid at first 6
5b. Cap more deeply or highly colored 7
6a. Cap spotting brown from handling ....
Leccinum insolens var. *brunneomaculatum*
Smith, Thiers & Watling

Cap 7-10 cm, dry, appressed fibrillose then glabrescent, becoming dingy tan in age; context bluish where touched with $FeSO_4$;

stipe 8-13 cm long, 1-2.3 cm near apex, surface pallid with dark brown points and dots over all or nearly so; spores $12\text{-}15 \times 4\text{-}5\ \mu$; caulocystidia mostly clavate-mucronate, more rarely fusoid-ventricose; cap cuticle of hyphae 5-18 μ wide, many with short cells some of which are subglobose, end cells often short and bullet-shaped, content in Melzer's homogeneous or rarely some hyphae showing small beads.

Under birch and aspen, Michigan, July.

6b. As in 6a but cap not spotting when bruised and some context hyphae near the cuticle showing some dextrinoid incrusting material .... *Leccinum insolens* Smith, Thiers & Watling var. *insolens*

7a. Caps reddish orange to ferruginous ....
............*Leccinum insigne* Smith, Thiers & Watling var. *insigne*

Caps 4-15 cm, dry becoming subviscid, fibrillose becoming glabrous; context spotting bluish with $FeSO_4$; pore layer with a sandy brown sheen at maturity if injured; young pores staining olive to yellow if lightly bruised; stipe 8-12 cm long, 1-3 cm thick above, up to 4 cm at base, ornamentation pallid to brown or reddish at times but finally black; spores $13\text{-}16 \times 4\text{-}5.5\ \mu$; caulocystidia mostly clavate, up to 20 μ broad; cuticle of cap of hyphae 4-8 μ wide, with a poorly developed epicutis of hyphae 12-20 μ wide, end cells of the latter bullet-shaped, hyphal cells long or short and some inflated, content when revived in Melzer's not rounding into globules.

Common under aspen, June and July, central United States.

7b. Caps orange-yellow or with gray to rusty brown overcast 8
8a. Cut surface of cap context staining yellow and then gray ....
.................*Leccinum luteocinerascens* Smith, Thiers & Watling

Cap up to 10 cm, tacky to the touch, orange-ochraceous; tubes weakly yellowish before maturing to grayish brown, pores small and pallid at first; stipe up to 11 cm long, 12 mm thick, staining yellow in cortex when cut, surface weakly ornamented with brown to blackish dots and lines; spores $12\text{-}15 \times 4\text{-}5\ \mu$; caulocystidia clavate, mucronate and fusoid-ventricose all intermingled; cuticle of cap of hyphae 6-18 (25) μ wide, short cells often present, end cells often bullet-shaped, content of cells when mounted in Melzer's showing some beads and globules 1-3 μ wide.

Solitary under birch, Michigan, July.

8b. Cut surface of cap context staining bluish gray directly; cap yellowish with an overlay of rusty brown epicuticular hyphae .... *Leccinum fuscescens* Smith, Thiers & Watling

Cap 4-9 cm, dry then subviscid; context bluish with $FeSO_4$; tubes staining fuscous when cut; pores olivaceous pallid, staining olive if lightly bruised; stipe 8-11 cm long, 1-2 cm thick, ornamentation present as coarse blackish squamules and reticulation; spores

12-15 × 3.8-4.5 μ; caulocystidia mostly elongate-mucronate; cuticle of cap of hyphae up to 20 μ wide, end cells bullet-shaped, some short cells present; in Melzer's the cell content not forming globules or only a few colorless globules finally showing in scattered cells.

Under aspen and birch, Michigan, August.

Section SCABRA

The margin of the cap is not appendiculate as in section *Leccinum* and the hyphae of the cuticle of the cap do not contain short, greatly inflated cells.

Key to Subsections

1a. Cap white, pallid or tinged pale crust brown on disc .... Subsect. *Pallida* p. 200

1b. Cap avellaneous, yellow-brown, grayish, gray-brown or blackish 2

2a. Context in apex of stipe when cut staining gray to fuscous (either with or without a change to reddish first) .... Subsect. *Fumosa* p. 203

2b. Context not changing to grayish or fuscous when cut but context may stain reddish, yellowish or brownish .... Subsect. *Scabra* p. 205

Subsection PALLIDA

Key to Species

1a. Pseudocystidia that are brown in either KOH or Melzer's present in the hymenium; on sandy soil under oak and aspen .... *Leccinum olivaceopallidum* Smith, Thiers & Watling

Cap 6-9 cm, convex, whitish to pale olive-buff, grayer in age; context soon vinaceous-gray when cut, with $FeSO_4$ pale blue; pores olive-buff staining vinaceous-brown when injured; stipe 11-14 cm long 10-13 mm thick, ornamentation coarse, tips of squamules brownish; spores 11-15 × 4-5 μ; cuticle of cap of hyphae 4-7 (10) μ wide, end cells tubular, hyphae tubular.

Under oak and large-toothed aspen, September, southern Michigan.

1b. Not as above 2

2a. Tubes staining rusty cinnamon when injured; odor strong of radish ....see *Leccinum parvulum* Smith, Thiers & Watling p. 205
2b. Not as above 3
3a. Cut context of stipe-apex staining reddish or lilaceous to violaceous and finally fuscous 4
3b. Cut context of stipe unchanging to slowly merely a dingy tan ..5
4a. Cut context staining reddish violet or lilac-gray to fuscous without a truly red preliminary phase; spores 16-18 $\times$ 5.5-6.2 μ........
....*Leccinum chalybaeum* Singer

Cap 4-8 cm, pulvinate, glabrous to unpolished, a pale buff to dingy cinnamon; context with $FeSO_4$ green; tubes becoming weakly yellowish before maturing; stipe 4-6.5 cm long, 1.3-2.1 cm thick, ornamentation white becoming brownish at least over lower half; spores 16.3-17.7 $\times$ 5.5-6.2 μ; caulocystidia fusoid-ventricose; cuticle of cap of hyphae 4-10 μ wide, tubular or nearly so.

In gardens, open woods, flatwoods, with oak, on sandy ground or humus, July, Florida.

4b. Cut context staining reddish before changing further ....
Leccinum holopus var. *americanum* Smith, Thiers & Watling

Cap 5-12 cm, glabrous to slightly areolate, subviscid in age, white at first, later vinaceous-buff over disc; context slowly reddish when cut; stipe 6-12 cm long, 10-15 mm thick, whitish beneath blackish brown fine ornamentation at maturity; spores 14-19 $\times$ 5-6 μ; caulocystidia mostly fusoid-ventricose; cuticle of cap of hyphae 4-8 μ, end cells tubular to cystidioid, cell content homogeneous in Melzer's.

On moss in and along edges of bogs and in low woods, Michigan, late summer and fall, common.

5a. Spores 3.5-5 μ wide ....
....................*Leccinum angustisporum* Smith, Thiers & Watling

Cap 3-5 cm, dry, plushlike, vinaceous-buff over disc, margin whitish; context white, scarcely changing, bluish with $FeSO_4$; pores pallid staining yellowish when lightly bruised; stipe up to 7 cm long, 1 cm thick, very fine brown punctations present as ornamentation; spores 14-20 $\times$ 4-5 μ; caulocystidia fusoid-ventricose; cuticle of cap of hyphae 5-12 μ wide, end cells somewhat cystidioid, content of cells homogeneous in Melzer's.

Under birch, Upper Peninsula, Michigan, July, rare.

5b. Spores 5-7.5 μ wide 6
6a. Caulocystidia lemon yellow in KOH (stipe spotting yellow on application of KOH when fresh); under dwarf birch in alpine northern habitats ....
..........*Leccinum rotundifoliae* (Singer) Smith, Thiers & Watling

Cap 2-6 cm, dry and unpolished, becoming subviscid white to pallid becoming pale tan to clay color on disc, rimulose at times in age; context spotting blue with $FeSO_4$, unchanging when injured; stipe 4-10 cm long, 5-12 mm thick at apex, ornamentation white slowly becoming brownish; spores 16-20 (26) $\times$ 5.5-7.5 (8) μ; cap cuticle of hyphae 3-5 μ wide, end cells tubular, flexuous, content of cells in Meldzer's lacking globules.

Scattered near dwarf birch in cold northern habitats or high mountain bogs.

6b. Not as above 7
7a. Cap slimy viscid ....
........................*Leccinum glutinopallens* **Smith, Thiers & Watling**
Caps 6-7 cm, glabrous, margin pallid, disc vinaceous-buff; context when cut slowly staining pinkish tan, spotting bluish with $FeSO_4$; pores pallid, when injured staining avellaneous then dingy brown; stipe 6-8 cm long, 10-15 mm thick, staining pinkish tan from handling, ornamentation very fine and at first pallid, in darkening merely becoming pinkish tan; spores 15-19 $\times$ 5-6.5 μ; caulocystidia clavate to fusoid-ventricose; cuticle of cap a layer of gelatinous hyphae 4-8 μ wide, the cells 30-300 μ long, end cells tubular to weakly cystidioid, content of hyphal cells in Melzer's homogeneous to granular.

Under birch, aspen, balsam, and spruce, Sugar Island, Michigan, July, rare.

7b. Not as above 8
8a. Many of the caulocystidia with a proliferated neck (fig. 214-c); spores 18-26 $\times$ 6-7.5 μ ....
..........................*Leccinum proliferum* **Smith, Thiers & Watling**
Cap 4-6 cm, dry to subviscid, white, spotted with minute brownish appressed squamules; context white, slowly grayish in stipe apex when cut; stipe 4-6 cm long, 8-11 mm at apex, 12-18 mm at base, pallid, overlaid with dull brown ornamentation; spores 18-26 $\times$ 6-7 μ; caulocystidia with neck often proliferated and hyphal-like (basically fusoid-ventricose to clavate); cuticle of cap of hyphae 4-10 μ wide, end cells tubular to slightly enlarged, hyphae tubular, content homogeneous as mounted in Melzer's.

On low ground under large-toothed aspen, northern Michigan, late summer and fall, not common.

8b. Not as above 9
9a. Spores 17-20 $\times$ 5.5-7 μ ....
........*Leccinum holopus* var. *lacteum* **Smith, Thiers & Watling**
Cap 4-7 cm, dry and dull, glabrous, milk white, disc finally vinaceous-buff to pale tan; context white, spotting olive with $FeSO_4$; pores pallid, if lightly bruised staining yellowish; stipe 9-12 cm long, 10-12 mm thick, surface oranmented with whitish scurf which darkens to pale crust brown, ground color pale tan in age; caulocystidia

mostly fusoid-ventricose, neck not proliferated; cuticle of cap of narrow (3-7 μ wide), tubular hyphae, end cells tubular or nearly so, hyphal content homogeneous as revived in Melzer's.

On hummocks under white cedar and black ash, Michigan, July.

9b. Spores 14-18 × 5-6 μ ....
................*Leccinum holopus* (**Rostk.**) **Watling**, var. *holopus*

Cap 3-10 cm, convex, glabrous, subviscid, dull white except for a vinaceous-buff disc; context unchanging when cut; pores whitish, staining yellowish when lightly bruised; stipe 8-14 cm long, 1-2 cm thick, ornamentation pallid but becoming brownish; caulocystidia fusoid-ventricose with neck elongated and somewhat flexuous, clavate cells also present; cuticle of cap of hyphae 4-7 μ wide, end cells tubular to weakly cystidioid, cell content homogeneous as revived in Melzer's.

Scattered in cold bogs, northern United States and Canada, summer and fall, uncommon.

Subsection FUMOSA

Key to Species

1a. Context in apex of stipe staining pinkish before changing to fuscous 2
1b. Stipe staining fuscous directly when sectioned near the apex ..3
2a. Spores 13-16.5 × 4-5 μ ....
.........*Leccinum murinaceo-stipitatum* **Smith, Thiers & Watling**

Cap 8-12 cm, glabrous, viscid, dark cinnamon-brown with a grayish overcast to blackish brown, margin yellowish at times; context white at first; tubes 1-1.5 cm deep, depressed, whitish then dark wood brown; pores small, olivaceous pallid, if bruised lightly staining olivaceous (if bruised severely staining vinaceous-buff); stipe 5-10 cm long, 2.5-3 cm at base, 1-2 cm thick at apex, drab to mouse-color over all as a result of the ground color and ornamentation both being gray; caulocystidia typically with a proliferated neck; hyphae of cap cuticle showing some pigment globules as revived in Melzer's.

Scattered in mixed woods containing both aspen and birch, July and August, Northern Michigan, rare.

2b. Spores 13-16 (19) × 4.5-6.5 (7) μ ....
.... see *Leccinum subleucophaeum* p. 210
3a. Spores 5-6.5 μ wide 4
3b. Spores 4-5 μ wide 5
4a. Cap glabrous and viscid when young ....
............*Leccinum olivaceo-glutinosum* **Smith, Thiers & Watling**

Cap 5-10 cm, glabrous, viscid to slimy, dull olive to olive-brown, becoming olive-green over marginal area; context pallid, slowly avellaneous when cut, instantly blue with $FeSO_4$; tubes 1-2 cm deep, pallid becoming wood brown; pores pallid, staining yellowish brown injured; stipe 9-15 cm long, 9-15 mm thick; pallid, tinged vinaceous or olivaceous at times near apex, ornamentation of blackish dots and squamules; spore deposit near "Argus brown" (rich yellow-brown); spores 16-19 $\times$ 5-6.5 μ; cuticle of cap of appressed tubular hyphae with end cells elongate-subfusoid, hyphal cells readily disarticutlating.

Scattered where birch is present, August, Upper Peninsula of Michigan, rare.

4b. Cap dry and streaked with dark fibrils ....
....see *Leccinum subleucophaeum*
5a. Cap fuscous to dark drab when young ....
........................*Leccinum griseonigrum* Smith, Thiers & Watling

Cap 4-9 cm, convex, fibrillose to subgranular, finally slightly areolate, bluish black to fuscous but finally paler to avellaneous or in age where exposed to sunlight bleaching to pale tan; context white, slowly blue when cut and in age changing to violaceous-gray; tubes 10-20 mm deep, white when young, then wood brown, slightly pinkish when cut; pores minute, pallid, when lightly bruised staining yellowish; stipe 5-11 cm long, 1-1.7 cm thick, finely ornamented with dark brown to dark gray squamules and points, wood brown around worm holes; spores 13-16 $\times$ 4-5.5 μ; cheilocystidia 28-42 $\times$ 8-12 μ, neck long and often crooked; caulocystidia ventricose with a crooked, filamentose elongated neck; cap cuticle of hyphae 4-8 (16) μ wide, tubular, walls smooth to rough, some short cells present, end cells bullet-shaped.

Gregarious under trembling aspen, apparently common under this tree but the distribution remains to be established.

5b. Cap pale tan to dark yellow-brown 6
6a. Tubes weakly yellowish when young ....
...........................*Leccinum huronensis* Smith, Thiers & Watling

Cap up to 10 cm, convex, subviscid, appressed-fibrillose, becoming only slightly areolate, dark yellow-brown but drying drab (near "hair brown"); context pallid, staining gray directly when cut; tubes weakly yellow then dark wood brown, 2 cm deep; pores small, staining olive when lightly bruised; stipe about 9 $\times$ 1 cm, cut surface soon fuscous, ornamentation of fine to coarse lines and squamules appearing blackish on a pallid ground color; spores 13-16 $\times$ 4-5 μ; caulocystidia clavate to fusoid-ventricose; cuticle of cap of appressed hyphae 3-9 μ wide, in Melzer's occasional cells showing pigment globules up to 6 μ wide.

Solitary, Yellow Dog River, Marquette county, Michigan, rare.

6b. Tubes white to pale olive-buff when young 7
7a. Context hyphae next to subcutis orange-red in Melzer's ....
...........................*Leccinum proximum* Smith, Thiers & Watling

Cap 3-7 cm, convex, dry and obscurely fibrillose, becoming glabrous and subviscid, color dingy yellow-brown to blackish brown; context white, thick, firm, slowly grayish when cut; tubes 8-12 mm deep, white, slowly wood brown; pores whitish at first, stained yellow when injured lightly; stipe 4-9 cm long, 8-13 mm thick at apex, slowly staining vinaceous-gray when cut in the apex, stained orange-buff in base in some; surface ornamentation brownish black on a pallid ground; spores 14-18 (20) $\times$ 4.5-6 μ; cap cutis of hyphae 3-5 μ wide in epicutis and 6-15 μ below, cells disarticulating, end cells 25-100 μ long, cystidioid.

Under birch, Michigan, rare, summertime.

7b. Context hyphae not colored as in above choice ....
....................*Leccinum disarticulatum* Smith Thiers & Watling

Cap 4-10 cm, convex, streaked with short appressed fibrils, becoming subviscid, dry and unpolished at first, color pale dingy tan near the margin, dingy cinnamon over the disc; context white, soon stained pinkish gray on cut surface, bluish gray with $FeSO_4$; tubes 10-12 mm long, white at first, pores white but dingy brown in age, staining yellow at white stage when lightly bruised, small; stipe 7-12 cm long, 10-20 mm thick, cut surface white then pinkish gray then finally fuscous, surface ornamentation brown to blackish below, paler above; spores 12-16.5 $\times$ 4.5-6 μ; cutis of cap of appressed hyphae 6-12 μ wide.

Scattered under birch and aspen, Cheboygan County, Michigan, July.

Subsection SCABRA

Key to Species

1a. Pores staining rusty cinnamon when bruised; odor when fresh strongly raphanoid ....
........................*Leccinum parvulum* Smith, Thiers & Watling

Cap 2.5-3.5 cm, obtuse then broadly convex or umbonate, viscid, pallid becoming pale tan, becoming minutely areolate at times; context white, when cut slowly grayish brown in old ones, with $FeSO_4$ slowly olive, with KOH brownish, taste mild, odor strongly of radish; tubes 1 cm deep, dull cinnamon mature, becoming nearly free; pores minute, dull cinnamon like the tubes, staining rusty cinnamon where bruised; stipe 6-8 cm long, 7-9 mm thick near apex, base with a napiform bulb, surface ornamented with dingy cinnamon elements not darkening much on aging; stipe interior white, slowly wood brown in apex when cut; spores 14-17 $\times$ 4.5-5.5 (6) μ; caulocystidia both clavate and fusoid-ventricose types mixed; cuticular hyphae of cap 5-11 μ wide, some terminal cells bullet-shaped, content not forming globules in Melzer's.

Scattered under oak and pine, Cheboygan County, Michigan, June, rare.
1b. Not as above 2
2a. Spores 10-15 × 3.5-4.5 μ; stipe becoming yellow over a considerable portion of its length ....
....*Leccinum flavostipitatum* **Dick & Snell**
Cap 6-10 cm, minutely fibrillose then glabrous, grayish black to paler, some tinged greenish; context white but when cut slowly pinkish; tubes nearly free, long, white at first and pores concolor; stipe up to 11 cm long, and 2 cm thick, ornamentation blackish, ground color mostly pale yellow and drying yellow, cortex when cut changing to pinkish, yellow and blue-green stains may also be present; caulocystidia clavate to fusoid-ventricose; hyphae of stipe cortex lemon yellow in KOH; cuticular hyphae of cap 4-10 μ wide, few short slightly inflated cells present, cell content not forming globules as revived in Melzer's.

Gregarious under spruce, Nova Scotia, Canada, apparently rare.
2b. Spores 5-7 μ wide 3
3a. Stipe in apex staining pink or redder when cut 4
3b. Stipe apex unchanging when cut or slowly becoming slightly brownish 6
4a. Cap coffee brown to dark rusty brown; cap cuticle of hyphae 4-6 μ wide and with numerous pigment globules as revived in Melzer's ....*Leccinum coffeatum* **Smith, Thiers & Watling**
Cap 5-10 cm, convex, glabrous, becoming viscid, dark coffee brown; context white, when cut slightly vinaceous; with $FeSO_4$ bluish; tubes 1-1.5 cm long, depressed, pallid becoming dark yellow-brown; pores small, pallid at first, staining yellowish cinnamon bruised; stipe 6-10 cm long, 1-2 cm thick, ornamented by fine brown points, ground color pallid above, grayish below; spores 15-19 (20) × 5-7 μ; caulocystidia mostly clavate to elliptic-pedicellate; cuticular hyphae of cap 3-6 μ wide.

Scattered under birch and aspen, Chippewa County, Michigan, July, rare.
4b. Not as above 5
5a. Cap dull cinnamon young and darker cinnamon when mature; stipe ornamentation fine and long remaining pallid ....
........................*Leccinum pallidistipes* **Smith, Thiers & Watling**
Cap 5-10 cm, convex, dry becoming viscid, glabrous, dull cinnamon; context pallid, reddish when cut, bluish with $FeSO_4$; tubes 1-2 cm deep, pallid to wood brown; pores grayish pallid staining yellow-brown to dark cinnamon; stipe 9-14 cm long, 1-2 cm thick, surface pallid, ornamentation fine and pallid, darkening only in age; spores 15-18 × 5-6 μ; caulocystidia clavate to fusoid; cuticular hyphae of cap 4-8 μ wide, content not forming globules in Melzer's, end cells clavate to weakly cystidioid.

Solitary to scattered under birch, Chippewa County, Michigan, July, rare.

5b. Cap pale pinkish buff becoming grayer; stipe ornamentation coarse .... *Leccinum rimulosum* **Smith, Thiers & Watling**

Cap 3-10 cm, convex, unpolished, subareolate, becoming subviscid, very pale crust brown (pale tan), with an overlay of grayish brown squamules; context when cut slowly vinaceous; tubes 1.5 cm long, pallid; pores readily staining dingy grayish brown; stipe 4-9 cm long, 1-3 cm thick at apex, clavate to fusiform, ornamentation sparse and coarse, pallid and darkening slowly; spores $15\text{-}18 \times 5\text{-}6$ μ; caulocystidia clavate to mucronate; cuticular hyphae of cap 5-9 μ wide, content not forming globules in Melzer's, end cells weakly cystidioid.

Under birch, Chippewa County, Michigan, July, rare.

6a. Caulocystidia often with a proliferated neck ....
........................*Leccinum singeri* **Smith, Thiers & Watling**

Cap 3-8 cm, convex, glabrous, viscid, gray-brown to bister; context when cut staining dingy pinkish tan, with $FeSO_4$ quickly bluish; tubes up to 2 cm long, wood brown mature, depressed; pores avellaneous staining yellowish bruised; stipe 6-12 cm long, 10-15 mm thick at apex, when sectioned staining red and/or yellow in some part usually near the base, ornamentation fine, weakly brownish to finally blackish at least near the base; spores $15\text{-}20 \times 5\text{-}6.5$ μ; caulocystidia mostly ventricose-mucronate and neck becoming proliferated; cuticular hyphae of cap 4-12 (15) μ wide, some cells disarticulating, content homogeneous in Melzer's, end cells on broad hyphae bullet shaped.

Scattered in mixed woods, Emmet County, Michigan, July, uncommon.

6b. Not as above 7
7a. Stipe ornamentation fine, pallid becoming orange to cinnabar but finally darkening in drying or in age ....
........................*Leccinum subpulchripes* **Smith, Thiers & Watling**

Cap 3-4.5 cm, convex, glabrous, viscid, pale tan; context pallid, unchanging when cut, with $FeSO_4$ instantly blue to grayish blue; tubes wood brown mature; pores staining yellow-brown bruised; stipe 3-5.5 cm long, 5-9 mm thick, when cut stained cinnabar in base, interior generally yellowish, surface furfuraceous from pallid ornamentation which becomes orange and finally cinnabar; spores 14-18 $\times$ 5-6.5 μ; caulocystidia mostly fusoid but apex more obtuse than acute; cuticular hyphae of cap 4-9 μ wide, content not forming globules in Melzer's, cells readily disarticulating, end cells narrowly cystidioidal.

Scattered under pine and alder, Luce County, Mich. August rare.

7b. Stipe ornamentation coarse over lower half of stipe and soon black over that area ....
.... *Leccinum scabrum* (Fr.) S. F. Gray

Cap 4-10 cm, convex, unpolished becoming viscid, glabrous at maturity, grayish brown to dingy yellowish brown but in age often olive tinted; context white, when cut unchanging; tubes 8-14 mm long, pallid, depressed, wood brown mature; pores pallid staining yellowish when lightly bruised; stipe 7-12 (15) cm long, 7-12 (16) mm thick, surface with coarse black ornamentation over lower part, paler and ornamentation finer above; spores 15-19 $\times$ 5-7 μ; caulocystidia mostly clavate-mucronate; cuticular hyphae of cap 6-15 μ wide, homogeneous to granular in Melzer's, some hyphae with one (or 2) short, slightly inflated cells.

Scattered under birch, throughout the range of the genus, apparently, at least, in conterminous United States, late summer and fall, not uncommon—but often misidentified.

Section LUTEOSCABRA

Cuticle of cap a cellular epithelium, or with inflated cells numerous but not compacted in a layer, or many hyphae with inflated to globose cells solitary or scattered in a filament; hymenophore often yellow (subsect. *Luteoscabra*) and cap typically smooth (appearing fibrillose in subsect. *Pseudoscabra*).

Key to Subsections

1a. Context and/or hymenophore yellow in some degree when young or upon being dried ... Subsection *Luteoscabra* p. 208
1b. Young tube layer pallid or only faintly yellow just before maturing to wood brown 2
2a. Cap cuticle a distinct cellular epithelium (it may collapse on old specimens); cap glabrous and shining by maturity as a rule .... Subsection *Albella* p. 209
2b. Cap cuticle of filaments containing some distinctly inflated cells or these rather numerous but not forming a layer, cap fibrillose .... Subsection *Pseudoscabra* p. 210

Subsection LUTEOSCABRA

Key to Species

1a. Spores 6-8 μ wide; cap often blackish on the disc ....
.... *Leccinum crocipodium* (Letellier) Watling

Cap 4-7.5 cm, margin obtuse, surface resinous to the touch and soon areolate; context staining vinaceous-gray when cut, green in

FeSO$_4$; tubes at maturity grayish brown; pores pale olive-ochraceous and staining brown where injured; stipe 5-7 cm long, 10-17 mm thick, usually red at base; context yellowish, surface resinous-furfuraceous, the particles discoloring to dull brown; spores 14-18 (20) $\times$ 6-8 μ; inflated cells of pileus cutis not forming a distinct layer.

Gregarious under hardwoods in thin woods, eastern North America to the Great Lakes region, summer and fall, rare.

1b. Spores 3.5-6.5 μ wide 2
2a. Cap uneven to pitted; stipe resinous to the touch ....*Leccinum rugosiceps* (Peck) Singer

Cap 5-13 cm, convex, yellow to orange-ochraceous, reddish when cut; tubes pale bright yellow young, not staining on pores when bruised; stipe 8-10 cm long, 2-3 cm thick, surface furfuraceous-punctate to obscurely reticulate; pleurocystidia 36-48 $\times$ 9-13 μ; spores (14) 16-21 $\times$ 5-6 μ.

Gregarious under hardwoods in thin woods, eastern North America west to the Great Lakes and southward, common southward.

2b. Cap smooth or slightly wrinkled; stipe not resinous to the touch 3
3a. Stipe ornamentation pallid becoming blackish; spores 17-20 $\times$ 5-6 μ ....*Leccinum luteum* Smith, Thiers & Watling

Cap 3-6.5 cm, glabrous, subvciscid, shallowly pitted at times, pale yellow becoming olive-brown; context pallid to flushed yellow, staining vinaceous-gray when cut; tubes pallid when young, about 15 mm long; pores 2-3 per mm; stipe 6-13 cm long, 8-10 mm thick above, pallid, yellow near base, ornamentation as fine blackish points; spores 17-20 $\times$ 5-6.5 μ; caulocystidia 50-120 $\times$ 10-20 μ, neck often proliferated.

Scattered under blue beech (Carpinus) on low ground, southeastern Michigan, rare.

3b. Stipe ornamentation soon amber to rusty colored; spores 10-14 $\times$ 3.5-5 μ ....*Leccinum brunneo-olivaceum* Snell, Dick & Hesler

Cap 5-9 cm, viscid or subviscid, glabrous, light brownish olive; context yellowish, with reddish stains when cut; tubes free from stipe, yellow, unchanging; pores 2-3 per mm; stipe 4-8 cm long, 7-12 mm thick, furfuraceous-scabrous, yellowish within, red stained; spores 10-14 $\times$ 3.5-4.5 μ; color in KOH pale golden yellow; cuticle of cap a poorly organized layer of cystidioid hyphal end cells.

Rare, known only from the south.

Subsection ALBELLA

Key to Species

1a. Cap yellow at first ....see *L. luteum*
1b. Cap yellow-brown to fuscous or whitish 2

2a. Context in apex of stipe (use young specimens) not staining when cut .... *Leccinum albellum* (Peck) Singer

Cap 3-6 cm, plano-convex, glabrous, smooth to pitted, in age often areolate, but occasionally velutinous at first, whitish to pale buff or tan or olive-buff, at times yellowish; context 1-1.5 cm thick, white, unchanging; tubes whitish at first, deeply depressed; pores about 1 mm broad, pallid and unchanging; stipe 5-8 cm long, 7-11 mm at apex, white to pale olive-buff, becoming scabrous and ornamentation darkening in age; spores (10) 15-19.5 (24) $\times$ 4-6 μ.

Common in southern United States but increasingly rare northward, summer and fall under hardwoods. There are a number of variants of this species in need of further study.

2b. Context in apex of stipe staining gray and finally blackish .... *Leccinum griseum* (Quélet) Singer

Cap 3-9 cm broad, glabrous, smooth becoming rugulose to pitted, areolate in age, dingy yellow-brown becoming olive-brown to olive along margin or in local areas; context pallid staining gray when cut; tubes 10-20 mm deep, becoming free, pallid becoming wood brown; tubes 10-20 mm deep; pores pallid avellaneous staining greenish when bruised; stipe 4-12 cm long, 8-15 mm thick, pallid to grayish, furfuraceous to scabrous, ornamentation gray-brown; spores 11-15 $\times$ 5.5-6 μ.

Gregarious to scattered, under hardwoods, Michigan, common early in the fall during wet seasons.

Subsection PSEUDOSCABRA

Key to Species

1a. Stipe apex or adjacent context of cap when cut staining reddish before changing to some other color 2

1b. Stipe apex when cut not staining as in above choice; cuticular hyphae of cap as revived in Melzer's showing some pigment globule formation ....
.... *Leccinum aberrans* Smith, Thiers & Watling

Cap about 7 cm, dry, subtomentose, dark grayish brown, pallid ground color showing beneath; context white, taste strongly acid at first, when cut becoming weakly pinkish tan in stipe apex; tubes 1.5 cm deep, depressed; pores minute, gray, staining cinnamon-brown where injured; stipe about 5 cm long, 1 cm thick, solid, equal, dark gray from closely spaced points and squamules; spores 16-22 $\times$ 5-7 μ; epicuticular hyphae of cap with end cells 15-30 μ wide.

Under birch, rare, south shore of Lake Superior, Chippewa County, Michigan.

2a. Color change in stipe apex progressing to gray or fuscous ....
.... *Leccinum subleucophaeum* Dick & Snell

Cap 3-10 (15) cm, convex, with dark appressed fibrils, often blackish over disc, grayish toward margin; context white, slowly becoming gray when cut; tubes whitish then avellaneous, 10-20 mm deep, deeply depressed; pores about 2 per mm; stipe 5-10 (15) cm long, 10-20 mm thick, surface covered with black scabrous points, staining greenish at base where handled; spores 13-16 (19) × 4.5-6.5 (7) μ.

Scattered to gregarious in sandy aspen-beech woods, New England, Michigan, summer and fall, not common.

2b. Color change to pink soon fading back to pallid or surface browning slightly 3
3a. Cap pallid at first, becoming pale crust-brown ....
....*Leccinum oxydabile* (Singer) Singer

Cap 2.5-3 cm, slightly fibrillose but soon glabrous; tubes white when young, becoming cream-buff when cut; stipe 6-7 cm long, 8-10 mm thick at apex, pallid, slowly staining vinaceous when cut, surface with fine ornamentation which is white at first but becomes avellaneous; spores 15-21 × 5-6.5 μ; pleurocystidia 48-75 × 9-16 μ, fusoid-ventricose with long narrow neck; cheilocystidia 18-32 × 6-10 μ; cap cutis of hyphae 7-15 wide, the end cells clavate to subglobose.

Under birch along roadsides, rare. Great Lakes region, summer.

3b. **Cap at first with an over-lay of blackish fibrils; caulocystidia often with a secondary septum distal to the ventricose part (fig. 214-c)**.................*Leccinum snellii* **Smith, Thiers & Watling**

Cap 3-9 cm, dry but subviscid in age, fibrillose with appressed fascicles of dark brown to blackish fibrils, in age minutely squamulose to nearly glabrous; pores white at first becoming grayish and staining dingy ochraceous when bruised; stipe 4-11 cm long, 1-2 cm thick at apex, even, pink to dull red in the apex when cut, blue in lower part, surface white with blackish spots; spores (15) 16-22 × 5.5-7.5 μ; fusoid-ventricose pleurocystidia lacking; cheilocystidia 28-42 × 7-12 μ, fusoid-ventricose; cap cutis of hyphae having few to many inflated cells.

Scattered to gregarious along roads under yellow birch, Great Lakes region, midsummer on into August during wet weather.

BOLETUS

Fruit bodies fleshy, typically centrally stipitate, hymenophore usually readily peeling away from context of pileus; spore deposit olive, olive-brown, olive-yellow, amber brown or fuscous brown; tube trama wtih hyphae somewhat divergent from central strand.

Key to Sections

1a. Spores ornamented by a loosely fitting outer layer which collapses to form warts and wrinkles; cap viscid; stipe more or less lacerate reticulate .... *Allospori*
One species. Fig. 216 .... *Boletus betula* Schweinitz

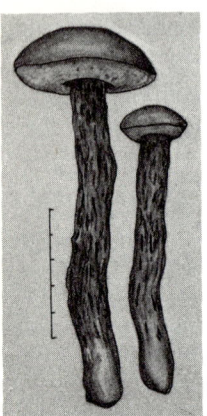

Fig. 216. *Boletus betula*.

Cap 3-9 cm, convex, reddish, orange-brown or yellow, yellow tints more evident in age; context greenish yellow near tubes but orange-yellow near cuticle, unchanging if injured; tubes depressed, dark greenish yellow; pores about 1 mm broad, pale yellow at first, greenish yellow in age, unchanging when injured; stipe 10-20 cm long, 7-16 mm thick, lacerate-reticulate, yellow upward and reddish downward but in age reddish over all; spores $15\text{-}18 \times 6\text{-}9 \mu$, apex with a distinct pore; cuticle of cap a trichoderium of hyphae 4-7 μ wide, the end-cells subclavate to nearly cylindric.

Scattered, most often under mixed pine and oak, but southeastern and southern but extending northward along the Atlantic coast, common during warm wet summer weather during some seasons but seldom found in quantity.

1b. Spores smooth though apex may be truncate or notched (fig. 162) 2

2a. Spores flattened (truncate) or notched (fig. 162 r) at apex .... *Truncati* p. 227

2b. Spores not with a modified apex 3

3a. Tubes in age tending to become pink to red throughout or in part; taste acrid in some species; cap subviscid or merely soft to the touch (see *Suillus castanellus* also p. 153) .... *Piperati* p. 213

3b. Not as above 4

4a. Pores some shade of orange, red dark brown to bay-brown when young .... subsect. *Luridi* of sect. *Boletus* p. 236

4b. Pores not colored as above when young 5

5a. Stipe typically reticulate (see fig. 241) at least near apex; pores are not stuffed when young (see sect. *Subtomentosi*) .... *Boletus* p. 235

5b. Stipe furfuraceous to pruinose or glabrous, at times coarsely ridged or with coarse wide-mished reticulation 6

6a. Cap unpolished to velvety or subtomentose .... Sect. *Subtomentosi* p. 214

NON-GILLED FLESHY FUNGI 213

6b. Cap glabrous and moist or viscid 7

7a. Stipe furfuraceous to punctate but ornamentation not darkening as in *Leccinum* .... Sect. *Pseudoleccinum* p. 229

7b. Stipe more or less pruinose to naked (see subsect. *Calopodes* of *Boletus* also.) .... Sect. *Pseudoboleti* p. 231

Section PIPERATI

Taste of raw flesh sharply acrid (mild in *B. rubinellus*), the tubes reddish to rose-red throughout at maturity or in age, cap soft to the touch and subviscid when wet.

Key to Species

1a. Taste mild; tubes soon red throughout. Fig. 217 ....
.... *Boletus rubinellus*

Cap 2-5 cm broad, soft and subviscid; tubes deep wine-red throughout; stipe 2-5 cm long, 5-7 mm thick, equal, pale yellow within, surface yellow to red in varying proportions; spores $9\text{-}13 \times 3.5\text{-}4\ \mu$; pleurocystidia $36\text{-}48\ (55) \times 9\text{-}15\ \mu$, fusoid-ventricose; cuticle of cap a trichodermium of hyaline (in KOH) subgelatinous hyphae.

Gregarious in mixed woods, including pine. Northeastern and north central North America, summer and fall, not common.

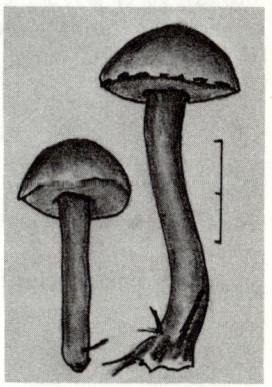

Fig. 217. *Boletus rubinellus*.

1b. Taste acrid; tubes sometimes finally becoming red over the pore surface as well as on the sides 2

2a. Pores staining blue when bruised ....
....*Boletus piperatoides* Smith & Thiers

Cap 3-6 cm, becoming nearly plane, dull orange-cinnamon, subviscid; taste slowly peppery; pores 2-3 per mm, dull yellow-brown where undamaged; stipe 4-6 cm long, 4-6 mm thick, honey-color above, lemon-yellow in base, base covered with lemon-yellow mycelium; spores $7\text{-}9\ (10) \times 3\text{-}3.5\ \mu$; cuticle of cap of appressed hyphae $4\text{-}8\ \mu$ wide; clamp connections absent.

Gregarious in low oak woods, Michigan, summer, during some seasons fairly frequent.

2b. Pores staining brownish slightly or not staining if injured (they may change color slowly from youth to age) taste acrid. Fig. 218 .... *Boletus piperatus* Fr.

Fig. 218. *Boletus piperatus*.

Cap 1.5-4 (10.5) cm broad, pellicle somewhat separable, subviscid moist, orange-cinnamon to clay-color or pale buff; tubes adnate becoming subdecurrent, ochraceous to brown when young, often becoming red to vinaceous-red in age (over the pores as well as the sides); stipe (2) 3-6 (8) cm long, 3-7 (12) mm thick, equal, solid, yellowish within and streaked reddish, surface concolorous with cap to reddish, base usually coated with yellow mycelium; spores 8.4-9 (12) $\times$ 4-4.5 μ; pleurocystidia and cheilocystidia similar, 43-60 $\times$ 8-13 μ, fusoid-ventricose to subcylindric, neck tapered; cutis of cap a tangled trichodermium of broad (10-17 μ), somewhat fusoid or cylindrical end cells.

Solitary to gregarious under hardwoods or conifers, northern U.S.A. and in Canada, summer and fall, often common.

Section SUBTOMENTOSI

Key to Subsections

1a. Fruit bodies attached to those of the gastromycete *Scleroderma*. Fig. 219 .... Subsect. *Parasitici*
Only one species included: .... *Boletus parasiticus* Fries

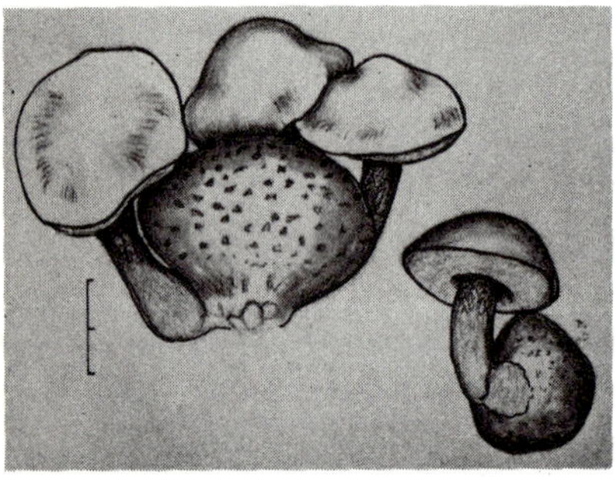

Cap 2-8 cm broad, unpolished to velvety, olivaceous to tawny-olive, with a narrow sterile margin; context pale lemon yellow, bluish black in Melzer's applied to the cut surface, instantly orange-ochraceous in KOH; tubes 3-5 (10) mm deep, adnate but with decurrent lines; pores honey-yellow slowly staining ochraceous when injured; stipe 2-6 cm long, 8-13 mm thick, pale yellow within, sur-

Fig. 219. *Boletus parasiticus*.

face obscurely fibrillose, instantly cinnabar-orange where KOH is applied; spores 12-18.5 × 3.5-5 μ; trichodermium of pileus of hyphae 4-9 μ wide with some inflated cells to 15-20 μ wide.

Widely distributed in North America but apparently common only in the southeastern states, summer and fall.

1b. Habitat terrestrial or lignicolous 2

2a. Spores short (7-9 × 3-3.5 μ); habitat on decayed wood ....
....Subsect. *Sulphurei*
Only one species treated here: ....*Boletus sphaerocephalus* **Barla**

Cap 5-10 cm broad surface soft and subviscid to the touch, unpolished, sulphur yellow fresh; veil lacking; context sulphur yellow, staining blue when cut; tubes 10-15 mm deep, pores 2-3 per mm, blue when injured; stipe 6-10 cm long, 1-2.5 cm thick, yellow and unpolished; spores 7-9 × 3-3.5 μ, bright yellow in KOH; cuticle of pileus of interwoven hyphae some cells of which are inflated to 8-12 μ in the midportion.

Clustered on sawdust piles, occasional in eastern North America but more widely distributed, summer.

2b. Not as above 3

3a. At least some spores in a mount notched or truncate at apex (fig. 162 r) .... see Sect. *Truncati* p. 227

3b. Not as above 4

4a. Spores often over 20 μ long; pileus granulose-squamulose at maturity .... Subsect. *Mirabiles* p. 216

4b. Spores smaller; pileus not as above 5

5a. Pileus dark to bright red when young; tubes yellow and pores staining blue (often slowly) when bruised ....
....Subsect. *Fraterni* p. 223

5b. Pileus differently colored when young 6

6a. Pores staining greenish to blue when injured (often slowly) ....
....Subsect. *Subtomentosi* p. 220

6b. Pores staining yellow to brownish or unchanging ....
.... **Subsect.** *Versicolores* **p. 216**

Subsection MIRABILES

1a. Growing on or beside decaying conifer logs; cap surface granulose-roughened. Fig. 220 .... *Boletus mirabilis* Murrill

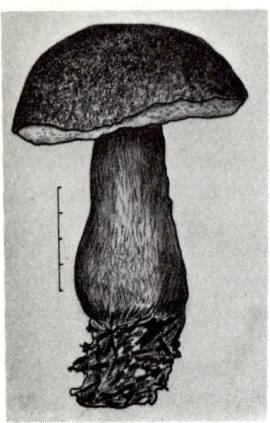

Pileus 5-16 (20) cm broad, dry, dark bay to dark grayish brown; pores staining yellow when bruised; stipe 8-12 (20) cm long, 1-3.5 cm thick, often with a wide coarse reticulum at apex, surface dull reddish brown; spores $19\text{-}24 \times 7\text{-}9$ μ; cap trichodermium of comparatively short cells ($26\text{-}80 \times 10\text{-}15$ μ), their pigment rapidly disintegrating in KOH.

Common in the Pacific Northwest but rare in the Great Lakes area, fall. Edible.

Fig. 220. *Boletus mirabilis*.

1b. Terrestrial, surface of young pileus subtomentose to subgranulose. Fig. 221 .... *Boletus projectellus* Murrill

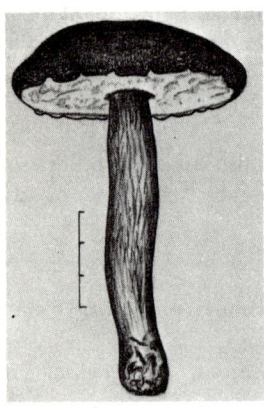

Pileus 4-15 cm broad, dry, subtomentose, soon areolate, reddish to dingy cinnamon; cut flesh slowly changing to yellow-brown; pores staining yellow when bruised; stipe 7-12 cm long, 1-2 cm thick, at times staining olive-brown when cut surface, exterior unpolished, shallowly reticulate at times; spores $18\text{-}33 \times 7.5\text{-}10$ (12) μ; trichodermium of cap soon collapsing, the hyphae 4-8 μ wide.

Scattered under 2- needle pines on sandy soil, southeastern states and Great Lakes area, common during very wet seasons, late summer or early fall. Edible.

Fig. 221. *Boletus projectellus*.

Subsection VERSICOLORES

1a. Spore deposit bright yellow-brown (amber brown) 2
1b. Spore deposit not as above 3

2a. Pileus rugulose at first, vinaceous-brown to yellow-brown, not spotted .... see *Boletus affinis* var. *affinis* Peck p. 233
2b. Pileus with pale spots; spores 9-16 × 3-5 μ ....
....see *Boletus affinis* var. *maculosus* Peck
3a. Stipe narrowed to base, reticulate and attached tenaciously to the substrate .... *Boletus tenax* Smith & Thiers

Pileus 4-10 cm, finally plane to depressed, buffy brown becoming red, NH$_4$OH on fresh cuticle quickly bright green, surface velvety; tubes yellow, decurrent; pores 1-3 mm radially, unchanging if injured; spores 9-12 × 4.5-5.5 μ; cuticle of pileus a trichodermium, some cells short and disarticulating; hyphae of subcuticular region with patches of weakly dextrinoid material adhering on them.

Under oak, September, during wet seasons in southern Michigan.

3b. Not as above 4
4a. Spores 8-11 × 3-5 μ 5
4b. Spores 10 μ or more long (see *B. mariae* also) 8
5a. Pleurocystidia 38-70 (100) × 9-16 μ, content dark brown in Melzer's, yellow in KOH .... *Boletus auriporus* Peck

Pileus 3-7 cm broad, dry, subpruinose, in age matted-fibrillose under a lens, dingy yellow-brown to dull reddish brown; context pale yellow, unchanging, taste slightly acid; tubes lemon-chrome (very bright), retaining this color dried; pores 2-3 per mm and widening to 1-2.5 mm near stipe; stipe 3-6 cm long, 1-1.5 cm thick, pale yellow to brownish, dark yellow-brown where handled, somewhat viscid when wet, faintly pruinose with yellow pruina when young; hyphae of pileus cuticle matted down, 6-12 (20) μ wide, content yellow in KOH but soon fading.

Scattered to gregarious under hardwoods, most abundant in our southeastern states but extending up the Atlantic Coast and northward to Michigan, summer or early fall after heavy rains.

5b. Pleurocystidia not dark brown or red in Melzer's ....•....6
6a. Pileus rusty red .... *Boletus roxanae* Frost

Pileus 3-8 cm, dry, granulose-roughened, glabrous in age; context buffy white, unchanging, odor weakly pungent, taste acid-disagreeable, FeSO$_4$ on cut surface grayish, KOH brownish; tubes 5-8 mm long, depressed around the stipe, pale yellow, unchanging; stipe 4-8 cm long, 8-12 mm at apex, cortex lemon yellow, surface yellow above and yellow-brown below, cuticle of pileus a trichodermium of hyphae 5-12 μ wide with some cells enlarged to 30 μ, yellow in KOH but soon hyaline.

Solitary to scattered in sandy oak woods, eastern North America late summer.

6b. Not as above 7
7a. Pileus olive to honey yellow ....
.... *Boletus mariae* Smith & Thiers

Cap 4-9 cm broad, dry and velvety to subtomentose, NH_4OH on cuticle immediately brown; tubes olive-yellow, unchanging if bruised; stipe 5-9 cm long, 8-15 mm thick, yellowish within, surface near apex with a faint wide-meshed reticulum, densely pruinose downward, the pruinosity brownish; spores 9-12 (13) $\times$ 3.5-4.5 μ; trichodermium of pileus of cells 9-16 (18) μ wide, short and often inflated, end cells bullet-shaped.

7b. **Pileus pale tan** .... *Boletus subilludens* Smith & Thiers

Cap 4-9 cm, glabrous and unpolished, finally somewhat areolate or diffracted-squamulose; context pale yellow, unchanging when cut; tubes bright yellow, drying olive-ochraceous, 1 cm long, depressed around the stipe, unchanging when injured; stipe 3-8 cm long, 6-12 mm thick, yellow within, brighter as dried, surface yellow-brown, naked; cuticle of pileus a tangle of hyphae 4-9 μ wide, end cells tubular, at least some cells readily disarticulating.

Gregarious in low wet hardwood forests, Great Lakes region, August, rare.

8a. **Trichodermium of pileus containing elements having some short inflated cells** 10
8b. **Trichodermium of pileus of hyphae with essentially tubular cells** 9
9a. **Spores 10-13 (14) $\times$ 3.5-4.2 μ; pileus olive-yellow to dull yellow-brown** ....*Boletus subpalustris* Smith & Thiers

Cap 3-5 cm, dry, velvety, NH_4OH on cuticle dull olive at first; context yellowish, unchanging if cut; tubes 1 cm deep, nearly free, dull yellow; stipe 3-6 cm long, 5-10 mm thick; pileus trichodermium of tubular cells 6-11 μ wide, short slightly inflated cells rarely present.

On wet ground under aspen, June, Great Lakes Area, probably not rare, summer and early fall.

9b. **Spores 9-12 (13) $\times$ 4-5 μ; pileus dingy pale cinnamon** ....see *Boletus alutaceus* Morgan in Peck p. 235

10a. **Spores (13) 14-17 $\times$ 4-5.5 μ; pileus vinaceous- brown or orange-brown** ......see *Boletus hoseneae* Smith & Thiers p. 235
10b. **Spores 10-14 μ long, pileus not as above** 11
11a. **Pores 1-2 per mm at maturity** 12
11b. **Pores 1-2 mm wide at maturity** 13
12a. **Terminal cells of cap trichodermal elements mostly bullet-shaped to cystidioid** ....*Boletus minutiporus* Smith & Thiers

Cap 4-6 cm broad, dry, subtomentose, olive-buff; context pallid to very pale yellow, when cut slowly staining slightly greenish blue; NH_4OH on cuticle dingy olive then (quickly) brownish; tubes 5-7 mm deep, adnate to short decurrent; pores 1.5-2.5 per mm, unchanging bruised; stipe 3.5-6 cm long, 9-14 mm thick, pallid within, with pale yellow mycelium near base, yellow above this and pale tan near apex; spores 10-13 × 4-5 μ.

Under hardwoods, early summer, northern Michigan, rare(?)

12b. Terminal cells of pilear trichodermal elements globose to dumbbell-shaped .... *Boletus brunneocitrinus* **Smith & Thiers**

Cap 3-5 cm broad, subtomentose, NH_4OH on cuticle dull brown immediately; tubes up to 15 mm deep, dull yellow; stipe 5-8 cm long, 5-8 mm thick, base covered with bright yellow mycelium, pruinose above iwth dark yellow-brown pruina; hyphae in subcutis of pileus with dextrinoid incrustations.

Solitary on very rotten conifer logs in waste areas, July, Great Lakes region, rarely collected.

13a. NH_4OH on fresh cap cuticle brillant green quickly changing to brown. Fig. 222 .... *Boletus illudens* **Peck**

Cap 3-9 cm broad, moist to subvelvety, not conspicuously areolate in age, pinkish cinnamon or a richer cinnamon drying with a strong yellow tone; context pallid then yellow, with $FeSO_4$ soon olive-black; tubes honey-yellow, becoming olive-yellow, adnate to decurrent; stipe 3-9 cm long (4) 6-13 mm wide, mustard yellow in cortex and around base, pallid to brownish to yellow over apical region; cap trichodermium of hyphae 4-12 μ wide, some cells 12-17 μ wide and globose or nearly so.

Fig. 222. *Boletus illudens.*

Densely gregarious to scattered under oak, late summer and fall, eastern North America and the Great Lakes area.

13b. NH_4OH on fresh cap; cuticle immediately purple then darkening .... *Boletus nancyae* **Smith & Thiers**

Cap 4-10 cm broad, subtomentose to tomentose or matted down and appressed-fibrillose-squamulose, dark yellow-brown; context yellow; tubes 9-13 mm deep, dull yellow; stipe 4-9 cm long, 8-15 mm thick, yellow within, surface coarsely reticulate and pruinose, pruina reddish, base coated with pale yellow mycelium; pilear trichodermial elements oval to subglobose, the cells often disarticulating; subcuticular hyphae with some dextrinoid pigment deposits on them.

Gregarious at edge of a bog, in a mixed forest, Great Lakes area, rare, early summer.

Subsection SUBTOMENTOSI

The chief distinguishing feature of this subsection is the slight to distinct change to blue or bluish green observed on the freshly bruised pore surface. It may take a few minutes for this to become evident.

Key to Species

1a. Cap olive-fuscous to blackish but with a hoary bloom at first, becoming various shades of olive to olive-brown or dingy yellow-brown, occasionally dull red. Fig. 223 .... *Boletus zelleri* **Murrill**

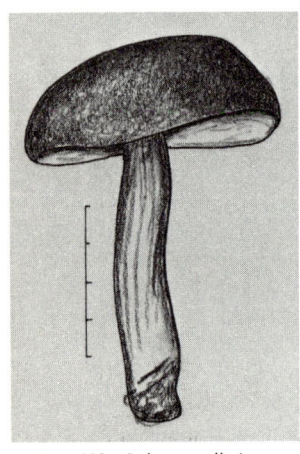

Fig. 223. *Boletus zelleri*.

Cap 5-12 cm, convex, smooth to rugulose, often unpolished to nearly velvety in age, finally areolate at times; context yellow, reddish in age at times under the cuticle; tubes yellow, blue if bruised, about 1 cm deep, pores small; stipe 5-10 cm long, 7-20 mm thick, dry, pruinose to punctate, yellowish with reddish overlay from pruina, or pruina lacking, redder in age; spores $12\text{-}15 \times 4\text{-}5.5$ μ; pleurocystidia $40\text{-}85 \times 10\text{-}13$ μ, clavate to mucronate or fusoid-ventricose; hyphae of cap cuticle forming a turf of inflated end cells.

Under cedar, alder, spruce and fir, Pacific Northwest, in California at times it appears to be associated with redwood, late summer, fall and through the winter if the weather is favorable, common. Edible.

1b. Not as above 2
2a. Cap olive, olive-yellow, rose or purplish, usually a mixture of these, the red more prominent in age; stipe often rose red in some part—often above the middle. Fig. 224 .... *Boletus smithii* **Thiers**

Cap 10-16 cm, convex to plane, dry, matted-fibrillose; context up to 3 cm thick, pallid yellow, with a red line beneath the cuticle, sometimes blue if injured; tubes 1-1.5 cm deep, yellow, blue if injured, pores small (1-2 per mm), yellow, in age obscurely reddish in places; stipe 10-16 cm long, 1-3.5 cm thick, yellow within, surface slightly appressed-fibrillose, rose red in some part—often near apex; spores 14-19 × 4-6 μ.

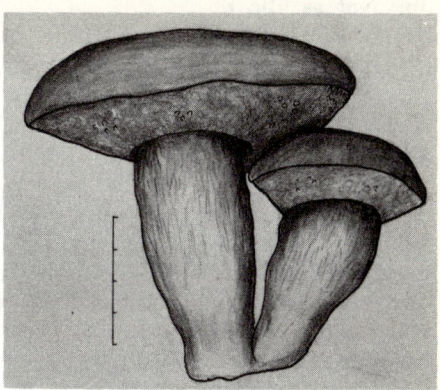

Fig. 224. *Boletus smithii.*

Solitary to gregarious in conifer forests, Pacific Northwest late summer and fall, fairly common.

2b. Not as above 3

3a. NH_4OH on cuticle dull brown; cuticular hyphae with dark yellow-brown walls as mounted in Melzer's; cap areolate, olive to olive-brown with red on margin and in the cracks of the cuticle. Fig. 225 ....*Boletus chrysenteron* **Fries**

Cap 3-8 cm, convex, finally plane, dry and velvety to subtomentose, dark olive to olive-brown but developing red tints variously; context whitish becoming yellow, slowly staining blue when cut, yellowish on blue areas with $FeSO_4$; tubes bright yellow becoming Isabella color, pores yellow, about 1 mm wide, staining blue; stipe 4-6 cm long, 5-10 mm thick, yellowish pallid at apex, purplish red in base, basal mycelium white, scurfy to pruinose over all; spores 9-13 × 3.5-4.5 μ; trichodermal hyphae with cells up to 20 μ wide, the walls dark yellow-brown in Melzer's, end cells cystidioid more or less.

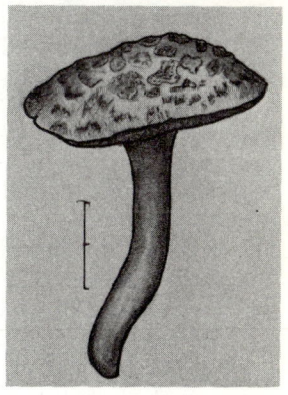

Fig. 225. *Boletus chrysenteron.*

Solitary to gregarious, summer and fall, on earth exposed around uprooted trees and along roads in the woods, common during some seasons, throughout eastern North America but rather rare in the western states.

3b. Not as above 4
4a. NH₄OH giving a green flash (or blue-green) when applied to the fresh cap (but see *B. minutiporus* also p. 218) ....
....*Boletus spadiceus* Fries

Cap 5-11 (18) cm, convex to nearly plane, dry, velvety, at times areolate in age, dark olive-buff to dingy yellow-brown, when wet reddish brown; context pallid yellow, rarely slightly blue if bruised, no reaction with FeSO₄; tubes 5-12 mm long, yellow-ocher, pores 1-2 mm wide; stipe 5-12 cm long, 1-3 cm thick, yellow within, surface unpolished and roughened, at times near apex with coarse lines (almost reticulate), tinged pinkish on a pallid ground color near apex, yellow lower down; spores (9) 11-14 × 4.5-5.5 μ; elements of cap trichodermium 6-12 μ wide, walls smooth and hyaline in KOH, lacking distinctly inflated short cells.

Solitary to gregarious on banks(especially along road cuts), late summer and fall, common in the Pacific Northwest, less common in eastern North America.

Var. *gracilis* with stipe 5-10 mm thick occurs in the Great Lakes area. Its spores are 9-12 (13) × 3.5-4.5 μ.

4b. NH₄OH giving a mahogany-red to dark brown reaction on cap 5
5a. Hyphae of the subcutis of the cap lacking rusty brown incrustations on the walls in Melzer's ....
....*Boletus tomentosulus* Smith & Thiers

Cap up to 12 cm, convex, granulose-rimose, yellow-ocher over all, context white, weakly yellow when dried; tubes 8-12 mm deep, decurrent, ocher-yellow, pores 1-1.5 mm wide; stipe 5-10 cm long, 15-20 mm thick, surface coarsely reticulate-ribbed or merely with longitudinal lines, yellow except for pinkish base which is partly covered by yellow mycelium; spores 11-14 × 3.8-4.8 μ; hyphae of cap trichodermium 6-15 μ wide, having some cells inflated to 20 μ.

Solitary to scattered on road banks, early summer, Michigan, rare.

5b. Hyhpae of subcutis having rusty brown incrustations on walls as seen mounted in Melzer's 6
6a. Hyphae of cap trichodermium with red content as mounted in Melzer's ....*Boletus subparvulus* Smith & Thiers

Cap 4-5 cm, convex, dark tobacco brown, glabrous, surface uneven; context pallid, slowly pale yellowish, with FeSO₄ slowly bluish gray; tubes dull yellow, pores weakly yellow; stipe 5-6 cm long, 8-10 mm thick, interior pale yellow above and rusty rose in the base, surface reddish pruinose on a yellow ground color above, downward rusty rose to yellowish at base; spores 10-13 × 4-4.5 μ; hyphae of the cap trichodermium heavily incrusted as seen in KOH mounts, incrusting material brown, end cells of hyphae clavate and up to 15 μ broad.

Solitary in hardwood slashings, northern Michigan, July, rare (?).
6b. Cuticular hyphae not as in above choice ....
....*Boletus subtomentosus* **Fries**

Cap 5-18 (20) cm, broadly convex, subtomentose, areolate in age, olivaceous to olive-yellow to yellow-brown, in age redder as cuticle collapses; context whitish becoming yellow; tubes 1-2.5 cm deep, variously attached (depresed, adnate or decurrent), pores 1-2.5 mm wide, yellow, olive-yellow in age; stipe 4-10 cm long, 1-2 (3) cm thick, surface pruinose to scabrous and variously reticulated with coarse lines at times, base sulphur yellow, pallid to dingy yellow beneath pruina above; spores 10-13 (15) $\times$ 3.5-5 μ; hyphae of cap trichodermium 8-14 μ wide; end cells merely obtuse (not enlarged), the hyphal cells elongate (4 times longer than broad or more).

Common in late summer and fall on road banks and hummocks in conifer forests but usually not in large numbers, northern U.S.A. and southern Canada.

A small variety (var. *perplexus* Fig. 226) with pallid basal mycelium and fairly numerous short cells in the trichodermal hyphae occurs in Michigan.

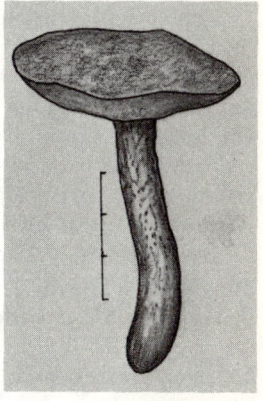

Fig. 226. *Boletus subtomentosus* var. *perplexus*.

Subsection FRATERNI

The species placed here have red to orange-red caps when young or freshly matured, the surface is typically velvety but it may be merely unpolished in some, and there is no significant reticulation on the stipe.

Key to Species

1a. Stipe 1-3 cm thick near apex 8
1b. Stipe 3-10 (15) mm thick near apex ..2
2a. Pores grayish olive; spores 7-8 $\times$ 4-5 μ Fig. 227 ....
........*Boletus tennessensis* **Smith & Snell**

Cap 6-9 cm broad, dry, unpolished; flesh whitish, quickly blue if cut (near tubes), tinged red around worm holes, taste very slightly bitterish (hardly distinctive); tubes adnate to decurrent, up to 7 mm long, cream-buff (yellowish) fresh, more olive

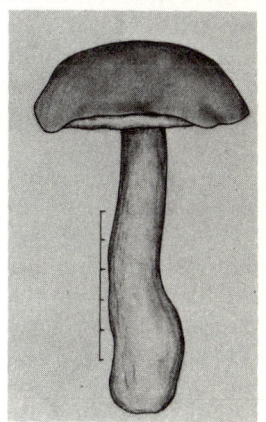

Fig. 227. *Boletus tennessensis*.

when mature, pores quickly blue if injured; stipe 8-10 cm long, 10-25 mm thick, furfuraceous to tomentose-areolate, extreme apex yellow, dingy pallid downward; spores subellipsoid; pleurocystidia 25-40 $\times$ 5-8 μ.

Solitary under mixed pine and oak, Tennessee, August, apparently rare.

2b. Not as above 3
3a. End cells of cuticular hyphae often with distinctive amyloid inclusions of amorphous material; inflated cells present in many epicuticular hyphae ....*Boletus flavorubellus* Smith & Thiers

Cap 2.5-8 cm, pulvinate to broadly convex, deep red, paler in age, finally fading to yellow; context flavous, gray in $FeSO_4$; tubes 4-5 mm deep, flavous, pores small (2-3 per mm), flavous; stipe 3-7 cm long, 5-11 mm thick, flavous within, surface flavous beneath reddish pruina or in portion the ground color reddish, base with yellow-ocher mycelium; spores 10-13 $\times$ 4-5 μ; hyphae of cap trichodermium 12-20 μ broad, 2-3 times as long as wide or some globose.

Scattered on wet earth, southern Michigan, late summer, rare.

3b. Not as above 4
4a. Spores 5-7 μ wide 5
4b. Spores 3.5-5 μ wide 6
5a. Pores large and angular; KOH not causing end cells of cap cuticle to be bright yellow .... *Boletus fraternus* Peck

Cap 2-4 cm, convex, deep red becoming duller, subtomentose becoming areolate; context yellow; tubes slightly depressed, pores large, yellow; stipe short, cespitose, 2.5-4 cm long 5-12 mm thick, subtomentose, often irregular, slightly velvety at base, paler near apex and base, yellow when young (within), changing to dark green where wounded; spores 12-16 $\times$ 5-6.5 μ; hyphae of trichodermium 7-15 μ wide, mostly of short inflated cells, end cells bullet-shaped or beaked.

This frequently misidentified species is southern in distribution. Its northern limits remain to be determined.

5b. Pores 1-2 per mm, end cells of cuticular hyphae bright yellow in KOH ....*Boletus campestris* Smith & Thiers

Cap 3-4 cm, convex, velvety, becoming merely unpolished, rose-red to pinkish red, areolate in age and yellow in the cracks; context yellow; tubes 6-8 mm deep, flavous young, greenish yellow in age, pores 1-2 per mm, bright yellow becoming greenish yellow; stipe 4-5 cm long, 5-10 mm thick, base flavous from mycelial coating, reddish pruinose upward, concolorous with pores near apex; spores 11-14 (15) $\times$ 4.5-6 (7) μ; hyphae of cap trichodermium 5-12 μ wide and tubular, end cells merely tapered to an obtuse apex.

In lawns, early summer, southern Michigan, rare (?).

6a. Stipe with white mycelium at base ....*Boletus rubeus* Frost

Cap 3-5 cm (estimated), nearly plane, appressed subtomentose, brick red, becoming mottled red and yellow; context yellow; tubes lemon yellow, stuffed when young, pores yellow or at times some of them reddish; stipe small often flexuous, brick red or mottled like the cap; spores 10-12.5 × 3-4 μ; cuticle of interwoven tubular hyphae 4-9 μ wide, very few short cells present, end cells tubular (Note: this account is based on the type).

The lack of a true trichodermium and the white mycelioid base of the stipe appear distinctive. It is closely related to *B. bicolor*.

Under hardwoods, central and eastern United States. Rare.

6b. Stipe with pale to rich yellow basal mycelium 7
7a. Cap cuticle an epithelium (cellular layer) of inflated cells but these not compactly arranged ....
....*Boletus harrisonii* Smith & Thiers

Cap 2.5-7 cm, convex, dry, dull, finally finely areolate, brick red to ocher-red; context yellow, odor pungent; tubes yellow, pores small; stipe 4-6 cm long, 4-10 mm thick, flexuous, yellow streaked brown within, surface yellow, midportion and base dull yellow-brown; spores 9-12 (13-18-22) × 4.5-5.5 (6-7.5) μ; hyphae of cap trichodermium 6-12 (15) μ wide, upper 3-4 cells subglobose and forming a loose layer.

Gregarious on grass near spruce trees, southern Michigan, July.

7b. Not as above ....*Boletus rubellus* Kromb.

Cap 3-8 cm, broadly convex, dry, velvety, finally areolate, brick red; context yellow staining blue; tubes deep yellow; pores ± 1 mm wide, staining blue; stipe 4-8 cm × 5-10 mm, equal, yellow within, surface red downward, yellow above; spores 10-13 × 4.5-5 μ; hyphae of pilear trichodermium 5-11 μ wide, walls smooth to minutely roughened, end cells cylindric to subcapitate, 8-25 μ broad where enlarged.

Great Lakes region, summer, not common. Var. *flammeus* has more inflated cells in the pilear trichodermium and a flame colored cap.

8a. Pores grayish olive when young, spores 7-8 × 4-5 μ ....
....See *Boletus tennessensis* page 223
8b. Not as above 9
9a. Pleurocystidia 26-38 × 12-18 μ, vesiculose or ventricose and apex broadly rounded .... *Boletus miniato-olivaceus* Frost

Cap 5-15 cm, vermillion fading to olivaceous, smooth, soft, spongy; tubes bright yellow, adnate to slightly decurved, pores small; stipe 6-15 mm thick, light yellow, smooth; spores 11-14 (14.5-16) × 3.5-5 (5.5-7) μ; hyphae of cap cuticle 6-10 μ wide, some cells inflated to 15 μ or more wide or short (1-3 μ as long as wide), end cells slightly inflated to subglobose-pedicellate and head up to 18 μ wide.

Borders of woods, July and August, New England.

9b. Pleurocystidia and end cells of cuticular hyphae not as above
....10

10a. Spores (11) 12-16 (17) × (3) 4-5 µ ....
.... *Boletus miniato-pallescens* **Smith & Thiers**
Cap 8-20 cm, convex, rarely shallowly depressed, glabrous but dull and indistinctly velvety, rimulose in age, deep rose-red fading in age to yellow; context pale yellow; tubes adnate to decurrent, 1-2 cm deep, rich yellow, pores 1-2 per mm, yellow or slowly reddish after being bruised (as blue fades out); stipe 6-14 cm long, 1-4.5 cm thick, not reticulate, yellow above, orange-red below, pruinose; hyphae of cap cuticle with end cells 30-60 × 9-14 µ and clavate to fusoid forming a tangled more or less hymeniform layer.

Gregarious in open oak woods, early fall, rather common in Michigan at times.

10b. Spores smaller than in above choice 11
11a. Pores wide and near stipe almost lamellate ....
.... *Boletus subfraternus* **Coker & Beers**
Cap 3-4.5 cm, convex, dry, velvety, dull rose-red fading to flame-scarlet and finally orange-buff; context buffy pallid, yellowish in drying, soft and fragile; tubes 1 cm deep, adnate becoming nearly free, dull yellow, pores greenish yellow; stipe 2.5-4 cm long, 1-1.5 cm thick, ochraceous near apex, pale scarlet over a yellow ground color below, faintly pruinose; spores 9-13 (14) × 4-5 (6) µ; hyphae of cap trichodermium with walls roughened by thin hyaline platelike particles hyaline in KOH and Melzer's, end cells 20-50 × 10-18 µ or these secondarily septate and the apical cell 8-10 µ wide and cylindric to ovate.

On soil along woods roads, northern Michigan and North Carolina, not common, late summer.

11b. Pores small (1-2 per mm) and round or nearly so 12
12a. Cap and stipe deep madder red. Fig. 228 ....
.... *Boletus bicolor* **Peck**

Cap 5-15 cm, convex to irregular, dry, unpolished becoming subtomentose and finally areolate; context pale yellow; tubes 5-10 mm deep, bright yellow, pores bright yellow, stuffed at first, 1-2 per mm, occasionally reddish over limited areas in age; stipe 5-10 cm long, 1-3 cm thick, surface dry, dull, smooth straw yellow at apex; spores 8-11 (12) × 3.5-4.5 (5) µ; cuticle of cap a tangled mass of hyphae 4-7 µ wide, sparginly septate, tubular, end cells tubular.

Fig. 228. *Boletus bicolor*.

12b. Cap and stipe not both deep red persistently 13

NON-GILLED FLESHY FUNGI

13a. Hyphae of cap cuticle containing many short cells up to 20 μ broad .... *Boletus pseudo-sensibilis* Smith & Thiers

Cap 6-14 cm convex, unpolished, dry, dull ferruginous to rusty red, finally fading to dingy cinnamon, becoming areolate, NH_4OH blue on cuticle becoming purplish; context yellow, quickly azure blue if cut; tubes 5-8 mm deep, adnate to decurrent, bright yellow, pores 1-3 per mm and yellow; stipe 8-16 cm long, 1.5-3 cm thick near apex, vinaceous-red in base, yellow above, surface naked and glabrous; spores 9-12 × 3-4 μ; hyphae of cap cuticle interwoven, 5-15 μ wide, with many end cells cystidioid.

Gregarious in oak woods, southern Michigan, summer, abundant during some seasons.

13b. Hyphae of cap cuticle tubular and cells elongate. Fig. 229 ....
.... *Boletus sensibilis* Peck

Cap 6-15 (30) cm, convex, dry and unpolished, brick red or darker, slowly becoming dull cinnamon (in age); context pale yellow instantly changing to blue when cut; tubes 1-1.5 cm, bright yellow, pores 1-2 per mm, bright yellow, but in age on old bruised areas reddish; stipe 8-12 cm long, 1-3 (4) cm thick near apex, surface brilliant yellow down to the dull red base, the extreme apex very obscurely reticulate; spores 10-13 × 3.5-4.5 μ; hyphae of cap cuticle 3-7 μ wide, intricately interwoven, end cells tubular and blunt.

Gregarious in sandy oak woods, eastern North America, abundant in Michigan, summer and early fall.

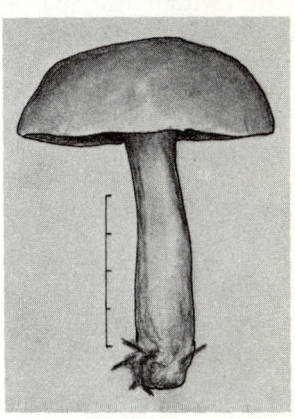

Fig. 229. *Boletus sensibilis.*

Section TRUNCATI

Spores truncate or notched at the apex (but see *Boletellus intermedius* also). *B. truncatus* resembles *B. chrysenteron* so closely in gross features that the experts have had difficulty in recognizing them.

Key to Species

1a. Spores 9-12 × 4-5 μ 2
1b. Spores 11-15 (17) μ long or 5-7 μ wide 3
2a. Stipe rhubarb red from pruinose covering ....
.... see *Boletellus intermedius* Smith & Thiers p. 253
2b. Stipe with yellowish brown pruina ....
.... *Boletus subdepauperatus* Smith & Thiers

Cap 3-5 cm, convex, velvety to subtomentose, olive-brown when young, dingy yellow-brown mature; context pallid buff (not distinctly yellow); tubes 10 mm deep, dingy yellow, staining bluish if bruised, pores about 1 mm wide, dingy olive yellowish; stipe 4-6 cm long, 6-8 mm thick, dingy yellow-brown; hyphae of cap cuticle in a trichodermium the elements having inflated end cells $25\text{-}80 \times 10\text{-}30$ μ, heavily incrusted by plates of pigment, mostly fusoid-ventricose.

Scattered on barren soil, beech-maple forest, southern Michigan, rare, summer.

3a. Taste of fresh context bitter to disagreeable; cut context staining blue then rose color .... *Boletus patriciae* Smith & Thiers

Cap 4-5 cm, convex to plane, unpolished, olive-brown becoming olive-gray; context yellowish pallid becoming olive-buff in age; tubes pale yellow aging to olive-buff, pores 2 per mm, yellow becoming yellowish olive; stipe 4-5 cm long, 9-12 mm thick, yellowish pallid within near apex, lower down dull rose color, surface rose-red and finely pruinose to apex, base coated with olive-buff mycelium; spores $11\text{-}15 \times 5\text{-}6.5$ μ, with a fleeting amyloid reaction, hyphae of cap trichodermium heavily incrusted and the incrustation colored brown in KOH and Melzer's, end cells cystidioid and not infrequently with secondary septa.

Gregarious under hardwoods during wet weather in late summer, southern Michigan.

3b. Taste mild, cut context staining blue directly and not reddening 4

4a. Cap soon showing red on margin or in the cracks of the cuticle, strongly areolate in age; $FeSO_4$ on context greenish gray. Fig. 230 .... *Boletus truncatus* (S. S. & D.) Pouzar

Cap 3-8 (11) cm, convex, dry, subtomentose, olive-brown, with red line under cuticle; context whitish then slowly yellowish; tubes olive-yellow, 7-15 mm deep, pores 1-2 per mm, finally about 2 mm wide; stipe 4-8 cm long, 4-12 mm thick, naked to pruinose, red below, yellow above, base surrounded by dingy ochraceous mycelium; spores $10\text{-}15 \times 4.5\text{-}6.5$ (7) μ; hyphae of cap trichodermium 8-14 μ wide with brown incrustations, end cells tapered to an obtuse apex.

Fig. 230. *Boletus truncatus*.

Solitary to gregarious along old roads and around uprooted trees where soil is disturbed, common in eastern North America, summer and fall.

4b. Not as above 5

NON-GILLED FLESHY FUNGI

5a. Spores amyloid (especially near apex) ....
.... see *Tylopilus amylosporus* **p. 179**
5b. Spores non-amyloid, 13-17 × 5-7 µ ....
.... *Boletus porosporus* (Imler) Smith

Cap 4-11 cm, convex, dry, densely tomentose (plushlike), buffy-brown to olive-brown; context pallid yellowish white, staining blue, pores angular and about 1 mm wide; stipe 4-10 cm long, 8-20 mm thick, surface pruinose-scurfy and reddish at maturity, yellowish above a dark yellow-brown base, base surrounded by grayish buff mycelium; spores weakly dextrinoid; hyphae of trichodermium 9-15 µ wide, incrusted with yellow-brown plates of pigment.

Scattered under conifers, Washington, late summer on wet years.

Section PSEUDOLECCINUM

Cap moist, glabrous or pubescent when young in one, viscid at times, stipe furfuraceous to punctate but ornamentation not darkening.

Key to Species

1a. Spores 16-21 × 5.5-7.5 µ, wall 0.5-1.5 µ thick ....
.... *Boletus rubropunctus* Peck

Pileus 2.5-5 cm, glabrous, reddish brown; context yellow, unchanging; tubes nearly plane, depressed at stipe, unchanging, bright golden yellow; stipe 2-5 cm long, 4-6 mm thick, tapered upward, yellow, punctate with reddish dots; cuticle of cap a thick layer of interwoven hyphae 4-10 µ wide, both long and short cells present, the cells tending to disarticulate, hyphae tubular or some cells slightly inflated, end cells cylindric to narrowly clavate or cystidioid.

Scattered under oak and chestnut, Quebec, New York and Georgia, summer, rare.

1b. Spores smaller (see *Boletus zelleri* also p. 220) 2
2a. Cap viscid, stipe having reddish dots in age ....
.... *Boletus longicurvipes* Snell & Smith

Cap 1.5-6 cm, obtuse to convex, cuticle separable, reddish orange to dingy ochraceous, often with a reddish brown reticulum; context white becoming yellowish, unchanging, $FeSO_4$ no reaction; tubes 9-12 mm deep, adnate to depressed, unchanging, pores small (about 2 per mm), pale yellow but in age greenish gray; stipe 5-9 cm long, 8-15 mm thick, whitish above, pinkish brown downward; spores 13-17 × 4-5 µ; cuticle of cap a turf of clavate cells 4-10 µ wide with a slime layer above them.

Scattered under oak in eastern United States, more common in the Southeast than in the Great Lakes area, summer and early fall.

2b. Cap moist to dry, stipe ornamentation not reddish 3

3a. **Terminal cells of elements of cap cuticle tubular and often secondarily septate, cap surface corrugated** ....
....*Boletus hortoni* **Smith & Thiers**

Cap 4-12 cm, umbonate to convex, dry, dingy ochraceous with reddish undertone; context yellow, slowly blue if cut; tubes about 8 mm deep, yellow, pores yellow, minute, bluish if bruised; stipe 6-10 cm long, 10-20 mm thick, smooth or nearly so, yellow within, surface pale yellow, brick red lower down in places; spores 12-15 × 3.5-4.5 μ; cuticle of cap a tangled trichodermium, the cells in many hyphae inflated to 20 μ wide.

Solitary in moist deciduous woods, summer, rare, Michigan and New England.

Peck named it *B. subglabripes* var. *corrugis* but the features of the cap cuticle and the corrugated surface of the cap justify its being recognized as a species.

3b. **Not as above** 4

4a. **Spores 14-18 × 5-6.5 μ; stipe pruinose** ....
....*Boletus sphaerocystis* **Smith & Thiers**

Cap 5-7 cm, convex to plane, unpolished, dingy cinnamon to clay-color; context yellowish; tubes dull olive, 1 cm long, honey-yellow, often stained orange; stipe 5-6 cm long, 1-1.5 cm thick, lemon chrome within, pruinose, lemon streaked reddish; cuticle of cap a trichodermium of chains of inflated cells, the cells up to 55 μ wide.

Scattered under oak, southern Michigan, September.

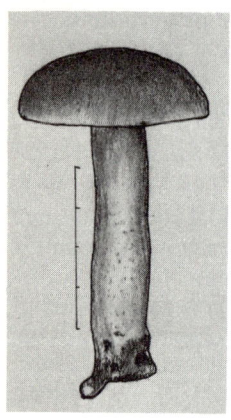

Fig. 231. *Boletus subglabripes.*

4b. **Spores 11-14 × 3-5 μ; stipe furfuraceous. Fig. 231** ....*Boletus subglabripes* **Peck**

Cap 4.5-10 cm, convex, glabrous, moist, surface often uneven, ochraceous to clay-color to dull cinnamon; context becoming pale yellow, rarely changing to slightly bluish when cut; tubes 10-15 mm deep, bright yellow, pores small, unchanging if bruised; stipe 5-10 cm long, 10-20 mm thick, cortex at times reddish in age, sometimes reddish stained at the base; cuticle of cap an epithelium of cells 10-24 μ wide.

Gregarious under birch, summer and early fall, common in the Great Lakes area, very rare in the Pacific Northwest, and not uncommon in eastern Canada and the U.S.A. generally where birch is present.

Section PSEUDOBOLETI

In this section the cap is glabrous and moist to subviscid, slimy, or matted-fibrillose and also distinctly viscid. The stipe is not reticulate and the pores stain blue more or less readily in most species (see also sect. *Substomentosi*, subsect. *Versicolores* if cap is velvety and pores do not stain).

Key to Species

1a. Context of cap when cut or broken changing instantly to blue 2
1b. Context not changing or if changing doing so more slowly 3
2a. Cap lemon yellow when young; pores 1-2 per mm. Fig. 232 ....
........*Boletus pseudosulphureus* Kallenbach

Cap 4-9 cm, pulvinate, margin sterile for 0.5-1 mm inward, surface unpolished at first, shiny at maturity; context lemon yellow; tubes about 1 cm deep, yellow, pores small, lemon yellow; stipe 8-12 cm long, 1-1.5 cm thick, yellow within, finally dark red in the base, surface lemon yellow above a reddish base, smooth and weakly pruinose; spores $10\text{-}14 \times 4.5\text{-}5 \times 5\text{-}6\ \mu$; hyphae of cap cuticle tubular, $3\text{-}6\ \mu$ wide, end cells tubular or nearly so.

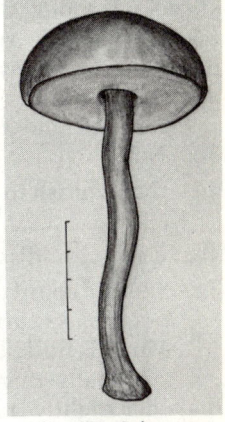

Fig. 232. *Boletus pseudosulphureus*.

Solitary to scattered in moist mixed woods, rare but to be expected in eastern North America, early summer.

2b. Cap dark yellow-brown to tobacco brown; pores 1-2 mm wide. Fig. 233 ....*Boletus pulverulentus* Opatowski

Cap 4-8 (12) cm, convex, dry, dull, slowly somewhat shiny and tacky to the touch, NH_4OH on cuticle giving a green flash; context soft, yellow; tubes 6-10 mm deep, adnate to subdecurrent, yellow, pores lemon yellow; stipe 4-8 cm long, 1-2.5 cm thick, surface yellow to orange-yellow above, reddish brown and pubescent below, apex faintly pruinose at first; spores $11\text{-}14\ (16) \times 4.5\text{-}6\ \mu$; caulocystidia often with an apical proliferation; cuticle of cap a tangled layer of hyphae $3\text{-}7\ \mu$ wide, end cells tubular.

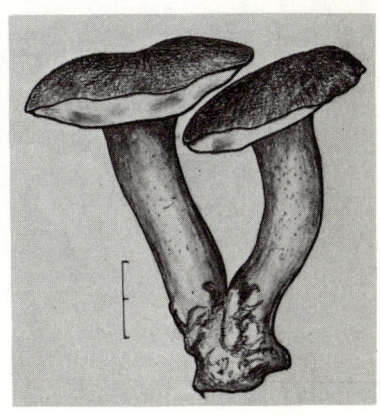

Fig. 233. *Boletus pulverulentus*.

Solitary to scattered on moist soil in woods, summer and early fall, eastern North America, not rare but seldom in quantity.

3a. Taste of pellicle bitter; spores 8-10 × 4-5 μ ....
.... *Boletus calvinii* Smith & Thiers

Cap 5-10 cm, convex, viscid, ferruginous-red; context scarcely changing color when bruised; tubes adnate then depressed, 10 mm deep, yellow, at length greenish, pores angular, about 1 mm wide; stipe 4-6 cm long, 6-15 mm thick, rufous to near the apex, apex pallid, faintly pruinose; spores obscurely inequilateral in profile; hyphae of cuticle of pileus 4-6 μ wide, embedded in a gelatinous matrix, apical cells tubular.

Scattered under oak, southern Michigan, August.

3b. Not as above 4

4a. Cap whitish to near maturity (but see *B. alutaceus* also p. 235)
....5

4b. Cap with distinct pigmentation 6

5a. Spore deposit bright yellow-brown ....
Boletus stramineus (Murr.) comb. nov. (*Gyroporus stramineus* Murrill, Bull. Torrey Club 67:63. 1940)

Cap finally tinged yellowish, glabrous; context white, unchanging, odor slightly fragrant, bluish gray in $FeSO_4$; tubes white to buffy cream; pores small, unchanging or slightly brownish bruised; stipe 3-6 cm long, 10-35 mm thick, white, with a faint reticulation over the upper part or not reticulate, mycelium white; spores (9) 10.5-14.5 × 2.5-3.5 μ.

Under oak and in rather open places along flatwoods or under scrub pine-oak, or on lawns and in gardens, Florida, Edible.

5b. Spore deposit olive-brown. Fig. 234 ....*Boletus pallidus* Peck

Cap dull alutaceous in age, 4.5-15 cm broad, convex, glabrous, unpolished, tacky in age when wet; context pallid or in age yellowish near tubes; tubes 1-2 cm deep, adnate to depressed or decurrent, pale yellow, finally olive-yellow; pores 1-2 mm wide, pallid yellowish; stipe 5-12 cm long, 8-30 mm thick, pallid within, surface smooth (or rarely faintly reticulate at apex), weakly yellow at apex, often flushed reddish near the base, spores 9-15.5 × 3-4.5 μ.

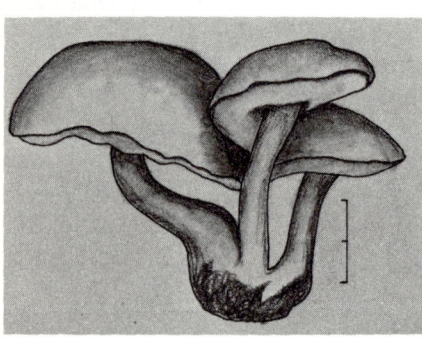

Fig. 234. *Boletus pallidus*.

Scattered to gregarious or cespitose, oak woods on sandy soil, often common, summer, eastern United States.

6a. Spore deposit bright yellow-brown (amber brown) 7
6b. Spore deposit olive, olive-brown or dingy yellow-brown 8
7a. Cap dark red to dark purplish red ....
Boletus purpureofuscus nom. nov. (*Xanthoconium purpureum* Snell & Dick, Mycol. 53:234. 1961)

Cap 3-7 cm broad, dull, glabrous, rarely with an occasional fibrillose patch; tubes whitish becoming ochraceous to rusty ochraceous; stipe 5-8 cm long, 7-15 mm thick, often curved, the extreme apex reticulate or striate, pallid yellowish to brownish yellow, tinged reddish in places, base pure white; spores (7) 9-13 (14) × 3-4 μ.

Under oaks, northeastern United States.

7b. Cap rich yellow-brown, at times with pallid spots; stipe at apex at times slightly reticulate. Fig. 235 ....
....*Boletus affinis* var. *affinis* Peck

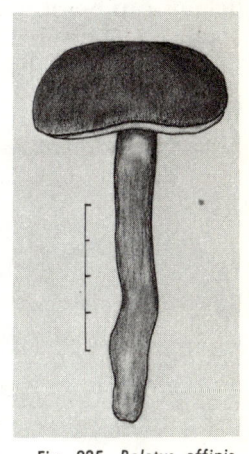

Cap 5-10 cm, convex, dry, rugulose to smooth, vinaceous-brown to yellow-brown; context white, unchanging; stipe 8-13 cm long, 1-2 cm thick, fawn-color or almost the color of the cap in the midportion, base whitish, apex pallid; spores 12-16 × 3-3.5 μ; pleurocystidia 36-42 (54) × 7-12 μ, fusoid-ventricose; cuticle of pileus a trichodermium with the end cells of the hyphae clavate and 24-36 × 10-12 μ.

Gregarious or scattered in hardwood forests, eastern North America to Michigan and Louisiana. It is often abundant along old logging roads during the summer and early fall.

Var. *maculosus* Peck has a cap variously decorated with pallid spots, the stipe often entirely pallid and lacking reticulation. It is more common in the western Great Lakes area than the type variety but occurs at the same time of the year and in the same habitats.

Fig. 235. *Boletus affinis*.

8a. Tubes lemon chrome in color; either pileus or stipe viscid 9
8b. Not as above (if yellow then not exceptionally bright) 10
9a. Cap viscid, chestnut brown; stipe not viscid, yellowish and smooth but stained brick red near the base at times ....
....*Boletus flaviporus* Earle

Cap 6-9 cm broad, thin; hymenophore depressed around the stipe but tubes often decurrent by lines; pores about 1 mm wide; stipe 6-9 cm long, 8-18 mm thick, often with a short pseudorhiza, smooth or marked with glutinous granules, solid; spores 14-17 × 5-6 μ, bright yellow in KOH; pleurocystidia 38-57 × 10-20 μ, content hyaline in KOH, thin-walled, fusoid-ventricose, apex obtuse to subacute; cheilocystidia pedicellate-clavate and with or without a slight mucro, hyaline in KOH; pileus cuticle a thick gelatinous trichodermium of hyphae 3-5 μ wide and hyaline in KOH; clamps not observed.

Scattered to gregarious under oak in California, not uncommon after the first few rainy periods in the fall.

9b. Cap viscid wet but soon dry, tawny olive to fulvous; stipe viscid (but a veil absent) ....see *Boletus auriporus* Peck p. 217

10a. Stipe clavate (1-3 cm at apex and up to 5 cm at base); pileus dingy cinnamon ....*Boletus huronensis* Smith & Thiers

Cap 8-14 cm, obtuse to convex, surface dry and unpolished; content pale yellow, grayish green to bluish gray with $FeSO_4$; tubes dull yellow, pores about 2 per mm, yellow, bluish then brownish after bruising; stipe 7-10 cm long, yellow above, paler below, unpolished, brownish where handled; spores 12-15 $\times$ 3.5-4.5 μ; hyphae of cuticle of cap 5-9 μ wide, tubular but apical cell narrowed to a flexuous neck and subacute apex.

Gregarious under hemlock, summer, northern Michigan.

10b. Not as above 11
11a. Cap 3-10 cm, subviscid if wet; pores staining blue weakly. Fig. 236 ....*Boletus badius* Fries

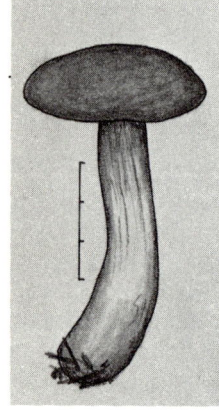

Fig. 236. *Boletus badius*.

Cap 3-10 cm, soon dry, NH_4OH on cuticle olive to green, color of surface dark yellow-brown to bay red; context whitish at first, soon yellow near the tubes, staining weakly vinaceous when cut in area above the stipe, bluish green in $FeSO_4$; tubes weakly yellow, depressed-adnate to decurrent, when mature greenish yellow; pores small (1-2 per mm), yellowish; stipe 4-9 cm long, 10-22 mm thick, cortex yellowish near apex, pinkish red below; spores 10-14 $\times$ 4-5 μ; cuticle of cap a tangled mass of hyphae 5-10 μ wide, cell content golden yellow in KOH, end cells tubular.

Solitary on old conifer logs and stumps and on humus, common, summer, eastern North America.

11b. Cap dry and tubes not staining blue when injured 12
12a. Cap bay red to vinaceous-brown (or orange-cinnamon) 13
12b. Cap dingy cinnamon to olive-brown or buff colored 14
13a. Cap and stipe bay red ....*Boletus albocarneus* (Pk.) Peck

Cap 2.5-6 cm, convex, subglabrous; tubes greenish yellow; pores small; stipe 2.5-5 cm long, 3-5 mm thick, glabrous; spores 12-15 $\times$ 4-5 μ; hyphae of cap cuticle 4-8 μ wide, end cells weakly cystidioid (up to 11 μ wide).

Known from New York, but its fruiting pattern and distribution remain to be determined.

13b. Cap vinaceous-brown to orange-cinnamon; stipe yellow above, red below .... *Boletus hoseneae* Smith & Thiers

Cap 5-6 cm, becoming rimose, surface moist and subhygrophanous; context with an olive line above the tubes, no reaction with $FeSO_4$; pores greenish yellow, about 1 mm wide; stipe 6-7 cm long, 10-12 mm thick, bright yellow above, striate from tube lines, vinaceous-red and unpolished below; cuticle of pileus a lax palisade of cells up to 20 μ wide and globose, clavate or cystidioid.

Southeastern Michigan, under hardwoods on sandy soil, rare, early fall.

14a. Spores 10-13 $\times$ 3-4 μ; stipe pallid but with an apical red zone .... *Boletus glabellus* Peck

Cap 7-12 cm, subglabrous; context white; tubes ochraceous-tinged with green; stipe 2.5-7 cm long, 1-2.5 cm thick, reddish at base, glabrous, even; hyphae of pileus cuticle 5-11 μ wide, short cells present in the chains.

Known from New York. Previously it was not clearly distinguished from other species.

14b. Spores 8-12 $\times$ 4-5 μ; stipe not as above 15
15a. Context yellow in both pileus and stipe .... see *Boletus subilludens* Smith & Thiers
15b. Context pallid in cap and stipe; stipe staining vinaceous buff when cut .... *Boletus alutaceus* Morgan in Peck

Cap 5-10 cm, convex, dry, subpruinose, if wet very slightly tacky; context unchanging when cut; tubes up to 15 mm deep, whitish becoming pale olive-buff or more olivaceous, unchanging; pores 1-1.5 mm wide, olive-pallid, in age brownish; stipe 6-8 cm long, 1-2 cm thick, smooth or above faintly striate with lines, pallid inside and out, brownish from handling.

Gregarious on swampy ground central United States, summer, rare in Michigan.

Section BOLETUS

Key to Subsections

1a. Pores when immature dark brown, orange or some shade of red .... Subsect. *Luridi* p. 236
1b. Not as above 2
2a. Stipe rather coarsely reticulate and pleurocystidia as revived in KOH with yellow to smoky yellow content (they are also yellow in water mounts of fresh material); if reticulum is wide-meshed or coarse see Section *Subtomentosi* .... Subsect. *Reticulati* p. 243
2b. Not as above 3

3a. Tubes yellow at first and not stuffed; taste often bitter; pores often staining blue when injured ... Subsect. *Calopodes* p. 244

3b. Tubes white at first and stuffed; taste usually pleasant; pores rarely staining blue if injured .... Subsect. *Boletus* p. 248

Subsection LURIDI

Key to Stirpes

1a. Pores when young brown to dark brown ....
.... Stirps *Vermiculosoides* p. 236

1b. Pores red to orange when young 2

2a. Stipe reticulate from slight to prominent ridges or veins of tissue which form the netted pattern ... Stirps *Luridus* p. 240

2b. Stipe not reticulate though pruina may be arranged in lines to form a faint netted pattern .... Stirps *Subvelutipes* p. 238

STIRPS VERMICULOSOIDES

Key to Species

1a. Stipe reticulate at least over the apical region ....
....*Boletus fagicola* Smith & Thiers

Cap 4-12 (18) cm broad, dry, velvety to subtomentose, becoming irregularly rimose to areolate; bright yellow on the young incurved margin, dull yellow to yellow-brown elsewhere; stipe 4-8 cm long, 1-2.5 cm thick, ochraceous shaded with gray or brown, often reddish at the base and dingy brown after handling (after blue has faded); spores 9-12 (14) $\times$ 3.5-5 μ thick, ochraceous-brown under microscope; pleurocystidia 35-55 $\times$ 7-10 μ, narrowly fusoid-ventricose, the neck often curved; pileus cuticle a trichodermium of narrow hyphae 4-7 μ wide, tubular.

Gregarious to scattered in oak woods and brushy places, eastern North America and the Great Lakes region, summer and fall, fairly common.

1b. Stipe surface even to the apex but usually pruinose to furfuraceous 2

2a. Spores 9-12 × 3-3.5 μ. Fig. 237 ....
.................................Boletus vermiculosoides **Smith & Thiers**

Fig. 237. Boletus vermiculosoides.

Cap 4-12 cm, convex, finally nearly plane, dry, dull, unpolished, bright yellow young, becoming snuff brown to bister; context bright yellow, dingier in age, margin at times lobed; tubes about 1 cm deep, pallid olivaceous, pores minute (2-3 per mm), dark sepia to amber brown; stipe 4-9 cm long, 1-2 cm thick, surface olivaceous-pallid to yellowish, dingy brown around base from handling; pileus cuticle of interwoven hyphae 2.5-5 μ wide, cell content orange-brown or darker in Melzer's.
Gregarious under oak, southern Michigan.

2b. **Not as above** 3

3a. **Odor of dried specimens strong and disagreeable; cap dingy yellow-brown** ....Boletus subgraveolens **Smith & Thiers**

Cap 8-13 cm broad, subviscid, dingy yellow-brown, glabrous, slightly mottled; context yellowish white, dull blue if bruised; taste mild; tubes 6-12 mm long, depressed around stipe, pale yellow, pores about 2 per mm, rich yellow-brown ("Sudan brown"); stipe 6-9 cm long, 2-3 cm thick reddish cinnamon in cortex, dull red in base, surface lemon yellow at apex, pallid and pruinose below; spores 10-13 × 3.5-4.5 μ; cuticle of cap a trichodermium but soon collapsing, the hyphae 3-6 μ wide, tubular, smooth or with a gelatinous sheath.
Under aspen, southern Michigan.

3b. **Odor not pronounced; cap grayish brown tinged red** ....
....Boletus vermiculosus **Peck**

Cap 4-12 cm, convex, when wet subviscid; context yellow; tubes greenish yellow, pores reddish brown, minute, readily staining bluish black; stipe 4-8 (9) cm long, 1-2 cm thick, yellow with a covering of brown pruina, context gradually becoming rose red; spores 10-13.5 × 4-5 μ (11-15 × 4.5-5 (6) μ in the type); cuticle of cap a trichodermium with hyphae 3-6 μ wide, end cells tubular.
Gregarious in woods and open places, New York to Michigan.

Stirps SUBVELUTIPES

Key to Species

1a. Cap dark red and with dark red fibrils; context not changing to blue when bruised ....*Boletus rubropictus* Snell & Smith

Cap 4-5 cm broad, convex, dry, fibrillose; context pale yellow, unchanging when bruised, red around the worm holes, taste acidulous; tubes yellowish, unchanging injured; pores dark red; stipe about 7 cm long, 1 cm thick, faintly reticulate above, punctate to fibrillose below, with reddish splashes of color, base whitish, yellow within; spores $7\text{-}12 \times 4\text{-}4.5\ \mu$.

Solitary under pine, southern U.S.A., summer, rare.

1b. Not as above 2

2a. Cap brilliant red; stipe at base thinly coated with yellow mycelium; pseudocystidia present in hymenium ....
....*Boletus subluridellus* Smith & Thiers

Cap 5-10 cm broad, dry and resinous to the touch, evenly colored, instantly dark violet where touched; context bright lemon yellow but instantly blue when cut; tubes yellow; stipe 4-9 cm long, 1.5-2.5 cm thick, lemon yellow, pruinose-furfuraceous; spores $10\text{-}13 \times 4\text{-}4.5\ \mu$; pleurocystidia filamentose, embedded in the hymenium or fusoid-ventricose and $36\text{-}44 \times 9\text{-}13\ \mu$; cap cuticle of tangled hyphae $3\text{-}6\ \mu$ wide.

Gregarious in grassy oak woods, southern Michigan, late summer.

2b. Not with above combination of features 3

3a. Spores $9\text{-}13 \times 4\text{-}5\ \mu$ ....*Boletus spraguei* Frost

Cap dark russet or brown, covered with velvety scurf; context white, changing to blue; tubes with dark maroon pores; stipe dark brown below, ochraceous above, smooth above, minutely velvety below; cap cuticle a tangled mass of hyphae $3\text{-}7\ \mu$ wide, tubular, the end cells tubular to weakly cystidioid.

Scattered in mixed forests (oak present), late summer, New England to Michigan.

3b. Spores $12\text{-}16\ \mu$ or more long 4

4a. Cap dark rose red; caulocystidia proliferated ....
....*Boletus roseobadius* Smith & Thiers

Cap up to 12 cm broad, dry and appressed fibrillose; context pallid before staining; tubes yellow, about 12 mm deep, pores flame scarlet; stipe about 10×1.5 cm, dark red with yellow streaks within, surface rose-pruinose above; spores $12\text{-}16 \times 5\text{-}6.5\ \mu$ cuticle of cap a matted layer of hyphae $2\text{-}4\ \mu$ wide.

Solitary to scattered, under hardwoods on low ground, southern Michigan.

4b. Not as above 5

NON-GILLED FLESHY FUNGI

5a. Stipe decorated with pustules and/or fibrils 6
5b. Stipe merely pruinose to nearly naked 7
6a. Spores 5.2-8 μ wide; stipe with lateritious granules and fibrils
  .... *Boletus puniceus* **Thiers**

Cap 6-10 cm broad, convex, surface dry, matted-fibrillose; context 1-2 cm thick, bright yellow, blue instantly on injury, odor and taste not distinctive; stipe 5-9 cm long, 1-3 cm at apex, surface dry to moist, glabrous at apex, tomentose to granulose toward the base, ground color yellow but below marked with red to lateritious granules or fibrils, yellow within, instantly bluing on injury; spores 11-16 × 5.2-8 μ.

Gregarious to scattered under oaks and manzanita in open hardwood forests, California, rare (?).

6b. Spores 4-5.5 μ wide; cuticle of cap a palisade of pileocystidia fusoid, clavate or filamentose in shape (all intermingled) ....
  .... *Boletus morrisii* **Peck**

Cap 5-10 cm, convex, dry, glabrous but glistening under a lens, citrine or somewhat metallic in tone, in age yellowish to reddish brown, sterile margin narrow but distinct; context yellow not changing to blue; tubes lemon yellow, pores 2 per mm, lemon yellow or some reddish brown; stipe 4-6 cm long, 1-1.5 cm thick, nearly equal, dry, solid, yellow within, surface lemon yellow beneath reddish dots, not reticulate.

Southeastern United States northward along the Atlantic coast.

7a. Cap olivaceous, matted-fibrillose, becoming squamulose at times in age. Fig. 238 ....
  .... *Boletus pseudo-olivaceus* **Smith & Thiers**

Cap 3-10 cm, dry; tubes 1 cm deep yellow; pores dark maroon-red but in age paler; stipe 8-12 cm long, 1-3 cm thick, yellow within before changing, deep rusty rose in the base, surface pruinose with reddish pruina often arranged in faintly reticulate pattern, olivaceous to olive-ocher at base, lacking strigosity; spores 13-16 × 5-6.5 μ; cuticle of cap of appressed non-gelatinous hyphae 3-6 μ wide.

Under hazelnut bushes and near maple and birch mixed, early summer, northern Michigan.

Fig. 238. *Boletus pseudo-olivaceus*.

7b. Not as above 8

8a. Cap pale yellow to cinnamon or reddish but drying yellow at least over a wide marginal area; stipe with dark red strigosity over the base. Fig. 239 .... *Boletus subvelutipes* **Peck**

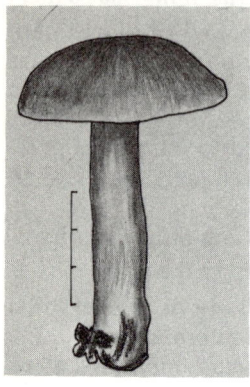

Fig. 239. *Boletus subvelutipes.*

Cap 6-15 cm broad, minutely fibrillose to velvety-tomentose, in age areolate, becoming reddish brown, often dark blue to blackish when bruised; context yellow but changing to blue at once when injured; tubes yellowish, the pores red; stipe 3-6 (10) cm long 1-2 cm thick, yellow at apex, becoming dark reddish at base; spores $11\text{-}16.5 \times 4.5\text{-}6.5\ \mu$; cuticle of cap a trichodermium.

Solitary to scattered under hardwoods; eastern North America to the Great Lakes region, early summer common but seldom abundant. In Michigan it is one of the first boletes to appear.

8b. Cap dark yellow-brown fresh and drying date brown (dark yellow-brown; stipe with yellow strigosity at base. Fig. 240 ......
....*Boletus erythropus* **Fries**

Fig. 240. *Boletus erythropus.*

Cap 8-15 cm broad, convex, dry, smooth to uneven, subtomentose, context 1-3 cm thick, yellow, quickly blue on injury, odor often pungent and unpleasant; tubes greenish yellow, blue on injury, pores brick red to orange-red; stipe 8-12 cm long, 1-3-3.5 cm, thick, clavate to equal, surface dry, glabrous to granulose or somewhat fibrillose but not reticulate, yellow but granules or pruina bright red; spores $13\text{-}16 \times 4.8\text{-}5.5\ \mu$.

Gregarious to solitary under hardwoods, California fall. This species is most likely to be confused with *B. subvelutipes.*

STIRPS LURIDUS

1a. Cap dark blood red, viscid; stipe blood red and coarsely reticulate. Fig. 241 .... *Boletus frostii* **Peck**

Cap 5-13 (15) cm broad, hoary at first but soon shining, fading and having yellowish areas when old; tubes yellow to olivaceous-

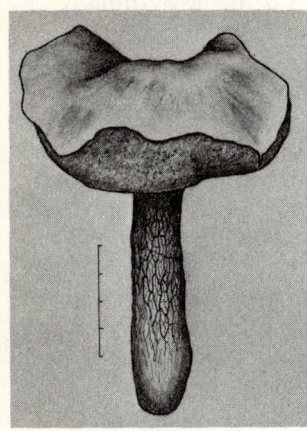

Fig. 241. *Boletus frostii.*

yellow, the pores deep red and their surface typically beaded with yellowish droplets when young; stipe 4-12 cm long, 1-2.5 cm thick at apex, very coarsely reticulate over all, often yellow to white at base; spores $11\text{-}15 \times 4\text{-}5\ \mu$; cap cuticle a thick gelatinous to matted down trichodermium, the hyphae 3-6 μ diam.

Scattered to gregarious in open oak woods, eastern North America to the Great Lakes region south to the Gulf, summer, common.

1b. Not as in above choice 2
2a. Cap and pores dark blood red; not staining blue anywhere ....
Boletus holoroseus **Smith & Thiers**

Cap 3-10 cm, convex, dry, vinaceous-red, finally olive-brown; context vinaceous-red at maturity, taste mild, with $FeSO_4$ olive; tubes about 12 mm deep, pallid becoming red throughout their length; pores vinaceous-red; stipe 5-11 cm long, 1-2 cm thick, dark red beneath a fine dull red reticulum, ground color dingy yellowish, pallid near apex at first; spores (9) $11\text{-}14 \times 5\text{-}7\ \mu$, ovate to elliptic in face view, subfusoid to obscurely kidney-shaped in profile; cap cuticle a turf of hyphae 4-6 μ wide.

Rich low woods of oak, beech and ash, late summer, southern Michigan.

2b. Not as above 3
3a. Cap pinkish on margin at first, whitish to pallid, olive buff at maturity. Fig. 242 ....*Boletus satanus* **Lenz**

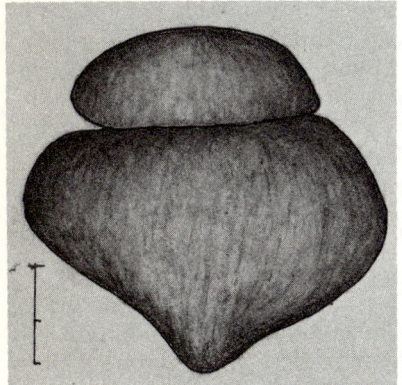

Fig. 242. *Boletus satanus.*

Cap 10-20 cm broad, convex, massive, dry, unpolished, rarely becoming scaly, sometimes rimose-areolate; context 2-5 cm thick, pale olive-buff to distinctly green and blue when injured, taste and odor not distinctive; tubes pale greenish yellow but blue when injured, pores dark blood red when young; stipe 6-12 cm long, bulb up to 12 cm broad when young, 3.5-7 cm broad at apex, conspicuously reticulate over upper part or over all; reticulations pink to vinaceous; spores 12-15 × 4-6 μ; pleurocystidia often imbedded in the hymenium.

Scattered to gregarious in humus under oaks, California, fall, rare.
3b. **Cap more highly colored** (see *B. auriflammeus* also; p. 244)... 4
4a. **Reticulum of stipe distinctly red** 5
4b. **Reticulum of stipe not red** (or faintly so in *B. vinaceobasis*)....6
5a. Cap dark red; stipe equal or nearly so. Fig. 243 ....
..................*Boletus rubroflammeus* Smith & Thiers

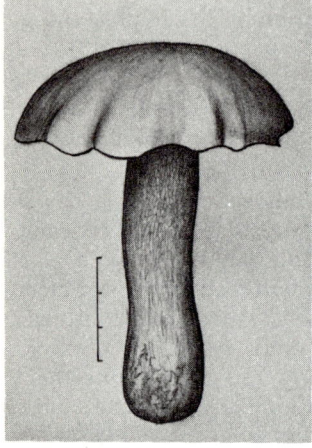

Fig. 243. *Boletus rubroflameus*.

Cap 6-12 cm broad, broadly convex, the margin projecting slightly beyond the tubes, surface dry and appearing appressed fibrillose or with matted grayish tomentum at first; context thick, yellow, quickly blue when injured, taste mild, odor slight; tubes yellow, blue if injured; pores deep maroon-red; stipe 6-8 cm long, 1-3 cm thick, yellowish within, quickly blue on injury; surface reticulate with a blood red reticulation; spores 10-14 × 4-5 μ.

Scattered to gregarious in rich deciduous woods, southern Michigan.

5b. Cap olive-buff to olive-brown, or reddish only on the margin; stipe massive when young (4-7 cm thick). Fig. 244 ....
..................*Boletus eastwoodiae* (Murr.) Saccardo & Trotter

Fig. 244. *Boletus eastwoodiae*.

Cap 10-30 cm broad, surface dry and unpolished; context thick, bright yellow quickly staining blue on injury, taste and odor not distinctive; tubes bright yellow with deep red pores when young, quickly blue if injured; stipe 8-20 cm long, up to 9.5 cm thick in bulb, dry, conspicuously reticulate with blood red reticulum on a background of yellow to apricot buff; spores 14-16 × 5-6.5 μ.

Solitary to gregarious in mixed hardwood-conifer stands in the river valleys of the Pacific Northwest, late summer and fall, rare.

6a. **Spores 9-12 × 5-6 μ**............*Boletus vinaceobasis* Smith & Thiers
Cap 4-10 cm, nearly plane, smooth, dry, ochraceous-brown becoming olivaceous-brown; context dull yellow before changing to

blue; tubes about 1.5 mm deep, yellow; pores dull red, vinaceous-red, reticulum distinct over upper half and only faintly reddish at the most; cuticle of cap a trichodermium of hyphae 3-6 μ wide.

Solitary in open oak woods, southern Michigan, not common.

6b. Spores 12-17 × 5.6-7 μ. Fig. 245 .... *Boletus luridus* **Fries**

Cap 5-12 cm broad, unpolished to shiny, matted-fibrillose or with minute fibrillose scales; context thick, up to 3 cm, yellow to reddish, with a red line above the tubes when freshly cut, blue when injured; tube pores deep red, soon fading to orange-red; stipe 6-15 cm long, 1-3 cm thick; spores amyloid when fresh; cuticle of cap a tangled trichodermium of narrow (3-5 μ) hyphae with slightly roughened walls.

Solitary to gregarious in open deciduous woods, eastern North America, summer and fall, common at times.

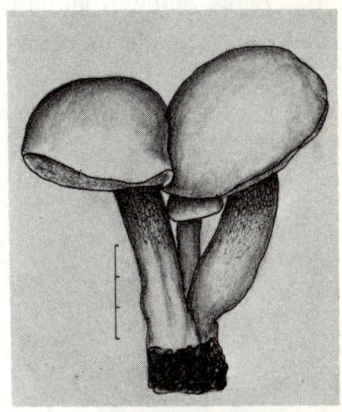

Fig. 245. *Boletus luridus*.

Subsection RETICULATI

Stipe strongly reticulate, pleurocystidia as revived with KOH having a yellow to smoky yellow content.

Key to Species

1a. Cap 5-12 (17) cm, convex, dry, subtomentose or the cuticle becoming matted down like felt, gray streaked with darker fibrils, often fuscous to drab-gray developing an ochraceous undertone in age. Fig. 246 ....
..................*Boletus griseus* Peck

Context pallid, where cut sometimes flushed dingy vinaceous with $FeSO_4$ bluish gray; tubes 8-15 mm deep, pores 1-2 per mm, pallid young; stipe 4-11 cm long, 1-2.5 (4) cm thick, greenish yellow in base at first, cortex

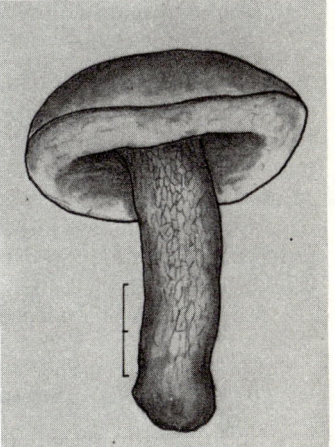

Fig. 246. *Boletus griseus*.

becoming yellow on aging, surface pallid at first, becoming yellow from base up; spores 9-12 (13) × 3.5-4 μ; cuticle of cap a trichodermium of hyphae 5-10 μ wide, cells broader and shorter near apex.

Solitary to scattered, grassy open oak woods, eastern North America and the Great Lakes region, summer, often common.

1b. Pores yellow from an early stage 2

2a. Context pale or clear yellow, becoming deep golden yellow when cut. Fig. 247 ....*Boletus ornatipes* **Peck**

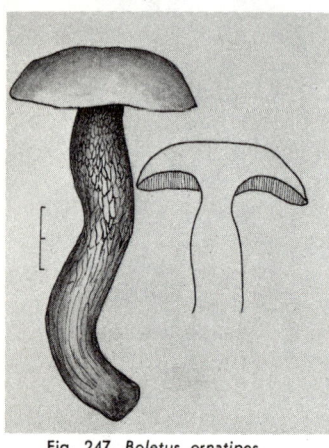

Fig. 247. *Boletus ornatipes.*

Cap 4-16 (20) cm broad, dull and unpolished to minutely tomentose, subviscid when moist, fuscous to violaceous-fuscous, at times yellowish brown in age; tubes lemon yellow, staining orange-yellow; stipe 8-15 cm long, 1-2 (3.5) cm thick, nearly equal, chrome yellow throughout, becoming darker orange chrome and finally dingy yellow over all; spores 9-13 × 3-4 μ; pleurocystidia 38-56 × 35-75 μ; cap cuticle a trichodermium with cylindric end cells, the elements 4-8 μ in diam.

Cespitose to scattered in sandy soil in second growth hardwoods along roads and on banks; eastern U. S. and Canada to Great Lakes and south to Alabama, summer, often abundant after heavy rains.

2b. **Context cream colored, sometimes with pinkish tints, unchanging when cut** ....*Boletus auriflammeus* **Berkeley & Curtis**

Cap 2-7 (10) cm broad, rich brownish orange at first becoming more chrome yellow, pulverulent and felted-tomentose, becoming finely areolate, slightly viscid young, becoming dry; tube pores 1-2 mm wide, deep chrome yellow then bright crimson over all or in splotches; stipe up to 8 cm long, 1.5 cm thick, subequal, pinched at base and with strong white mycelial plates and cords, chrome yellow, pulverulent, strongly reticulated at least above; spores 8.5-11 × 3.7-4.5 μ.

In deciduous or mixed pine woods, southeast, summer.

Subsection CALOPODES

Stipe typically reticulate and often bulbous when young; taste frequently bitter, flesh frequently staining blue when bruised; tubes yellow at first and not stuffed when young.

NON-GILLED FLESHY FUNGI

Key to Species

1a. Cap whitish to pale buff or fuscous-olive to dark olivaceous or olive-brown 2
1b. Cap red or reddish (when young often pallid but soon becoming red, the red color often persisting along the margin in age) 5
2a. Cap whitish when mature; stipe bright red in midportion or over all (see *B. rubripes* also p. 246). Fig. 248 ....
.... *Boletus inedulis* Murrill

Cap 4-11 cm broad, densely cottony tomentose, often becoming areolate with the white flesh prominent, often pale glaucous gray to avellaneous; context white to yellowish, becoming blue if injured; stipe 6-9 (12) cm long, 8-20 mm thick, equal or slightly enlarged downward, reticulate over upper 3/4 or nearly smooth except at apex, yellow above, pinkish below, soon sordid reddish brown or blackish at base from handling; spores 9-12 × 3.5-4.5 μ; cap cuticle a tangled trichodermium of hyphae 4-7 μ diam, soon collapsing.

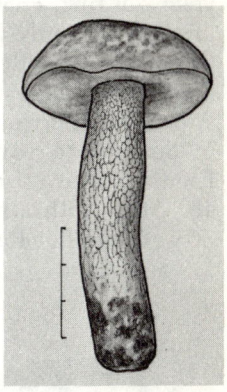

Fig. 248. *Boletus inedulis*.

Solitary to gregarious around woodland pools in oak-hickory forests and during wet seasons in upland forests generally; Great Lakes region, summer and early fall common during some seasons. A very beautiful species.

2b. Not as above 3
3a. Cap olive-fuscous, dark olivaceous or olive-gray, usually some shade of olivaceous when collected; stipe lacking red or pinkish tints. Fig. 249 .... *Boletus coniferarum* Dick & Snell

Pileus 10-30 cm broad, unpolished to subtomentose, becoming areolate in age at times; context pallid to yellowish, standing blue if injured; tubes yellow staining blue; stipe bulbous becoming nearly equal, massive (to 6 cm thick), pale yellow or olivaceous-yellow, soon blue from handling; spores 11-14 × 3.5-5 μ.

Gregarious to solitary in the conifer forests of the

Fig. 249. *Boletus coniferarum*.

Pacific Northwest, fall, not common, but sometimes found north of Upper Priest Lake in northern Idaho.

This is a gigantic species much like *B. calopus* but lacking red tints on the stipe and the stipe usually less reticulate.

3b. Not as above **4**

4a. Stipe lacking a distinct reticulum (use handlens); taste bitter; cap some shade of olive-buff ....*Boletus rubripes* **Thiers**

Pileus 6-25 cm, convex, with a narrow sterile margin, dry, velvety, olive-buff, soon areolate; context thick, instantly blue when cut, pale yellow at first, $FeSO_4$ olive-gray; tubes to 2 cm deep, depressed, yellow but instantly blue where bruised; stipe 7-20 cm long, 1-5 cm thick, surface with variously disposed areas, lower part dingy olive-brown after injury; spores $12.5\text{-}17.6 \times 4\text{-}5\ \mu$; cuticle of pileus of appressed interwoven hyphae.

Solitary to scattered under conifers, Sitka spruce especially, Pacific Northwest in the fall.

4b. Stipe with a pallid reticulum; taste bitter; cap olive-brown to olive-buff, often deeply areolate. Fig. 250 ....
....*Boletus calopus* **Fries**

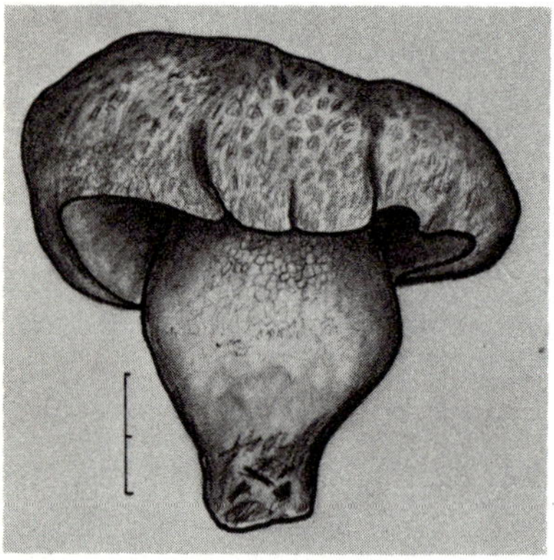

Cap 10-30 cm broad, unpolished to subtomentose, becoming areolate in age if exposed to the sun, finally appearing matted-fibrillose context yellow fading to whitish, instantly blue if injured; stipe (6) 10-15 (20) cm long, (2.5) 3-7 cm thick, bulbous or nearly equal, bright red in some portion of surface, quickly blue if injured; spores $13\text{-}19 \times 5\text{-}6\ \mu$.

Solitary to scattered in virgin conifer forests, Pacific Northwest late summer and fall, rather frequent. It is rare in the Great Lakes region.

Fig. 250. *Boletus calopus*.

5a. Cap cuticle of appressed-interwoven hyphae; red color often remaining only on cap margin; taste mild ....
....*Boletus pseudopeckii* **Smith & Thiers**

Cap 4-11 cm broad, broadly convex, dry and unpolished, at times tinged red only along the margin, often with a grayish overtone generally from a thin coating of fibrils; context thick, pale yellow, blue when injured; tubes grayish yellow to yellow, pores yellow or sometimes (near stipe) slightly reddish; stipe 4-12 cm long, 1-3 cm thick, yellow within, staining blue when cut, often a red zone at apex or variously over upper part, base usually yellow; spores 10-14 × 3.4-4.5 μ.

Scattered to gregarious in eastern North America, also in the Great Lakes region, summer, rare. It seems to be associated with beech (*Fagus*).

5b. Cap cuticle a trichodermium often collapsed in age 6
6a. Spores 9-12 (13) × 3.5-5 μ; taste of raw flesh bitter; pileus red but soon changing to buffy brown ....
....*Boletus peckii* Frost in Peck

Pileus 5-10 cm broad, convex, surface dry and minutely tomentose; tubes yellow turning blue where wounded; stipe 6-10 cm long, about 10 mm thick, strongly reticulate, red with the apex yellow (the color brighter than the pileus and retained longer); cuticle of pileus a distinct trichodermium, the hyphae 4-8 (10) μ wide.

In deciduous woods; Sand Lake, New York. Its distribution remains to be determined.

6b. Spores longer; taste not bitter 7
7a. Spores 11-16 × 4-5 μ; context and pores staining blue only slightly when injured ....*Boletus regius* Krombholz

Pileus (4) 8-20 cm broad, uneven to pitted, yellowish becoming red by maturity; context bright yellow; tubes bright yellow; stipe 7-12 cm long, 2.5-5 cm thick; cuticle of pileus a turf but this soon collapsing.

Under oak and manzanita, central California soon after the rainy season begins, not common.

7b. Spores 10-15 × 3.5-4.5 μ; taste mild; context and pores readily staining blue. Fig. 251 ....
....................*Boletus speciosus* Frost

Pileus 8-15 cm broad, convex, dry, unpolished, persistently brilliant deep rose red; context yellow, quickly blue when cut; pores quickly staining blue when injured; stipe 5-13 cm long 1.5-4 cm thick, pinched off at the base to enlarged slightly, surface finely reticulate, light yellow with red at the base; pileus cuticle a trichodermium collapsing to form a matted layer.

In the late summer and fall in open oak woods in particular, rare but widely distributed east of the Mississippi River.

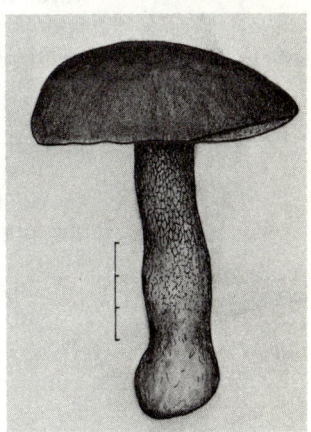

Fig. 251. *Boletus speciosus*.

Subsection BOLETI

Tubes stuffed when young, (the pores are overgrown by a weft of white hyphae), stipe reticulate by fine reticulation, context of cap white at first, a change to blue on injury rarely showing. As far as known all in this subsection are edible.

Key to Species

1a. Tubes brownish yellow when mature; spores variable in size $13\text{-}17 \times 4\text{-}5.5 \mu$ ($17\text{-}25 \times 6.5\text{-}12 \mu$) .... Boletus gertrudiae Peck

Cap 5-12 cm, glabrous, soft, dry, orange-yellow to brownish yellow; context unchanging; tubes bright yellow when young, pores minute; stipe rather long, equal, glabrous, yellow above, white below; spores (the abnormal ones) with walls 1-2 μ thick; cuticle of cap a trichodermium with the end cells of the elements clavate to cystidioid and arranged in a loose palisade, weakly yellow in Melzer's.

New England, rare.

1b. Not as above 2
2a. Cuticle of cap more or less a palisade of pileocystidia, some large end cells with secondary septa present. Fig. 252 ....
.... Boletus separans Peck

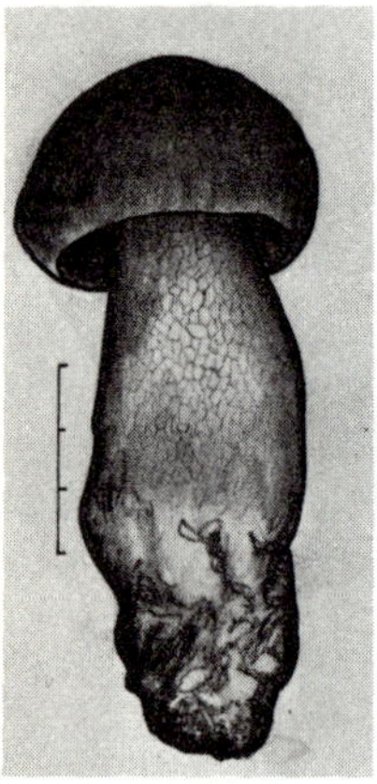

Cap 6-15 (20) cm, surface dry, tacky after rains, glabrous, dark red to liver brown or bay-brown; tubes whitish becoming yellowish (not olivaceous); pores pale yellow when mature, 1-2 per mm; stipe 6-15 μ long, 10-25 mm thick, clavate becoming equal, concolorous with cap; spores $12.5\text{-}16 \times 3.5\text{-}4.5 \mu$; end cells of the elements of the trichodermium $40\text{-}80 \times 12\text{-}18 \mu$ forming the loose palisade of pileocystidia.

Scattered in deciduous woods, eastern and central United States, summer, rare.

We have a variety of this species, var. *subcaeruleus* (Dick & Snell) Smith & Thiers in which the pores change to blue slightly when injured.

Fig. 252. Boletus separans.

2b. End cells of cap cuticular hyphae not forming a palisade as in above choice, or cuticle of appressed hyphae 3
3a. Cap lemon yellow splashed ferruginous to vinaceous-tawny; pores staining vinaceous-cinnamon when bruised ....
.... Boletus chippawaensis Smith & Thiers

Cap 6-7 cm, convex, glabrous, slightly viscid but soon dry; context olive-gray with $FeSO_4$; tubes pale greenish yellow becoming olive-ochraceous; pores bright yellow about 1-2 per mm; stipe 6-10 cm long, 2-3.5 cm thick, solid, surface pinkish buff to cinnamon buff;

spores 11-16 × 5-7 µ; cap cuticle a trichodermium with end cells 10-22 × 6-12 µ and clavate to mitten-shaped.

Scattered in mixed conifers and hardwoods, Michigan, summer, rare (?).

3b. Not as above 4
4a. **Spores 12-15 × 3.8-4.5 µ; content of trichodermial hyphae reddish in Melzer's, clamp connections occasional on hyphae of basidiocarp** .... *Boletus insuetus* **Smith & Thiers**

Cap 3-8 cm, convex, dry, glabrous, in age areolate, pale tan to tawny but with yellow tones in age; context white; tubes yellow, unchanging; pores yellow, unchanging or slowly yellowish brown if injured; stipe 6-9 cm long, 10-16 mm thick, clavate at first, base whitish splashed yellow, grayish brown to avellaneous above, reticulate over upper half with a fine pallid network; cuticle of cap a trichodermium of thin-walled readily collapsing hyphae 6-10 µ wide, end cells typically cystidioid.

In mixed woods, northern Michigan, August, apparently rare.

4b. Not as in above choice 5
5a. Cap dry and velvety to unpolished when young 6
5b. Cap viscid or shiny when young 7
6a. Trichodermial hyphae roughened; spores 10-14 × 3.5-4.5 µ ....
.... *Boletus atkinsoni* **Peck**

Cap 6-10 cm, convex, grayish brown to yellowish brown, rimulose-areolate in age at times; tubes becoming yellow, pores minute, soon yellow; stipe 5-10 cm long, 1-2.5 cm thick, pallid beneath a pale brownish reticulum; cuticle of cap of hyphae 4-7 µ wide, tubular, cells elongate, walls roughened by minute plates of material, end cells scarcely inflated.

Our data are from the type. It is apparently an eastern species and not too well known, having been confused with *B. variipes*.

6b. **Cap blackish brown to smoky brown or crust brown, typically becoming strongly areolate; spores 12-17 (18) × 3.5-5.5 µ. Fig. 253** ....
........*Boletus variipes* **Pk.**

Cap 6-20 (30) cm, convex to plane; context white; tubes 1-3 cm deep, soon yellow; pores 1-2 per mm, becoming yellow by maturity, unchanging if injured; stipe

Fig. 253. *Boletus variipes*.

8-15 cm long, 1-3.5 cm thick, finely reticulate above with a pallid reticulum, colored like the cap or paler; cuticle of cap of hyphae 4-9 μ wide, end cells 30-60 $\times$ 5-9 μ, tapered to a blunt apex, the hyphae smooth as revived in KOH, walls thin.

Gregarious and often abundant in thin oak woods or in beech-maple stands; common during wet warm summer weather in eastern North America and the Great Lakes area.

Var. *fagicola* is blackish brown at first and fades only slowly. Also, its spores are slightly amyloid.

7a. Cap black to blackish brown when young and then with a hoary bloom; reticulum of stipe mostly brown in age ....
.... *Boletus aereus* Fries

Cap 8-15 (20) cm, various shades of date brown when older (often unevenly); context thick, white to pallid, odor and taste agreeable; tubes stuffed and white at first, greenish yellow mature, not staining appreciably when injured; stipe 8-15 cm long, 2-4 cm thick, enlarged downward, solid, white within; surface white at first as is the fine reticulum; spores 12-15 $\times$ 4-5 μ.

Solitary to gregarious under oak, in the fall. California. It is not as common as most collectors wish since it is one of our very best edible species.

7b. Not with a blackish cap having a hoary bloom at first 8

8a. Cap pale to dark crust brown; clamp connections absent; cuticle of pileus a collapsing trichodermium of hyphae 8-15 μ wide with walls gelatinous in KOH. Fig. 254 and 355 ....
.... *Boletus edulis* Fries var. *edulis*

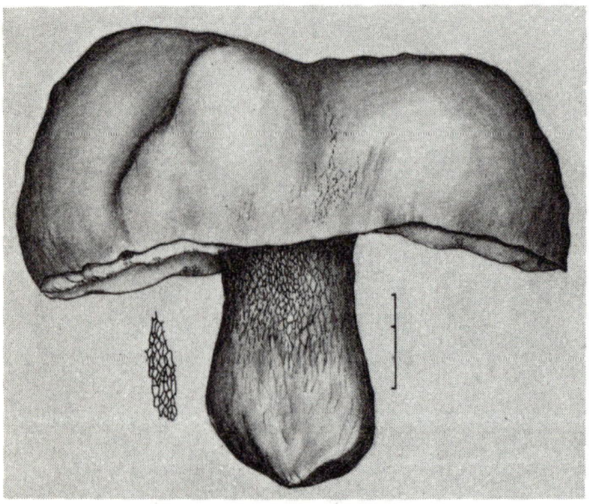

Pileus 8-25 cm broad, convex; context 2-4 cm thick, taste nutty; tubes up to 3 cm deep, greenish yellow in age; stipes massive 10-18 cm long, 2-4 cm thick, base up to 10 cm thick at times; spores (13) 14-17 (19) $\times$ 4-6.5 μ; a fleeting amyloid reaction on hymenophoral tissue present on revived material.

Scattered to gregarious under conifers, summer and fall, especially in the Rocky Mountain area and Pacific Northwest: this the typical variety is rare in eastern North America, but some of the following varieties are fairly common.

Fig. 254. *Boletus edulis*.

8b. Pileus not colored as in above choice 9
9a. Cuticular hyphae with diverticulae on many of them; cap ochraceous at all stages .... *Boletus edulis* var. *ochraceus* Smith & Thiers
9b. Not as above 10
10a. A "fleeting amyloid" reaction absent on tissue of the hymenophore as revived in Melzer's (as viewed on a glass plate over a white paper no bluish or bluish tint develops in the crushed material) .... *Boletus edulis* var. *clavipes* Peck
10b. Hymenophoral tissue revived in Melzer's giving the above described reaction 11
11a. Cap dark rose red; pores staining light cinnamon when bruised .... *Boletus edulis* var. *aurantioruber* f. *roseus*
11b. Cap ferruginous-red to bay-red; pores staining yellowish olive when bruised ..*Boletus edulis* var. *aurantioruber* Dick & Snell

Boletus pinicola Vitt. and *Boletus nobilis* Peck are additional taxa in this group. Peck's species is described from under hardwoods (oak). Much more study on the stirps Edulis is needed in North America.

PULVEROBOLETUS Murrill

Fleshy pore fungi with a dry floccose bright yellow veil with the fibrils intergrown with the tissue of the stipe rather than separate from it (as in the genus *Suillus*), and the spores unornamented. This concept is narrower than that of Singer, and in our area embraces only one species.

1a. Fig. 255 ....*Pulveroboletus ravenelii* (B. & C.) Murrill
Cap (1) 2-6 (10) cm, appearing pulverulent at at times from veil remnants, often subviscid when wet, disc reddish, remainder bright yellow; context slowly bluish when cut and then later yellowish to dark brown; tubes bright yellow; pores 2-3 per mm, bright yellow; stipe 4-9 (15) cm long, 4-16 mm thick, slowly pinkish where injured, yellow - fibrillose from veil and at times faintly anulate; spores 8-10.5 × 4-5 μ; cuticle of cap of hyphae 2.5-6 μ wide, yellow to hyaline in KOH, rusty brown in Melzer's; clamps absent.

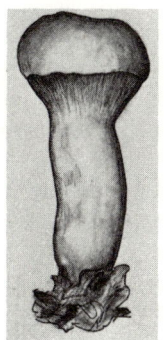
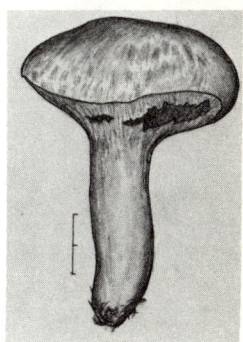

Fig. 255. *Pulveroboletus ravenelii*.

Solitary to gregarious in both hardwood and conifer forests, summer and early fall, most abundant in the southeastern states but occurring northward to the Lake Superior shore and eastward; generally rare.

BOLETELLUS Murrill

Spores under the microscope ornamented with more or less longitudinally arranged wings, ridges or striations.

Key to Species

1a. Veil present; cap squamulose, the scales coarse and imbricate
....*Boletellus ananus* (Curt.) Murr.
Cap 4-10 cm, subglobose becoming convex, color deep red becoming more dingy yellow in age; context pallid to yellowish; tubes yellow, staining blue, finally reddish brown over all, depressed around the stipe; pores yellow becoming broad and angular; stipe 6-14 cm long, 8-15 mm wide, white or pallid, with a reddish zone near apex, somewhat fibrillose, rarely with an annular zone; spores 16-20 (23) × 7.5-9.5 μ.

Often around the bases of trees, especially pine and oak, southern and southeastern but extending north up the Atlantic coast, not common.

1b. Veil lacking 2
2a. Stipe lacerate-reticulate. Fig. 256 ....
....*Boletellus russellii* (Frost) Gilbert

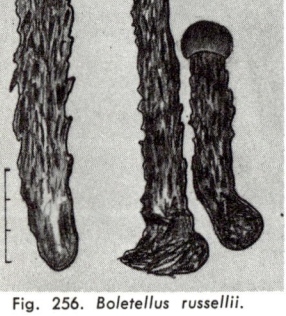

Fig. 256. *Boletellus russellii*.

Cap 3-10 (13) cm, convex, dry, soon conspicuously areolate, buffy brown to olive-gray or at times cinnamon-brown to rufous (reddish); context yellow unchanging; tubes yellowish olive to olive-green; pores olive-yellow to olive-green, large and angular; stipe 10-18 cm long, 1-2 cm thick, interior yellow, typically dull red or reddish brown; spores 15-20 × 7-11 μ; cuticle of cap a trichodermium of wide inflated cells (10 μ or more wide).

Solitary to scattered on humus usually under oak, Great Lakes region eastward and southward, during warm wet weather in late summer; rarely collected in large numbers.

2b. Stipe surface not lacerate-reticulate 3

3a. Spores 9-12 × 4-5 μ, weakly striate; cap bright red to olive-gray. Fig. 257 ....*Boletellus intermedius* Smith & Thiers

Cap 4-10 cm, broadly convex, bright red becoming olive-gray and areolate in age; context staining blue; tubes 7-12 mm long, bright yellow; pores 1-2 per mm; stipe 6-12 cm long, 8-17 mm thick, smooth to longitudinally striate, rhubarb red from pruina, yellow at apex, basal mycelium pallid; cap trichodermium of heavily incrusted hyphae as revived in KOH.

Scattered in thin oak woods in southeastern Michigan in September; rare.

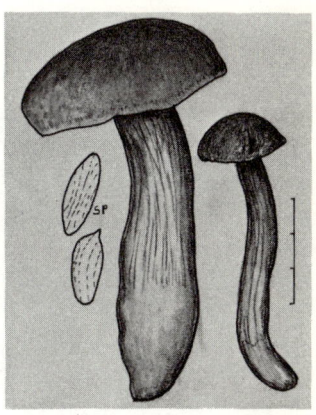

Fig. 257. *Boletellus intermedius*.

3b. Spores larger and conspicuously striate 4

4a. Cap dark brown; stipe surface becoming squamulose-furfuraceous. Fig. 258 .... *Boletellus chrysenteroides* (Snell) Singer

Cap 3-6 cm, convex, velvety to tomentose, dark vinaceous-brown, becoming areolate-cracked and the pale yellowish white context showing; tubes bright yellow becoming sordid greenish yellow; stipe 2-4 cm long, 8-12 mm thick, apex yellowish, lower portion dull reddish becoming dingy where handled, appearing almost reticulate at times from the scurf; spores (10) 12-16 (22) × 4.6-7.5 (8) μ; pleurocystidia 36-60 × 8-14 μ, fusoid-ventricose with acute or capitate apex; cheilocystidia fusoid-ventricose with acute to capitate apex or clavate to mucronate; cuticle of cap a trichodermium with short cells near the tips of the hyphae and the subapical cell often inflated.

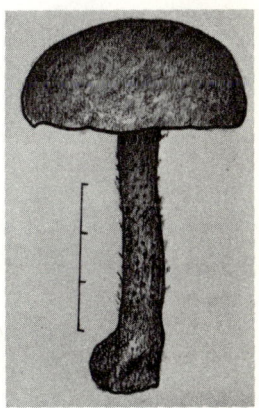

Fig. 258. *Boletellus chrysenteroides*.

Single to gregarious in oak woods, especially around very old logs and stumps, from the Great Lakes region eastward and southward, usually rare to uncommon.

4b. Cap red; stipe red-pruinose to scurfy. Fig. 259 ....
.......................*Boletellus pseudochrysenteroides* **Smith & Thiers**

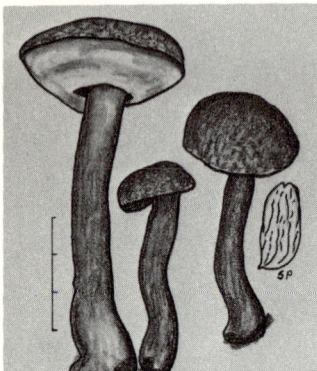

Fig. 259. *Boletellus pseudochrysenteroides.*

Cap 5-10 cm, convex, subtomentose becoming areolate, dark red; context yellow, changing to deep blue when injured; tubes 8-12 mm long, yellowish, soon blue where injured; pores 1-1.5 mm wide, yellow; stipe 6-9 cm long, 9-14 mm thick, apex yellowish, base coated with dingy honey yellow mycelium; spores deposit dark olive-fuscous; content of hyphae of the trichodermium of the cap dark orange-brown as revived in Melzer's.

Scattered under beech in beech-maple woods in southeastern Michigan in late summer and early fall, rare.

STROBILOMYCES

Cap coarsely fibrillose squamulose to finely squamulose, fibrils gray to blackish; tubes pallid to cinereous, blackening in age; spore deposit blackish brown; spores subglobose and ornamented.

Key to Species

1a. Spores reticulate. Fig. 260 ....
....*Strobilomyces floccopus* (Fr.) **Karsten**

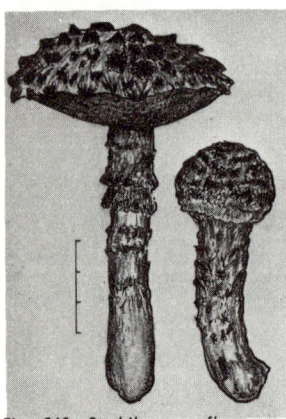

Fig. 260. *Strobilomyces floccopus.*

Cap 4-15 cm, pulvinate to broadly convex, gray to blackish, margin usually decorated with veil remnants; context pallid, staining reddish then blackish, stained red with KOH; tubes 12-15 mm deep, staining reddish then black; pores angular, pallid, staining reddish then black if injured; stipe 5-12 cm long, 12-25 mm thick, with a thick woolly sheath from the soft veil; spores 9.5-15 $\times$ 8.5-12 μ; pleurocystidia 17-90 $\times$ 8-26 μ, content brown in age.

Solitary to scattered in hardwood forests, common but not found in large numbers, occurring east of the Great Plains. Not recommended for the table.

NON-GILLED FLESHY FUNGI

1b. Spores echinate to verrucose at times with a partial reticulum in addition .... *Strobilomyces confusus* Singer

Cap decorated by very acute erect spines or squamules as compuared to the soft more or less appressed scales of the above species.

Great Lakes region and New England, generally rare.

KEY TO GENERA OF LYCOPERDALES
(The True Puffballs)

See fig. 261.

1a. Fruit body opening up to exhibit a star-shaped structure with a spore sac at the center of the star 2

1b. Not as above 3

2a. Spore sac opening by an apical pore or slit or a distinct peristome; sac atached by a single short stalk to the center of the star (see *Astreus* also p. 288) .... *Geastrum*

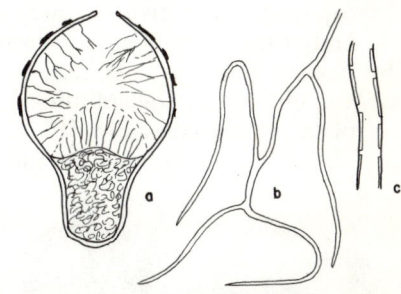

Fig. 261. (a) longitudinal section through a fruit body of *Lycoperdon* showing the sterile base, the gleba above it and the wall (peridium) enclosing the whole; (b) capillitial thread; (c) same enlarged to show pits in the wall.

2b. Spore sac opening by several pores (salt shaker-like); sac attached by several slender stalks. Fig. 262. ....
.... *Myriostoma coliformis* (**Pers.**) **Corda**

Fruit body at first hypogeous and subglobose, when opened 1.5-7 (10) cm broad; outer surface smooth or nearly so, outer layer splitting as in *Geastrum*; spore sac minutely roughened, silvery brown; spores 4-6 μ, globose, warty; capillitium of long slender tapered threads 2-5 μ wide, the walls thickened.

On sandy or loam soil, along woods borders, in old fields, etc., late summer and fall, rare but widely distributed.

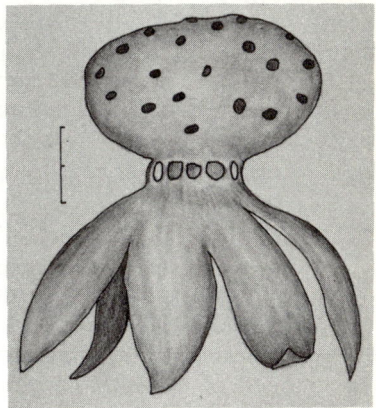

Fig. 262. *Myriostoma coliformis.*

3a. Endoperidium persistent, membranous (it is the wall of the spore sac), at some stage in development covered by the remains of an outer layer (exoperidium) in the form of patches, warts or spines; opening by an apical pore or peristome 4
3b. Endoperidium breaking up with the exoperidium or rupturing in an irregular manner 7
4a. Capillitium threads much-branched from a main shaft of axis, branches slender and with tapered pointed ends; spores with long pedicels .... Bovistella p. 271
4b. Capillitium threads without a conspicuous main axis and lacking a distinct system of branches 5
5a. Exoperidium separating from the endoperidium circumscissilly exposing about half or more of the endoperidium (the fruit body then resembling an acorn in its cup) ... Disciseda p. 272
5b. Not as above 6
6a. Capillitium (paracapillitium) accompanied by membranous plates at maturity. Fig. 263 ....
.... Morganella subincarnata (Pk.) Kreisel & Dring

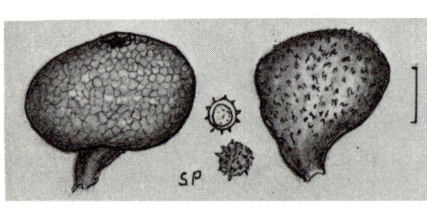

Fig. 263. Morganella subincarnata.

Fruit body 1-3 cm broad, globose to pear-shaped, remains of exoperidium in the form of brown spines and warts with tips connected to form groups, connected at first basally with brownish scurf, endoperidium pitted when spines have fallen away; gleba grayish or tinged purplish at maturity; sterile base rudimentary to well-developed; spores 3.5-4 μ, globose, ornamented as in *Lycoperdon*, apedicellate (but broken pedicels present in mounts); capillitium of hyaline (or nearly so) threads with relatively thin walls and much incrusting debris, sparingly branched, frequently septate, 4-7 μ wide.

Gregarious to scattered on moist mossy logs of hardwood species, late summer and fall. It is not uncommon some seasons on the slash of maple, beech and birch in the Great Lakes region.

6b. Capillitium typical as to type (thick-walled and brown in KOH) .... *Lycoperdon* p. 273
7a. Capillitium much branched (having a main axis and branches from it with ends of branches tapered to points), the threads arising from the inner peridium and the base 8
7b. Threads of capillitium lacking a conspicuous main axis (and not conspicuously branched) 10
8a. Thread of capillitium aggregated into a ball which is fairly persistent .... *Lanopila bicolor* (Lév.) Pat.

Fruit body "Bovista-like" (a true puffball), 2-8 (10) cm broad, outer peridium white and flaking off; inner peridium violaceous to grayish lilac, more or less sloughing off with the exoperidium leaving a ball of tightly interwoven glebal elements; capillitium of threads 2-6 μ wide tapered to acute tips, branching occasional, color violaceous to violaceous-brown (as in *Calvatia cyathiformis*); spores 4-6 (7) μ, ornamented as in *Lycoperdon*. The species described here is to be regarded as an American variant.

Gregarious on soil in Texas in the fall.

8b. Gleba becoming powdery or a flocculent mass (not held together as a cushion until late maturity) 9

9a. Fruit body 4-20 cm or more in diam; main axis of capillitial threads 20-30 μ wide; spore case hard and about 2 mm thick. Fig. 264 .... *Mycenastrum corium* **(Guers.) Dev.**

Fruit body at first covered by a felted whitish layer (exoperidium) soon cracking into block-like areas and falling away exposing the hard thick spore case; spores 8-12 μ wide, globose; branches of capillitium with spines.

Gregarious to solitary on soil—on areas where cattle are fed, in pastures, etc., summer and fall, widely distributed, but common in the Rocky Mountain states.

9b. Fruit body 2-10 cm wide; spore case less than 1 mm thick as dried (papery to membranous) .... *Bovista* p. 270

10a. With a papery to parchment-like membrane separating the sterile base from the gleba. Fig. 265 ....
.... *Vascellum depressum* **(Bon.) Smarda**

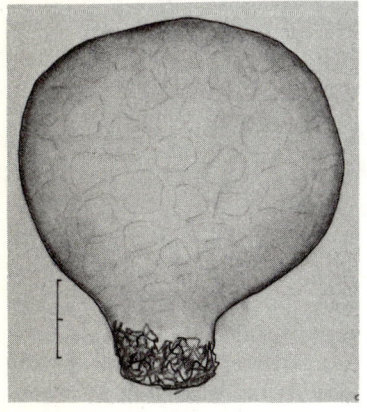

Fig. 264. *Mycenastrum corium*.

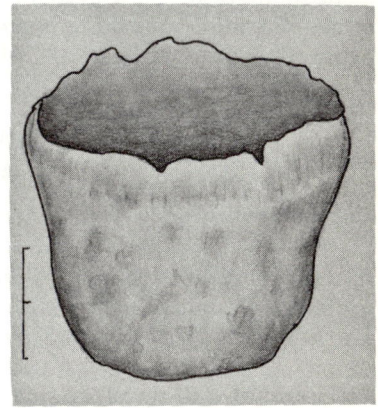

Fig. 265. *Vascellum depressum*.

Fruit body turbinate, bowl- or urn-shaped, 2.5-5 cm high 2-4 cm broad, white to pale buff, inner peridium metallic brownish, shining, opening by stellate lobes later partly breaking away wall but persistent over lower half (to form a bowl), exoperidium of soft spines and granules, both types deciduous; subgleba prominant, chambers large; gleba brownish olive; capillitial threads 3.3-6.6 μ, septate, sparingly branched, walls not pitted, breaking into short sections; spores 3-5.5 μ nearly smooth.

On lawns, in pastures, on golf courses, etc., common in the Pacific Coast states but widely distributed over the Northern Hemisphere.

10b. Not as above 11
11a. Capillitium with thorn-like branches reminding one of *Bovista*.
Fig. 266 ....*Calbovista subsculpta* Morse

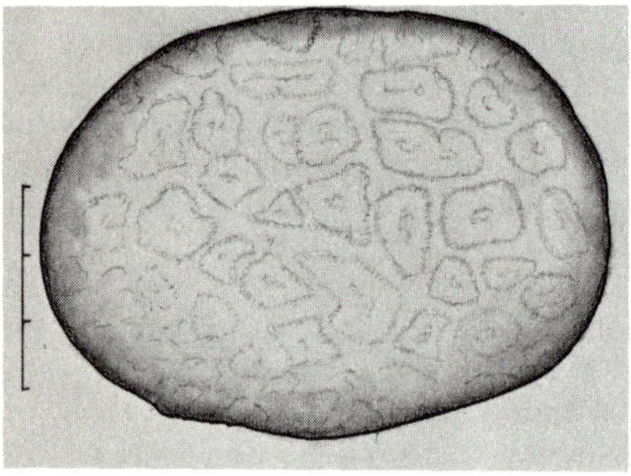

Fruit body pallid to dingy, the tips of the scales often grayish; exoperidium thick, felt-like, breaking up into areolate patches or pyramids 5-8 mm thick in places; inner wall (endoperidium) thin and shiny; sterile base one fourth to one third of the size of the gleba; gleba dark umber, somewhat purplish on weathering; spores globose, 3-5 μ.

Fig. 266. *Calbovista subsculpta*.

Usually single to gregarious in subalpine habitats in open areas, along borders of the forest, or along roadsides, April to August, Rocky Mountains and coast ranges where it is one of the most abundant of the large puffballs at higher elevations.

11b. Not as above ......*Calvatia* (including *Langermannia*) p. 258

CALVATIA
Key to Stirpes

1a. Gleba distinctly violaceous at maturity ....
....*Stirps Cyathiformis* p. 259
1b. Gleba reddish brown, olive-brown, umber brown or ochraceous 2
2a. Peridial wall hard and *Scleroderma*-like at maturity ....
....*Stirps Pachyderma* p. 260
2b. Peridial wall disintegrating completely or remaining as a cup-like wall around the margin of the sterile base 3
3a. Peridial wall more or less persistent around margin of sterile base; subgleba cellular and violaceous or purplish ....
....*Stirps Tatrensis* p. 265
3b. Not as above 4

4a. Peridium breaking up into conspicuous polygones or cones; sterile base usually present .... Stirps *Sculpta* p. 261
4b. Not as above 5
5a. Fruit body large (8-40 cm); sterile base reduced or absent .... Stirps *Gigantea* p. 263
5b. If of large size then a sterile base present 6
6a. Gleba powdery at maturity .... Stirps *Bovista* p. 269
6b. Gleba a cottony mass more or less persistent .... Stirps *Craniiformis* p. 266

STIRPS CYATHIFORMIS

1a. Peridium becoming spotted red; spores strongly verrucose and dextrinoid .... *Calvatia rubrotincta* Zeller
   Basidiocarps 4-7 cm broad, 3-4 cm high, sulcate below, base with several cord-like rhizomorphs; surface whitish at first; endoperidium easily broken along the ridged reticulations, sterile base about 1/10 the volume of the gleba, large-celled; gleba powdery; capillitium 2.2-6 μ diam., the branches fork-like, subacute at tips, wall to 1 μ thick and with small round pits, threads breaking readily. Spores 5-6.5 (7.7) μ.
   Under ponderosa pine in Oregon, rare as far as known.
1b. Not as above 2
2a. Sterile base inconspicuous ....*Calvatia cyathiformis* f. *fragilis* (Vitt.) Smith
   Growing scattered to gregarious on the open prairies and pasture land, widely distributed but common over the Great Plains.
2b. Sterile base well developed 3
3a. Spores distinctly ornamented. Fig. 267 ....*Calvatia cyathiformis* f. *cyathiformis* (Bosc.) Morgan

Fruit body 7-16 cm broad, 9-20 cm high, often areolate over upper surface; pallid becoming brownish to dingy purple-drab; sterile base chambered, remaining intact after spores are dispersed; capillitial threads 2.2-8 μ wide; spores 4.5-7.7 μ, pale tawny in Melzer's.

On the ground in grasslands, widely distributed but common in pastures in the midwest and over the Great Plains.

3b. Spores smooth or practically so 4

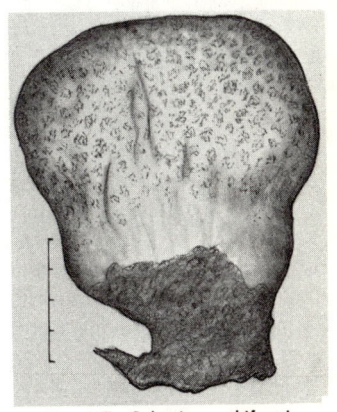

Fig. 267. *Calvatia cyathiformis*.

4a. Spores long-pedicellate; endoperidium subcoriaceous and with a ferruginous-brown lining ....
.... *Calvatia sigillata* (Craign.) Morgan

Fruit body 10-14 cm broad, top-shaped, narrowed to a stem-like base, soon marked into polygonal areas by depressed lines; capillitium slightly branched, rarely pitted; spores 3.5-5.5 μ.
On the ground in grass land, Great Plains, rare.

4b. Spores lacking a pedicel or with only a stump of one; endoperidium ochraceous and velvety .... *Calvatia leiospora* Morgan

Fruit body 6-9 cm tall, 4-6 cm wide, oblong to obovoid, base thick and plicate, exoperidium smooth, very thin, reticulately marked; sterile base about the size of the gleba; capillitium 2.5-3.5 (4) μ wide, sparingly branched; spores 3.5-4 μ.
On grass land, northern Great Plains.

STIRPS PACHYDERMA

1a. Pits of capillitial threads slit-like 2
1b. Pits of capillitial thread more or less isodiametric 4
2a. Spores distinctly verrucose at maturity. Fig. 268 ....
.... *Calvatia fumosa* Zeller var. *fumosa*

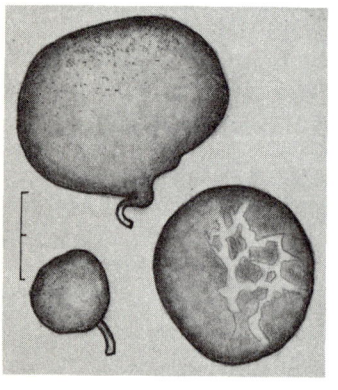

Fig. 268. *Calvatia fumosa*.

Fruit body 3-10 cm wide, subglobose, smooth to slightly furfuraceous, wrinkled in drying, rarely inconspicuously areolate, where exposed to the light, soon smoke gray to umber brown; peridium of 2 layers almost inseparable, 1-2 mm thick, hard and persistent; subgleba lacking to rudimentary; gleba very dark brown and powdery; capillitial threads 2.2-18 μ wide, in long or short segments, sparsely branched, branches often Y-shaped, the tips subacute, aseptate, walls 1-1.5 μ thick, broken edges jagged; spores (4.5) 5-7.7 μ, dark olive-brown in KOH, tawny in Melzer's.

Solitary to gregarious in dense spruce-fir forests in the mountains in the summer and early fall, common at times.

2b. Mature spores smooth or indistinctly ornamented 3
3a. Peridial surface smooth or nearly so ....
.... *Calvatia hesperia* Morgan

Fruit bodies 4-8 cm broad, depressed, white to pearl gray; peridium of two adherent layers, coriaceous, slowly breaking up to release spores; sterile base absent; gleba clay color to greenish yellow, finally chocolate color, pulverulent; capillitium 4.4-7.7 μ wide, more or less flexuous, tips blunt, walls about 2 μ thick; spores 4.4-5.5 (6.6) × 4-5 μ, tawny in KOH or Melzer's.

Sandy soil in southern California, rare.

3b. Peridium with upper surface consisting of cones or warts with gray to fuscous tips. Fig. 269 .... *Calvatia subcretacea* Zeller

Fruit body 2-7 cm broad, 1.5-4 cm high, sterile base absent to rudimentary, surface chalky white, tips of warts often becoming smoke gray; warts up to 7 mm across the base, breaking away individually; gleba powdery, buff to burnt umber; capillitial threads 2.2-13 μ wide; spores 4-6.5 μ, nearly smooth, tawny in Melzer's.

In duff in spruce-fir and hemlock forests in the mountains, widespread in our western mountains in the summer and early fall.

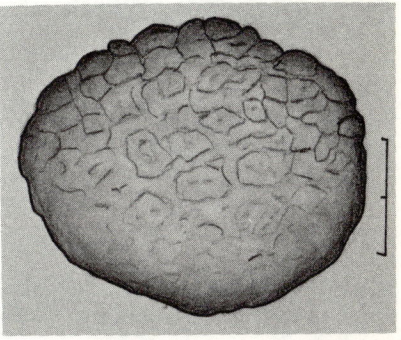

Fig. 269. *Calvatia subcretacea*.

4a. Many spores ellipsoid to ovate; fruit bodies 4-17 cm broad ....*Calvatia pachyderma* (Pk.) Morgan

Fruit bodies 7-12 cm high, 3-17 cm broad, variously shaped; peridial wall 2-4 mm thick; exoperidium smooth to slightly furfuraceous, white to brownish, thin (about 1 mm) and rind-like, often peeling from the endoperidium in thin patches; endoperidium tan to dark olive-brown, umbrinous to faintly purplish, powdery at maturity; sterile base absent; capillitial threads 3.3-13 μ wide, abundantly branched, flexuous, interwoven, walls up to 2 μ thick, pits rare to occasional, round to elliptic; spores 3.5-6.5 (7.5) × 3.5-5.5 μ, smooth to finely warted, yellowish tawny in Melzer's.

In open places in arid regions, the Southwest and California.

4b. Spores regularly globose; pits of capillitium isodiametric; threads frequently branched ....
.............................*Calvatia fumosa* var. *idahoensis* Smith

STIRPS SCULPTA

1a. Pits of capillitial threads slit-like; spores nearly smooth ....
....see *Calvatia subcretacea*

1b. Pits of capillitial threads more or less isodiametric or if they are slit-like then a sterile base present 2

2a. Threads of capillitium with walls 1-2 μ thick; exoperidial spines often curved or coiled; subgleba well developed. Fig. 270 ....
.... *Calvatia sculpta* (Hark.) Lloyd

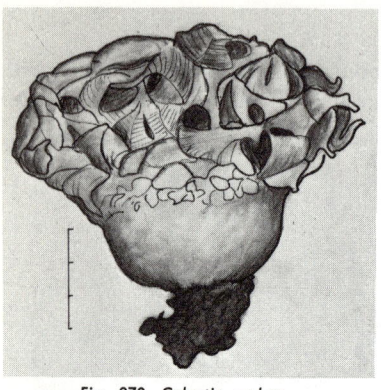

Fig. 270. *Calvatia sculpta*.

Fruit body 4-10 cm broad, obovate, turbinate or pear-shaped; exoperidium breaking up into large warts often with longitudinal lines or parallel lines, in age the warts dividing vertically but remaining attached by their apices; gleba yellow to olive-brown and finally powdery; capillitium threads 2.2-7.7 μ wide, branches attentuated at apex, abundantly septate; spores 3.3-5.5 (6.5) μ pale brown in Melzer's, very minutely ornamented.

In duff under conifers at high elevations summer and fall, mountains of our western states.

2b. Not as above 3
3a. Spores practically smooth; warts of the exoperidium neither coarse nor ornamented by lines ...... *Calvatia owyheensis* Smith

Fruit body about 5 × 3 cm, with a mycelioid rooting base, surface evenly areolate warty and often with a central spine on each wart; endoperidium thin and adhering to exoperidium; sterile base slight; gleba olive-brown, more or less powdery; capillitial threads yellow-brown in KOH, walls 1-1.5 (2) μ thick, threads 1.5-8 μ wide, ends of some branches needle-like; spores 3.5-6 μ, pedicel short.

3b. Spores distinctly ornamented 4
4a. Fruit body 10-12 cm broad; threads of capillitium often incrusted .... see *Calvatia cretacea* p. 264
4b. Fruit body up to 6 cm broad; capillitial threads smooth ....
.... *Calvatia arctica* Ferdin. & Winge

Fruit body about 3 cm high; exoperidium white then cinnamon, breaking into pyramidal warts ornamented by parallel lines and also vertical lines; endoperidium thickish, pale olive-buff; gleba rather pulverulent, dark yellow-brown; sterile base very inconspicuous, chambers minute, their walls pallid; capillitial threads honey yellow, fragmented and thin-walled (up to 0.7 μ), with scattered round pits, main threads 3-8 μ wide; spores 4.7-5.2 (6.3) μ, honey yellow, with low warts (0.4 μ high).

Found in arctic regions.

STIRPS GIGANTEA
(Langermania of some authors)

1a. Fruit body smooth to near maturity; capillitial threads with round pits; spores practically smooth. Fig. 271 ....
....Calvatia gigantea (Pers.) Lloyd

Fig. 271. Calvatia gigantea.

Fruit body 20-50 cm, subglobose, with cord-like root, surface with the texture of a kid glove when young; exoperidium breaking into flakes and falling away from the endoperidium at maturity; endoperidium thin and fragile, gradually breaking up; gleba yellow to olivaceous-brown; sterile base absent to rudimentary; capillitial threads 2.2-8.8 μ wide, branches attenuated at the tips, frequently septate, walls of threads up to 1.5 μ thick; spores 3.3-5.5 μ yellowish to tawny in Melzer's.

Solitary or in arcs or gregarious under brush along woods borders, in meadows, along drainage ditches, etc., late summer and fall, throughout eastern North America, common.

1b. Not as above 2
2a. Spores smooth or practically so; exoperidium forming warts up to 2 cm high at times. Fig. 272 ....Calvatia booniana Smith

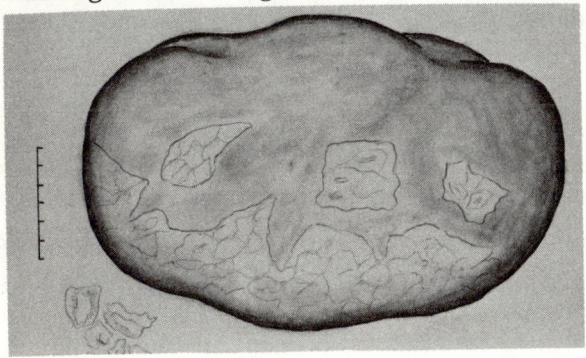

Fig. 272. Calvatia booniana.

Fruit bodies depressed-globose, up to 60 cm broad, 7-30 cm high; endoperidium 1-2 mm thick, entire wall 2-4 mm thick; gleba olive-brown; sterile base rudimentary to absent; capillitial threads 3.3-8.8 μ wide, threads branched, septate, breaking at the septa, walls up to 2 μ thick, bright olive-yellow in KOH, rarely pitted; spores 4-6 (6.5) × 3.3-5.5 μ, subglobose to globose.

Under sagebrush in arid situations, Idaho, Oregon and Nevada, summer.

2b. Spores distinctly verrucose 3
3a. Surface of fruit body embossed but not scaly; capillitial threads not pitted to any extent; exoperidium corky and about 2 mm thick as dried ....*Calvatia lepidophora* (E. & E.) Coker & Couch

Fruit body 15-20 cm broad; exoperidium as a thin glazed rind inseparable from a corky layer about 2 mm thick, surface areolate, the areolae duller colored at maturity; endoperidium papery thin and dark brown; capillitial threads 2.2-5.5 μ wide, elongate, slightly interwoven, branched rather commonly, tips of branches pointed; septate, walls up to 1 μ thick, pits rare, round, minute; spores (4.5) 5.5-6.5 × (5) 5.5-6 μ, subglobose, densely verruculose, with a hyaline envelope, olive-brown in KOH, ochraceous tawny in Melzer's; pedicels absent or inconspicuous.

Scattered on grassy soil in prairie regions, South Dakota, Indiana, etc.

3b. Not as above 4
4a. At least some threads of the capillitium encrusted with debris
.... *Calvatia cretacea* (Berk.) Lloyd

Fruit body 10-12 cm broad, brownish gray when mature; exoperidium thick and breaking up into polygones or warts, peeling off in large flakes with part of the endoperidium, the remainder of the latter glabrous, polished, and horn gray; gleba rather dark brown; subgleba rudimentary to fairly prominent, chambered, dark olive-brown often tinted lilaceous; threads of capillitium 3-13 μ thick, aborted branches rare, septa rare, pits puncture-like (opening to outside), edges irregular from a slight tearing effect; spores 4-7.5 μ, yellow-brown in Melzer's, with a short stump of a pedicel.

On grassy areas and dry heaths in open arctic areas of Canada.

4b. Capillitial threads smooth .... *Calvatia polygonia* Smith

Fruit bodies 8-16 cm, exoperidium continuous then broken into polygonal warts which may show some horizontal lines; endoperidium adhering to warts and breaking up and falling away with them; gleba cottony, dingy brown, maintaining its shape for a time after peridium has sloughed off; subgleba absent to rudimentary; threads of capillitium 3-8 μ wide, pale ochraceous-brown in KOH, bright fulvous in Melzer's, wall 0.5-1.2 μ thick, pits scattered, nearly isodiametric, branches subacute; spores 3.5-6.5 μ, bright yellow to pale tan in Melzer's, strongly ornamented, lacking a pedicel.

On prairie sod, Colorado, summer.

STIRPS TATRENSIS

1a. Spores 9-12 μ globose, reticulate; capillitium breaking up into S-shaped or very sinuous fragments ....*Calvatia paradoxa* Smith

Fruit body 2-6 cm broad, 2-3.5 cm high, glabrous, becoming rimose over upper suface, outer layer adherent to inner layer and both together forming a leathery spore case opening widely by radial tears across the upper part (as in *Scleroderma flavida*); subgleba none to rudimentary; gleba powdery, dark sepia at maturity, soon entirely dispersed; threads of capillitium with walls 0.4-1 μ thick, smooth; spores dark umber brown in KOH.

On soil in pastures and on waste land in mountainous areas, Colorado and Idaho.

1b. Not as above 2
2a. Capillitial threads incrusted, very thick-walled, not pitted, the broken ends often lacerate-fibrillose ....*Calvatia lacerata* Smith

Fruit body about 7 cm broad; exoperidium a thick felty layer, pallid becoming brownish, sloughing off in patches leaving a thin pallid to brownish inner peridium, finally dehiscing by radial tears into triangular segments; gleba a somewhat cottony mass not becoming completely dispersed, very dark brown; subgleba none present; threads of capillitium 2-7 μ wide, rarely septate, not pitted, thick-walled (to exclusion of cell cavity at times), surface incrusted; spores 3.5-5 μ, ornamented by plugs extending into a hyaline sheath up to 1 μ thick, bister in Melzer's, pedicel lacking.

Solitary in a young Douglas fir area, Rhododendron, Oregon, fall.

2b. Capillitium not as above 3
3a. With a distinct membrane between the gleba and subgleba; capillitial threads not pitted ....
.................See *Vascellum depressum* (Bon.) Smarda p. 257
3b. Not as above 4
4a. Gleba a cottony discrete mass ....
....*Calvatia lloydii* Zeller & Coker

Fruit body 3-8 cm wide, slowly becoming areolate with the areolae finally forming prominent warts or obtuse spines; exoperidium not separating readily from the endoperidium which is papery thin; gleba a light to dark olive-brown; subgleba concave and extending up from around the lower edge of the gleba to form a cup, chambered, purplish brown, with a metallic luster; threads of capillitium 2.2-9 μ wide, much-branched, fragmented, umbrinous in KOH pale tawny in Melzer's, wall about 1 μ thick, with abundant slit-like pits; spores 4-5.5 μ, olive-brown in KOH, minutely echinulate, ochraceous tawny in Melzer's.

In dry conifer forests, California and Idaho.

4b. Gleba powdery and soon completely dispersed. Fig. 273 .... *Calvatia tatrensis* **Hollis**

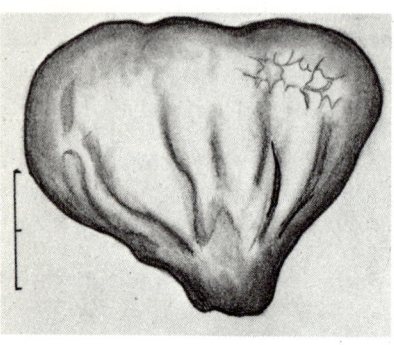

Fig. 273. *Calvatia tatrensis*.

Fruit body 4.5-9 cm broad, 5-7 cm high, obvate; exoperidium thick, breaking into deciduous plaques; endoperidium chamois to dull tawny, firm becoming papery, splitting irregularly to form a broad mouth with tattered edges; gleba powdery and chocolate brown to dark olive-brown; subgleba plicate to furrowed, occupying the lower fourth of the fruit body, chambered, with the walls violaceous to olivaceous; capillitial threads 2.2-10.8 μ wide, flexuous, frequently branched, subacute at the tips, aseptate, breaking readily, pits slit-like, walls up to 2 μ thick, dark yellow-brown in Melzer's; spores 4.5-7.7 × 4.4-6.6 μ subglobse, almost smooth, tawny in Melzer's.

On waste land, often under sagebrush in the western states.

Var. *gruberi* lacks plications at the base and has heavier exoperidial ornamentation.

STIRPS CRANIIFORMIS

1a. Exoperidium dark brown to blackish; gleba dark cocoa color at maturity .... *Calvatia umbrina* **Lloyd**

Fruit body 4-6 cm broad; exoperidium and endoperidium not easily separable; endoperidium very thin and fragile, breaking up over upper part first; sterile base none; gleba dark umber; threads of capillitium septate, sinuous, smooth, wall about 1 μ thick, pitted, dark brown in KOH, 3-10 μ wide; spores 4-9 μ wide, smooth.

On the ground, California.

1b. Not as above 2
2a. Sterile base absent or nearly so 3
2b. Sterile base well developed 4
3a. Spores smooth; gleba ochraceous .... *Calvatia diguetii* **Hark & Pat.**

Fruit bodies 4-6 cm wide, 2 cm high, surface ochraceous, minutely furfuraceous, peridium thin, breaking into fragments, gleba ochraceous, cottony; capillitial threads fragile, branched, 3-6 μ wide, pale ochraceous; spores 3-4 μ, smooth, with a stump of a pedicel.

On sandy soil on the California Coast.

3b. Spores verruculose; gleba dark olive-brown ....
....*Calvatia lycoperdoides* **Smith**

Fruit body 1.5-4 cm high, 1.7-5 cm broad; exoperidium and endoperidium adherent, exoperidium furfuraceous to spinulose, or warted over the top, peridium breaking into large flakes; subgleba absent; gleba cottony, remaining intact a long time, dark olive-brown; capillitial threads branched, interwoven, tapered to the tips, aseptate or septa rare, broken edges ragged, walls about 1 μ thick, pits slit-like to isodiametric; spores 4-6.5 μ, pale tawny in Melzer's, verruculose.

In open places in conifer woods, California, Washington and Idaho, late summer and fall.

4a. **Fruit body when fresh quickly staining yellow when injured, drying ochraceous to orange-red in places; spores nearly hyaline in KOH. Fig. 274** .... *Calvatia rubroflava* **(Cragin.) Morgan**

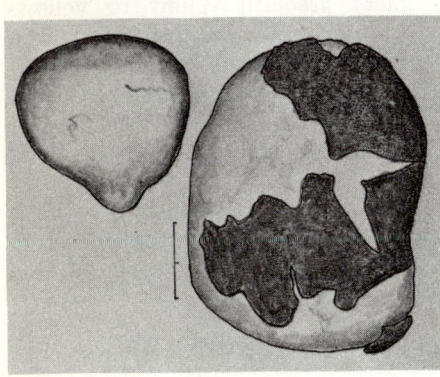

Fig. 274. *Calvatia rubroflava*.

Fruit body 2-10 cm wide, 1.5-5 cm high; peridium thin and practically one-layered, breaking up and falling away; subgleba not cellular at maturity, occupying about 1/3 of fruit body and extending up the sides as a thin layer; gleba yellow to olive-yellow to olive-orange; capillitial threads 2.2-6.6 μ thick, somewhat flexuous, branched, scarcely attenuated to tips, with many septa, walls -1.0 μ thick, pits 1-3 μ wide, nearly hyaline in KOH and Melzer's; spores 3-5 (5.5) × 3-5 μ, subglobose, weakly ornamented, hyaline in KOH and only faintly tawny in Melzer's.

Usually on cultivated soil, widely distributed but more typically southern than northern.

4b. Not as above 5

5a. **Spores 5.5-7.7 × 5.5-7 μ, usually flattened on one side; threads of the capillitium hyaline** .... *Calvatia ochrogleba* **Smith**

Fruit body 7-9 cm broad, smooth to furfuraceous; dull reddish brown; exoperidium very thin, not easily separable, both layers breaking up together; gleba of fine texture not readily dispersed, pale orange-yellow to orange-buff; threads of capillitium 2.2-6.5 μ wide, with scattered round pits, sparsely branched; frequently septate; spores 5-7.5 × 5.5-7 μ, hyaline in KOH, yellowish tawny in Melzer's, asperulate.

Known only from Oregon.

5b. Not as above 6

6a. Surface smooth to nearly smooth, threads of capillitium with numerous large pits. Fig. 275 ....
....*Calvatia craniiformis* (Schw.) Fr.

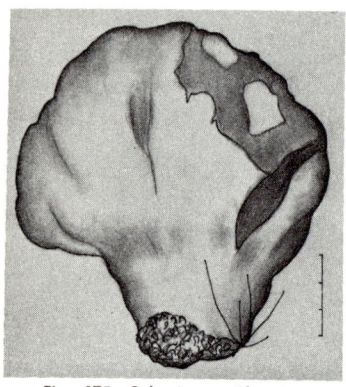

Fig. 275. *Calvatia craniiformis*.

Fruit body 8-20 cm broad, 6-20 cm high; subgleba occupying the stalk-like base; exoperidium scaling off as thin plates; endoperidium breaking up after the exoperidium; gleba cushion like (remaining intact) greenish yellow to yellow-brown; capillitial threads 2-7.5 μ wide, attenuated gradually to 1.1 μ wide, walls -1.0 μ thick, yellowish in KOH; spores (2.2) 3.3-4.4 μ, nearly smooth; yellowish in KOH and Melzer's.

On ground in brushy low areas or upland woods, wide-spread in the Southwest and east of the Rocky Mountains.

6b. Surface of fruit body granular to furfuraceous 7

7a. Spores distinctly ornamented (orn. 0.5-1 μ high) ....
......*Calvatia excipuliformis* (Pers.) Perdek. var. *excipuliformis*

Fruit bodies 6.5-8 cm high, fertile heads 3.5-4.5 cm wide, sterile stalk widest at apex and containing the subgleba; exoperidium thin, breaking into plates; endoperidium yellowish to chamois, thin and papery; gleba cottony, somewhat enclosed over lower edge by the cuplike subgleba, purplish brown; threads of capillitium 1.1-7.7 μ, strongly tapered to the tips, aseptate or septa rare, walls about 1 μ thick, pits occasional, roundish, pale olive-brown in KOH; spores 3.5-5.6 μ, globose, tawny in Melzer's.

On grassy waste ground, pastures, lawns, etc. It is widely distributed but not common.

7b. Spores with indistinct ornamentation. Fig. 276 ....
.... *Calvatia elata* (Massee) Morgan

Fruit body long-stipitate, subgleba occupying the stipe, 9 cm long and 4 cm wide for the stipe, head 4-7 cm wide; exoperidium pale brown to leather color at maturity, thin, granular; endoperidium thin, breaking into fragments; gleba brown to olive-brown; threads of capillitium (1.1) 2.2-5.5 (6.5) μ ornamentation about 0.25 μ high, olive-brown in KOH, pale tawny in Melzer's.

On low ground in brushy places such as bog edges or on grassy to mossy wet areas, eastern North America.

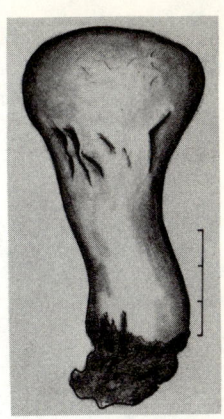

Fig. 276. *Calvatia elata*.

STIRPS BOVISTA

1a. Pits in walls of capillitial threads small and round; gleba passing through an orange stage; spores asperulate, ornamentation 0.5-1.1 μ high ....*Calvatia candida* (Rost.) Hollos

Fruit bodies 1.7-6 cm broad, 1.5-6 cm high, chalky white; exoperidium up to 1 mm thick; endoperidium papery, breaking into plate-like areas or peeling away from gleba; subgleba occupying a fourth of the fruit body; gleba umbrinous and powdery at maturity; capillitial threads 2.2-6.6 μ tips attenuated, branches Y-shaped, walls flexuous and up to 1 μ thick, pits minute and round; spores 5-6.5 (7.5) μ yellowish olive in KOH; ochraceous tawny in Melzer's.

On soil in arid places, under sagebrush etc., summer and fall, western U.S.A.

1b. Pits in capillitial threads elliptic to slit-like 2

2a. Spores distinctly ornamented .... *Calvatia pallida* Smith

Fruit body 1.5-5.5 cm wide, 1-2.5 cm high, exo- and endoperidium adherent, thin (-1.0 mm), brittle, surface finely wrinkled; base plicate; subgleba poorly developed, cavities small; gleba powdery and soon dispersed, olive-brown with a purplish tinge; threads of capilltium 2.2-9 μ wide, sinuous, attenuated at the tips, septate, septa rare to occasional, pits lenticular to slit-like; spores (4.4) 5.5-7.7 μ, ochraceous tawny in Melzer's.

Open woods in meadows, etc., at high elevations, summer and fall, Idaho and Washington.

2b. Spores smooth or practically so.
Fig. 277 ....*Calvatia bovista*
(Pers.) **Kambly & Lee**

Fruit body 5-15 cm broad, substipitate, exoperidium breaking up into areolate pieces; endoperidium thin; subgleba occupying the stipe, chambered; gleba olive to brownish olive, powdery but not soon dispersed; capillitial threads 2-12 (18) μ wide; spores (3.3) 4-6.6 (7.7) × 3.3-6 (6.8) μ, pale tawny in Melzer's.

On waste soil, roadsides, pastures, etc., widely distributed summer and fall. The name *C. utriformis* Pers. is currently used for this species in Europe.

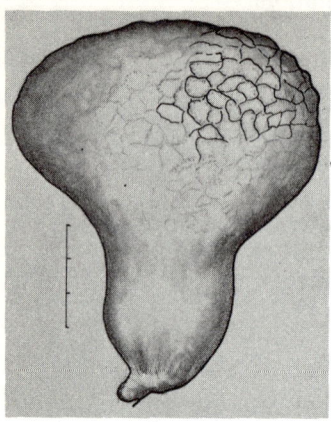

Fig. 277. *Calvatia bovista*.

BOVISTA

Surface at first covered with a thin, smooth to unpolished covering which flakes off at maturity exposing the smooth polished wall of the spore sac, opening at times by a pore enlarging to a rupture, or developing several openings, becoming detached from the ground and often blown about by the wind, sterile base lacking; capillitium composed of separate free-branching units.

Kreisel uses a much broader concept, including in the genus many species generally referred to other genera.

1a. Fruit body attached to the soil by a drab patch of fibers; wall of spore sac at maturity bluish to purplish umber.
Fig. 278 ....*Bovista plumbea* **Pers.**

Fruit body developing on the surface of the ground, 1-3 (8) cm wide; gleba dark brown at maturity; spores 5-7 × 4-5 μ oval with a long pointed pedicel (9-14 μ), appearing finely echinuate under an oil immersion lens; main threads of capillitial units 15-20 μ wide.

Open pastures, golf courses, parks, lawns, etc., summer and fall, widely distributed.

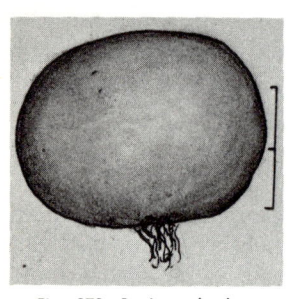

Fig. 278. *Bovista plumbea*.

1b. Not as above...2
2a. Fruiting body 3-9 cm wide, attached by a small cordlike rhizomorph which breaks at maturity; developing above ground ......
....*Bovista pila* **Berk. & Curt.**

Surface white at first, staining pinkish to alutaceous when handled, this layer flaking off to expose the dark brown to bronze wall of the spore sac which usually has a metallic luster, opening at the apex by an irregular fissure; spores globose to subglobose, 3.5-4.2 μ smooth, pedicel usually only a stub; main axis of capillitial units 10-12 μ wide.

Solitary, scattered to gregarious or subcespitose in pastures, pastured woods, around stables, or where cattle have been wintered. It develops during the late summer and fall but is durable and persists through the winter. It is widely distributed in the United States and Canada.

2b. **Fruit body 1-3.5 cm wide, with a broad basal area of attachment; developing in early stages underground but finally partly exposed** .... *Bovista minor* Morgan

White when young and with considerable adherent trash, when outer coat disappears surface dark reddish brown, spore-sac wall non-rigid, often dented and wrinkled; gleba olivaceous-brown; spores 4-5 × 3.5-4 μ, oval, pedicel up to 15 μ long, surface finely echinulate when seen under oil immersion lens, smooth under low power; capillitial units with the main axis 10-20 μ wide.

In conifer plantations, on banks, etc., fall, Great Lakes region southward generally rare but abundant at times. As the fruit bodies mature they develop a sweet aromatic odor which is lost upon drying.

BOVISTELLA

Fruit body subglobose to turbinate, surface covered by a coating of spines or particles or granules, spore case opening by an apical pore; sterile base present; capillitial units of a main axis with frequent branches, the main axis (or filament) as wide or wider than the diameter of the spores.

1a. **Fruit body small (5-8 mm), attached by a pad or knot of fibrils** ....*Bovistella echinella* (Pat.) Lloyd

Fruit body white when young, covered by a loose floccose coating aggregating into floccose patches and gradually falling away; spore sac dark brown, papery, the pore apical and becoming lacerated; gleba olive-brown; sterile base rudimentary (absent at times); spores 5-6 μ, minutely punctate, rusty brown in Melzer's, pedicel 4-8 μ long; capillitial units of separate threads, septa numerous, more sparsely branched than in *Bovista* main axis 5-6 μ wide. On sandy soil in pastures, east of Rocky mountains, probably much more abundant than the records show, summer and early fall.

Note: Kreisel includes this species in Bovista.

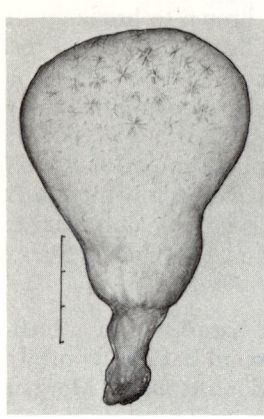

Fig. 279. Bovistella radicata.

1b. Fruit body 3-7.5 (14) cm broad; with a thick well developed pseudorhiza. Fig. 279 ....Bovistella radicata (Mont.) Pat.

Fruit body covered by a coating of slender spines often united at their tips, much granular to furfuraceous material between them; spore sac papery, opening by a pore or slit gradually widening to expose most of the gleba; gleba yellow-brown; sterile base well developed; spores oval, 4-5 × 3.5-4.5 μ pedicel 6-11 μ long; capillitial units much-branched and branches often gnarled, main axes 8-10 μ wide.

Scattered in fields, pastures, waste ground, etc. It seems to favor cultivated fields, summer and fall, widely distributed in the Northern Hemisphere.

DISCISEDA

Fruit bodies depressed-globose, peridium 2-layered; exoperidium in the form of a membrane or a sand case, fragile and deciduous in part (usually with remnants as a submedial disc or cup causing the fruit body to resemble an acorn in its cup); endoperidium papery-tough, opening either by a basal or apical pore depending on the species; sterile base none; capillitium present; spores colored and ornamented.

1a. Spores 3-6 μ, globose, smooth or nearly so. Fig. 280 ....
....Disciseda candida (Schw.) Lloyd

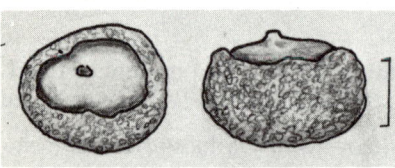

Fig. 280. Disciseda candida.

Fruit body acorn-like, 2-3.5 cm when mature; exoperidium adhering over upper portion, lower half separating from endoperidium thus freeing the spore sac from any attachment; gleba with basidia arising from strings of threads (hymenial cavities poorly formed and irregular), finally olive-brown to purplish; spores with a short pedicel; capillitial threads 3-5 μ thick, irregular, rarely branched, finally breaking into short pieces.

Scattered to gregarious on waste ground. Common in some areas east of the Rocky Mountains. The populations occurring over the Great Plains need critical study.

1b. Spores larger 2

2a. Spores 6-8 μ, globose, distinctly warty. Fig. 281 ....
................................*Disciseda subterranea* (Pk.) Coker & Couch

Fruit body 1-2 cm, acorn-like; spore sac unpolished, with a bluish to glaucous gray coating over a dull ground color; gleba dull cinnamon; spores coarsely echinulate; capillitial threads flexuous, readily breaking, septa numerous, branching frequent.

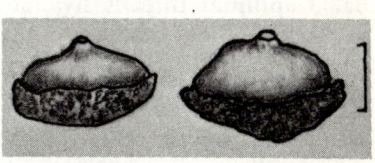

Fig. 281. *Disciseda subterranea*.

On sandy soil, eastern North America, rare (apparently).

2b. Spores 10-12.5 μ ....
....*Disciseda muelleri* (Berk.) Cuninngham

Fruit body up to 2.5 cm, with a short stout rooting base; exoperidium soon umber, with minute pale subpersistent warts; endoperidium firm and rather thick, brown; gleba reddish brown; capillitial threads flaccid, pale, sparsely branched; spores coarsely spinulose, apedicellate, epispore reddish umber in KOH.

Described from Australia but apparently occurring rarely in the Great Lakes area on exposed sand plains where temperatuers are high in the summer.

LYCOPERDON

Fruit body typically globose to pear-shaped, composed of two layers, the outer layer consisting of spines, warts, granular or felty floccose material which usually sloughs off at maturity, inner wall forming the rather rigid spore case and at maturity somewhat membranous or papery; typically opening at the apex by a pore through which the spores escape; gleba colored and with typically thick-walled colored threads; sterile tissue (often chambered) termed the subgleba or sterile base; spores globose, subglobose or rarely ellipsoid, with or without a pedicel, usually surrounded by a thin hyaline envelope into which small needle-like projections or warts may extend (seen only under a high power oil-immersion lens), in some species the wall smooth.

1a. Sterile base not chambered and usually greatly reduced in size or it is absent; if slightly chambered the cavities less than 0.5 mm wide 2

1b. Sterile base typically well developed 7

2a. Fruit body with a pitted surface after spines have fallen away; when young colored vinaceous-gray; on wood of hardwoods ....see *Morganella subincarnata* **p. 256**

2b. Not as above 3

3a. Capillitial threads hyaline in KOH; on grassy ground; fruit body 1-2 cm broad .... *Lycoperdon curtissii* **Berkeley**

Fruit body covered with spines at first; lacking conspicuous rhizomorphs; gleba olivaceous, powdery at maturity; capillitial threads 3-7 μ wide, thin-walled; often with incrusting debris; spores 3-3.5 μ olivaceous in KOH, rsuty brown in Melzer's, minutely ornamented.

Densely gregarious on grass land, widely distributed, fall or late summer, throughout North America.

3b. Not as above 4

4a. Fruit body brilliant to golden to lemon yellow when immature .... *Lycoperdon coloratum* **Peck**

Fruit body 1.5-4 cm, pinched off at base, attached by rhizomorphs, color slowly becoming bronze to dull brown by maturity, covered with minute harsh discrete darker warts and nodules, finally glabrous at least around the pore; gleba white to olive to coffee brown; sterile base poorly developed; spores 3-4.2 μ, minutely ornamented, rusty brown in Melzer's; capillitial threads olive-brown in KOH, 3-6.5 μ wide, walls up to 0.7 μ thick.

Eastern North America, solitary to gregarious on humus and debris, summer and fall.

4b. Not as above 5

5a. Lacking a sterile base, small (1-2 cm); spores globose .... *Lycoperdon pusillum* (**Pers.**) **Schwn.**

Fruit body globose or nearly so, pinched off at base and rooting slightly, white at first, surface floccose becoming covered by closely arranged small warts and granules, finally falling away; endoperidium pale brown to dark dull brown and obscurely spotted, apical pore 3-5 mm wide, margins lobed; gleba yellow to olive-brown to coffee brown; sterile base none; capillitial threads 2.5-6 μ wide, thick-walled, yellow-brown in KOH, rather crooked, tapered to apex, widest threads pitted; spores 3.5-4.5 μ, apedicellate, minutely ornamented.

Densely gregarious to clustered on waste soil, pastures, etc., summer and fall, common and widespread.

Note: Some authors place this species in *Bovista*.

5b. Not as above 6

6a. **Sterile base rudimentary, the chambers not conspicuous; spores ellipsoid. Fig. 282** .... *Lycoperdon oblongisporum* **Berk. & Curt.**

Fruit body 1-3 cm, attached by a persistent rhizomorph; exoperidium in the form of a thin layer of granular-fibrous material breaking up into minute patches eventually sloughing off exposing the smooth wood brown endoperidium; mouth nearly round and usually lobed to crenate on the margin, rather large; gleba yellow to olive-brown and finally darker; capillitial threads flexuous, 3-5 μ wide, septa rare, branching infrequent, olive toned in KOH, tapered gradually; spores 5-6 $\times$ 3.5-4 μ, ellipsoid, apedicellate, smooth to obscurely ornamented.

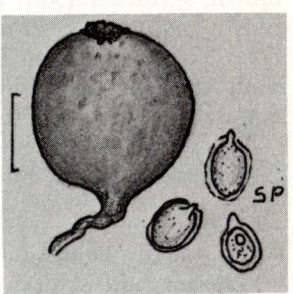

Fig. 282. *Lycoperdon oblongisporum.*

Gregarious on exposed soil or around bases of trees, summer, rare but widely distributed, Michigan to Cuba.

6b. **Sterile base typically well-developed; spores globose, 3.7-4.2 μ**
.... *Lycoperdon ericetorum* **Persoon var.**
cepaeforme (**Pers.**) **Bowerman**

Fruit body 1-3.5 cm wide, 2-4.5 cm high, base rooting or attached by a rhizomorph, surface covered by a sparse coating of short spines to minute warts, or granules, becoming glabrous, endoperidium olive-brown at maturity, apical pore round or nearly so; gleba olive-brown when mature; sterile base only slightly developed and lacking distinct chambers; capillitial threads much branched, main branches 5-7 μ wide, tapered to apices, olive-brown in KOH; spores 3.7-4.2 μ, olive-brown in KOH, rusty brown in Melzer's, minutely ornamented.

Densely gregarious to scattered on humus in woods and on waste soil, eastern North America, fall.

Note: This species was previously treated under the name *L. polymorphum* var. *cepaeforme* in North America.

7a. **Exoperidial remnants soon blocked out into warts with sharp tips and when separating from the endoperidium adhering to each other in sheets or chunks. Fig. 283** ....
.... *Lycoperdon marginatum* **Vitt.**

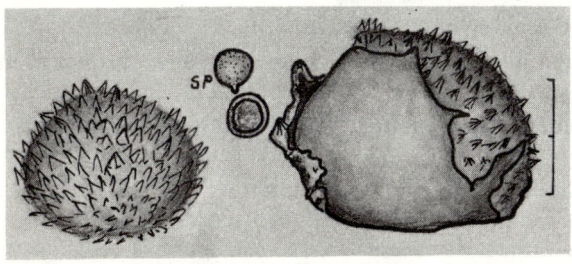

Fig. 283. *Lycoperdon marginatum*

Fruit body 1-5 cm broad, flattened, in age plicate on under side, with a short rooting base at times; endoperidium pale to dark olive-brown, surface smooth to obscurely pitted; gleba olive to grayish brown, pallid in age after removal of spores; sterile base well-developed, chambers about 1 mm wide; capillitial threads 3-6 μ wide, walls thickened and finally dark yellow-brown; spores 3.5-4.2 μ, minutely ornamented, rusty brown in iodine.

On sandy soil, summer and fall, very common and widespread. *L. candidum* Persoon is very similar.

7b. Not as above 8
8a. **Typically lignicolous; spores smooth; exoperidial remnants adhering and in drying causing surface of endoperidium to become roughened. Fig. 284** ....*Lycoperdon pyriforme* **Persoon**

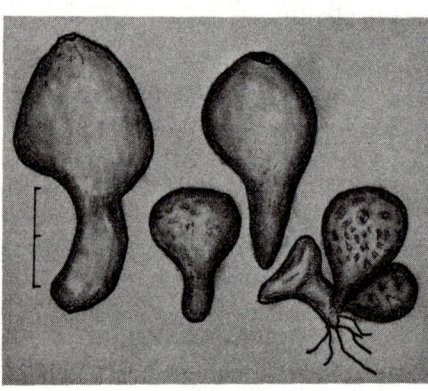

Fig. 284. *Lycoperdon pyriforme*.

Fruit body pyriform to subglobose, 1.5-3 (4.5) cm wide, 24.5 cm wide, surface pallid to crust brown, darker in age, smooth at first, roughened in age from outer layer breaking into particles or small spines and adhering to the endoperidium, eventually falling away (by spring), pore slow to form and often a slit 1 cm long; gleba olivaceous to olivaceous-brown; sterile base of small chambers; attached by conspicuous white rhizomorphs; spores 2.8-3.5 μ olivaceous to olive-brown; capillitial threads olive to dull brown in KOH, sparingly branched, even to flexuous, bright rusty brown in iodine.

Scattered to cespitose on wood (on sawdust piles often in clusters larger than a loaf of bread), fall (but the fruit bodies persist until spring or longer).

Edible when white clear through.

8b. Not as above 9
9a. Gleba olive to olive-brown or dull yellow-brown at maturity ....
10
9b. Gleba in fully mature fruit bodies dull violaceous to purple-drab 16
10a. **Capillitial threads with numerous small round pits; gleba pale dull cinnamon when mature; sterile base prominent** ....
 ....*Lycoperdon dakotensis* **Brenckle**

Fruit body 2-5 cm wide; exoperidium as fine granulose warts adherent over sides but not over upper surface, pallid drying to pale dingy tan; endoperidium papery, pale grayish tan, opening by a slit; sterile base distinctly chambered, chambers small (use a hand lens); broadly attached to the substrate; spores 3.2-4.5 μ, smooth to very minutely punctate, yellow-brown in KOH and the same in Melzer's but in addition showing an oil globule, lacking a pedicel; capillitial threads 2-6 μ wide, walls up to 1 μ thick, smooth, sparingly branched, tapered to a narrow crooked filament about 1 μ thick, walls yellow-brown in KOH.

On wet prairie sod, South Dakota, fall.

Note: This species is a typical *Lycoperdon*, but not to be confused with *L. oblongisporum* which is amply distinct on spore shape.

10b. Not as above 11
11a. Spores subglobose to broadly oval and with a long persistent pedicel ....*Lycoperdon pedicellatum* Peck

Fruit body 2-5 cm broad, 3-6 cm high, attached by numerous rhizomorphs; exoperidium as spines 1-2 mm long, single or in groups with tips converging, falling away to expose the obscurely pitted to reticulate endoperidium which is dull brown to grayish; apical pore slit-like; gleba olive to dull cinnamon; sterile base well developed, chambers up to 1 mm wide, pallid to brownish; spores 3.5-4.5 $\times$ 4-5 μ, pale cinnamon in KOH, dark rusty brown in Melzer's, finely ornamented, pedicel 10-18 μ long; capillitial threads 4-6 μ wide, sparingly branched.

Scattered to gregarious on humus rich in lignin or on very rotten wood, fall, widely distributed in eastern North America.

11b. Not as above 12
12a. Fruit body with yellow tones at maturity; capillitial threads with numerous pits; spines of exoperidial layer pale brown (but see *L. muscorum* p. 278 and *L. foetidum* p. 278 also) .... *Lycoperdon flavotinctum* Bowerman

Fruit body 1-3 cm high, 1.3-3.5 cm broad, usually broader than tall, slightly plicate around the base, exoperidium present as slender spines converging at tips or of separate spines and granules, these falling away; inner peridium shiny and pale colored, pore apical; gleba olive-brown, with a small pseudo-columella; subgleba well developed, chambered, convex at the gleba; capillitial threads with walls up to 0.8 μ thick, tapered to a blunt apex, branched, (2.5) 3.5-5 (6) μ wide; spores 4-4.5 (5) μ, minutely ornamented.

On the ground in open places, August to October, Great Lakes region especially in Canada.

12b. Not as in above choice 13

13a. Growing on deep moss. Fig. 285 ....
....*Lycoperdon muscorum* Morgan

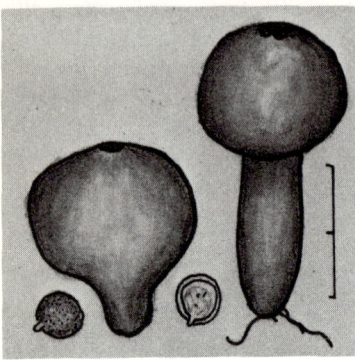

Fig. 285. Lycoperdon muscorum.

Fruit body pyriform to stipitate-subcapitate, (1.2) 1.7-3 cm high and 1.4-1.8 cm broad; sterile base greatly variable in length, chambered; exoperidium as granules and some spines or of small simple spines, at times the tips convergent; inner peridium where showing shiny, pore apical; fruit body slightly yellowish toned or olive yellowish when fresh; gleba olive-brown at maturity; capillitial threads 2-6.5 μ wide, with pitted walls up to 0.8 (1) μ thick, occasionally septate, branched, readily fragmenting, yellow-brown in KOH; often irregular in outline; spores (3.5) 4-5 μ, rusty brown in Melzer's; minutely punctate-echinulate.

Scattered on deep moss, rare, apparently northern in distribution.

13b. Not as above 14
14a. Spiny coating tinged lavender in immature stages; spines split at the base into 2-4 parts but the tips united ....
....*Lycoperdon peckii* Morgan

Fruit body 1.5-4 cm broad, 3 cm high, exoperidial spines 1-1.5 mm long, readily deciduous leaving pale smooth circular spots outlined by minute granules, buffy brown at maturity; subgleba occupying about a third of the fruit body; capillitial threads up to 6 μ wide, sparingly branched; gradually tapered to the apex; spores 3.6-5 μ, olive-brown in KOH.

On the ground, in fall, eastern North America, probably more common than the records indicates.

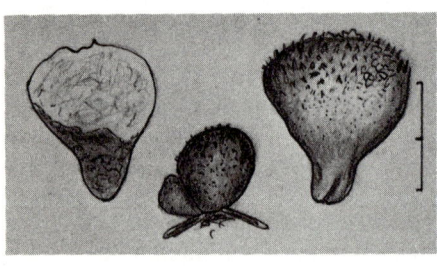

Fig. 286. Lycoperdon foetidum.

14b. Not colored as above and spines not as above 15
15a. On fresh immature and mature specimens the exoperidial spines fine and fuscous to black, the ground color at maturity with a yellowish tone. Fig. 286 ....
...*Lycoperdon foetidum* Bonarden

Fruit body 1-3 cm broad, 2-3.5 cm high, pear-shaped to globose; sterile base well-developed, chambers obvious; exoperidial spines very fine and pointed, densely spaced over upper part and surrounded by granular material; endoperidium smooth in age, papery, opening by a pore, grayish tan in color and with a slight yellow tone; gleba dull cinnamon (snuff brown to sepia); spores 4-5 μ, minutely echinulate, Isabella color in KOH, ochre in Melzer's; capillitial threads 4-6 μ wide, branches narrower (1.5-2.5 μ near the tips), undulating to crooked, Y-branches present, walls to 1.5 μ thick and yellow-brown in KOH.

On duff and debris in dense conifer forests, Pacific Coast region of the United States and Canada, common at times. This species has also been known under the name *L. nigrescens*.

15b. Spines of fruit body cone-like, not fuscous, leaving distinct spots on surface where they have fallen away, ground color not yellowish. Fig. 287 ....*Lycoperdon perlatum* **Pers.**

Fruit body 1.5-6 (9) cm, obovoid to turbinate; sterile base well developed, often plicate to wrinkled along the margin, white when immature, spines brownish in age before falling away, furfuraceous between the spines; endoperidium with spots from the large spines but in age smooth, opening by a pore, grayish in age; gleba olive-toned to olive-brown at maturity; spores 3.5-4.5 μ, apedicellate, olive-brown in KOH, yellow to rusty brown in Melzers; minutely echinulate-punctate; capillitial threads thick-walled, yellow-brown in KOH slightly pitted, filaments flexuous to crooked, 3-7 μ wide, tapered to apex.

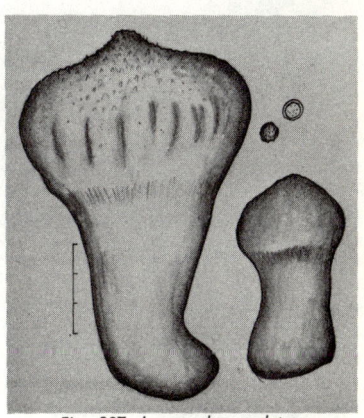

Fig. 287. *Lycoperdon perlatum.*

Solitary to cespitose on humus, in forests, along roadsides, etc. throughout North America, late summer and fall, common. A variant with wood brown spines is common at times in the Pacific Coast area.

16a. Outer coating smooth, finally sloughing off in thin flakes; spores 5.5-8 μ. Fig. 288 ....*Lycoperdon rimulatum* **Peck**

Fruit body 1-5 cm broad, usually deeply plicate, around the base; surface grayish to

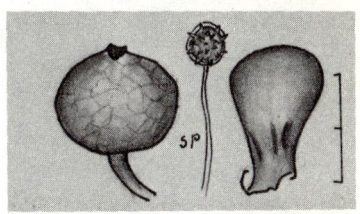

Fig. 288. *Lycoperdon rimulatum.*

drab, soon weakly rimose-areolate and the layer finally separating from the endoperidium; endoperidium purplish gray to brownish, with an apical pore; gleba finally purplish; spores with a pedicel 2-3 times as long as the pore; capillitial threads 3-7 μ wide, sparingly septate.

On soil and duff in woods and along their borders or on sandy soil on waste land with a few trees present, eastern North America but not common, late summer and fall.

16b. Not as above 17
17a. The exoperidial remnants in the form of spines 2-6 mm long..18
17b. The exoperidial remnants shorter or less rigid than in the above 19
18a. Surface reticulated at least for a time after spines have fallen off. Fig. 289 ....*Lycoperdon echinatum* **Persoon**

Fruit body 2-5 cm broad, with white rhizomorphs, surface covered with spines 3-6 mm long often with convergent tips, white becoming brown; endoperidium pale to dark purple-brown; gleba purplish; sterile base not well developed, chambers small; spores 4-4.5 to 4.8-6 μ, in some collections broken pedicels littering the mount; capillitial threads 6-8 μ wide, branched, crooked and contorted, pitted.

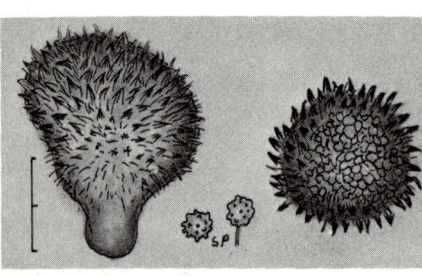

Fig. 289. *Lycoperdon echinatum*.

On humus in woods in the fall, eastern Canada and the United States, abundant at times.

18b. Surface smooth when spines have fallen off. Fig. 290 ....
....*Lycoperdon pulcherrimum* **Peck**

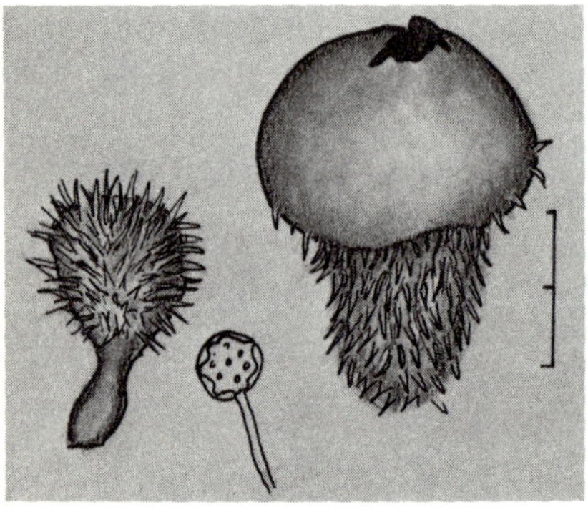

Fruit body 2-5 cm wide, 3-4.5 cm high; spines 4-6 mm long, remaining whitish even in drying; endoperidium purple-brown in age, pore with a torn lobed margin; gleba finally dark purple-brown; sterile base about one third the volume of the gleba, chambers distinct, purple-brown in age; spores 4-4.5 μ, pedicel 10-13 μ long; capillitial threads branched slightly pitted, 6-7 μ wide for main branches.

Fig. 290. *Lycoperdon pulcherrimum*.

On humus in hardwoods, widely distributed in eastern and southern United States but generally rare.

19a. **Exoperidial remains in the form of lax delicate flocculent spicules with granules between, these soon wearing away** ....*Lycoperdon floccosum* **Lloyd**

Fruit body pear-shaped, (2) 3-8 (10) cm wide, (3) 4-10 (12) cm high, often plicate at the base, and below enlarged part; inner peridium finally glabrous, papery, pore as in *L. umbrinum;* subgleba well developed, chambers large; capillitium with walls up to 1 μ thick, sparsely pitted, branched, threads 4-9 μ wide for the main axes; spores 3.5-4.5 (5-6) μ, smooth to minutely ornamented pedicels breaking off and littering the mount.

On conifer duff, solitary to gregarious, fall, widely distributed but abundant locally on occasion, especially in the Great Lakes area.

19b. Not as above 20
20a. **Spores 5.5-7 μ (incl. orn.)** ....*Lycoperdon glabellum* **Peck**

Fruit body 2-3 cm high, 1.5-2.5 cm broad, obovoid, attached to substrate by white-fibrous mycelium; exoperidial remains as granules and small warts giving surface a furfuraceous aspect; inner peridium ordinarily glabrous only in patches, pore apical, slit-like (up to 7 mm long); subgleba occupying about half the fruit body, chambered; capillitial threads 2.4-6.5 μ wide, walls 0.5-1 μ thick, pits rare, branching frequent, septa occasional; spores apedicellate but broken pedicels numerous in the mount.

On the ground, southeastern Canada and eastern United States, area.

20b. **Spores smaller than in the above, (3.6) 4.0-5.2 μ, Fig. 291** ....*Lycoperdon molle* **Pers.**

Fruit body stipitate to pear-shaped, 1-4 cm broad and up to 6 cm high, typically grayish brown to "cafe au lait" with spines merging into granules; endoperidium opening by a rather large pore; pseudo-columella present; spore deposit dark brown typically tinged purplish; spores strongly verrucose, pedicels litter the mount; capillitial threads up to 6 μ wide, pits small and not abundant, wall fairly thick.

On soil and humus in either hardwoods or conifer forests, late summer and fall, often frequent but not in

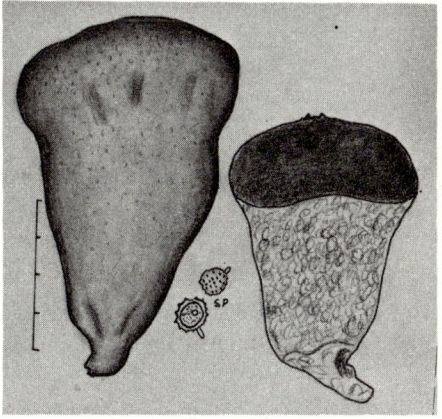

Fig. 291. *Lycoperdon molle.*

great quantity, widely distributed. This species is included as part of the *L. umbrinum* complex by some authors. For the fungus with the olive-brown gleba and yellowish tints in the endoperidium at maturity see *L. flavotinctum* Bowerman.

GEASTRUM
Earth Stars

Fruit bodies globose to subglobose but pointed at the apex, hypogeous at first or epigeous throughout their development, rounded or stalk-like below, the wall layered, the outer layer opening and splitting to form rays arranged star-like, the spore sac (inner wall) papery, thin, opening by a single apical pore or peristome; spores globose, colored, typically ornamented; capillitium of simple long thick-walled threads.

1a. Rays hygroscopic (expanding when moistened; curving over the spore sac when dried) 2
1b. Rays not hygroscopic 5
2a. Spores 6-7.5 µ diam (if larger, see *Astreus hygrometricus* p. 288). Fig. 292 ....*Geastrum campestre* (Morgan) Kambly & Lee

Fig. 292. *Geastrum campestre*.

Fruit body 2.5-5 cm wide as expanded; rays 6-12, fleshy layer chocolate to umber colored, soon wrinkled-rimose; spore case sessile or nearly so, ashy gray from an asperulate covering; gleba chocolate color; spores dark brown in KOH, verruculose, apedicellate; capillitial threads 3-5 µ wide, pale yellowish in KOH, aseptate, rarely branched, walls thickened.

Gregarious in sandy pastures, October-November, eastern North America, widely distributed but not common.

2b. Spores smaller than in above choice 3
3a. Peristome not sulcate (present merely as a puncture or slit) ....
.... *Geastrum floriforme* Vitt.

Fruit body 2-2.5 cm wide as expanded, at first covered with soil and debris, becoming smooth and pale; spore sac with a poorly defined opening. Spores 2.5-3.4 µ, verrucose; capillitial threads up to 10 µ wide, thick-walled (often appearing solid), subhyaline to very pale brownish.

On sandy soil, western United States and in Florida.

NON-GILLED FLESHY FUNGI

3b. Peristome sulcate to grooved or radially fimbriate 4
4a. Peristome truly sulcate. Fig. 293 ....
.................................*Geastrum umbilicatum* Fr. sensu Morgan

Fig. 293. *Geastrum umbilicatum*.

Fruit body 1-2 cm wide, fragile, light brown, with much adhering debris when fresh; spore sac about 1 cm wide, whitish from a thin farinose coating which finally wears away; mouth area delimited by a depressed dark brown zone; rays ascending with tips recurved, slowly spreading out when moist; spores wood brown in KOH, minutely warted; capillitial threads wavy, pallid to wood brown, some with incrustations.

Closely gregarious on sand and debris, eastern North America, fall, not common.

4b. Peristome lacerate-fimbriate ....
........................*Geastrum recolligens* (Woodw. ex Sow.) Desv.

Fruit body 2-3.5 cm, covered over all with a thin felt, soon glabrous, the exterior becoming whitish; fleshy layer smooth and very dark brown; spore sac brown, sessile; spores 3.5-4.2 μ, verrucose, warts 0.3 μ high, non-cyanophilic; capillitial threads 5-7 μ wide, nearly solid.

On waste land in arid regions, apparently common in southeastern Idaho. In the desert sun the outer surface of the rays bleaches to whitish rather soon.

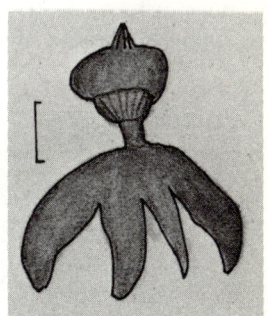

Fig. 294. *Geastrum pectinatum*.

5a. Pedicel of spore sac sulcate where attached to the sac; spores 4.5-6 μ in diam. Fig. 294 ....
..............*Geastrum pectinatum* Persoon

Fruit body 1-2 cm wide unopened, exterior with considerable adherent debris; rays wood brown to cinnamon-brown and upper surface cracked into irregular patterns; spore case purplish drab beneath a hoary sheen, peristome sulcate-striate; mouth area not sharply separated from the spore sac proper; spores bister in KOH, verruculose; capillitial threads 4-7 μ wide, rarely branched.

On soil in thin woods, eastern North America, rare.

5b. Not as above 6
6a. Peristome long-striate to strongly longitudinally wrinkled 7
6b. Peristome not as above 8
7a. Spore sac with a distinct but short pedicel elevating it when the fruit body is expanded .... *Geastrum nanum* Persoon

Fruit body 5-8 mm when unopened, globose with a bluntly conic apex, pallid and with adhering trash; opening by splitting into 4-6 rays; fleshy layer of rays continuous but cracking in drying; spore sac pallid to brownish drab, papery, with a whitish bloom, peristome continuous with, or only slightly delimited from, the remainder of the spore sac proper by a slight depression; spores 3.5-4.2 μ, bister in Melzer's; capillitial threads pallid to yellowish in Melzer's, 3-6 μ wide, walls very thick.

On rich humus in hardwood forests, not uncommon, summer and fall, eastern North America. It was previously known under the name *G. schmideli*.

7b. Spore sac practically sessile and remaining seated in a bowl much as in *G. saccatum* Fig. 297 ...... *Geastrum morgani* Lloyd

Fruit body 1-2.5 cm broad, outer surface vinaceous-buff to wood brown, with some trash adhering, fleshy layer of the rays thick (3 mm), soft, watery pallid to pinkish, reddish brown as dried; spore sac about 1 cm broad, wood brown or darker, surface felted and unpolished; mouth area delimited by a circular line; spores 3-4 (4.5) μ, near bister in KOH; capillitial threads 4-8 μ wide, wavy, hyaline to yellowish brown, thick-walled.

On soil often around stumps, September, October, central United States, rare.

8a. Typically large (5-10 cm as expanded) 9
8b. Usually not over 5 cm broad when expanded .. 11
9a. Fleshy layer of rays thick, breaking so as to leave the spore sac sitting in a saucer-like base. Fig. 295 ....
....*Geastrum triplex* Jungh.

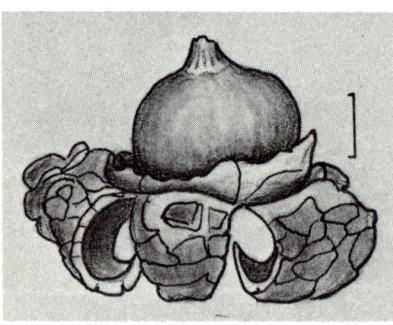

Fig. 295. *Geastrum triplex*.

Rays of fruit body thick and fleshy at first; spore sac sessile, pale to dark avellaneous, unpolished, mouth delimited by a circular paler area, distinctly radially fibrillose, mouth lacerate-fibrillose;

spores 3.5-4.5 μ, pale cinnamon-brown in KOH; capillitial threads somewhat incrusted, 3-6 μ wide, thick-walled, hyaline to yellowish in KOH, yellowish in Melzer's.

Gregarious on rich humus in low hardwood forests, common, summer and fall, widely distributed.

9b. Not as above 10
10a. Mouth area paler than remainder of spore sac, outer layer of fruit body separating leaving underside of rays clean ....
.... *Geastrum limbatum* **Jungh.**

Fruit body almost clean of trash, fleshy layer of rays dull cinnamon when dried and irregularly rimose; spore sac dark wood brown to drab, short-pedicellate (pedicel pallid), mouth area pallid and fibrillose; spores 3.5-4.5 μ, pale bister in KOH; capillitial threads thick-walled, hyaline to dull brown, smooth to slightly incrusted.

On soil in waste places, central and southern United States, rare.

10b. Mouth area not sharply delimited; outer surface of fruit body with much trash adhering to it and not separating from it cleanly. Fig. 296 .... *Geastrum rufescens* **Persoon**

Spore case on a short thick stalk, surface dull brownish to unpolished to granular-velvety; mouth slightly elevated and fibrous, becoming fimbriate, lacking a definite peristome; gleba bister or darker; fibrous layer of rays toned vinaceous when debris is removed; spores 3-4.2 μ; capillitial threads 3.5-6 μ wide, unbranched, thick-walled, pallid to brown in KOH, smooth to incrusted.

Gregarious to clustered or the clusters gregarious, eastern North America, late summer and fall, common in some localities.

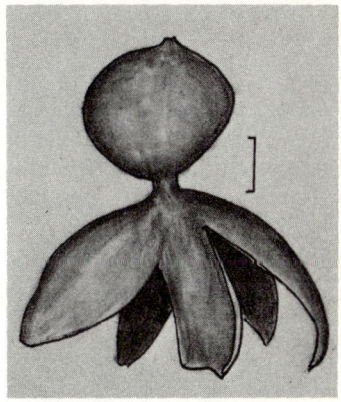

Fig. 296. *Geastrum rufescens.*

11a. Mouth area sharply delimited by a circular ridge or depression 12
11b. Mouth area not distinct from remainder of spore sac 13
12a. Spores bister in KOH ....
.... *Geastrum fimbriatum* **Fr. f.** *fimbriatum*

Fruit body 0.8-2 cm wide before opening, outer mycelial layer pallid to pale tan; rays 5-8 (12), with acute tips, sinuses extending half way to the base, mycelial (outer) layer peeling off, fleshy inner layer smooth in the bowl; spore sac 8-15 mm wide, tan to dark brown, mouth fibrillose, not sharply delimited from the remainder of the spore sac; gleba fuscous brown; spores 3-3.5 µ; capillitial threads nearly hyaline in either KOH or Melzer's, thick-walled, 4-7 µ wide.

On rich humus under deciduous trees, fall, fairly common, eastern North America.

12b. As above but spores hyaline ....
.... *Geastrum fimbriatum* f. *pallidum* Smith

13a. Spore sac sessile in a bowl-like depression. Fig. 297 ....
.... *Geastrum saccatum* Fr.

Fig. 297. *Geastrum saccatum*.

Fruit body 6-12 (20) mm broad, 8-15 mm high, expanding to 2-5 cm across the rays; outer surface with little adhering trash, buff to pale tan; inner fleshy layer pallid to avellaneous, continuous over the bowl, and often over the rays; spore case 0.5-2 cm wide, papery, wood brown to purple drab; peristome conic, fibrillose, delimited by a circular raised or depressed line, often paler than remainder of spore sac; gleba coffee-colored; spores 3.5-4.5 µ, pale date brown in KOH; capillitial threads yellowish to brownish, 4-8 µ wide, incrusted, very thick-walled.

Gregarious on rich humus, around stumps, etc., late summer, not common but often abundant under junipers, widely distributed in eastern North America.

13b. Spore sac pedicellate, wall roughened with minute particles giving it a hoary sheen. Fig. 298 ....
.... *Geastrum quadrifidum* Persoon

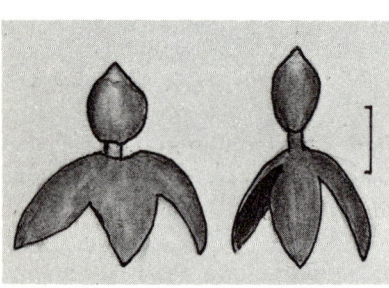

Fig. 298. *Geastrum quadrifidum*.

Fruit body 0.5-3 cm wide as expanded, outer wall splitting into 4-8 rays which become arched upward with the tips remaining attached to the mycelial "cup" remaining on the ground; fleshy layer avellaneous to pallid or finally wood brown, often scaling away in part at least; spore sac pedicellate, wall papery and surface roughened with particles giving it a hoary sheen on dark ground color; mouth distinctly fimbriate from radial fibers forming a pointed cone, mouth area outlined by a distinct groove and paler than the remainder of the sac; gleba chocolate brown; spores 3.5-5 µ; threads of capillitium very thick-walled, yellowish in KOH.

Common in conifer woods, especially plantations, Great Lakes region of North America, but more widely distributed. It is generally known under the name *G. coronatum* in the older literature.

Geastrum minimum is not fornicate (standing on the tips of the rays as described above) and occurs in waste sandy soil. Both have an asperulate spore sac.

SCLERODERMATALES

Fruit body with the basidia distributed symmetrically in the young gleba or in nests or in cavities arising from dissolution of the ground tissue, but not in a well organized hymenium; gleba powdery at maturity and borne in a spore case which opens (dehisces) in various ways.

See Figs. 300, 301 for illustrations of the type of fruit body included here. Many in this group are desert fungi.

Key to Families

1a. Gleba divided into pea-like structures (peridioles) in which the spores are produced. Fig. 299 ....*Pisolithaceae*
Pisolithus tinctorius ....(Pers.) Coker & Couch

Fruit body large, 5-18 (25) cm high, 4-10 (15) cm wide, usually with a thick fibrous-rooting base, rarely sessile, outer wall very thin and breaking away to expose the pea-like peridioles; peridioles whitish to yellowish to brownish becoming watery vinaceous (an inky fluid is present in the fresh fruit body), at maturity the peridioles breaking into a powder (the spores); spores 8-12 µ in diam., warty with a hyaline envelope.

In road cuts, clay soil, well drained gravelly and sandy soil, old fields, cultivated fields, etc., summer and fall. It is widely distributed but is most abundant in the southeastern states and the Pacific Northwest. Most people regard it as one of the most unattractive of the fungi.

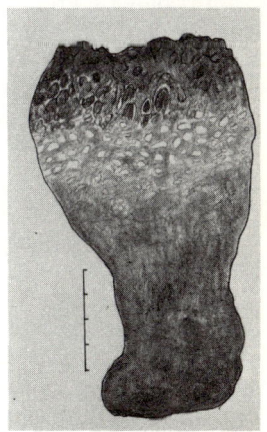

Fig. 299. *Pisolithus tinctorius.*

1b. Not as above 2

2a. Outer layer of spore case splitting into rays which open out as in *Geastrum* when moist .... *Astreaceae*
Fig. 300 .... *Astreus hygrometricus* (Pers.) Morgan

Fig. 300. *Astreus hygrometricus*.

Fruit body 1-4 cm wide when open, arising from black hairlike rhizomorphs some of which may adhere to the base of the fruit body as appressed hairs; outer wall splitting into 7-15 pointed rays which bend backward when wet and curve inward over the spore sac when dry; spore sac sessile, pallid grayish, opening by a slit or tear or with an irregular pore; gleba white when young, cocoa brown at maturity; spores 7-10.5 μ in diam., globose, brownish cinnamon in KOH.

In colonies, gregarious to scattered, developing just under the soil surface and becoming exposed at maturity. It is characteristic of sandy areas, dunes, old fields, etc. It is common and widely distributed over North America. In *Astreus pteridis* the fruit body is 10-15 cm wide when expanded; the spore sac opens by rupturing. It is known from the Pacific Northwest.

2b. Not as above 3
3a. Stalk composed of anastomosed strands forming a rough lacunose stem usually quite gelatinous when fresh ....
.... *Calostomataceae* p. 295
3b. Not as above 4
4a. Stalk woody and hard or soon becoming so ....
.... *Tulostomataceae* p. 291
4b. Fruit body sessile; gleba violaceous or dark colored and shot through with pallid veins at first; in some species with a mycelial "root" .... *Sclerodermataceae* p. 288

SCLERODERMATACEAE

Fruiting bodies mostly above ground, subglobose, ovoid or pyriform, sessile or on a false stipe consisting of a mass of fibrous my-

NON-GILLED FLESHY FUNGI

celium binding together so much sand, soil or debris that it forms a fairly firm structure but not one which elevates the spore case; wall of spore case thick and hard, persistent, usually a single layer, breaking open irregularily or in lobes; spores globose, ornamented; capillitium lacking or rudimentary; saprophytic on soil or rotten wood.

SCLERODERMA

Key to Species

1a. Habit in sand, often on dunes; with a long stalk-like base made up of a mass of mycelium and sand; outer layer of the spore case nearly smooth; spore case opening irregularly; spores 10-20 μ in diam., spines 1-2 μ long ...... *Scleroderma macrorhizon* Wallroth

Late summer and early fall, widely distributed in the Northern Hemisphere.

1b. Not as above 2
2a. Fruiting body splitting into large coarse lobes opening outward somewhat as in *Geastrum* when mature 3
2b. Not splitting as in above choice 4
3a. Fruit body 4-10 cm wide, the spore-case wall thick and roughened .... *Scleroderma polyrhizon* Persoon

Exterior nearly white, then yellow or straw color, the gleba deep brown when mature; spores 6.5-10 μ, with a hyaline sheath and warts projecting into it to produce a verrucose-subreticulate pattern, the hyaline covering readily sloughing off.

In hard ground or on sandy soil, late summer and fall, Michigan southward, more common in the southeastern states.

3b. Fruit body 2-5.5 cm wide, the spore case wall thinner than in above choice, smooth when young but often the surface broken into flat scales. Fig. 301 .... *Scleroderma flavidum* E. & E.

Fig. 301. *Scleroderma flavidum.*

Young specimens buried in the sand, becoming exposed by maturity, pallid yellowish to straw color, finally dingy pale yellow-brown, opening by splitting into segments which recurve slightly, not splitting clear to the base; gleba yellowish brown; spores 9-13 μ in diam. including ornamentation, the spines 1-1.5 μ long.

Scattered to gregarious in soil or (especially) on sand, common on waste soil such as old fields, late summer and fall, common. The old spore cases often persist through the winter.

4a. **Fruit body with outer layer soon forming distinct inherent scales which often have a smaller central wart; spores strongly reticulate. Fig. 302** .... *Scleroderma citrinum* **Persoon**

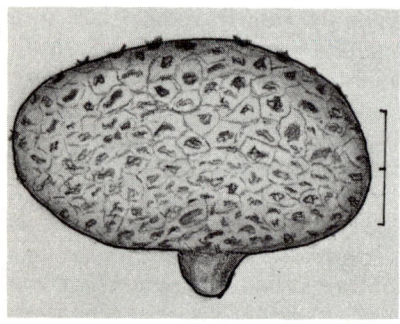

Fig. 302. *Scleroderma citrinum*.

Fruit body 3-12 cm wide, yellowish brown, wall turning pink when fresh material is cut, cracking at the apex into irregular lobes which do not open outward; gleba soon dark violaceous to nearly black, at first with pallid lines through it, powdery when mature; spores 9-13 μ in diam., including the ornamentation.

Solitary, gregarious, scattered or cespitose around old stumps and around and on very decayed logs in low rich woodlands, on hummocks in bogs, etc., in most any type of northern forest, summer and fall. It is the commonest of the hard-skinned puffballs. It is widely known under the name *S. aurantium*. It is frequently parasitized by *Boletus parasiticus*.

4b. Not as above 5
5a. Fruit body 1.5-4 (5) cm wide; having a false stipe or at least a strong tuft of mycelium at area of attachment ....
.... *Scleroderma areolatum* **Ehrenb.**

Stipe enlarged upward from a fibrous-mycelioid mass, surface of spore case dotted especially on upper surface, with distinct inherent darker brown scales, wall thin and fragile when dried, opening by an irregular slit; gleba watery cream color becoming purplish to olive-brown before becoming powdery; spores 10-18 μ, (incl. ornamentation), spines 1.4-1.6 μ high.

Gregarious to subcespitose on humus or along decayed logs, especially common along hedge rows and around plantings of shrubs, late summer and fall, Eastern North America, common.

5b. Not as above 6
6a. Fruiting body 3-9 cm wide, sessile or merely with a slight false stipe or tuft; spores 15-20 μ, reticulate ....
.... *Scleroderma arenicola* **Zeller**

NON-GILLED FLESHY FUNGI

Fruit body subglobose, sometimes quite irregular, surface smooth to matted-fibrillose but developing some small flat spot-like scales, wall very thick and hard, finally opening by a slit, gleba dark yellowish brown to blackish.

Scattered to gregarious under hardwoods or conifers on poor soil, late summer and fall, apparently widely distributed but not common.

6b. **Fruit body hypogeous, covered with scurfy to branlike scales** .... *Scleroderma texense* **Berkeley**

Fruit body white becoming clay color or brownish; gleba soon black, marbled with white veins; spores (7) 9-12.5 μ, echinulate, ornamentation 0.8 μ high.

In sandy soil, fall, Texas and the Pacific Northwest.

TULOSTOMACEAE

Fruit body hypogeous at first, spore case becoming elevated by the elongation of a stalk or a pseudo-stalk of fibrous structure; peridium duplex, outer layer partly evanescent, the remains forming a cup-like volva to the base of the stalk, inner layer thin, dehiscing by an apical pore, several pores or circumscissilly; gleba without typical chambers when young; basidia evenly distributed in the glebal tissue or forming a rudimentary hymenium; capillitium well developed; spores ornamented.

Key to Genera

1a. Endoperidium dehiscing circumscissilely or through numerous pores; basidia in a rudimentary hymenium ...*Battarraea* **Persoon** Fig. 303 ....*Battarraea stevenii* **(Liboshitz) Fr.**

Stalk 10-25 (35) cm high, 5-15 (20) mm thick, at base with a 2-layered non-gelatinous volva, surface with long ragged over-lapping scales brownish in color; spore case depressed-globose, 2-3 cm high, up to 6 cm wide, at first consisting of 2 membranes, the outer flaking off and the inner separating circumscissilly so that the top part falls off as a lid or calyptra; gleba pulverulent, capillitial threads of 2 types: (1) simple hyaline threads and (2) fusiform or cylindric "elators" with inner wall having annular to spiral thickenings; spores 5.7 μ, pale brown, punctate, wall about 1 μ thick.

Solitary to scattered on soil in arid regions, generally rare, but in southwestern Idaho relatively common for a desert-type fungus.

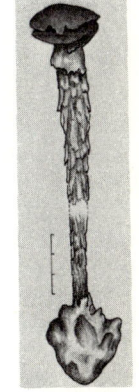

Fig. 303. *Battarraea stevenii.*

1b. **Spore case not dehiscing as in above choice 2**

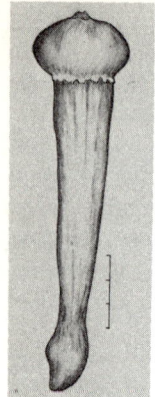

Fig. 304. Chlamydopus meyenianus.

2a. With a distinct volva at the base of the stalk ....Chlamydopus Speg. Fig. 304 ....
....Chlamydopus meyenianus (Klotzch) Lloyd

Stalk 5-35 cm long, (6) 12-35 mm thick, somewhat woody, silky fibrillose or somewhat scaly, narrowed below and seated in a 2-layered volva; peridum 1-2 cm high and 1.5-3.5 cm wide, exoperidium a mixture of soil and hyphae (and soon falling away); endoperidium tough, membranous, yellowish to pallid, smooth to slightly roughened; gleba ochraceous to brownish, pulverulent at maturity; capillitial threads long and hyaline; spores 6-9 (10) μ, yellowish, echinulate.

Solitary to scattered on waste soil in arid regions, Southwest, rare.

2b. Not as above 3
3a. Spore case opening by the breaking up of the endoperidium over the supper surface ....Phellorina Berk. Fig. 305 ....Phellorina strobilina Kalchbrenner

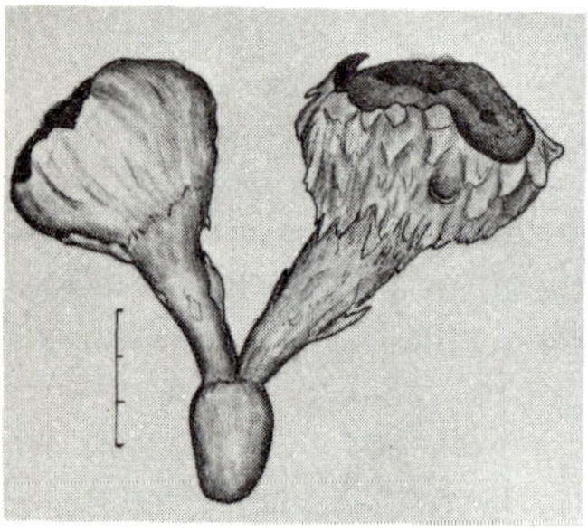

Fruit body 6-9 cm high, shaped like a wine glass; stipe solid and woody, coarsely scaly from an outer layer that sloughs off, and where the stipe expands to form the spore case more adherent (but finally falling away) and in the form of coarse, large, imbricate scales; endoperidium thin and finally breaking up across the flattened apical surface to expose the rusty cinnamon gleba; base of stipe typically enlarged into a hardened mass of soil and mycelium resembling a sclerotium and at times giving rise to 2-3 fruit bodies; capillitial threads thick-walled (0.7-1.2 μ), pale ochraceous-cinnamon, rarely septate, not abundant; spores 5-7 $\times$ 4.5-6 μ, globose to subglobose, verrucose, pale ochraceous-cinnamon in KOH.

Fig. 305. Phellorina strobilina.

On desert soils, solitary or 2-3 in a cluster, Texas, rare.
3b. Spore case opening by an apical stoma (pore) ....
....Tulostoma Persoon

TULOSTOMA

Spore case becoming elevated by the elongation of the stipe; peridium duplex, outer layer partly evanescent wtih the remains forming a cup around the base of the spore case, the latter opening by a pore; capillitium well developed; spores ornamented; basidia evenly distributed in the glebal tissue.

Key to Species

1a. Spores ornamented with distinct ridges; outer layer of peridium often surrounding the base of the spore case as in an acorn and its cup. Fig. 306 .... *Tulostoma striatum* **Cunningham**

Fruit body 1.5-2.5 cm high, with a basal mycelial bulb, a short stalk (1-2 cm), and a spore case about 1 cm wide, outer layer of spore case soon flaking off except for the cup around the base; endoperidium pallid tan, minutely furfuraceous; the mouth area distinct, raised, and fibrillose; opening by a pore; gleba ferruginous-salmon; stalk 2-3 mm thick; dingy tan; spores 6-8 × 4-7 μ, ellipsoid to ovoid; capillitial threads 4-8 μ wide, thick-walled, hyaline in KOH.

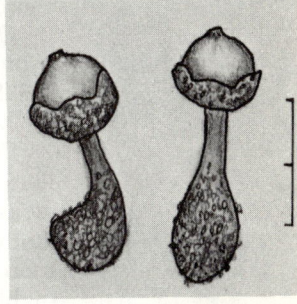

Fig. 306. *Tulostoma striatum*.

On soil, often in cultivated fields, typically rare but known from both the southern and northern hemispheres.

1b. Not as above 2

2a. Mouth of spore case delimited by a narrow membranous collar in most basidiocarps 3

2b. Mouth a pore often with lacerated margin 4

3a. Spore case persistently covered by sand particles. Fig. 307 ....
.... *Tulostoma simulans* Lloyd

Fruit body 2-4 cm high, stalk 1.5-3 cm long and 3-4 mm thick, base bulbous from adhering mycelium; spore case acorn-like, 10-15 mm wide, dark reddish brown when fresh but color all but obscured; stipe with a surface covering of rusty brown lacerate scales, grayish in age; spore case in drying shrinking away from the stalk leaving a collar; spores 4-6 μ wide, ornamented from plugs extending into a hyaline layer, yellowish in KOH; capillitial threads 4-6 μ wide, thick-walled, hyaline.

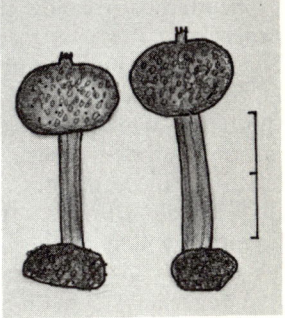

Fig. 307. *Tulostoma simulans*.

On sandy soil often near white pine or juniper, widely distributed from the Great Lakes region southward.

3b. Spore case soon glabrous or nearly so. Fig. 308 ....
....*Tulostoma brumale* **Persoon**

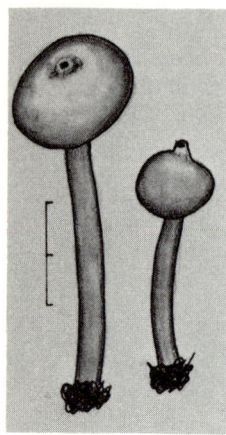

Fig. 308. *Tulostoma brumale.*

Fruit body 1-1.5 cm high, 1-5 cm long, 2.5-4 mm thick, spore case 1-2 cm wide; stipe usually pallid, slender, lacerate scaly to nearly smooth; capillitial threads 4-7 μ wide, hyaline; spores 3-5 μ, minutely verrucose, some with short pedicels.

On sandy soil in waste places; widely distributed in North America and Europe.

4a. Spores very minute (2-3 μ wide) ....
.................................*Tulostoma finkii* **Lloyd**

Fruit body 1.5-3 cm high, stalk 3-4 mm thick; spore case 0.7-1.5 cm wide; spore case mouse gray when faded; outer peridium a sandy cortex eroding to leave a basal cup; spore case opening by 1-4 pores, edges raised slightly in some cases; surface minutely lacerate scaly; spores globose to slightly angled; capillitial threads 3-4 μ wide, swollen ends up to 12 μ thick.

Upland woods in a pasture, February, North Carolina.

4b. Spores larger 5

5a. Spores 4.5-6.2 μ, verrucose ....*Tulostoma campestre* **Morgan**

Fruit body with spore case 10-20 mm wide, 10-15 mm high; stalk 2-5 (6) cm long, 2.5-5 mm thick; sand layer breaking into small adherent warts which ultimately fall away; spore case wall pale tan to gray, opening by a pore with a lobed to lacerate margin; spores near ochraceous-tawny in Melzer's; capillitium of thick-walled, up to 7 μ wide filaments hyaline in KOH.

Scattered in sandy fields, widely distributed in eastern North America.

5b. Spores smooth or nearly so ....*Tulostoma fibrillosum* **White**

Stalk 5-8 cm long, 3-5 mm thick; spore case 10-15 mm broad; spore case whitish to ashy, smooth or obscurely pitted, sand adhering on the base, mouth area indistinct, opening by a pore with a lobed fibrillose margin; stipe pulling away from the sand case, at first loosely fibrillose from coarse fibrils; capillitium of hyaline threads swollen at the septa, 4-7 μ wide; spores 5-7 $\times$ 4.5 μ to 5-7 μ.

Gregarious to scattered in sand, widely distributed in eastern North America but rare.

NON-GILLED FLESHY FUNGI

CALOSTOMATACEAE

Fruit bodies hypogeous at first, subglobose, at maturity raised on a rooting netlike gelatinous stalk; spore case opening by an apical pore; gleba powdery at maturity, columella lacking; spores smooth or ornamented; capillitium present. Growing on soil.

CALOSTOMA

Key

1a. Outer surface of inner wall cinnabar red when the outer wall falls away, inclosed spore sac light clear yellow; lattice-like rooting stalk stout short, scarcely lifting the spore sac above the ground, gelatinous when fresh; exoperidium when fresh a thick slimy coating; mouth composed of about 5 elevated ridges deep red in color; spores $14\text{-}20 \times 6\text{-}9\ \mu$. Fig. 309 ....
.... *Calostoma cinnabarina* Desv.

Late summer in the southern states, often along road banks.

1b. Red color confined to the pore region; spore sac bright yellow; rooting stalk up to 6 cm long, lifting the spore sac well above the ground; spores $6\text{-}8\ \mu$ in diam., globose, pitted ....
.... *Calostoma lutescens* (Schw.) Burnap

Later summer and fall, also southern in distribution but not as common as the above.

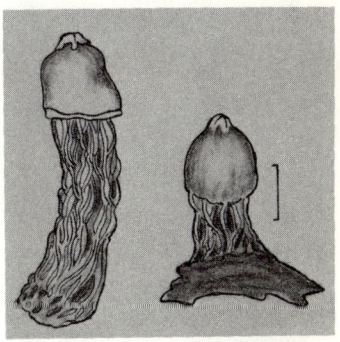

Fig. 309. *Calostoma cinnabarina*.

PODAXALES

This order contains fungi in which the basidia occur in a true hymenium but the spores are not discharged from the basidia at maturity. The fruit bodies resemble mushroom fruit bodies with the exception that they do not (typically) open up, and of course they do not have the hymenium borne on lamellae. The group connects up to the Hymenogastrales through the Secotiaceae (or secotioid fungi). For the treatment of these in this work see the Hymenogastrales.

1a. Spores $10\text{-}16 \times 9\text{-}12\ \mu$ or larger. Fig. 310 ....
.... *Podaxis pistillaris* (Pers.) Morse

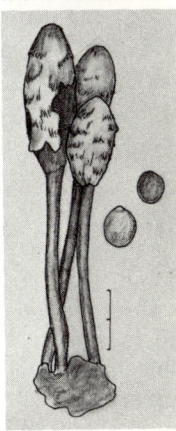

Fig. 310. *Podaxis pistillaris*.

Fruit body 6-20 cm tall; spore case 2-10 cm long, 1-4 cm wide, ovate to narrowly elliptic, exterior fibrillose scaly to nearly glabrous; endoperidium membranous, pallid to buff or brownish ochraceous, rarely darker, opening irregularly; stalk 4-12 cm long, 2-10 mm thick, whitish and at first squamulose, becoming smooth or longitudinally striate (twisted at times), lacking a true volva; columella percurrent as a continuation of the stipe; gleba finally dark brown to black; capillitial threads olivaceous to reddish brown in KOH, sparingly septate, rarely branched, when old sometimes coiled spirally; spores with wall 2-3 μ thick, typically with an apical pore.

Scattered in desert areas after rains, it is the most frequently collected and the most characteristic fungus of our southwest desert. It occurs as far north as Idaho. In stature it remainds one of the shaggy mane, *Coprinus comatus*.

1b. Spores 6-7.5 $\times$ 5-6.5 μ. Fig. 311 ....
....*Longia texensis* (**B. & C.**) **Zeller**

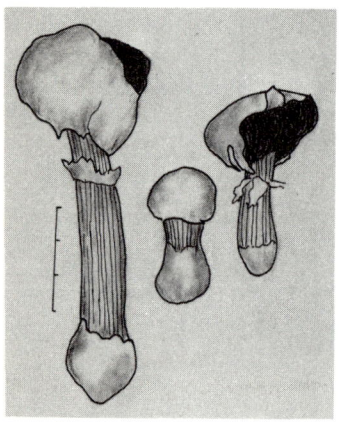

Fig. 311. *Longia texensis*.

Fruit body agaric-like; spore case subglobose to depressed-globose, 3-9 cm broad, 2-7 cm high; stalk stout, 3-8 cm long, 2-3.5 cm thick near the base, becoming woody, solid, smooth or striate; partial veil present and forming an annulus on the stalk (the veil at first continuous with the outer layer of the pileus) surface scaly becoming smooth or nearly so, pallid to brownish but soon dark from the spores; gleba sublamellate, convoluted into chambers, free from the stalk; spores subglobose dark brown in KOH (spore dust blackish).

On soil in waste places in arid regions, late fall and winter in our Southwest, northward to Idaho and Oregon.

NIDULARIALES (Bird's Nest Fungi)

Fruit bodies small, usually less than 2 cm high and up to 1.5 cm broad; globose, obovoid, subcylindric, cup-shaped, or vase-shaped; with or without a lid (the epiphragm) covering the apex, when the lid falls away the interior is seen to contain a number of pill-like objects causing the fruit body to resemble a minute bird's nest with "eggs" (the peridioles) in it; spores smooth, capillitium lacking. Growing on soil, wood or dung. There are a number of species in the order but only 3 are treated here as examples of the group.

1a. **Peridioles imbedded in a mucilage (and not attached to the wall of the peridium by a cord). Fig. 312...** *Nidula candida* **Peck**

Fig. 312. *Nidula candida.*

Fruit body 5-20 mm high, 3-8 mm broad, when young and in good growing condition dull cinnamon from a scurfy covering over basal part, and over the epiphragm; peridioles light brown; new fruit bodies often develop from old ones.

On rotting wood, old berry canes and on the ground. It is common in the Pacific Northwest.

Note: The name "candida" means shining white. The only white specimens I have seen of this species were old bleached out ones.

1b. Not as above 2

2a. **Peridioles whitish; wall of fruit body a single layer. Fig. 313** .... *Crucibulum levis* **(DC) Kambly & Lee**

Fig. 313. *Crucibulum levis.*

Fruit body 5-10 (12) mm high, 5-10 mm wide, sessile; surface velvety to unpolished and tan to cinnamon-brown, margin of cup erect or flared slightly; epiphragm soon disappearing; peridioles 1-2 mm broad, lenticular, with a cord; spores (4) 7-10 $\times$ 4-6 μ, thick-walled.

On ligneous and vegetable debris, fall, common, widely distributed.

2b. Not as above 3

3a. **Peridioles gray to black; wall of fruit body 3-layered. Fig. 314** .... *Cyathus stercoreus* **(Schw.) de Toni**

Fig. 314. Cyathus stercoreus.

Fruit body 5-15 mm high, 4-8 mm at apex, at times with a basal brownish pad of mycelium, vase-shaped, outer surface fibrillose and pallid to brown when young, nearly glabrous in age and then at times with depressed circular zones, inner surface smooth, pale to dark lead color; epiphragm soon evanescent; spores (22) 25-30 (35) × (18) 20-27 (35) μ, nearly hyaline.

Scattered to cespitose on dung, manured ground, around sawdust piles, etc., common and widespread.

3b. **Fruit bodies lacking an epiphragm; wall of fruit body thin and fragmenting at maturity** .... *Nidularia* **Fries**

This genus is the type of the family and order, but is poorly represented in North America.

PHALLALES (The Stink Horns)

Fruiting body at first consisting of a white to pinkish elastic, egg-shaped or nearly globose body which has 2-3 wall layers, the inner being gelatinous, the outer layer(s) present at base of receptaculum which may be stalk-like or branched, the stalk or the head (if present) bearing the slime mass (gleba); wall of the egg remaining at the base of the stalk as a volva; gleba typically dark colored and very foul smelling; spores olivaceous or green, smooth, small.

The soft, gelatinous eggs always arouse much interest, they may occur solitary or in clumps and unless they are sectioned they may be mistaken for true puffballs. The very marked offensive odor of the expanded fruit body attracts insects which carry away the sticky spore-bearing slime on their legs. Dispersal of the species is gained in this manner.

Key to Families

1a. Receptaculum branched at least near the apex or unbranched and bearing a subglobose headlike structure at the apex; the gleba (spore slime) borne on the inner surface of the branches of the receptatculum .... *Clathraceae* **p. 299**

1b. Receptaculum stalk-like, unbranched tapered at apex or with a pileus either smooth or reticulate; gleba borne on the outer surface of the pileus or receptaculum ....*Phallaceae* **p. 300**

CLATHRACEAE

Key to Species

1a. Receptaculum a single distinct stalk bearing a subglobose head-like structure at the apex. Fig. 315 ....
....*Simblum sphaerocephalum* **Schlect**

Stalk 7-9 cm high, 1-1.6 cm thick, bright red above, pale below; spores 3.7-4.4 × 1.4-2 μ.
Eastern United States, but more abundant southward.
A second species which is yellow and has spores 7 × 3 μ is reported from Texas: *S. texense*.

1b. Not as above 2

2a. Receptaculum composed of 2-5 stout columns arising separately from the base and fused above. Fig. 316 ....
.... *Clathrus columnatus* **Bosc.**

Fruit body rosy red above, pale at the base; volva watery white; spores 3.7-4.8 × 1.8-2.4 μ.
Southeastern United States, generally considered rare.

2b. Not as above 3

3a. Receptaculum composed of a short stalk which divides into 3 arms, the arms fused at their tips. Fig. 317 ....
....*Pseudocolus schellenbergiae* **Sumstine**

Fruiting body orange above, white below, volva dark brown, smooth, 2-3 cm wide; gleba dark green; spores 4.5-5.5 × 2-2.5 μ.
Eastern United States, rare.

3b. Not as above..4

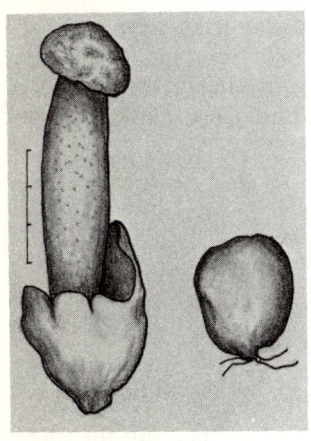

Fig. 315. *Simblum sphaerocephalum.*

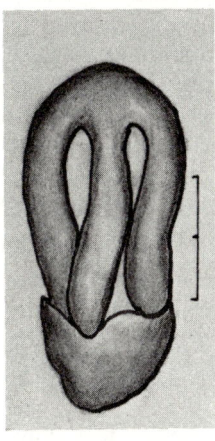

Fig. 316. *Clathrus columnatus.*

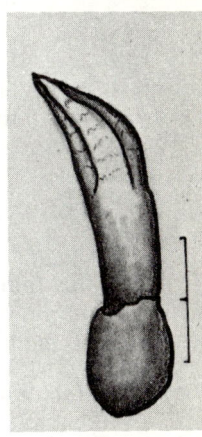

Fig. 317. *Pseudocolus schellenbergiae.*

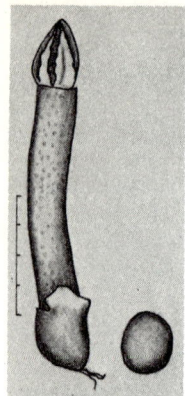

Fig. 318. *Anthurus borealis*.

4a. Stalk divided above into usually 5 (4-6) arms, the arms incurved and meeting above, but not fused at the tips. Fig. 318 ....
................................*Anthurus borealis* Burt

Fruiting body 10-12 cm tall, stalk white, the arms pale flesh color on the backs; gleba brownish olive-green; spores $3\text{-}4 \times 1.5\ \mu$, 5-8 on a basidium, the latter constricted at intervals so as to appear like a string of beads.

Solitary or subcespitose, United States, occasionally abundant in California.

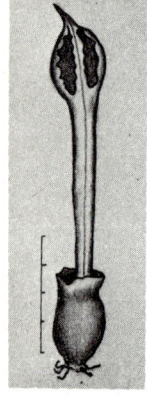

Fig. 319. *Lysurus mokusin*.

4b. Arms usually joined at their tips and forming a tapering spire. Fig. 319 ....
................................*Lysurus mokusin* (L.) Fr.

Fruiting body up to 15-16 cm tall, stalk bright pink above, paler below, arms nearly blood red, gleba borne in the spaces between the arms, light brown at first, becoming dark brown and finally when dry almost black; spire up to 5 mm thick at base, 2-23 mm long, often bent down; spores nearly hyaline $3.6\text{-}4.2 \times 15\text{-}18\ \mu$.

In gardens and lawns. Reported from southern United States. It has also been reported from greenhouses (Illinois). Fruiting during every month of the year in southern California but most abundant from May to October.

PHALLACEAE
Stinkhorn

In this family we have the true stink horns. Its members are more common northward in the United States and southern Canada than are the members of the preceding family.

1a. Receptaculum an elongate stalk bearing a pileus at the apex 2

1b. Receptaculum tapering to a pointed tip and bearing the gleba (slime mass) on the upper part of the stalk itself 4

NON-GILLED FLESHY FUNGI

2a. Receptaculum with a distinct latticed skirtlike structure (indusium) hanging from beneath the pileus. Fig. 320 ....
.... *Dictyophora duplicata* (Bosc.) **Fisher**

Pileus thin above, upper surface reticulate and bearing the slimy glebal remains, under surface smooth, white; the indusium white, net-like, hanging down below the pileus for 3-6 cm; stalk white; egg globular to flattened, 4-6 × 5-7 cm, white or tinged flesh color.

Solitary or in groups, often near uprooted trees, around the base of dead trees or on humus. Late summer and fall, eastern United States.

2b. Not as above 3

3a. Outer surface of pileus distinctly reticulated. Fig. 321 ....
.... *Phallus impudicus* **Persoon**

Fruit body up to 25 cm high, cap 1.5-4 cm broad, its depressions filled with the olivaceous glebal slime; indusium thin and not extending appreciably below the pileus margin; stalk 2.5-3 cm thick, white at apex; egg whitish to pinkish, 3.5-6 × 3-4.5 cm; spores 3.7-4.2 × 1.3-2 μ.

On the ground, usually around trees and shrubs, fall, Great Lakes region southward.

3b. Outer surface of cap granular. Fig. 322 ....
.... *Phallus ravenelii* **Berk. & Curt.**

Fruit bodies up to 16 cm high, stalk 1.5-3 cm thick, yellowish, fading to white; egg large 3-5 × 2-3.5 cm, whitish, pinkish or pinkish lilac, rhizomorphs pinkish lilac; spores 3-3.5 × 1.5 μ.

Densely gregarious, scattered or (rarely) solitary on sawdust piles, around rotten logs, etc., late summer and fall, eastern North America, common in the Great Lakes region.

4a. Stalk 6-10 cm long, equal nearly to the abruptly rounded apex. Fig. 323 .... *Mutinus caninus* (Pers.) **Fr.**

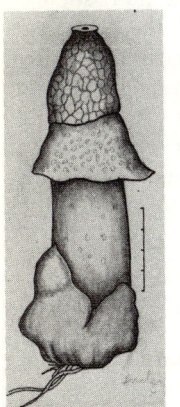
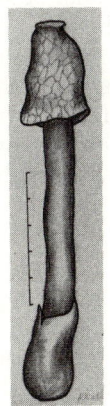
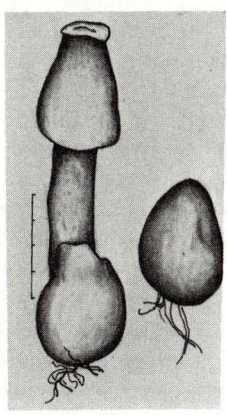
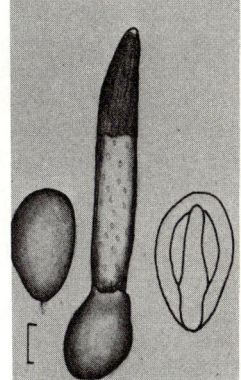

Fig. 320. *Dictyophora duplicata*. Fig. 321. *Phallus impudicus*. Fig. 322. *Phallus ravenelii*. Fig. 323. *Mutinus caninus*.

Fruit bodies up to 10 cm high, the stalk red to orange-red (white in var. *albus* Zeller) at the apex, paler below; gleba olivaceous-brown, covering the upper 2-3 cm of the stalk except for the extreme apex; eggs white, 1-2 cm long, 1-1.5 cm in diam., white; spores 3.5-5 $\times$ 1.5-2 μ.

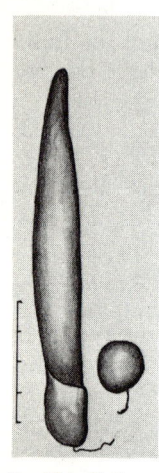

Fig. 324. *Mutinus elegans*.

Gregarious to solitary on soil or very rotten wood. Late summer and fall, eastern North America where it is not uncommon but to be expected in the western states also.

4b. Stalk 10-17 cm long, tapered from about the middle to the apex and downward to the base. Fig. 324 ...... *Mutinus elegans* (Mont.) Fischer

Stalk pinkish red above, paler to whitish below; gleba on the upper third; eggs globose to ovoid, white with a pinkish tinge.

On or around decaying wood, on rich soil, humus, etc.; summer and fall during warm wet weather. Great Lakes area and the Southeast, abundant at times. The eggs are slow in "hatching," at times taking up to two weeks.

THE HYMENOGASTRALES (OR FALSE TRUFFLES AND RELATED FUNGI)

Fruit bodies mostly hypogeous but many epigeous, globose, ovoid, ellipsoid, irregular, or "tuberlike," sometimes stalked and then epigeous; with or without a columella (a column of sterile tissue extending into or through the fertile tissue (the gleba), the stipe and the columella continuous if both are present and the combined structure termed a stipe-columella; gleba lacking capillitium, remaining firm and intact throughout the life of the fruit body or becoming reduced to slime, or in some finally reduced to a powder; peridium (the wall of the fruit body) remaining intact throughout the life of the fruit body, or breaking open in some manner to release the spores.

The genera treated in the following keys are treated unevenly. The basic idea is to have one (the most common) representative of each genus, but where our knowledge justifies it, treatments in various degrees of detail are included, the most elaborate being that of *Rhizopogon*, the largest genus in the order in North America. As pointed out elsewhere the true truffles are Ascomycetes, and are very rare in North America.

Key to the Genera of the Hymenogastrales

1a. Stipe (or stipe-columella) present. Fig. 325 2
1b. Stipe (or stipe-columella) absent, but a columella (simple or branched) and typically less than 3 mm thick may be present 17
2a. Stipe-columella stump-like with narrow branches leading from the apex of the stump; fruit body pale greenish yellow; stipe-columella usually not evident until fruit body is sectioned. Fig. 325 .... *Truncocolumella citrina* Zeller

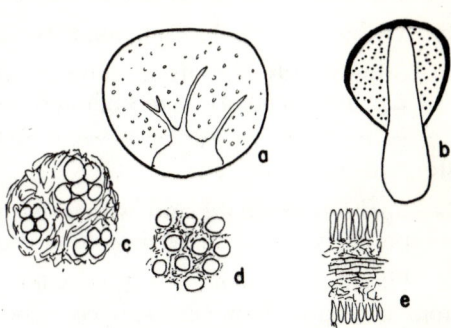

Fig. 325. Hymenogastrales: (a) section of a fruit body showing a cushion like columella with branches (see *Truncocolumella* and *Hymenogaster*); (b) longitudinal section through *Nivatogastrium* showing "stipe-columella" (the part in contact with the gleba is the columella); (c) heteromerous tissue as found in *Macowanites*; (d) tramal tissue (tramal "plates") and cavities (which are lined by hymenium as shown in e, in such genera as *Rhizopogon* (they are indicated as circular in section here for diagramatic purposes, more often they are elongate and irregular in outline).

Fruit bodies 2-5 (7) cm, broad, 1.5-5 cm high, becoming yellow-ochre to (finally) olive-fuscous, whitish only before exposed to light and still immature, stump-like base of stipe-columella citrine yellow; spores 6.5-9.7 $\times$ 3.5-4.5 μ, smooth, yellowish in KOH, slightly darker in Melzer's; hyphae of the peridium 3-15 μ wide, tubular more or less, walls yellowish and smooth in KOH; clamps present.

Associated with Douglas fir in the Pacific Northwest, fairly common in the fall on the coast, and in the summer in the northern Rocky Mountains.

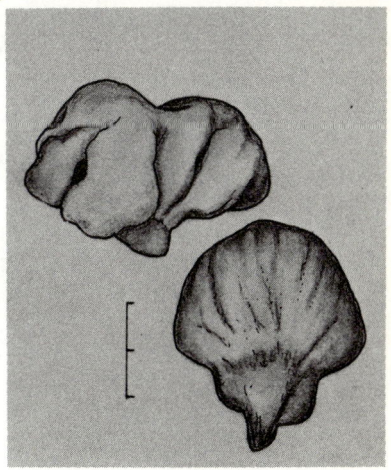

Fig. 326. *Truncocolumella citrina*.

A variety (var. *separabilis* Smith) is known from Idaho in which the gleba separates somewhat from the stipe-columella.

2b. Not as above 3

3a. Gleba yellow-brown, tan or rusty brown when mature 4
3b. Gleba (and spores) some other color 11
4a. Gleba at least somewhat powdery at maturity 5
4b. Gleba not powdery at maturity 7
5a. Stipe woody and often scaly; growing in desert regions; "cap" narrowly oval, 4-15 cm high and not expanding ....
 .... see *Podaxis pistillaris* p. 295
5b. Not as above 6
6a. Spores dextrinoid and with a germ pore; gleba only slightly powdery .... *Neosecotium macrosporium* (Lloyd) Singer

"Pileus" 1-3 cm high, 1-2 cm wide, the margin not separating from the stipe-columella, surface smooth, avellaneous or whitish; gleba chambered at first but becoming somewhat powdery when fully mature, brownish, not separating from the columella; stipe-columella percurrent; spores globose and 13.5-18 μ or 14-18 $\times$ 12-15 μ, surface appearing areolate-ornamented at maturity.

On grassy sandy soils in the Great Plains, early summer.

6b. Spores dextrinoid and lacking a germ pore; ....
 .... see *Endoptychum agaricoides* p. 313
7a. Gleba essentially poroid as in *Boletus*. Fig. 327 ....
 .... *Gastroboletus turbinatus* (Linder) Singer

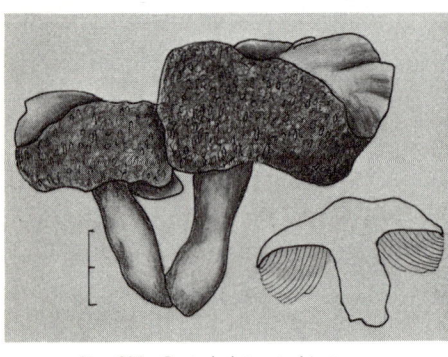

Fig. 327. *Gastroboletus turbinatus*.

Fruit body 2-5 cm broad, resembling an aborted bolete, dry and velvety, golden yellow or with a reddish tinge; gleba tubulose, separating readily from the pileus; context yellow and quickly staining blue on exposure, the pores red to orange at times; stipe-columella short, 1-2 cm long, 8-20 mm thick, extending to near apex of pileus, yellow to reddish, typically staining blue where injured and later these areas red; spores 14.5-18 $\times$ 6.5-9.5 μ.

On humus under conifers, along mountain trails and roadsides, Missouri and the Pacific Northwest, summer and fall, under conifers, not uncommon.

7b. Not as above 8

8a. Growing on conifer wood in cold wet situations in the mountains; hymenial cystidia 60-100 × 15-25 μ. Fig. 328 ....
.... *Nivatogastrium nubigenum* (Hark) Sing. & Smith

Fruit body 1-2.4 cm broad, 1.5-4 cm high, larger at times, surface smooth, somewhat viscid, ochraceous fading to white or whitish, the wall remaining attached to the stipe-columella; gleba loculate, the chambers elongated vertically (as convoluted lamellae), dull cinnamon-brown; columella and veil white, the veil fibrillose and evanescent; spores 7.5-9 × 5.5-6.3 μ, smooth, ochraceous in KOH.

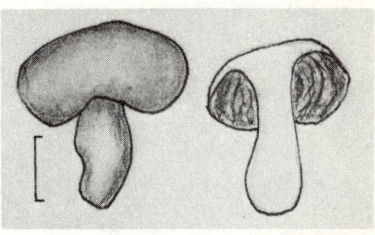

Fig. 328. *Nivatogastrium nubigenum*.

Solitary to clustered, epigeous on conifer logs and chips often at the edge of snow banks, Rocky Mountain and Pacific Northwest.

8b. Terrestrial, often in the conifer duff 9

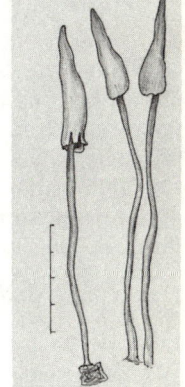

9a. Hymenophore lamellate; stip slender elongate; fruit body epigeous. Fig. 329 ....
....*Galeropsis cucullata* (Shope & Seaver Zelle)

Fig. 329. *Galeropsis cucullata*.

Pileus conic, 6-10 mm wide, 2.5-4 cm tall, yellowish to grayish buff, subviscid, glabrous; gleba pale fulvous to fulvous, lamellae often crisped and contorted; stipe 10-12 cm long, 1-2 mm thick, bulbous at base, dingy buff, glabrous or nearly so; spores 12-16 × 8-10 μ, tawny in KOH, smooth, with an apical pore.

Gregarious to scattered among grasses in wet areas often at elevations of 10,000 ft. in the Rocky Mountains, summer.

9b. Stipe short and thick; gleba lacunose to sublamellate 10
10a. Growing under spruce and fir in the mountains; spores inamyloid, warty-rugulose and fulvous in KOH. Fig. 330 ....
............................*Thaxterogaster pingue* (Zeller) Sing. & Sm.

NON-GILLED FLESHY FUNGI

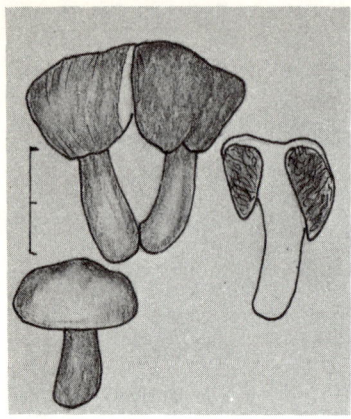

Fig. 330. *Thaxterogaster pingue.*

Fruit body 1-5 cm broad, margin at times separating from the stipe-columella, olive-yellow darkening to deep dingy brown, slimy if wet or only slightly viscid; gleba cinnamon (pale to dark), chambers irregular; stipe 1-4.5 cm long, 8-25 mm thick, always well-developed, slimy below when wet, violaceous (pale purple-drab); columella continuous with stipe but usually narrower; spores 14-16.5 × 8-9.5 μ.

Solitary to gregarious, under the duff or pushing through it, June to October, Rocky Mountains and the Pacific Northwest, common at times.

10b. Under Eucalyptus or oak; spores ornamented by canals through the thick spore wall ....
.... *Setchelliogaster tenuipes* (**Setchell**) **Pouzar**

Fruit body 1-3 cm tall and broad; stipe up to 2 cm tall, thin and often bent or flattened; pileus yellow-brown to red-brown, margin separating from the stipe to expose the gleba; gleba ochraceous-brown, chambered to gill-like; volva none (veil line superior, fibrillose and evanescent); spores 14-19 × 9.5-12.5 μ.

Growing subhypogeously on earth and humus, California in the rainy season (in June in Oregon).

11a. Gleba pallid to yellow 12
11b. Gleba mostly yellowish clouded gray, chocolate color or blackish 15
12a. Growing on hardwood logs in wet places such as swamp borders; spores hyaline smooth, inamyloid. Fig. 331 ....
................................."*Lentodium squamosum*" **Morgan**

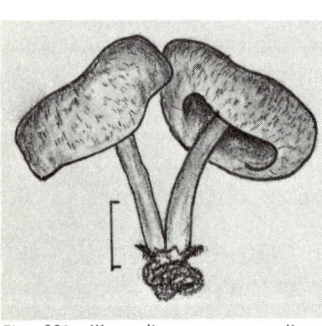

Fig. 331. *"Lentodium squamosum."*

Pileus 3-7 cm broad, dry, minutely sqaumulose around the disc the squamules dull brown, ground color pallid to dingy ochraceous, gleba vertically lacunose or gill-like; stipe 2-6 cm long, 3-7 mm thick; spores 5.5-6 × 2-2.6 μ.

Scattered to clustered, often after heavy fall rains, Midwest, common at times. It has been shown that this "species" is merely a variant of the American form of *Lentinus tigrinus*.

12b. Growing on duff and humus; spores with amyloid ornamentation 13
13a. Latex present (check young fruit bodies at apex of "stipe" spores often reticulate. Fig. 332 .... *Arcangeliella* p. 374
13b. Latex absent 14

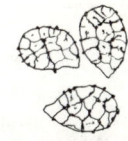

Fig. 332. *Arcangeliella lactarioides.*

14a. Cuticle of peridium of pseudoparenchyma-type cells; leptocystidia present in the hymenium *Cystangium sessile* ....
.... (Massee & Rodway) Singer and Smith

Fruit body to 20 × 10 mm, depressed-globose, smooth, cream-colored; gleba labyrinthiform and very fragile as dried, exposed at apex of stipe, ochraceous; stipe-columella with stipe portion 3-5 × 1-2 mm, smooth, hollow; spores 9.7-15 × 9.2-13.5 μ, wall ± 1.2 μ, thick, ornamentation 0.8-2.2 μ high, of isolated spines not always completely covered by amyloid material; leptocystidia 77-115 × 16-27 μ.

C. sessile is the type of the genus, but is not known from North America.

14b. Cuticle of pileus various (but not as in 14a); hymenial cystidia mostly as pseudocystidia or macrocystidia ....
.... *Macowanites* p. 374

15a. Gleba more or less lamellate, rarely exposed around the stipe; hymenial cystidia 60 μ or more long; spores large and "boletoid" in shape. Fig. 333 ... *Brauniellulua nancyae* Smith

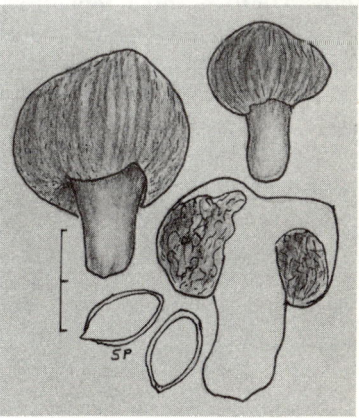

Fig. 333. *Brauniellula nancyae.*

Fruit body 1-5 cm, margin irregular and connected to stipe until late maturity, fibrillose, the fibrils grayish to dark drab over an ochraceous ground color, in age becoming purplish red; gleba ochraceous becoming drab; stipe-columella ochraceous at first, vinaceous-red in age; spores 16-20 × 6.5-9 μ.

Solitary to clustered in duff under lodgepole pine, central Idaho, late summer.

15b. Not as above 16
16a. **Cap practically lacking, exposing black gill-like plates elevated on a stipe at maturity. Fig. 334** ....
.... *Montagnea arenarius* (DC) **Zeller**

Fruit body 8-30 cm tall, cap merely an expanded disc of the stipe-columella, white or grayish; gleba—the plates attached to the margin of the disc-like pileus—black at maturity; stipe white, almost woody on drying, volva usually double, the outer part white and covered with sand, the inner composed of tough fibrous strands; spores blackish, $20\text{-}28 \times 10\text{-}14\ \mu$.

Growing in sandy places in semiarid regions scattered to gregarious, Texas, California, Oregon, Itah, Idaho, etc.

The volva is usually lost in the process of removing the specimens from the soil, since the stipe originates deep in the soil.

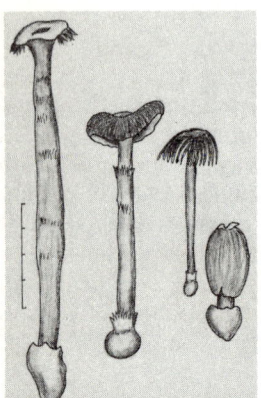

Fig. 334. *Montagnea arenarius*.

16b. **Not as above. Gleba blackish, becoming somewhat powdery; stipe-columella short; volva lacking** ....
.... see *Endoptychum* p. 313
17a. Gleba slimy at maturity 18
17b. Gleba cartilaginous, firm, or finally powdery 20
18a. **Gleba divided into sectors by the branches of the columella; fruit body with an elongated tapered sterile base—overall shape elongate-pear-shaped. Fig. 335** ....
.... *Phallogaster saccatus* **Morgan**

Fruit body 2.5-5 cm high, up to 3 cm wide, whitish tinged vinaceous or lilac, rupturing in a star-shaped manner; gleba consisting of a number of green separate masses with a disagreeable odor, rhizomorphs white to lilac; spores subcylindric, $4\text{-}5 \times .5\text{-}1.8\ \mu$.

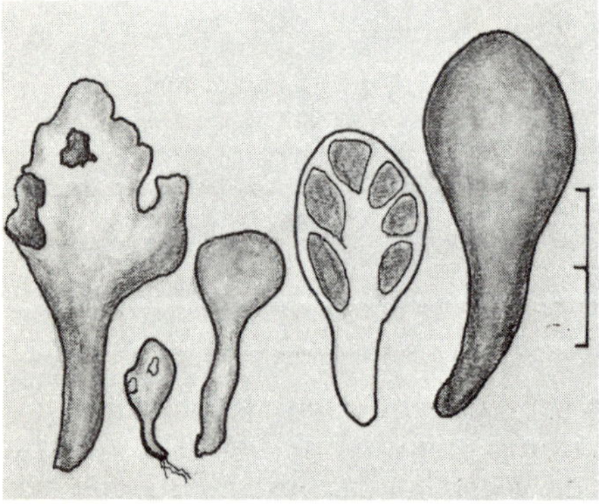

Solitary, scattered or in small clusters from a single rhizomorph, late spring to mid summer eastern United States.

Fig. 335. *Phallogaster saccatus*.

18b. Not as above 19

19a. Peridium readily cracking and becoming free from the gleba if fruit body is compressed; gleba gelatinous-cartilaginous, olivaceous; columella distinct and often branched. Fig. 336 ....
....*Hysterangium separabile* Zeller

Fruit bodies up to 3 cm diam., globose or nearly so, often irregular generally irregular as dried, white to pale flesh color, pinkish where bruised; columella prominent; gleba green when fresh then olive; peridium glabrous and unpolished; spores olivaceous in masses, lanceolate, 12-19 × 6-8 μ, odor offensive at maturity, taste mild when young.

Hypogeous under conifers and deciduous trees and shrubs common in the western mountains but widely distributed.

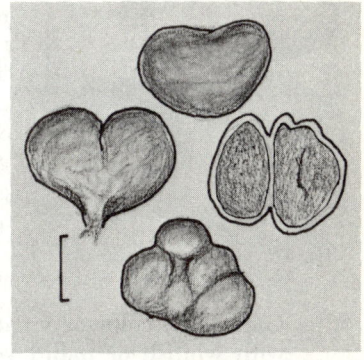

Fig. 336. *Hysterangium separabile.*

19b. Peridum not as above; columella absent or rudimentary; gleba gelatinous only in age .... see *Rhizopogon* p. 320

20a. Peridium thick and hard; gleba a black powder at maturity; columella nearly globose. Fig. 337...*Radiigera atrogleba* Zeller

Fruit bodies 3.5-5 cm, globose, embedded in a mass of mycelium; columella 10-15 mm wide at widest point; gleba of plate-like fascicles of hyphae, capillitium not branched; spores 5.5-6.5 μ.

In duff under conifers, Pacific Northwest, summer and fall, also in the northern Rocky Mountains in the early summer often on the shoulders of logging roads.

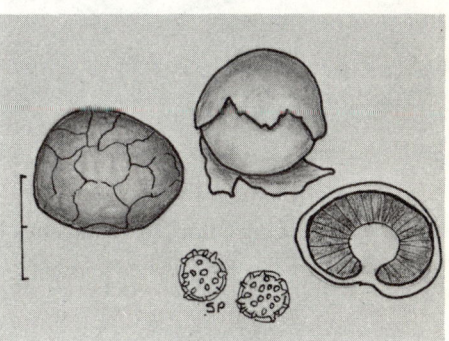

Fig. 337. *Radiigera atrogleba.*

20b. Not as above 21

21a. Basidia not in a well defined hymenium, cavities soon filled with gel 22

21b. Basidia in a distinct hymenium, cavities empty but becoming filled with spores 24

22a. Gleba white to pallid or creamy at maturity; spores globose to broadly ellipsoid and inamyloid. Fig. 338 ....
..................................Leucogaster rubescens Zeller & Dodge

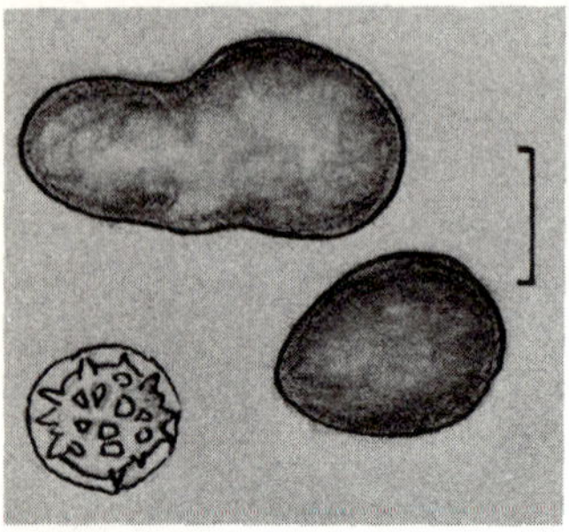

Fruit body 1-3.5 cm, subglobose, whitish at first to flesh pink, brick red to brownish, surface viscid when moist; gleba cream color as dried, cavities about 2 per mm, filled with a clear gel; basidia pyriform, 15-25 × 8-14 μ, with pedicels 50-125 μ; spores globose to oblong, 11-15 μ, including gelatinous sheath, warty-reticulate, inamyloid.

Fig. 338. *Leucogaster rubescens*.

In duff and humus, Pacific Northwest, spring.

22b. Gleba clay-color or vinaceous-brown to black, often marbled with whitish or pallid veins 23
23a. Gleba black, marbled with whitish veins. Fig. 339 ....
..................................*Melanogaster variegatus* (Vitt.) Tulasne

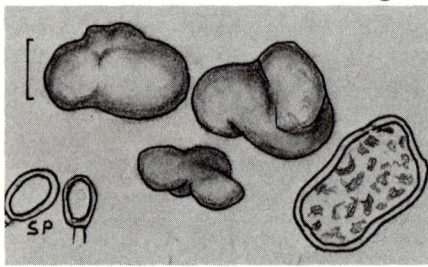

Fruit body 1-3 cm, globose, rusty brown; gleba black with thin pallid to yellow-orange veins; spores 7.5-10 × 5-7.5 μ, ellipsoid, very dark brown.

Solitary to gregarious in the duff in conifer or hardwood forests, widely distributed, but generally rare in North America.

Fig. 339. *Melanogaster variegatus*.

23b. Gleba clay-color to vinaceous-brown, marbled with pallid veins. Fig. 340 ....*Alpova cinnamomeus* Dodge

Fruit body 1-3.5 cm, nearly glabrous, white to pale cinnamon to dark rusty brown finally; glebal cavities soon filled with gel; spores 4-5.3 (7) × 2-2.5 (3) μ, ellipsoid, pale brown in groups. See *Rhizopogon diplophloeus* also p. 321.

In soil and duff, Great Lakes area and Pacific Northwest, common in the Northwest in the fall (in relation to other species in the order).

Fig. 340. *Alpova cinnamomeus*.

24a. Spore ornamentation non-amyloid or practically so; clamps present on hyphae of the fruit body; spores globose to broadly ellipsoid ...... *Hydnangium roseum* (Harkness) Singer & Smith

Fruit body irregularly lobes, 1-3 cm, pale rose color; gleba chambered, lacking a columella or sterile base, deeper colored within than on the surface, the latter fibrillose-roughened; spores globose, 10-15 μ ornamented with cones 1.3-1 × 1.3-2 μ (very coarse); basidia 2-spored; epicutis of peridium of appressed-interwoven hyaline hyphae not sharply differentiated from the hyphae of the context, no sphaerocysts or laticiferous hyphae seen but oleiferous hyphae present.

Under oaks, California, January.

24b. Not as above 25
25a. Spore ornamentation inamyloid; clamps absent; a latex present or absent; spores globose to broadly ellipsoid .... *Octavianina* p. 361
25b. Not as above 26
26a. Latex present; spore ornamentation amyloid; spores globose to ellipsoid, columella weakly developed .... *Zelleromyces* p. 372
26b. Not as above 27
27a. Spores ornamented with a thin amyloid crust as an outer layer covering at least part of the spore, thick inner layer traversed by fine canals. Fig. 341 .... *Mycolevis siccigleba* Smith

Fruit body 1-4 cm, white becoming yellowish and finally grayish olive, with scattered rhizomorphs; neither KOH or FeSO$_4$ causing a color change in the peridium; Melzer's causing it to stain copper-green to bluish on white portions; gleba white, consistency very dry, light of weight, finally becoming olivaceous; spores 9-12 × 8-11 μ (18 × 16 μ),

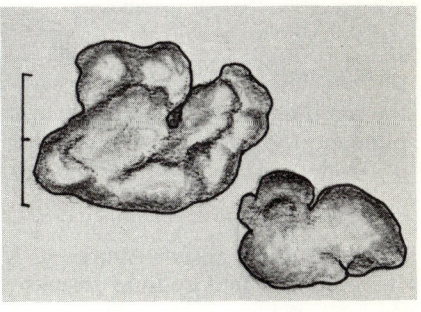

Fig. 341. *Mycolevis siccigleba*.

a thin outer layer extending away from the apiculus and blue to violet in Melzer's, in some breaking into flakes, inner wall 2 μ thick and traversed by fine canals; basidia 4-spored; cystidia none; peridial epicutis a tangled turf of hyphae 2.5-5 μ; clamps none.

In duff under conifers, northern Idaho, July.

27b. Not as above 28
28a. Spore ornamentation amyloid 29
28b. Spore ornamentation inamyloid 30
29a. Mediostratum of tramal plates containing sphaerocysts; peridium poorly developed to lacking .... *Gymnomyces* p. 368

29b. Mediostratum of tramal plates lacking sphaerocysts; peridium well developed ....*Martellia* p. 362
30a. Spores longitudinally grooved, rusty brown in KOH; peridium absent or poorly developed (see *Chamonixia* and *Hymenogaster* also p. 313) ....*Gautieria* p. 319
30b. Not as above 31
31a. Peridium well-developed and when fresh staining blue where injured; spores rusty brown in KOH and obscurely grooved to rugulose. Fig. 342 ....
....*Chamonixia brevicolumna* Smith & Singer

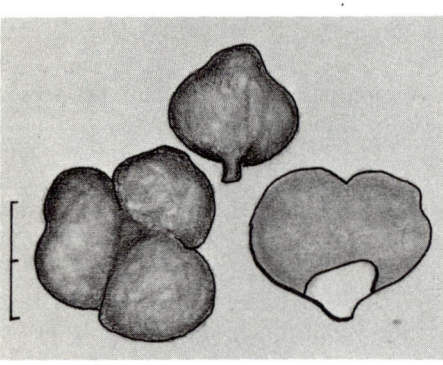

Fig. 342. *Chamonixia brevicolumna*.

Fruit body 1.8-2.5 cm, subglobose, unpolished, at times with scattered fine rhizomorphs, olive-ochre but soon stained blue where bruised, having a distinct basal point of attachment, gleba chambers minute, reddish cinamon when cut, soon stained blue, columella a rounded basal plug extending into the gleba up to a third of its thickness, unbranched, soon stained blue where cut; spores 15-18 $\times$ 10-13 μ; peridium duplex, its outer layer a trichodermium of septate elements having some cells 16-20 $\times$ 15-18 μ, inner region of the peridium bright lemon to chrome yellow in KOH from dissolved pigment, the hyphae 2.5-5 μ wide; clamps absent.

Under spruce-fir stands central Idaho, August.

31b. Not as above 32
32a. Peridium absent; spores in Melzer's smooth but with darker colored longitudinal streaks ....*Protogautieria lutea* Smith

Fruit body about 2 $\times$ 1 cm, soft and fleshy in consistency, surface alveolate from chambers of exposed gleba (peridium absent), pale bright greenish yellow, dingy brownish from handling, with KOH brown, $FeSO_4$ no reaction; odor peculiar but soon vanishing; taste mild; columella rudimentary, dendroid; gleba pale yellow; spores 14-19 $\times$ 9-12 μ, ellipsoid, smooth (in KOH) pale cinnamon buff, in Melzer's reddish brown and showing darker longitudinal bands of a still darker red-brown color; basidia 35 $\times$ 15 μ, 4-spored. Cystidia about 100 $\times$ 20 μ, vinaceous-red in KOH and with red incrustations; peridium absent but exposed ridges of the gleba with a palisade of cells reddish to purplish in KOH. Clamps present.

Under Douglas fir and larch, Cusick, Washington, early July.

32b. Peridium present; spores typically large, rusty brown in KOH and warty-wrinkled or with a loosely enveloping outer sac (utricle) .... *Hymenogaster* p. 313.

ENDOPTYCHUM

Key to Species

1a. Gleba blackish, somewhat powdery when mature; spores dark brown in KOH. Fig. 343 ....
...................................*Endoptychum depressum* **Singer & Smith**

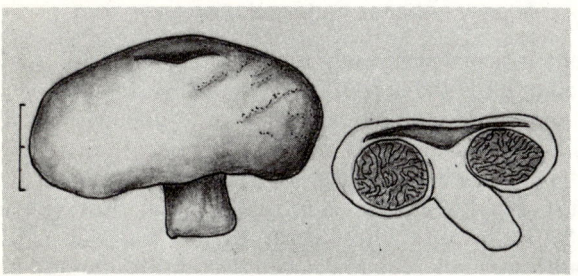

Fig. 343. *Endoptychum depressum.*

Fruit body 3-9.5 cm broad, white to dingy pallid, lower part tending to stain vinaceous; gleba nearly gill-like (of greatly elongated chambers); stipe 1-3 cm × 8-20 mm, whitish, the columella percurrent; context white, tending to stain yellow; spores 6-8 × 5.3-7.7 μ.

Hypogeous becoming epigeous, often in clumps, on soil under conifers, aspen often present also, late summer and fall central Idaho.

1b. Gleba pale brown and not powdery. Spores 6.5-8 × 5.5-7 μ, subhyaline in KOH, dextrinoid ....
....*Endoptychum agaricoides* **Czerniaiev**

Fruit body 1-7 cm wide and 2-10 cm high, appressed fibrillose, white becoming dingy to pale tan, in age scaly at times; gleba pale brown at maturity, not or only slightly powdery, sublamellate when young; columella percurrent, the gleba not becoming exposed.

Scattered to gregarious on soil, waste land, pastures, lawns, etc., throughout the United States but abundant at times in the Great Basin states of the West after wet weather, summer and fall.

It is edible when young, but becomes fibrous in age. *E. arizonicum* is a closely related species from our Southwest with spores 8.5-15 × 4.5-7 μ.

HYMENOGASTER

This genus, *Chamonixia*, and *Gautieria* form a related group of fungi with (mostly) large rusty brown spores more or less coarsely ornamented, and a columella percurrent to greatly reduced in size, or absent. This unit of three genera is still very much in need of critical study here in North America.

We recognize two subgenera: Subgenus Dendrogaster, in which the spores are less than 15 μ long and the gleba showing a percurrent to well-developed columella (or a pulvinate base), or columella absent in a few species. Subgenus Hymenogaster features a greatly reduced columella and spores mostly more than 15 μ long.

Subgenus DENDROGASTER
Key to Selected Species

1a. Outer surface of fruit body viscid (the hyphae 2-3 μ wide, gelatinized as mounted in KOH) .... *Hymenogaster idahoensis* Smith

Fruit body 2-3.5 cm subglobose, evenly yellowish olive-buff to olive-argillaceous; with KOH no reaction, FeSO$_4$ no reaction, odor and taste mild; gleba of plates radiating from a small stumplike columella, colored dull cinnamon, with FeSO$_4$ dingy olive; spores 13-16 $\times$ 8-10 μ, oval to ellipsoid, strongly ochraceous in KOH, verrucose-roughened, the subapical ornamentation darker; basidia 2-spored, many ochraceous in KOH; peridium 2-layered, the subcutis of hyphae 4-15 μ wide; clamps present.

Under spruce-fir stands, central Idaho, August.

1b. Not as above 2
2a. Fruit body with lilac to violaceous tints at least when young 3
2b. Fruit body never with above colors or never staining blue or purplish when injured 6
3a. Fruit body staining purplish to blue when injured 4
3b. Not staining as above 5
4a. Context of peridium and tramal plates strongly gelatinous, surface flecked with red on a white ground color ....
.... *Hymenogaster ruber* Harkness

Spores 9-12 $\times$ 6.5-8 μ, dingy yellow-brown in KOH; apical beak inconspicuous; inner wall about 2 μ thick; ornamentation warty-rugulose; peridium thick, dingy brownish yellow in KOH, soon gelatinizing; clamps present.

California, rare.

4b. Context of peridium not gelatinous; peridium white, gradually bluish from handling .... *Hymenogaster subcaeruleus* Smith

Fruit body 1-2 cm, globose, fibrillose, dry, with KOH slowly brown; FeSO$_4$ no change; gleba pale dull cinnamon-brown when mature; columella absent, consistency crumbly; spores 9-12 $\times$ 6.5-8 (-9) μ, ellipsoid, finely verrucose; clamps none.

Under fir, northern Idaho, summer, N. J. Smith collector.

5a. Spores 11-13 $\times$ 6.5-8 μ .... *Hymenogaster sublilacinus* Smith

Fruit body 2-5.5 cm, globose; columella branched; surface dingy ochraceous where handled; gleba cinnamon-brown when mature; odor sweetly fragrant; spores ellipsoid, verruclose; basidia 4-spored; peridium 2-layered, the epicutis about 100 μ thick, the hyphae 4-10 μ wide, walls hyaline; the inner layer fulvous in KOH, the hyphae 4-15 μ wide; clamps present.

In deep duff under Engleman spruce, central Idaho, July.

5b. Spores 9-11 × 5-6.5 × 5-6.5 μ. Fig. 344 ....
....Hymenogaster diabolus Smith

Fruit body 1-2.5 cm, subglobose, surface unpolished, purplish at first, dull buff colored as dried; sterile base pulvinate, 1.5-2.5 mm broad, with radiating lines of sterile tissue as columella; gleba cinnamon at maturity; odor pungent; spores ellipsoid, ornamentation warty-rugulose; peridium one-layered, hyaline or nearly so, lacking incrustations, 4-9 μ wide; clamps present.

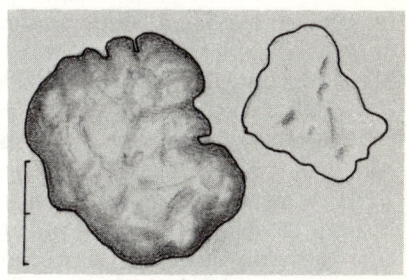

Fig. 344. Hymenogaster diabolus.

Under pine, Seven-Devils Mts., Idaho, July.

6a. Outer layer of peridium of thick-walled hyphae ....
....Hymenogaster subborealis Smith

Fruit body 4-12 mm, globose, whitish dry and fibrillose on aging the fibrils yellowish; KOH or FeSO₄ no color change; lacking a definite point of attachment; gleba soon dark vinaceous-brown; columella present only as thickened tramal plates; spores 7-9 × 4.5-5.5 μ, ellipsoid, minutely verrucose; peridium of interwoven hyphae 4-15 μ wide, the walls 2-3 μ thick and hyaline in KOH; inner layer of thin-walled hyphae; some cells inflated to 5-12 (16) μ; clamps not found.

Under hemlock-Thuja stands, northern Idaho, September.

6b. Not as above 7

7a. KOH lemon yellow on peridium (fresh or dried).
Fig. 345 Hymenogaster subochraceus Smith

Fruit bodies 1-3.5 cm, dry, matted-fibrillose, ochre-yellow becoming paler, dark reddish brown where cutis is worn away; gleba soon rusty cinnamon, odor and taste mild; columella pulvinate with

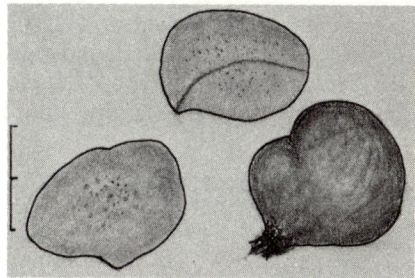

Fig. 345. Hymenogaster subochraceus.

a few branches extending from it; spores 8-11 × 6-7.5 (8) μ, verrucose, ellipsoid; basidia 4-spored; peridium with epicutis of hyphae 2-3.5 μ wide; in central area hyphae 4-15 μ wide; clamps none.

In duff under spruce, central Idaho, August.

7b. Not lemon yellow in KOH 8
8a. Fruit body white, silky, slowly brown from handling; odor aromatic ....*Hymenogaster brunnescens* Smith

Fruit body 1-4 cm, globose; gleba rusty cinnamon when mature; columella dendroid and percurrent, white to grayish and cartilaginous; spores 10-13 × 6.5-8 μ, ellipsoid, warty-rugulose; peridium of interwoven hyphae; clamps present.

In duff under spruce, central Idaho, August.

8b. Fruit body pallid olive-buff, becoming yellowish; odor of pine pitch ....*Hymenogaster subolivaceus* Smith

Fruit body 2-5 cm, dry, unpolished; gleba cinnamon when mature; columella rudimentary; spores 8-11 × 4.5-6.6 μ, rusty brown in KOH, warty-rugulose; basidia 4-spored; peridium a single layer of hyaline to ochraceous thin-walled hyphae with inflated cells only near the subhymenium; clamps present.

In stands of lodgepole pine, Pole Mountain, near Laramie, Wyoming, July.

Subgenus HYMENOGASTER

Key to Selected North American Species

1a. Peridium with an hymeniform epicutis, the elements 9-17 μ broad ....*Hymenogaster mcmurphyi* Zeller & Dodge

Fruit body 1-1.5 cm, yellow, darker as dried; fibrillose; sterile base small and pulvinate; gleba yellow to yellow-brown (dark vinaceous-brown in the herbarium); spores 14-17 × 11-15 μ, globose, golden yellow in KOH, the inner wall up to 2.5-4 μ thick, ornamented with closely set warts up to 2 μ high; basidia 4- and 2-spored, dingy yellow-brown in KOH from a granular content; tramal plates of interwoven pale ochraceous non-gelatinous hyphae; cells of the peridial epicutis 26-38 × 9-17 μ, with granular to wrinkled ochraceous content as revived in KOH; clamps present but rare.

In sandy soil, under ash and oak, California, February and March.

1b. Not as above 2
2a. Peridium white, staining inky black from handling ....
....*Hymenogaster nigrescens* Smith

Fruit body 1-3 cm, silky, dry, white, drying pallid to brownish but where handled inky black, with $FeSO_4$ olive; odor none; gleba avellaneous to wood brown (gray-brown) or tinged purplish, as dried dingy pallid; columella none; spores 17-22 × 10-13 μ, broadly fusoid, distinctly beaked, rusty brown in KOH, irregularly rugulose;

basidia 4-spored; hyphae of the tramal plates 4-9 μ wide and yellowish in KOH; hyphae of the peridial epicutis 2-5 μ wide but sphaerocysts in groups 8-12 μ diam. in the central portion; clamps none.

In conifer duff, northern Idaho, July.

2b. Not as above 3
3a. Fruit body pale tan flecked with red; context of peridium of thin-walled inflated cells some of which are in pockets; clamps present but often rare ....
....Hymenogaster occidentalis **Zeller & Dodge**

Fruit body 1-2 cm; clay color as dried; spores 20-25 × 14-18 μ, lacking a beak, bister in KOH, wrinkled-warty inner layer about 2 μ thick; basidia 2- and 4-spored; peridial epicutis of hyphae 4-7 μ wide, walls yellowish in KOH.

Under oak and conifers, California and Oregon, March to May.

3b. Not as above 4
4a. Hymenial cystidia present 5
4b. Hymenial cystidia absent 6
5a. Central portion of peridium (beneath the epicutis) of inflated thin-walled hyaline to yellowish hyphal cells ....
....Hymenogaster subalpinus **Smith**

Fruit body 5-12 mm, appressed fibrillose, dry, dull white; dingy yellow from handling and finally purplish brown; $FeSO_4$ on surface weakly olive, KOH yellow-brown; gleba grayish becoming violaceous-brown; columella rudimentary; spores 17-27 × 10.15 μ, dark rusty in KOH, warty-roughened; basidia 2-spored; cystidia 20-30 × 10-15 μ, the apex obtuse to subacute, thin-walled; peridium with a thin epicutis of hyphae 3-7 μ wide, yellow in KOH; clamps absent.

Under cedar-hemlock, northern Idaho, June.

5b. Inner region of peridium of ochraceous-brown hyphae with somewhat thickened walls, the hyphae 8-16 μ wide with many cells inflated to 25-30 μ ....
....Hymenogaster boozeri **Zeller & Dodge**

Fruit body with a cheese like odor fresh; color white staining brown where injured; spores 26-35 (-40) × 9.5-15 μ, elongate-fusoid, wrinkled longitudinally on the outer layer; basidia 2-spored; hymenial cystidia 30-40 × 8-12 μ, thin-walled, apex acute; peridium with an epicutis of hyphae 3-6 μ wide, yellowish in KOH; clamps absent.

Under oak, Oregon, April.

6a. Fruit body grayish to pale dull grayish brown fresh; taste decidedly farinaceous ....Hymenogaster farinaceus **Smith**

Fruit body 10-15 mm, surface furrowed to point of attachment; gleba dull cinnamon; columella rudimentary, pulvinate, greenish gray in $FeSO_4$; spores 13.5-18 (-20) × 10-13 μ, ovoid, verruculose-wrinkled; basidia mostly 2-spored; subhymenium cellular (2-4 cells deep); epicuticular region of peridium of smooth hyphae 3-6 μ wide, the inner region heteromerous (the sphaerocysts to 25 μ) and with walls yellowish in KOH in some; clamps absent.

Under hardwoods (oak, maple and basswood mixed) with pine and hemlock near by, July, Michigan.

6b. Not as above 7
7a. Spores mostly 20 μ or more long 8
7b. Spores (most of them) under 20 μ long 13
8a. Spores 24-31 × 14-18 μ ....
.... *Hymenogaster gardneri* **Zeller & Dodge**

Fruit body 1-1.5 cm, soon checked or cracked at the surface, dingy white becoming brown, surface smooth to flocculent; gleba brown, firm, watery; basidia 2-and 4-spored; spores rusty brown in KOH, ellipsoid to subfusoid, more or less beaked, scarcely longitudinally wrinkled (but coarsely wrinkled generally); peridium of interwoven non-gelatinous hyphae yellowish in KOH; clamps absent.

In clay soil under *Quercus,* California, March.

8b. Not as above 9
9a. Spores not showing longitudinal wrinkles or grooves 10
9b. Spores showing longitudinal wrinkles 12
10a. Spores 18-25 × 13-17 μ. Fig. 346 ....
.... *Hymenogaster parksii* **Zeller & Dodge**

Fig. 346. *Hymenogaster parksii.*

Fruit bodies 0.5-1.5 cm, white to gray becoming cinnamon buff to clay color; gleba grayish drying dark vinaceous-brown; spores with a distinct pedicel and prominent beak, pale fulvous in KOH, outer wall wrinkled; peridium of appressed-interwoven hyphae 3-8 μ wide, some cells in midportion inflated; clamps absent (?).

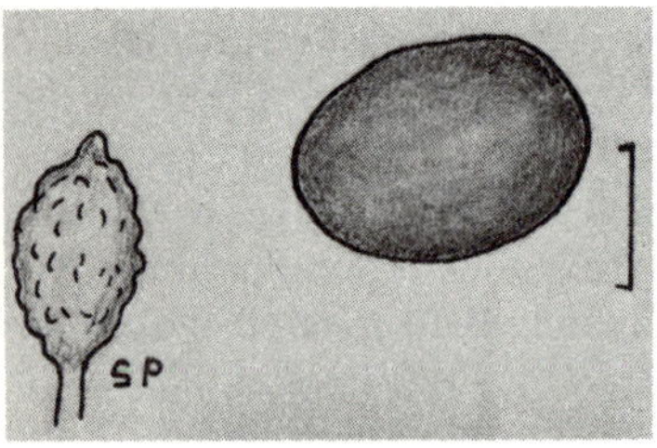

Under *Quercus* and *Heteromeles,* California, November to April.

Note: *Dendrogaster megasporus* Zeller & Dodge is close to *H. parksii* but should differ in having a well developed columella and a blackish brown gleba as dried as well as 1- and 2-spored basidia.

10b. Not as above 11
11a. Gleba dark umber when fresh ....
.... *Hymenogaster gilkeyae* **Zeller & Dodge**

Fruit body 1-2.5 cm, snow white to grayish, drying cartridge buff, smooth, silky; sterile base pulvinate to conic; gleba drying snuff brown; spores 16-22 × 11-14 μ, ellipsoid to subfusoid, outer wall pale ochraceous in KOH, inner wall rusty-ochraceous; basidia 2-

spored; epicutis of peridium of hyphae 2-5 μ wide with some free ends projecting (but not forming a trichodermium); inner layer with some hyphae with cells enlarged and scattered or in groups; clamps absent.

Under buckeye and oak, Oregon and California, November and April.

11b. Gleba pallid becoming grayish brown (fresh) ....
....*Hymenogaster alnicola* Smith

Fruit body 1-1.5 cm, shape irregular, surface at first white-cottony, later variegated snuff-brown and pallid olivaceous-yellow, odor faintly fragrant; $FeSO_4$ green on peridium. KOH brownish; gleba dull cinnamon as dried; columella pulvinate and branches coming off from it; spores 16-20 (24) × 8-12 (13) μ, broadly fusoid, very dark bay-brown in Melzer's; basidia 2- and 4-spored; epicutis of hyphae 4-7 μ wide, cells 2-3 times as long as broad, with yellow incrustations on the walls; clamps present (but rare).

12a. No species treated here since the group needs critical study in relation to other genera. *H. caerulescens* Z. & D. stains blue.
12b. Species of *Gautieria* with some degree of peridial development key here.
13a. When bruised staining blue (when fresh) see *Chamonixia* p. 312 also ....*Hymenogaster pyriformis* Zeller & Dodge

Fruit body 1-2 cm, white but brown where exposed in situ, drab to olive-brown as dried; sterile base prominant; gleba gray, bluish where cut, drying fuscous; spores 14-18 × 9-11 μ, with 5-8 longitudinal furrows; epicuticular zone of peridium of hyphae 4-9 μ wide, yellowish to hyaline in KOH.

Under oak, California, October.

13b. Not staining blue. A number of species as yet not critically restudied will key out here but are not included since some may require new combinations.

GAUTIERIA

1a. Under hardwood trees; glebal cavities 0.5-1 cm broad at maturity; peridium absent (glebal cavities and their partitions form the fruit body) ....*Gautieria morchelliformis* Vitt.

Fruit body 1-5 cm wide; lining of glebal cavities rusty cinnamon; columella often indistinct; spores 12-24 × 8-12.5 μ; rusty brown in KOH.

Solitary or in clusters, late summer and early fall, often abundant after heavy early September rains but generally rare. Widely distributed.

1b. Under conifers; glebal cavities finally up to about 0.25-0.5 cm wide. Fig. 347 ....*Gautieria graveolens* Vittadini

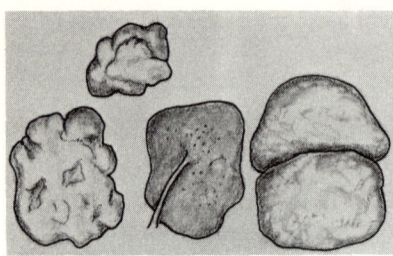

Fig. 347. *Gautieria graveolens*.

Fruit body 1-5 cm, globose or nearly so, light brown to rusty brown or pallid if very immature; columella distinct, often reaching the center of the fruit body; attached by a rhizomorph; walls of glebal cavities cinnamon at maturity; peridium absent but exposed edges of glebal plates furnished with a palisade of rusty-ochraceous (in KOH) pyriform to clavate cells; spores $15\text{-}20 \times 11\text{-}13\ \mu$, with 7-10 prominent ridges.

Solitary or in groups under spruce-fir in the western mountains, summer and early fall. This is our common western *Gautieria* and I have collected a market basket full of it in a half day's collecting in central Idaho. The odor develops as the specimens mature and is very strong as they approach old age.

RHIZOPOGON

Fruit bodies globose to variously irregular in shape, typically covered with an inconspicuous to distinct outer layer of rhizomorphs and generally lacking a distinct basal attachment; the gleba chambered and the chambers typically irregular and sinuous (use a hand lens); columella lacking or (in a few species) rudimentary; spores smooth to (rarely) very obscurely ornamented and hyaline to ochraceous to brown under the microscope; hymenium lining the chambers; basidia of various shapes, 1-, 4-, 6- or 8-spored, the spores sessile or borne on sterigmata.

Type species *R. luteolus* Fr.

This genus is more abundant in North America than anywhere else in the world, but is still in need of intensive further study.

1a. Gleba virgate ....Subg. *Rhizopogonella* 2
1b. Gleba and peridium not as above ....Subg. *Rhizopogon* p. 321....5

Subg. RHIZOPOGONELLA

2a. Clamp connections present on hyphae of the peridium 3
2b. Clamps absent and a latex present (on fresh specimens) 4
3a. Fruit body with a copious covering of rhizomorphs ....
....*Rhizopogon pachyphloeus* Zeller & Dodge

Spores $4.5\text{-}5.5 \times 2\text{-}2.5\ \mu$, ellipsoid, not amyloid; groups of enlarged cells up to $40\ \mu$ wide present in peridium; gleba rather gelatinous; peridium ochraceous isabelline (dingy ochraceous), becoming dark rusty brown.

Southeastern (New York, Carolina, Virginia and Jamaica). In soil, its tree-associate(s) remain to be determined.

3b. Fruit body surface nearly glabrous ....
....*Rhizopogon diplophloeus* **Zeller & Dodge**

Spores $4.5\text{-}5.5 \times 2.3\text{-}2.8\ \mu$, ellipsoid, amyloid when young but not when mature; peridium formed by large cells (up to 25 μ broad); gleba soon gelatinous; peridium clay-color at first becoming dark rusty cinnamon.

Western and northern in distribution (California, Oregon, Washington, Utah, Wyoming; in Canada: Northwest Territory and Newfoundland). The tree associate is not known for certain.

4a. Spores 2.5-3 μ wide; gleba vinaceous-brown when dried ....
....*Rhizopogon olivaceoniger* **Smith**

Fruit bodies 1.5-2.5 cm, brownish olive young but darkening from handling, dirt gray when dried; latex pinkish buff and sticky; odor fruity; spores 6-9 μ long, inamyloid; gleba soon gelatinized.

Under red pine (*P. resinosa*), Nova Scotia in Canada.

4b. Spores 3-4 (5) μ wide; gleba pallid at maturity ....
....*Rhizopogon olivaceotinctus* **Smith**

Fruit bodies 2-4.5 cm, yellow-brown fresh, tinged with olive as dried, epicutis of peridium with cells having yellow walls in KOH; spores 8-10 (-12) μ long; hymenium soon gelatinizing completely.

Tree associate not known; known only from northern California.

Subg. RHIZOPOGON
Key to Sections

5a. Sections of peridium mounted in KOH showing an outer thin layer (epicutis) of hyphae with dark brown walls ....
....*Sect. Villosuli* **p. 322**

5b. Not as above **6**

6a. With one or both of the following characters: (1) Spores amyloid at some stage in their development. (2) Sections of the peridium when mounted in KOH showing olive, green or bluish olive over all or in restricted areas ...*Sect. Amylopogon* **p. 327**

6b. Not as above **7**

7a. With one of the two, (or both) of the following characters: (1) The base of the spore (in optical section) with 2 prongs (base inverted cup-like). (2) Spores 3 μ or more wide and the gleba more or less fulvous at maturity when fresh ....
....*Sect. Fulvigleba* **p. 332**

7b. Spores not with basal "claws" as seen in optical section, or gleba olivaceous to olive-brown at maturity if the spores are 3 μ or more broad at maturity ....*Sect. Rhizopogon* **p. 340**

SECTION VILLOSULI

It should be noted that the color of the walls of the epicuticular hyphae is for most species a color change induced by the KOH used as a mounting medium. Sections mounted in Melzer's do not exhibit the same color changes.

Key to Species

1a. Spores 3 μ or more wide 2
1b. Spores typically less than 3 μ wide 6
2a. Spores 6-8 μ long ....*Rhizopogon gilkeyae* Smith

Fruit body 10-15 mm, unpolished, cinnamon-gray, drying cinnamon-brown, no rhizomorphs evident; peridium scaling off in patches pallid areas; with $FeSO_4$ olivaceous; gleba grayish cinnamon-buff, consistency firm but not hard; spores 6-8 $\times$ 3.3-4.2 μ, base obscurely truncate; peridium of tawny hyphae in KOH, with thick-walled hyphae over the surface but setae and flagellate hyphal ends also present; no green to olive stains anywhere in KOH.

Collected by Dr. Helen Gilkey at Corvallis, Oregon in April.

2b. Spores (7) 8-12 μ long or longer (see *R. clavitisporus* also p. 333) 3
3a. Peridium staining red when injured (on fresh young specimens) ....*Rhizopogon rogersii* Smith

Fruit body 1-2.5 cm, matted fibrillose, the fibrillose layer easily wearing away to expose pallid inner layer; presumably staining red when injured; $FeSO_4$ on epicutis olive-black; gleba not hard when dried; spores 8-10 $\times$ 2.8-3.6 (-4) μ; epicutis of peridium with some enlarged cells up to 20 μ wide and flagellate hyphal ends present; in KOH much dark green pigment in the area bordering the gleba. Wallowa County, Oregon, July.

3b. Not as above 4
4a. Subhymenium of branched filaments gelatinous in KOH ....
....*Rhizopogon zelleri* Smith

Fruit body 8-15 mm, unpolished, scurfy, color wood brown but as dried cinnamon-brown (paler where epicutis has been removed); gleba cinnamon-buff to (when mature) avellaneous, firm but not hard as dried; spores 9-12 $\times$ 3.5-4 μ; epicutis of peridium thin, flagellate hyphal ends present but no thornlike projections seen.

In duff under conifers, Oregon and Idaho, April in Oregon, July and August in Idaho.

4b. Subhymenium cellular in mature fruit bodies 5
5a. Subcutis of peridium staining dull blue on bruising in fresh material; fruit bodies 1-2.5 cm thick ....
....*Rhizopogon villescens* Smith

Fruit bodies fibrillose, dark yellow-brown ("sepia") when fresh; KOH bluish black on subcutis, $FeSO_4$ dull olivaceous; gleba dull violet around the worm holes, green in KOH but quickly fading; spores 7-10 (11) × 3-3.8 μ; epicutis of peridium with flagellate hyphal ends.

Under fir and pine, northern Idaho, July.

5b. No color change on subcutis of peridium if bruised when fresh; fruit bodies 3-8 cm thick; spores 9-12 × 3.5-4.5 μ ....
....Rhizopogon ponderosus Smith

Fruit bodies pallid becoming gray-brown, dry and fibrillose but outer fibrils easily rubbed off, on dried specimens KOH gives an olive to green stain and $FeSO_4$ stains the surface olive-black; gleba pallid becoming olive-buff, drying pale cinnamon; epicutis of peridium thin, flagellate ends present; cells of the epicuticular hyphae versiform (irregular in shape).

In duff under lodgepole and ponderosa pine, Oregon and California, October and November.

6a. Subcutis of the peridium staining blue to violet-drab on injury
.... 7
6b. Subcutis of peridium (or epicutis) not staining as above 11
7a. Spores 5.5-6.5 × 2.3-3 μ (see R. umbrinoviolascens also p. 324)
....Rhizopogon parksii Smith

Fruit bodies 1-3 cm, pallid with an overlay of dark fibrils, becoming dull brown, unpolished to loosely appressed-fibrillose, the outer layer separating to expose the pinkish ground color (which soon stains blue and finally umber), as dried showing vinaceous-brown areas between the fuscous patches; KOH on peridium inky fuscous, $FeSO_4$ dark olive; spores subellipsoid subhymenium cellular, the cell walls gelatinous at maturity; peridium with flagellate hyphal ends; subcutis a thick layer reddish in KOH on revived material.

Under sitka spruce in particular, California, Oregon and Washington. It is the most abundant Rhizopogon in the sitka spruce zone along the coast.

7b. Spores typically 6.5-8 μ long 8
8a. Fresh fruit body blackening quickly when handled ....
.... Rhizopogon collosus var. nigromaculatus
8b. Fresh fruit body staining violaceous on the subcutis where handled 9
9a. Peridium pallid becoming dark yellow-brown to dull cinnamon; gleba with russet to rusty yellow stains around worm holes ......
.... see Rhizopogon rudus in section Amylopogon p. 328
9b. Not as above 10
10a. Fruit body cinnamon-brown fresh ....
....Rhizopogon pseudovillosulus Smith

Fruit body 9-16 mm, dry, fibrillose, KOH instantly olive on peridium, $FeSO_4$ instantly olive; gleba olive brown; spores $6.5\text{-}8.5 \times 2\text{-}2.5\ \mu$; hyphae of epicutis containing many "knee-joint" cells and also flagellate hyphal ends.

Under spruce-fir with some larch present, central Idaho and northward.

10b. Fruit body violaceous-brown ("Benzo brown" to "cinnamon-drab") .... *Rhizopogon umbrinoviolascens* Smith

Fruit body 1-3 cm, dry and unpolished, lacking any reddish stains or tints; gleba olive-buff when mature; spores $6\text{-}7.5 \times 2\text{-}2.5\ \mu$; hyphae of epicutis of peridium of cells 9-15 μ wide, many inflated-versiform cells present, flagellate hyphal ends present.

Under Douglas fir and larch, eastern Washington and northern Idaho summer and fall.

11a. Lacking any olive coloration when sections of the peridium are mounted in KOH (of either fresh or dried material) 12
11b. KOH producing olive stains, these often localized 15
12a. Paraphyses (brachybasidioles) 8-12 μ wide and with yellow-brown walls (at least in locules near the peridium) ....
.... *Rhizopon brunneifibrillosus* Smith

Fruit bodies 3 cm, fibrillose, dark cinnamon-brown, darker brown with KOH, $FeSO_4$ slowly black on peridial surface; gleba firm as dried (sectioning readily); spores $7\text{-}8.5 \times 2.2\text{-}2.5\ \mu$; hyphae of tramal plates hyaline to slightly yellow-brown; subhymenium not gelatinous; epicutis of peridium with some cells up to 50 μ wide, flagellate hyphal ends rudimentary.

Eastern slope of the Cascade Mts. in Oregon and in Idaho, rare, summer and fall.

12b. Not as above 13
13a. Peridium with a dull cinnamon-brown epicutis over a subcutis which is vinaceous in dried specimens ....
.... *Rhizopogon quercicola* Smith

Fruit bodies 2-3 cm, epicutis a cinnamon-brown fibrillose layer tending to slough off in places, with only a single basal rhizomorph; gleba near cinnamon-buff as dried, soft and readily sectioned (as dried); spores $5.5\text{-}7 \times 2\text{-}2.2\ \mu$; brachybasidioles thin-walled, vesiculose to clavate; hyphae of tramal plates not gelatinous, 3-6 μ wide; subhymenium cellular; hyphae of epicutis with some cells up to 40 μ wide.

Under chinquapin oak (*Castanopsis*), October, Oregon.

13b. Not as above 14
14a. Peridium olivaceous fresh, becoming olivaceous-black ....
.... *Rhizopogon viridis* Zeller & Dodge

Fruit bodies 1-2 cm, very dark brown as dried; gleba deep olive to olive-brown (as dried); spores $6.5\text{-}8 \times 2\text{-}2.5\ \mu$; subhymenium cellular but cells developing mucilaginous wall thickenings; hyphae of epicutis in a tangled turf, thin-walled, no flagellate hyphal ends observed.

In duff under pine, northern Idaho.

14b. Peridium pallid becoming ivory, grayish brown as dried, deep reddish brown with KOH .... *Rhizopogon molallaensis* **Smith**

Fruit bodies 2.5-4.5 cm, appressed-fibrillose, becoming decorated with olivaceous to umber squamules and patches, with KOH reddish brown becoming blackish; with $FeSO_4$ faintly grayish, odor of Swiss cheese; gleba drying olivaceous; spores $5.5\text{-}7 \times 2.4\text{-}3\ \mu$; epicutis of hyphae with some cells thick-walled, no flagellate hyphal ends seen. Gregarious near Douglas fir, Oregon, November.

15a. Fresh peridium staining bister when bruised; in KOH rusty brown; wet in appearance when mature .... *Rhizopogon florencianus* **Smith**

Fruit body 1-4 cm, pallid at first, soon dingy yellow-brown, staining bister from handling, with $FeSO_4$ olive-black; gleba dingy cinnamon as dried; spores $7\text{-}9 \times 2.3\text{-}2.6\ \mu$, cells of subhymenium and of some tramal hyphae readily disarticulating; hyphae of epicutis often with flagellate hyphal ends.

Under fir and spruce, central Idaho, August.

15b. Not as above 16
16a. Subcuits of peridium vinaceous as dried, staining pink when fresh specimen is cut open 17
16b. Not staining as in above choice 19
17a. End cells of epicuticular hyphae 8-15 μ wide and clavate to cystidioid, flagellate hyphal ends absent .... *Rhizopogon subareolatus* **Smith**

Fruit body 1-6 cm, dry and unpolished, becoming areolate, pallid at first, becoming dingy vinaceous and as dried dark dingy yellow-brown (rarely with bluish fuscous areas), with $FeSO_4$ dark olive, in KOH inky black in old ones, when young staining vinaceous; gleba olivaceous drying ochraceous; spores $6\text{-}7 \times 2\text{-}2.3\ \mu$; hyphae of epicutis with some cells 8-15 μ wide.

Under pine, Oregon, during the fall rainy season.

17b. Not as above 18
18a. Spores $5.5\text{-}6.5 \times 2\text{-}2.3\ \mu$ .... *Rhizopogon mutabilis* **Smith**

Fruit body 1-3 cm, whitish, vinaceous-fuscous as dried; KOH olivaceous on cut peridium; $FeSO_4$ olive-brown; peridium of distinct fuscous-brown walled hyphae 3-8 (13) μ wide, or some cells 10-15 μ and variously shaped.

Under lodgepole pine, central Idaho, August.

18b. Spores $6.5\text{-}8 \times 2.2\text{-}2.8\ \mu$ .... *Rhizopogon hawkeri* **Smith**

Fruit body 1-4 cm, dry, wood brown to vinaceous-fuscous over a whitish ground color, changing to bright pink where injured; with $FeSO_4$ dark olive; KOH quickly pale olive; gleba nearly fuscous in age; cystidia 26-30 × 8-10 μ, projecting 10-15 μ beyond the basidia; epicutis of hyphae with versiform cells 2-11 μ wide, many setalike cells present, flagellate hyphal ends also present.

In very rotten wood, central Idaho, August.

19a. Odor pungent-fragrant on fresh material; gleba cinnamon-brown when mature .... *Rhizopogon fragrans* **Smith**

Fruit body 18 mm, subtomentose, cinnamon-brown fresh, drying russet or darker; epicutis chipping off; gleba dark cinnamon-brown; spores 6.5-8 × 2-2.8 μ; epicutis of crooked dark brown (in KOH) hyphae 4-15 μ wide, "knee-joint" cells present, flagellate hyphal ends also present.

Under spruce and fir, central Idaho, August.

19b. Not as above 20

20a. Brachybasidioles soon thick-walled; fruit bodies 8-25 mm thick .... *Rhizopogon villosulus* **Zeller**

Fruit body arising from a rhizomorph, slightly villose, bister brown when fresh and about the same as dried; $FeSO_4$ olive; KOH olive; spores 6-8 × 2-2.5 μ; epicutis of loosely interwoven hyphae with cinnamon-brown walls, very few flagellate hyphal ends present.

Under spruce and fir and Douglas fir, June to September, not rare in the Pacific Northwest.

20b. Not as above 21

21a. Epicuticular hyphae mostly thick-walled; fruit bodies wood brown as dried ...... *Rhizopogon colossus* var. *colossus* **Smith**

Fruit body 1.5-9 cm, fibrillose, pallid and gradually darkening to wood brown to dull cinnamon-brown, no color change on handling (possibly slightly more brownish); gleba pallid then olivaceous to dark olive, drying ochraceous; spores 6-7.5 × 2.2-2.7 (3) μ; epicutis poorly developed, of brown hyphae and hyphal segments (in KOH), "knee-jointlike" cells and globose cells up to 40 μ wide present, flagellate hyphal ends rare.

Cespitose-gregarious under lodgepole pine, Oregon, fall.

See also *R. colossus* var. *nigromaculatus* p. 323.

21b. Epicuticular hyphae mostly thin-walled; dried fruit bodies fuscous .... *Rhizopogon sepelibilis* **Smith**

Fruit body 1-5 cm dark fuscous; gleba pallid buff as dried, not hard; spores 6-7.5 × 2-2.5 μ, epicutis of orchraceous (in KOH) hyphae with only slightly thickened walls, the cells versiform and often cystidial (and 10-15 μ wide), greatly inflated cells up to 25 μ wide present, flagellate hyphal ends also present.

Mt. Rainier National Park, Washington, October.

SECTION AMYLOPOGON

See *R. albiroseus* (p. 341) which also has the immature spores slightly amyloid. *R. semitectus* with non-amyloid spores is also keyed here. See p. 330.

Key to Species

1a. Hyphae of tramal plates as revived in KOH containing masses of amorphous brown to cinnamon pigment; spores 6-8.5 × 3.5-4.5 μ, some of them dark violet in Melzer's .... *Rhizopogon anomalus* Smith

Fruit body 1-2 cm, dingy ochraceous, as dried cinnamon-brown or darker; gleba grayish brown when dried and consistency bone-like; hyphae of peridium mostly with dark brown content (as revived in KOH) and much amorphous material between the hyphae; in Melzer's (revived) staining some large pigment globules orange-brown.

Known from vicinity of Copeland, Idaho, in a stand of mixed conifers.

1b. Not as above 2
2a. Fresh fruit bodies with violaceous-umber stains on a dull white ground color; sections of fresh or recently dried material bright vinaceous-red in KOH; spores 7-9 × 2.6-3.2 μ .... *Rhizopogon semireticulatus* Smith

Fruit bodies 4-6.5 cm, with an over lay of numerous distinct rhizomorphs; with $FeSO_4$ on surface dark olive-brown; gleba pallid becoming grayish brown; spores very weakly amyloid to inamyloid as they reach maturity.

Under Douglas fir and larch, eastern Washington, late fall.

2b. Not as above 3
3a. Basidiocarps becoming cinnamon to gray toned with yellow or tan, as dried cinnamon to ochraceous tones evident 4
3b. Fruit body white becoming grayish fuscous to dark vinaceous-brown in drying 9
4a. Spores 6-7.5 × 2.2-2.5 μ 5
4b. Spores 7-9 × 2.8-3.7 μ 7
5a. Fruit body tan when fresh; epicutis of peridium a turf (trichodermium) which collapses in age .... *Rhizopogon griseovinaceus* Smith

Fruit body 2-3.5 cm, dry, minutely areolate, vinaceous-gray as dried; gleba olive buff as dried and very soft and friable (it crumbles easily); spores yellowish in Melzer's when mature; epicutis of peridium of hyphae 9-15 (20) μ wide, the cells often short, walls greenish in KOH at first.

Under conifers, Lane County, Oregon, October.

5b. Not as above 6
6a. Fruit body pallid, becoming brown from handling; epicutis of peridium of appressed hyphae 1-3 hyphae deep, some cells thick-walled and fulvous in KOH .... *Rhizopogon rudus* Smith

Fruit body up to 5 cm, subcutis staining bluish fuscous when bruised, olive with $FeSO_4$; some giant cells 25-75 μ scattered through the peridium.

Near Douglas fir, Priest River, Idaho.

6b. Odor strong of carmel; subhymenium and tramal plates with non-gelatinous hyphae with cells often 20-40 μ wide and readily disarticulating .... *Rhizopogon fragmentatus* Smith

Fruit body about 3 cm, peridium duplex, inner layer white, outer layer lateritious to dark brown; gleba rusty brown as dried; spores 6-8 × 3-3.7 μ, pale cinnamon in KOH; peridium of interwoven hyphae 4-15 μ wide.

Under conifers, Mt. Adams, Washington, October.

7a. Gleba dull green; peridium slowly staining red from handling .... *Rhizopogon arctostaphyli* Smith

Fruit body 2-5 cm, grayish with yellow tints, grayish ochraceous as dried; spores 7-9 × 2.8-3.5 μ, amyloid (pale blue over all); peridium lacking sphaerocysts.

Humboldt County, California.

7b. Not as above 8
8a. In Melzer's some spores dark violet over part (half) of the spore and paler elsewhere .... *Rhizopogon milleri* Smith

Fruit body 1-2.5 cm, whitish becoming cinnamon buff and drying this color; gleba pale cinnamon when young, cinnamon when mature; spores 6.5-8.5 (9.2) × 3-4 μ; peridium with subcutis red in KOH.

In a larch pine stand, northern Idaho, September.

8b. Spores weakly amyloid when young, inamyloid when mature .... *Rhizopogon salebrosus* Smith

Fruit body 1-3 cm, yellow-brown to cinnamon-brown with an overlay of vinaceous-brown rhizomorphs, $FeSO_4$ dark olive on the cutis; KOH on cut peridial surface vinaceous; spores 7-9 (10) × 2.8-3.5 (4) μ; inflated cells present in the peridium as cut ends cells.

Under fir and pine, central Idaho, August.

9a. Spores (at least some of them) dark violet in Melzer's 10
9b. Spores inamyloid or weakly but evenly amyloid 15
10a. Spores from interior chambers inamyloid; spores from chambers near the peridium strongly amyloid ....
....*Rhizopogon chamaleontinus* Smith

Fruit body 1-2 cm, white, fuscous as dried; KOH on surface olive going to black; hyphae of subhymenium with candelabra-type branching; spores 6-9 × 3-4.5 (5) μ, hyphae of peridium 5-12 μ wide.
Under conifers, Priest Lake, Idaho, September.

10b. Not as above 11
11a. Spores 5.5-6.5 (7) × 2-2.5 μ ....*Rhizopogon pedicellus* Smith

Fruit body 15 mm, white, slowly staining pinkish, dark vinaceous fuscous as dried; $FeSO_4$ staining peridium olivaceous; freshly cut gleba staining vinaceous; peridium a single layer of interwoven hyphae.
Under pine, Warm Lake, central Idaho, August.

11b. Not as above 12
12a. Fruit body 1-3.5 cm, white staining shell pink from handling; gleba green and drying bone-hard in mature specimens ....
...................*Rhizopogon atroviolaceus* Smith

Spores 6-8 × 3-3.6 μ or 7-9 × 3-4 μ, mostly dark violet in Melzer's and many minutely punctate-ornamented.
Under pine, spruce and fir mixed, central and northern Idaho, summer and fall.

12b. Not as above 13
13a. Spores 7-10 × 3.5-5 μ ....*Rhizopogon kauffmanii* Smith

Fruit body 1.5-6 cm, white, slowly fuscous from handling; with $FeSO_4$ quickly deep blue; gleba hard when dried; in mounts of the peridium in Melzer's some globules with amyloid content are present, some hyphal segments of peridial hyphae with thickened strongly amyloid segments also present.
Under conifers, Copeland, northern Idaho, September and in the Salmon River region.

13b. Spores mostly under 3.5 μ wide 14
14a. Peridium with cells up to 20 μ wide in the inner region ....
...................*Rhizopogon fallax* Smith

Fruit body 10-65 mm, white becoming fuscous, with $FeSO_4$ dark olive; with KOH on the peridium vinaceous-fuscous to inky black; spores variable in size (6-10 × 2-3.5 μ) in a single fruit body.
Under lodgepole pine, Wyoming, August and September.

14b. Peridium of hyphae 4-10 μ wide ....
...................*Rhizopogon subpurpurascens* Smith

Fruit body 1-4 cm, white overlaid with fibrils, slowly staining brownish and finally purplish red; spores variable, some with a "pistol grip" from the manner in which the apiculus is attached; consistency of the fresh fruit body distinctly rubbery.
Under lodgepole pine and alpine fir, Sawtooth Mts., Idaho and also in the Seven-Devils Mts. near Hell's Canyon, summer and fall.

15a. Spores 5.5-7.2 × 2-2.5 μ ....see *Rhizopogon pedicellus* p. 329
    Note: See *R. parksii* and *R. nitens* also as the spores may be doubtfully amyloid and the characteristic epicutis of the peridium not yet well developed.

15b. Spores longer and/or wider than in the above 16
16a. Spores 9-12 μ or longer 17
16b. Spores 6-9 (10) μ long 20
17a. Spores weakly amyloid when young; peridium dull vinaceous-brown as revived in KOH ....*Rhizopogon subbadius* Smith

    Fruit bodies 1-2.5 cm, glabrous, white, becoming overlaid with drab matted fibrils, $FeSO_4$ negative, KOH causing a dingy vinaceous stain on the surface; cut peridium pallid slowly staining brownish vinaceous (on fresh material); spores 9-12 (14) × 3.5-4.5 (5) μ.

    Under lodgepole pine, Sawtooth Mts., central Idaho, Priest River in northern Idaho, and in Wyoming.

17b. Not as above 18
18a. Spores 10-18 × 4-8 μ (see *R. clavitisporus* also p. 333) ....
    ....*Rhizopogon alkalivirens* Smith

    Fruit body 1-3 cm, pallid, in age vinaceous-brown, KOH green on peridium then black, $FeSO_4$ bluish olive; gleba firm but sectioning easily (in dried material); peridium with giant cells up to 30 μ wide and with thickened walls.

    Under conifers, Boulder Creek, near New Meadows, central Idaho.

18b. Spores smaller than in above choice 19
19a. Hymenium soon becoming entirely gelatinized ....
    ....*Rhizopogon subgelatinosus* Smith

    Fruit body 8-30 mm, white, the fibrils becoming wood brown (gray-brown), $FeSO_4$ olive on the peridium, KOH dark olive on peridial surface; gleba bone hard when dry; spores (8) 9-12 × (2.5) 3-4 μ, inamyloid; hyphae of peridium mostly with thickened translucent walls in KOH.

    Under stands of mixed conifers, Salmon River area of Idaho, August.

19b. Hymenium not gelatinizing ......*Rhizopogon semitectus* Smith

    Fruit body 2-2.5 cm, white, with fine rhizomorphs, surface fibrils gradually cinnamon-brown, where handled staining vinaceous-brown; $FeSO_4$ olive-fuscous on surface, KOH greenish fuscous on surface but reddish near the cavities; gleba white then gray, in age cinnamon-brown, cartilaginous, rubbery and hard when dry; peridium with cells 15-20 μ in the epicutis, their walls yellow in KOH when fresh and greenish as revived, spores inamyloid.

    Under cedar and hemlock, Priest Lake, northern Idaho, September.

20a. Spores 6-7 × 2.5-3 μ ....
.... *Rhizopogon tephroleuca* **Harrison & Smith**

Fruit bodies 0.8-2.5 cm, pallid beneath slightly olivaceous rhizomorphs, darkening and appearing watery when handled, often beaded with yellowish drops; peridium up to 1 mm thick (and preserving the shape of the fruit body after the gleba has gelatinized), KOH on surface olivaceous, the inner layer vinaceous; $FeSO_4$ on surface olivaceous-fuscous to a gray to black reaction; peridium with some cells inflated to 20 μ in cross section.

Under ponderosa pine and other conifers, New Mexico.

20b. Not as above 21
21a. Peridium white when young, gradually becoming overlaid with vinaceous-brown fibrils and in age dark vinaceous-brown over all .... *Rhizopogon subcaerulescens* **Smith**

This is a cartilaginous, common species very difficult to identify. The spores are 7-9 × 2.3-3.5 μ. One variety stains green on the peridium with $FeSO_4$ (var. *viridescens*), others stain olive to bluish and the type variety usually stains slowly to somewhat bluish on handling. Var. *subpannosus* in the variant which becomes entirely dark vinaceous-brown in age from an epicutis of colored fibrils (but these are not dark brown in KOH). This collective species is found throughout the Pacific Northwest.

21b. Not as above 22
22a. Under pinyon pine, New Mexico; peridium staining yellowish when broken .... *Rhizopogon pinyonensis* **Harrison & Smith**

Fruit body 2-5 cm, white with vinaceous-brown fibrils over the surface; spores 7-9 × (3) 3.2-4 (4.5) μ, amyloid; gleba very gelatinous-cartilaginous and drying very slowly.

22b. Not as above 23
23a. Spores 7-9 × 2.5-3 μ .... *Rhizopogon idahoensis* **Smith**

Fruit body 1-6 cm white, slowly becoming wood brown to somewhat fuscous, where injured slowly staining dingy lilac-vinaceous, $FeSO_4$ on peridium greenish then inky black; KOH staining the surface purplish to vinaceous-fuscous; gleba olivaceous-gray; hyphae of peridium 3-9 μ wide; spores evenly and distinctly amyloid when mature.

In duff under conifers in areas where Douglas fir is present, common at times in Idaho and eastern Washington, late summer and fall.

23b. Spores 3-4.5 μ wide 24
24a. Spores mostly inamyloid when mature ....
.... *Rhizopogon vestitus* **Harrison & Smith**

Fruit bodies 6-14 mm, whitish then dingy cinnamon-brown and finally duller (wood brown), droplets often forming on surface, $FeSO_4$ olive-fuscous, KOH olive to olive-black; gleba drying to a hard consistency; spores 8-11 (12) × 3-4 μ; peridium with some hyphal cells up to 35 μ wide in cross section.

Under Ponderosa pine, New Mexico.

24b. Spores 7-9 × 3-4 μ, walls distinctly but weakly amyloid at maturity ....*Rhizopogon ellenae* Smith

Fruit bodies 1-6 cm, white, when handled slowly becoming avellaneous to fuscous; $FeSO_4$ olive in peridium; KOH on peridium muddy vinaceous-brown; gleba pallid then dark bister, drying olive-brown; subhymenium of inflated cells broader than the basidioles; hyphae of peridium 4-8 μ wide, local groups of short cells up to 14 μ wide also present.

Under mixed conifers, Idaho.

SECTION FULVIGLEBA

Key to Species

1a. Spores 9-18 μ long, often irregular shape 2
1b. Spores rarely up to 11 μ long and mostly oblong to ellipsoid or ovoid 10
2a. Groups of spores hyaline in KOH; KOH on the fresh peridium yellowish then reddish 3
2b. Not as above 4
3a. Spores 9-12 × 3.8-5 μ ....
....*Rhizopogon canadensis* Harrison & Smith

Fruit body up to 1.5 cm, whitish with cinnamon-buff areas and as dried cinnamon-buff over all, with an obscure overlay of fine rhizomorphs; peridium thin and transparent; gleba with a watery juice when fresh, as dried cinnamon-buff and sectioning readily (not hard); subhymenium of inflated cells 12-30 μ wide.

Under conifers, Sheep Lake, near Nelson, B. C. Canada.

3b. Spores 11-14 × 4.5-6.5 μ ....
....*Rhizopogon hysterangioides* Smith

Fruit bodies 1-3 cm, nodulose to irregular, dry, dull white, yellowish in the depression, no rhizomorphs present; gleba of a dry firm consistency; $FeSO_4$ slowly pale bluish on the peridium; spores yellowish in Melzer's; basidia clavate to subglobose above a wavy pedicel; cystidia none; peridium compactly interwoven hyphae 3-8 μ wide, no sphaerocysts present.

In duff under spruce and fir, central Idaho, August.

4a. Young gleba pallid but changing to dark yellow-brown when cut; peridium not staining red when injured ....
....*Rhizopogon variabilisporus* Smith

Fruit body 2-4 cm, attached by a cluster of basal rhizomorphs, surface rough and fibrillose, whitish with the fibrils soon dingy vinaceous-brown, drying blackish brown; gleba concolorous with peridium in old fruit bodies; spores 12-20 × 5-8 µ, versiform; subhymenium cellular; peridium with inflated cells scattered or in groups, the filamentous tissue reddish in KOH; epicuticular hyphae hyaline in KOH.

In conifer duff July and August, Idaho, rare.

4b. Not as above 5
5a. **Fruit body white with yellowish areas and staining dingy carmine where bruised** ...*Rhizopogon hymenogastrosporus* Soehner

Fruit body drying dull brown, with a tuft of hairs at the base and a few reddish brown rhizomorphs near the apex; peridium very thin; gleba white then dingy yellow and then toned greenish yellow, when dried gray-greenish brown; basidia with 3-5 sterigmata; spores 8-10 × 5-6 µ and numerous *Hymenogaster*-like spores 10-13 × 7-9 µ also present, the latter versiform.

Known from Europe.

5b. Not as above 6
6a. Gleba some shade of yellow before maturity 7
6b. Gleba pallid to gray or olivaceous before maturity 8
7a. **Gleba rusty brown at maturity; spores reddish cinnamon in Melzer's** .... *Rhizopogon subclavitisporus* Smith

Fruit body 1-2 cm, dry and fibrillose, whitish then rose-purplish and finally dingy clay color, dull vinaceous as dried, KOH red on young specimens, garnet brown on old ones; spores 9-13 × 4.5-7 µ, base truncate and cupped; becoming thick-walled; brachybasidioles with ochraceous walls in KOH; epicutis with giant cells to 40 µ, scattered in it (their walls 2-3 µ thick), some epicuticular hyphae fulvous in KOH and ochraceous flagellate hyphal ends also present.

In duff under conifers, northern Idaho, July.

7b. Not as above .... see *Rhizopogon ventricosporus* p. 342
8a. **KOH on fresh peridium red to vinaceous (no olive tints present on fresh or on revived sections); fresh fruit body staining vinaceous where bruised** .... *Rhizopogon griseogleba* Smith

Fruit body 10-15 mm, dry, nearly glabrous, with scattered rhizomorphs, pale to dark wood brown; $FeSO_4$ on peridium dark olive; gleba grayish brown, drying drab; consistency hard and bonelike; spores versiform and variable in size (12-18 × 6-12 µ), possibly many of them conidia.

Dug from ashes of an old campfire, Valley County, Idaho.

8b. Not as above (KOH giving both olive and red stains) 9
9a. **Spores 11-18 × 5-9 µ** .... *Rhizopogon clavitisporus* Smith

Fruit body 10-25 mm, covered with a thin coating of cinnamon-brown fibrils and these easily pulling away from the subcutis which dries dingy vinaceous-fuscous, $FeSO_4$ on surface of peridium olive-gray to (as dried) grayish buff, firm but not hard when dried; epicutis of peridium of dark brown hyphae (in KOH) and flagellate hyphal cells present.

Under conifers (ponderosa pine mostly), Idaho and Oregon, July to November.

9b. Spores 9-12 × 3-4.5 μ ... see *Rhizopogon semitectus* Smith p. 330

Note: *R. ponderosus*, *R. zelleri* and *R. superiorensis* may key out here also.

10a. Spores as viewed on an optical section, apparently with two basal projections 11
10b. Spores merely truncate at base or basal scar not evident 19
11a. Basidiocarp bright yellow to orange-yellow 12
11b. Fruit body duller in color 15
12a. Gleba fuscous in age; spores 6-8 × 3-3.5 μ ....
.... *Rhizopogon cokeri* Smith

Fruit body 0.5-1 cm, bright sulphur yellow, lemon chrome or brighter, not changing on injury, $FeSO_4$ no reaction, KOH no reaction; brachybasidioles with amorphous inclusion as revived in KOH; epicutis of peridium a weak trichodermium of long narrow filaments.

Under white pine, North Carolina, Nova Scotia and Idaho, summer, apparently not rare in northern Idaho.

12b. Not as above 13
13a. Spores 8-11 (12) × 3-4.5 μ .... *Rhizopogon superiorensis* Smith

Fruit body 10-15 mm, bright orange-yellow, KOH on fresh peridium vinaceous-red going to rusty brown, $FeSO_4$ olive-black; gleba streaked dingy yellow, subhymenium of narrow interwoven hyphae; peridium of interwoven hyphae 4-8 μ wide, much reddish debris around them in KOH amounts.

Under red pine, Lake Superior area, Michigan, August.

13b. Spores smaller 14
14a. Fruit body deep chrome to orange mottled mahogany red, drying bay-red over all .... *Rhizopogon lowii* Smith

Fruit body 1.5-2 cm, gleba bone hard as dried; spores 7-9 × 3-4 μ; peridium of interwoven hyaline hyphae 3-8 (14) μ broad, amorphous pigment between them magenta red in KOH.

In soil in a mixed woods, North Carolina, October.

14b. Fruit body pure white then yellow to dull yellow not staining red when bruised ....
........*Rhizopogon atlanticus* Coker & Dodge in Coker & Couch

Fruit body 1-4 cm, dingy yellow-brown in drying, odor fragrant; spores 7-9 × 3.5-4 μ; subhymenium of parenchyma-like cells about 2 deep; peridium of hyaline smooth hyphae 3-6 μ diam., thin-walled; smooth; epicuticular region of more compactly interwoven hyphae.

Under pine, South Carolina and Florida.

15a. Fruit body white then vinaceous-red; spores (5.5) 6-7 (8) × 3-4 (4.5) μ ....*Rhizopogon vinicolor* Smith

Fruit body 1-3 cm, surface dry and appressed fibrillose; $FeSO_4$ on peridium merely slightly olive-brown, KOH staining it purplish; gleba becoming dark olive-brown; subhymenium cellular; peridium a thin layer of interwoven fibrils; interior hyphae reddish in KOH, in the epicutis the hyphal walls cinnamon-buff in KOH.

Under conifers, Priest Lake area, Idaho, July.

15b. Not as above 16

16a. Tramal plates gelatinizing before or soon after spores mature; a grayish epicutis slowly developing over the white to vinaceous ground color ....*Rhizopogon gelatinosus* Smith

Fruit body 6-12 mm, white but soon flushed vinaceous-tan, then pale orange-cinnamon, developing a thin overlay of grayish fibrils; with KOH reddish to rusty-brown, with $FeSO_4$ olive becoming blackish; gleba finally dark yellow-brown; spores 7-8.5 × 3-4.5 μ; peridium of interwoven hyhae 3-6 μ wide, lacking vesiculose-inflated cells; as revived in KOH most of the layer remarkably clean.

In duff under jack pine, Luce County, Michigan, August.

16b. Not as above 17

17a. Gleba in mature specimens staining fuscous when specimen is cut open; mounts in Melzer's (fresh or dried) not showing amyloid globules ....*Rhizopogon olivaceofuscus* Smith

Fruit body 1-3.5 cm, white becoming pale tan then progessing to clay color, often with reddish areas, slowly staining reddish brown to reddish from handling on immature stages; KOH staining cutis garnet brown; with $FeSO_4$ olive-black, odor pungent in age; spores 6.5-7.5 × 3.3-4 μ, pale cinnamon in KOH; peridium a single layer of appressed hyphae 3-9 μ wide, ochraceous-tawny or paler in KOH (as revived), no inflated cells observed.

Under mixed conifers (spruce, fir and pine), Priest River district, northern Idaho, not uncommon in the area.

17b. Not as above 18

18a. **Peridium where handled slowly staining inky-fuscous but with an intervening red stage; mounts in Melzer's (fresh or revived) showing amyloid globules** ....*Rhizopogon inquinatus* **Smith**

Fruit bodies about 2 cm, whitish to pallid buff, FeSO$_4$ olive to blackish on the peridium; gleba olive, when cut olive-brown to blackish; odor none; spores 6.5-7.5 (8) × 3-3.5 µ, yellowish in KOH singly; peridium of appressed hyphae 3-5 µ wide, lacking greatly inflated cells, amyloid globules in mounts often large (up to 30 µ wide).

Under cedar-hemlock, Priest River district, Idaho, June.

18b. **Fresh peridium not staining where injured; amyloid granules absent in mounts of fresh or dried material** ....
....*Rhizopogon pinicola* **Smith**

Fruit bodies 8-27 mm, unpolished to silky, snow white, slowly yellowish tan, finally near snuff brown (pale dingy date brown); KOH no reaction on peridium of white (young) stage, lilaceous on older ones; FeSO$_4$ no reaction; spores 6-7 × 3-3.5 µ, yellow-brown in KOH; peridium of narrow (3-5 µ) hyaline hyphae, hyaline to yellowish globules present in mounts in Melzer's.

Under lichens in openings of a mature stand of Norway Pine (*P. resinosa*), northern Michigan, late summer.

19a. Spores 3.8-5 µ wide 20
19b. Spores 2-3.5 (-4) µ wide 26
20a. Spores 8-10 × 4-5 (6) µ 21
20b. Spores 6-8 µ long 25
21a. **Gleba pallid when young, soon cadmium yellow when cut** ....
....*Rhizopogon lutescens* **Smith**

Fruit bodies 1-2.5 cm, some with basal attachment, pallid at first, soon flushed buff, finally dingy ochraceous over some areas; with FeSO$_4$ slowly black; with KOH dingy purplish but on ochraceous areas more rusty brown; spores in groups near orange-ochraceous in KOH; peridium of interwoven hyphae 2-6 µ wide, lacking greatly inflated cells, those in the interior of the peridium rusty-vinaceous in KOH.

In a rotten conifer log, central Idaho, July and August.

21b. Not as above 22
22a. **Gleba orange-buff, when dried buff with a tint of reddish in the ochraceous ground color** ....
....*Rhizopogon armeniacus* **Harrison & Smith**

Fruit body 1-2 cm, color apricot to apricot buff, drying dingy vinaceous-brown; staining strongly vinaceous when handled; KOH vinaceous-lilac on peridium and FeSO$_4$ slowly fuscous; gleba brittle as dried, with a short columella; spores hyaline in KOH, 8-10 × 4-5

μ; peridium separable, of hyphae 6-15 μ wide, at surface first arranged in a loose turf but this collapsing; the cells short but not inflated, end cells 12-17 μ wide, ovate to oval.

Under pinyon pine, New Mexico, October.

22b. Not as above 23
23a. Gleba hard as bone when dried and not easily sectioned; peridial surface wet when fresh and soon dingy brown from handling .... *Rhizopogon subcinnamomeus* Smith

Fruit body 1-2.5 cm, pale grayish tan finally near cinnamon-brown; $FeSO_4$ olive-black on surface; KOH dark garnet red; gleba pallid to croceus to dark rusty brown finally; spores 7-10 × 4-5 (6.5) μ, truncate at base, groups in KOH strongly cinnamon-colored; peridium of a loosely tangled outer layer of hyphae 3-5 μ wide having dark cinnamon pigment incrustations; subcutis (and central region) clean, red in KOH, no nests of sphaerocysts observed.

In duff under conifers, Priest Lake area of Idaho, July.

23b. The dried gleba sectioning readily; peridial surface not as above 24
24a. Peridium whitish, when handled staining lilaceous to purplish and soon this color over all .... *Rhizopogon parvulus* Smith

Fruit body 7-14 mm, red on application of KOH, olivaceous with $FeSO_4$; gleba white then yellowish and in age fulvous; spores in groups in KOH dull rusty brown; peridium with central area dull magenta as revived in KOH, no greatly inflated cells noted.

Under Douglas fir and larch, northern Idaho, July.

24b. Peridium pale ochraceous; soon rusty brown from handling .... *Rhizopogon ochraceisporus* Smith

Fruit body 2-3.5 cm, with $FeSO_4$ slowly dark olive, on the gleba soon dark olive, KOH instantly dark rusty brown on the peridium; spores 7-9 × 8.8-4.5 μ, ochraceous in KOH when fresh; peridium of appressed interwoven hyphae yellow in KOH, 4-12 μ wide, much-branched, fascicles of short crooked hyphae form a loose epicutis.

In duff under fir, Idaho and Washington, summer and fall.

25a. Odor farinaceous; basidia with 4 prominent sterigmata often with pale cinnamon walls in KOH ....
.... *Rhizopogon exiguus* Zeller & Dodge

Fruit body 2-10 mm, white with ochraceous mottling, becoming pale date brown; peridium a single layer of compactly interwoven hyphae bright rusty cinnamon in KOH.

Under hemlock, Pierce County, Washington.

25b. Basidia 6-8 spored; spores sessile; odor not distinctive ....
.... *Rhizopogon diabolicus* Smith

Fruit body 1-3 cm, dry, whitish then flushed vinaceous but soon ochraceous tones pervading over all, KOH dull lilaceous on white stage, rusty brown on old specimens, $FeSO_4$ no reaction on white stage, olive-black on brown specimens; gleba yellowish becoming russet; spores 6.3-8.4 × 3.5-4.5 μ, truncate; peridium with an epicutis of loosely interwoven hyphae incrusted with dull cinamon pigment in KOH, the hyphae 4-9 μ wide; with a central region of closely interwoven hyphae and an innermost zone in which the glebal cavities form, the latter region heavily pigmented as seen in Melzer's.

Under conifers, Seven-Devils Mts., Idaho, summer.

26a. Spores (7) 8-10 × 2.3-3.5 (4) μ 27
26b. Spores 6-8 μ long 30
27a. Cuticle of peridium duplex, the inner layer of hyphae with thickened (1.5 μ) walls olivaceous-brown in KOH ....
.... *Rhizopogon inversus* **Harrison & Smith**

Fruit body to 2.5 cm, pale date color, with a basal cluster of dark brown rhizomorphs; surface blackish brown with KOH, with $FeSO_4$ olive-fuscous; gleba blackish brown at maturity (fresh), rather hard as dried; basidia with olive to olive-brown walls near the peridium, paler in inner cavities; epicutis of peridium of loosely interwoven hyphae 8-17 μ wide, many of the cells short and some inflated to 25 μ, walls ochraceous to pale tawny in KOH.

Solitary under mixed conifers, New Mexico, September.

27b. Peridium not as above 28
28a. Spores 6-10 × 2-2.5 μ ....*Rhizopogon thaxteri* **Zeller**

Fruit body about 1 cm, white staining reddish when fresh; gleba dark rusty brown as dried; peridium of hyphae 1.5-3 μ wide, pale cinnamon in KOH; context hyphae 4-8 μ wide.

Kittery Point, Maine.

28b. Spores wider than in above choice 29
29a. Fruit bodies cinnamon when fresh, soon darker brown where touched and finally blackish; cut peridium when fresh staining red with KOH ....
................................*Rhizopogon cinnamomeus* **Harrison & Smith**

Fruit body 1-2 cm, soon dark olive-fuscous with $FeSO_4$; gleba dark brown and tough but sectioning easily when dried; spores 7-9 × 3-4 μ, yellowish singly in KOH; subhymenial hyphae filamentous; peridium of appressed interwoven hyphae (3) 4-10 (14) μ wide, the layer reddish in KOH.

Under mixed conifers near Balfour, British Columbia, Canada, July.

29b. Fruit body 1-1.5 cm, yellowish when young, then ochraceous buff, finally brownish, not changing color from handling; KOH lilac on the surface of the peridium, $FeSO_4$ merely dull buff (negative); gleba as dried blackish brown; almost crumbly, easily sectioned...*Rhizopogon singularis* **Harrison & Smith**

Spores 7-9 × 3-3.5 μ truncate to cupped; subhymenium almost absent; peridium a layer of interwoven hyphae not appreciably inflated.

Under ponderosa pine, New Mexico, September.

30a. Fruit body 1-1.5 cm, white, drying pallid, tending to become rimose; staining reddish slightly then brownish where handled, purple with KOH, $FeSO_4$ soon drab ....
....*Rhizopogon amoenus* **Harrison & Smith**

Spores 6-7 × 2.8-3.2 μ, truncate at base, ochraceous in KOH; peridium with an epicutis of hyphae 3-5 μ wide, their content ochraceous, walls hyaline to ochraceous in KOH; hyphae of context 3-8 μ wide with some cells 12-18 μ wide, the walls swelling (in KOH) to 0.4-1.25 μ thick.

Under ponderosa pine, New Mexico, October.

30b. Not as above 31

31a. Gleba when fresh dark vinaceous-brown, as dried hard and olive-brown ....*Rhizopogon columbianus* **Harrison & Smith**

Fruit body about 2 cm, pallid becoming dingy brown, then with a slight cinnamon tint; slightly vinaceous with KOH, with $FeSO_4$ no reaction; spores 6.5-8 × 3-3.8 μ, truncate, pale cinnamon in KOH; peridium of appressed hyphae 4-9 μ wide, cells short to long but none greatly inflated; epicutis merely of appressed hyphae.

Under Douglas fir and ponderosa pine, near Nelson, British Columbia, Canada, summer, Harrison.

31b. Not as above 32

32a. Fruit body staining red from handling ....
....*Rhizopogon vesiculosus* **Smith**

Fruit body 1-2.5 cm, dry, white becoming dingy saffron, KOH red on the epicutis, $FeSO_4$ fuscous; gleba white to pale yellow to (at maturity) blackish brown, as dried dark yellow-brown; spores 6-6.5 × 3.2-3.6 μ, ovate-truncate, yellowish in KOH peridium of hyphae 5-10 μ wide and with scattered yellow-brown (when young) inflated cells up to 50 μ wide in the layer.

Under lodgepole pine, eastern Washington and adjacent Idaho, July.

32b. Basidiocarp not staining readily when bruised ....
...........................see *Rhizopogon olivaceofuscus* **Smith p. 335**

SECTION RHIZOPOGON
Key to Subsections

1a. Spores 3-5 µ wide .... Subsect. *Rhizopogon* p. 341
1b. Spores 1.6-3 µ wide .... Subsect. *Angustispori* p. 357

Subsect. Rhizopogon
Key to Stirpes

1a. Peridium red when injured .... Stirps *Rubescens* p. 341
1b. Peridium not staining red .... Stirps *Luteolus* p. 343

Subsect. Angustispori
Key to Series & Stirpes

1a. Fruit body developing yellow tones at some stage in the development of the fruit body .... Series *Lutei* p. 347
   (a) Staining red where injured .... Stirps *Vulgaris* p. 352
   (b) Not staining red from injury ... Stirps *Ochraceorubens* p. 347
1b. Fruit bodies variously colored but not yellow. Series *Versicolores* p. 357..2
2a. Fruit body pale to bright peach-pink to salmon pink or white, often fading to whitish, at times pinkish ochraceous, rhizomorphs salmon-buff to dingy vinaceous-buff ....
.... Stirps *Subsalmonius* p. 358
2b. Not as above 3
3a. Fruit body dark cinnamon fresh, blackish brown from handling and black and shiny as dried ... Stirps *Brunneiniger* p. 357
3b. Not as above 4
4a. Spores 5-6.5 µ long .... Stirps *Bacillosporus* p. 359
4b. Spores 6-8 µ long 5
5a. Fruit body staining red where injured .... Stirps *Evadens* p. 359
5b. Fruit body not staining as above 6
6a. Fruit body grayish vinaceous to vinaceous-brown ....
.... Stirps *Maculatus* p. 357
6b. Not as above 7
7a. Fruit body white to whitish and drying gray to whitish ....
.... Stirps *Albidus* p. 358
7b. Fruit bodies variously colored but not as above ....
.... Stirps *Brunnescens* p. 357

Subsection Rhizopogon
Stirps Rubescens

1a. Gleba exuding a hyaline viscous latex when cut; odor resembling that of rotten eggs (with a strong sulphur component) ....*Rhizopogon succosus* Smith

Fruit body about 1 cm thick, pale cream color becoming reddish and drying bay-brown; taste sweetish; gleba as dried very hard; spores $7\text{-}10 \times 3\text{-}4.2\ \mu$; hymenium soon gelatinized; peridium with red amorphous material (in KOH) between the hyphae, some sphaerocysts $12\text{-}20\ \mu$ wide scattered in the layer, most hyphae $3\text{-}8\ \mu$.

In soil, North Carolina.

1b. Not as above 2
2a. Fruit body lacking yellow color at all times in its development 3
2b. Fruit body with a yellow stage in its development 5
3a. $FeSO_4$ on fresh surface olive-black; spores $8\text{-}10 \times 3.5\text{-}4\ \mu$ ($9\text{-}11 \times 5\ \mu$) ....*Rhizopogon pseudoroseolus* Smith

Fruit body 10-15 mm, white slowly becoming vinaceous, with KOH bright rose-color, drying vinaceous-red; peridium of loosely arranged hyphae $5\text{-}15\ \mu$ wide, encrusting debris of hyphae mineral red in KOH.

Under lodgepole pine, central Idaho, July.

3b. Not as above 4
4a. Fruit body white when young, soon entirely rose color ....*Rhizopogon roseolus* Corda sensu A. H. Smith

Fruit body 1-2 cm, KOH intensifying the rose color; gleba finally olive; spores $6.5\text{-}8 \times 2.8\text{-}3.2\ \mu$; peridium of appressed hyphae $4\text{-}10\ \mu$ wide, in KOH the entire layer diffused with rose pigment, as revived vinaceous-brown.

Under lodgepole pine, Idaho, July.

4b. Fruit body dull white to brownish at maturity ....*Rhizopogon albiroseus* Smith

Fruit body 1-3 cm, stained areas soon fading to white again, color finally dingy grayish; KOH red on white surface, gleba buffy brown, in Melzer's bluish gray; spores $7\text{-}9 \times 2.8\text{-}3.3\ \mu$, weakly amyloid when immature; peridium of appressed-interwoven hyphae red in KOH, sections clean (not much debris present), some cells short and inflated to $12\text{-}15\ \mu$ (these are not sphaerocysts).

Under alpine fir, northern Idaho, July.

5a. Spores 9-12 × 3-5 μ or larger 6
5b. Spores 7-10 × 2.8-3.5 (4) μ 7
6a. Spores 9-12 × 3-5 μ ....*Rhizopogon abietis* Smith

Fruit body 1-4 cm, with a basal rhizomorph; white, soon lemon yellow to more ochraceous; KOH vinaceous to reddish brown on the surface; gleba becoming dark olive; peridium of appressed interwoven thin-walled non-gelatinous hyphae 5-10 μ wide, with many inflated cells to 15 μ or more broad; epicutis typically a turf with elements having clavate terminal cells to 14 μ wide.

In duff in stands of alpine fir (some spruce also present), Idaho and Wyoming, summer.

6b. Spores 9-13 × 6-8 μ .... *Rhizopogon ventricosporus* Smith

Fruit body 1-3 cm, appressed fibrillose, ochre-yellow, peridium near saffron yellow when cut; gleba grayish becoming honey yellow; hyphae 4-8 μ wide, some cells to 12 μ or more wide, groups of inflated cells present next to the gleba.

Under spruce and white-bark pine, Seven-Devils Mts., western Idaho, August.

7a. Fruit body white to yellowish to olive and with blackish stains at maturity; spores 7-9 × 2.8-3.5 μ ....
....*Rhizopogon subaustralis* Smith

Fruit body 1-3 cm thick, FeSO$_4$ on surface dark olive; color of dried specimens cinnamon buff to dingy cinnamon, retaining blackish area in drying, gleba dingy tawny when mature; peridium a thick layer of interwoven hyphae 3-12 μ wide, no groups of inflated cells observed.

Under pine, North Carolina, July.

7b. The yellow stage more pronounced than in the above species, lacking blackish stains 8
8a. Gleba drying to the hardness of bone, dark yellow-brown at maturity ....*Rhizopogon ochroleucoides* Smith

Fruit body 1-5 cm, matted-fibrillose; FeSO$_4$ on peridium olivaceous; KOH dull vinaceous-red; cut peridium red on young specimens but croceous on old ones; spores 7-10 × 2.8-3.3 μ; peridium with an inner layer dark cinnamon in KOH from amorphous pigment, some cells 15 μ or more wide; outer layer yellowish in KOH.

Under conifers, Idaho and Washington, summer and fall.

8b. Gleba drying fragile and easily sectioned, olive-tawny to olive-buff. The "Rubescens Complex" keys here. These are the commonest members of the genus in North America and the most difficult to identify.

Rhizopogon luteorubescens stains red and the stained portions fade back to the original color more or less. It has a strong olive FeSO$_4$ reaction.

NON-GILLED FLESHY FUNGI

Rhizopogon rubescens var. *rubescens* (Fig. 348) has spores 8-10 × 3.2-4.2 μ and the spores are subfusoid in shape.

Rhizopogon rubescens var. *pallidimaculatus* has the gleba in dried specimens with paler yellow streaks and spots causing a mottled appearance.

Rhizopogon rubescens var. *rileyi* has spores 6.5-8 × 2.5-3 μ and lacks a positive $FeSO_4$ reaction.

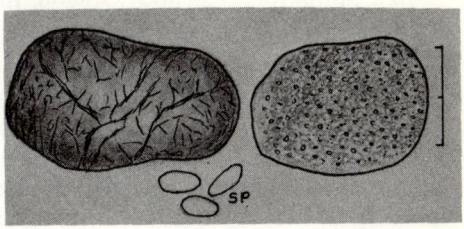

Fig. 348. *Rhizopogon rubescens*.

Rhizopogon rubescens var. *ochraceus* the fruit bodies have a basal attachment and the spores are more oblong than fusoid.

STIRPS LUTEOLUS

1a. Cystidia 40-80 × 7-12 μ abundant at least in the glebal cavities near the peridium ....*Rhizopogon pannosus* Zeller & Dodge

Spores 7-9 × 3-3.5 μ, pale cinnamon in groups as seen in KOH, basal scar distinct; cystidia narrowly fusoid-ventricose to subcylindric, hyaline in KOH; hymenium in Melzer's orange-brown to orange-red; peridium of one layer of hyphae, the hyphae 4-16 μ wide, tawny to pale cinnamon in KOH.

Mariposa County, California.

1b. Not as above 2
2a. Fruit body golden yellow with inner layer brick red (when fresh); gleba not hard as bone as dried ....
....*Rhizopogon brownii* Smith

Fruit body 8-15 (30) mm, staining rusty brown where bruised; rusty brown as dried; gleba olive-buff; spores 7-10 × 3-4.5 μ, elliptic to subfusoid; peridium a thick layer with a dark red-brown outer zone (as revived in KOH) and a paler innermost zone (note the difference in color in the zones from the fresh to dried condition).

In a pine woods, Livingston Parish, Louisiana.

2b. Not as above 3
3a. Spores 5.5-7.5 μ long 4
3b. Spores 7-10 μ long 6
4a. Giant inflated cells present in the peridium, the latter sublateritius as dried; spores 6-7.5 × 3.5-4 μ ....
....*Rhizopogon subalpinus* Smith

Fruit body 1-2.5 cm, dingy vinaceous-red as dried, $FeSO_4$ olive-black (on dried specimens); gleba firm but not hard (as dried), cinnamon buff; subhymenium cellular; peridium with some thick-walled brown hyphae over the surface but not forming a layer; KOH showing rusty brown pigment deposits in area near the gleba.

In a campground, central Oregon, July.

4b. Not as above 5

5a. Spores 5-5.6 × 2.8-3.5 μ; fruit bodies pale cinnamon-brown as dried .... *Rhizopogon oregonensis* Smith

Fruit body 2-7 cm, ochraceous-tawny to cinnamon-brown, $FeSO_4$ or KOH not reacting on dried peridium; gleba pinkish buff as dried (young) but umber brown (old), as dried friable and readily sectioned; peridium a single layer, the hyphae 4-10 μ wide, some inflated cells up to 15 μ wide present, in KOH with yellow-brown pigment in the cell sap.

In duff under conifers, southwestern Oregon.

5b. Spores 6-7.5 × 3.3-3.5 μ; fruit body blackish as dried ....
.... *Rhizopogon reaii* Smith

Fruit body 1.5-3 cm, pale tan at first, more or less covered by blackish rhizomorphs; $FeSO_4$ (on dried specimens) olivaceous but the stain soon fading, KOH not leaving a permanent stain; gleba olive-brown when mature, consistency as dried almost crumbly; odor rather strong (Rea); peridium of hyphae 4-11 μ wide, some inflated cells present but none in groups as sphaerocysts.

Epigeous on ground under oak, Santa Barbara, California.

6a. Fruit body when fresh staining olive where handled; gleba dark olive and hard as bone when dried ....
.... *Rhizopogon subolivascens* Smith

Fruit body about 15 mm thick, dull rusty ochraceous when fresh; with KOH dingy vinaceous (on fresh material), $FeSO_4$ slowly dark olive (no reaction on dried specimens); gleba dark olive when mature; spores 7-8.5 × 3.5-4 μ, ochraceous in KOH, in Melzer's rusty red (where collected along the hymenium); peridium of hyphae 4-10 μ wide, no sphaerocysts seen.

In duff under conifers (spruce, fir and pine), McCall, central Idaho, July.

6b. Not as above 7

7a. Peridial hyphae in the epicutis densely coated with minute colorless granules (mount in KOH) .... *Rhizopogon baxteri* Smith

Fruit bodies 5-12 mm, clay color at first, then flushed pinkish pale-cinnamon to ochraceous-cinnamon, yellow-brown as dried; staining olivaceous with $FeSO_4$ on dried specimens, with KOH dull fulvous; gleba firm, cinnamon-buff to dull cinnamon; odor of leeks when fresh; spores 7-9.5 (10.5) μ × 3-3.8 μ; subhymenium cellular; peridium of hyphae 3-6 μ wide, the layer pale tawny in KOH, lacking distinctly inflated cells.

In a nursery of pine seedlings, Ann Arbor, Michigan.

7b. Not as above 8
8a. **Fruit body pale yellow, becoming yellow-brown from handling** 9
8b. Not staining as in above choice 10
9a. **Gleba hard and firm-cartilaginous when fresh** ....
....*Rhizopogon brunneicolor* Smith

Fruit body 1-2 cm, $FeSO_4$ applied to surface of fresh specimens staining them pale gray, KOH on the yellow surface staining it cinnamon-brown; gleba yellow-brown when fresh and mature; spores $7\text{-}9 \times 2.8\text{-}3.8\ \mu$; peridium in sections (sub. mic.) with an olive-black layer next to the gleba in $FeSO_4$ (the same layer reddish in KOH); epicutis ochraceous in KOH, hyphae $4\text{-}12\ \mu$ wide but more distinctly inflated cells also present.

Under conifers, summer, Idaho, not common.

9b. **Gleba soft and almost sticky when fresh** ....
....*Rhizopogon molligleba* Smith

Fruit body 1-2.5 cm, ocher-yellow, yellow-brown from handling or this color overall finally, as dried near cinnamon-brown in places; $FeSO_4$ plus ethanol quickly dark oilve on fresh surface; gleba dark yellow-brown, with a cheese-like consistency in dried mature specimens; spores $7.5\text{-}9 \times 2.8\text{-}3.3\ \mu$; subhymenium cellular; peridium of appressed-interwoven hyphae, with rusty brown debris as revived in KOH, some hyphae up to $15\ \mu$ wide but groups of sphaerocysts are lacking.

Under alpine fir and white-bark pine, Heaven's Gate Ridge, Seven Devils Mts., Hell's Canyon, Idaho, August.

10a. **Fruit body when young covered by a heavy white tomentum; gleba blackish brown and bone hard as dried** ....
....*Rhizopogon oswaldii* Smith

Fruit body 2-5.5 cm, date brown (rather dark), honey yellow around the base, where covered by debris olive-green to greenish brown, when dried blackish brown; gleba olive when fresh and mature, oozing a viscous liquid when cut; odor earthy then pungent-disagreeable (finally of spoiled garlic); spores $7.5\text{-}9 \times 3\text{-}3.6\ \mu$; peridium separable from gleba and 2-layered, the white outer layer (on young specimens) dingy ochraceous in KOH, lower layer fuscous-brown in KOH, hyphae $4\text{-}11\ \mu$ wide, no greatly inflated cells present.

Under mixed conifers, rare, Washington and Oregon, fall.

10b. Not as above 11
11a. **Gleba marked out into distinct areas by tramal plates; spores $7\text{-}11 \times 2.9\text{-}3.7\ \mu$, obscurely angular to variously shaped** ....
....*Rhizopogon piceus* B. & C. sensu Coker & Couch

Fruit body about 1.5 cm, glabrous, greenish yellow becoming dingy yellow and then blackish from handling, rhizomorphs present;

gleba hard as dried, brownish yellow fresh, toughish, elastic; odor described as "suggesting walnuts or wine"; spores olivaceous individually, many obscurely angular to subtriangular; peridium of hyphae 3-5 μ thick, interhyphal spaces filled with masses of rusty brown to yellow-brown amorphous pigment.

Under pine in the winter, North Carolina.

11b. Not as above 12
12a. Fruit body pale yellow fading to whitish in age; peridium 2-layered .... *Rhizopogon luteoalbus* Smith

Fruit body 1-3 cm, glabrous beneath scattered rhizomorphs, dingy Isabella-color as is that of the gleba which shows through the peridium, staining olivaceous with $FeSO_4$, in KOH brownish and ethanol staining it vinaceous, not changing color when bruised; gleba crumbly as dried; spores 7-9 (10) $\times$ 2.8-3.5 μ; subhymenial elements filamentous; peridium 2-layered as revived in KOH, epicutis pale sulphur to hyaline, inner layer rusty in KOH, epicutis pale sulphur to hyaline, inner layer rusty brown, lacking inflated cells or sphaerocysts.

Under lodgepole pine, central Idaho, summer and fall.

12b. Not as above 13
13a. Peridium one-layered; gleba bone hard as dried; rhizomorphs copious over the peridium when fresh; spores 7-10 $\times$ 2.5-3.5 μ
....*Rhizopogon luteolus* Fr.

Fruit body 1-4 cm, dry, fibrillose, yellow-ochre to golden tawny, rhizomorphs often tawny at first, $FeSO_4$, KOH, or ethanol—none producing a significant color change; gleba olivaceous at maturity; spores 7-10 $\times$ 2.5-3.5 (4) μ; peridium of appressed hyphae 5-12 μ wide, vinaceous as revived in KOH, slowly fading to fulvous, inflated cells, both scattered and in pockets, present.

Solitary in duff under fir trees, Idaho, summer, rare.

13b. Not as above 14
14a. When dried the gleba spotted with pallid yellowish areas and its consistency not bone hard; spores 6.5-9 $\times$ 3-4 μ ....
....*Rhizopogon laetifulvus* Smith

Fruit body 1-2.5 cm, fibrillose, rhizomorphs rare, yellowish to canary yellow, dull pale yellow as dried, not staining when injured, KOH on dried specimens dull vinaceous, $FeSO_4$ slightly olivaceous, ethanol staining peridium vinaceous; spores 6.5-9 $\times$ 3-4 μ; peridium with an epicutis of appressed greenish yellow to hyaline hyphae 4-12 μ wide, both long and short cells present and some inflated; subcutis rusty brown in KOH.

14b. Gleba not speckled and not hard as dried; fruit bodies small (mostly 2-5 mm); spores 8-10 $\times$ 3-3.5 μ ....
.................................*Rhizopogon parasiticus* **Coker & Totten**

Fruit body light ochraceous salmon to warm buff; spores ochraceous in KOH, oblong to subfusoid; peridium of loosely arranged hyphae 2-5 μ wide and with some yellowish amorphous pigment in the layer between the hyphae.

On pine roots, North Carolina. There is a question as to whether it is parasitic on the pine roots.

SECT. RHIZOPOGON
Subsect. Angustispori
Series Lutei
Stirps Ochraceorubens

1a. Hyphae of tramal plates thick-walled as revived in KOH 2
1b. Hyphae of tramal plates thin-walled (under 0.5 μ thick) as revived in KOH 3
2a. Mature gleba yellow-brown; peridium clay colored fresh ....*Rhizopogon argillaceus* Smith

Fruit body 1-4 cm, with numerous white rhizomorphs; bister to olive-brown as dried; gleba exuding hyaline droplets when cut; spores 6.5-8 $\times$ 2.8-3 μ; peridium white in section (fresh) and not appreciably discoloring, hyphae 8-12 μ wide, walls ochraceous in KOH, 2-3 layered, pockets of sphaerocysts present in the lower layer (the cells up to 20 μ wide), the layer purplish in places in KOH.

In duff under conifers, Idaho and Washington, August and September.

2b. Mature gleba olive-gray; peridium olive-yellow ....*Rhizopogon isabellinus* Smith

Fruit body 1-3 cm, Isabella color, dry and fibrillose, retaining this color in drying, not staining red where injured; KOH on surface yellow-brown, $FeSO_4$ olivaceous; gleba as dried firm but not hard; spores 5.5-7 $\times$ 2.3-3 μ ellipsoid; peridium of appressed-interwoven hyphae olive-yellow in KOH, the layer clean.

3a. Peridium subviscid fresh, staining orange to reddish brown before becoming black ....*Rhizopogon nigrescens* Coker & Couch

Fruit body 2-6 cm, bright yellow, soon russet where exposed and finally blackish; in KOH purplish (burnt orange on dried specimens in 2 percent KOH), $FeSO_4$ dark olive; gleba clay color becoming olive and drying dull fulvous; spores 6-7.5 $\times$ 2-2.5 μ; peridium of hyphae 4-10 μ, interwoven, appressed, no inflated cells seen, the layer bright red in Melzer's after a short time.

Under pines, all year, common southeastern States.

3b. Not as above 4

4a. Fruit body dull orange, drying vinaceous-brown; epicuticular hyphae with ochraceous incrustations ....
.... *Rhizopogon aurantiacus* Smith

Fruit body 1-2.5 cm, dry, rhizomorphs dull brown, blackening in drying; KOH on surface slowly reddish to reddish brown, $FeSO_4$ gray to blackish, not staining when cut or bruised; gleba honey yellow; spores 6.5-8 × 2.2-2.5 μ; peridium with an epicutis of ochraceous incrusted hyphae, inner layer red in KOH, no sphaerocysts present. Gregarious under spruce and fir, central Idaho.

4b. Not as above 5
5a. Spores 5.5-6.5 × 2-2.5 μ (see *R. sordidus* also p. 351) 6
5b. Spores 6-10 × 2.2-3 μ 9
6a. Fruit body typically with a basal short rooting group of rhizomorphs; giant inflated cells present in the peridium ....
.... *Rhizopogon subradicatus* Smith

Fruit body 3-9 cm, rhizomorphs yellowish to cinnamon-buff in age clay-color; ground color lemon yellow to dingy sulphur, fading to cinnamon-buff, not staining where injured, with KOH on surface becoming yellow-brown, with $FeSO_4$ slightly olive yellowish; gleba dry, stained ochraceous around the worm holes, grayish olive to olive-brown when mature; peridium of appressed interwoven hyphae 3-10 μ wide, inflated cells to 40 μ wide present.

Under ponderosa pine, Roosevelt Lake, Washington, November.

6b. Not as above 7
7a. Sybhymenium showing candelabra-type branching ....
.... *Rhizopogon willamettensis* Smith, nom. nov.[*]

Fruit body up to 5 cm, copiously covered with cinnamon-brown rhizomorphs over a dingy ochraceous ground color; not changing color where injured; KOH brick red then red-brown on suface, $FeSO_4$ slowly dark olive-brown; gleba olive-buff; peridium of appressed hyphae 5-12 μ wide, not showing any sphaerocysts.

Under conifers, Williamette River, Oregon, fall.

7b. Not as above 8
8a. $FeSO_4$ staining surface of peridium dark green to inky black ....
.... *Rhizopogon libocedri* Smith

Fruit body 1-3 cm, grayish tan fresh, drying dingy cinnamon, KOH staining it a darker brown; gleba pale tan; peridium of hyphae 4-10 μ wide forming a very thin layer, ochraceous-tawny in KOH as revived, clean, no sphaerocysts present.

Under *Libocedrus decurrens*, Del Norte County, Calfornia.

8b. $FeSO_4$ staining fruit body pale olivaceous slowly ....
.... *Rhizopogon flavofibrillosus* Smith

Fruit body 3-5.5 cm, pallid with straw yellow fibrils at first, at maturity greenish yellow with rose colored areas, attached by a basal cluster of rhizomorphs; KOH on fresh peridium dull purplish red,

[*] *Rhizopogon brunneofibrillosus* Smith, 1968. *Elisha Mitchell Sci. Soc.* 84: 275.

sectioned fresh peridium not staining; gleba olivaceous; peridium with an epicutis at first a trichodermium of short branched hyphae with end cells 26-40 $\times$ 5-9 μ, subclavate, and thin-walled; subcutis of interwoven hyphae reddish in KOH as revived (from a dissolved pigment), scattered groups (cut ends of rhizomorphs) of larger cells present.

Under Douglas fir and ponderosa pine, central Idaho, July.

9a. **Peridium a single thick layer of somewhat pseudoparenchymatous cells** .... *Rhizopogon sipei* Smith

Fruit bodies 3-9 cm, pallid to dingy tan becoming blackish brown; gleba dingy tan as dried; spores 6-7.5 $\times$ 1.8-2.2 μ, basal scar distinct; large oleiferous hyphae present in the tramal plates; peridium with dense masses of interhyphal pigment yellowish brown in KOH.

Under Douglas fir, McKenzie River Valley, Oregon.

9b. Not as above 10
10a. **Peridium russet where bruised, readily separable in flakes** ......
.... *Rhizopogon separabilis* Zeller

Fruit body 1.5-4 cm, white to yellowish, with vinaceous spots, becoming pale yellow, drying a dingy vinaceous-brown, gleba buffy-citrine; odor of raw potatoes to subfarinaceous; spores 6-8 $\times$ 2.5-3 μ; peridium in KOH fulvous in outer zone, nearly hyaline near gleba, with many inflated cells to 20 μ, most hyphae (in the colored zone) 3-7 μ wide.

Under lodgepole pine, Oregon.

10b. Not as above 11
11a. **Dried fruit body with a lemon buff ground color overlaid by blackish rhizomorphs; spores 7-7.5 $\times$ 2.5-3 μ** ....
.... *Rhizopogon fuscorubens* Smith

Fruit bodies 1-3 cm, $FeSO_4$ on ochraceous areas staining them olive; gleba olivaceous in age; brachybasidioles thin-walled; subhymenium cellular; tramal plates of non-gelatinous hyphae; peridium of rhizomorphs interwoven with much-branched hyphae, as revived in KOH magenta to fuscous-red, the hyphae 4-12 μ wide, no sphaerocysts present.

Known from Oregon.

11b. Not as above 12
12a. **Spores 7-9 $\times$ 1.8-2.3 μ, rod-shaped; peridium lacking sphaerocysts; rhizomorphs inconspicuous** ....
.... *Rhizopogon burlinghamae* Smith

Fruit body 2-4 cm, reddish tawny as dried, with $FeSO_4$ on dried specimen no reaction; gleba pale tan as dried, consistency firm but not hard (as dried); spores on short sterigmata; peridium of appressed interwoven hyphae 3-8 μ wide, no sphaerocysts seen, sections revived in KOH fulvous at first but slowly becoming clean as the debris goes into solution.

Under pine (?), Pacific Grove, California.

- 12b. Not as above 13
- 13a. Not staining brown when handled 14
- 13b. Soon staining brown when handled 17
- 14a. KOH soon staining fresh peridium rusty brown ....
....*Rhizopogon alpestris* Smith

Fruit body 1-3.5 cm, pallid beneath rhizomorphs at first, slowly becoming dull ferruginous and finally dull brown as dried (in silica gel), dingy vinaceous as dried over heat; rhizomorphs inconspicuous as dried; $FeSO_4$ on surface of peridium slowly gray to blackish; gleba finally dark yellow-brown; spores 6-8 $\times$ 2.3-3 μ; peridium a thin layer of appressed hyphae dark reddish brown in KOH fresh and dark magenta as revived, many hyphal cells inflated somewhat but sphaerocysts lacking.

Under conifers (spruce-fir), central Idaho, August.

- 14b. **KOH staining fresh peridium red to ferruginous or scarcely staining it at all** 15
- 15a. **Columella distinct in fresh specimens** ....
....*Rhizopogon arenicola* Smith

Fruit body 1.5-2.5 cm, bright yellow overlaid with brown rhizomorphs, not staining when injured; KOH on cuticle maroon red darkening to bay-brown, $FeSO_4$ giving no significant reaction; gleba olive-gray when mature; spores 6-8 $\times$ 2.2-2.5 μ; subhymenium cellular; peridium of rhizomorphs and separate interwoven hyphae, red in KOH.

Under lodgepole pine, Priest Lake, northern Idaho, fall.

- 15b. **Columella lacking, fruit body white then pale ochraceous then slowly lateritius; KOH on peridium ferruginous to carmine red** 16
- 16a. **Fruit body slowly becoming lateritious with some yellow still showing in age; KOH on fresh specimens ferruginous** ....
....*Rhizopogon sublateritius* Smith

Fruit body 1-6.5 cm, rhizomorphs present over surface and often a cluster at the basal attachment, white then yellow and finally lateritious over much of surface, not changing color where bruised; KOH on surface slowly ferruginous, $FeSO_4$ slightly olive-yellow but if ethanol is added quickly olive; gleba olive-gray at maturity; spores 5.5-8 $\times$ 2-2.3 μ; peridium of interwoven appressed mostly hyaline hyphae 4-10 μ wide, some groups of cells present, the cells up to 18 μ broad, in the epicuticular zone the hyphae walls tawny to brick red in KOH and also in Melzer's, interior of peridium clean.

Under ponderosa pine, Oregon and Washington and Idaho, fall.

- 16b. **Fruit body slowly becoming ochraceous; spores 6-8.5 $\times$ 2.5-3 μ** ....*Rhizopogon monticola* Smith

Fruit body 2-5 cm, often with dingy lilaceous to reddish stains at time of collection (but not staining soon after injury), more or less covered with yellowish to clay-colored rhizomorphs; KOH on surface carmine red, $FeSO_4$ olivaceous slowly; peridium a thin layer of appressed hyphae as an epicutis, this layer clean and hyaline to yellowish in KOH, subcutis dull red with KOH and amorphous interhyphal debris present (clean in KOH when fresh), many hyphal cells inflated but no groups of sphaerocysts present.

In duff in spruce-fir zone, central Idaho, late summer.

17a. Fruit body at first orchraceous, overlaid with brown rhizomorphs; hyphal incrustations and interhyphal debris magenta in KOH ....*Rhizopogon ochraceorubens* Smith

Fruit body 2-8 cm, golden yellow to tawny or in age russet, often tending to stain fulvous where injured, as dried and in contact with naphthalene (in the herbarium) vinaceous-red to vinaceous-brown; peridium tending to slough off in patches, $FeSO_4$ on surface greenish to dark olive, KOH slowly reddish brown; gleba olive to olive-brown; spores 6-8 × (1.7) 2-2.5 (3) μ, subhymenium cellular; peridium of rhizomorphs incorporated in a layer of appressed hyphae; hyphal incrustations and interhyphal debris vinaceous-red in KOH, some cells inflated to 20 μ but no pockets of sphaerocysts seen, ground hyphae (excluding those of the rhizomorphs) 3-10 μ wide.

Under lodgepole pine, summer and fall, Idaho, Washington and Oregon, a common species in the Northwest.

17b. Not as above—mostly without conspicuous rhizomorphs 18
18a. Cut surface of fresh peridium staining saffron yellow ....
....*Rhizopogon ochraceobrunnescens* Smith

Fruit body about 15 mm, ocher-yellow, staining brown from handling, KOH dingy reddish brown on surface, $FeSO_4$ brownish; gleba at maturity olive-gray, hard when dry; spores 6.5-7.5 × 2.5-3 μ; peridium 2-layered, the epicutis of hyphae 4-10 μ wide and ochraceous in KOH, subcutis (inner layer) red in KOH, interhyphal material rusty brown.

In conifer duff, Idaho, rare.

18b. Not as above 19
19a. Spores 6.5-7.5 × 2.2-2.5 μ; pockets of inflated cells present in the peridium ....*Rhizopogon sordidus* Smith

Fruit body 1-3.5 cm, very few rhizomorphs evident, yellow-ochre fresh, soon dingy brown from handling, dark dingy brown as dried; KOH on surface pinkish cinnamon and soon fading; $FeSO_4$ no reaction; peridium when cut with inner layer staining red; gleba finally dingy yellow-brown; not hard to section when dry; peridium with an epicutis of appressed-interwoven hyphae 3-8 μ wide, inner layer with heavy concentration of yellow-brown pigment and debris.

Under ponderosa pine eastern Washington and adjacent Idaho, July.
19b. Not as above 20
20a. Surface of fruit body staining yellow-brown with KOH ....
.... *Rhizopogon olivaceoluteus* Smith

Fruit body 1-2.5 cm, dull greenish yellow, wet to the touch and matted-fibrillose, soon dull brown where handled, with KOH dull yellow-brown to dull cinnamon; gleba hard as bone when dried; spores 7-9 × 2.6-3 μ; peridium of appressed interwoven hyphae 4-10 μ wide, some enlarged cells up to 15 μ but no nests of sphaerocysts seen.

Under alpine fir, Gisborne Mt., Priest River Exp. Forest, Priest River, Idaho, July.
20b. Surface of basidiocarp red in KOH when fresh 21
21a. FeSO$_4$ no reaction on fresh peridium; gleba bone hard when dried .... *Rhizopogon luteoloides* Smith

Fruit body 1-3 cm, yellow-ochre fresh, quickly staining yellow-brown at maturity (dull cinnamon as dried); spores 7-9 × 2.5-3 μ; peridium with an epicutis of hyphae 4-12 μ wide, the cells often inflated, the layer pale ochraceous in KOH; the lower layer rusty brown in KOH, most cells somewhat inflated.

Under white bark pine, Seven Devils Mts., Idaho.
21b. FeSO$_4$ quickly olive-black on peridium; gleba firm but as dried sectioning readily (not hard) ....
.... *Rhizopogon argillascens* Smith

Fruit body 1-3.5 cm, pale grayish tan, slowly yellow-brown from handling dingy clay color as dried; attached basally by a cluster of rhizomorphs, staining reddish slightly on subcuticular layer; KOH dark red on surface; gleba dingy yellow-brown; spores 6-8 × 2.3-3 μ; peridium 2-layered, the inner with inflated cells in poorly defined areas and staining heavily in KOH; outer layer of appressed hyphae 3-10 μ wide, walls pale ochraceous in KOH and little interhyphal debris present.

Under lodgepole pine, eastern Washington and northern Idaho, July.

STIRPS VULGARIS

1a. Spores 10-13 × 2-2.5 μ .... *Rhizopogon cylindrisporus* Smith

Fruit body 3-5 cm, ochraceous over all, rhizomorphs fairly numerous, peridium separable in patches, FeSO$_4$ no reaction, KOH a dark red-brown; gleba olive-buff to yellow-brown; basidia 2- and 4-spored; peridium similar to that of *R. ochraceorubens* (red in KOH, many rhizomorphs incorporated in the layer).

In duff, central Idaho, October.
1b. Spores shorter 2

2a. Fresh fruit bodies subviscid to lubricous 3
2b. Fresh fruit bodies with an essentially dry fibrillose surface 5
3a. Peridium staining orange to reddish and then black from handling .... see *Rhizopogon nigrescens* p. 347
3b. Not as above 4
4a. FeSO$_4$ on peridium dark olive ...*Rhizopogon butyraceus* Smith

Fruit body 1-3 cm, rich ochre-yellow, surface subviscid to wet; with KOH dull vinaceous; gleba of minute chambers, dark olive in age; firm when dried but not hard; spores 7-8.5 × 2-2.5 μ; peridium of appressed non-gelatinous hyphae 4-12 μ wide, short cells present in the broader hyphae, vinaceous-red in KOH in outer layer, a narrow hyaline (in KOH) inner layer present, some cells in it up to 18 μ wide, lower layer red in Melzer's.

In a Douglas fir area in the duff, Valley County, Idaho, July and in the Seven Devils Mountains.

4b. FeSO$_4$ not causing a color change on the peridium ....
....*Rhizopogon udus* Smith

Fruit body 1-3 cm, lubricous, rich ochre-yellow, inner layer of peridium staining red when cut, surface red-brown in KOH; odor fragrant; gleba olive-brown, hard like bone as dried; spores 7-8 × 2.5-3 μ; peridium of appressed hyphae 8-12 μ wide but some cells up to 23 μ wide, walls yellowish in KOH, incrusting material along the hyphae of the inner layer.

Under spruce and pine, Idaho, summer.

5a. KOH on fresh peridium causing no color change ....
....*Rhizopogon defectus* Smith

Fruit body 1-3.6, cm dingy ochraceous, soon red when bruised but finally brownish, when dried dingy ochraceous with vinaceous areas, glabrous (free of rhizomorphs) except for a basal tuft, FeSO$_4$ slowly faintly olivaceous, columella short (8 mm more or less) but distinct; spores 6.5-8 × 2.2-2.7 μ; peridium of appressed hyphae 4-9 (-15) μ wide, large oleiferous hyphae up to 15 μ wide also present, in sections of fresh material in KOH the outer layer of hyphae (epicutis) is clean; the inner layer red to red-brown in KOH due to amorphous interhyphal debris and masses of pigment, lacking distinct groups of sphaerocysts.

Under mixed conifers including lodgepole pine, northern Idaho, July.

5b. KOH on fresh peridium causing a color change 6
6a. KOH staining peridium brown (see *R. sordidus* also p. 351)..7
6b. KOH staining peridium lilac to red 8
7a. Pockets of enlarged cells present in lower zone of peridium ......
....*Rhizopogon ochroleucus* Smith

Fruit bodies 2-6 cm, pallid, slowly yellow, drying ocher-buff, staining pink slightly when injured; FeSO$_4$ no reaction on surface when fresh, olivaceous on dried peridium; gleba olivaceous fresh, dingy ochraceous as dried; spores 6-8 × 2.3-3 μ; peridium one-layered, of appressed interwoven hyphae 8-15 μ but with pockets of larger cells near the gleba, yellow near the surface and fulvous in the interior of the layer.

Under conifers, late summer and fall, Idaho and Oregon.

7b. Peridium not showing pockets of enlarged cells ....
.... *Rhizopogon subcitrinus* Smith

Fruit body 8-15 mm, no obvious rhizomorphs present, dull ochre-yellow, slightly pink if injured, drying olive-buff, $FeSO_4$ merely brownish; gleba dark olive when mature and bone hard when dried; spores 7.5-9 × 2.5-3 μ; peridium of hyphae 3-9 μ wide, the layer dull rusty brown in KOH, many cells short and irregular and also enlarged at the septa.

Warm Lake, central Idaho, under ponderosa pine, August.

8a. Fruit body apricot color fresh; brachybasidioles with 1-2 highly refractive globules revived in KOH ....
.... *Rhizopogon subcroceus* Smith

Fruit body 5-30 mm, rhizomorphs fine and darker in color than the fibrillose surface, sectioned peridium (fresh) staining apricot-salmon; $FeSO_4$ dark olive on revived sections; gleba dark olive-brown mature; spores (5.5) 6-7 (8.5) × 2-2.7 μ, tramal plates of hyphae 2.5-5 μ wide but some cells up to 10 μ and versiform; peridium of hyphae 3-5 (10) μ wide, hyaline to ochraceous in KOH fresh, some cells in lower zone 15 μ or more broad (note that cut ends of some hyphae are the same width), with very little interhyphal debris or pigment as revived in KOH.

Gregarious under pine; near New Meadows, central Idaho.

8b. Not as above 9
9a. Peridium lacking groups of inflated cells in the interior zone but individual cells may be inflated 10
9b. Peridium showing groups of inflated cells in the inner region of the lower layer 15
10a. Gleba cheesy when fresh, bone-hard as dry ....
.... *Rhizopogon deceptivus* Smith

Fruit bodies 8-20 mm, white and cottony, then cream color or yellower to ochraceous, $FeSO_4$ on surface dark olive-brown, with KOH pale dingy vinaceous; gleba dark sepia; spores 6-7.5 × 2.6-3 μ; epicutis of fresh peridium a weak trichodermium, the hyphae 4-9 μ, the layer vinaceous-brown revived in KOH; some cells barrel-shaped and about 15 μ broad.

Under conifers, summer, Idaho, not rare.

10b. Gleba when fresh cartilaginous, when dried sectioning readily
....11

11a. Fruit bodies with a basal cluster of rhizomorphs; with copius pigment in the peridium as revived in KOH ....
................................*Rhizopogon vulgaris* (Vitt.) M. Lange

Fruit body up to 4 cm, cream color to ochraceous and often yellowish brown where exposed; rhizomorphs brownish; gleba pallid then olive-gray, odor slight; spores $5.5\text{-}8 \times 2\text{-}2.6$ μ, many subfusoid; peridium of appressed hyphae, no pockets of vesiculose cells seen, in KOH finally fulvous near the surface and nearly hyaline toward the gleba.

Under mixed conifers, Idaho, apparently rare.

11b. Not as above 12
12a. Hymenial elements 4-6 μ wide, mostly narrowly clavate ....
....*Rhizopogon cusickiensis* Smith

Fruit body 10-15 mm, ochre-yellow, KOH on surface reddish, $FeSO_4$ olivaceous; rhizomorphs mostly basal; gleba white then honey-tan, fairly hard as dried; spores $7\text{-}9$ $(10) \times 2.2\text{-}2.8$ (3) μ; peridium of interwoven hyphae 3-8 (12) μ wide, scattered pockets of inflated cells noted, as revived in KOH rusty cinnamon near the gleba.

Under Douglas fir, July, Cusick, eastern Washington.

12b. Hymenial elements 6-11 μ broad 13
13a. Fruit bodies salmon buff to apricot-buff to pallid, with vinaceous-buff rhizomorphs over the surface ..see *R. subsalmonius*
13b. Not as above .... p. 358 14
14a. Fruit body 1-6 cm, yellow and as dried covered with brown rhizomorphs (see *R. sublateritius* the immature stages also p. 350) ....*Rhizopogon occidentalis* Zeller & Dodge

Fruit body whitish at first, near lemon yellow at maturity, peridium staining red when cut, surface staining yellow to orange or reddish brown slowly on handling, $FeSO_4$ on dried peridium olive; gleba olive drying cinnamon-buff; spores $5.5\text{-}7 \times (2)$ $2.3\text{-}2.6$ (3) μ; peridium one-layered, of appressed hyphae 3-8 μ wide; oleiferous hyphae present, also inflated hyphal cells 10-20 μ but not in groups.

Under mixed conifers, Idaho, Oregon and California.

14b. Basidiocarps pale olive-buff to olive-buff as dried; peridium up to 2 mm thick when fresh ....
..............................*Rhizopogon pachydermus* Harrison & Smith

Fruit bodies 1.5-5 cm, ochraceous-buff to apricot-buff, sections of peridium blackish when mounted in KOH, with $FeSO_4$ olive-fuscous, red in Melzer's; gleba honey yellow to olive-buff; spores $6\text{-}7 \times 2\text{-}2.5$ μ; peridium of appressed interwoven hyphae 4-12 μ wide, the inner two thirds greenish hyaline in KOH, outer layer near amber brown; no sphaerocysts observed.

Under pinyon pine, near Santa Fe, New Mexico, October.

15a. Fruit body usually with a basal cluster of rhizomorphs; peridium separable at maturity (see *R. argillascens* also p. 352) .... *Rhizopogon pseudoaffinis* Smith

Fruit body 1-4 cm, snow white and cottony, becoming yellowish and where injured purplish red, with $FeSO_4$ slowly pale olivaceous, with KOH plus ethanol vinaceous; gleba olive yellowish mature; spores 6.5-8 × 2.5-3 μ; subhymenium cellular; peridium soft at first, the hyphae 4-11 (20) μ wide, groups of inflated cells present with a colored zone in KOH which is vinaceous in fresh specimens and rusty brown as revived.

Under spruce and fir, west-central Idaho, summer, uncommon.

15b. Not as above 16
16a. Gleba pinkish where cut or bruised ....
.... *Rhizopogon couchii* Smith

Fruit bodies 2-6 cm, unpolished, $FeSO_4$ on peridium no reaction; rhizomorphs few to lacking, white to yellow to brownish and in drying showing blackish areas; gleba white then olivaceous, drying pale tan, staining pink in fresh sectioned specimens; spores 5.5-7 × 2.2-2.5 μ; peridium a single layer of appressed interwoven hyphae 3-10 μ wide, many with intracellular pigment but interhyphal pigment also present, red in KOH in freshly dried material, tawny in herbarium specimens after a few years; some enlarged cells scattered in the layer.

Under pine, southeastern states and northern Michigan, usually abundant when it fruits.

16b. Gleba not staining when cut 17
17a. Spores 5-6.5 μ long; epicutis of peridium in the form of a trichodermium .... see *Rhizopogon flavofibrillosus* p. 348
17b. Spores 6-9 μ long; epicutis not a trichodermium 18
18a. Gleba olive to olive-brown when fresh (and mature); cut peridium staining reddish ....
.... see *Rhizopogon rubescens* var. *rileyi* p. 343
18b. Gleba gray (avellaneous) when fresh and mature; cut peridium staining ochraceous to pinkish ochraceous ....
.... *Rhizopogon luteoalboides* Smith

Fruit body 1-3 cm, staining pinkish where handled but stain soon fading, wax-yellow to ochre-yellow, duller as dried; KOH pinkish on fresh cutis, $FeSO_4$ dull brown but add ethanol and it goes to black; gleba dingy ochraceous as dried; spores 7-9 × 2.4-3 μ; peridium of a layer of ochraceous interwoven hyphae 4-12 μ wide as an epicutis, a rusty brown lower layer (as revived in KOH) of hyphae 8-18 μ wide, and some inflated cells present in it as well as oleiferous hyphae 8-14 μ wide.

Under alpine pines and fir and spruce, Seven-Devils Mts., western Idaho, summer.

SUBSECT. ANGUSTISPORI

Series Versicolores
Key to Stirpes

1a. Fruit body pale to bright peach-pink to salmon-pink or white, often fading to whitish, at times pinkish ochraceous; rhizomorphs salmon-buff to dingy vinaceous-buff .... Stirps *Subsalmonius* p. 358
1b. Not as above 2
2a. Basidiocarp dark cinnamon fresh, blackish brown from handling and black and shiny as dried .... Stirps *Brunneiniger*
Only one species: *Rhizopogon brunneiniger* Smith

Fruit body 1-3 cm, glabrous and shiny, dark fulvous fresh, attached at base to a single rhizomorph or a group; gleba white then yellow to yellowish olivaceous, hard when dried and near clay-color; peridium a single layer of closely interwoven hyphae having coagulated blackish content (no olive or green color in mounts revived in KOH); no sphaerocysts seen.

Under alder and hemlock, Oregon, rare.

2b. Not as above 3
3a. Spores 5-6.5 μ long .... Stirps *Bacillosporus* p. 359
3b. Spores 6-8 μ long or longer 4
4a. Fruit body staining red where injured ... Stirps *Evadens* p. 359
4b. Fruit body not staining as above 5
5a. Fruit body grayish vinaceous to vinaceous-brown ....
.... stirps *Maculatus*
Only one species: *Rhizopogon maculatus* Zeller & Dodge

Fruit body 1-2 cm, dark vinaceous-brown as dried and mottled with pallid patches where peridium has sloughed off, fine rhizomorphs present and vinaceous-brown as dried; gleba grayish when mature; hard and bone-like in consistency when dried; spores 7-9 × 2-2.5, yellowish in Melzer's; peridium as revived in KOH with an orange-brown layer near the gleba, outer region yellowish to brownish.

In sand under conifers, California, spring.

5b. Not as above 6
6a. Fruit body white to whitish and drying gray to whitish ....
.... Stirps *Albidus*
6b. Not as above (variously colored) .... Stirps *Brunnescens*
Only one species: *Rhizopogon brunnescens* Zeller

Fruit body small, 10-15 mm, white to pinkish, yellow-fulvous to cinnamon-brown in drying; gleba white to slightly buff; spores 6.5-8 × 2.5-3 μ; peridium duplex; epicutis of dark brown interwoven hyphae; inner layer of lighter brown prosenchyma and pseudoparenchyma (Zeller). As dried the gleba is bone-hard and difficult to section, and no epicutis is evident.

In conifer duff, Mt. Shasta, California, July.

STIRPS SUBSALMONIUS

One collective species is included but five apparently distinct variants have been recognized and are keyed out as follows:

1a. Injured places on peridium lacking a color change, KOH pinkish lilac on parts of fresh peridium which are pink to salmon before testing ....
.......................*Rhizopogon subsalmonius* var. *subsalmonius* Smith
1b. Not as above 2
2a. Basidiocarp surface staining pinkish at least slightly when injured 3
2b. Not staining as above 4
3a. Some pockets of enlarged cells present in the peridium; sections of peridium revived in KOH with debris (interhyphal) in the epicuticular zone; spores somewhat dextrinoid ....
.............................*Rhizopogon subsalmonius* var. *similis* Smith
3b. Peridium lacking pockets of inflated cells ....
.............................*Rhizopogon subsalmonius* var. *persicinus* Smith
4a. KOH slowly lilac-gray on peridial surface ....
.............................*Rhizopogon subsalmonius* var. *griseolilascens* Smith
4b. KOH causing no color change on the fresh peridium ....
.............................*Rhizopogon subsalmoius* var. *roseitinctus* Smith

This collective species is very common at times in the mountains of Idaho in the spruce-fir zone after heavy rains in August.

STIRPS ALBIDUS

1a. Gleba when dry hard and when sectioned rather crumbly (not like bone); odor when fresh unpleasant (with a strong sulphur component) .... *Rhizopogon pseudoalbus* Smith

Fruit body 1-2.5 cm, few rhizomorphs present, no appreciable color change when cut or injured by rubbing, KOH pink on fresh surface, $FeSO_4$ olive; gleba olive-brown, gelatinous; spores $6-7 \times 2-2.3$ μ; peridium a clean layer in KOH (or Melzer's), hyphae 5-12 μ wide, appressed-interwoven, lacking groups of sphaerocysts.

In spruce-fir stands, central Idaho, summer.

1b. Fruit body white, drying pallid, loosely enveloped by numerous rhizomorphs ....*Rhizopogon albidus* Smith

Fruit body 1×3 cm, with $FeSO_4$ olivaceous; gleba pallid becoming olive-brown, when dried sectioning easily; spores 6.5-7.5 (-8.2) $\mu \times$ 2.2-2.8 (3) μ, oval to oblong; peridium of appressed-interwoven hyphae in one layer, enlarged cells only in area where cavities are forming; hyphae 3-12 μ wide, hyaline in KOH; some ochraceous interhyphal debris present as revived in KOH.

Under alpine fir and white-bark pine, central western Idaho, late summer.

STIRPS BACILLOSPORUS

1a. Fruit body white drying cinereus; peridium readily separable in flakes ....*Rhizopogon cinerascens* Smith

Fruit body 1-2.5 cm, dull, glabrous, dry, slowly brownish from handling, drying cinereous (in silica gel), cut peridium staining red; KOH rose-red on the surface, $FeSO_4$ no reaction; gleba olive-buff when mature, rather dry in consistency; spores dull brownish in groups in KOH; peridium thick, epicuticular zone in KOH with patches of cinnamon pigment, lower zone nearly hyaline and with some groups of enlarged cells (the layer rather clean).

Under conifers, northern Idaho, summer.

1b. Not as above 2
2a. Fruit body pallid fresh but fuscous as dried; brachybasidioles becoming thick-walled ....*Rhizopogon nitens* Smith

Fruit bodies 1-2.5 cm, attached by a basal rhizomorphs, glabrous, possibly subviscid fresh; gleba finally wood brown (gray-brown); peridium with heavy incrustations of pigment-debris osbcuring hyphal detail as mounted in KOH, some pigment intracellular, KOH on surface of peridium staining it dark olive to olive-brown, in Melzer's the layer (the peridium) orange-brown in color but pigment globules not formed.

Under conifers, Washington, late summer and fall.

2b. Fruit body pallid fresh, merely dingy buff as dried; brachybasidioles remaining thin-walled ....
....................................*Rhizopogon bacillisporus* Smith

Fruit body up to 5 cm, not staining when injured, with $FeSO_4$ olive on dried surface, with KOH vinaceous-brown; gleba ochraceous-buff as dried; spores 5-6 × 1.7-2 μ; peridium a single layer, the hyphae appressed 4-9 μ wide, ochraceous-tawny, some cells more or les inflated, golden ochraceous pigment deposits present (in KOH) on the hyphae often as droplets.

Alpine, under alpine fir, Oregon and Wyoming, rare.

STIRPS EVADENS

1a. Spores 8-10 × 2.2-3 μ 2
1b. Spores 5-8 × 2-2.5 μ 3
2a. $FeSO_4$ on fresh specimens slowly pale olive ....
....................................*Rhizopogon obscurus* Smith

Fruit body 1 × 2.5 cm, glabrous, slowly red from handling, KOH on surface staining latter pink; gleba olivaceous, greenish in KOH, pinkish in KOH; peridium with an epicutis of hyphae 4-12 μ wide, near surface with ochraceous incrustations (in KOH) both in fresh and revived material, groups of enlarged cells present in subcutis and this region hyaline in KOH as revived; scattered ochraceous oleiferous hyphae present; many large plate-like crystals in the layer as revived in KOH.

Under lolgepole pine, central Idaho, summer.

2b. FeSO$_4$ bluish black on fresh peridium ....
....*Rhizopogon proximus* **Smith**

Fruit body 2-3 cm, matted-fibrillose, slowly brownish on exposed areas, staining red if injured; KOH on cutis red; gleba not staining when cut; peridium of appressed-interwoven hyphae 3-9 μ wide, laticifers 8-12 μ wide also present, no groups of sphaerocysts seen; layer dingy cinnamon in KOH as revived, pigment particles present and often very fine.

Under larch and Douglas fir, eastern Washington, October.

3a. KOH or FeSO$_4$ (neither one) causing a color change on fresh specimens ....*Rhizopogon masonae* **Smith**

Fruit body 2-4 cm, covered by numerous coarse rhizomorphs; surface staining red when bruised; clay-color as dried; gleba olivaceous, when dried firm but not hard; columella present at times; peridium indistinctly 2-layered, enlarged cells present in the lower layer; vinaceous-brown intracellular pigment bodies present (sections of fresh specimens in KOH), these bodies rusty brown in KOH on revived material.

Under Douglas fir and hemlock in mixed conifer-hardwood area, Oregon, October, *M. Mason*.

3b. KOH or FeSO$_4$ (or both separately) causing a color change on the fresh peridium 4
4a. Odor none; spores 5-6 × 2-2.3 μ ....
....see *Rhizopogon cinerascens* p. 359
4b. Odor distinctive 5
5a. Odor sweetly fragrant; gleba olive-fuscous when mature ....
....*Rhizopogon odoratus* **Smith**

Fruit body 2-6 cm, with loosely appressed rhizomorphs, red stains developing from handling and slowly discoloring to brown; peridium not readily separable, KOH on surface staining it red, FeSO$_4$ no reaction; gleba dark olive; spores 6.5-7.5 × 2-2.5 μ; peridium of hyaline non-incrusted hyphae (in KOH or in Melzer's); no greatly inflated cells seen.

Under ponderosa pine, San Poil Creek, Roosevelt Lake, northeastern Washington, October.

5b. Odor metallic-disagreeable; gleba merely olivaceous when mature (see *R. thaxteri* also p. 338).....*Rhizopogon evadens* **Smith**

This collective group of variants, classified as R. *evadens*, has spores 6-8 (10) × 2-2.5 μ; peridium red with KOH when fresh but as revived in the medium shows none of the usually vinaceous-brown debris associated with the reaction of the mounting medium in other species.

These variants occur mostly under lodgepole and whitebark pine in the west, but the species is also known from Nova Scotia in Canada.

ASTEROSPORALES

OCTAVIANINA

Fruit body globose to irregular, usually less than 5 cm diam., surface typically unpolished, peridium with or without sphaerocysts; peridial epicutis usually not clearly defined; columella reduced or none; spores non-amyloid, ornamentation typically coarse; clamp connections absent; latex present or absent.

Key to North American Species

1a. Spores 17-23 × 12-15 μ; ornamentation as spines 1-1.5 × 0.5 μ, yellowish in Melzer's .... *Octovianina macrospora* Singer & Smith

Fruit body about 1 cm, white when fresh; gleba of open chambers, presumably white when fresh; sterile base present; spores with inner wall 1.5-2 μ thick, pale buff in KOH, pale ochraceous in Melzer's basidia 1- and 2-spored; cystidia none; epicutis of peridium a collapsed turf of clavate to cystidioid cells 18-27 × 4-8 μ, or 20-30 × 3-5 μ if fusoid; peridial context of interwoven subgelatinous (in KOH) hyphae 3-6 μ wide.

Under hemlock, Oregon, August.

1b. Spores globose to subglobose and smaller 2
2a. Fruit body white, soon blackening where handled 3
2b. Fruit body not blackening .. 4
3a. Context of peridium containing sphaerocysts. Fig. 349 ....

......*Octavianina asterosperma* var. *potteri* Singer & Smith

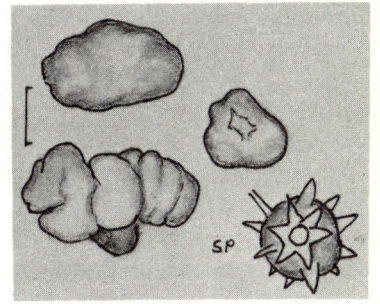

Fig. 349. *Octavianina asterosperma*.

Fruit body 1-2 (4) cm, glabrous, unpolished; gleba watery white drying rusty brown; columella present as a pulvinate sterile base; spores 12-16 (18) μ, ornamentation of blunt warts 2.5-3.5 × 2-3 μ, dextrinoid; basidia 2-, 3-, and 4-spored; latex absent; epicutis thin, of appressed hyphae, yellowish in KOH; context of hyaline heteromerous tissue.

In humus under hardwoods, Great Lakes region, summer.

3b. Context of peridium entirely filamentose ....
........................*Octavaianina nigrescens* (Zeller) **Singer & Smith**

Fruit body 2-4 cm, attached by a single rhizomorph, white, soon blackening, fuscous as dried; gleba cinnamon-brown; columella none; spores 12-16.5 × 10-14 μ, wall about 2 μ thick and tawny in KOH or Melzer's, ornamented with coarse warts with fine horizontal striations; basidia 2, 3, and 4-spored; subhymenium filamentous and subgelatinous; peridial epicutis of appressed rusty brown (in KOH) hyphae 3-7 μ wide.

Mixed woods near Ithaca, New York.

4a. Latex absent ....*Octavianina rogersii* **Singer & Smith**

Fruit body 1-2.5 cm, white, drying whitish to pale buff, surface unpolished as dried; gleba pale tan as dried; columella rudimentary; spores 14-19 μ globose, wall about 2 μ thick and pale orange-yellow in Melzer's; ornamentation inamyloid, of rods and spines 1.5-3 × 0.6-1 μ; basidia 1-spored; cystidia 60-80 × 7-11 μ, narrowly clavate to fusoid; epicutis continuous with context of peridium, the hyphae 2-4 μ wide; some sphaerocysts present in the context.

Under Douglas fir, May, Oregon.

4b. Latex present, cream colored and abundant ....
............................*Octavianina papyracea* **Singer & Smith**

Fruit body about 1 cm, cream color, hard, unchanging if bruised; gleba pale tan; columella lacking; spores 14-17 μ, globose, wall 1 μ or more thick, orange-yellow in Melzer's, ornamented with spines 2-3 × 0.5-1 μ, inamyloid; basidia 1- and 2-spored; cystidia scattered, 40-60 × 10-13 μ, mucronate at apex; peridial epicutis of hyphae 3-4 μ, ochraceous in KOH and with free ends ascending; context of hyaline subgelatinous hyphae, lacking sphaerocysts in the layer.

Under Sequoia, northern California, November.

MARTELLIA

Key to North American Species

1a. Spore ornamentation mainly in the form of a reticulum or a broken reticulum 2
1b. Spore ornamentation of separate spines, warts or granules or these connected into small groups 6
2a. Hymenial cystidia present 3
2b. Hymenial cystidia absent 4
3a. Spores 11-13 μ, globose ....
........................*Martellia alba* (Harkness) **Singer & Smith**

Fruit body about 1 cm, pale cinnamon-brown (as preserved); spore ornamentation as chains of connected warts, the prominences

0.4-0.8 (-1) μ; basidia 1-, 2-spored; cystidia 20-40 $\times$ 10-13 μ, more or less embedded in the hymenium; peridium one-layered but in the epicuticular zone somewhat gelatinized in KOH, the hyphae 2-6 μ wide and hyaline.

In the forest, California, spring.

3b. Spores 8-10 (11) μ ....
.................*Martellia setigera* (Zeller & Dodge) Singer & Smith

Fruit body 5-15 mm, dry and velvety, white to light brown; gleba creamy white, becoming light brown; columella and sterile base none; spore ornamentation about 0.25 μ high; basidia 1-, 2-, and 4-spored; cystidia 34-52 $\times$ 7-11 μ, fusoid, apex acute, filamentous pseudocystidia also present, these 30-40 $\times$ 3-5 μ; peridial epicutis a turf of cystidia (10) 15-30 $\times$ (3) 5-8 (10) μ, clavate, subfusoid, setalike, etc.

Oregon, March, under conifers.

4a. Columella absent; spores 7-9 (10) μ ....
....*Martellia subochracea* Smith

Fruit body 1-4 cm, dry and unpolished, white, slowly flushed cinnamon-buff to tawny, lacking rhizomorphs, KOH on surface dark tawny, $FeSO_4$ no change; odor none; gleba white, slowly flushed dingy cinnamon; spore ornamentation of rods and spines 0.8-1.2 μ long, many fused at base to form a broken reticulum; basidia 2- and 4-spored; subhymenium of cells up to 20 μ wide, peridial epicutis a weak turf of cystidia 20-36 $\times$ 3-7 μ, narrowly fusoid to almost aciculate, hyaline to ochraceous in KOH.

In duff under Abies, central Idaho, August.

4b. Columella present; spores slightly larger 5
5a. Peridium when fresh with a readily separable outer layer ....
..........................*Martellia monticola* (Harkness) Singer & Smith

Fruit body 10-35 mm, white, pinkish buff only in age, glabrous; gleba white, on maturing becoming pale cinnamon, loculate; columella varying from percurrent to reduced; spores 10-12.5 $\times$ 9.5-12 μ, prominences of the ornamentation 0.5-1.1 μ high; basidia 2- and 4-spored; peridial epicutis in the form of a lax turf of hyphal ends and cystidioid elements, the terminal cells 24-41 $\times$ 4.5-8.5 μ, versiform.

Under alpine fir, Hell's Canyon, Nez Perce National Forest, western Idaho, August.

5b. **Peridium not readily separating into 2 layers (see *M. cremea* also p. 364)** ....*Martellia subalpina* Smith

Fruit body 1-3.5 cm, glabrous but unpolished, dull white to yellowish to cinnamon-buff, KOH or $FeSO_4$ each negative; gleba white becoming pale tan, finally with dull brown stains; spores 8-10 (11) $\times$ 7.5-10 (11) μ, ornamentation with prominences 0.2-0.4 μ high; basidia 2-spored (rarely 4-spored); peridial epicutis a poorly formed turf of terminal cells 20-36 $\times$ 5-9 μ, many pseudocystidial hyphae also present; subcutis a layer of compactly interwoven non-gelatinous hyphae about 100 μ thick.

Under alpine fir, central Idaho, August.

6a. Spores seldom reaching (or not reaching) 12 μ in diam. or length 7
6b. Spores mostly over 12 μ in greatest dimension 15
7a. Spore ornamentation with prominences 0.2-0.5 μ high ....
....*Martellia californica* Singer & Smith

Fruit body about 1 cm, unpolished, dull croceus (yellow) becoming dull cinnamon; gleba cinnamon-color; spores 9-12 × 7.5-9 μ, in KOH with an ochraceous-orange content; basidia 2- and 4-spored; cystidia 36-52 × 8-13 μ, scattered; epicutis of peridium orange-brown in KOH, basically a turf of crooked interwoven elments, cell walls with short proliferations; hyphae of context 3-8 μ, their walls slightly thickened and subgelatinous.

Near Guadeloupe, California, April.

7b. Spore ornamentation 0.5-2 μ high 8
8a. Hymenial cystidia abundant to scattered 9
8b. Hymenial cystidia absent or rarely present as imbedded pseudocystidia 12
9a. Odor of fresh material vanilla-like ....see *Martellia fragrans*
9b. Odor absent or not as above 10
10a. Hymenial cystidia with the refractive content (as revived in KOH) of chrysocystidia ....*Martellia fallax* Singer & Smith

Fruit body 1-2 cm, white, staining rusty brown; gleba nearly white; basidia 2-spored (rarely 4-spored); cystidia 38-50 × 12-17 μ; epicutis of peridium of interwoven hyphae hyaline to yellowish in KOH and their walls thickened and translucent; surface with scattered cystidia or these in scattered fascicles, the cells 20-30 (40) × 4-8 μ.

Under oak, California.

10b. Not as above 11
11a. Columella percurrent ....
.................*Martellia creamea* (Zeller & Dodge) Singer & Smith

Fruit body up to 2 cm, light buff to cinnamon-buff, pallid yellowish as dried; spores 10-12 × 9-12 μ; basidia 2- and 4-spored; cystidia 35-46 × 12-17 μ, ventricose-mucronate; peridial epicutis of hyaline interwoven hyphae 3-5 μ wide.

In duff, under oak, Oregon, March.

11b. Columella absent ....*Martellia foetans* Singer & Smith

Fruit body about 3 cm, smooth, glabrous, dull tawny drying cinnamon-brown; gleba pallid staining dull cinnamon; odor resembling that of *Russula foetans*, taste slightly disagreeable; spores 8-11 × 7-9 μ; basidia mostly 4-spored (some also 1, 2, and 3-spored);

cystidia 30-40 × 3.5-8.2 μ, cylindric, clavate or fusoid-ventricose; hyphae in epicuticular region dark fulvous-brown in KOH.

Under lodgepole pine, central Idaho, August.

12a. Spores pale cinnamon in KOH 14
12b. Spores hyaline or nearly so in KOH 13
13a. Context of peridium of gelatinized hyphae ....
....*Martellia brunnescens* **Singer & Smith**

Fruit body 10 × 25 mm, white, glabrous, surface uneven to tuberculate or alveolate, in age brownish as if stained; gleba white staining brown; spores 8-11 × 8-9 μ; basidia 2- and 4-spored; peridial epicutis a turf of seta-like cells 22-36 × 3-7 μ, the walls thickened and yellowish in KOH; context hyphae 2-4 μ wide, hyaline in KOH, smooth.

Under conifers, Oregon, May.

13b. **Hyhpae of context of peridium not gelatinous; the hyphae ochraceous to rusty brown in KOH** .... *Martellia fragrans* **Smith**

Fruit body 1-4.5 cm, dry, glabrous, unpolished, pallid slowly becoming cinnamon-brown, KOH on surface russet, $FeSO_4$ no reaction; gleba dry and firm (like styrofoam), pallid to whitish staining cinnamon; spores 8-11 × 7.5-10 μ; basidia 4-spored; cystidia rare, filamentose and usually embedded in the hymenium; peridial epicutis of cystidia 18-27 × 4-8 μ, many brown to ochraceous in KOH.

Under alpine fir, central Idaho, August.

14a. **Lacking sphaerocysts in the peridium and lacking a fragrant odor** ....*Martellia subfulva* **Singer & Smith**

Fruit body 8-15 mm, glabrous; gleba dull cinnamon; columella none; spores 9-12 × 8-11 μ, pale cinnamon in KOH; basidia mostly 2-spored, content in KOH cinamon to yellowish (preserved material); peridial epicutis a turf of clavate to fusoid cells with ochraceous content revived in KOH.

In conifer duff, Oregon, June.

14b. **Odor strong of burnt sugar; sphaerocysts present in inner portion of the peridium** ....*Martellia fulvispora* **Smith**

Fruit body 1.5-3 cm, surface dry and pubescent, white but soon stained cinnamon-brown, KOH on surface quickly russet, $FeSO_4$ no reaction; gleba white then stained like the peridium; columella weak, dendroid; spores 9-12 × 8-10 μ, hyaline in white parts of gleba, fulvous in the brown parts (in KOH); basidia mostly 2-spored; hymenial cystidia very inconspicuous, embedded; peridial epicutis a turf of cystidia 18-27 × 3-6 μ, some pseudocystidia 2-6 μ wide also in the layer, epicutis rusty brown in KOH as revived.

Under conifers (spruce-fir), central Idaho, summer.

15a. Hymenial cystidia present 16
15b. Hymenial cystidia absent 18

16a. Spores 15-18 × 10-15 μ ....
........................*Martellia oregonensis* (Zeller) **Singer & Smith**
Fruit body 10-20 mm, white, smooth, staining brownish; gleba white, becoming pink and then brownish vinaceous; odor farinaceous; spores with spines 4-7 μ × 1.5-2.5 μ; basidia 1-spored; cystidia 42-54 × 7-11 μ; fusoid; peridial epicutis a cellular zone 3-6 cells deep, the cells 8-20 μ broad, small cystidia project from the layer.
Oregon, April.
16b. Not as above 17
17a. Surface of peridium (fresh) ribbed to wrinkled or variously uneven, white to pallid or only slightly discolored in age, drying pallid. Fig. 350 ....*Martellia idahoensis* **Singer & Smith**

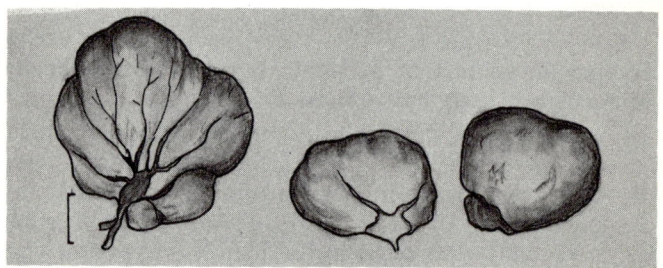

Fig. 350. *Martellia idahoensis*.

Fruit body 8-50 cm; gleba white, pale cinnamon-buff in age, dry in consistency when cut (fresh); columella poorly developed; spores 10-13 × 9-11.5 μ; basidia 1, 2, 3, and 4-spored; cystidia 40-50 × 9-10 μ (as macrocystidia), leptocystidia rare, 30-37 × 12-15 μ; peridial epicutis over 200 μ thick as dried, in structure it is a trichodermium of elements with enlarged cells, the end cells clavate.
In duff in spruce-fir forests, central Idaho, summer.
17b. Peridial surface very smooth, yellowish and drying tawny; gleba antimony yellow as dried ....
..................*Martellia scissilis* (Zeller & Dodge) **Singer & Smith**
Fruit body about 3 cm broad; odor strong of witch hazel; columella thin, extending about halfway through the gleba; spores 10-14 μ, globose, with spines 0.7-1 × 0.5 μ, amyloid at tips; cystidia abundant, 40-55 × 9-16 μ, obventricose-mucronate; peridium a thick subgelatinous layer of interwoven hyphae; clamps none.
Under conifers, northern California, November.
18a. Spores 15-20 (23) × 12-15 (16) μ ....
........................*Martellia ellipsospora* (Zeller) **Singer & Smith**
Fruit body 1-1.3 cm broad, 1-2 cm tall, smooth but outer layer flaking off, white to pale ochraceous; occasionally with white rhizomorphs over surface; gleba cream color becoming ochraceous-buff; columella absent; basidia 1-spored (rarely 2-spored); peridial epicutis hardly distinct from the peridial trama, the hyphae 3-6 μ wide.

Under conifers, Oregon, June to August.
18b. Not as above 19
19a. Epicutis of peridium a cellular layer (epithelium) often 2-3 cells or more deep 20
19b. Peridial epicutis not as above 22
20a. Subhymenium gelatinous in KOH; gleba soon stained brown; surface of peridium uneven to alveolate ....
....*Martellia maculata* **Singer & Smith**

Fruit body 1-2 cm, pallid, soon with brown stains; columella absent; basidia 2- and 4-spored; spores 10-15 × 8.5-11 µ, the spore ornamentation amyloid only at the tips of the spines; hyphae of peridial context gelatinous.

Under incense cedar, California (?).
20b. Not as above (subhymenium cellular) 21
21a. Elements of spore ornamentation grouped (and connected) to form ridges and crests, in some giving impression of a broken reticulum ....*Martellia variabilispora* (**Zeller**) **Singer & Smith**

Fruit body about 15 mm, white, drying alutaceous; gleba white drying cinnamon-buff; spore ornamentation strongly amyloid at the tips; basidia 1-spored; peridial epicutis 4-6 cells deep; peridial context of hyphae 3-5 µ wide and hyaline.

Mary's Peak, Benton County, Oregon, October.
21b. Elements of ornamentation of the spore mostly unconnected
....*Martellia vesiculosa* **Singer & Smith**

Fruit body 1-2 cm, white; gleba creamy and unchanging; spores 10-14 × 8-11 µ, wall about 1 µ thick, ornamentation very readily deciduous (many spores in a mount nearly glabrous); basidia mostly 2-spored; cells of peridial epicutis 18-50 µ wide.

Under incense cedar, Comstock, western Oregon, October.
22a. Elements of spore ornamentation as spines or cones 3.5-5 µ high and 1-2.5 µ wide at base ....
.................*Martellia gilkeyae* (**Zeller & Dodge**) **Singer & Smith**

Fruit body 2-4.5 cm, glabrous, in age with veins forming a reticulum, buff with brownish stains; pale tawny as dried; gleba white becoming creamy pinkish buff as dried; basidia 1-spored; subhymenium filamentous hyphae 3-6 µ wide; peridial epicutis a loose tangled turf of hyphal ends 2-4 µ wide, and mostly pale ochraceous and having granular content.

Under *Corylus californicus*, Oregon, May.
22b. Elements of spore ornamentation about 1-1.5 µ high 23
23a. Columella present ....*Martellia occidentalis* **Singer & Smith**

Fruit body about 1 cm, blackish, wrinkled, consistency hard (in dried specimens); spores 11-14 (17) × 10-13 (15) µ, ornamentation strongly amyloid; basidia 4-spored; peridial epicutis a gelatinous layer up to 200 µ thick, of more or less interwoven hyphae.

Under oak, California, March.

23b. Columella absent .... *Martellia parksii* **Singer & Smith**
Fruit body about 10 mm, as dried dull cinnamon-brown; gleba also cinnamon-brown; consistency rubbery-tough as revived (or preserved in liquid); spores 10-14 (18) × 9-12 (14) μ; basidia 2-spored; subhymenium cellular; peridial epicutis a turf of small clavate to filamentose cells (4-8 × 3-6 μ and 4-12 × 1.5-3 μ respectively), the elements incrusted with amorphous material; context of narrowed (1.5-4 μ) gelatinous hyphae.

Comstock, western Oregon, November.

GYMNOMYCES

Fruit body more or less globose, peridium thin and evanescent to well formed, if present often having sphaerocysts in the peridium; columella absent to rudimentary; spores ornamented and ornamentation amyloid to partly amyloid.

Key to North American Species

1a. Fruit body white becoming rose-tinted in places; spores with a heavy deposit of amyloid material at the base of or partly surrounding the sterigmal appendage ....
............................*Gymnomyces roseomaculatus* **Singer & Smith**

Fruit body more or less globose, peridium thin and evanescent to coloring to brownish over all; gleba white, becoming tan; odor penetrating (resembling that of witch hazel); columella none; spores 14-17 × 12-16 μ, ornamentation of closely set rods 1-1.5 × 4.6-1 μ, strongly amyloid; basidia 2-spored; cystidia 43-62 × 12-18 μ, apex obtuse to subacute; subhymenium cellular; peridial epicutis of hyphae 4-10 μ and ochraceous in KOH; peridial context heteromerous.

Central California, March, under oak.

1b. Not as above 2
2a. Basidia ochraceous tawny as revived in KOH ....
............................*Gymnomyces cinnamomeus* **Singer & Smith**

Fruit body 10-25 mm, glabrous, cinnamon-brown; gleba chambered, pale cinnamon-brown; columella lacking; spores 9-12 μ (orn. excl.), ornamentation of spines up to 1 μ long; basidia 4-spored; cystidia none; subhymenium cellular; peridium with a thick epicutis of subgelatinous hyphae 3-10 μ wide; sphaerocysts present in a poorly defined inner zone.

Under oak, Berkeley, California, January.

2b. Basidia hyaline in KOH (or nearly so) 3
3a. Spores with inamyloid spines and a low broken amyloid reticulum between them; peridium evanescent ....
............................*Gymnomyces alveolatus* **Singer & Smith**

Fruit body 3-5 cm, pale dull ochraceous tawny as dried, peridium thin (glebal chambers showing through); gleba pale tan; columella slight; spores 9-12 μ; basidia 2-spored; cystidia 30-37 × 4-8 μ, occurring embedded in the hymenium as crooked filaments; subhymenium of loosely woven much-branched filaments; hyphae of peridium 4-10 μ wide; sphaerocysts rare.

Under oak, Oregon, May.

3b. Not as above 4
4a. Epicutis of appressed interwoven hyphae 5
4b. Epicutis in the form of a trichodermium 6
5a. Columella percurrent; gleba rose pink when fresh ....
..........................*Gymnomyces socialis* (Harkness) Singer & Smith

Fruit body 10-20 mm or more, smooth, cream-color, pinkish cream or as dried ochraceous to clay-color; sterile base distinct (a rudimentary stipe-columella present); gleba rose pink, drying "pinkish buff"; spores 9-14 × 8-10 (11) μ, globose, ornamentation 1.2-2 × 0.9-1.2 μ, as cones, strongly amyloid; basidia 4-spored; cystidia rare, 26-30 × 10-14 μ, fusoid-ventricose; peridium with a filamentose interwoven epicutis, beneath this zone of heteromerous tissue.

Hypogeous under *Eucalyptus, Pasania densiflora*, etc., California.

5b. Columella none; gleba white at first ....
.................................*Gymnomyces compactus* Singer & Smith

Fruit body 1-2 cm, white with brownish spots, uneven to wrinkled; gleba staining brown; spores 10-14 × 9-12 μ, ornamentation heavily amyloid and present as warts arranged in lines, about 1 μ high; basidia 4-spored; epicutis of peridium a decumbent turf of cystidia 18-30 × 4-7 μ, mostly fusoid to clavate; context hyphae 4-7 μ wide, subgelatinous; sphaerocysts only near the subhymenium.

Under spruce and fir, summer, central Idaho.

6a. Spores 12-14 (18) × 9-12 (15) μ; peridium white changing to brown. Fig. 351 ....*Gymnomyces ferruginascens* Singer & Smith

Fruit body 7-50 mm; gleba white, pallid when mature, tawny to darker as dried; odor slightly disagreeable; prominences of ornamentation 1-1.5 μ high; basidia 2- and 4-spored; pseudocystidia imbedded in the hymenium up to 7.5 μ broad; peridial epicutis a palisade of versiform elements, hyaline at first, brown in stained areas, FeSO$_4$ on peridium olivaceous; with KOH quickly rusty brown.

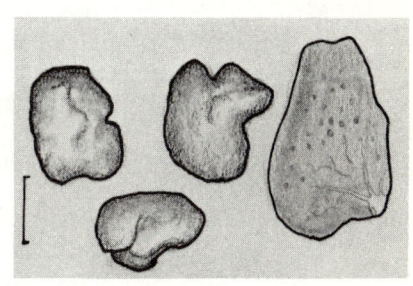

Fig. 351. *Gymnomyces ferruginascens.*

Under spruce-fir, central Idaho, summer.

6b. Spores 8-11 × 7-9 μ, peridium white and unchanging ....
....*Gymnomyces parksii* Singer & Smith

Fruit body 10-15 mm, with a hollow stipe-like base not penetrating the gleba; spores with spines 2-2.5 μ long, amyloid at apex;

basidia 2- and 4-spored; cystidia rare, about 50 × 11 μ, subfusoid; peridial epicutis a trichodermium of septate hyphae 6-11 μ, sphaerocysts present in the inner layer.

Under oak, California.

ELASMOMYCES

This genus differs from *Martellia* in possessing a stipe-columella. It is intermediate between *Martellia* and *Macowanites* to some extent.

Key to North American Species

1a. Peridium of fruit body a single layer, not a turf of hyphal end cells and no trichodermium present 2
1b. Peridium with a differentiated cuticle or at least a turf of dermatocystidia or a trichodermium (check immature specimens) 3
2a. Spores 15-20 × 12-15 μ, ellipsoid; odor of ethyl acetate when fresh .... *Elasmomyces odoratus* **Singer & Smith**

Fruit body 10-20 mm, whitish and unpolished; stipe-columella percurrent but reduced in width; gleba pallid becoming pinkish cinnamon; basidia 1- and 2-spored; subhymenium cellular; peridial epicutis of hyphae 3-5 μ, ochraceous in KOH, merging into the context; no sphaerocysts present.

Under Douglas fir and hemlock, Mt. Rainier National Park, Washington, July.

2b. Spores 8-11 × 7-9 μ (excl. apiculus); peridium and gleba salmon-color when fresh ....
....*Elasmomyces echinosporus*(Zeller & Dodge) **Singer & Smith**

Fruit body about 15 mm, smooth, delicate; stipe-columella not percurrent (merely projecting into the gleba); basidia 2- and 4-spored; subhymenium cellular; sphaerocysts present in inner portion of peridium.

Under oak, San Francisco Bay area, California.

3a. Hymenial cystidia present 4
3b. Hymenial cystidia absent ....
.... *Elasmomyces zellerianus* **Singer & Smith**

Fruit body 15-25 mm; peridium yellowish white, pruinose; gleba light ochraceous fresh, drying tawny to wood brown; stipe columella short and thick in the stipe part, narrower and percurrent for columella part; basidia 2-spored; subhymenium cellular; peridial epicutis poorly defined, the hyphae more or less decumbent and with versiform end cells.

Under conifers, Washington, October.

NON-GILLED FLESHY FUNGI

4a. Odor of dried fruit body sweetly fragrant; spore ornamentation as a broken reticulum ....
.................................*Elasmomyces camphoratus* **Singer & Smith**

Fruit body 6-12 mm pallid to dark tan or rusty brown; glabrous, dull; gleba near cinnamon-buff; spores 7.5-11 (12) × 6.5-8 (10) μ; basidia 1- to 4-spored; cystidia 32-43 × 9-13 μ, fusoid-ventricose; subhymenium filamentous; peridial epicutis compactly arranged trichodermium of crooked filaments, and both clavate and fusoid end cells; peridial context with only an occasional sphaerocyst; oleiferous hyphae hyaline but distinct.

Under conifers, western Washington, November.

4b. Not as above 5
5a. Stipe portion of stipe-columella lacking (merely a sterile base present) ....
...............*Elasmomyces pilosus* (**Zeller & Dodge**) **Singer & Smith**

Fruit body 3-4.5 cm, whitish becoming reddish brown, olive shades present as dried; unpolished to pubescent; sterile base giving rise in the gleba to a dendroid columella; spores 8-11.5 × 8-10 μ; basidia 4-spored; cystidia 35-50 × 7-12 μ; subhymenium filamentous and gelatinous; peridium 2-layered, epicutis a palisade of cystidia, the cells 30-60 × 6-9 μ; inner layer of gelatinous hyphae 3-8 μ wide, no sphaerocysts present.

Hypogeous under oak, California, February to April.

5b. Stipe portion of the stipe-columella continuous with columella portion and peridium showing bright red pigmentation 6
6a. Peridial context heteromerous. Fig. 352 ....
....*Elasmomyces roseipes* **Singer & Smith**

Fruit body 18-40 mm broad, 12-20 mm high, disc often diffracted scaly, whitish areas often present on peridium; gleba sublamellate, ochraceous; stipe-columella 7-15 × 3-8 mm; spores 8.8-12 × 7.5-10 μ; peridium 3-layered; epicutis with a diffuse pink pigment (in KOH) and consisting of a palisade of cystidioid cells clavate to capitate and 17-31 × 3-9 μ; subcutis of appressed interwoven hyphae; innermost layer of heteromerous tissue; basidia 1, 2, 3, and 4-spored; cystidia 39-55 × 5.5-10 μ.

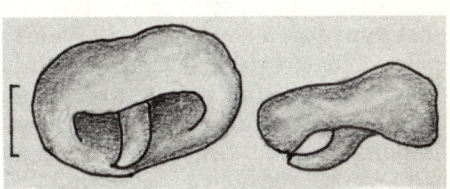

Fig. 352. *Elasmomyces roseipes.*

In spruce woods, July and August, California.

6b. Context lacking sphaerocysts (not heteromerous) ....
....*Elasmomyces russuloides* **Setchell**

Fruit body 10-15 mm broad, 10-12 mm high, glabrous, white with bright red dominating; gleba white, sublamellate; stipe-columella short fairly robust; percurrent, unpolished; spore ornamentation in the form of widely spaced heavily amyloid bands in a broken reticulum; basidia 2-spored; cystidia 40-60 × 10-12 μ; subhymenium of narrow (2-3 μ wide) branched hyphae; peridial epicutis a turf (decumbent in age) of cystidia up to 130 × 12 μ; context lacking sphaerocysts, the hyphae 4-5 μ wide.

Under oak and other broad-leaved trees, Berkeley, California.

ZELLEROMYCES

Fruit body globose or angular from external pressures, usually with a well-defined columella, the gleba chambered and not gelatinous or cartilaginous in consistency; exuding a latex when cut; spores globose to ellipsoid and usually large, with amyloid ornamentation; peridium with heteromerous tissue at least where it joins the tramal plates.

Key to Species

1a. Spores typically ellipsoid; sphaerocysts absent from the mediostratum of the tramal plates 2
1b. Spores typically globose to subglobose or sphaerocysts present in the mediostratum of the tramal plates 3
2a. Fruit body cinnabar red fresh; spores 14-17 × 11-13 μ ....
    .... *Zelleromyces cinnabarinus* **Singer & Smith**

Fruit body 1-4 cm, sessile but attached by a pad of mycelium, dull cinnabar red when fresh, dark reddish brown as dried; gleba pale cinnamon-buff; columella absent or rudimentary and the branches radiating from the slight sterile base; latex white; spore ornamentation forming a knotty reticulum, the prominences up to 1 μ high, bands 0.6-1 μ wide; cystidia 26-30 × 9-13 μ, broadly fusoid, with refractive content.

Under pine, Gulf Coast area and the region bordering the Gulf of St. Lawrence, summer in the north, winter in the Gulf Coast area.

2b. **Fruit body pale cream color to pale clay color fresh; spores 10-13 × 8-11 μ** ....*Zelleromyces oregonensis* **Singer & Smith**

Fruit body 10-30 mm, cinnamon-buff to dingy pale tawny as dried, unpolished; columella dendroid, the branches pale buff; latex clear whitish; spores with ornamentation in the form of closely spaced but unconnected rods 1-1.25 × 0.4-0.5 μ, amyloid over all or just the upper part; basidia 4-spored; cystidia 46-48 × 9-11 μ, fusoid-ventricose to clavate content not oily-refractive in KOH; epicutis of fruit body a turf of dermatocystidia 28-45 × 4-9 µ; hypodermal layer yellow in KOH; clamps absent.

Under incense cedar, Oregon, October.

3a. **Peridium with a medial gelatinous layer and pockets of globose cells to the interior of it. Fig. 353** ....
................................*Zelleromyces ravenelii* (B. & C.) Singer & Smith

Fruit bodies 2-4 cm, pallid to light fawn as dried; sterile base not prominent; columella slender and percurrent; latex white and aromatic; spores 12-17 µ, ornamentation a heavy small-meshed reticulum, ridges about 1 µ wide and 1-1.5 µ high; cystidia 48-60 × 10-15 µ, clavate with an apical mucro; small dermatocystidia cover the surface of the peridium, these 18-26 × 3-7 µ and irregular in outline.

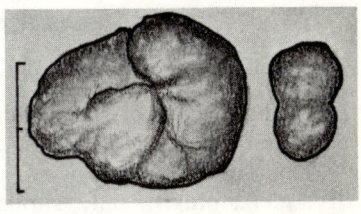

Fig. 353. *Zelleromyces ravenelii.*

Hypogeous, southern United States.

3b. **Not as above** 4
4a. **Spores 9-12.5 (15) × 6.5-8.5 (10) µ, ellipsoid** ....
........................*Zelleromyces gardneri* (Z. & D.) Singer & Smith

Fruit body 8-25 mm diam., cream color to yellow (preserved in alcohol), columella dendroid; gleba cream color to clay color as dried; latex white; spore ornamentation strongly amyloid, 0.25-0.5 µ high, in the form of crooked ridges and warts fused into crests and these at times connected to give the effect of a broken reticulum; basidia 4-spored. Hymenial cystidia 24-35 × 10-16 µ; tramal plates with sphaerocysts in the central stratum; peridium present as a thin layer of appresed hyphae; clamps absent.

Under leaves of *Quercus agrifolia* (oak) in California.

4b. **Not as above, spores globose** 5
5a. **Spores 10-16 µ, ornamentation in the form of spines with the apex amyloid** ....*Zelleromyces gilkeyae* Singer & Smith

Fruit bodies 2-5 cm, globose, appressed fibrillose, pallid becoming reddish fulvous, uneven to wrinkled; gleba pale to rich cinnamon; latex milky white; spines on the spores 2-3 × 0.7-1 µ (long and narrow); basidia 2-spored; hymenial cystidia 46-62 × 10-14 µ, elongate-mucronate; epicutis of peridium a trichodermium the elements closely packed to form a cellular layer, the end cells ochraceous-brown revived in KOH; clamps absent.

In duff in conifer forests, Oregon, fall.

5b. **Spores 9-12 µ diam., ornamentation of broad warts entirely covered by amylaceous material** ....
..........*Zelleromyces glabrellus* (Zeller & Dodge) Smith & Smith

Fruit body 10-15 mm, globose, smooth, white to brownish; columella percurent; gleba white, drying ivory-yellow to cream-buff; latex present; spore ornamentation 1-1.5 (2) μ high; basidia 4-spored; hymenial cystidia 50-70 $\times$ 14-20 μ, broadly fusoid; peridium with a cellular epicutis the cells thin-walled and hyaline in KOH; clamps none.

ARCANGELIELLA

Key to North American Species

1a. Sphaerocysts of the peridium with refractive somewhat thickened walls .... *Arcangeliella crassa* Singer & Smith

Fruit body about 3.5 cm, pale pinkish buff, glabrous, moist to dry; gleba pinkish buff, sublamellate, pale pinkish buff; stipe 5-8 mm thick, 1 cm high; spores 8-11 $\times$ 6.5-8 μ, ornamentation a small-meshed reticulum or a broken reticulum, prominences about 0.25 μ high; basidia 4-spored; cystidia 52-65 $\times$ 7-12 μ, flexuous, often pointed; epicutis of peridium of appressed hyphae 3-6 μ wide, laticiferous hyphae numerous.

In conifer duff, Stanislaus National Forest, Oregon.

1b. Sphaerocysts of peridium all thin-walled 2
2a. Cystidia present merely as ends of laticiferous hyphae extending into the hymenium .... *Arcangeliella lactarioides* Zeller

Fruit body 25-30 mm, peridium innately fibrillose, yellowish, brownish as dried; gleba white becoming creamy, sublamellate; spores 8-11 $\times$ 6-7 μ, ornamentation a reticulum with prominences 0.3-0.5 μ high; basidia 4-spored; epicutis a gelatinous layer with dermatocystidia present.

Mt. Shasta California, under fir.

2b. Cystidia 33-48 $\times$ 9-12 μ, somewhat fusoid ....
.... *Arcangeliella tenax* Smith & Wiebe

Fruit body to 7 cm broad, 5.5 cm high, pale buff very slightly tacky when fresh but appearing unpolished, unchanging on injury; context pale buff, when cut very slightly pinkish or unchanging; gleba pale ochraceous lacunose; stipe-columella 4.5 $\times$ 2.5 cm, solid, pale buff; latex white, milky-opaque, unchanging, taste quickly and strongly acrid; spores 8.5-10.3 $\times$ 6.5-7.5 (8) μ, ornamentation a complete to broken reticulum with prominences 0.3-0.5 μ high; basidia 2-, 3-, and 4-spored; epicutis of peridium 200 μ or more thick, of appresed-interwoven hyphae 3-6 μ broad, non-gelatinous.

Mt. Hood, Oregon, October.

MACOWANITES

Hymenophoral trama heteromerous; pseudocystidia present (similar to the type referred to as "macrocystidia" of *Russula*) but not blackening in sulfobenzaldehyde in all species; spores globose to broadly ellipsoid, with amyloid ornamentation, hyaline to yellowish under the microscope; gleba basically lamellar in type but mostly convoluted to loculate; aspect of fruit body that of an unexpanded *Russula;* spores not forcibly discharged from basidia.

Key to North American Species

1a. Spore ornamentation in the form of a reticulum or broken reticulum or numerous short branched lines (some unconnected particles may be found over the spore surface also 2
1b. Spore ornamentation in the form of unconnected rods, spines, or warts or some of these united into short lines or crests 13
2a. Spore ornamentation with highest prominences 0.8-1.5 μ high ..3
2b. Prominences of spore ornamentation 0.8 μ or less high 6
3a. Odor pungent-offensive in old caps; columella 10-30 mm thick; peridium reddish brown ....
..............................*Macowanites magnus* Parks in Zeller & Dodge

Fruit body 3-14 cm, conic to nearly plane, viscid, pale tan to dark brown drying to vinaceous-brown or tan; gleba white drying warm buff, sublamellate; stipe-columella 3-7 cm long, about 3 cm thick, white throughout; spores 8.5-13.5 $\times$ 7.5-12.3 μ; basidia 1, 2, 3, and 4-spored; cystidia 60-80 $\times$ 10-14 μ, narrowly clavate to fusoid; epicutis of peridium a gelatinized layer of hyphae 3-4 μ wide.

Santa Clara County, California.

3b. Not as above 4
4a. Taste of raw flesh nauseous; peridium dull vinaceous-red ....
....*Macowanites nauseosus* Smith

Fruit body 1.8-2.3 cm, convex, glabrous, viscid, brownish vinaceous, context white, exceedingly fragile; gleba sublamellate, adnexed, pinkish buff to ochraceous; stipe-columella 1-1.5 cm long, 4-7 mm thick, pallid within, cortex pinkish buff, $FeSO_4$ on cortex vinaceous, surface white and not staining; spores 9-13 $\times$ 7-9 μ, ornamentation in the form of broken short irregular lumpy lines; basidia 4-spored; cystidia 43-65 $\times$ 10-15 μ, subfusoid-mucronate to clavate or clavate-mucronate; epicutis of peridium a gelatinous trichodermium of branched hyphae 80-120 μ long and 3-5 μ wide, many pseudocystidia in the layer also.

Gregarious under fir, South Fork of Lake Fork Creek, central Idaho.

4b. Taste not distinctive; peridium some other color 5
5a. Stipe staining fulvous around the base; peridium crust brown ....
....*Macowanites pinicola* Smith

Fruit body 2-4 cm, glabrous, viscid, pallid slowly becoming pale tan context white, thin, fragile, $FeSO_4$ pinkish gray; gleba attached at apex of stipe-columella, distinctly yellowish ("warm buff"), lacunose; stipe-columella 1-3 cm long, 1-1.5 cm thick, white, fulvous around the base where handled; spores 9-11.5 μ, ornamentation in the form of a wide-meshed partial reticulum; basidia 2- and 4-spored; cystidia rare, 32-44 × 10-16 μ, ventricose-mucronate, with an amorphous refractive inclusion as revived in KOH; epicutis of peridium a gelatinous trichodermium of hyphae 50-100 × 3-6 μ.

Under *Pinus contorta*, Dry Creek, central Idaho, October.

5b. Stipe not staining rusty; peridium lemon yellow ....
....*Macowanites citrinus* Singer & Smith

Fruit body 2-4 mm convex, slightly viscid, in age grayish along the margin; gleba chambered to sublamellate, yellowish pallid, slowly slightly grayish on exposure; stipe-columella 10-15 mm long, 8-11 mm thick, white, spores 9-11 (14) × 8-10 (12) μ, ornamentation a broken reticulum; basidia 4-spored; cystidia rare, 48-64 × 9-11 μ, mucronate; epicuticular region of peridial cutis a turf of filaments 3-7 μ wide with frequent septa; $FeSO_4$ gray on context of stipe on gleba soon grayish, on context of peridium no reaction.

Under *Pinus contorta*, Sawtooth Mts., Idaho, summer.

6a. Stipe-columella staining rusty in some part 7
6b. Stipe-columella not staining rusty (finally only slightly so around the worm holes) 9
7a. Peridium vinaceous-red; peridial epicutis very gelatinous ....
....*Macowanites vinicolor* Smith

Fruit body 1-3 cm, viscid, dingy vinaceous-red in some with a slightly olive tinge, margin with ochraceous stains; context white, taste mild; gleba milk white, slowly stained cinnamon-buff where bruised; stipe-columella 1-1.5 cm long, 8-12 mm thick, white staining rusty; spores 10-13 × 7.5-10 μ, ornamentation mostly of short branched lines; basidia 4-spored; cystidia 56-80 × 10-17 μ subfusoid to clavate; epicutis of pileus a turf 40-60 μ deep, the hyphae 3-6 μ wide, with a gelatinous layer 25-50 μ deep above this which is penetrated by long pseudocystidia up to 200 μ long and 4-8 μ wide.

Solitary under conifers, Brundage Mt., McCall, central Idaho, August.

7b. Not as above 8
8a. Peridium fuscous-violaceous; spores 7-10 × 6-8.5 μ ....
................................*Macowanites fuscoviolaceus* Singer & Smith

Fruit body up to 30 mm, glabrous, viscid, violaceous becoming violaceous-fuscous, margin with pallid areas; gleba scarcely lamellate, milk white except for tawny stains around worm holes, free from stipe-columella; stipe-columella 2-3 cm long, up to 12 mm thick, solid, surface white, rusty stained around the base; context white, brittle, taste mild; spores 7-10 × 6-8.5 μ, ornamentation not forming a complete network; basidia 4-spored; cystidia 40-65 × 9-16 μ, narrowly clavate to fusoid-ventricose; epicutis of peridium a turf of hyphae up to 100 μ long and 2.5-4 μ wide embedded in a mass of slime (in KOH mounts).

Under alpine fir central Idaho, summer.

8b. **Peridium pallid; spores 9-15 × 7-12 μ** ....
.................................*Macowanites fulvescens* **Singer & Smith**

Fruit body 2-3 cm, whitish, smooth then becoming areolate, the areolae becoming clay-color; gleba pallid tan, sublacunose; columella 4 mm wide, not continued into a stipe in some; odor and taste not distinct; spores 9.5-15.2 × 7-12 μ, ornamentation a partial reticulum; basidia 2- and 4-spored; cystidia (pseudocystidia) 63-110 × 13-18 μ; leptocystidia 48-64 × 18-24 μ also present; epicutis of peridium consisting of a turf of pseudocystidia and hyphal ends, not gelatinized, the cystidial elements with contents blackening in sulfobenzaldehyde.

Under spruce and fir, central Idaho, summer.

9a. **Taste slowly acrid; gleba typically milk white** ....
............................*Macowanites albidigleba* **Singer & Smith**

Fruit body 10-30 mm, dry, unpolished pallid at first, slowly pale dull rose color; gleba white until old age, sublamellate; stipe about 10 mm long and 8-10 mm thick, white; spores 7.5-11 × 7.5-9.7 μ, ornamentation a broken reticulum; basidia 2- and 4-spored; cystidia 40-72 × 12-18 μ, fusoid to clavate; epicutis of peridium a turf containing pseudocystidia with blackening content in sulfobenzaldehyde among the hyphal ends in a loose arrangement in a subgelatinous matrix.

Under alpine fir central Idaho, summer.

9b. **Not as above** 10
10a. **Peridium bright red (as in *Russula emetica*)** ....
..................................*Macowanites pseudoemeticus* **Smith**

Fruit body 2-3.5 cm, glabrous, subviscid, splitting along margin, often with pallid areas; context white, fragile, taste mild; gleba sublamellate, the lamellae crowded, thickish, fused to form chambers, pallid to pale pinkish buff; stipe-columella short (1-2 cm long), 5-10 mm thick, white; spores 8-9 (10) × 7-8 (9) μ, ornamentation a broken reticulum; basidia 2- and 4-spored; cystidia 40-65 (70) × 9-16 μ, epicutis of cap a turf of greatly elongated pseudocystidia (60-200 × 4-7 μ), hyphal elements of turf 40-60 × 2.5-6 μ, often branched.

Under spruce, central Idaho, August.

10b. **Peridium not colored as above** 11
11a. **Peridium with grayish lilac colors; odor when fresh very peculiar** ....*Macowanites lilacinus* **Smith**

Fruit body 2-3 cm, glabrous, slimy viscid, rimose in age, pellicle separable to disc; context exceedingly fragile, thin, watery lilac gray, dingy vinaceous in $FeSO_4$; gleba free, sublamellate, pale ochraceous when mature, not staining when injured; stipe columella 2 cm long 8 mm thick, white; spores 8-10 × 7-9 μ, ornamentation essentially a broken reticulum; basidia 4-spored; cystidia numerous, 50-73 × 9-16 μ, subfusoid to subclavate and mucronate; epicutis of peridium a short turf of subgelatinous elements 60-100 μ high and 2-5 μ wide, also present are pseudocystidia up to 100 μ long, 5-8 μ wide, some with an apical capitellum.

Under spruce, central Idaho, August.

11b. Not as above 12
12a. Peridium pinkish cinnamon; odor of cherry pits, very strong on young fresh material .... *Macowanites olidus* Smith

Fruit body 3-4.5 cm, convex-depressed, glabrous, slimy, pellicle not separable, color pinkish cinnamon over all or disc olive tinged, context thin, fragile, white, taste mild, $FeSO_4$ on stipe faintly pinkish, gleba sublamellate, soon ochraceous-buff or yellower, apparently never enclosed by the peridium; stipe-columella 2-3 cm long, 8-11 mm thick, not staining; spores 9-12 × 7-8.5 μ, ornamentation a partial reticulum, basidia 4-spored; cystidia 40-60 × 10-16 μ, clavate-mucronate; epicutis of peridium a turf of gelatinous hyphae and pseudocystidia the latter 100-150 long (the depth of the layer), the hyphal ends of the turf hyphae clavate to cystidioid and 7-12 μ wide; subcutis also gelatinous.

12b. Peridium milkwhite to yellowish or grayish olive; odor none
.... *Macowanites subolivaceus*

Fruit body 2-6 cm, convex, slimy, cutis cracking into irregular pieces, taste mild; gleba milk-white becoming yellowish; stipe-columella 2-4 cm × 10-20 mm, white; spores ± globose, ornamentation 0.4-0.8 μ high, not forming a reticulum; subhymenium cellular (2-5 cells deep); pilear epicutis a turf of branched hyphae 3-6 μ wide, gelatinous, 3rd and 4th cell from tip short and 6-11 μ wide; pseudocystidia present in hymenium.

Gregarious under spruce, central Idaho, late summer.

13a. Prominent spore ornamentation less than 0.5 μ high 14
13b. Prominent spore ornamentation more than 0.5 μ high 17
14a. Peridium dingy rose-color; staining ochraceous where injured
.... *Macowanites subrosaceus* Smith

Fruit body up to 3.5 cm, subviscid but soon dry, becoming areolate, developing ochraceous stains over the squamules; context whitish, fragile, taste mild; gleba adnate to apex of columella, lacunose, pale ochraceous not staining; stipe-columella short (2 cm × 8 mm), stained ochraceous at base; spores 9-12 × 8-10 μ; basidia 2- and 4-spores; cystidia 36-58 × 9-15 μ, fusoid to clavate-mucronate, also present are pseudocystidia 20-35 × 5-8 μ; epicutis of peridium of interwoven subgelatinous hyphae ochraceous in KOH and 2-4 μ

wide, at times forming a weak turf; context with rusty brown (in KOH) oleiferous hyphae.

Solitary under spruce, central Idaho, August.

14b. Not as above 15
15a. Taste slowly acrid; spore ornamentation 0.3-0.7 μ high; odor none or slight .... **Macowanites luteolus** Smith & Trappe

Fruit body 1-3 cm, viscid but soon dry and unpolished, evenly pale cream-color but gradually darker and duller, yellowish as dried; context pallid, odor slight; gleba lamellate to lacunose cream-buff, not staining; stipe-columella 1-1.5 cm long, 4-7 mm wide buffy pallid dry, unchanging; spores 7-9 $\times$ 6.5-7.5 (10-12 $\times$ 8-10) μ; basidia 2- and 4-spored; cystidai numerous 46-62 $\times$ 10-16 μ, narrowly clavate-mucronate to narrowly ellipsoid-pedicellate and some mucronate; epicutis of peridium a turf of subgelatinous elements with terminal cells 4-6 μ wide, the cells narrowly clavate to cystidioid, some narrow pseudocystidial hyphae extending through the layer; subcutis a thick layer of interwoven hyphae 5-10 μ wide with scattered enlarged cells in it.

Under hemlock and spruce, Oregon coast.

15b. Not as above 16
16a. Spore ornamentation 0.25 μ or less high; peridium pale tawny .... **Macowanites setchellianus** Singer & Smith

Fruit body 10-30 mm broad, glabrous, near pale ochraceous tawny; gleba paler than peridial surface, lacunose; stipe-columella percurrent, concolor with peridial surface (data from dried specimens); spores 7-10 (11) $\times$ 6-7.5 (8) μ; basidia 4-spored; cystidia 42-63 $\times$ 8-12 μ, subcylindric to narrowly clavate, hyaline to yellowish in KOH; cuticle of peridium complex; subcuticular layer cellular and the cells catenulate, turf structure more obvious near the surface where the terminal cells often give rise to versiform dermatocystidia.

West-central, California.

16b. Spore ornamentation 0.3-0.5 μ high; peridium pallid yellow to dingy ochraceous .... **Macowanites chlorinosmus** Smith & Trappe

Fruit body 2.5-5.5 cm, subviscid but soon dry, cuticle splitting in age, color ivory to pallid yellow, disc more dingy ochraceous, pellicle somewhat separable; context whitish, odor of chlorine, taste very unpleasant; gleba adnate to stipe to apex, up to 2 cm deep, pale ochraceous becoming orange-ochraceous; stipe-columella 1-3 cm long, 6-9 mm thick, solid, fragile, surface white to pallid, unchanging; spores 8-9.5 $\times$ 6.5-7.5 μ; basidia 4-spored; cystidia 50-65 $\times$ 10-15 μ, subclavate-mucronate; epicutis of peridium a compact subgelatinous trichodermium of versiform elements, the component hyphae with cells up to 20 μ broad at the ends and clavate to fusoid in shape; dermatopseudocystidia scattered to rare.

Scattered to gregarious under spruce and hemlock, Cape Lookout State Park, Tilamook County, Oregon, November.

17a. Taste acrid; peridium dull grayish vinaceous ....
....Macowanites acris **Singer & Smith**

Fruit body up to 5 cm, dry and unpolished, dull grayish vinaceous to violaceous-brown; gleba sublamellate, pinkish buff, firm; stipe 3 cm long, 20 mm at apex, stained faintly ochraceous at base; spores 8-12 × 7-10 μ; basidia 4-spored; cystidia 70-111 × 6-13 μ; epicuticular zone of peridium a turf of hyphal ends loosely arranged and 2-3 μ wide, somewhat gelatinized in KOH.

Under spruce, central Idaho, July.

17b. Taste mild; color of peridium not as above 18
18a. Spores 10-15 μ (globose) or 11-16 × 9.5-13 μ; peridium white when fresh ....Macowanites mollis **Singer & Smith**

Fruit body 1-3 cm, depressed-globose, white and soft to the touch, lubricous, drying cinnamon-buff to alutaceous; gleba white to buff drying paler than peridium; stipe-columella present but greatly reduced, stipe portion 4-6 × 2-3 mm; spores with ornamentation as small spines discrete or connected; basidia 1- and 2-spored; cystidia 38-56 × 5-8 μ, narrowly clavate-mucronate to subfilamentose; cuticle of peridium a basal cellular layer, the cells 8-15 μ wide and from these there is a turf of dematopseudocystidia mixed with branched hyphal filaments versiform—clavate, fusoid or contorted.

Lower Tahoma Creek, Mt. Rainier National Park, Washington.

18b. Not as above 19
19a. Odor of iodiform; clavate to capitate cells 8-15 μ broad scattered in the peridial epicutis ....
.....................................Macowanites iodiolens **Smith & Wells**

Fruit body 2.5-3.5 cm, smooth, pellicle separable, surface dry to moist, unpolished to pruinose or subvelvety, in age at times areolate over disc, color pale ochraceous or disc at times tinged pinkish to

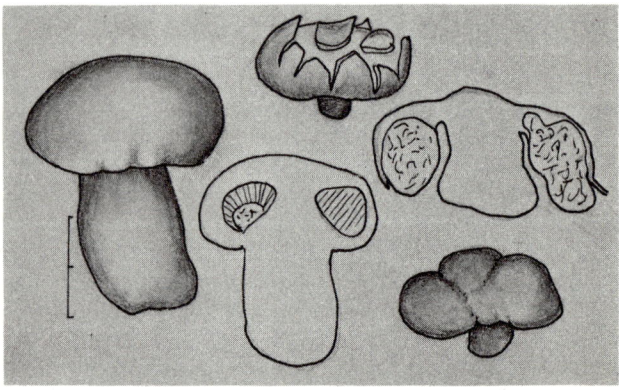

Fig. 354. Macowanites americanus.

pinkish lilac; gleba ochraceous, as dried pallid buff, stipe-columella 15-20 mm long, 5-8 mm thick extending another 5-10 mm below the peridial margin, surface yellowish; spores 9-11 × 8-9.5 μ; basidia 4-spored; cystidia 45-60 × 8-13 μ, many with a needle-like projection at apex; peridial epicutis a turf of clavate to flagellate pseudocystidia up to 50 × 7.5 μ, many pedicellate-clavate cells also present the enlarged part 8-15 μ broad, up to 35 (45) μ long; filliform to versiform elements also present in the turf.

Solitary to gregarious Cape Lookout State Park, Oregon, October.

19b. Lacking both of the above features. Fig. 354 ....
.............................*Macowanites americanus* **Singer & Smith**

Fruit body 1-5 cm, smooth and viscid at first, soon breaking up variously over the disc, colors variable (yellow, olive-vinaceous purplish or lilaceous in varying proportions); taste mild; odor not distinct; gleba white at first but soon pale to rich ochraceous; stipe-columella 10-30 × 4-12 mm, white; spores 8.7-13.2 × 8.2-11.8 μ; basidia mostly 4-spored; cystidia 40-90 × 7-11.5 μ; peridial epicutis at first a palisade of pseudocystidia 25-85 × 4-8 μ.

Gregarious to cespitose under spruce and fir, Pacific Northwest, summer common.

GLOSSARY

allantoid (of spores), sausage-shaped in profile view.
alveolate (of a surface), with broad shallow depression
amorphous, lacking any characteristic shape or structure.
amylaceous, any material giving a blue to violet reaction (color change) with iodine.
amyloid, a cell wall is said to be amyloid when it turns blue with iodine. It also applies to particles of an organic nature in or outside of a cell.
annulate, having a ring of sterile tissue (remains of a veil) present on the stipe above the base.
annulus, the ring of veil tissue left on the stipe (in heavily veiled species) when the veil breaks away from the cap margin.
apedicellate, lacking a pedicel.
apiculus, a short projection on either end of a spore.
apiculate, furnished with an apiculus.
apothecium, the cup-like or saucer-shaped to urn-shaped fruit body of a fungus in the order Pezizales (Ascomycetes).
applanate, flattened or horizontally expanded.
areolate (of a surface), cracked in areas much resembling in shape those observed in a drying out mud-flat.
argillaceous (a color term), clay-brown (a pale dingy yellow-brown).
ascocarp, the fruit body in which or on which the asci are produced.
ascomycete, any fungus in which the spores are produced in asci.
ascospore, the spore produced in the ascus as the result (typically) of reduction division (the division in which the number of chromosomes is reduced by half in the daughter nuclei).
ascus (asci), the cell in which reduction division occurs followed by the formation (typically) of 8 spores (ascospores) *in* the ascus.
asperulate, roughened by very small adhering particles, as on a spore.
basidiomycete, a fungus in which the spores of the sexual state (in which reduction divison occurs) are borne on short projections outside of the spore-mother cell (the basidium).
basidiocarp, any fungous fruit body bearing basidia.
basidium (basidia), the cell *in* which reduction divison typically occurs and *on* which the resulting spores develop.
basidiole, a young basidium on which spores have not yet started to form.
basidiospore, a spore produced on a basidium.
beaked, with an abrupt terminal projection (as when the apex of a spore is abruptly narrowed and extended.
bifurcate, forking by twos (dichotomously forked).
bister (a color term), a dingy yellow-brown (a medium date-brown).
bolete, a common name to designate the fruit body of the fleshy porefungi (members of the *Boletaceae*).
boletoid (of spores), shaped like the spores of most boletes, fig. 162 k.

brachybasidioles, inflated cells in the hymenium which form the support for the sporulating basidia. They are much more inflated than the basidioles and are present only in speices with highly specialized hymenia. They might also be defined as a sterile inflated basidiole.

bulbous (fig. 355), a bulb-like enlargement.

cap, the expanded apex of the stipe on the underside of which the hymenophore is produced (technically, the *pileus*).

capillitium, sterile specialized hyphae which with the spores form the gleba (spore-mass) in a gasteromycete.

capillitial, of the capillitium, *i.e.,* "capillitial hypha."

capitate, with a head (the fertile enlarged part of a fruit body sharply distinct from the stalk, and globose or nearly so).

cartridge buff (a color term), a very pale dull yellow.

catenulate, cells in a linear series, in a sense somewhat as in a chain.

caulocystidia, cystidia borne on the stalk of a fruit body.

cerebriform, shaped like a brain.

cespitose (caespitose), occurring in clusters.

chrysocystidia, cystidia in which the content strongly absorbs certain stains, or in which the content coagulates to form an amorphous mass when the fruit body is dried. The mass in easily demonstrated by reviving the cells in KOH (2.5%).

circumscissle, opening by a circular or equatorial line (as in the breaking of a volva when the part covering the cap adheres to the latter when the stipe elongates.

clamp connection, see fig. 162 a. They occur at the cross walls of hyphae of Basidiomycetes generally, but are absent in many species—even among closely related species.

clamps, slang for clamp connection.

clavate, club-shaped: of a stipe (stalk), the thick end is at the base and it is in this sense that the term is used here as applied to the stipe; in a cystidium the thick end is at the apex.

colliculose, having a surface interrupted by several to numerous irregular protrusions ("little hills," literally).

columella, the sterile tissue projecting through or into a pore mass. In a gasteromycete often a continuation of the stalk.

concolor (concolorous), of the same color, *i.e.,* lamellae and pileus concolorous.

concrescent (of caps), several grown together.

connate (of stipes), arising from a point, hence several stipes narrowed to a point below.

connivent (of cap margin), bent in so that the edge of the cap points toward the stipe at the horizontal level.

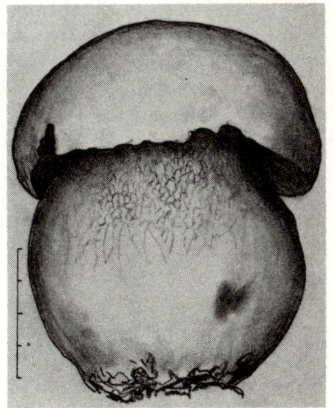

Fig. 355. *Boletus edulis.*

context (of cap or stalk), the interior, or the flesh. Context is a general term which can be applied irrespective of the texture of the species at hand—gelatinous, woody or fleshy.

contextual, pertaining to the context, *i.e.*, contextual hyphae.

cortex, the outer rind of the stalk.

cristate, crested: from *crista* (a ridge or line), usually referring to interrupted segments of spore ornamentation which are longer than wide.

cyanophilous, strongly absorbing a blue dye.

cystidia, sterile cells scattered in the hymenium. They are often named in relation to where they occur: *pleurocystidia* on sides of tubes or gills (lamellae); *cheilocystidia* on edges of tubes; *pileocystidia* for scattered cells on the pileus; *caulocystidia* for non-basidium-like cells on the stipe.

cystidioid, shaped like a cystidium, fig. 3 k.

daedaleoid, having the featuers of *Daedalia*: especially having the pores elongated variously to give a pattern resembling a labyrinth.

decorticated, with the bark removed (as on a dead tree or log).

dehiscing, the act of opening to disperse the spores in a gasteromycete.

dendroid, with tree-like branching.

dermatocystidia, cystidia occurring on sterile surfaces such as those of cap and stalk. Especially useful when where there is no cap or stalk as in some gasteromycetes.

dermatopseudocystidia, an unfortunate attempt to combine two systems of cystidial nomenclature into one term. For the first part see dermatocystidia; for the second, see pseudocystidia.

dextrinoid, a wine-red to red-brown reaction of a spore wall or content to iodine.

dichotomous, forking in pairs, as the gills of *Cantharellus*.

disarticulating, coming apart, as the cells in a hypha separating from each other.

discomycete, an Ascomycete with a cup-like or saucer-like fruit-body (fig. 1 j).

divaricate, sharply diverging, as a secondary elongation from a cell.

duplex (of context), of two distinct textures.

echinulate, with sharp spines (usually contrasted with verrucose which means warty.

echinate, with coarse spines.

effused-reflexed (of a fruit body), usually having much of the upper surface adhering to the substrate but with the margin free and curved out as if to form a pileus.

ellipsoid, a 3-dimensional term used to describe a spore which resembles an ellipse in both profile and face views.

endoperidium, the inner layer (if two are present) in the wall of a gasteromycete.

epicutis, the outermost layer of the cap (not counting veil remnants).

epicuticular, pertaining to the epicutis.

epigeous, fruiting bodies at maturity with the hymenophore above ground (literally, above ground in contrast to hypogeous, underground).

epiphragm (in bird's nest fungi), a tissue covering the "eggs" in the "nest."

esculent, any edible fungus of good flavor.

NON-GILLED FLESHY FUNGI

excentric, off center, as the stipe in *Boletinellus*.
exoperidium, the outer layer in the wall of a puffball.
farinaceous, used here in the sense of a mealy taste (freshly ground meal), but by some authors used to indicate a granular surface.
fascicle, a bundle, fasciculate means in bundles (or cespitose).
fibrillose, as if having a distinct covering of hairs or fibrils (in contrast to being glabrous *i.e.*, bald).
fimbriate (of pileus margin), fringed with distinct hairs or fibrils which project.
floccose, dry and loosely arranged or organized.
flocculent, in the form of small soft particles.
frondose, of trees: broad-leafed trees.
fructification—fruit body—fruiting body, in this work these terms apply to the spore-producing state of the fungus plant and they are either ascocarps or basidiocarps.
fruit body, see fructification.
fulvous (a color term), bright rusty brown much as in powdered cinnamon.
furfuraceous, roughened with small particles.
fuscous (a color term), about the color of a dark storm cloud.
fusoid, of a spore or cystidium—tapered at both ends.
germ pore, a soft spot in the wall of the spore, usually at the apex and a feature of most thick-walled spores. The germ tube grows out through it in the process of spore germination.
glabrous, bald.
globose, in the shape of a sphere.
gregarious (of fruit bodies), growing in groups close together but not attached at the base.
hardwood, wood of broad-leaved trees regardles of its specific gravity or strength.
heteromerous (of context of a fruit body), of two kinds of tissue: it consists of groups of globose cells surrounded by filamentous hyphae (fig. 325 c).
hyaline, lacking color and being translucent.
hymeniform, in the form of a hymenium (a palisade of cells, not hyphae) of either Ascomycetes or Basidiomycetes.
hymenium, the palisade layer of spore producing cells in an Ascomycete or Basidiomycete.
hymenial, of the hymenium.
hymenophore, the tissue bearing the hymenium.
hypha (hyphae), the thread-like unit of the fungous plant, and the basic unit of structure of the fruit body though in the latter the hyphal cells often become greatly modified.
hyphal peg, bundles of hyphae extending through the hymenium.
hypogeous, fruiting under ground (as in the truffles).
hygroscopic, taking up moisture from the air.
imbricate (of scales), arranged in an overlapping manner like shingles on a roof.
inamyloid, not giving a blue or dark red color with iodine.
involute, the margin of the pileus curled inward (see *Helvella*).
isabella color, a sordid yellowish brown tinted with olive.
krauty, taste ± of sauerkraut.

lamella (lamellae) (of a mushroom), the thin blade-like pieces of tissue that extend from the stalk to the margin of the cap (they form, *in toto*, the hymenophore).

lamellate, bearing lamellae.

  Sublamellate, a condition in which the outline of the lamellae is obscured by the anastomosing and or forking of the lamellae.

lamprocystidium (ia), a cystidium with a thick wall, (0.7- 2 μ or more thick).

lanceolate (mostly of cystidia): long and narrow with an acute apex.

lateral (of stipe), attached at margin of cap, *i.e.*, the cap margin is not continuous around it.

latex, a milk-like substance (but in no way related to milk), mostly white but also of various colors depending on the species, and often changing color on exposure to air.

lateritious (a color term), brick red (a dull red).

laticiferous, applied to the hyphae in a fruit body which contain latex.

lignicolous, of fruit bodies, attached to wood, and hence presumed to be living on the wood as a source of nourishment.

loculate, full of cavities.

leptocystidia (ium), thin-walled cystidia lacking distinctive content.

macrocystidia in the (Hymenogastrales), very large pointed cystidia often with globular content.

melzer's, the mounting medium known as Melzer's sol., for formula see p. 15.

mycelioid, moldy in texture (as if covered with mycelium).

mycelium (ia), a term for the hyphae comprising a single fungous plant. Naturally it is merely a mass of threads, or these may be aggregated into strands. When the plural (mycelia) is used it refers to a number such fungous plants.

mucronate (of a spore or cystidium), with a short abrupt, blunt to pointed apical projection (the mucro).

napiform, turnip-shaped (wide above and narrowed below).

nodulose (of spores), covered with small bumps or nodules.

obovate (of spores or cystidia), ovate in reverse—with the enlargement at the apex instead of the base as in "egg-shaped."

oleiferous (of hyphae), those hyphae in which waste materials (presumably) are deposited. They are often of more irregular appearance and opaque compared to the regular hyphae.

ornamentation, the material and the pattern of its disposition over the surface in question.

ornamented, decorated in some way such as the scales of the pileus or the warts, spines, or lines on the surface of a spore.

ovate, more or less egg-shaped as seen in a two-dimensional frame-work.

ovoid, as above but in a three-dimensional frame-work.

pallid, a dull off-white to grayish white.

paracapillitium, threads thin-walled, septate, and hyaline.

paraphyses, sterile structures produced in the hymenium of Ascomycetes (Discomycetes) in this work.

parasite, an organism living on and deriving its sustenance from a second one.

pedicel (of a spore), the remains of the sterigma that remain attached to the spore when the latter is mature (used mainly in gasteromycetes) where spores are not discharged from the sterigmata.

percurrent (in gasteromycetes), used to describe a columella which extends through the gleba to the upper wall of the fruit body.

peridioles (in the Nidulariales), the packages of spores resembling pills that are found in the nest-like fruit body.

Peridium, a wall. But also applied to the puff-ball fruit body in some works.

peridial, pertaining to the peridium, as peridial ornamentation.

peristome (of a gasteromycete), the opening, as well as any specialized tissue around it, through which the spores escape.

pileus (pilei) the cap of a mushroom-type fruit body.

pleurocystidium, a cystidium on the face of the hymenophore if the latter is differentiated into face and edge.

plicate (of pileus margin), folded deeply as in a fan.

polychromatic, of many colors.

proliferated, elongated secondarily, as in the neck of a cystidium (fig. 214 c).

pruinose, appearing as if frosted lightly by minute particles.

pseudocystidia, filamentose sterile structures with an opaque oily content found in the hymenium of some Basidiomycetes.

pseudoparenchymatic, a tissue of hyphal origin but the cells closely compact and more or less isodiametric.

pulvinate (of a columella), shaped like a cushion.

pyxidate, a type of branching in coral-fungi, see fig. 87.

pyriform, pear-shaped.

radicating, with a rootlike extension of the stalk.

receptaculum (of stink horns), the structure on which the gleba is displayed for spore dispersal.

repand, spread out.

resupinate, adhering to the substrate over entire surface of fruit body.

reticulum, with a netting (reminding one of a tennis net, *i.e., reticulate*.

rhizoid, a rootlike strand of mycelium.

rhizomorph, a complex strand of modified hyphae appearing as a cord or coarse string (often found under the bark of fallen trees).

rivulose, with many small cracks over the surface often in a somewhat concentric pattern.

rugulose, wrinkled.

sac (spore sac) of a puffball, the endoperidium containing the gleba.

saprophyte, a plant obtaining sustenance from non-living organic materials.

sclerotium, a compact mass of mycelium of definite shape in a resting state. They often germinate and produce fruit bodies—as in *Sclerotinia* of the Discomycetes.

secotioid, shaped as in *Sectium* (like an unexpanded mushroom).

septa, the partitions in a hypha (sing. *septum*).

septate, having septa.

septal, pertaining to a septum, as a septal pore (a hole in the septum).

sessile, lacking a stalk.

setae, greatly elongated and pointed lamprocystidia often with colored walls.
simple, non-septate, or without complications, in a coral-fungus, *unbranched*.
sinuous, crooked or in outline irregular.
spathulate, flattened (like a spathula).
sphaerocyst (sphaerocyte), a greatly enlarged to globose hyphal cell.
spinulose, bearing spines.
spore, the reproductive body (cell or cells) of the fungi and other lower plants. Asexual spores are termed conidia or sporangiospores depending on how they are borne. Spores associated with the sexual stage are zygospores, ascospores and basidiospores. The last two are most important to this work.
sporocarp, the fruit body which bears spores; it may be either an ascocarp or a basidiocarp.
squamule, a small scale.
squamulose, bearing squamules.
stellate, star-shaped (see *Astreus* or *Geastrum*).
sterile, not producing spores such as an hymenium that fails to produce spores.
sterigma (sterigmata), the spicule on a basidium on which the basidiospore forms.
stipe-columella, used in the secotioid fungi when the gleba is free from the columella and no sharp line exists to separate the "stipe" from the "columella."
stipitate, furnished with a stipe.
stirps, a central species and its sattelites. It bears the name of the central species and indicates that the author considers all the species grouped there to be clearly related by descent. The category is not recognized by the official rules of nomenclature, so that no record of the use of the name needs to be kept. Each author can propose his own grouping for the same central species.
strigose, with radiating hairs (around base of stipe), or having coarse upright hairs on the pileus.
subcutis, a layer immediately beneath the cuticle of the pileus (not present in all sporocarps). Also the lower layer in a 2-layered cuticle, the upper being the epicutis.
subcylindric, with the approximate shape of a cylinder.
sublammellate, the lamellae somewhat obscured in outline because of forking or anastomosing of the lamellae, *i.e.*, not clearly lamellate.
substratum (substrata), the non-living material from which a fungus derives its sustenance (if the material is living, the fungus is termed a *parasite*).
subventricose, slightly swollen in the mid-portion as in most leptocystidia.
sulcate, deeply creased.
sulfobenzaldehyde, see p. 16 for formula.
terete, round in cross section.
tomentose, covered with soft hairs.
trama, the interior tissue of pileus, lamellae or stipe.
trichodermium (of cuticle), consisting of more or less upright hyphal ends or branches but each consisting of more than one cell.

NON-GILLED FLESHY FUNGI

truffles, Ascomycete fruit bodies related to the Discomycetes but growing under ground and highly prized as food.
truncate, (of spores), cut off at the end, flattened at the apex.
tuber-like, shaped like a small potatoe.
tubercle, a lump of tissue (in *Hericium* giving rise to a frame work of branched).
tuberculate, bearing small tubercles or warts.
turbinate, shaped like a top.
umbrinous, darkly shaded, usually used to modify a stated color.
ungulate, hoof-shaped.
unpolished (of a surface), not shiny (but not with particles of sufficient size to cause it to appear furfuraceous or granular).
utriform, bladder-shaped, (widest below and with a broad apex).
versiform, variable in shape, or, of cystidia, many different shapes on one fruit body.
verrucose, warty.
verruculose, covered with small warts.
villose, covered with soft hairs.
virgate, streaked.
volva, the remains of an outer veil left around the base of the stipe when the outer veil breaks. Figs. 320, 321, 322.

INDEX

A

Agaricales, 146
Albatrellus, 111
 caeruleoporus, 111
 confluens, 113
 cristatus, 112
 flettii, 111
 ovinus, 112
Aleuria
 aurantiaca, 28
Alpovah
 cinnamoeus, 310
Anthopeziza
 floccosa, 31
Anthurus
 borealis, 300
Aphyllophorales, 101
Archangeliella
 crassa, 374
 lactarioides, 374
 tenax, 374
Artist's Fungus, 108
Ascomycetes, 20
Ascotremella
 fagineae, 24
Astreaceae, 288
Astreus
 hygrometricus, 288
 pteridis, 288
Auricularia
 auricula, 70

B

Bankera, 132
 carnosa, 133
 fuligineo-alba, 133
Basidiomycetes, 66
Battarraea
 stevensii, 291
Bear's Head, 127
Bird's Nest Fungi, 296
Boletaceae, 146
Boletellus, 252
 ananus, 252
 chrysenteroides, 253
 intermedius, 253
 pseudochrysenteroides, 254
 russellii, 252
Boletinellus
 merulioides, 148
Boletopsis
 griseus, 104
 leucomelas, 104
Boletus, 211

Sect.
 Boletus, 235
 Piperati, 213
 Pseudoboleti, 231
 Pseudoleccinum, 229
 Subtomentosi, 214
 Truncati, 227
Stirps
 Luridus, 240
 Subvelutipes, 238
 Vermiculoisoides, 236
Subsections
 Boleti, 248
 Calopodes, 244
 Fraterni, 223
 Luridi, 236
 Mirabilis, 216
 Parasitici, 214
 Reticulati, 243
 Sulphurei, 215
 Subtomentosi, 220
 Versicolores, 216

affinis, 233
 var. affinis, 233
 var. maculosus, 233
albocarneus, 234
alutaceus, 235
areus, 250
atkinsoni, 249
auriflammeus, 244
auriporus, 217
badius, 234
betula, 212
bicolor, 226
brunneocitrinus, 219
calopus, 246
calvinii, 232
chippawaensis, 248
chrysenteron, 221
coniferarum, 245
eastwoodiae, 242
edulis
 var. aurantioruber, 251
  clavipes, 251
  edulis, 250
  f. roseus, 251
  ochraceus, 251
erythropus, 240
fagicola, 236
flaviporus, 233
flavorubellus, 224
fraternus, 224
frostii, 240
gertrudiae, 248

glabellus, 235
griseus, 243
harrisonii, 225
holoroseus, 241
hortoni, 230
hoseneae, 235
huronensis, 234
illudens, 219
inedulis, 245
insuetus, 249
longicurvipes, 229
luridus, 243
mariae, 217
miniato-olivaceus, 225
miniato-pallescens, 226
minutiporus, 218
mirabilis, 216
morrisii, 239
nancyae, 219
ornatipes, 244
pallidus, 232
patriciae, 228
peckii, 247
piperatus, 214
porosporus, 229
projectellus, 216
pseudo-olivaceus, 239
pseudopeckii, 246
pseudo-sensibilis, 227
pseudosulphureus, 231
pulverulentus, 231
puniceus, 239
purpureofuscus, 233
regius, 247
roseobadius, 238
roxanae, 217
rubellus, 225
rubeus, 224
rubinellus, 213
rubripes, 246
rubroflammeus, 242
rubropictus, 238
rubropunctus, 229
satanus, 241
sensibilis, 227
separans, 248
smithii, 220
spadiceus, 222
sphaerocystis, 230
speciosus, 247
spraguei, 238
stramineus, 232
subdepauperatus, 227
subfraternus, 226
subglabripes, 230
subgraveolens, 237
subilludens, 218
subluridellus, 238
subpalustris, 218
subparvulus, 222
subtomentosus, 223
    var. perplexus, 223

subvelutipes, 240
tenax, 217
tennessensis, 223
tomentosulus, 222
truncatus, 228
variipes, 249
    var. fagicola, 250
vermiculosoides, 237
vermiculosus, 237
vinaceobasis, 242
zelleri, 220
Bondarzewia, 110
berkelyi, 110
montanus, 111
Bovista, 270
minor, 271
pila, 270
Bovistella, 271
echinella, 271
radicata, 272
Brain-fungi, 43
Brauniella
nancyae, 307
Bulgaria, 24
melastoma, 24
mexicana, 25
rufa, 25

C

Calbovista
subsculpta, 258
Calocera
viscosa, 70
Caloscypha
fulgens, 25
Calostoma
cinnabarina, 295
lutescens, 295
Calostoma
cinnabarina, 295
lutescens, 295
Calostomataceae, 295
Calvatia, 258
  Stirps
    Bovista, 269
    Craniiformis, 266
    Cyathiformis, 259
    Gigantea, 263
    Pachyderma, 260
    Sculpta, 261
    Tatrensis, 265
arctica, 262
booniana, 263
bovista, 270
candida, 269
craniiformis, 268
cretacea, 264
cyathiformis
  f. cyathiformis, 259
  f. fragilis, 259
diguetii, 266

INDEX

elata, 269
excipuliformis
  var. excipuliformis, 268
fumosa
  var. fumosa, 260
  var. idahoensis, 261
gigantea, 263
hesperia, 260
lacerata, 265
leiospora, 260
lepidophora, 264
lloydii, 265
lycoperdoides, 267
ochrogleba, 267
owyheensis, 262
pachyderma, 261
pallida, 269
paradoxa, 265
polygonia, 264
rubroflava, 267
rubrotincta, 259
sculpta, 262
sigillata, 260
subcretacea, 261
tatrensis, 266
umbrina, 266
Cantharellaceae, 92
Cantharellales, 70
Cantharellus, 95
  Sect. Cantharellus, 97
    Excavatus, 96
    Mesopus, 99
bonari, 96
cibarius, 99
cinnabarinus, 98
convolvulatus, 100
floccosus, 97
kauffmanii, 97
infundibuliformis, 101
lateritius, 98
lutescens, 100
odoratus, 99
purpurascens, 98
sphaerosporus, 100
subalbidus, 97
subperforatus, 99
tubaeformis, 100
Chamonixia
  brevicolumna, 312
Chanterelle, 95
Chlamydopus
  meyenianus, 292
Clathraceae, 299
Clathrus
  columnatus, 299
Clavaria, 72
amethystina
  var. lilacina, 77
appalachiensis, 75
atkinsoniana, 73
cinerea, 78
corniculata, 77

cristata, 78
fumosa, 74
fuscoferruginea, 73
fusiformis, 76
gracillima, 76
helvola, 75
luteotenerrima
  var. borealis, 76
miniata, 75
mucida, 72
ornatipes, 77
phycophylla, 72
purpurea, 74
pulchra, 76
rosea, 75
rubicundula, 74
umbrinella, 78
vermicularis, 73
zollingeri, 77
Clavariaceae, 71
Clavariadelphus
borealis, 90
cokeri, 91
ligula, 91
lovejoyae, 89
mucronatus, 89
pistillaris, 90
sachalinensis, 91
subfastigiatus, 91
truncatus, 89
unicolor, 90
Clavicorona
avellanea, 88
divaricata, 88
piperata, 88
pyxidata, 88
Coltrichia, 116
cinnamomeus, 117
greenei, 116
montagnei, 116
perennis, 117
Cordyceps, 60
capitata, 61
clavulata, 63
entomorrhiza, 62
fracta, 61
gracilis, 62
macularis, 65
michiganensis, 63
militaris, 65
myrmecophila, 62
ophioglossoides, 61
paludosa, 64
ravenelii, 64
sphecocephala, 63
stylophora, 64
superficialis, 64
tuberculata, 63
unilateralis, 64
valliformis, 61
variabilis, 65

Craterellus
  caerulofuscus, 95
  calyculus, 94
  cinerelus
    var. multiplex, 95
  cornucopioides, 94
  fallax, 93
  foetidus, 94
Crucibulum
  levis, 297
Cryptoporus
  volvatus, 102
Cudonia
  circinans, 59
  grisea, 59
  lutea, 58
  monticola, 59
Cyathus
  stercoreus, 297
Cystangium
  sessile, 307

D

Daedalea, 122
  ambigua, 123
  confragosa, 123
  quercina, 123
  unicolor, 122
Dendrogaster
  megasporus, 318
Dentinum, 131
  albidum, 132
  albo-magnum, 132
  repandum, 132
    var. album, 132
  umbilicatum, 131
Dictyophora
  duplicata, 301
Discina
  perlata, 28
Disciseda, 272
  candida, 272
  muelleri, 273
  subterranea, 273

E

Earth Stars, 282
Earth Tongues, 50, 54
Echinodontium
  tinctorium, 103
Elasmomyces, 370
  camphoratus, 381
  echinosporus, 370
  odoratus, 370
  pilosus, 371
  roseipe, 371
  russuloides, 371
  zellerianus, 370
Endoptychum
  agaricoides, 313
  arizonicum, 313
  depressum, 313

F

False Truffles, 302
Favolus
  alveolaris, 104
Fomes, 118
  everhartii, 121
  fomentarius, 120
  igniarius, 120
  juniperinus, 118
  officinalis, 118
  pini, 120
  pinicola, 119
  rimosus, 121
  roseus, 119
Fuscoboletinus, 171
  Sect. Fuscoboletinus, 173
    Grisellii, 175
    Palustres, 172
    Pseudosuillus, 176
  aeruginascens, 175
  glandulosus, 174
  grisellus, 176
  ochraceoroseus, 172
  paluster, 175
  serotinus, 175
  sinuspaulianus, 174
  spectabilis, 173
  weaverae, 176

G

Galeropsis
  cucullata, 305
Ganoderma, 108
  applanatum, 108
  lucidum, 110
  oregonense, 110
  tsugae, 109
Gastroboletus
  turbinatus, 304
Gautieria
  graveolens, 319
  morchelliformis, 319
Geastrum, 282
  campestre, 282
  coronatum, 287
  fimbriatum
    f. fimbriatum, 285
    f. pallidum, 286
  floriforme, 282
  limbatum, 285
  minimum, 287
  morgani, 284
  nanum, 284
  pectinatum, 283
  quadrifidum, 286
  recolligens, 283
  rufescens, 285
  saccatum, 286
  schmideli, 284
  triplex, 284
  umbilicatum, 283

INDEX

Geoglossaceae, 50
Geoglossum, 54
  affine, 55
  alveolatum, 56
  cohaerens, 55
  difforme, 55
  fallax, 56
  glabrum, 55
  glutinosum, 54
  intermedium, 56
  nigritum, 55
    var. heterosporum, 55
  pumilum, 56
  pygmaeum, 56
  simile, 55
Geopyxis
  cupularis, 26
Gomphus, 92
  clavatus, 93
  pseudoclavatus, 93
Gymnomyces, 368
  alveolatus, 368
  cinnamomeus, 368
  compactus, 369
  ferruginascens, 369
  parksii, 369
  roseomaculatus, 368
  socialis, 369
Gyromitra, 43
  caroliniana, 45
  esculenta, 44
  gigas, 45
  infula, 44
  montana, 46
  underwoodia, 44
Gyroporus, 149
  castaneus, 150
  cyanescens, 149
  purpurinus, 150
  subalbellus, 150
  umbrinisquamosus, 150

H

Hapalopilus
  nidulans, 107
Helvella, 38
  acetabulum, 38
  atra, 42
  californica, 41
  corium, 39
  costifera, 38
  crispa, 41
  elastica, 43
  lactea, 41
  lacunosa, 40
  macropus, 40
  pezizoides, 42
  queletii, 38
  sphaerospora, 41
  stevensii, 43
  villosa, 40
Helvellaceae, 37

Hen of the Woods, 110
Hericium, 126
  abietis, 127
  coralloides, 128
  erinaceus, 127
  ramosum, 127
Hydnaceae, 125
Hydnangium
  roseum, 311
Hydnellum, 138
  Stirps aurantiacum, 141
    Caeruleum, 138
      Spongiosipes, 142
  aurantiacum, 141
  caeruleum, 140
  conigenum, 141
  cruentum, 139
  cumulatum, 145
  cyanodon, 140
  cyanopodium, 139
  diabolus, 143
  earlianum, 142
  ferrugipes, 140
  frondosum, 145
  humidum, 144
  longidentatum, 142
  mirabile, 144
  multiceps, 145
  peckii, 143
  pineticola, 143
  suaveolens, 139
  piperatum, 144
  regium, 138
  scrobiculatum, 145
  spongiosipes, 142
  suaveolens, 139
  subsuccosum, 144
  subzonatum, 140
  zonatum, 140
Hydnum, 133
  calvatum, 138
    var. odoratum, 138
  crassum, 137
  cristatum, 136
  cyanellum, 134
  fennicum, 135
  fuligineo-violaceum, 134
  fumosum, 137
  fuscoindicum, 134
  imbricatum, 135
  lanuginosum, 136
  martioflavum, 136
  rimosum, 134
  scabrosum, 135
  stereosarcinon, 137
  subfelleum, 137
  subincarnatum, 137
  ustale, 136
Hymenogaster, 313
  Subgenus Dendrogaster, 314
      Hymenogaster, 316
  alnicola, 319

boozeri, 317
brunnescens, 316
caerulescens, 319
diabolus, 315
farinaceus, 317
gardneri, 318
gilkeyae, 318
idahoensis, 314
mcmurphyi, 316
nigrescens, 316
occidentalis, 317
parksii, 318
pyriformis, 319
ruber, 314
subalpinus, 317
subborealis, 315
subcaeruleus, 314
sublilacinus, 314
subochraceus, 315
subolivaceus, 316
Hymenogastrales, 302
Hypomyces
  lactifluorum, 21
  transformans, 84
Hysterangium
  separabile, 309

I

Ischnoderma
  resinosum, 108

J

Jelly-fungi, 67

L

Laetiporus
  sulphureus, 102
    var. semialbinus, 102
Lanopila
  bicolor, 256
Leccinum, 187
  Sect. Leccinum, 188
    Luteoscabra, 208
    Scabra, 200
  Stirps
    Atrostipitatum, 192
    Aurantiacum, 193
    Rufescentoides, 195
  Subsect.
    Albella, 209
    Fumosa, 203
    Lactiflua, 188
    Luteoscabra, 208
    Obscura, 190
    Pallida, 200
    Pseudoscabra, 210
    Scabra, 205
    Velosi, 188
    Versicolores, 197
    Vulpina, 189
  aberrans, 210
  albellum, 210
  ambiguum, 192
  angustisporum, 201
  arctostaphylos, 194
  atrostipitatum, 193
  aurantiacum, 194
  boreale
    var. boreale, 196
    var. microspora, 196
  brunneo-olivaceum, 209
  chalybaeum, 201
  cinnamomeum, 197
  clavatum, 197
  coffeatum, 206
  crocipodium, 208
  discolor, 195
  fallax, 194
  fibrillosum, 196
  flavostipitatum, 206
  fuscescens, 199
  glutinopallens, 202
  griseum, 210
  holopus
    var. americanum, 201
      holopus, 203
      lacteum, 202
  idahoensis, 189
  imitatum, 198
  incarnatum, 196
  insigne
    var. insigne, 199
  insolens
    var. brunneomaculatum, 198
      insolens, 199
  laetum, 196
  luteocinerascens, 199
  luteum, 209
  murinaceo-stipitatum, 203
  obscurum, 191
  ochraceum, 197
  olivaceo-glutinosum, 203
  olivaceopallidum, 200
  oxydabile, 211
  pallidistipes, 206
  pellstonianum, 193
  ponderosum, 190
  proliferum, 202
  rimulosum, 207
  rotundifoliae, 201
  rufescentoides, 195
  rugosiceps, 209
  singeri, 207
  snellii, 211
  subatratum, 190
  subfulvum, 189
  subleucophaeum, 210
  sublutescens, 189
  subpulchripes, 207
  subrobustum, 195
  subspadiceum, 191
  subtestaceum, 198
  testaceoscabrum, 192

INDEX

uliginosum, 191
vinaceo-pallidum, 193
vulpinum, 190
Lentaria patowillardii, 81
Lentinus tigrinus, 306
"Lentodium
  squamosum," 306
Lenzites, 121
  betulina, 121
  saepiaria, 122
  trabea, 122
Leotia
  atrovirens, 57
  lubrica, 57
  viscosa, 58
Leucogaster
  rubescens, 310
Longia
  texensis, 296
Lycoperdales, 255
Lycoperdon, 273
  candidum, 276
  coloratum, 274
  curtissii, 274
  dakotensis, 276
  echinatum, 280
  ericetorium
    var. cepaeforme, 275
  flavotinctum, 277
  floccosum, 281
  foetidum, 278
  glabellum, 281
  molle, 281
  muscorum, 278
  oblongisporum, 275, 277
  peckii, 278
  pedicellatum, 277
  perlatum, 279
  polymorphum var. cepaeforme, 275
  pulcherrimum, 280
  pusillum, 274
  pyriforme, 276
  rimulatum, 279
Lysurus mokusin, 300

M

Macowanites, 374
  acris, 380
  albidigleba, 377
  americanus, 381
  chlorinosmus, 379
  citrinus, 376
  fulvescens, 377
  fuscoviolaceus, 376
  iodiolens, 380
  lilacinus, 377
  luteolus, 379
  magnus, 375
  mollis, 380
  nauseosus, 375
  olidus, 378
  pinicola, 375
  pseudometricus, 377
  setchellianus, 379
  subrosaceus, 378
  vinicolor, 376
Martellia
  alba, 362
  brunnescens, 365
  californica, 364
  cremea, 364
  ellipsospora, 366
  foetans, 364
  fragrans, 365
  fulvispora, 365
  gilkeyae, 367
  idahoensis, 366
  maculata, 367
  monticola, 363
  occidentalis, 367
  oregonensis, 366
  parksii, 368
  scissilis, 366
  setigera, 363
  subalpina, 363
  subfulva, 365
  subochracea, 363
  variabilispora, 367
  vesiculosa, 367
Melanogaster
  variegatus, 310
Microglossum
  arenarium, 60
  atropurpureum, 60
  fumosum, 60
  olivaceum, 60
  rufum, 59
  viride, 60
Microstoma
  protracta, 32
Mitrula
  abietis, 58
  gracilis, 58
  paludosa, 58
Montagnea
  arenarius, 308
Morchella, 46
  angusticeps, 48
  crassipes, 49
  deliciosa, 48
  esculenta, 49
  semilibera, 47
Morels, 46
  Beefsteak Morel, 44
  Black Morel, 48
  Common Morel, 49
  Delicious Morel, 48
  Early Morel, 46
Morganella
  subincarnata, 256
Multiclavula, 72
Mutinus
  caninus, 301
    var. albus, 302

elegans, 302
Mycenastrum
    corium, 257
Mycolevis
    siccigleba, 311
Myriostoma
    coliformis, 255

N

Neosecotium
    macrosporium, 304
Nidula
    candida, 297
Nidularia, 298
Nidulariales, 296
Nivatogastrium
    nubigenum, 305

O

Octavianina, 361
    asterosperma var. potteri, 361
    macrospora, 361
    nigrescens, 362
    papyracea, 362
    rogersii, 362
Otidea, 33
    abietina, 34
    alutacea, 34
    auricula, 34
    cantharella, 34
    grandis, 34
    kauffmanii, 35
    leporina, 33
    onotica, 33
    rainierensis, 35
Oxyporus, 117
    nobilissimus, 118
    populinus, 117

P

Pachyella, 35
Peziza, 35
    badioconfusa, 36
    clypeata, 35
    proteana, 35
    repanda, 36
    venosa, 36
    violacea, 36
Pezizaceae, 23
Pezizales, 22
Phaeolus
    schweinitzii, 103
Phaeobulgaria
    inquinans, 24
Phallaceae, 300
Phallales, 298
Phallogaster
    saccatus, 308
Phallus
    impudicus, 301
    ravenelii, 301
Phellodon, 129
    atratus, 129
    confluens, 130
    melaleucus, 130
    niger
        var. alboniger, 131
        niger, 131
    tomentosus, 130
Phellorina
    strobilina, 292
Phlogiotis
    helvelloides, 68
Pisolithaceae, 287
Pisolithus
    tinctorius, 287
Plectania
    nannfeldtii, 31
Podaxales, 295
Podaxis
    pistillaris, 295
Polyozellus
    multiplex, 92
Polypilus
    frondosus, 110
    umbellatus, 110
Polyporaceae, 102
Polyporus, 113
    arcularis, 114
    brumalis, 114
    elegans, 114
    ellisii, 115
    fagicola, 115
    giganteus, 111
    pescaprae, 116
    picipes, 113
    radicatus, 115
    squamosus, 114
Polystictus
    tomentosus, 105
Protogautieria
    lutea, 312
Pseudocolus
    schellenbergiae, 299
Pseudohydnum
    gelatinosum, 68
Pseudoplectania
    melaena, 31
    nannfeldtii, 31
    nigrella, 30
Pulveroboletus, 251
    ravenelii, 251
Pustularia
    bronca, 29
Pycnoporus
    cinnabarinus, 107
    sanguineus, 107

R

Radiigera
    atrogleba, 309
Ramaria
    abietina, 82
    acris, 80
    apiculata, 80

aurea, 85
botrytis, 84
botrytoides, 87
brunnea, 85
byssiseda, 81
cacao, 84
caulifloriformis, 87
conjunctipes, 86
fennica, 83
flaccida, 83
fumigata, 83
gelatinosa, 83
gracilis, 82
grandis, 85
obtusissima, 87
ochraceo-virens, 81
pusilla, 83
sanguinea, 84
secunda, 85
stricta, 81
subbotrytis, 86
subspinulosa, 86
suecia, 82
Ramariopsis
  crocea, 79
  kunzei, 79
  pulchella, 79
Rhizina
  inflata, 25
Rhizopogon, 320
  Sect. Amylopogon, 327
    Fulvigleba, 332
    Rhizopogon, 340
    Villosuli, 322

S

Sarcoscypha
  coccinea, 31
  occidentalis, 32
Sarcosoma
  globosa, 23
Sarcosphaeria
  crassa, 27
Scleroderma
  arenicola, 290
  areolatum, 290
  aurantiacum, 290
  citrinum, 290
  flavidum, 289
  macrorhizon, 289
  polyrhizon, 289
  texense, 291
Sclerodermataceae, 288
Sclerodermatales, 287
Scutellinia
  hemisphaerica, 33
  scutellata, 32
Sepultaria
  arenicola, 27
Series
  Lutei, 347
  Versicolores, 357

Setchelliogaster
  tenuipes, 306
Simblum
  spherocephalum, 299
  texense, 299
Slippery Jack, 164
Spathularia, 56
  flavida, 57
  spathulata, 56
  velutipes, 57
Spongipellis
  unicolor, 106
Spragueola
  irregularis, 52
Steccherinum, 128
  adustum, 129
  crassiusculum, 129
  septentrionalis, 128
Stinkhorns, 300
Stirps
  Albidus, 358
  Bacillosporus, 359
  Brunneseens, 357
  Evadens, 359
  Luteolus, 343
  Maculatus, 357
  Ochraceorubens, 347
  Rubescens, 341
  Subsalmomeus, 358
  Vulgaris, 352
Strobilomyces, 254
  confusus, 255
  floccopus, 254
Subgenus
  Rhizopogon, 321
  Rhizopogonella, 320
Subsection
  Angustispori, 357
  Rhizopogon, 341
    abietis, 342
    albiroseus, 341
    alkalivirens, 330
    alpestris, 350
    amoenus, 339
    anomalus, 327
    arctostaphyli, 328
    armeniacus, 336
    atlanticus, 335
    flavofibrillosus, 348
    fragmentatus, 328
    fragrans, 326
    fuscorubens, 349
    gelatinosus, 335
    gilkeyae, 322
    griseogleba, 333
    griseovinaceus, 327
    hawkeri, 325
    hymenogastrosporus, 333
    hysterangioides, 332
    idahoensis, 331
    inquinatus, 336
    inversus, 338
    isabellinus, 347

kauffmanii, 329
laetifulvus, 346
libocedri, 348
lowii, 334
luteoalboides, 356
luteoalbus, 346
luteolus, 346
luteorubescens, 342
lutescens, 336
maculatus, 357
masonae, 360
milleri, 328
molallaensis, 325
molligleba, 345
monticola, 350
mutabilis, 325
nigrescens, 347
nitens, 359
obscurus, 359
occidentalis, 355
ochraceisporus, 337
ochraceorubens, 351
ochroleucoides, 342
odoratus, 360
olivaceofuscus, 335
olivaceoniger, 321
oregonensis, 344
oswaldii, 345
pachyphloeus, 320
pannosus, 343
parasiticus, 346
parksii, 323
parvulus, 337
pedicellatus, 329
piceus, 345
pinicola, 336
pinyonensis, 331
ponderosus, 323
proximus, 360
pseudoaffinis, 356
pseudoroseolus, 341
pseudovillosulus, 323
quercicola, 324
reali, 344
rogersii, 322
roseolus, 341
rubescens, 341
  var. luteorubescens, 342
        ochraceus, 343
        pallidimaculatus, 343
        rileyi, 343
        rubescens, 343
rudus, 328
salebrosus, 328
semireticulatus, 327
semitectus, 330
separabilis, 349
sepelibilis, 326
singularis, 339
sipei, 349
sordidus, 351
subalpinus, 343
subareolatus, 325
subaustralis, 342
subbadius, 330
subcaerulescens, 331
  var. subpanosus, 331
      viridescens, 331
subcinnamomeus, 337
subcitrinus, 354
subclavitisporus, 333
subcroceus, 354
subgelatinosus, 330
sublateritius, 350
subpurpurascens, 329
subradicatus, 348
subsalmonius, 358
  var. griseolilascens, 358
      persicinus, 358
      roseitinctus, 358
      similis, 358
      subsalmonius, 358
subviolascens, 344
succosus, 341
superiorensis, 334
tephroleuca, 331
thaxteri, 338
umbrinoviolascens, 324
variabilisporus, 332
ventricosporus, 342
vesiculosus, 339
vestitus, 331
villosulus, 326
vinicolor, 335
viridis, 324
vulgaris, 355
willamettensis, 348
Suillus, 151
Sect. Boletinus, 152
     Paragyrodon, 151
     Suillus, 159
acerbus, 169
acidus, 166
albidipes, 162
albivelatus, 163
americanus, 161
appendiculatus, 156
borealis, 160
brevipes, 169
brunnescens, 160
caerulescens, 155
castanellus, 153
cavipes, 152
cothurnatus, 165
decipiens, 154
flavogranulatus, 168
flavoluteus, 171
floridanus, 154
glandulosipes, 161
granulatus, 170
grevillei, 158
hirtellus, 171
  var. cheimonophilus, 171
      thermophilus, 171

INDEX

hololeucus, 157
imitatus, 156
lakei, 155
   var. pseudopictus, 153
lithocarpi-sequoiae, 157
lutescens, 164
luteus, 164
megaporinus, 163
pallidiceps, 167
pictus, 153
pinorigidus, 166
placidus, 167
ponderosus, 156
proximus, 158
pseudobrevipes, 158
pseudogranulatus, 157
punctatipes, 168
punctipes, 170
pungens, 162
ruber, 159
sibiricus, 162
solidipes, 154
sphaerosporus, 151
subaureus, 169
subluteus, 165
subolivaceous, 166
subvariegatus, 159
tomentosus, 159
umbonatus, 164
Sulphur Shelf, 102

T

Thaxterogaster
  pingue, 305
Tremella
  concrescens, 69
  foliacea, 70
  reticulata, 69
Tremellales, 67
Tremellodendron
  schweinitzii, 69
Trichoglossum
  confusum, 53
  farlowii, 53
  hirsutum, 53
  octopartitum, 53
  tetraporum, 54
  varibile, 54
  velutipes, 54
  walteri, 53
Truncocolumella
  citrina, 303
     var. separabilis, 303
Tulostoma, 292
  brumale, 294
  campestre, 294
  fibrillosum, 294
  finkii, 294
  simulans, 293
  striatum, 293
Tulostomataceae, 291

Tylopilus, 177
  alboater, 181
  amylosporus, 179
  atrofuscus, 179
  badiceps, 183
  ballouii, 183
  chromapes, 177
  cyaneotinctus, 180
  eximius, 181
  felleus, 186
  fumosipes, 181
  gracilis, 177
  humilis, 184
  indecisus, 185
  intermedius, 185
  minor, 185
  olivaceobrunneus, 178
  peralbidus, 182
  plumbeovilaceous, 186
  porphyrosporus, 179
  pseudoscaber, 178
  rhoadsiae, 186
  rubrobrunneus, 182
  sordidus, 180
  subpunctipes, 184
  subunicolor, 183
  tabacinus, 183
  umbrosus, 180
Tyromyces, 123
  albellus, 125
  caesius, 124
  guttulatus, 124
  perdelicatus, 124
  spraguei, 124
  tephroleucus, 125

U

Underwoodia
  columnaris, 22
Urnula
  craterium, 30
  geaster, 29

V

Vascellum
  depressum, 257
Verpa bohemica, 46
  conica, 47
Vibrissia
  truncorum, 52

W

Wynnea
  americana, 26

X

Xylaria
  polymorpha, 21

Z

Zelleromyces, 372
  cinnabarinus, 372
  gardneri, 373
  gilkeyae, 373
  glabrellus, 373
  oregonensis, 372
  ravenelii, 373